Symantec C++ Programming for the Macintosh

Symantec C++ Programming for the Macintosh

Neil Rhodes
Julie McKeehan

Brady

New York London Toronto Sydney Tokyo Singapore

Brady Publishing
A Division of Prentice Hall Computer Publishing
15 Columbus Circle
New York, NY 10023

ISBN: 1-56686-049-0

Library of Congress Catalog No.: 93-1660

Printing Code: The rightmost double-digit number is the year of the book's printing; the rightmost single-digit number is the number of the book's printing. For example, 93-1 shows that the first printing of the book occurred in 1993.

96 95 94 93 4 3 2 1

Manufactured in the United States of America

Limits of Liability and Disclaimer of Warranty

The authors and publisher of this book have used their best efforts in preparing this book and the programs contained in it. These efforts include the development, research, and testing of the theories and programs to determine their effectiveness. The authors and publisher make no warranty of any kind, expressed or implied, with regard to these programs or the documentation contained in this book. The authors and publisher shall not be liable in any event for incidental or consequential damages in connection with, or arising out of, the furnishing, performance, or use of these programs.

Trademarks

Most computer and software brand names have trademarks or registered trademarks. The individual trademarks have not been listed here.

To my mother, Mary, who taught me to always take a book wherever I go. Books have provided me a lifetime of reward, as has she.

Neil Rhodes

To my parents, Gloria and Richard McKeehan, who taught me to finish what I start, even if it's harder than I thought. And, to my best friend, Barbie who mothered my children, fed my dogs, and did a thousand things without hesitation to ensure I would have a life to come back to.

Julie McKeehan

Credits

Publisher
Michael Violano

Managing Editor
Kelly D. Dobbs

Developmental Editor
Perry King

Production Editor
Kristin Juba

Editorial Assistant
Lisa Rose

Book Designers
Michele Laseau
Kevin Spear

Cover Designer
HUB Graphics

Indexer
Jeanne Clark
Craig Small

Production Team
Diana Bigham
Katy Bodenmiller
Julie Brown
Tim Cox
Mark Enochs
Sean Medlock
Linda Seifert
Greg Simsic
Beth Rago
Carrie Roth

Acknowledgments

Writing a book about prerelease software is a bit like skydiving with a prototype parachute. Even though you would not jump without enormous faith in the parachute manufacturer, you still are filled with spine tingling tension until you pull the cord and everything goes according to plan. We had the same experience writing this book. Symantec has produced consistently excellent Macintosh software in the past, so we had confidence that this product would be no different. But, in the midst of working with the prerelease versions of Symantec C++, we many times thought ourselves fools for writing about how to use something that was not yet usable. Not that there was anything unusual about Symantec C++—any prerelease software contains such bumps and kinks. Otherwise, it would not be prerelease.

This all goes to say that, although we tried to ensure that no mistakes crept into the text, there are doubtless some. While the presence of any errors is solely our responsibility, we would be grateful if you report any you find in the text or in the programs. We also will gratefully acknowledge you in the next edition if you find an error we do not know about already.

This book is the product of many peoples' labors besides our own, and these people deserve recognition for their contributions. Many thanks go especially to Perry King, our editor at Brady, for all his efforts under a tight deadline. This work has been much improved by the touch of his skilled hand—from suggestions on content to the review of each chapter. Likewise, our production editor, Kristin Juba, worked just as valiantly. We consider ourselves fortunate to have worked with such professionals. Thanks also to Tracy Smith (the then acquisitions editor) at Brady, who approached us about writing this book. Gratitude as well to Carole McClendon, our agent at Waterside Productions, for making the contract negotiation an almost painless process.

Many thanks also go to Phil Shapiro at Symantec. He quickly responded to all our questions about Symantec C++, even with a very busy schedule of his own. He is a bright guy, and Symantec is lucky to have him. To all the other people on the Symantec C++ team, from the product manager to the programmers to the manual writers, our thanks for producing a product we are proud to write about.

We owe a special debt of gratitude to Dave Wilson for his willingness to contribute programming time to this book. Dave is not only a fine teacher but a good friend as well. As the original impulse behind Neil's getting into the programmer training business, he cannot be thanked enough.

Thanks to all of our students, but particularly to Neil's students at Apple Developer University. No teacher could ask for a better, brighter bunch to learn from.

In the more general realm, we also would like to thank Apple Computer for producing the PowerBook and DuoBook on which this entire book was written. We can hardly wait to see what they will cook up next. Thanks also to Joel West for getting us into the Macintosh software business and for being the impetus behind our striking out on our own.

Last, but not least, our heartfelt gratitude goes to Loring and Barbie Fiske-Phillips. It is only because of their generosity and unceasing labors on our behalf that this book was finished on time. No one could ask for better friends.

Contents

Introduction

"C++ is the programming language of the future." This is, no doubt, a remark you have heard repeated so often your ears are numb. In the past, if you were a Macintosh programmer and wanted to ride the C++ wave into the future, you quickly encountered a tsunami—Macintosh Programmer's Workshop (MPW). From Apple, MPW may support C++, but it also comes with a learning curve the shape of Mt. Everest and compile times the speed of cold molasses. Faced with this situation, many programmers decide to live without C++.

Symantec, the creators of the most popular development environment for the Macintosh, THINK C, have thoughtfully provided you with a better alternative, Symantec C++ for Macintosh. This new programming environment is a sleek, brilliantly fast vehicle for C++. It is just the right mode for just the right language.

Why are we so sure that C++ is the right language and that you should learn it? Here are some pretty compelling reasons:

- You want a job as a programmer.
- You already have a programming job, but want a raise.
- You do not want to be replaced by a C++ programmer.
- You want to develop state-of-the-art software.

Of course, knowing C++ well enough to write good programs is not enough to bring about any of above (except maybe getting a job—there is a high demand for C++ programmers); however, it is guaranteed to help do so. Here are just two of the reasons why the advantages of learning C++ should be as obvious to you as it is to most Macintosh software developers:

- Bedrock, the new Windows and Macintosh application framework from Apple and Symantec, is expected to have a major impact on program development and is due out shortly. The notion of capturing the combined Macintosh and Windows market with one development effort can reasonably be expected to make most developers salivate. Knowing this, you should not be surprised when Macintosh development shifts to Bedrock. What if you are a programmer, who wants to be part of this group? The catch is that you have to do Bedrock coding in C++.

- Pink, the new object-oriented operating system from Taligent (the joint Apple and IBM venture), may be distributed to developers as early as next year. Pink, if it turns out as anticipated, is expected to metamorphosize the PC and Macintosh worlds. Imagine being one of the application developers for this new system. The catch? You have to write your applications in C++.

The New C++ from Symantec

Should you learn C++? Only you can decide that. But, if you do, here are some reasons why Symantec C++ is the right compiler to use:

- The new project manager. Symantec C++ for Macintosh is not just new a C++ compiler in an old framework. Symantec also has opened up the Project Manager, the program's development environment, by decoupling it from the compiler. This new multilingual Project Manager enables multiple translators within the same project—part of your project can be written in C, and part in C++.
- Source code control. The new environment also supports source code control. Using Apple's SourceServer (shipping with Symantec C++), you can have the same capabilities MPW users possess for managing project source code. One-person projects are a snap in THINK C; but now, you can develop a large project with a multi-programmer team in Symantec C++ just as easily.
- A resource compiler. Symantec C++ for Macintosh also comes with THINK Rez, a compiler for Apple's Rez language. Rez is a language that is particularly useful for describing resources in a textual format. Thus, you can create your resources visually in ResEdit, textually with Rez, or using a combination of the two.
- An on-line reference system. Also from Symantec, THINK Reference is an on-line reference program that you can access from the Project Manager with a few clicks of the mouse. Do you have a routine for which you need the parameters? When you click twice, THINK Reference provides a detailed listing of that

routine and its parameters. This tool makes coding unfamiliar territory far easier.

There also are a host of new little niceties that make using Symantec C++ for Macintosh better. The following are just a few of them:

- A multiple-file search can produce a list of all matching lines, rather than just finding lines sequentially.
- The compiler no longer stops at the first error it finds. Instead, errors and warnings can be logged to a window. This way you can fix a group of syntax problems before trying to rebuild a project.
- The shift left and shift right commands now work the way they do in MPW.
- You can add word processor or picture documentation files to a project.
- The Project Manager faithfully remembers the windows settings of your project when you last used it. When you go back to a project, it reopens the windows the way they were when you closed the project.

These features are by no means all that is new. It should be just enough to convince you that Symantec C++ for Macintosh is the right program to use to learn C++ on the Macintosh. After you decide to program with C++, you should realize why this book is essential.

What This Book Has To Offer

Should you read this book? If you want to write C++ programs using Symantec C++ for Macintosh, the answer is yes. After you read it, you should be able to the following:

- Use Symantec C++ for Macintosh to develop applications. This is not a theoretical book about C++; instead, it is a practical one. The goal is to turn you into a C++ programmer, not a C++ theoretician.
- Design your programs as a collection of objects to make them easier to write, modify, and maintain.

- Use C++ as a more effective C and as a complete object-oriented language.
- Begin to write C++ code like a veteran, using efficient and idiomatic C++ structures.
- Use application frameworks, primarily the THINK Class Library. Application frameworks are more wonderful than freshly baked bread. They shorten your development time, while giving your application more features than it normally would have.

Here are a few examples of why you might need this book:

- You may be a committed THINK C programmer who wants to learn C++ because you are convinced it is the language of the future. If you are, you can take comfort from Symantec's approach to C++: It is quick and intuitive. You also get an easy transition path for your existing projects because parts of your project can be written in C++ while other parts can remain in C.
- You might be a MPW C++ programmer who is tired of plodding compiles and long linking in MPW. If you are, you should be pleasantly surprised. You can make a change to your code, recompile it, and run it in a matter of seconds. Contrast this process with the minutes spent on an MPW compile. Furthermore, having slogged through the long learning curve of MPW, you should be overjoyed with Symantec C++ for Macintosh. The program has a tightly integrated, intuitive interface, and it only takes hours to become familiar with the environment rather than the days or months needed to become proficient with MPW.
- You might be a programmer interested in learning C++ because you know that object-oriented programming is a better way to write and maintain code. Symantec C++ for Macintosh is a great environment in which to make the transition to object-oriented programming.
- You may have been waiting for the right C++ for the Macintosh—one that did not require extraordinary amounts of time or money. With Symantec C++ for Macintosh, you can start writing and debugging C++ code within an hour or two.

If any of these descriptions apply to you, this book is worth your time.

What You Should Know

You need to know how to program in C. It helps to have at least some knowledge of how to program on the Macintosh. You do not need to know C++ and you do not need to know how to use THINK C. However, if you do know either of these, all the better.

What Is in This Book

Here is the book in a nutshell: You learn the environment and then the language. Then you use both with the THINK Class Library to write different programs.

Part 1 focuses on getting you up and running in the Symantec C++ environment. This section's introduction provides a summary of the chapters, along with the history of Symantec C++ for Macintosh and its relation to other Symantec products. Do not worry if some of the terms and concepts listed here are new to you; they are explained within the chapters.

Chapter 1 teaches you how to use the Project Manager and the C/C++ compilers. Chapter 2 continues with a multiple-file project, which you create and run. In Chapter 3, you learn how to interpret compiler errors and warnings. C++, in particular, has many warning messages. Chapter 4 is where you learn about the complexities of debugging. In Chapter 5, you learn how to build resource files using the resource utilities available in Symantec C++. Along with other useful information, in Chapter 6 you learn how to build applications. In Chapter 7, you see how precompiled header files help speed up compiles.

After creating projects in the Symantec C++ environment in Part 1, you are ready to immerse yourself in C++. In Part 2, you go from an introduction of the language, including the history, to a detailed discussion of objects. Objects, of course, are C++'s fundamental code constructs that make C++ an object-oriented language.

Chapter 8 compares C with C++. You see how C++ has added features to C that make it a better procedural language. In Chapter 9, you learn about object-oriented design. Writing code in an object-oriented language is very different from writing code in a procedure-based language. If you try to write code in C++ clothed in a procedural skin, you lose most of the power and advantage of C++. Plus, it is not very much fun. This chapter helps you avoid that trap. After you have learned about some of the principles of object-oriented design, you can start doing some object-oriented programming using C++, as detailed in Chapter 10. You learn more about the features of C++ objects in Chapter 11. After you have mastered some of the most important elements of C++, you learn more about writing good C++ code in Chapter 12. In Chapter 13, you learn how to use the THINK Class Browser. The Symantec C++ compiler has a lot of options. Furthermore, they are hidden in several THINK Project Manager panels, so you learn about where they are and how to use them in Chapter 14.

Now that you have learned C++, you are ready to start writing some applications, as detailed in Part 3. A fundamental principle is the basis of this section: The best way to learn a language is to read and write code in it—then do it some more and then some more. You can see how to use C++ and application frameworks to speed your development.

Chapter 15 contains descriptions of application frameworks, particularly the THINK Class Library. Chapters 16, 17, 18, 19, 20, and 21 discuss the following programs RandomRectangle, TextTyper, PICTPeeker, Tick-Tock, C++ Calc, and AddressBook, respectively.

There are also several appendices you can look in to find detailed information on some other important topics, including compatibility and porting as well as SourceServer and ToolServer. You also can find complete source listings as well as a bibliography. Finally, Appendix F explains how to use the disk packaged with this book.

How You Should Read This Book

Here are some suggestions to help you focus your reading:

- If you have used the THINK C environment, you do not need to read all of Part 1. Instead, read the introduction to this section to find out where the new features of Symantec C++ are covered. You can then skip to that material.

- If you already know C++ programming, you do not need to read all of Part 2. Start with Appendix A to learn how the Symantec C++ compiler differs from other C++ compilers. Chapters 13 and

14 contain the rest of the information you need to know about using the Symantec C++ environment.

- If you already know how to use the THINK Class Library, you may not need to read all of Part 3. Chapter 15 offers an introduction to frameworks. There is detailed discussion of the TCL. Read Chapters 16-21 if you want to see some C++ sample programs that use the TCL. If other application frameworks besides the TCL interest you, read Chapter 15.
- If you have never used C++ or the Symantec environment before, the book was written with you in mind. Read it straight through.

PART 1

The Symantec C++ Environment

Symantec C++ for Macintosh has a long and varied history. The environment sprang from THINK C, while the compiler started life as Zortech C++. The following figure shows what that lineage looks like.

Back in the early years of the Macintosh, there was a small company with an idea of pairing a C compiler with an exciting development environment. The company was THINK Technologies, and the idea became THINK C, the most popular development environment for the Macintosh. Unlike other environments, THINK C had a Macintosh look and feel—it threw out the command line for a graphical interface. THINK quickly captured the market for third-party C compilers and was acquired by Symantec after a few years.

Zortech developed a successful C++ compiler for DOS that was one of the first true C++ compilers—it did not use C as an intermediate language, but generated object code directly.

LightspeedC 1.0
THINK Technologies
1985

LightspeedC 2.0
THINK Technologies
1986

THINK C 3.0
Symantec
1988

Zortech C++ for Macintosh 2.1.1
Zortech
1991

THINK C 4.0
Symantec
1989

THINK C 5.0
Symantec
1991

Zortech C++ for Macintosh 2.1.3
Symantec
1992

THINK C 6.0
Symantec
1993

***Symantec C++ for Macintosh* 6.0**
Symantec
1993

Symantec C++ for MPW 1.0
Symantec
1993

Geneaology of Symantec C++ for Macintosh

Although Zortech ported this compiler to MPW, it never caught on very well. When Symantec acquired Zortech, they had the raw ingredients for what finally turned into Symantec C++ for Macintosh: THINK C and Zortech C++.

Only time can tell whether Symantec C++ for Macintosh will rival THINK C in popularity. But the ingredients are all there: Symantec C++ is fast, functions graphically, and contains a C++ compiler that points the way to the future as well as its C compiler that maintains the present.

This section shows you how to use Symantec C++ within the THINK environment. You learn everything from creating that first source file to building a final stand-alone application. You do it faster, and have more fun, than you ever could have in MPW.

If you already are familiar with THINK C and want to read about the new features of the THINK Project Manager, read Chapters 2, 3, 4, and 5. Chapter 2 discusses mixing C and C++ in one project. Chapter 3 deals with errors and warnings. Chapter 4 discusses the THINK Debugger, which has some new features. Chapter 5 discusses THINK Rez.

1

Creating a Project

There are few traditions as sacrosanct within the computer programming world as that of starting a C or C++ tutorial with the Hello World program. Not one to break with such tradition, this chapter shows you how to build Hello World using Symantec C++. The information presented here should give you enough of an introduction to the Symantec C++/THINK environment to be able to navigate through a simple project. In this chapter, you do the following:

- Set up project folders (as well as briefly see what is included with Symantec C++).
- Use the THINK Project Manager and the Symantec C++ compiler by creating a new project (Hello World) and adding source files to it.
- Compile and link the Hello World project.
- Learn some of the option settings and what certain error messages mean.

The Symantec C++ Folders

There are a number of folders and files that come with Symantec C++. Figure 1.1 shows you what the topmost folder looks like after installing the software.

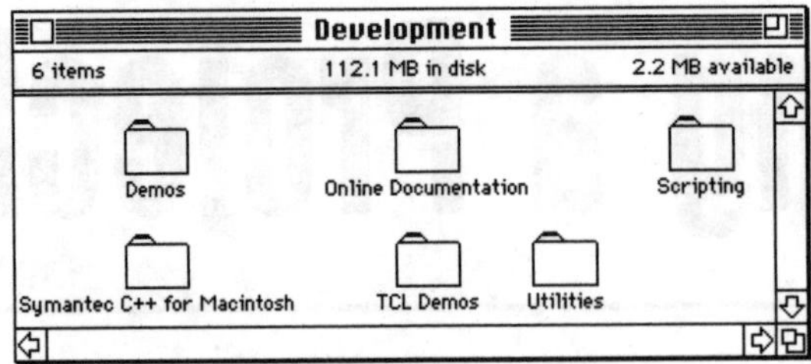

Figure 1.1. The main folder.

Table 1.1 provides brief descriptions of the contents of each folder.

Table 1.1. Contents of the Topmost Folder after Installing Symantec C++

Folder	Contents
Demos	Sample C++ programs
Online Documentation	The THINK Reference program with documentation for standard libraries and C++ iostreams
Scripting	Sample scripts to control the THINK Project Manager using AppleScript and UserLand Frontier
Symantec C++ for Macintosh	The Project Manager, compilers, header files, and libraries; the contents of this folder are shown in figure 1.2
TCL Demos	Sample THINK Class Library (TCL) programs
Utilities	Useful programs, including ResEdit

When you open the Symantec C++ for Macintosh folder, you see that it contains the folders shown in figure 1.2.

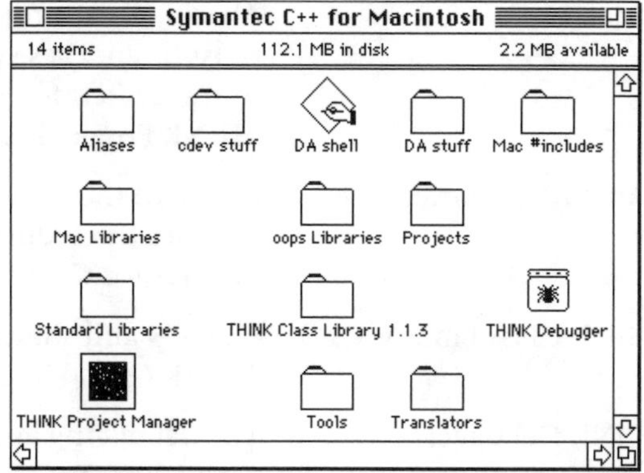

Figure 1.2. The contents of the Symantec C++ for Macintosh folder.

This is obviously the folder of interest. Its contents are detailed in table 1.2.

Table 1.2. Contents of the Symantec C++ for Macintosh Folder

Folder	Contents
Aliases	Aliases to the header files and libraries you want in a standard search path
cdev stuff	Useful code for writing control panels
DA shell	An application for testing desk accessories
DA stuff	Useful code for writing desk accesso-ries
Mac #includes	Macintosh-specific headers for C, C++, and Rez
Mac Libraries	Macintosh-specific libraries for C and C++
oops Libraries	Libraries (with source code) for C+ objects

continues

Table 1.2. Continued

Folder	Contents
Projects	Aliases to the projects you use the most often; these projects are added to the Switch to Project menu in the THINK Project Manager
Standard Libraries	Standard (not Macintosh-specific) libraries (including source code) and headers for C and C++
THINK Class Library 1.1.3	Headers and source files for the THINK Class Library (TCL)
THINK Debugger	The debugging application you use with Symantec C++; it launches automatically when you debug
THINK Project Manager	The application you use to access the Symantec C++ compiler; it is where you create, edit, compile, and build your applications
Tools	Contains SourceServer (see Appendix A for more information); you put aliases to ResEdit and THINK Reference in this folder so that the THINK Project Manager can launch them as necessary
Translators	The THINK C and Symantec C++ compilers as well as THINK Rez and other translators

Installing Symantec C++

To set up Symantec C++, follow the installation instructions that come with the product. There are some other things worth arranging as well:

1. Locate THINK Reference in the Online Documentation folder and create an alias to it.

2. Locate ResEdit in the Utilities folder and create an alias to it.
3. Put both aliases in the Tools folder.

Creating a New Project

The THINK Project Manager manages all aspects of the project from beginning to end. Everything—from creating source files to rolling the object files into an application—is done from within the Project Manager. The obvious first step, then, is learning to use the Project Manager.

Begin by creating a new folder to contain your project and its source file. Name the folder Hello.

IMPORTANT

Make sure that your project directories are not in the Symantec C++ folder or any of its subfolders. If you put project folders in there, the Project Manager has to search through all of your project folders every time it looks for standard include files.

Figure 1.3 shows you a fairly standard arrangement that you might use for your Hello folder and other project folders as well.

After you have created your new project folder and arranged it to your taste, launch the THINK Project Manager. Upon launching, the Project Manager displays the dialog shown in figure 1.4.

You create a new project by clicking the New button. The THINK Project Manager then displays a dialog for you to name the project. Name the new project Hello. .

You create the   character by pressing the option-P key combination. Save Hello. in the Hello folder you created earlier (see fig. 1.5).

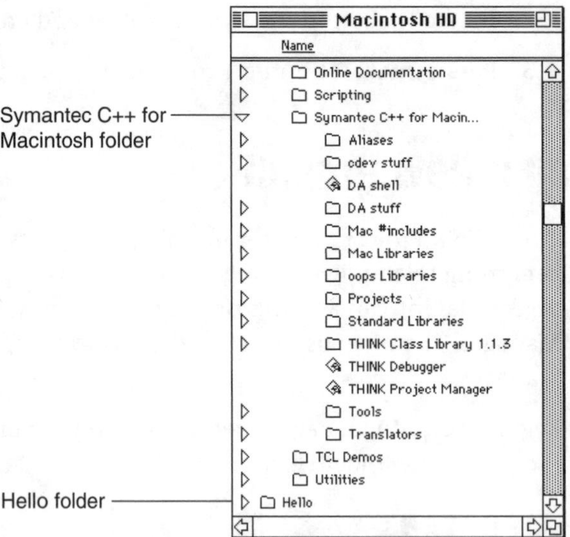

Figure 1.3. Location of your Hello folder.

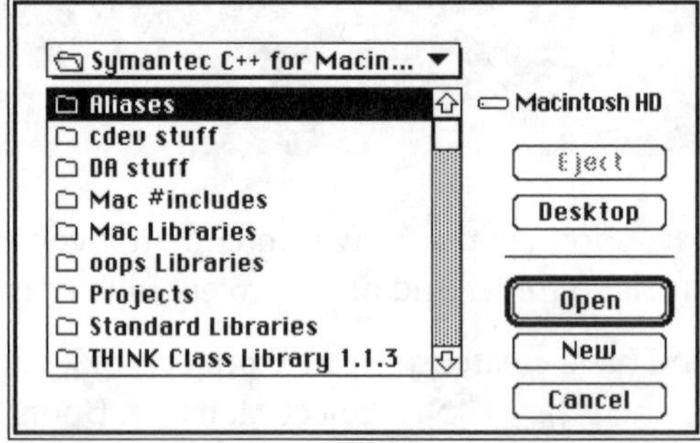

Figure 1.4. The THINK Project Manager initial dialog.

NOTE

Although it is not required, most projects end with the pi character ( ). One reason to follow this convention is that it makes it easy to distinguish project files from source files. Here is a mimetic aide to help you with the rule: Think of the three p's: project, pi, and option-P.

Figure 1.5. Creating the Hello. project.

After you have created the new project, the THINK Project Manager shows you the Project window and its accompanying menus (see fig. 1.6). The Project window also displays a list of all the files in the project; because you have not put any files in the project, the list is empty.

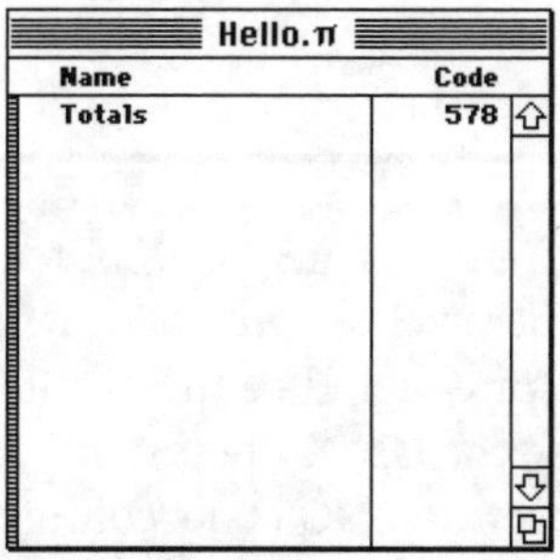

Figure 1.6. The Project window.

Creating a Source File

Create a new untitled window using New from the File menu and type the following source code in it:

```
#include <stdio.h>

void main()
{
    printf("Hello, world!\n");
}
```

After you are finished, save the file in your Hello folder (see fig. 1.7). Name the file Hello.cp.

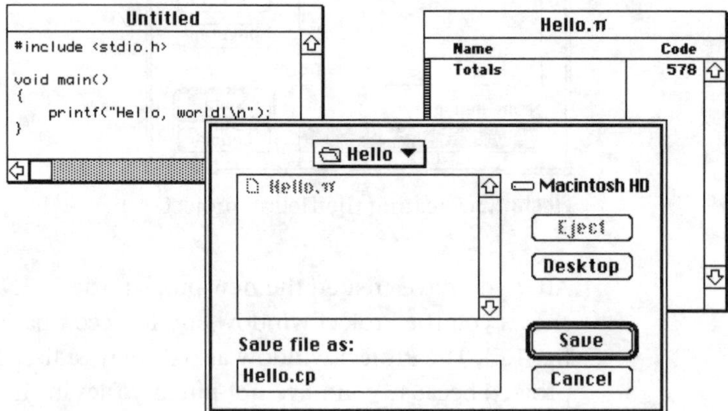

Figure 1.7. Saving Hello.cp.

NOTE

In most development environments, C source files are identified with the suffix `.c`. There is less agreement within the community on the proper suffix for C++ source files. UNIX platforms commonly use `.C` because the UNIX file system differentiates between upper- and lowercase. DOS C++ compilers typically adopt `.cpp` (for C plus plus). On Macintosh, you commonly use `.cp` (for CPlus, the name of the MPW C++ compiler).

With Symantec C++, you can use any suffix you desire, although `.cp` is most common. Chapter 2 describes how to modify your file suffixes to something other than `.cp` or `.cpp`.

Adding a Single Source File to the Project

There are two ways to add files to the project:

- ▼ Use Add Window from the Source menu.
- ▼ Use Add Files from the Source menu.

The first method, Add Window, is somewhat misleading. The menu only displays Add Window when it cannot be used. For example, when the Project window is frontmost, the Add Window item is dimmed (see fig. 1.8).

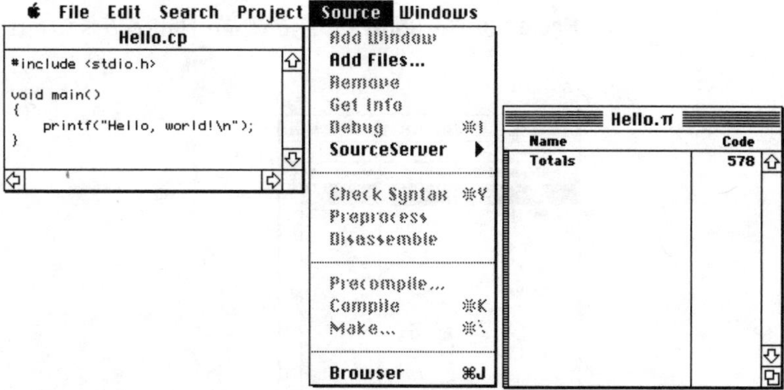

Figure 1.8. The Source menu when the Project window is frontmost.

On the other hand, if your frontmost window is a file that can be added to the project (like the C++ file Hello.cp), the Add Window menu item changes its name. The new name reflects the name of this frontmost window (see fig. 1.9).

Click on the Hello.cp window to make it frontmost and then choose Add 'Hello.cp' from the Source menu to add it to the project. The Project window is updated to reflect the newly added file, as shown in figure 1.10.

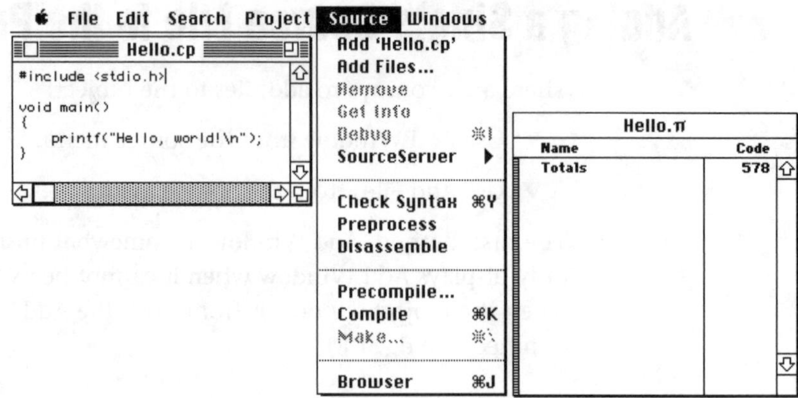

Figure 1.9. The Source menu when Hello.cp is frontmost.

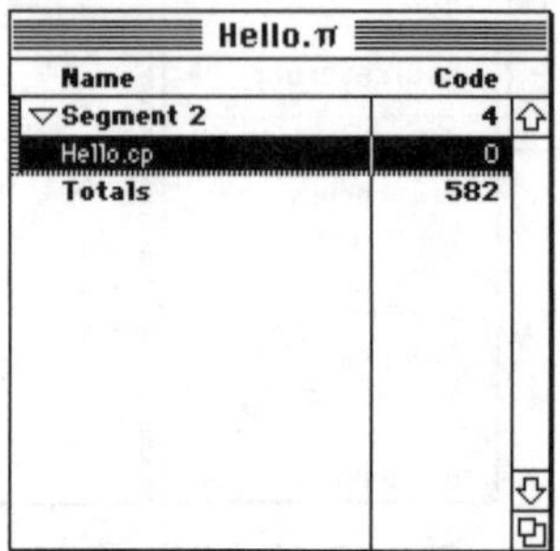

Figure 1.10. The Project window after adding Hello.cp.

Adding Libraries or Multiple Files to the Project

Your program does not link correctly unless you add the necessary libraries to the Hello. project. To do so, select Add Files from the Source menu (see fig. 1.11).

Figure 1.11. Add Files in the Source menu.

The Add Files Dialog

After Add Files is selected, it brings up a dialog. In this dialog, you can add one or more source or library files to the project (see fig. 1.12).

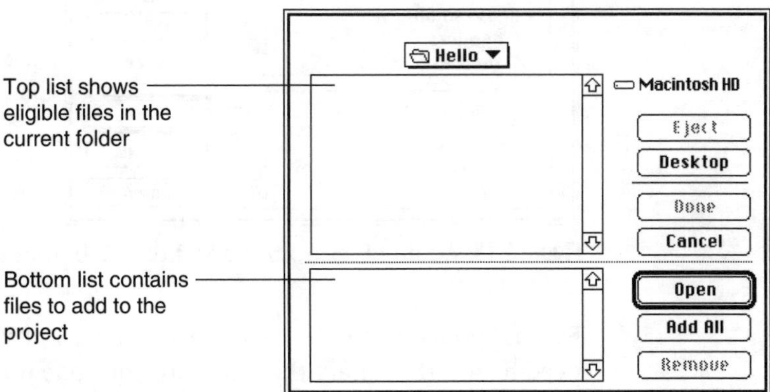

Figure 1.12. The Add Files dialog.

The buttons in the Add Files dialog perform the following actions:

- The Open/Add button moves the selected file from the top list to the bottom list (if a file in the top list is selected) or opens the selected folder (if a folder in the top list is selected).

- The Add All button moves all the files from the top list to the bottom list.
- The Remove button removes the selected file from the bottom list.
- The Done button quits the dialog and adds the files in the bottom list to the project.

Adding Libraries to Projects

After you have selected the Add Files dialog, you need to move to the folder that contains the correct library file. Using the pop-up menu, switch to the Standard Libraries folder, as shown in figure 1.13.

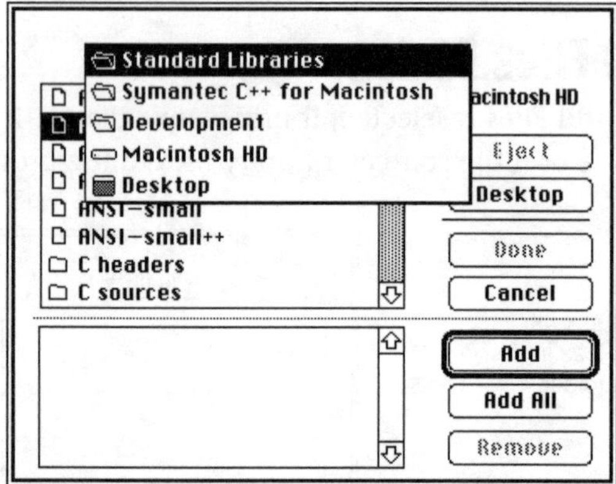

Figure 1.13. Adding files from the Standard Libraries folder.

Because your source file, Hello.cp, contains a `printf` statement, you need to add the library that contains the code for it to the project. The `printf` code is located in the ANSI++ library.

NOTE

By convention, C++ libraries end with the ++ characters.

Select ANSI++ and choose Add (or double-click on ANSI++). The dialog should now look like the one in figure 1.14. Click on Done to add the ANSI++ library and go back to the project.

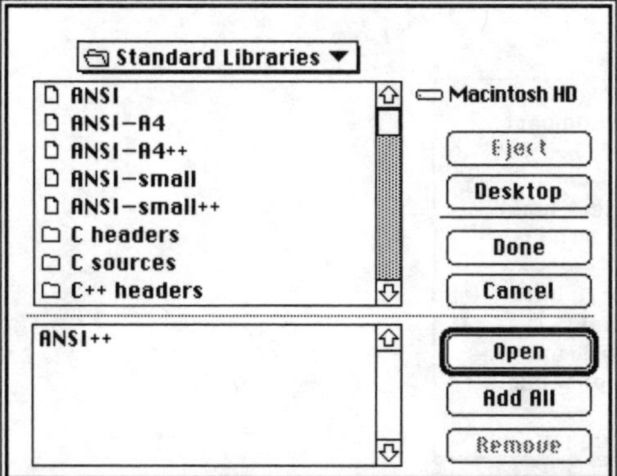

Figure 1.14. The Add Files dialog with ANSI++ in the bottom list.

Source Files in the Project Window

Your Hello. Project window should now have both the ANSI++ and the Hello.cp files in it (see fig. 1.15).

Hello.π

Name	Code
▽Segment 2	4
ANSI++	0
Hello.cp	0
Totals	582

Figure 1.15. The Project window after adding ANSI++.

You do not need any other libraries to link successfully, so it is time to run the program.

Running the Program

You run all programs in the THINK Project Manager the same way: Select Run from the Project menu (see fig. 1.16).

Figure 1.16. Using Run to run your program.

In this case, your program's source files have not been compiled and linked. In such cases, the THINK Project Manager displays the dialog shown in figure 1.17, asking if you want to bring the project up to date before running it.

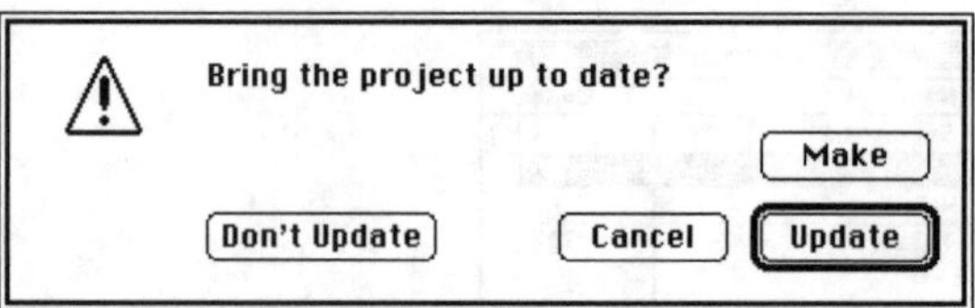

Figure 1.17. The dialog shown when a program needs compiling.

Selecting Update (the default) tells the Project Manager to compile and link the program.

While compiling, the THINK Project Manager displays a progress dialog that it updates as it deals with each file in turn (see figs. 1.18 and 1.19).

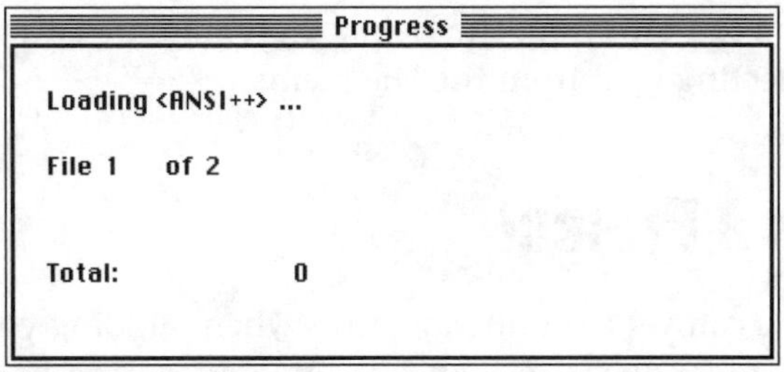

Progress

Loading <ANSI++> ...

File 1 of 2

Total: 0

Figure 1.18. The Progress window showing progress on ANSI++.

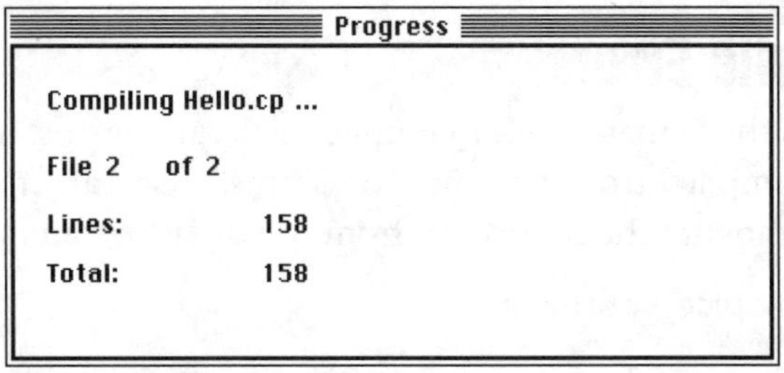

Progress

Compiling Hello.cp ...

File 2 of 2

Lines: 158

Total: 158

Figure 1.19. The Progress window showing progress on Hello.cp.

After successfully compiling each file, the Project Manager runs the program (if it does not, read on about errors). The ANSI++ library sends standard output to a console window (see fig. 1.20).

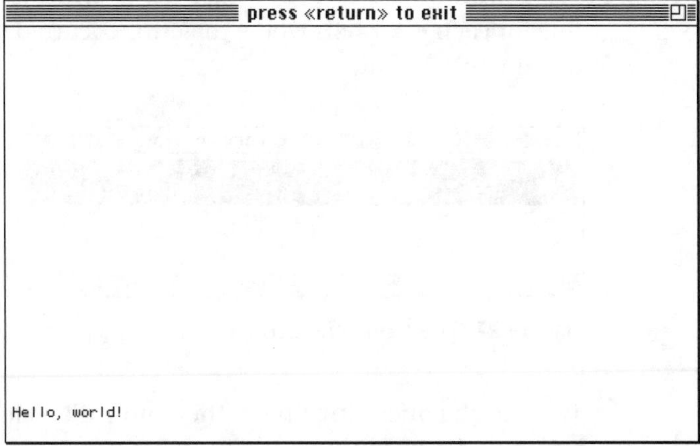

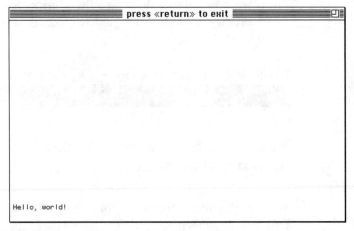

Figure 1.20. Output from running the Hello.cp program.

You can quit from the Hello.cp program by either pressing return or selecting Quit from the File menu.

Errors in a Project

You can get a number of errors when building your program. The compiler may report an error in your source file, or the linker may report an error when linking together all the compiled code.

Compile Errors

As the Symantec C++ compiler generates errors, it puts them in a Compile Errors window. To see this, create an error in Hello.cp by removing the semicolon from the `printf` statement:

```
#include <stdio.h>

void main()
{
    printf("Hello, world!\n")     /* semicolon gone */
}
```

Try to run the program, making sure to click Update when the Project Manager asks you about bringing the project up to date. The Compile Errors window appears showing a list of errors (see fig. 1.21). The first line for each error tells where the error occurred, and the second line describes the error.

Figure 1.21. The Compile Errors window.

To go to the offending line in the source file, select the error and press return or double-click on it. This takes you to the line where the compiler thinks the error occurred (see fig. 1.22).

Figure 1.22. Going to the line with the error.

As commonly happens with compilers, the selected line is the one immediately following the line with the actual error. Fix the error by adding the deleted semicolon and save the file.

Link Errors

The linker links together calls to functions with the code for those functions. Thus, if you call a function whose code is not present in the project, the linker reports an error. To see this in action, select ANSI++ in the Hello. Project window. Choose Remove from the Source menu (see fig. 1.23).

Figure 1.23. Using Remove to remove a file from the project.

Having assured yourself of failure, try to run the program (click Update to bring the project up to date). The linker displays an alert (see fig. 1.24) that tells you that the link failed. You can click on the link alert to make it go away. The THINK Project Manager displays a Link Errors window that describes exactly why the link failed.

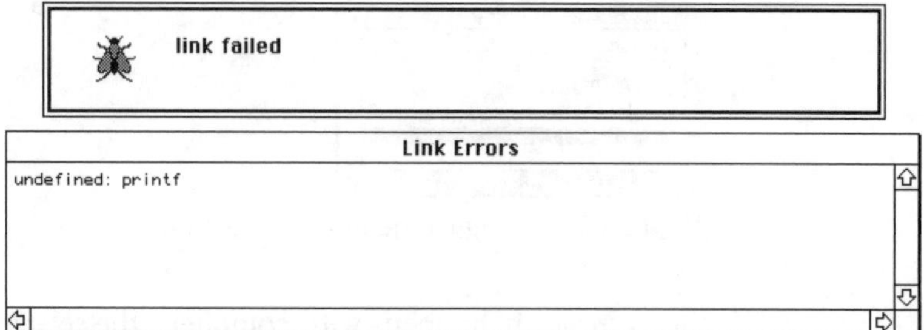

Figure 1.24. A link failure.

The error message, `undefined: printf`, in the window indicates that the source for the `printf` call could not be found. Add ANSI++ back to your project, and run your program again to get everything in working order.

NOTE

If you get the `undefined: main` link error, this means that the file containing your `main` function is not in your project.

Avoiding Dialogs

Using the THINK Project Manager preferences dialog, you can turn off confirmation dialogs you find unnecessary (or annoying). Select THINK Project Manager from the Options item in the Edit menu (see fig. 1.25).

Avoiding the Project Update Dialog

To turn the Project Update dialog off, go to the Preferences panel in the THINK Project Manger Options dialog. Uncheck Confirm project updates, as shown in figure 1.26. The THINK Project Manager now automatically brings your project up to date before running it.

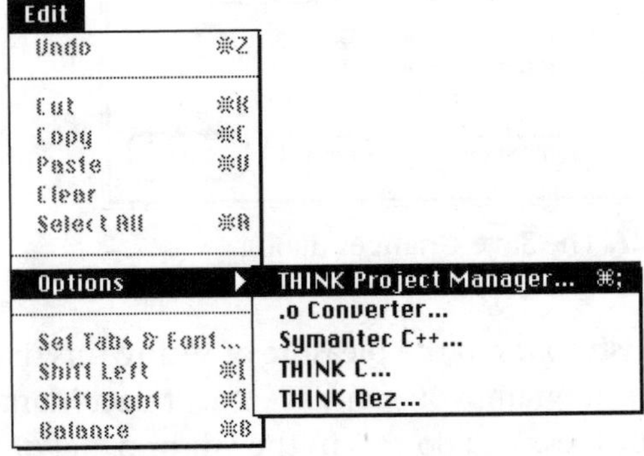

Figure 1.25. Setting options for the THINK Project Manager.

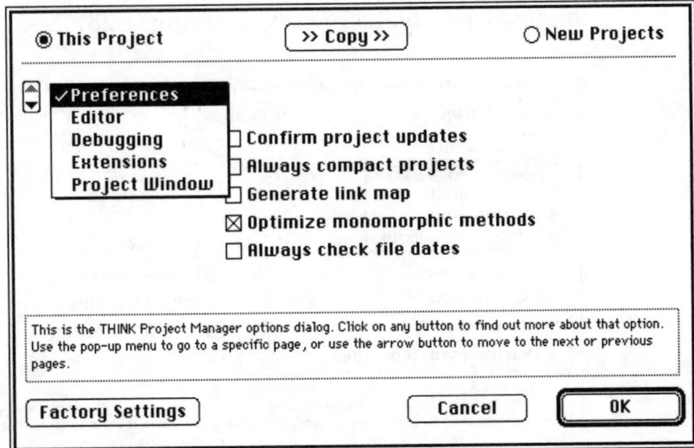

Figure 1.26. The Preferences panel of the THINK Project Manager Options dialog.

Avoiding the Save Changes Dialog

Before your program is actually run, but after it is built, the THINK Project Manager asks if you want to save changes to any modified source files (see fig. 1.27). The reasoning behind such an offer should be obvious: If your program crashes forcing a reboot, you lose any changes to unsaved files.

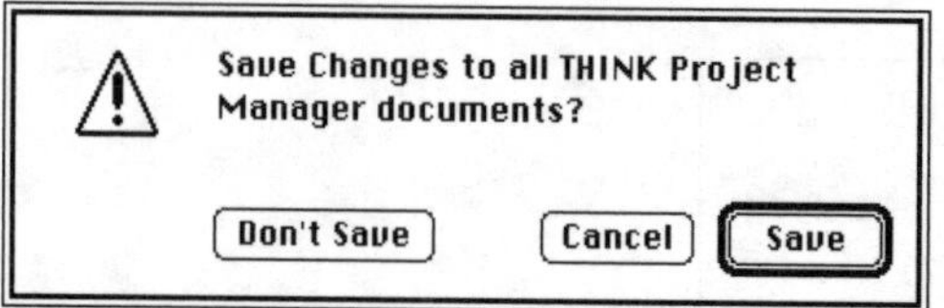

Figure 1.27. The Save Changes dialog.

If you wish to forgo the pleasure of seeing this dialog every time you run your program, you can have the Project Manager automatically save your files. You do this in the Editor panel of the THINK Project Manager Options dialog. Use the panel pop-up to select Editor. After you uncheck the Confirm saves check box, the Project Manager no longer alerts you before saves (see fig. 1.28).

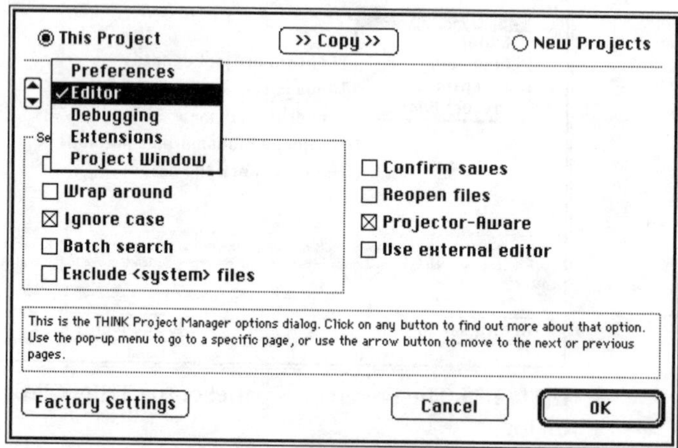

Figure 1.28. The Editor panel of the THINK Project Manager Options dialog.

Project-Building Shortcuts

The following are some shortcuts you can use in a project to help make life easier:

▼ When the Project window is frontmost, you can type the name of a file to select it (this works the same as the Finder).

- ▼ To open a file that is selected in the Project window, double-click on it or press return.
- ▼ Option-clicking on the title bar of a source file brings up a pop-up menu of its include files. For example, option-clicking anywhere on the Hello.cp title bar shows you its two include files: size_t.h and stdio.h (see fig. 1.29). To open an include file, select it from this pop-up menu.

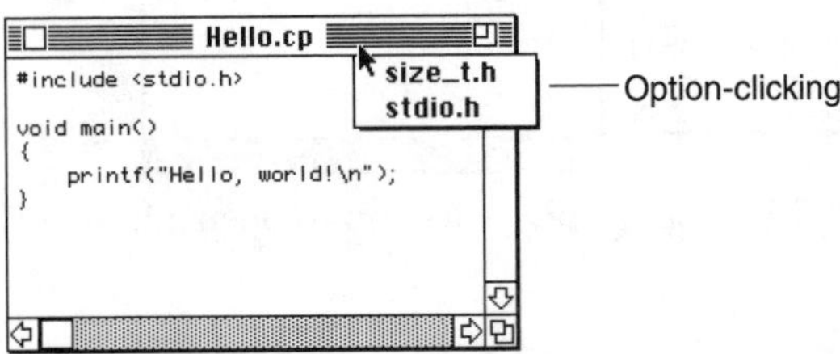

Figure 1.29. Option-clicking on the title of a source file.

- ▼ Option-clicking anywhere on the title bar of the Project window brings up a pop-up menu of the include files used by all the source files (see fig. 1.30). You can open any include file by selecting it.

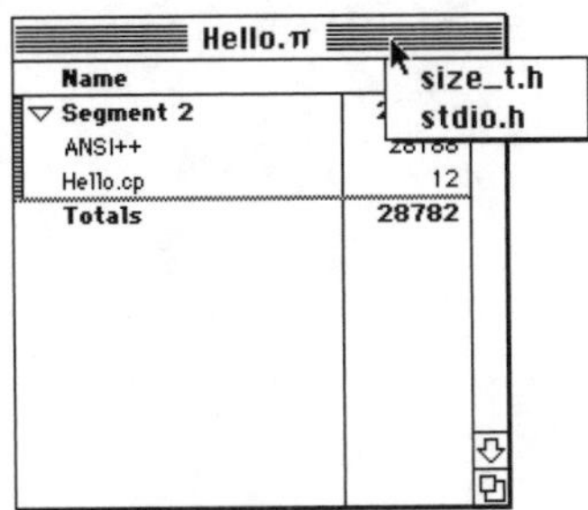

Figure 1.30. Option-clicking on the title of the Project window.

- ▼ Another way to open an include file is to select its name in a source file and then choose Open Selection from the File menu (see fig. 1.31).

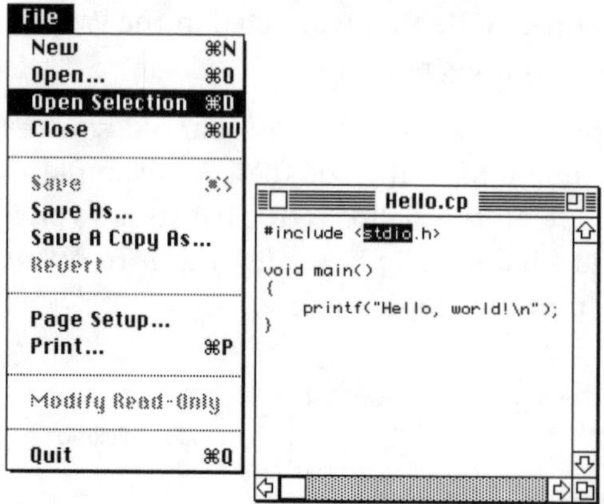

Figure 1.31. Using Open Selection to open a header file.

Summary

You should now feel fairly comfortable with the THINK Project Manager and its accompanying windows for viewing source files and listing errors. You also should know how to select certain options to lessen the number of interrupts during the running of your project. Next, you learn to use the THINK Project Manager to work with a larger project—one with multiple files and segmentation.

2

A Multiple-File Project

In a large, multiple-file project, there are a number of tasks you have to perform. The most obvious task—writing the source files—is only the beginning. Before you are through, you also need to know how to do the following:

- Add libraries to the project, including knowing which ones to use and where to find them.
- Use `#include` file syntax to take advantage of the THINK Project Manager's file-searching rules.
- Compile just one file.
- Check for syntax errors without having to do a costly compile.
- Slim down your projects when you need to send them to someone else or free up space on your drive.
- Search through files to find routines that you and time have forgotten.
- Segment your project.
- Use both the THINK C and Symantec C++ compilers on the same project.

You eventually may encounter each of these situations as the size of your projects grow. This chapter explains when you might encounter each problem and how to handle it in a multiple-file project. This chapter does not, however, contain an exhaustive treatment of the Symantec C++ project environment or multiple-file issues for that matter. For more information, you should refer to the program documentation.

You cannot progress further, however, until you get a bunch of source files created and put in a project.

Adding More Files to a Project

Either create a new MultipleFiles. project or open the MultipleFiles. project on the source file disk. The seven files that make up the project are: Main.cp, Reverse.h, Reverse.cp, Factorial.h, Factorial.cp, Average.h, and Average.cp. The code is provided below for your reference.

Here is the code for Main.cp:

```
#include <stdio.h>
#include "Factorial.h"
#include "Reverse.h"
#include "Average.h"

void main()
{
    int    i;
    char   s[] = "Neil Rhodes";
    char   palindrome[] = "Madam, I'm Adam";
    double values[] = {3.1, 4.1, 5.9, 15.6, 16.3, 15.7};

    for (i = 0; i < 14; i++)
        printf("Factorial(%i) = %ld\n", i, Factorial(i));

    printf("Reverse(\"%s\") = ", s);
    Reverse(s);
    printf("\"%s\"\n", s);

    printf("Reverse(\"%s\") = ", palindrome);
    Reverse(palindrome);
    printf("\"%s\"\n", palindrome);
```

```
    printf("Average() = %lf\n",
      Average(values, sizeof(values) / sizeof(values[0])));
}
```

The code for Reverse.h is as follows:

```
#pragma once

void Reverse(char *s);
```

The code for Reverse.cp is as follows:

```
#include "Reverse.h"
#include <string.h>

static void Swap(char *c1, char *c2)
{
        char tmp;

        tmp = *c1;
        *c1 = *c2;
        *c2 = tmp;
}

void Reverse(char *s)
{
    int length = strlen(s);
    int midPoint = length / 2;
    int i;

    for (i = 0; i < midPoint; i++)
        Swap(&s[i], &s[length - i - 1]);
}
```

Listed below is the code for Factorial.h:

```
#pragma once

unsigned long Factorial(unsigned long n);
```

Following is the code for Factorial.cp:

```
#include "Factorial.h"

unsigned long Factorial(unsigned long n)
{
    unsigned long result = 1;
    unsigned long i;

    for (i = 2; i <= n; i++)
        result *= i;
    return result;
}
```

Here is the code for Average.h:

```
#pragma once

long double Average(double *values, int numValues);
```

Here is the code for Average.cp:

```
#include "Average.h"
#include <SANE.h>

long double Average(double *values, int numValues)
{
    long double total = 0.0;
    int         i;

    for (i = 0; i < numValues; i++)
        total += values[i];
    if (numValues > 0)
        return total / numValues;
    else
        return 0.0;
}
```

Using Add Files in the Source menu, add the .cp files to the MultipleFiles. project. When complete, it should match the project shown in figure 2.1.

If you try and run the project at this point, without adding the necessary libraries, you get the link error shown in figure 2.2.

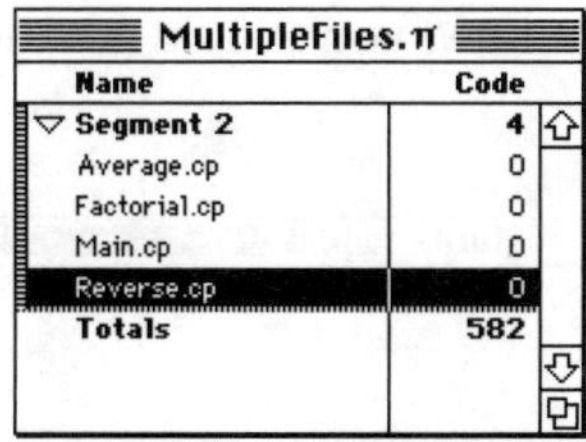

Figure 2.1. The Project window with source files.

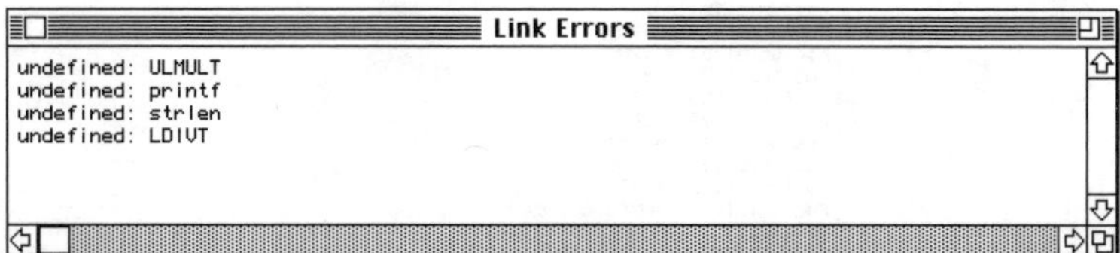

Figure 2.2. Link error due to missing libraries.

Add the necessary libraries so that the program runs. The `printf` and `strlen` routines used in Main.cp and Reverse.cp are defined by ANSI C. As you might have guessed, they are found in the ANSI++ library.

Reviewing the source code reveals that it never directly calls `ULMULT` and `LDIVT`. Instead, these routines are called by the compiler to do unsigned long multiplication and long division. Because the 68000 does not have instructions to implement these operations, you need to get the subroutines that support them from a library. Which library are they in?

Gaining knowledge about library contents is not an overnight process. If you are not a library expert, here are some of the solutions to which you might resort:

- Read through the product documentation on each library and its contents (the speed-reader's solution).
- Use trial and error by trying each library in turn (the solution for programmers who disdain documentation).
- Ask the resident library expert or just memorize that the CPlusLib library contains the necessary routines (the pragmatic solution).

Now that you know what libraries fix the problem, add them to the project. Using Add Files, put CPlusLib and ANSI++ in your project (both are found in the Standard Libraries folder).

Try running the program now; you should get the output shown in figure 2.3.

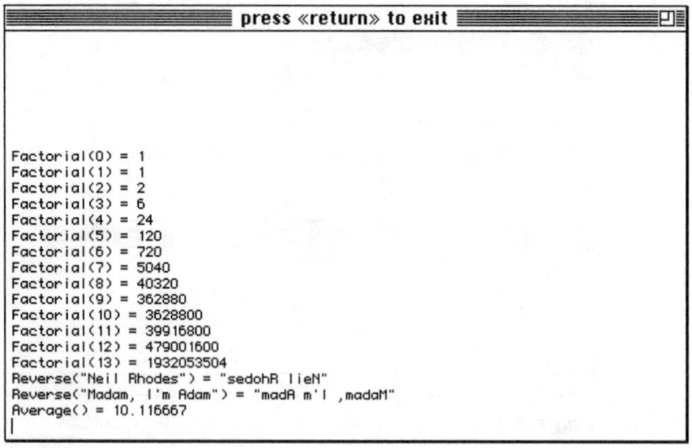

```
press «return» to exit

Factorial(0) = 1
Factorial(1) = 1
Factorial(2) = 2
Factorial(3) = 6
Factorial(4) = 24
Factorial(5) = 120
Factorial(6) = 720
Factorial(7) = 5040
Factorial(8) = 40320
Factorial(9) = 362880
Factorial(10) = 3628800
Factorial(11) = 39916800
Factorial(12) = 479001600
Factorial(13) = 1932053504
Reverse("Neil Rhodes") = "sedohR lieN"
Reverse("Madam, I'm Adam") = "madA m'I ,madaM"
Average() = 10.116667
```

Figure 2.3. Output of the MultipleFiles program.

Adding Include Files

If you look again at the include statements in the source files, you see two variations in syntax. Symantec C++ (like most C and C++ compilers) differentiates between #include statements that use <> and those that use " ".

If you use the #include <File.h> syntax in a source file, the compiler looks for File.h in the THINK tree. That is, the compiler starts searching in the THINK Project Manager folder and looks through all of the subfolders there.

If you use the #include "File.h" syntax, the compiler searches for File.h in the project tree. It starts looking in the folder containing the current project and then looks through all subfolders. If it does not find File.h there, it looks through the THINK tree.

Because of this search order, follow the two rules below for faster compiles.

RULE

Use #include `<_>` for standard include files (like `stdio.h` or `Quickdraw.h`). Otherwise, the compiler unnecessarily looks through your project tree for files it finds in the THINK tree.

RULE

Do not put your projects in the THINK tree. This way the compiler does not have to search additional include files in the THINK tree when doing an `#include` from another project.

The THINK Project Manager also searches when it looks for source files. This is a refinement that enables you to keep your project headers and your project sources in whatever folder structure you wish. (The file location must remain within the project tree, however.) Figure 2.4 shows a sample rearrangement of the files of the MultipleFiles project. Even if you use such a subfolder arrangement, the project still compiles and runs.

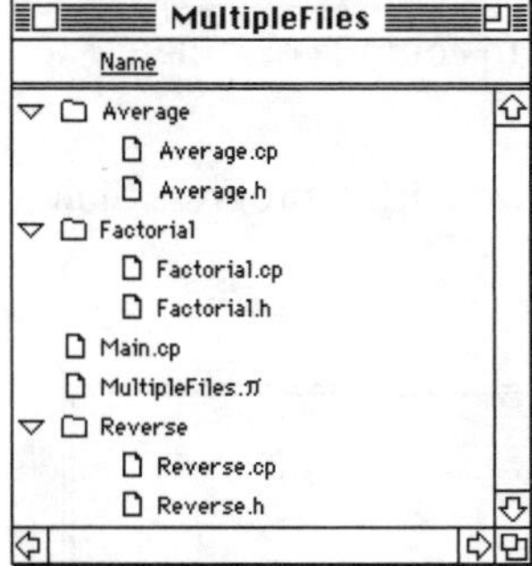

Figure 2.4. Moving files into subfolders.

Compiling a Single File

When you have a large project, you may not want to build the whole program; instead, you may want to compile just one file. For instance, if you have not written all your source code, doing a build may produce link errors. The THINK project manager enables you to compile a single file by using the Compile command from the Source menu.

To see how this operates, open Average.cp and make it frontmost. Select Compile (see fig. 2.5) and watch what happens.

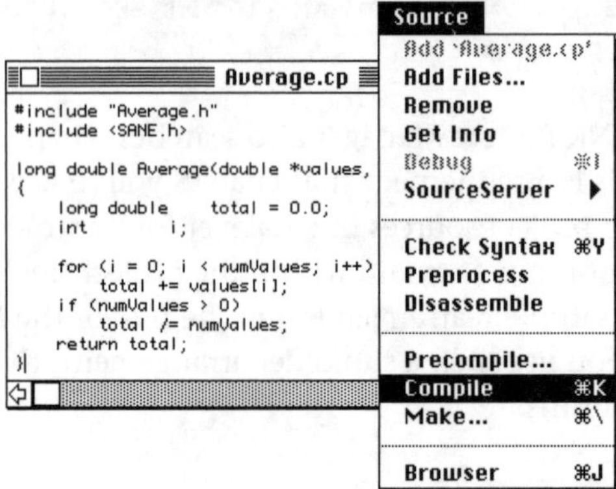

Figure 2.5. Using Compile to compile one file.

The compiler presents you with a progress dialog, as shown in figure 2.6.

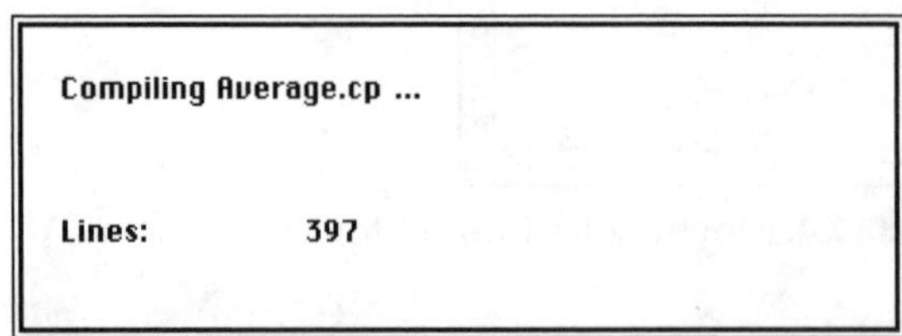

Figure 2.6. The Progress dialog when compiling one file.

This is the best way to compile single files in a project. However, it is not the only shortcut you can take; there is an even briefer route.

Checking for Syntax Errors

As is often the case on a project, you compile only to find syntax errors. You may not be finished writing the code for a file, but may want to snag any bugs introduced so far. If this is the case, then you want to use the Check Syntax command. This choice enables you to run through the compilation process without generating any object code. It is quicker than a compile because there is no code to generate, but it still provides the same errors and warnings.

To try this command, open Average.cp and remove a semicolon. Now that you have doomed yourself to failure, choose Check Syntax from the Source menu (see fig. 2.7).

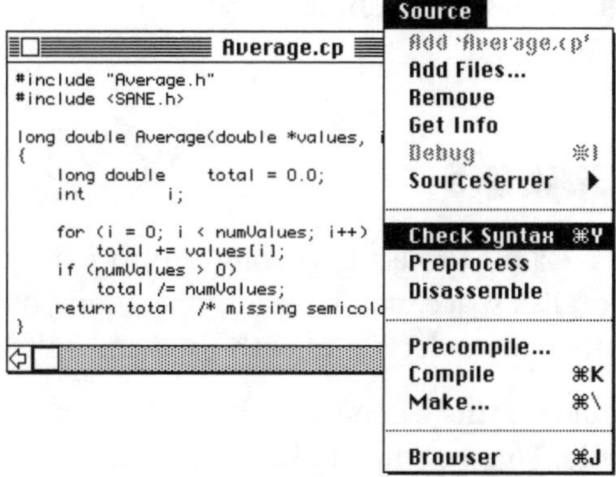

Figure 2.7. Running Check Syntax on a file.

This syntax check generates an error in the Compile Errors window, as shown in figure 2.8.

Before going further, put the semicolon back where it belongs.

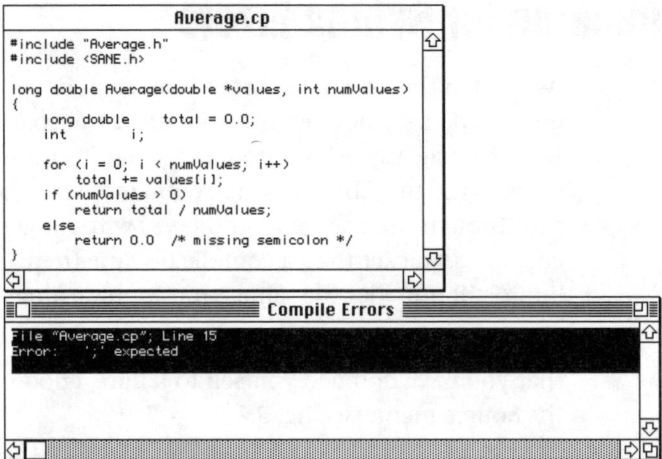
Average.cp
#include "Average.h"
#include <SANE.h>
long double Average(double *values, int numValues)
{
long double total = 0.0;
int i;
for (i = 0; i < numValues; i++)
total += values[i];
if (numValues > 0)
return total / numValues;
else
return 0.0 /* missing semicolon */
}
Compile Errors
File "Average.cp"; Line 15
Error: ';' expected

Figure 2.8. The results of Check Syntax.

Removing Objects

If you have a big project that you want to send to someone else or you are out of disk space, you have a problem on your hands. The solution is to remove the objects files with the Remove Objects command.

You should do this whenever you need to reduce the size of your project file. To give you an idea of the change in size, look at the MultipleFiles project before and after removing objects. Before removing the objects, the file size was 136K. This goes down to a slim 12K after the objects are eliminated.

To give this a try, select Remove Objects from the Project menu, as shown in figure 2.9.

You get a confirmation dialog (see fig. 2.10) that indicates the next build has to start from scratch.

Figure 2.9. Removing all objects from the project.

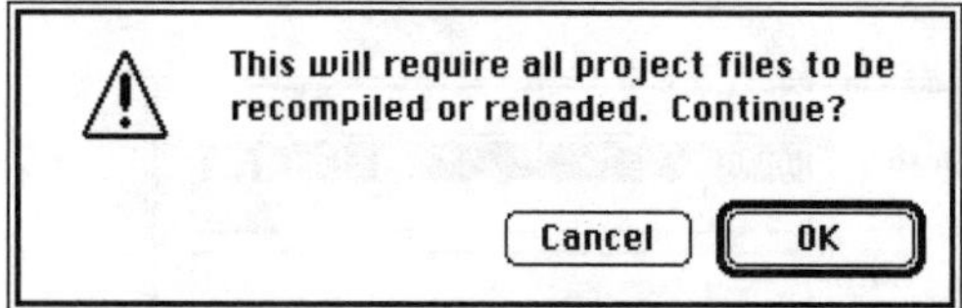

Figure 2.10. The Remove Objects confirmation dialog.

Searching through Multiple Files

Another aspect of a large multiple-file project is that only those lucky few with eidetic memory can remember where every routine is located. The THINK Project Manager provides sophisticated search facilities for the rest of the population. As well as searching through the current window, the Project Manager searches through multiple files.

To see how the search facility works, select Find from the Search menu (see fig. 2.11).

This brings up a dialog that has a place to enter the search string, as well as various search options (see fig. 2.12).

To conduct a multiple-file search, check the Multi-File Search check box. This, in turn, brings up a dialog in which you select the files you want to search (see fig. 2.13).

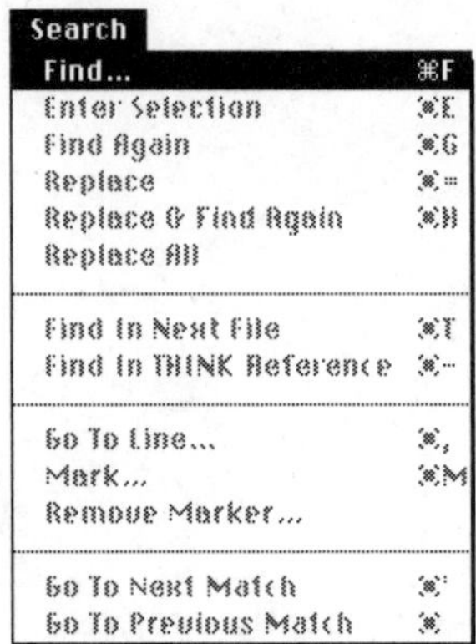

Figure 2.11. Using Find from the Search menu.

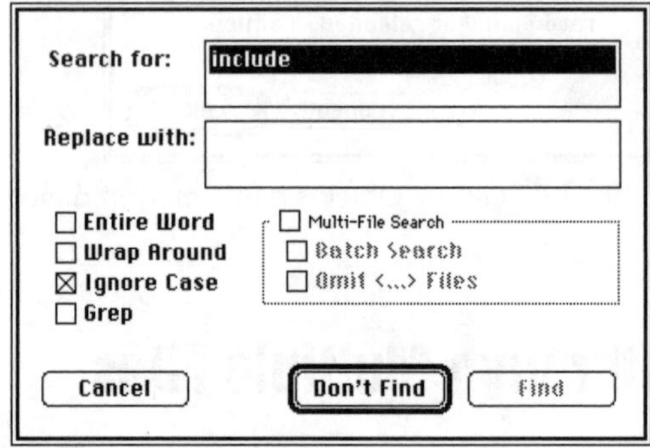

Figure 2.12. The Find dialog.

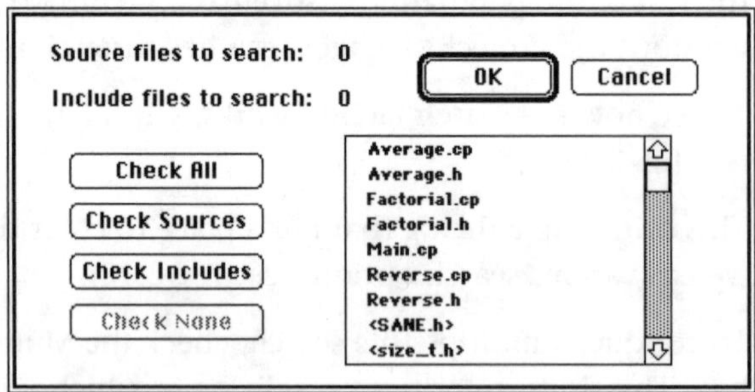

Figure 2.13. The Multi-File Search dialog.

Click on a file in the list to checkmark it. All checkmarked files are searched. You also can use the buttons on the left as shortcuts:

- The Check All button checks all files.
- The Check Sources button checks only source files.
- The Check Includes button checks only include files.
- The Check None button unchecks all files.

For your purposes, you want to click Check All (or press command-A) to checkmark all the files (see fig. 2.14). Click OK to return to the Find dialog.

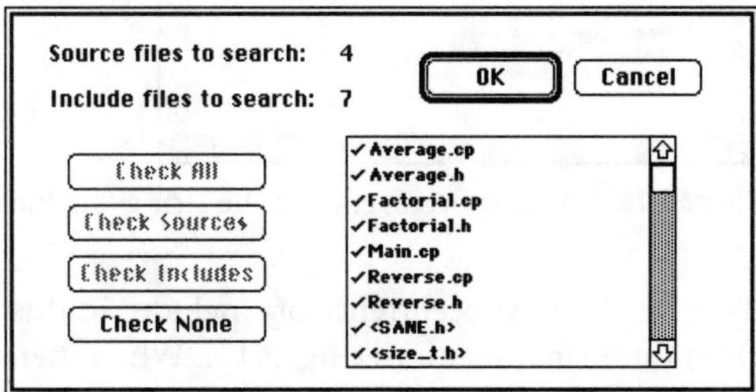

Figure 2.14. After pressing Check All.

When you click on the Multi-File Search check box, it brings up the Multi-File window. After someone plays with the option awhile, the same question is always asked: How do you turn the check box off if the Multi-File Search dialog always comes up? The answer is that you option-click on it. A shortcut for turning it on (and selecting all files) is to type command-A in the Find dialog.

You perhaps noticed the two check boxes under the Multi-File Search check box. When you select the Omit <...> Files option, the search skips any files in the THINK tree and only searches through files in your project. The other option, Batch Search, has to do with the two ways the THINK Project Manager has of presenting the results of searches. Both of these ways are covered in the following sections.

One-at-a-Time Searches

If Batch Search in the Find dialog is not checked, the THINK Project Manager presents the matching lines one at a time. To try this, click on the Find button in the dialog (making sure you are searching for "include"). The Project Manager opens the first file in which it finds the string "include" (see fig. 2.15).

```
Average.cp
#include "Average.h"
#include <SANE.h>

long double Average(double *values, int numValues)
{
    long double     total = 0.0;
    int             i;

    for (i = 0; i < numValues; i++)
        total += values[i];
    if (numValues > 0)
        return total / numValues;
    else
        return 0.0;
}
```

Figure 2.15. The first occurrence of the string "include."

To go to the next occurrence of "include" in this file, use Find Again from the Search menu (see fig. 2.16). When there are no more occurrences in a file, Find Again beeps. To find the next file containing the string, use Find In Next File from the same menu (see fig. 2.16).

Figure 2.16. The Search menu while a multiple-file search is in progress.

Batch Searches

The other alternative is for the THINK Project Manager to output a list of matching lines in a window. To do this sort of search, check the Batch Search check box in the Find dialog. Figure 2.17 shows you the window that results from a batch search of "include."

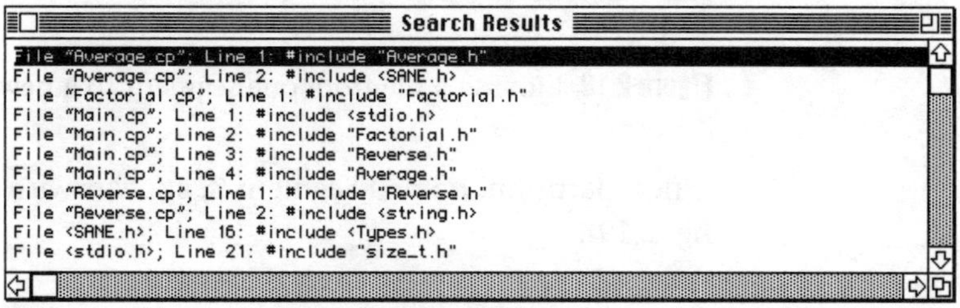

```
Search Results
File "Average.cp"; Line 1: #include "Average.h"
File "Average.cp"; Line 2: #include <SANE.h>
File "Factorial.cp"; Line 1: #include "Factorial.h"
File "Main.cp"; Line 1: #include <stdio.h>
File "Main.cp"; Line 2: #include "Factorial.h"
File "Main.cp"; Line 3: #include "Reverse.h"
File "Main.cp"; Line 4: #include "Average.h"
File "Reverse.cp"; Line 1: #include "Reverse.h"
File "Reverse.cp"; Line 2: #include <string.h>
File <SANE.h>; Line 16: #include <Types.h>
File <stdio.h>; Line 21: #include "size_t.h"
```

Figure 2.17. The Search Results window.

To go from a matching line shown in the window to the file containing that line, select the line in the window and press return (or just double-click on it). The THINK Project Manager opens the file at that line. You also can sequence through each of the lines by using the Go To Next Match and Go To Previous Match choices in the Search menu.

Segmenting Your Program

On the Macintosh, you break your code into code segments. These segments are loaded on demand and then unloaded with the Toolbox call UnloadSeg. The size of each of these segments needs to be less than 32K. The THINK Project Manager enforces this restriction at link time.

When you start a new THINK project, all of your code is in one segment. You create a new segment by doing the following:

1. Select the file you want to place in a new segment and hold the mouse button down on it.
2. Drag the file below the wavy line that follows the last filename.

Try that now with the Average.cp file. Create a new segment by dragging the file below the line under Reverse.cp (see fig. 2.18).

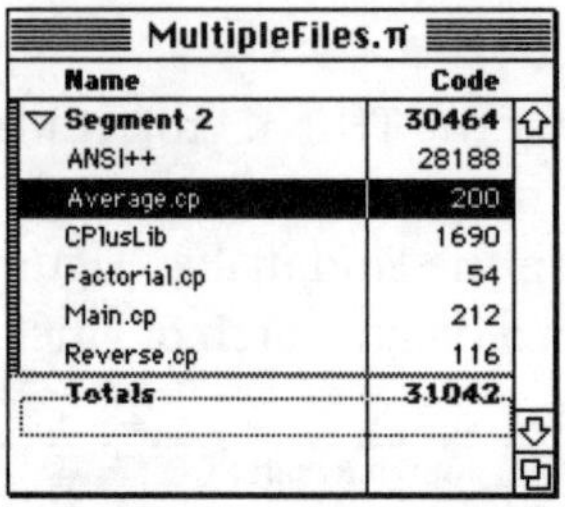

MultipleFiles.π

Name	Code
▽ Segment 2	30464
ANSI++	28188
Average.cp	200
CPlusLib	1690
Factorial.cp	54
Main.cp	212
Reverse.cp	116
Totals	31042

Figure 2.18. Moving a file from one segment to a new segment.

A new partition, named Segment 3, appears with Average.cp in it (see fig. 2.19).

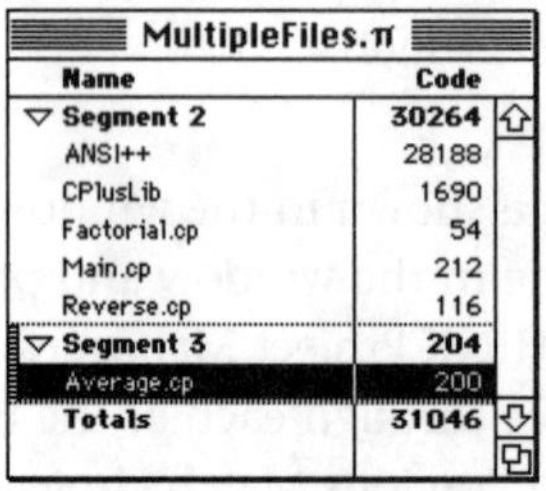

MultipleFiles.π

Name	Code
▽ Segment 2	30264
ANSI++	28188
CPlusLib	1690
Factorial.cp	54
Main.cp	212
Reverse.cp	116
▽ Segment 3	204
Average.cp	200
Totals	31046

Figure 2.19. After creating a new segment.

A dotted line separates one segment from another. Notice also that within each segment the files are alphabetized. If you want to move a file from one segment to another, just drag it to the other segment. To create another new segment, drag a file below the last segment.

A real problem arises in your project if you let a segment get too big. This impels the linker to notify you with an error message like the one in figure 2.20. To fix the problem, move some of the files from that segment to a different segment. To reduce the segment size correctly, you need to concentrate on the files with the largest size. The code size of each file is provided in the Project window (see fig. 2.19 above) to help you decide on the rearrangement.

Figure 2.20. Linker error if a code segment exceeds 32K.

Using Both C and C++

With the advent of Symantec C++, the THINK Project Manager enables you to mix both C and C++ in your project. There are some situations that might be ideal for this setup:

- You have a large C code base. Although C++ is mostly a superset of ANSI C, there are certain C language constructs that C++ does not accept (for instance, C++ requires function prototypes). While it is easy to write new C code that can be compiled with both C and C++, it can be tedious to update old C code. Thus, if you have a large C code base that does not compile with C++, it may be easier to have a multiple-compiler project.
- You want to use in-line assembler. Symantec C++ does not support in-line assembler. Because THINK C does, any function that needs in-line assembler needs to be done in C.

If you are going to have a multiple-language project, there are two critical issues that affect the structure of your project:

- You need to make sure that the right compiler is used. File extension configuration is necessary because the THINK Project Manager chooses the compiler based on the file extension (or suffix). If you use the extension `.c` for your C files and `.cp` for your C++ files, the right compiler will be used.
- Calling between C and C++ requires some C++ code modification. You need to make some changes to your C++ code to be able to call a C routine or to enable C to call your C++ routine. For each call from C++, or vice versa, the routine declaration needs to be modified to signify to the C++ compiler that a cross-language call will occur.

For the C++ compiler, add the following line before the declaration:

```
extern "C" {
```

And, add the following line after the declaration:

```
}
```

Here is an example of the change:

```
extern "C" {
void MyCRoutine(const char *s);
}
```

This special C++ syntax is usually within an `#ifdef` statement (the `cplusplus` symbol is automatically defined by Symantec C++). This way the header file containing the declaration can be shared between C and C++.

```
#ifdef __cplusplus
extern "C" {
#endif

void MyCRoutine(const char *s);

#ifdef __cplusplus
}
#endif
```

Create a new duo-language project (ideal for midnight DuoBook compiles). Name the project GoodnightMoon. . Listed below are the sources for the program. Pay special attention to code that calls C from C++ and vice versa:

Here is the code for Main.cp:

```
#include "CRoutine.h"

void main()
{
    CRoutine("Goodnight, moon");
}
```

Listed below is the code for CRoutine.h:

```
#pragma once

#ifdef __cplusplus
```

```
extern "C" {
#endif

void CRoutine(const char *s);

#ifdef __cplusplus
}
#endif
```

The code for C++Routine.h is as follows:

```
#pragma once

#ifdef __cplusplus
extern "C" {
#endif

void CPlusPlusRoutine(const char *s);

#ifdef __cplusplus
}
#endif
```

Here is the code for CRoutine.c:

```
#include <stdio.h>
#include "CRoutine.h"
#include "C++Routine.h"

void CRoutine(const char *s)
{
    printf("CRoutine: got %s\n", s);
    CPlusPlusRoutine(s);
}
```

The code for C++Routine.cp is as follows:

```
#include <stdio.h>
#include "C++Routine.h"

void CPlusPlusRoutine(const char *s)
{
    printf("CPlusPlusRoutine: got %s\n", s);
}
```

File Extensions

Symantec C++ for Macintosh also contains some other translators besides C and C++. A translator is responsible for taking a file from the project and translating it in a way appropriate for the final application.

Following is a list of the translators included with Symantec C++:

Symantec C++	This compiles C++ source code to 68000 object code.
THINK C	This compiles C source code to 68000 object code.
THINK Rez	This compiles Rez source code to resources.
Resource Copier	This copies a resource file to the resource fork of the program.
«none»	This does nothing—quite usefully. It is for a project file that might be used for documentation but still must reside in the project. With this file extension, the file can stay in the project without affecting the final program.
.o Converter	This converts an MPW .o object file to THINK Project Manager 68000 object code.

The THINK Project Manager uses these suffixes (or extensions) to determine which compiler to use. If you do not use the default extensions, as shown in table 2.1, you may need to change the settings.

Table 2.1. Default Extensions and Their Associated Translators

Extension	Translator
.cp and .cpp	Symantec C++
.c and .asm	THINK C
.r	THINK Rez
.rsrc	Resource Copier
.o	.o Converter
.note	«none»

To change extension settings or create your own extension types, select the THINK Project Manager from the Options dialog. From the Extensions panel of that dialog, you can see the default mappings and change them (see fig. 2.21).

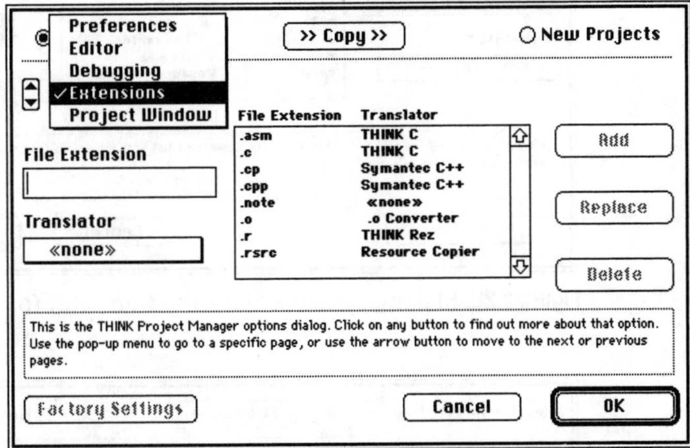

Figure 2.21. The Extensions panel of the THINK Project Manager Options dialog.

Practice changing the extensions and the translator. Start by changing the translator for .c files from THINK C to Symantec C++. Here is how you do it:

1. Select .c from the extensions list.
2. Select Symantec C++ from the Translator menu.
3. Click Replace (see fig. 2.22).

Now, create a new extension to use with documentation files. (This is done by adding a «none» translator for .doc extensions.) Do the following:

1. In the Extensions panel, type .doc in the File Extension text box.
2. Select «none» from the translator pop-up and click Add (see fig. 2.23).

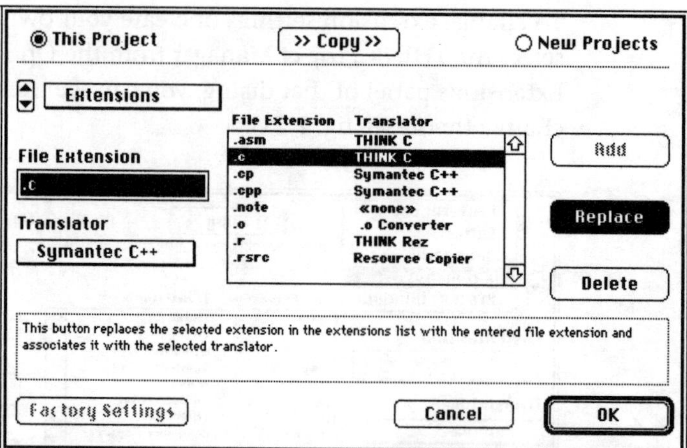

Figure 2.22. Making Symantec C++ the translator for .c files.

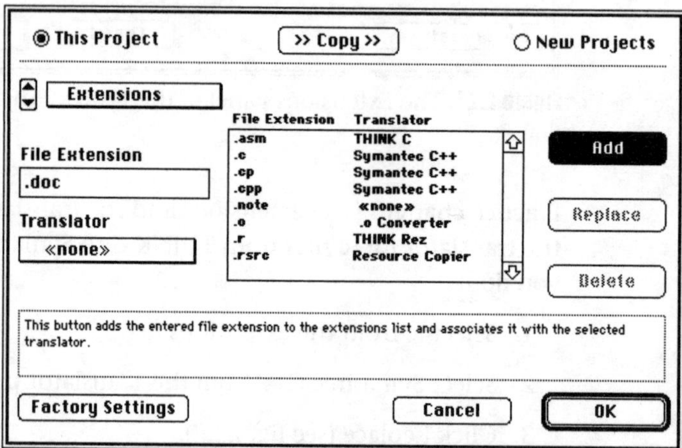

Figure 2.23. Making «none» the translator for .doc files.

You should now see a new extension for <<none>>, as shown in figure 2.24.

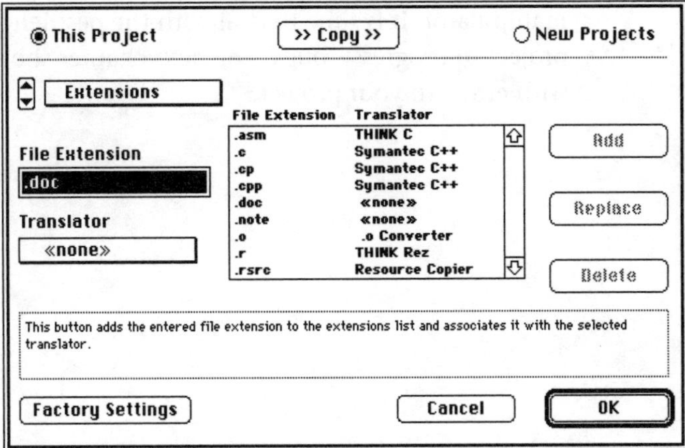

Figure 2.24. <<none>> with a new file extension.

Summary

At this point, you should have a fairly good understanding of all of the following:

- Adding multiple files to a project.
- Figuring out which libraries are needed for a project.
- Writing `#include` file syntax in-line with THINK Project Manager searching rules.
- Compiling just one file or checking for syntax errors without doing a full build.
- Removing objects from projects to slim down their sizes.
- Searching through project files to find a forgotten routine.
- Segmenting your projects properly using the rules described.
- Creating a multiple-language project that uses both THINK C and Symantec C++ compilers.

If you are not completely comfortable with these skills, you can either review the related section of the chapter again or look at the Symantec C++ documentation. Now, that you are a THINK Project Manager manipulator, it is time to deal with the pestilence that attacks any project in progress—bugs. The next chapter shows you how to deal with errors in your project.

3

Interpreting Error Messages

Like other compilers, the Symantec C++ compiler generates error messages whenever your code is not syntactically correct. Unlike some, Symantec C++ also provides warning messages whenever your code is slightly sloppy. Because the compiler goes to the trouble of generating these warning messages, you should do something with them. While it is true that warnings need not be eliminated for a successful compile, they do point out possible problems in your code. Thus, this chapter focuses on teaching you the following:

- Symantec C++'s method of presenting compile and link error messages.
- Understanding the error messages you get.
- Determining the number of error messages that the compiler reports.

- Understanding warning messages.
- The rationale for modifying code that produces warnings.
- How to configure the compiler so that is does not send you warning messages.

Before you can learn to fix errors and warnings, however, you need a sample program that produces a plethora of them.

An Error-Ridden Sample Program

Following is an example program that generates a number of errors and warnings. You can either create a new project named Errors. with the following source files or open the project file on the source code disk. Your project should consist of five source files: Main.cp, Reverse.h, Average.h, Reverse.cp, and Average.cp. For reference, the source listings of these files with each error commented are listed below.

The code for Main.cp is as follows:

```
#include <stdio.h>
#include "Reverse.h"
#include "Average.h"

void main()
{
    int     i;
    char    s[] = "Neil Rhodes";
    char    palindrome[] = "Madam, I'm Adam";
    double  values[] = {3.1, 4.1, 5.9, 15.6, 16.3, 15.7};

    printf("Reverse(\"%s\") = ", s);
    Reverse(s);
    printf("\"%s\"\n", s);

    printf("Reverse(\"%s\") = ", palindrome);
    Reverse(palindrome);
    printf("\"%s\"\n", palindrome);
```

```
    printf("Average() = %lf\n", Average(values,
      sizeof(values) / sizeof(values[0])));
}
```

Here is the code for Reverse.h:

```
#pragma once

void Reverse(char *s);
```

Here is the code for Average.h:

```
#pragma once

long double Average(double *values, int numValues);
```

Listed below is the code for Reverse.cp:

```
#include "Reverse.h"
#include <string.h>

static void Swap(char *c1, char *c2)
{
    char tmp;

    tmp = c1;     /* should be *c1 */
    c1 = c2;      /* should be *c1 and *c2 */
    c2 = tmp;     /* should be *c2 */
}

void Reverse(char *s)
{
    int length = strlen(s);
    int midPoint = length div 2;    /* should be /, not div */
    int i;

    for (i = 0; i < midPoint; i++)
        Swap(&s[i], &ss[length - i - 1]); /*should be s, not ss*/
}
```

The code for Average.cp is as follows:

```
#include "Average.h"
#include <SANE.h>

long double Average(double *values, int numValues)
{
    long double total = 0.0;
    int         i;

    for (i == 0; i < numValues; i++) /* should be =, not == */
        total += values[i];
    if (numValues > 0)
        return total / numValues;
    else
        return;                         /* should be return 0.0 */
}
```

After the project files are added, your Project window should look like the one in figure 3.1.

Errors.π

Name	Code
▽ Segment 2	2130
Average.cp	158
CPlusLib	1690
Main.cp	162
Reverse.cp	116
Totals	2708

Figure 3.1. The Errors. Project window.

The Compile Errors of an Error-Ridden Program

Try to build the program (by using Run or Bring Up To Date in the Project menu). As the files compile, the Compile Errors window should begin listing the following error messages:

```
_File "Average.cp"; Line 9
Warning: value of expression is not used

_File "Average.cp"; Line 14
Error:   no return value for function 'Average'
```

```
_File "Reverse.cp"; Line 8
Error:   cannot implicitly convert
from:<*>char
to  :char

_File "Reverse.cp"; Line 10
Error:   cannot implicitly convert
from:char
to  :<*>char

_File "Reverse.cp"; Line 16
Error:   '=', ';' or ',' expected

_File "Reverse.cp"; Line 20
Error:   undefined identifier 'ss'
```

As you can see, the compiler tries to compile each file even after it finds the first error—it examines the entire file. Even if it finds errors in one file, the compiler still tries to compile the rest. After the compiler completes its task, you can turn to the Compile Errors window and look at the results of its hard work. You can double-click on each error (see fig. 3.2) or select it and press Return. This takes you to the file and line on which the error occurred.

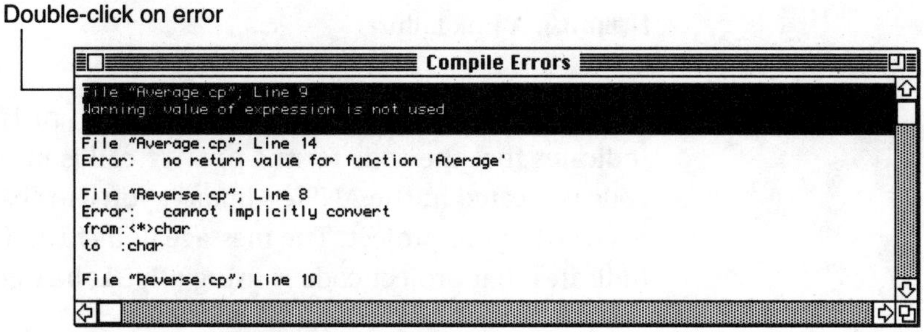

Double-click on error

Compile Errors

```
File "Average.cp"; Line 9
Warning: value of expression is not used

File "Average.cp"; Line 14
Error:   no return value for function 'Average'

File "Reverse.cp"; Line 8
Error:   cannot implicitly convert
from:<*>char
to  :char

File "Reverse.cp"; Line 10
```

Figure 3.2. The Compile Errors window.

You can use the up and down arrow keys to move up and down through the list of errors. You also can use Go To Previous Error and Go To Next Error menu items (in the Search menu) to take you backward and forward through the listings.

If you have a number of errors in a file, you might want to adopt the strategy of starting with the last error and working your way backward. Because fixing an error can involve adding or deleting lines, the earlier error line numbers stay correct if you work in reverse order.

Link Errors

The linker connects calls to functions with their code. It also connects the uses of globals with their definitions. Thus, if you call a function that does not have code in the project, the linker reports an error. It also displays an alert (for example, see fig. 3.3) that tells you that the link failed. Just click on the link alert to make it disappear and go to the Link Errors window to learn the cause of failure.

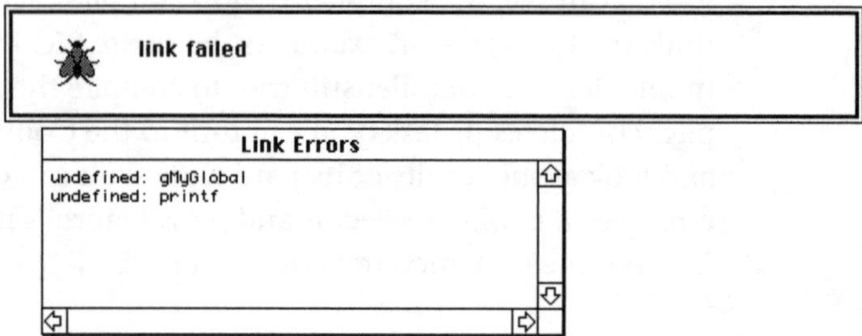

Figure 3.3. A link failure.

In this case, the error message `undefined: printf` in the window indicates that the code for the `printf` call is missing. Because this code is located in the ANSI++ library, you can fix this error by adding ANSI++ to your project. The message `undefined: gMyGlobal` indicates that project code is using `gMyGlobal` even though it has not been defined.

You can get link errors from any of the following:

- Missing code for a function.
- Missing the definition of a global variable.
- A segment is too large.

Examine these three cases:

- Link error from missing function code. A function can be missing code if you fail to add a library or a source file. Link errors also can happen if you have a name or argument type mismatch between the call of the function and its definition.

- Link error from a missing global variable definition. When you create a global variable, you should declare it in an include file with an `extern`:

  ```
  extern int gMyGlobal;
  ```

  In one source file, you should then define it this way:

  ```
  int gMyGlobal;
  ```

  The problem occurs if you declare the global in the include file, but fail to define it in a source file. In this case, the linker notifies you that the global is undefined.

- Link error from a large code segment. On the Macintosh, you must break your code into code segments. These segments are loaded on demand and then unloaded with the Toolbox call `UnloadSeg`. The size of each segment needs to be less than 32K. The THINK Project Manager enforces this restriction at link time by giving you an error if your segment is too large.

Choosing the Number of Errors To Report

Symantec C++ gives you control over how many errors are reported per file. To configure this setting, bring up the Symantec C++ options dialog by selecting Symantec C++ from the Options menu in the Edit menu (see fig. 3.4).

Then, use the pop-up menu to select the Debugging panel, as shown in figure 3.5.

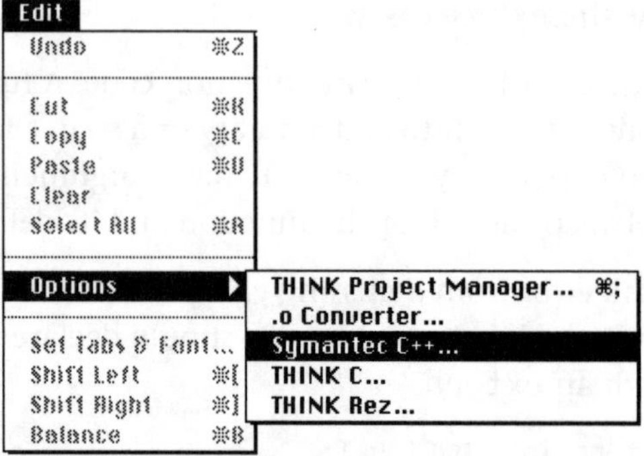

Figure 3.4. Bringing up the Symantec C++ options dialog.

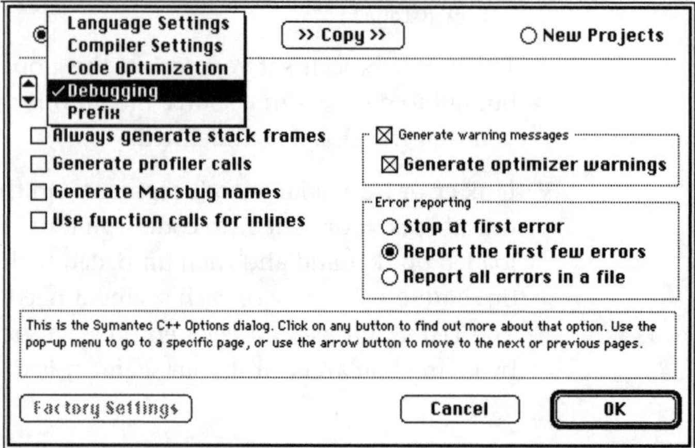

Figure 3.5. The Debugging panel of the Symantec C++ Options dialog.

In the error-reporting section of the panel, you get three separate choices. You can report only the first error in a file, the first few errors, or all of them. The wisest choice usually is to select the Report the first few errors option. Choosing the Stop at first error option only enables you to fix one error per file per build—usually a rather time-consuming method. On the other hand, choosing the Report all errors in a file option can inundate you with an avalanche of errors. This is especially true because compilers commonly get confused by a single error and generate many spurious ones as a result.

Getting Rid of Warnings

Symantec C++ generates numerous warning messages as well as error messages. The intention of a compiler warning is different from an error message, however. A warning points to code that the compiler believes may have an error. As a result of this flexibility in interpretation, some programmers routinely ignore warnings. They figure that, if the warning were really important, it would have been an error message. Other more cautious programmers examine the code that generates warnings. They either find an actual error and fix it or, more likely, find that the warning is spurious and ignore it. Then there is the final class of programmers who examine the code that causes warnings and fix it all. If there is an error they fix it; if the warning is spurious, they modify the code so that it no longer produces the warning.

Establishing a Philosophy about Warnings

You should strive to be in this last class, with code that compiles with no warnings. There are three important benefits to this approach:

- Satisfaction in a job well done. It is inherently more satisfying to have the compiler accept your code without argument. It is no different than building a house. Although it may be sufficient to pass code, you have no source of pride when the building inspector says "Well, it will pass code, but I really don't like the way you hung the drywall, or the way you strung the Romex, or the way you vented this fan."
- The increased capability to notice new warnings. If your project compiles with 43 warnings, are you really going to notice when the 44th warning appears? Warnings are mostly chaff with a sprinkle of wheat thrown in. By removing spurious warnings, you easily can notice the appearance of new warnings that could be serious.
- Others have an easier time maintaining your code. Programmers are more secure working on code without warnings. Someone new to the code especially needs to be able to notice new warnings that they might introduce—something much harder to do if it is the 44th warning.

The Three Rules of Warning Elimination

Now that you are filled with renewed vigor to produce warningless code, it is time to learn the right method for doing so. Follow the rules listed below:

1. Determine whether the warning is an actual error or spurious.
2. Fix the actual errors.
3. Rewrite the code that produces spurious warnings so it no longer produces warnings.

See how you should use these rules. Start with the first one. For example, when Symantec C++ thinks a semicolon is added incorrectly, it generates this warning:

```
Warning: possible extraneous ';'
```

The following generates the warning for an `if` statement:

```
if (i == 3);
    i++;
```

This generates one for a `while` loop:

```
while ((*s)++ != '\0');
```

In the above examples, the `if` statement is certainly a real error—the semicolon closes the `if`, so `i` always is incremented. The `while` loop, however, is probably not an error—it increments `s` until it reaches the end of the string.

If the warning signifies an actual error, follow the second rule and fix it. For the `if` statement, the fix is to remove the extra semicolon:

```
if (i == 3)
    i++
```

If the warning does not signify an actual error, follow the third rule and modify the code so that it does not generate a warning. For the `while` loop, an adequate fix is as follows:

```
while ((*s)++ != '\0')
    ; /* do nothing */
```

An even better fix is available, however:

```
while ((*s)++ != '\0')
{
    /* do nothing */
}
```

Either modification not only keeps the compiler from producing a warning, but more clearly communicates the intention of the `while` loop to the code reader.

If you simply cannot stand warnings, Symantec C++ does enable you to turn them off. Go to the Debugging panel of the Symantec C++ Options dialog (see fig. 3.6) to do so.

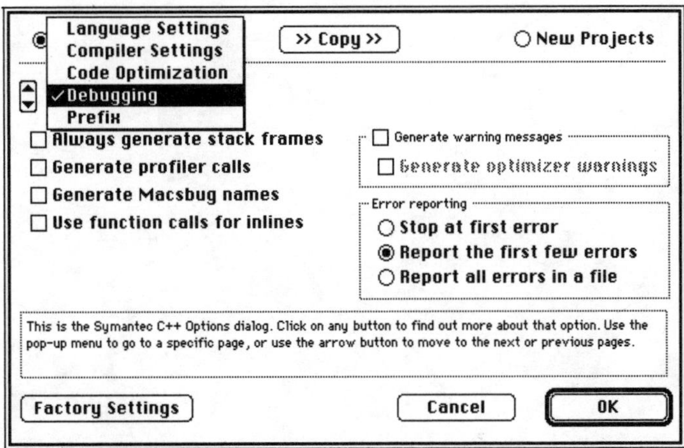

Figure 3.6. The Debugging panel of the Symantec C++ Options dialog.

If you uncheck the Generate warning messages check box, you will not receive any warnings. If you uncheck the Generate optimizer warnings check box, you will not receive the warnings based on information from the optimizer. (For details on the exact messages, see Chapter 14.)

While turning warnings off can never be condoned, it can be argued that programmers who never look at warnings in the first place do not need to see them at all.

Summary

You now should be ready to handle the error and warning messages you receive when building your programs. You also can determine how many error messages you want to see for each file—a feature sorely missed by earlier users of THINK C. You also should have a clear understanding of the need to clean up your code so that it does not produce spurious warning messages. And, though no one wanted to tell you, you now know how to turn the warnings off.

4

Debugging a Program

Symantec C++ provides a debugging resource to help you find code errors in your applications. This resource, the THINK Debugger, is a source-level debugger well worth the small amount of time it takes to learn. This chapter describes how to use the Debugger to do the following:

- ▼ Walk through your code statement by statement.
- ▼ Move through or display the entire call chain of a function.
- ▼ Move from the Debugger into the Source window to edit code.
- ▼ Set breakpoints in the Debugger and in your code.
- ▼ Examine variable values and call functions from within the Debugger.
- ▼ Configure your code to use a low-level debugger, such as MacsBug, when using the THINK Debugger is not feasible.

Having mastered each of these skills, you should be able to use the THINK Debugger effectively. But, because you cannot debug in the dark, the first topic is obvious—turning the Debugger on.

Turning On the Debugger

If you are ready to debug your source files, select Use Debugger from the Project menu (see fig. 4.1).

Figure 4.1. Selecting Use Debugger from the Project menu.

A check mark appears next to Use Debugger, as shown in figure 4.2.

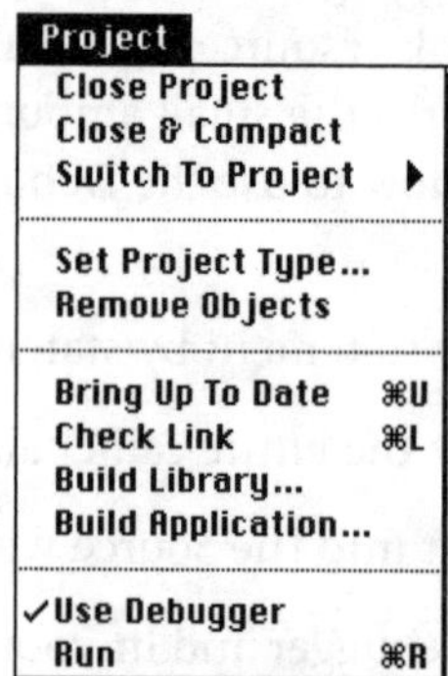

Figure 4.2. The Debugger is active.

The Project window also slightly alters because it reserves room on the left side of each source file for a diamond symbol (see fig. 4.3).

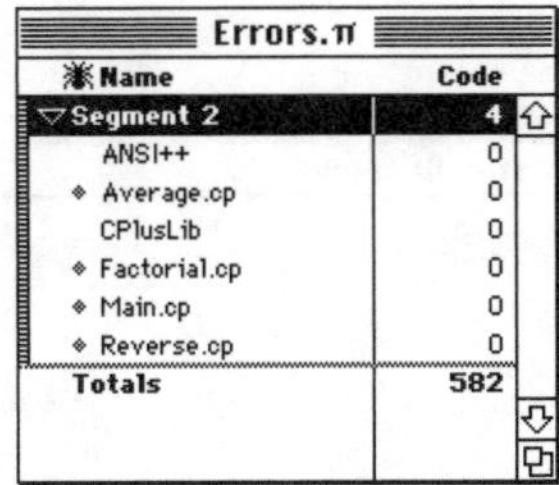

Figure 4.3. Main.cp, Reverse.cp, Factorial.cp, and Average.cp can be debugged.

The diamond signifies that the THINK Debugger can debug a source file. To enable debugging of a file, click to the left of the filename in the Project window. This toggles the diamond symbol. If the diamond is present, the file can be debugged; if it is not present, the file cannot be debugged. To turn debugging on or off for all source files simultaneously, option-click to the left of any filename.

NOTE

You normally want all compiler optimization off while debugging because it can rearrange when and how the code gets executed. One example of the influence of optimization is that multiple source statements can execute as one statement in the debugger. To turn off optimization, select the Code Optimization panel from the Symantec C++ Options dialog and uncheck Use Global Optimizer.

Starting Programs with the Debugger Activated

After Use Debugger is turned on, select Run. The THINK Project Manager immediately launches the THINK Debugger, and the Debugger window appears. The first line of your program is displayed in the Debugger window (see fig. 4.4). Because the Debugger actually is an application that the THINK Project Manager launches, it has its own menu bar.

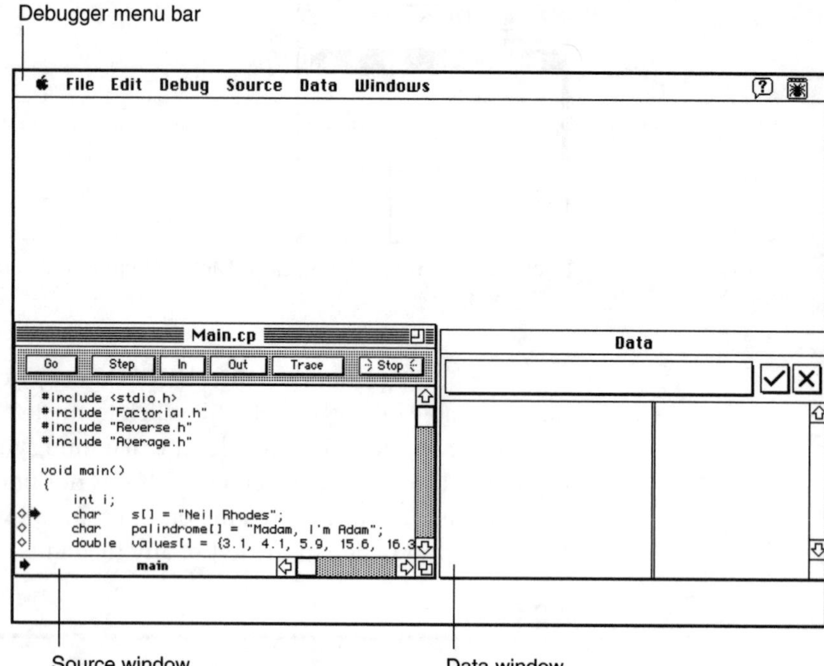

Figure 4.4. The THINK Debugger screen.

Command Options

If you look at the window where the source code is displayed, you see the Go, Step, In, Out, Trace, and Stop buttons. These are the commands that enable you to control the execution of your program. Along with these commands, the window also displays information about the running program. Look at figure 4.5 to see the Source window and the titles of its parts.

The current statement arrow points to the statement that executes next. You use the Status panel buttons to control program execution. The readouts show what is happening in your program. If the Go button is selected, your program is running; if the Stop button is selected, your program has stopped. In figure 4.5, the Stop button is selected.

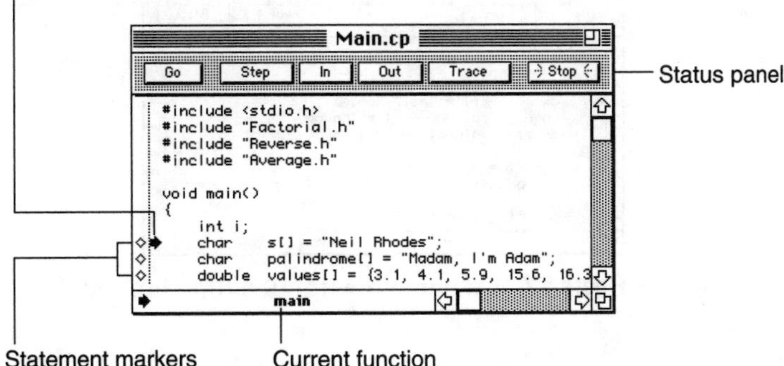

Figure 4.5. The Source window.

As an alternative to pressing a button, each command can be selected in the Debug menu and has command key equivalent (see fig. 4.6).

Debug	
Go	⌘G
Step	⌘S
Step In	⌘I
Step Out	⌘O
Trace	⌘T
Stop	⌘.
Go Until Here	⌘H
Skip To Here	
Monitor	⌘M
ExitToShell	

Figure 4.6. The Debug menu.

The Step Command

If you select Step, the current statement gets executed, and the Debugger stops. All function calls in the statement are stepped over (that is, ignored). If you are at the end of a function, Step returns you to the calling function. Figures 4.7 and 4.8 show before and after stepping over a statement without a function call.

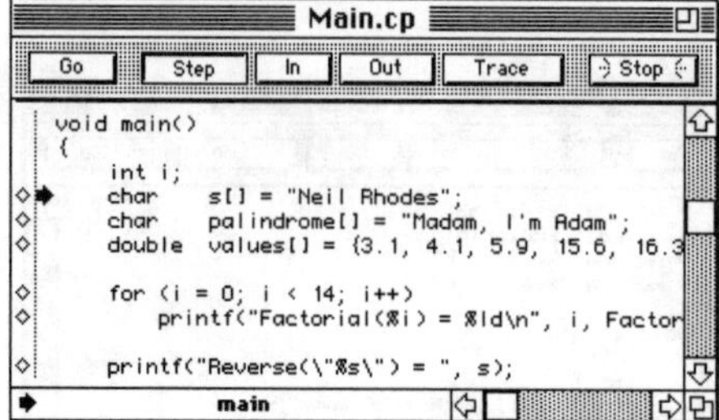

Figure 4.7. A statement without a function call.

```
{
    int i;
    char    s[] = "Neil Rhodes";
    char    palindrome[] = "Madam, I'm Adam";
    double  values[] = {3.1, 4.1, 5.9, 15.6, 16.3

    for (i = 0; i < 14; i++)
        printf("Factorial(%i) = %ld\n", i, Factor

    printf("Reverse(\"%s\") = ", s);
    Reverse(s);
```

Figure 4.8. After stepping over the statement.

As mentioned above, the stepping action steps over statements that have function calls. Figures 4.9 and 4.10 show before and after stepping over a function call statement.

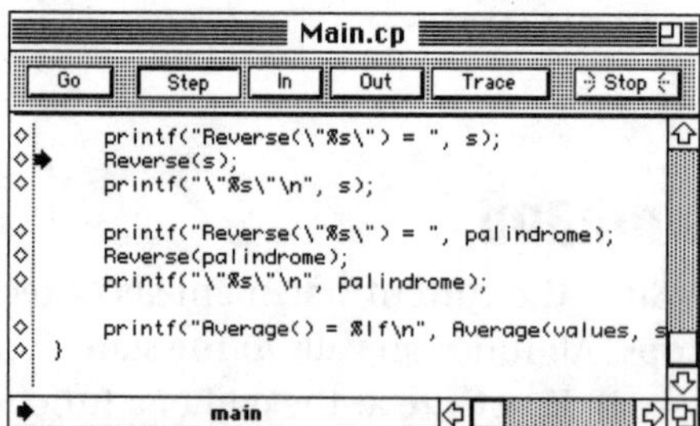

Figure 4.9. Before stepping over a function call.

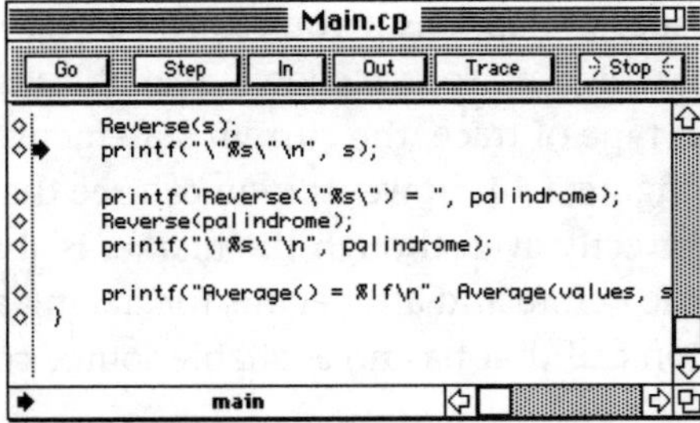

Figure 4.10. After stepping over a function call.

The Trace Command

If you select Trace, the Debugger still executes one statement and then stops. If the current statement contains a function call, however, the Debugger moves to the called function code and stops at the first statement there. Figures 4.11 and 4.12 show how tracing works on this kind of statement.

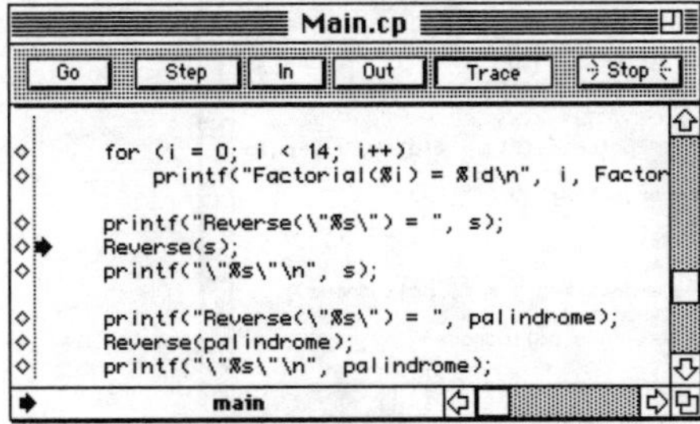

Figure 4.11. Before tracing into a statement with a function call.

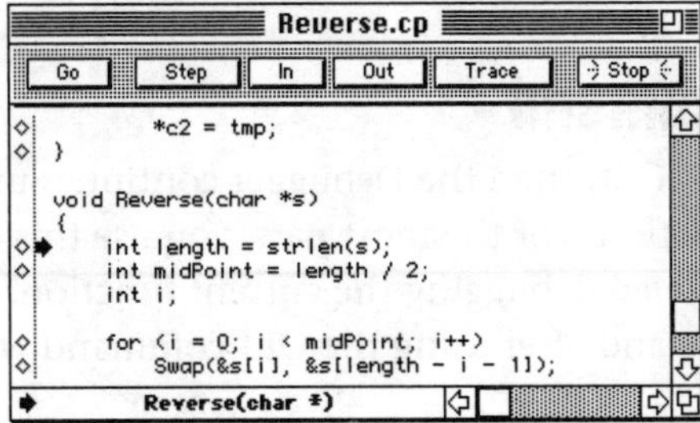

Figure 4.12. After tracing into a function call.

Something special happens if you request a Trace command on a function for which no source code is available, such as a library. If you perform this type of trace, the current statement marker disappears. If you look at figure 4.14, however, you can see that the current file is displayed correctly even though the marker is absent. Figures 4.13 and 4.14 show the before and after status for tracing a statement containing a function call that has no available source code.

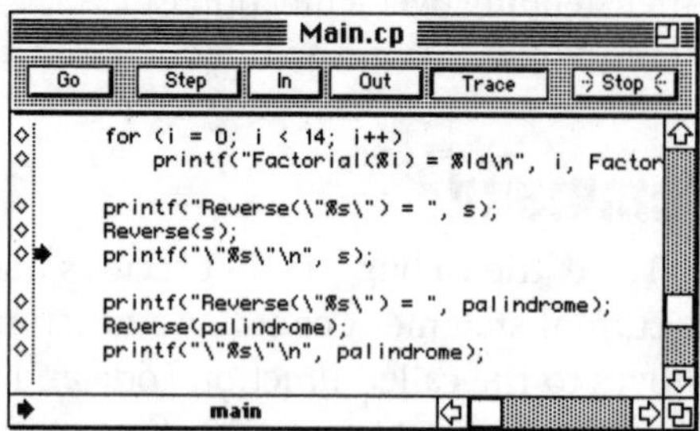

Figure 4.13. Before tracing into a function call with no source code.

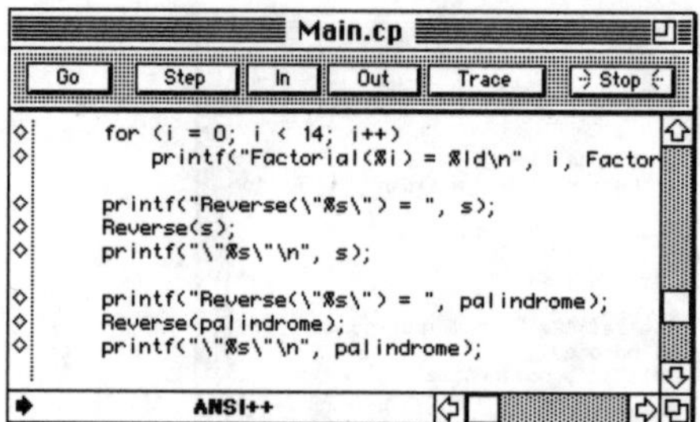

Figure 4.14. After tracing into a function call with no source code.

The Out Command

If you select Out, then the Debugger continues until it steps out of the current function. For the most part, you use this command when you have completed debugging the current function. Figures 4.15 and 4.16 show before and after using the Out command while in a function.

```
Reverse.cp
Go  Step  In  Out  Trace  Stop

}

void Reverse(char *s)
{
    int length = strlen(s);
    int midPoint = length / 2;
    int i;

    for (i = 0; i < midPoint; i++)
        Swap(&s[i], &s[length - i - 1]);
}

Reverse(char *)
```

Figure 4.15. Before stepping out of a function.

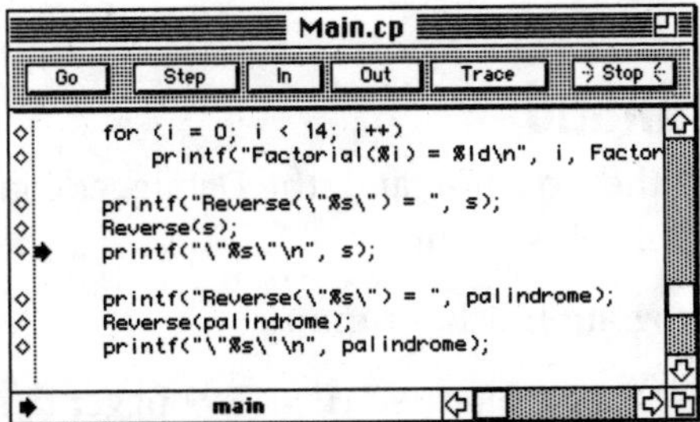

Figure 4.16. After stepping out of a function.

The In Command

If you select the In command, the Debugger steps until it reaches the next statement that has a function call. After entering the called function, it stops at the first statement. Figures 4.17 and 4.18 show what happens before and after using the In command to step into a function.

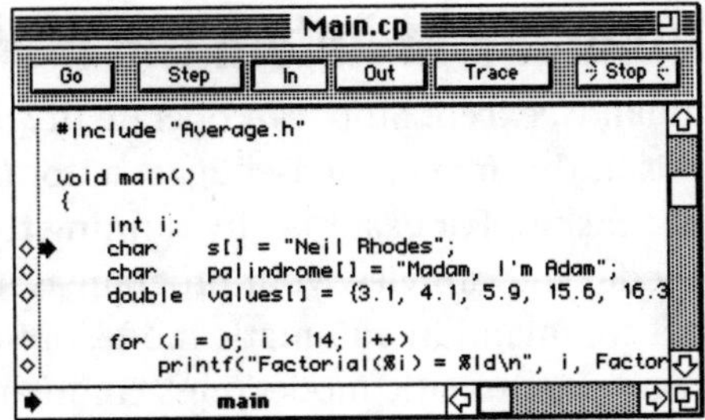

Figure 4.17. Before stepping into a function.

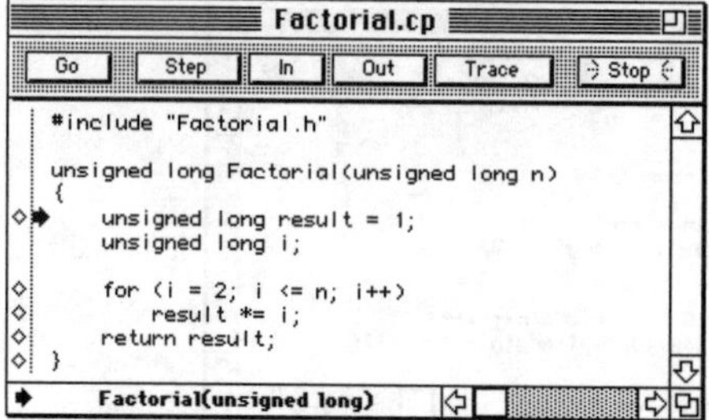

Figure 4.18. After stepping into a function.

The Go Command

If you select the Go command, the Debugger continues executing until one of the following occurs:

- The program finishes running.
- You use Stop from the THINK Debugger to stop the program.
- It reaches a breakpoint.
- A Debugger or DebugStr call gets executed.
- The program causes a system error (like a bus, address, or divide by zero error).

The Stop Command

If you select the Stop command, the Debugger stops at the next call to `GetNextEvent` or `WaitNextEvent`.

Putting a Command in Automatic Mode

All the commands, except Stop, can operate in *automatic mode*. When a command is in this mode, the Debugger automatically reexecutes it every time it finishes. For example, by running the Trace command in automatic mode, you can view your program as it executes line by line. To run a command in automatic mode, option-click on its button. To cancel automatic mode, press command-shift-period or double-click the Stop button.

Showing the Call Chain

The Source window can show you more than just the currently executing function. It also can display the chain of functions that leads to the current call, all the way back to the main program. Figure 4.19 shows the Call Chain pop-up menu. To see this pop-up, press on the current function name.

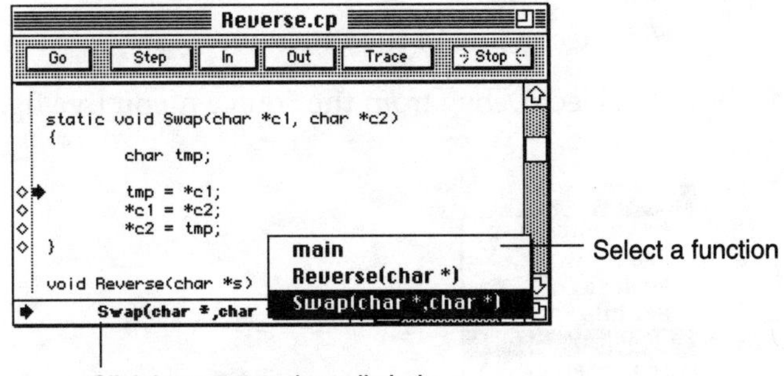

Figure 4.19. The Call Chain pop-up menu.

If you want to move to one of the call chain functions, select the function name in the Call Chain pop-up menu (see fig. 4.19). The function is then displayed in the Source window. The highlighted line shows where the current function returns (see fig. 4.20).

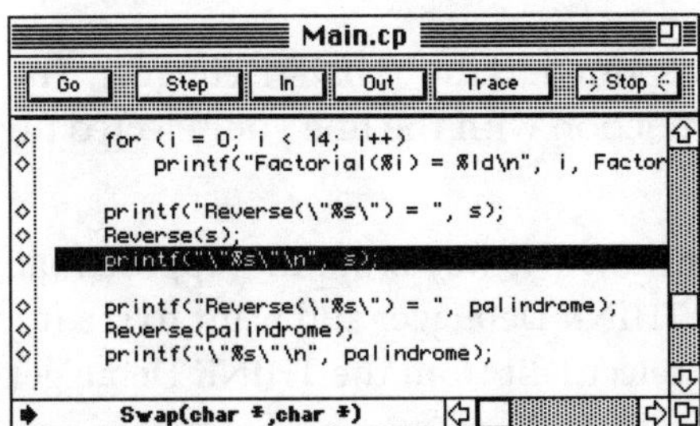

Figure 4.20. After selecting main from the Call Chain pop-up menu.

Examining Functions in the Source Window

If you want to look at a function in the Debugger Source window that currently is not displayed there, you need to open it in the THINK Project Manager. To do that, follow these steps:

1. Go to the THINK Project Manager.
2. Open the source file that contains the function.
3. Select a line in the function.
4. Select Debug from the Source menu (see fig. 4.21).

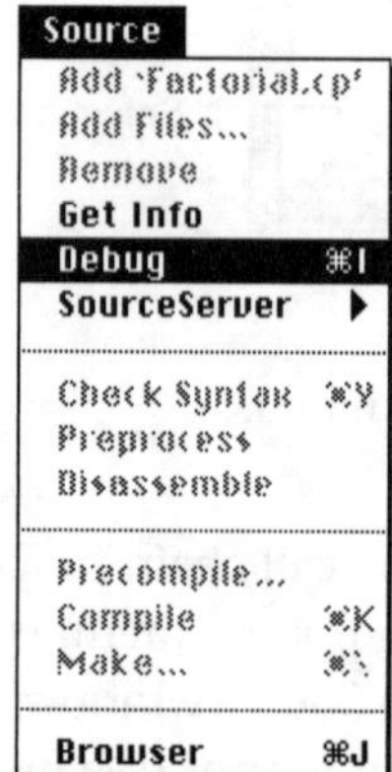

Figure 4.21. Using Debug from the THINK Project Manager.

You are transported to the THINK Debugger. The Source window shows the function with the line you selected highlighted (see fig. 4.22).

What about the other way around? Suppose that you are looking at code in the THINK Debugger and want to see it in the project source file. Simply select Edit from the THINK Debugger Source menu, as shown in figure 4.23.

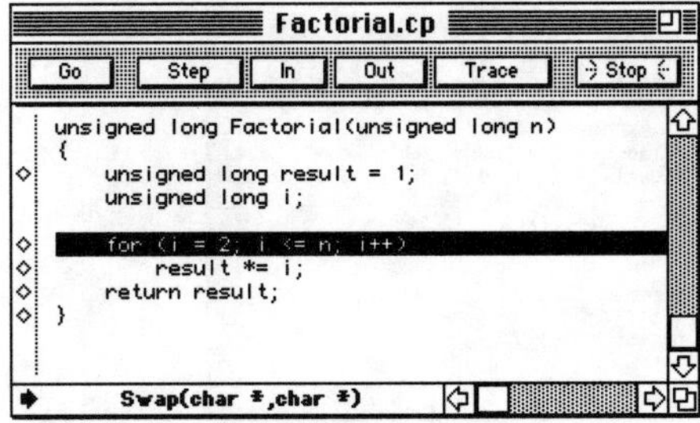

Figure 4.22. The THINK Debugger after selecting Debug from the Project Manager.

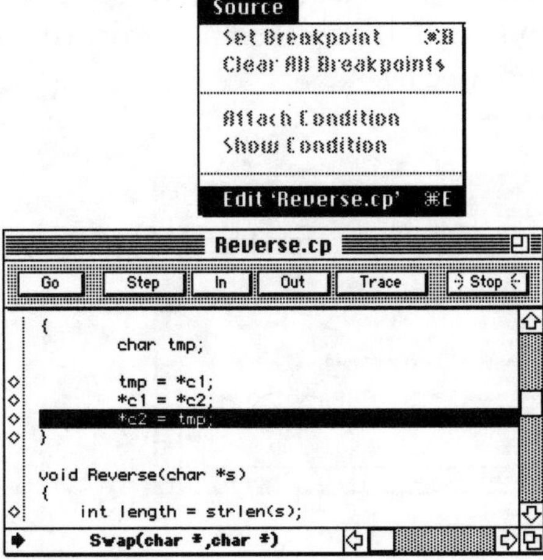

Figure 4.23. Using Edit from the THINK Debugger to open a function in the THINK Project Manager.

Using Breakpoints

You also can set breakpoints in your code in the THINK Debugger. To set a breakpoint at a particular statement, click on the statement marker. The marker changes from a hollow to a filled diamond (see fig. 4.24).

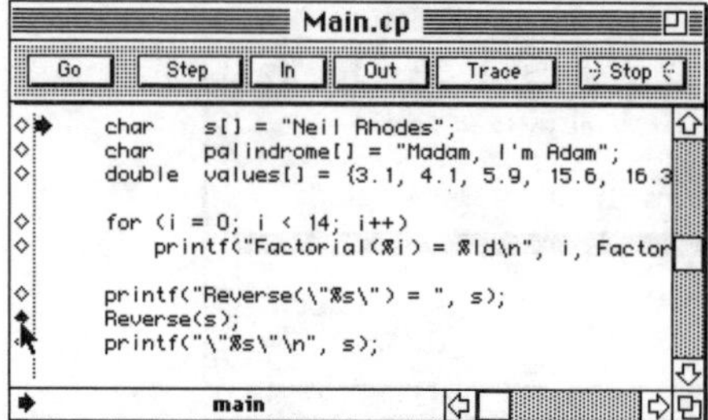

Figure 4.24. Setting a breakpoint.

With the breakpoint in place, you can use the Go command. Execution continues until the breakpoint is reached. At that point, the program stops (see fig. 4.25).

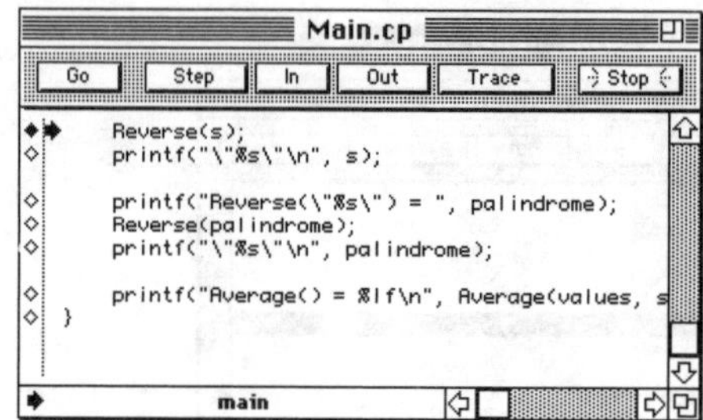

Figure 4.25. Stopping at a breakpoint.

You do not have to make the breakpoint permanent, however. To set a temporary breakpoint, option-click on the statement marker. The THINK Debugger then goes until it reaches that statement. It sets the breakpoint, executes until it gets to the statement, and then removes the breakpoint.

Examining and Setting the Values of Variables

When you want to look at variable values, you use the Data window in the Debugger. Figure 4.26 shows what it looks like.

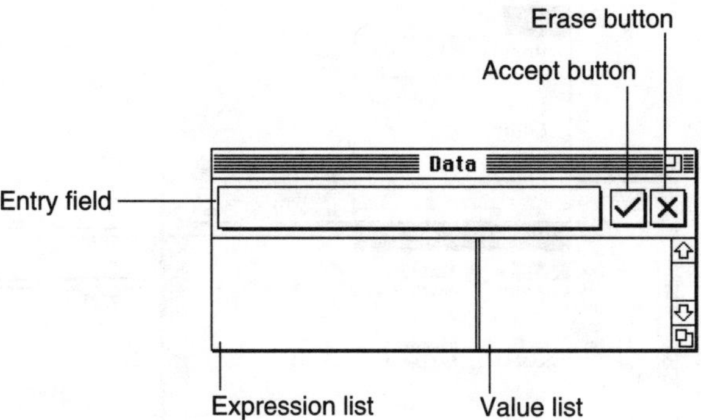

Figure 4.26. The Data window.

To examine a variable value, just type an expression into the entry field of the Data window and press Return (see fig. 4.27). You can enter a variable or a more complicated expression if you prefer.

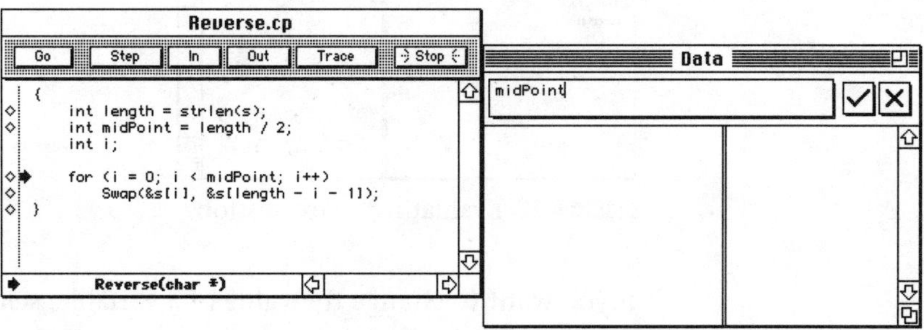

Figure 4.27. Entering an expression from the keyboard.

There is a shortcut for slow typers: Select an expression in the Source window and then choose Copy To Data from the Debugger Edit window (see fig. 4.28).

In either case, the expression is shown in the expression list on the left. The value of the expression is shown in the value list on the right (see fig. 4.29).

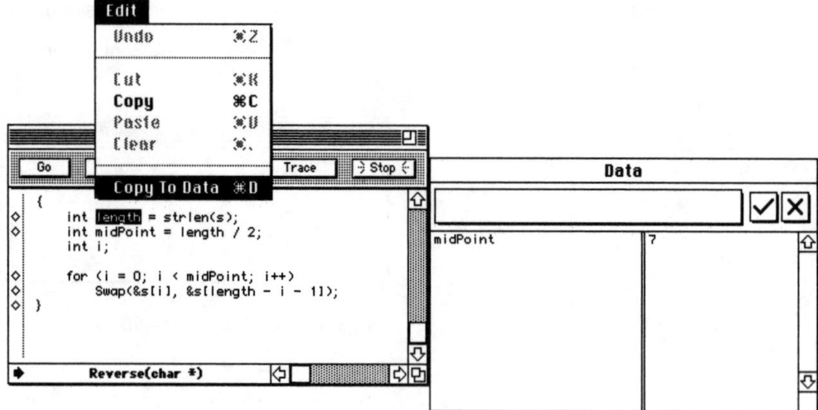

Figure 4.28. Entering an expression from the Source window.

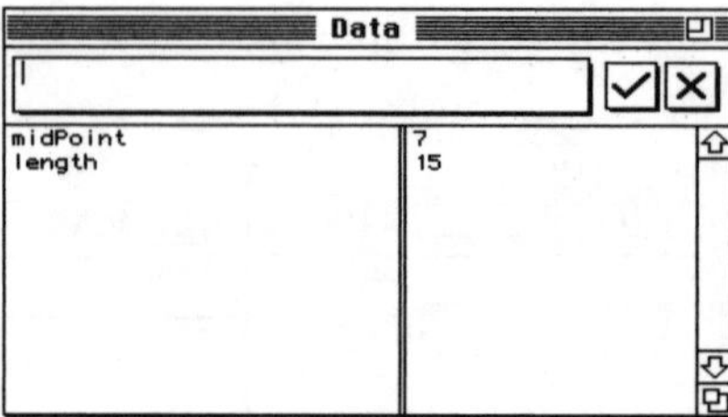

Figure 4.29. Evaluating an expression.

If you want to change the value of a variable, select its current value in the value list. Type a new value and press Return or click the check mark button when you have finished (see fig. 4.30).

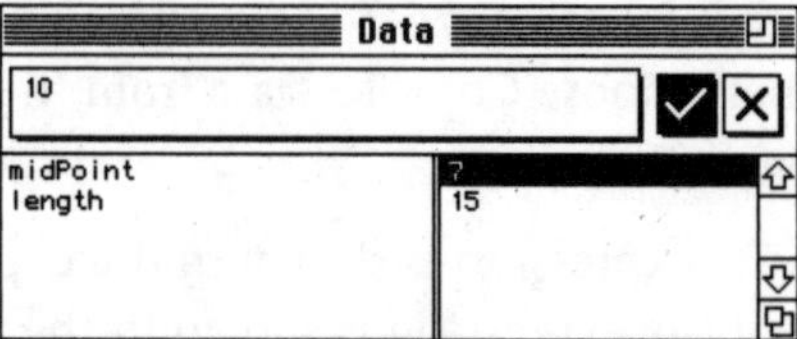

Figure 4.30. Changing the value of a variable.

Double-clicking in the right value column also enables you to do either of the following:

- Look at the contents of a structure or an array.
- Dereference a pointer.

If you want to do a double dereference, just shift-double-click. Figure 4.31 shows an example of an array with its contents displayed.

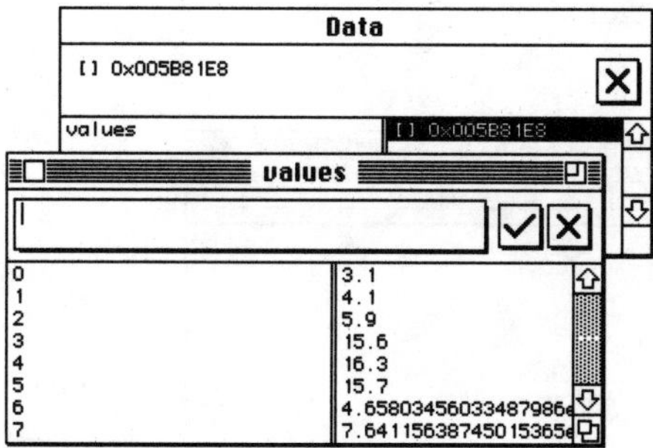

Figure 4.31. Displaying the contents of an array.

Each time you enter the Debugger, the expressions in the Data window are reevaluated. If you no longer want a particular expression reevaluated, select it and then choose Locked from the Data menu. To clear an expression, select it and choose Clear from the Edit menu. To clear them all at the same time, go to the Data menu and select Clear All Expressions.

Using Debugger Statements in Programs

The Toolbox calls Debugger or DebugStr can be called from within your code. If called, they cause your program to break into the THINK Debugger. If your program is not running with the THINK Debugger, the calls break into your low-level debugger (MacsBug, TMON, or TMON Pro). If you are not running a low-level debugger, the calls snarl up everything and cause a system error (ID 10).

Here is an example function that calls both `Debugger` and `DebugStr`:

```
void Foo()
{
    int i;
```

```
    i = 5;
    Debugger();
    i = 10;
    DebugStr("\pAfter i = 10");
}
```

Figure 4.32 shows what happens upon reaching the function's `Debugger` call.

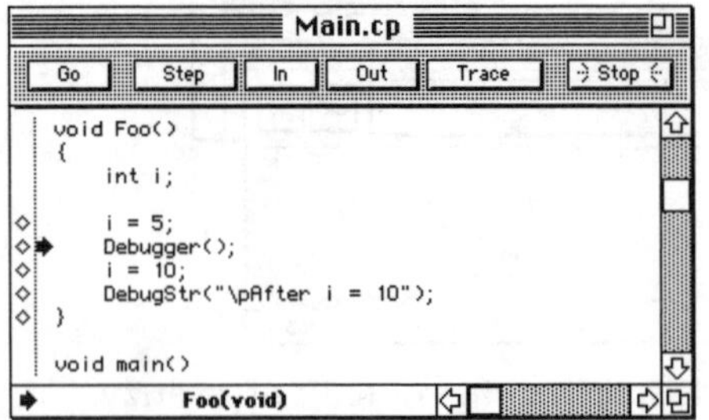

Figure 4.32. The effect of a Debugger call.

Similarly, figure 4.33 shows what happens when the `DebugStr` call is reached.

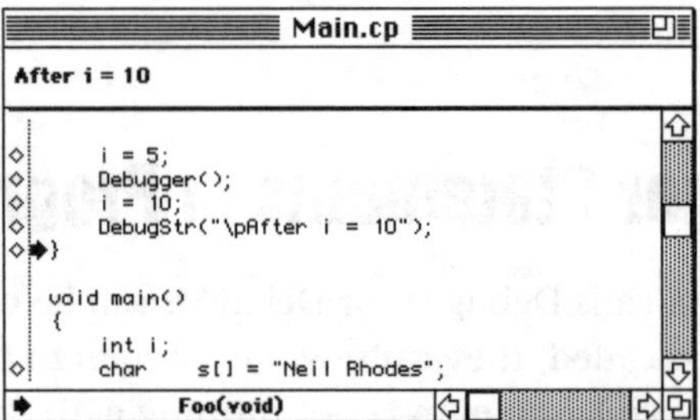

Figure 4.33. The effect of a DebugStr call.

Calling Functions from the THINK Debugger

You can do more than just evaluate variables in the Data window—you can call functions. Caution must be exercised when using this feature, however. If the function has a side effect, like changing a global variable value, then the Data window does not display the global variable correctly. Worse yet, if the function exits the program (with `exit` or `ExitToShell`), havoc ensues.

There also are restrictions on the kinds of functions you can call. This, coupled with the danger of side effects, is the reason this option is not available automatically. To specifically enable such calls, use the Debugging panel of the THINK Project Manager Options dialog and check Allow dataview function calls (see fig. 4.34).

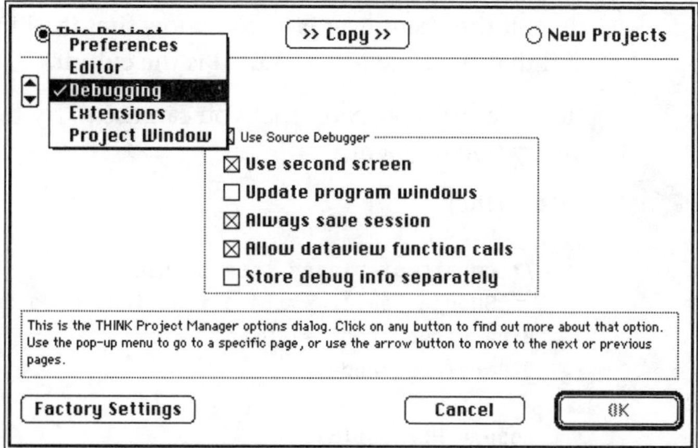

Figure 4.34. The Debugging panel of the THINK Project Manager Options dialog.

A particularly valuable use of this feature is to call data validation routines that check a data structure. For instance, if you have a binary tree, you can write a routine that checks to make sure the tree sorts correctly:

```
Boolean CheckBinaryTree(BinaryTree *aTree)
{
    if (aTree == NULL)
        return true;
    if (aTree->left != NULL) {
        if (aTree->left->value > aTree->value)
            return false;
        if (!CheckBinaryTree(aTree->left))
            return false;
```

```
    }
    if (aTree->right != NULL) {
        if (aTree->value > aTree->right->value)
            return false;
        if (!CheckBinaryTree(aTree->right))
            return false;
    }
    return TRUE;
}
```

You then can call this function as you step through your program, keeping an eye on the result of the CheckBinaryTree call the whole time. If the result ever is 0, you know that the binary tree is invalid and that the code just executed is the culprit.

Here is a main program that you can use to try this feature out on a binary tree problem:

```
void main()
{
    /* construct binary tree by hand.
       Should really write a function to do it */
    BinaryTree *root = NULL;
    BinaryTree *node;

    node = NewNode(5);
    root = node;

    node = NewNode(3);
    root->left = node;

    node = NewNode(4);
    root->left->left = node;  /* should be root->left->right */

    node = NewNode(8);
    root->right = node;
}
```

Now that you have the code to debug, it is time to call a function. Just type a call in the entry field of the Data window (see fig. 4.35).

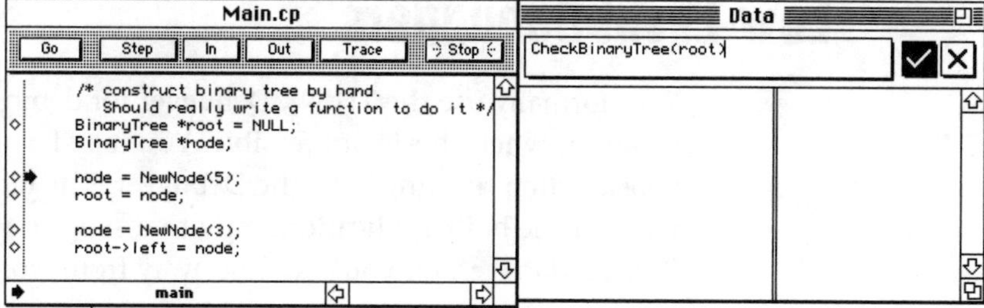

Figure 4.35. Calling a function from the Data window.

Expressions are evaluated each time you enter the Debugger. Thus, by single-stepping through the function, at every statement the binary tree is checked. Figure 4.36 shows the Debugger before the line that makes the tree invalid; figure 4.37 shows the Debugger after that line has executed.

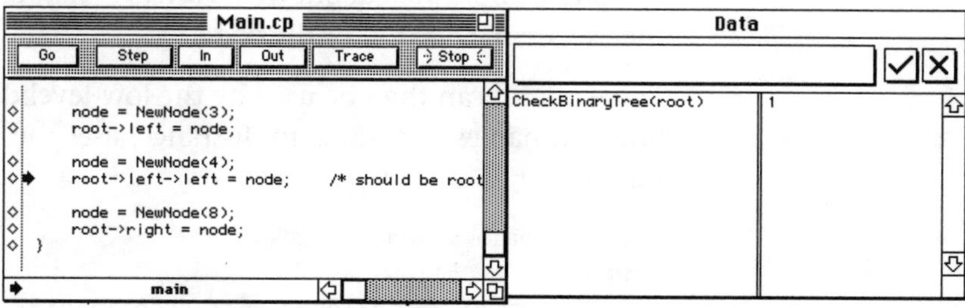

Figure 4.36. Before invalidating the binary tree.

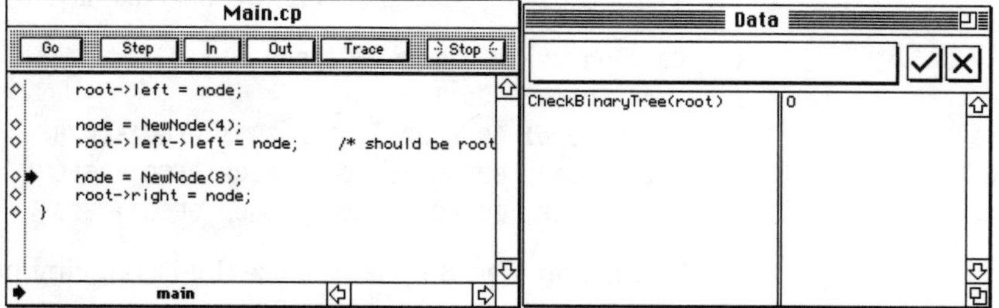

Figure 4.37. After invalidating the binary tree.

Low-Level Debuggers

You normally use the THINK Debugger for debugging. There are cases, however, when this is not feasible. You may have a bug that does not appear when running with the Debugger. The bug might appear when you run the built application, only to disappear when run from the Project Manager. Or you could be away from work and not have the source code with you.

The Symantec C++ compiler can help you when you cannot use the THINK Debugger. As a source-level debugger, the THINK Debugger gets function names from symbolic information created by the compiler. A low-level debugger, like MacsBug, TMON, or TMON Pro, does not have access to additional symbolic information. Fortunately, there is a way for the compiler to give low-level debuggers displayable function names. It can place *MacsBug names* at the end of the function. There is nothing complicated about this: Function names are just placed after the executable portion of the code.

These names can then be used by the low-level debugger to display function names. MacsBug, for instance, uses the names to display a stack crawl as follows:

```
Calling chain using A6 links
  A6 Frame   Caller
  top level 0059820C 'CODE 0001 0FCC'+0078
  005FABA8  005A0348 main+0066
  005FAB2C  005A0424 Reverse(char *)+003A
```

Without them, MacsBug is reduced to displaying the following:

```
Calling chain using A6 links
  A6 Frame   Caller
  top level 0059820C 'CODE 0001 0FCC'+0078
  005FABA8  005A0338 'CODE 0002 0FCC'+755C
  005FAB28  005A0402 'CODE 0002 0FCC'+7626
```

To turn on MacsBug names, use the Debugging panel of the Symantec C++ Options dialog (see fig. 4.38). Check the Generate MacsBug names check box.

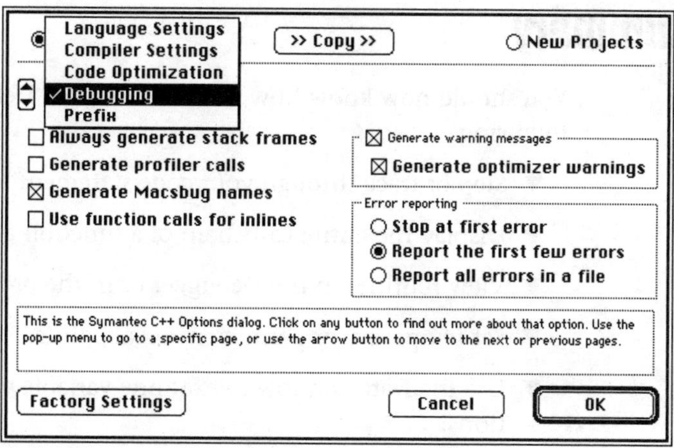

Figure 4.38. The Debugging panel of the Symantec C++ Options dialog.

Using Two Screens

If you have a multiple-monitor Macintosh, you can place the THINK Debugger windows on a second screen. This way they do not obscure the windows of the project files. Although you could do this manually, be lazy and let the THINK Debugger place your windows for you. To use automatic placement, check Use second screen in the Debugging panel of the THINK Project Manager Options dialog (see fig. 4.39).

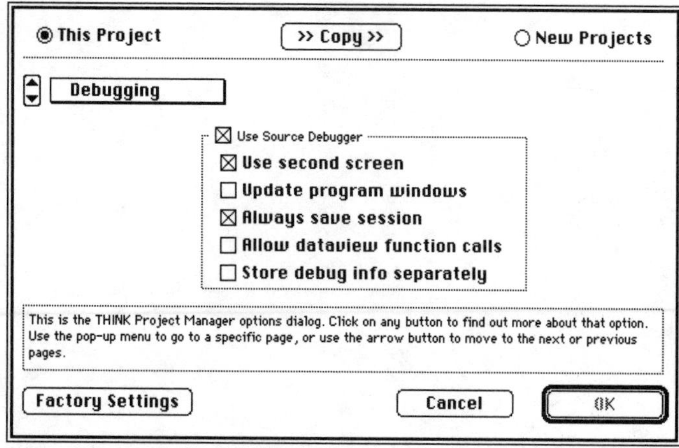

Figure 4.39. The Debugging panel of the Project Manager Options dialog.

Summary

You should now know how to use the THINK Debugger to do the following:

- Step or trace through your code statement by statement.
- Display the entire call chain of a function and move within it.
- View routines in the Debugger or in the project source files.
- Set temporary or permanent breakpoints.
- Use the Data window to examine variable values and call functions.
- Append MacsBug names to your code to make low-level debugging easier.

With the THINK Debugger, you make a formidable terminator.

5

Using Resource Utilities

An innovative aspect of the Macintosh interface is that it can easily be tailored to the native language of the user. A Quebec resident can expect to buy a Macintosh application and see not just French, but French Canadian displayed in the dialogs. Macintosh keeps this task easy for programmers by storing all the information required for localization in resources. Thus, you can modify the information in the resources (like strings, dialogs, menus, and icons) without touching the executable code.

Programmers new to Macintosh often are startled by this strict separation of code and data. It rarely takes them long to move from consternation to approval, however, because separation is a better way to design applications for an international world.

Development environments differ in how they get these resources into the program. Symantec C++ supports two different methods. One approach is to create them using ResEdit, Apple's graphical resource editor. The other approach is to use THINK Rez, a tool that converts the resource information in a text file into resources. This chapter shows you how to use both methods.

Writing a Program That Uses Resources

Before you can create resources, you need a program that uses them. Look at one that has resources to help create words.

Creating the Project

Make a new project called Alphabet. or open the one on the source code disk. This project contains the Main.cp and ResourceDefinitions.h source files.

The code for Main.cp is listed below:

```
#include <stdio.h>
#include <Types.h>
#include <OSUtils.h>
#include <string.h>
#include <ToolUtils.h>
#include "ResourceDefinitions.h"

#define kMaxInputLine     512

/* prompt for character input */
char gPrompt[256];

/* if they type an invalid character */
char gBadCharacter[256];

/* output if they type a valid character.  This is used as the
  first argument to printf */
char gCharIsForWordTemplate[256];

Boolean FindIndexOfCharacter(char c, int *ip)
{
    const  kCaseSensitive = true;
    const  kDiacriticalSensitive = true;
```

```
    Str255 entry;
    int    index = 0;
    Str255  charAsString;

    charAsString[0] = 1;
    charAsString[1] = c;

    do {
        GetIndString(entry, kCharsResourceID, ++index);
    } while (Length(entry) != 0 &&
      !EqualString(charAsString, entry,
      !kCaseSensitive, !kDiacriticalSensitive));
    *ip = index;
    return Length(entry) != 0;
}

/* returns false if no more input */
Boolean HandleOneInteraction()
{
    int c;
    char    inputLine[kMaxInputLine];

    printf("\n%s", gPrompt);
    if (fgets(inputLine, sizeof(inputLine), stdin) == NULL)
        return false;
    else {
        int i;

        if (!FindIndexOfCharacter(*inputLine, &i))
            printf("%s\n", gBadCharacter);
        else {
            Str255 word;

            GetIndString(word, kWordsResourceID, i);
            printf(gCharIsForWordTemplate, *inputLine,
              p2cstr(word));
            putchar('\n');
        }
        return true;
    }
}
```

```
void InitializeStrings()
{
    Str255  s;

    GetIndString(s, kMiscStringsID, kPromptItem);
    strcpy(gPrompt, p2cstr(s));

    GetIndString(s, kMiscStringsID, kBadCharacterItem);
    strcpy(gBadCharacter, p2cstr(s));

    GetIndString(s, kMiscStringsID, kTemplateItem);
    strcpy(gCharIsForWordTemplate, p2cstr(s));
}

void main()
{
    InitializeStrings();

    while (HandleOneInteraction())
    {
        /* do nothing */
    }
}
```

Following is the code for ResourceDefinitions.h:

```
#define kWordsResourceID 1024
#define kCharsResourceID 1025

#define kMiscStringsID   1026
#define kPromptItem            1
#define kBadCharacterItem      2
#define kTemplateItem          3
```

After you have added all the appropriate source files and libraries, you should have a project that looks like the one in figure 5.1.

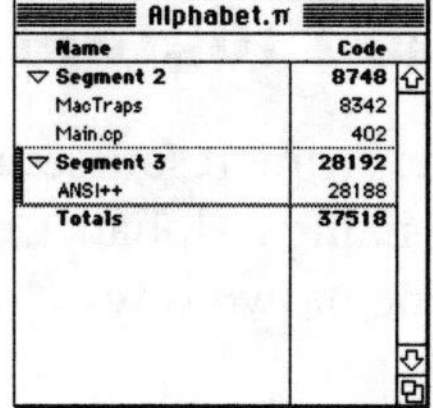

Figure 5.1. The Alphabet.π Project window.

What the Program Does

The program queries the user for a character. It then returns a word that begins with that character. Here is some output to give you an idea of the interaction (the user input is in italics):

```
Character? a
a is for Alexander

Character? d
d is for Daddy

Character? M
M is for Mommy

Character? u
u is for Unicornfish

Character? j
j is for Jagular

Character? ;
Invalid character
```

This program uses string resources in three different ways: as a list of valid characters, to find a corresponding string, and as utility strings for prompts and messages.

Including Resources in the Program

Before the program can run, the string resources need to be in the right place. This place is in file named Alphabet.π.rsrc. You can get the resources into a .π.rsrc file in one of two ways. The first method is to use ResEdit.

Creating Resources with ResEdit

You can create a new .rsrc file with ResEdit, Apple's graphical resource editor.

NOTE

The following discussion of ResEdit assumes that you already are familiar with ResEdit. Because no attempt is made to tutor you in its use, you might want to refer to the ResEdit documentation if this is new material.

To create the resources for the Alphabet program, you need to do the following:

1. Launch ResEdit.
2. Create a new file Alphabet.π.rsrc and put it in the project folder.
3. Create an `'STR#'` resource with ID 1024 that contains a list of words that start with the letters A through Z.
4. Create an `'STR#'` resource with ID 1025 that contains the letters A to Z.
5. Create an `'STR#'` resource with ID 1026 that contains the following strings:

```
"Character? "
"Invalid character"
"%c is for %s"
```

Figure 5.2 gives you a view of ResEdit in the act of creating these resources.

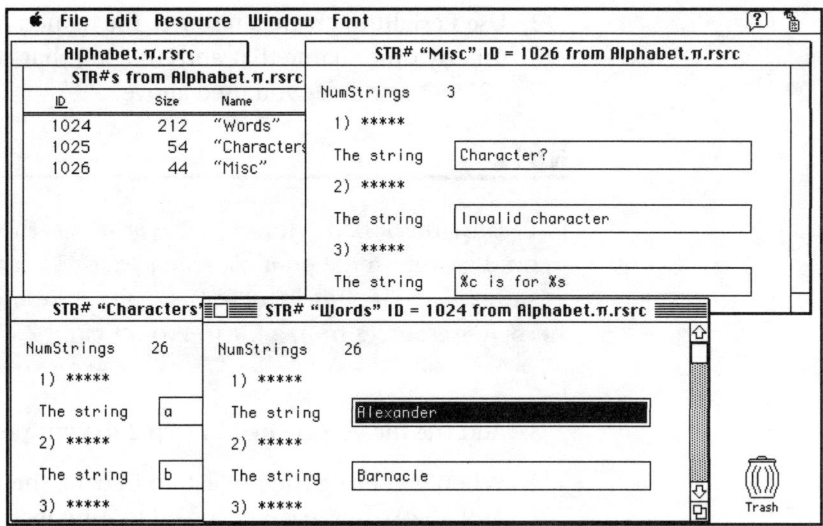

Figure 5.2. Using ResEdit to edit Alphabet.π.rsrc.

NOTE

The THINK Project Manager always looks for resources in a file with exactly the same name as the project but with a .rsrc appended. Thus, the filename you use for these resources must be Project.rsrc. In this case, the name of the project is Alphabet.π, so the resource file is named Alphabet.π.rsrc. Make sure you put the .rsrc file in the project folder.

Adding Resources Directly

A better use of ResEdit is to explicitly add .rsrc files to your project using the Add Files dialog. The next time you bring the project up to date, the THINK Project Manager copies the resources to the Alphabet.π.rsrc file.

To take this approach, do the following:

1. Start out with a clean slate by deleting the current Alphabet.π.rsrc.

2. Use ResEdit to create a resource file named AlphabetStrings.rsrc (or any other name that ends in .rsrc) that contains the same `'STR#'` resources you used above.

NOTE

Because the THINK Project Manager selects the translator based on the extension, you must name your resource files with the suffix .rsrc. The translator for .rsrc files is Resource copier, which copies resources from a file to Project.rsrc.

3. Add the file you created in step 2 to your project (see fig. 5.3).
4. When you bring the project up to date, the resources in AlphabetStrings.rsrc are copied to Alphabet.π.rsrc

Alphabet.π

Name	Code
▽ Segment 2	8748
MacTraps	8342
Main.cp	402
▽ Segment 3	28192
AlphabetStrings.rsrc	0
ANSI++	28188
Totals	37518

Figure 5.3. A resource file in the project.

There are two specific advantages to this approach:

- You can organize your resources in different files.
- If you open a .rsrc file from the project list, it opens the file in ResEdit. It even launches ResEdit for you (as long as you have an alias to it in the Tools folder of your THINK tree).

Creating Resources with THINK Rez

ResEdit is a graphic tool for adding resources to a program. The second approach to creating resources with the THINK Project Manager involves the use of the text-based tool, THINK Rez. This tool compiles a textual resource description into a file of resources. (MPW has a similar tool, the Rez tool.)

THINK Rez stores your text file full of resource infor-mation in the project. THINK Rez then converts its contents into resources. To see how this is done, look at a text file first.

Here is an Alphabet.r text file that contains THINK Rez descriptions of the string resources:

```
#include "Types.r"
#include "ResourceDefinitions.h"

resource 'STR#' (kCharsResourceID, "Characters", purgeable)
{
    {
        "a", "b", "c", "d", "e", "f", "g",
        "h", "i", "j", "k", "l", "m", "n",
        "o", "p", "q", "r", "s", "t", "u",
        "v", "w", "x", "y", "z"
    }
};

resource 'STR#' (kWordsResourceID, "Words", purgeable)
{
    {
        "Alexander",   "Barnacle", "Cornelius",
        "Daddy",       "Elephant", "Fox",
        "Gazelle",     "Horse",    "Iguana",
        "Jagular",     "Kanga",    "Limpet",
        "Mommy",       "Nicholas", "Ostrich",
        "Peacock",     "Quetzal",  "Richard",
        "Shere-kan",   "Thomas the Train", "Unicornfish",
        "Vulture",     "Walrus",   "Xirces",
        "Yo-yo",       "Zebra"
    }
};

resource 'STR#' (kMiscStringsID, "Misc", purgeable)
{
    {
```

```
                "Character? ",
                "Invalid character",
                "%c is for %s"
        }
};
```

Alphabet.r uses the same ResourceDefinitions.h file included by Main.cp. By setting up the information in this manner, both files can share the definitions of the resource IDs.

Before you can use Alphabet.r, however, you need to add it to the project. Remember to remove AlphabetStrings.rsrc at the same time. Your project window should look like the one in figure 5.4 when you are done making the changes.

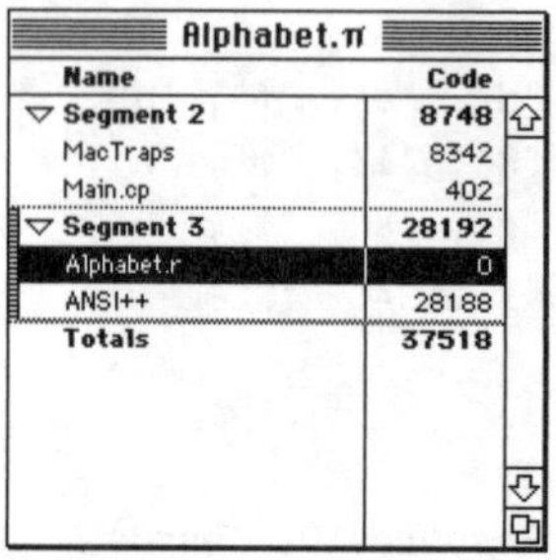

Alphabet.π

Name	Code
▽ Segment 2	8748
MacTraps	8342
Main.cp	402
▽ Segment 3	28192
Alphabet.r	0
ANSI++	28188
Totals	37518

Figure 5.4. Alphabet.r in the project.

NOTE

The THINK Project Manager uses the .r extension to indicate that the THINK Rez translator is used. Your Rez files always should end with the .r extension.

Comparing THINK Rez with ResEdit

You may be asking yourself whether you should take the THINK Rez or ResEdit road to creating resources. Each of the approaches has its benefits.

THINK Rez Advantages

Here are the advantages of using THINK Rez files:

- ▼ They print out easily. A text format is better for printing, particularly for use in a project notebook, magazine article, or book.
- ▼ You can share include files that define resource identifiers. You are guaranteed to have identical IDs for the resource ID and the one that is used when the code is accessed. You thus can avoid inconsistencies when you change IDs.
- ▼ You can use the preprocessor to conditionally include or exclude particular text. THINK Rez is great if you want to maintain one .r file that generates different resources depending on the state of preprocessor variables. For instance, the following code selects different text strings depending on the language being used:

```
#define qEnglish
#undef qPigLatin
resource 'STR#' (1028)
{
    {
#if defined(qEnglish)
        "Boat",
        "Car"
#elif defined(qPigLatin)
        "OatBay",
        "ArCay"
#endif
    }
};
```

- ▼ You can define your own resource types. For more information, on how to do this, see the THINK Rez documentation.

ResEdit Advantages

ResEdit is not without its advantages as well:

- ▼ It is a better design tool. As a graphical environment, ResEdit enables you to see the effects of your actions immediately. If you change a dialog, you can look at it without a new build.

- You can copy resources from other files. For example, you might want to copy a cursor from the system file to use in your application.

Exercise

Make the alphabet program Script Manager compatible. Make sure it handles scripts that have more than one byte per character. This is a hard task, but one that makes the program fully localizable for languages like Kanji that use multi-byte scripts.

6

Building an Application

During a development cycle, you usually run the program from within the Symantec C++ environment. Eventually, however, you have something that is ready for testing or, better yet, for that golden day when you produce a master release. Building the stand-alone version of your application does require setting some particular options. This chapter discusses these options and the other aspects of creating the final application. You learn how to set all of the following:

- ▼ The creator type.
- ▼ The application partition size.
- ▼ Certain important SIZE flags.
- ▼ The Far DATA and Far CODE options.
- ▼ The Smart Link option for your builds.

Except for the Smart Link option, all of these settings are located in the same area of the Project menu. You examine these options in the following sections.

Setting Build Options

The options that affect your stand-alone application are accessed from the Set Project Type menu item in the Project Menu (see fig. 6.1).

Figure 6.1. Using Set Project Type to bring up the Set Project Type dialog.

The Set Project Type dialog is shown in figure 6.2.

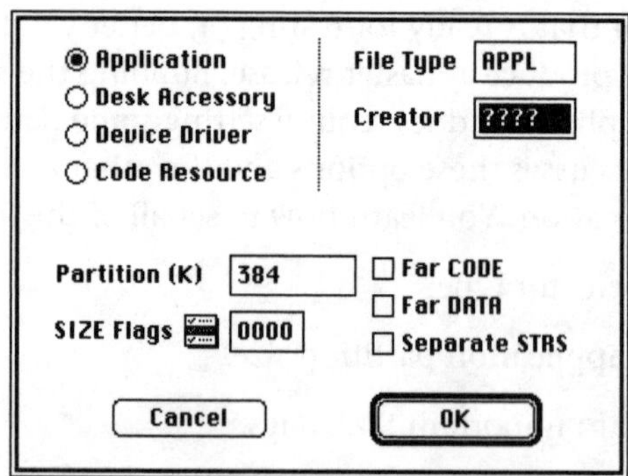

Figure 6.2. The Set Project Type dialog.

This dialog contains four different types of information that you must specify about your program:

Program type	The buttons in the upper-left area of the dialog box distinguish what kind of program it is. You can create a desk accessory, device driver, code resource, or application.
File type	Normally APPL, the file type and creator settings are used to identity and differentiate your program from every other program.
Memory	The settings in the lower-left area of the dialog box set how much memory the program needs to run and how it takes advantage of special System 7 and MultiFinder features.
Size settings	The options in the lower-right area of the dialog box include special settings reserved for bulky applications.

Each choice in the dialog, starting with the most important, is discussed below.

Creator

By far themost important thing to do in this dialog is to set the four-character creator in the Creator edit box. It also is the step that takes the most planning.

IMPORTANT

Every application should have a unique creator. The Finder uses this value to display the correct application icon and to launch the right application when a document is opened. To guarantee uniqueness for your programs, you must register your proposed creator with Apple's Developer Support Center. To obtain a registration form, write to Developer Support Center, Attn: C/F Type Administrator, 20525 Mariani Ave., M/S 75-3T, Cupertino, CA 95014. You also can use AppleLink (DEVSUPPORT) or Internet (DEVSUPPORT@applelink-apple.com).

You can use any characters you want in the four-character sequence. Your creator cannot consist entirely of four lowercase letters, however, because they are reserved for Apple programs.

Program Type

By selecting the appropriate radio button, you can make your program one of four types: application, desk accessory, device driver, or code resource.

Application is the most common choice. Historically, desk accessories (such as the Scrapbook) were the only items that appeared in the Apple menu and they only could be accessed from there. The distinction between applications and desk accessories has blurred with the advent of System 7 because you can put applications in the Apple menu and run desk accessories from the desktop.

Device drivers typically interact with hardware. Some examples include drivers for NuBus cards and the LaserWriter driver for PostScript printers. Code resources are blocks of code used in various situations. For example, start-up documents (INITs) and window definition procedures (WDEFs) are included in the code resource category.

Partition Size

You alsomust set the partition size of your program in the Partition (K) edit box. A typical application has a default value between 384 and 2,500K. The default value of 384K is suitable for small to medium applications, but you may need a larger value. You want to avoid setting the default value too low because your application can easily run out of memory and otherwise annoy the user. The number you set is used for all three partition sizes the user sees in the Finder (see fig. 6.3).

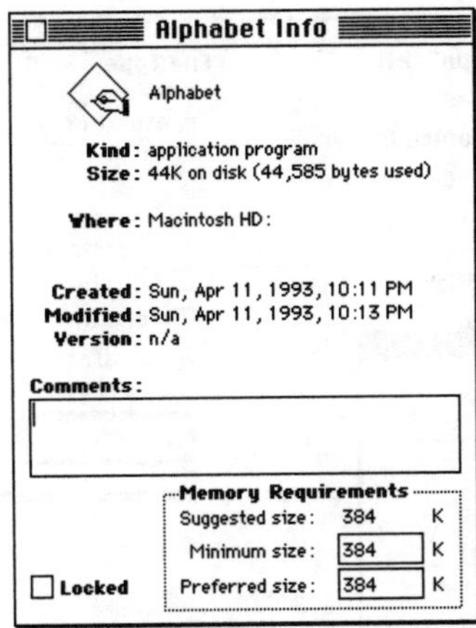

Figure 6.3. Partition sizes in the Finder.

The SIZE Flags

You also must set the SIZE flags. At build time, they are stored in the `'SIZE'` resource with ID –1 in the application. They provide information to the operating system about the application's capabilities. Although you can set the bits by hand (by typing in the hex value for the flags), it is much easier to use the SIZE flags pop-up menu (see fig. 6.4).

When you select a flag, the dialog places a check mark in the pop-up and calculates the appropriate value for the combined flags (see fig. 6.5).

These flags fall into three categories of information about your application's MultiFinder and System 7 support.

1. How well your application follows MultiFinder and System 7 guidelines. (The MultiFinder-Aware, Background Null Events, and Suspend & Resume Events flags.)
2. If it runs in the background and can receive application information from the Finder. (The Background Only, GetFrontClicks, and Accept ChildDiedEvents flags.)

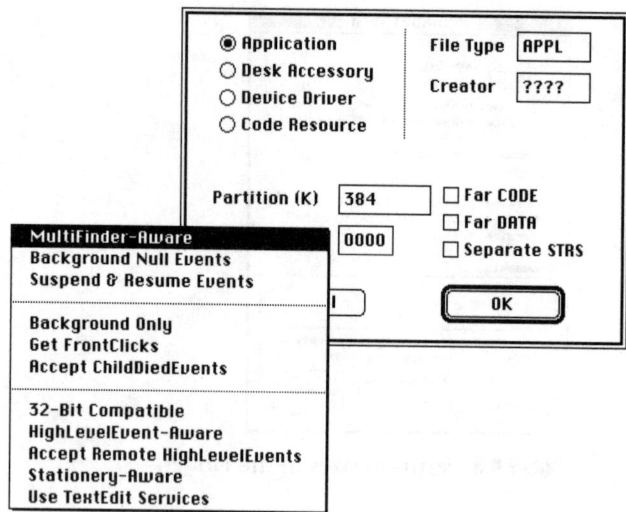

Figure 6.4. Using the SIZE flags pop-up menu.

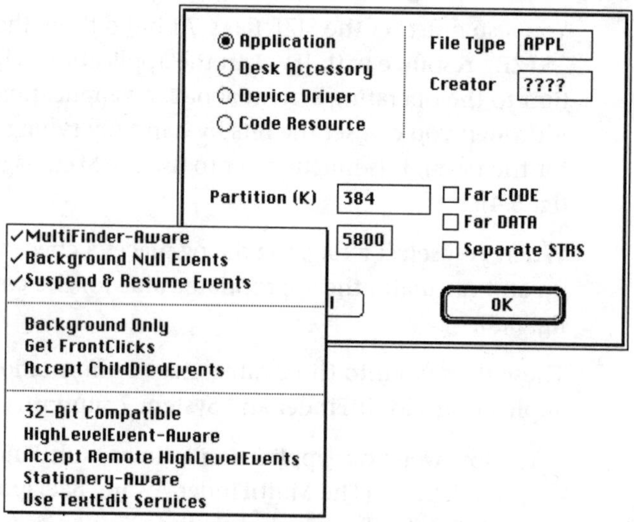

Figure 6.5. Setting SIZE flags using the SIZE flags pop-up.

3. Whether your application is 32-bit clean, can receive high-level events (like AppleEvents) both locally and remotely, can create stationery, and can use Script Manager in-line text entry. (The 32-Bit Compatible, HighLevelEvent-Aware, Accept Remote High-LevelEvents, Stationery-Aware, and Use TextEdit Services flags).

NOTE

> If you are using the THINK Class Library, you should set the MultiFinder-Aware, Suspend & Resume Events, and High-LevelEvent-Aware flags.

For a complete description of each flag, see the Symantec C++ product documentation.

Far CODE and Far DATA

Calls to functions in different segments of the project are made using the jump table. Each function called by another one in a different segment must have a jump table entry. Functions for which you take addresses must each have a jump table entry as well (because these functions could be called from anywhere). Finally, virtual member functions take a jump table entry.

With so many functions requiring entries, the jump table can fill up quickly. If it does, check the Far CODE option to make the jump table larger.

If Far CODE is unchecked, the references to the jump table are made using 16-bit (positive) values. Because each jump table entry is 8 bytes, this limits the number of jump table entries to 4,096.

If Far CODE is checked, references to the jump table are made using 32-bit values. This increases the number of jump table entries dramatically. Before you get your finger poised above the button, remember that there is a price to pay for such ample leg room. Your application becomes somewhat larger because it takes more code to use 32-bit values. Programs with the Far CODE setting checked have an average 6 percent increase in the size of the code.

You encounter the same issues with global variables. These variables (variables defined outside any function, static variables within a function, and static data members) are accessed by a method similar to jump table entries.

If the Far DATA option is off, globals are accessed by 16-bit (negative) values. This limits the size of global space to 32K. If the Far DATA option is on, globals are accessed using 32-bit values, which makes the size of global space essentially unlimited. The price you pay is that your code becomes slightly bigger.

NOTE

> If you combine code that uses the Far CODE or Far DATA options with libraries that do not use these settings, you need to consult the Symantec C++ documentation for instructions.

Separate STRS

Normally, string constants(like "Hello" or "\pWorld") are stored in global space. If Separate STRS option is on, string constants are stored in a special STRS component instead.

This option exists for compatibility with earlier versions of THINK C—do not use it for new code. This option is an artifact from the time when you could only have 32K of globals. There were some programs with large numbers of string constants that exceeded the 32K limit. The STRS components were the kludge that resulted. Times are better now, and you can use Far DATA if you need to exceed 32K of globals.

Building the Application

Now that every setting is configured properly, you can build your application by selecting Build Application from the Project menu. If your project is not up to date, you receive the familiar `Bring the project up to date` message (unless you have made updates automatic).

After your source files have compiled and your libraries have loaded, you have to decide where to place the application and what to name it (see fig. 6.6).

After clicking Save, the THINK Project Manager begins linking your application (see fig. 6.7).

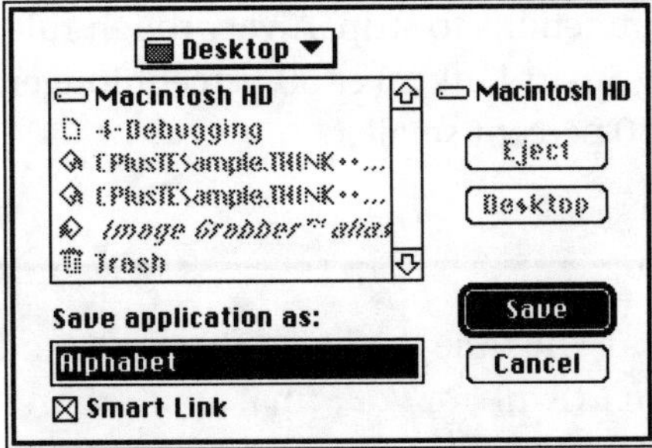

Figure 6.6. Specifying the name and location of your application.

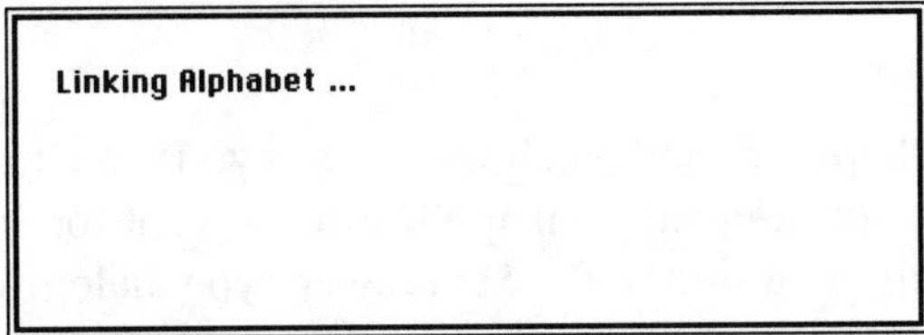

Figure 6.7. The linking progress dialog.

After the application is linked, the Project Manager copies the resources (from Project.rsrc) into your application (see fig. 6.8).

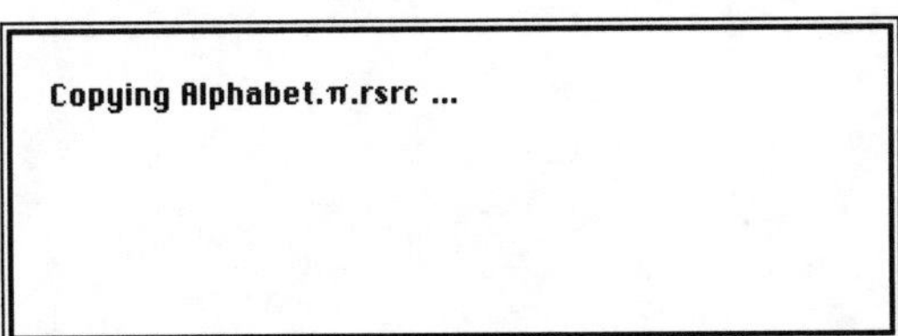

Figure 6.8. The resource copying progress dialog.

Quit the THINK Project Manager and give your application a whirl.

Smart Link

The Smart Link option makes your code smaller by removing functions that are never referenced. For example, it is common to have unreferenced functions when using libraries because you rarely use all of the functions they contain. Smart Link has its price; it takes time to decide what functions to strip. A very rough rule of thumb is that linking using Smart Link takes 50 percent longer, but makes your application 50 percent smaller.

NOTE

Regardless of the time it adds to the build, you always should turn on Smart Link for your final application build.

Summary

This chapter described all the aspects you have to consider when it is time to create your final application. Except for Smart Link, all of these options are found in the Set Project Type dialog. You also learned not to wait to the last minute to send your file creator type to Apple. It would be tragic if all that stood between you and a shrink-wrapped package were four characters.

7

Using Precompiled Headers

Symantec C++ is a quick compiler inside an efficient environment, but the way to get your compiles flying is to use precompiled headers. These files provide a way of storing the information from a number of header files in a compiled format. The Symantec C++ compiler then can read this compiled format in the twinkling of an eye and thereby forgo reading the individual header files.

To use precompiled headers in your source files, replace your standard include files with one `#include` of the precompiled file. This chapter shows you how to do this. You also learn how to use the standard precompiled headers provided with Symantec C++ and how to make your own versions. You also are shown some of the pitfalls to avoid when making modifications to header files or to the files that use them.

Using Precompiled Headers

There are a couple of rules for using precompiled headers, but they are easy to remember.

RULE

The `#include` statement for the precompiled header must precede everything but comments in your source file.

You can have other `#includes` in your file, but they must follow the precompiled header. This also is true of the declarations. Thus, your files generally look like this:

```
#include <myPrecompiledHeaderfile++>
#include <Quickdraw.h>

void Foo()
{
    Rect r = {10, 20, 50, 100};
    FrameRect(&r);
}
```

Or, they can look like this:

```
// Here is the main program

#include <myPrecompiledHeaderfile++>
#include "Foo.h"

void main()
{
    printf("%d %d\n", kFoo, kBar);
}
```

RULE

Only one precompiled header file is allowed per source file.

Different source files can include different precompiled headers, however. But be careful: If you put the precompiled header file in the project prefix, you cannot add any other precompiled header files to individual source files.

Standard Precompiled Header Files

Symantec C++ comes with two already built precompiled headers: MacHeaders++ and TCL++. MacHeaders++ contains about 30 different standard Macintosh header files. TCL++ is for use with the THINK Class Library. It contains commonly used Macintosh header files and some, but not all, of the TCL header files. If you are using the THINK Class Library, you probably want to include TCL++.

By default, Symantec C++ automatically includes MacHeaders++ in every source file. It does this via the Prefix panel, which is located in the Symantec C++ Options dialog in the Edit menu (see fig. 7.1). By using the Prefix panel, you can add information to the beginning of each source file; normally, this is an include of a common header file. The default setting in the panel is to include MacHeaders++.

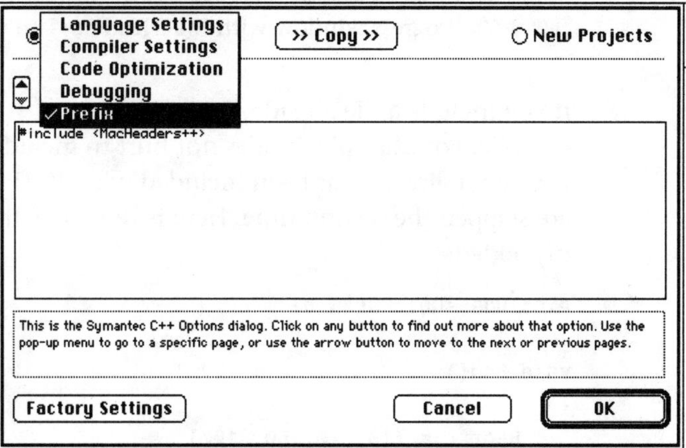

Figure 7.1. The Prefix panel of the Symantec C++ Options dialog.

Effects of Compiling with Precompiled Headers

Listed below is a small sample file that demonstrates the advantages of automatic inclusion of MacHeaders++:

```
void Foo()
{
    Rect r = {10, 20, 50, 100};
    FrameRect(&r);
}
```

First, the Prefix panel ensures that MacHeaders++ is included when this source file is compiled. Because MacHeaders++ includes QuickDraw.h, Foo.h does not have to include it explicitly in the declaration of `FrameRect`. When this file is compiled, the Progress window shows a five-line compile (see fig. 7.2).

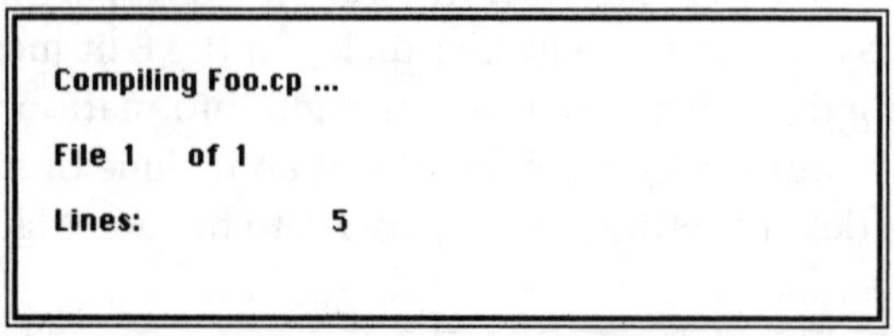

Compiling Foo.cp ...	
File 1 of 1	
Lines:	5

Figure 7.2. Progress window with MacHeaders++ in the Prefix panel.

If you include a file already in MacHeaders++, it does not affect your compile. For example, it does not hurt to include QuickDraw.h. Because it already has been included (via MacHeaders++), its contents are skipped the second time. Here is the file with QuickDraw.h explicitly added:

```
#include <QuickDraw.h>

void Foo()
{
    Rect r = {10, 20, 50, 100};
    FrameRect(&r);
}
```

When you compile this example, the Progress window shows a seven-line compile—one additional line for the #include and a blank line (see fig. 7.3). Had the compiler also compiled QuickDraw.h, many more lines would have been added.

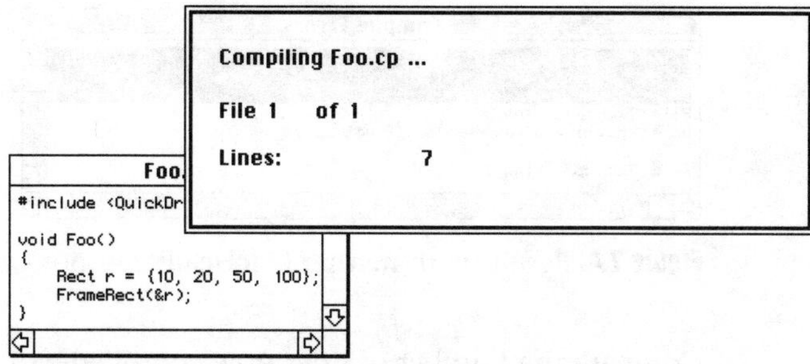

Figure 7.3. Progress window with MacHeaders++ in the Prefix panel and include of QuickDraw.h.

If you remove the #include of MacHeaders++ from the Prefix window, it is another story altogether. The compile gives an error if you forget to include QuickDraw.h:

```
void Foo()
{
    Rect r = {10, 20, 50, 100};
    FrameRect(&r);
}
```

Both Rect and FrameRect are now undefined without MacHeaders++ (see fig. 7.4).

You also can include QuickDraw.h without using MacHeaders++. The following file compiles correctly:

```
#include <QuickDraw.h>

void Foo()
{
    Rect r = {10, 20, 50, 100};
    FrameRect(&r);
}
```

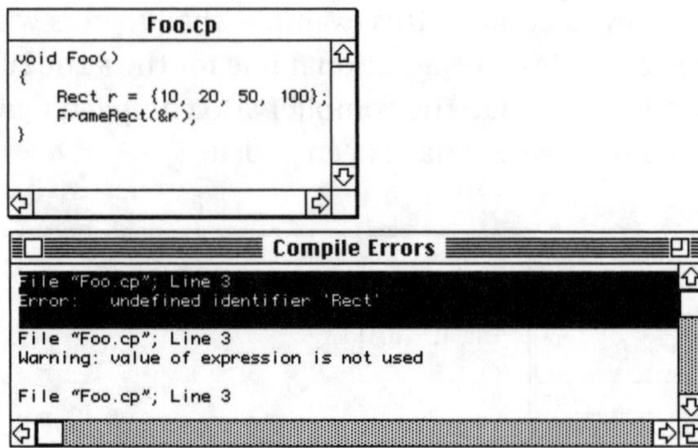

Figure 7.4. Results with neither MacHeaders++ nor QuickDraw.h.

Compare the number of lines now compiled with the earlier examples (see fig. 7.5).

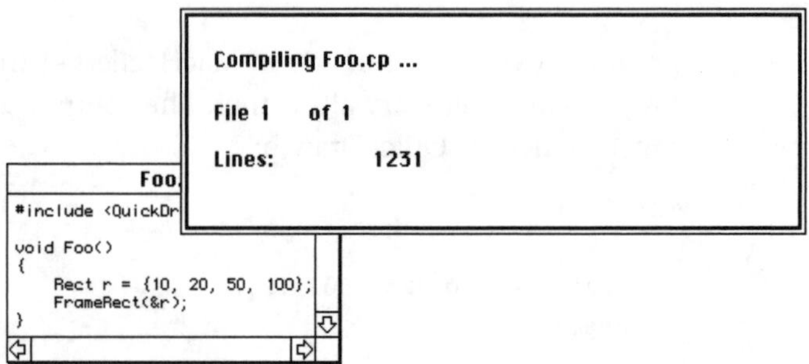

Figure 7.5. Progress window without MacHeaders++ but with include of QuickDraw.h.

Now imagine the even more common situation wherein you include more than one standard Macintosh header file. The difference between compile times for files using MacHeaders++ and those that rely on standard `#includes` can be staggering—like driving a Lotus at moped speeds.

Using Precompiled Headers in Individual Files

As long as you remove MacHeaders++ from the Prefix panel, you can include it or some other precompiled header file in any individual source file:

```
#include <MacHeaders++>

void Foo()
{
    Rect r = {10, 20, 50, 100};
    FrameRect(&r);
}
```

If you were to compile this, the Progress window would again show a seven-line compile.

You also might have a situation wherein you want to use MacHeaders++ on one source file and a special precompiled header file on another source file.

Creating Precompiled Headers

There comes a time when you want a custom precompiled header file that contains your own set of header files. For instance, MacHeaders++ does not include PrintTraps.h. If you want to print, you either can include PrintTraps.h in a source file or, faster yet, create a custom version of MacHeaders++ that includes the file.

If you find that a number of standard project header files that are lengthening your compile times, they are good candidates for inclusion.

The most important rule for precompiled header files also is pretty obvious.

RULE

> Do not precompile header files that change often.

If your precompiled header files are not fairly stable, they will require precompiling often. Situations like this negate the very benefits of precompiled headers.

Changing Header Files

There is a substantial problem with the way in which the THINK Project Manager deals with precompiled header files. The situation is made worse by how well it handles standard header files.

The problem is that changes to header files are not reflected automatically in the precompiled header file that includes them. The THINK Project Manager marks neither the precompiled header file nor the source file as out of date.

Walk through some source and header files to see how this problem affects the code. If you change a header file that is included by a source file, the THINK Project Manager nicely marks the source file as being in need of compilation. For instance, look at the following example files.

Listed below is the code for Foo.h:

```
#include "Bar.h"
#define kFoo 5
```

Here is the code for Bar.h:

```
#define kBar 10
```

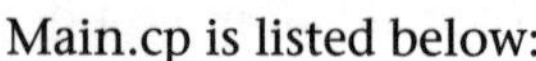

Main.cp is listed below:

```
#include <stdio.h>
#include "Foo.h"

void main()
{
    printf("%d %d\n", kFoo, kBar);
}
```

If you modify Foo.h, the THINK Project Manager marks Main.cp as needing recompilation because it includes Foo.h. Similarly, if you modify Bar.h, the THINK Project Manager marks Main.cp as needing recompilation because Main.cp includes Foo.h that includes Bar.h.

Precompiled headers are not handled the same way. For example, here is the same program using a precompiled header file, FooBar++, that includes Foo.h and Bar.h. Main.cp is similarly modified to include FooBar++:

```
#include "FooBar++"
#include <stdio.h>

void main()
{
    printf("%d %d\n", kFoo, kBar);
}
```

Now, modify Foo.h and Bar.h. Listed below is the code for Foo.h:

```
#include "Bar.h"
#define kFoo 500  //changed the value
```

Here is the code for Bar.h:

```
#define kBar 1000  //changed the value
```

In this case, the THINK Project Manager does not mark FooBar++ as needing a new precompilation. Therefore, FooBar++ still contains the old Foo.h and Bar.h. If you do not precompile FooBar++ over again, the program erroneously prints out:

```
5 10
```

The only bright spot here is that the THINK Project Manager marks files correctly if you do your own precompiling. In the above example, if you rebuild FooBar++, the THINK Project Manager realizes that Main.cp needs to be recompiled.

This situation gives rise to another rule to remember when working with precompiled header files.

RULE

It is up to you to precompile a file whenever one of its included header files changes. If you don't, mysterious things happen.

Creating a Precompiled Header File

Creating a precompiled header file is a fairly straightforward process:

1. Create a .cp file that `#includes` all the headers you want in the precompiled header file. For example, create a new file named

FooBar.cp (or anything else, as long as it ends in .cp). Then, add the following `#includes`:

```
#include "Foo.h"
#include "Bar.h"
```

2. Precompile the .cp file by choosing Precompile from the Source menu (see fig. 7.6).

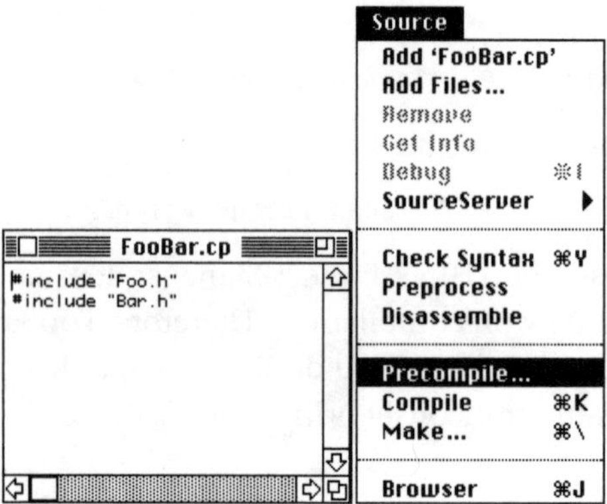

Figure 7.6. Precompiling headers.

WARNING

A common mistake programmers make is attempting to precompile a .h file instead of a .cp file. The Precompile command only works on .cp files and only is enabled when a .cp file is frontmost. Try as you might, you can never precompile a .h file.

While the .cp file precompiles, the THINK Project Manager shows a Progress window (see fig. 7.7).

After the precompile is complete, you get a dialog requesting the name and location of the new precompiled header file (see fig. 7.8).

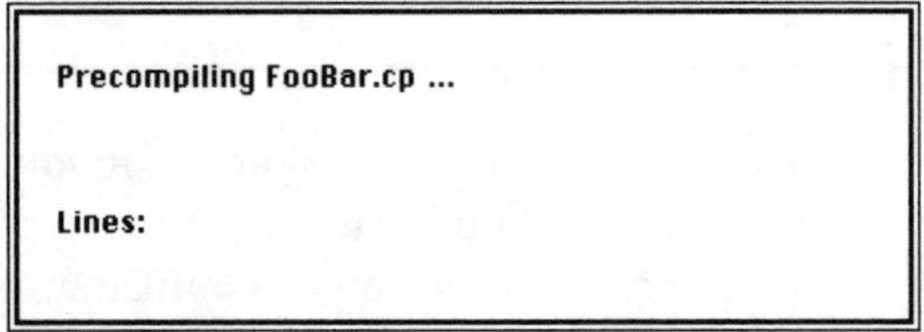

Figure 7.7. Progress window while precompiling.

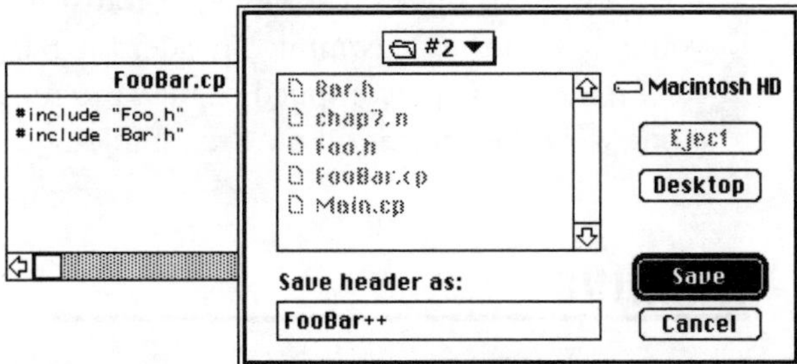

Figure 7.8. Saving the precompiled header.

3. Name the precompiled header file, making sure to include the ++ ending. A precompiled header file specific to a project should be stored in the project tree. If the header file is used by many projects, store it in the THINK tree.

IMPORTANT

The ++ on the end of the precompiled header file is a convention that indicates the header file is a C++ compilation. Although both THINK C and Symantec C++ support precompiled headers, the format they use is different. Do not use a header file created by one compiler with the other compiler.

4. Place the .cp file in a location that enables easy access. If any of the header files change, then you can open the .cp file and choose Precompile again. When you are prompted to save the precompiled header file, replace the old version with the new one.

NOTE

You can add the .cp file to your project if you want. This can be both good and bad. You have easy access to the file if you have to modify it. This method can be confusing, however. You may be tempted to think the project uses the file or, worse yet, takes it into account when updating the project files.

If you store a project on a floppy, or transmit it electronically, you may find the precompiled header file rather bulky. In this case, remove the precompiled header and provide instructions along with the project on how to rebuild it.

WARNING

The precompiled headers are built with the compiler settings of the current project. If you use the precompiled header in a later project with different compiler settings, the header could conflict with the project. In particular, if you change the 8-byte doubles option, you get the `Different configuration for precompiled header` error message. To fix this, just rebuild the precompiled header with the later project's compiler options.

Customizing MacHeaders++ or TCL++

Both MacHeaders++ and TCL++ have corresponding source files. For MacHeaders++, the source file is Mac #includes.cpp and it is located in the Mac #includes folder in the THINK tree. Its contents are as follows:

```
/*
 * Mac #includes.cpp - source to MacHeaders++
 *
 */

#include "Mac #includes.c"
```

The Mac #includes.c file contains all the actual `#includes` of the Toolbox files. By having two files—one included in the other—you can keep the same header file list for both. You then can precompile one file to get a THINK C precompiled header and the other to get a Symantec C++ precompiled header.

You can change which files are included in Mac #includes.c and then compile Mac #includes.cpp. You probably should give the resulting precompiled header a different name than MacHeaders++. If you don't, your MacHeaders++ will be different from the standard, and you or someone else may find this creates problems when swapping projects.

The sources for TCL++ are found in TCL #includes.cp in the THINK Class Library folder. This file includes commonly used Macintosh headers and some, but not all, of the TCL header files.

Summary

You now should know all you need to know about precompiled headers. Armed with your newfound knowledge of precompiled header files and the rest of the project environment, you should be ready to tackle C++ in force.

PART 2

The Elements of C++

C++ has derived its wide range of capabilities from its rich heritage. On one hand, it is a direct descendant of C, a language that provides both the structures of a high-level language and the operations that enable low-level machine access. Adding to this base, C++ also has benefited from the object-oriented concepts found in Simula and Smalltalk.

It is to this language that you now turn. First you learn how to use C++ simply as a better C. Next, you get an overview of C++ object-oriented programming and design. After getting a feel for the important elements of this type of programming, you are introduced to the most important C++ construct, the class. You learn how the class construct enables you to combine data and the routines that operate on that data. You then turn to the powerful C++ features of polymorphism and multiple inheritance. Having been rooted in these elements of the language, you learn some rules of thumb to help you write good C++ programs. Finally, the discussion returns to the Symantec C++ environment, where you learn about the THINK Class Browser and the various settings of the C++ compiler.

What this section does not do is teach you every important aspect of C++. Having completed this material, however, you can start writing C++ programs. This section also prepares you for more advanced material on C++ (refer to the bibliography in Appendix E for further reading). You have probably heard that C++ is not an easy language to learn or to use well. While there is a certain grain of truth to these statements, it is not a language you want to pass over. Writing good C++ programs takes practice, but the same is true of most worthwhile endeavors.

8

C++: An Enhanced C

Many of the changes made to C were done to make it a better language. With C, it is fairly easy to fling random syntactic changes in here and there and still have code that compiles; however, that has no more hope of working than a pig of singing.

C++, a more disciplined language, allows far less nonsense. A C++ compiler catches many more errors at compile time; these errors are not allowed to become run-time errors. The catch, of course, is that for the compiler to find the errors you have to spend much more time preparing your code for the compiler. It also takes you longer to get a clean compile. Rest assured, this additional effort offers you more than just the smug assurance of being more disciplined than your fellow C programmers. You know that, if your C++ program compiles, it may work and might even do what you wanted it to do.

Why should you read this chapter and implement the changes discussed? You should do so because you can become a better programmer than if you just use C. Furthermore, you can make these changes without committing yourself to becoming a full-fledged C++ programmer, which would require you to become an object-oriented programmer. Learning about object-oriented programming is dealt with in later chapters. In this chapter, you just learn a little grammar, you do not change your whole programming style.

Overview

What are the changes made to C++ that make it a better C? The following list highlights the improvements included in C++:

- The stream library replaces the stdio routines for standard I/O. This gives you fewer chances for error as well as providing extensibility.
- There is new and easier comment format (`//` comments instead of `/* */`).
- Declarations can be mixed with executable statements.
- Structs no longer need to be declared with the `typedef` statement.
- Functions can have default arguments.
- C++ provides more rigorous error checking, including special warnings and compile-time type checking.
- Functions can be overloaded. This feature enables two different functions to have the same name as long as their parameters are different.
- Memory allocation and deallocation functions are handled by the built-in operators `new` and `delete` instead of by the C library routines `malloc` and `free`.
- `Const` variables and inline functions replace the use of `#define`.
- References can be used to pass argument parameters by address instead of by value.

The following sections take a look at each of these improvements in turn.

Standard Input/Output

The standard I/O statements used in C changed in C++ for two reasons:

1. To help eliminate errors.
2. To add user extensibility.

Eliminating Errors in I/O Operations

The problem with standard C I/O operations is that, when you call standard I/O routines, you must specify the type of variable you will be outputting or inputting. The following call encodes the types of the items to be printed with `%d` and `%f`:

```
printf("%d %f", i, x);
```

Enforcing the encoding of variable types when the compiler already knows about them not only begs the programmer to type them in wrong, but is harder to read as well. With C++, the same code can be written this way:

```
cout << i << x;
```

Here, the compiler, knowing the types of `i` and `x`, sees to it that they are output appropriately. This first reason for changing C should be easy enough to appreciate.

The stream library that provides this new method for handling I/O works like this: A stream is created that refers to standard output or input, a file, or a string in memory. The syntax for outputting or inputting is the same, regardless of the source or destination. Here is the syntax:

```
stream << expression1 << expression2 ... << expressionN
```

The following C++ elements may be new to you:

`<<` This is an example of an *overloaded operator*. When used with streams, << is called the *insertion operator*. Similarly, >> is called the *extraction operator*.

`cout` This is a stream that is connected to standard output. Similarly, `cin` is a stream connected to standard input.

Here is an example of the syntax in use:

```
cout << "3 * 5 = " << 3 * 5 << '\n';
```

The line outputs the following:

```
3 * 5 = 15
```

Overloading functions and operators are discussed in more depth later in this chapter.

NOTE

> In C, operators are overloaded as well: You just cannot modify them yourself. For example, * when applied to integers means integer multiplication and when applied to floating-point numbers means floating-point multiplication—two different operations. In C++, you have access to this overloading capability through your own routines. The operator << is usually the left bit-shift operator, but the stream library overloads << to mean stream output.

Although youcan still use the `printf`/`scanf` family (stdio), you really should use streams. Unlike streams, the stdio library uses different routines for outputting to standard output, files, and strings (`printf`, `fprintf`, and `sprintf`, respectively). Similarly, input from standard input, files, and strings uses three different routines (`scanf`, `fscanf`, and `sscanf`). Obviously, trading six routines for two simplifies the code and reduces the chances for errors. The bounty of the stream library's benefits should become even clearer by looking at some comparative code examples.

Here is a small integer-producing program written using `stdio.h`:

```
#include <stdio.h>

void main()
{
    int i = 3;
    printf("i = %d\n", i);
}
```

Now, here it is using `stream.h`:

```
#include <stream.h>

void main()
{
    int i = 3;
    cout << "i = ", << i << '\n';
}
```

Both of these routines output the following:

```
i = 3
```

Using streams, each expression is output in order, and the way it is printed depends on the type of the expression. Look at the following line from the example above:

```
cout << "i = ", << i << '\n';
```

The first expression, `"i = "`, is a string; the second, `i`, is an integer; and the third, `'\n'`, is a character. Each one prints as expected.

Using `stdio` routines, if you have an integer, you use `%d`; if you have a floating-point number, you use `%f`. This is the source of numerous errors in programs. For instance, there is nothing in C to prevent you from writing the following:

```
printf("i = %f\n", i);
```

At run time, the compiler dutifully tries to interpret `i` as a floating-point number and outputs the following:

```
i = 0.000000
```

This is an error you would not enjoy finding in a complex program.

Streams Enable User Extension

As well as having unified syntax, the stream library also enables user extensibility. With stdio, suppose that you have the following structure:

```
struct MyStruct {
    int i;
    int j;
} s;
```

To print out `s`, you need to print out each field within it. Below is what the stdio code looks like:

```
printf("%d %d", s.i, s.j);
```

Whereas, after having written a routine that can output a `MyStruct` to a stream, all you have to write is the following:

```
cout << s;
```

More Examples of Streams

Now that you have examined why standard I/O has been changed in C++, look at some more code examples.

The Hello World program, which you originally learned in Chapter 1, is a good place to start. The new C++ way of coding this program using streams is shown below:

```
#include <stream.h>

void main()
{
    cout << "Hello, world!\n";
}
```

The original C version looks like the following:

```
#include <stdio.h>

void main()
{
    printf("Hello, world!\n");
}
```

Below is an example of a program that takes two integers as input:

```
#include <stream.h>

void main()
{
    int i;
    int j;

    cin >> i >> j;
}
```

Using `stdio`, the same program looks like this:

```
#include <stdio.h>

void main()
{
    int i;
    int j;

    scanf("%d %d", &i, &j);
}
```

You should agree that the first example, although unfamiliar, appears more natural than the second.

As you have seen, C++ I/O using streams reduces errors and adds extensibility. The age-old principle of Occam's razor demands that you choose the simpler solution.

The New Form of Comments

C++ gives you a new syntax for comments: the double slash, //, which can be used instead of `/* */`. The `//` characters begin a comment that terminates at the end of the line. Below is an example that uses the new comment style:

```
// Returns the maximum of two integers
int Max(int a, int b)
{
    if (b > a)          // could be >= instead
        return b;
    else                // if a tie, we return a
        return a;
}
```

If you already have been using THINK C, then you have had `//` comments available for some time and may have experienced their numerous benefits. For the rest of you who have had to do without `//` comments until now, it is easy enough to explain the greatest single advantage of this new form of comment: It is *auto-terminating*.

NOTE

Although // comments are not part of ANSI C, the THINK C compiler allows them anyway. Check in the Language Settings panel of the THINK C Options dialog box to make sure that Language Extensions are on. MPW C also accepts // comments.

A recurring C programming error is to forget to close a comment. This is not always easy to find. Even the best C programmer has had something like the following disaster strike:

```
/* Returns the maximum of two integers */
int Max(int a, int b)
{
    if (b > a)          /* could be >= instead
        return b;
    else                /* if a tie, we return a */
        return a;
}
```

Now this is the stuff of which dreams are made—bad ones. Here is what happens: The above code no longer computes the maximum value correctly because the second comment (`could be >= instead`) is not terminated. However, no error is generated because the closing `*/` of the third comment closes the second comment. So the code compiles and runs, but acts as though you wrote the following:

```
int Max(int a, int b)
{
    if (b > a)
        return a;
}
```

This is what is left after removing the comments; the code does not do what it is supposed to do. In conclusion, // comments are preferable to the older C-style comments, if not for ease of use, then for a good night's sleep.

Declarations Mixed with Executable Statements

C requires that all variable definitions within a function occur at the beginning of a block. C++ relaxes these rules. Variable definitions can occur anywhere.

NOTE

> C and C++ make a distinction between declarations and definitions. *Declarations* state that a variable exists; *definitions* also reserve space for the variable.

The following example shows a C++ function that includes some variable definitions within the block:

```
float Foo()
{
    int i;
    float total;
    float f;

    f = sin(1.0) / 5.0;
    total = 0;
    for (i = 0; i < 10; i++) {
        float g;

        g = f * i;
        total = g * g;
    }
    return total;
}
```

Note that the definition of `g` occurs within the `for` loop, which is reasonable because it is only used there. C++ enables you to go one step further, however, by immediately preceding the `for` loop with the declaration of the variable `i`:

```
float Foo()
{
    float total;
    float f;
```

```
    f = sin(1.0) / 5.0;
    total = 0;

    int i;
    for (i = 0; i < 10; i++) {
        float g;

        g = f * i;
        total = g * g;
    }
    return total;
}
```

You now have executable statements intermingled with variable definitions. C++ enables you to define this variable even closer to where it is used; you can move the definition of `i` into the `for` statement:

```
float Foo()
{
    float total;
    float f;

    f = sin(1.0) / 5.0;
    total = 0;

    for (int i = 0; i < 10; i++) {
        float g;

        g = f * i;
        total = g * g;
    }
    return total;
}
```

Defining the loop variable within the `for` statement is a common C++ idiom. This useful C++ idiom is quirky, however. If you are not careful, you may make mistakes using it until you master one particular idiosyncrasy due to the scope of variables. The following rule explains the problem.

RULE

> The variable scope extends from the point where the variable definition occurs to the end of the block in which the variable is defined.

Put another way, the scope of a variable defined within a `for` statement extends from that `for` statement to the end of the block in which the `for` statement occurs, not to the end of the `for` loop. It is an error to write the following code because `i` already is defined when you reach the second `for` loop:

```
for (int i = 0; i < 10; i++) {
    Foo();
}
for (int i = 0; i < 10; i++) {     // error, i already defined
    Bar();
}
```

Figure 8.1 presents a diagram that should clarify the relationships.

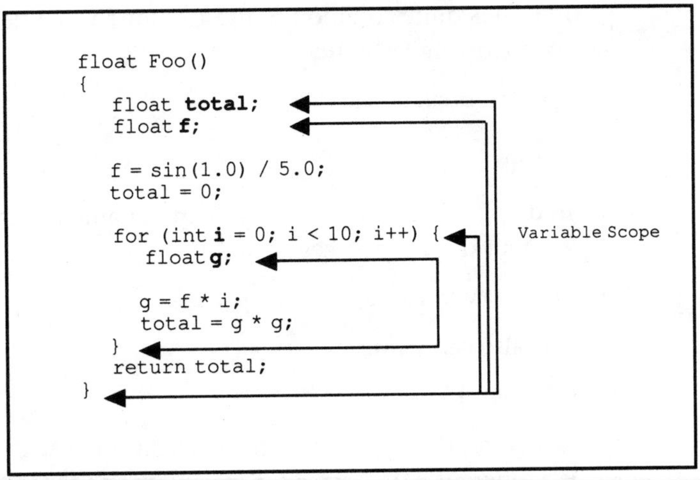

```
float Foo()
{
    float total;
    float f;

    f = sin(1.0) / 5.0;
    total = 0;

    for (int i = 0; i < 10; i++) {
        float g;

        g = f * i;
        total = g * g;
    }
    return total;
}
```

Variable Scope

Figure 8.1. The scope of variables.

NOTE

As you might imagine, forgetting the variable's scope is a common source of errors. There are two reasons why variables in a `for` loop are scoped as they are. First, many C programmers occasionally use the value of a `for` loop variable after the `for` loop to determine whether the loop finished iterating. Second, it is a mistake—as Ellis and Stroustrup say "it would probably have been better to introduce a special rule to limit the scope of a name introduced in the initializing statement of a *for-statement* to the *for-statement*, but now much code exists that depends on the general rule."

If you remember this rule of variable scope you should be fine. You certainly should find that this problem is far outweighed by C++'s more flexible approach to variable declaration.

Typedefing and Structs

In C, it is quite common to use `typedef` when declaring structures in the following fashion:

```
typedef struct MyStruct {
    ...
} MyStruct;
```

In doing so, you can use the structure named `MyStruct` either with or without the `struct` keyword:

```
struct MyStruct s;
```

You also can write:

```
MyStruct s;
```

C requires the `typedef` in the declaration of `MyStruct` because there is a different name space for structures and types. The above example is the way around this: The `typedef` causes the structure name also to be defined as a type name.

In C++, there is only one name space, and declaring a structure automatically declares a type with that name. This removes the dubious possibility that you have in C, in which you can cause `struct Foo` and `Foo` to be two totally different types. Thus, you can write the following:

```
struct MyStruct {
    ...
};
```

You then can use:

```
struct MyStruct s;
```

Or, you can use:

```
MyStruct s;
```

C++ still accepts the `typedef` to define a type name equivalent to a corresponding `struct` name. Thus, if you forget and still use the `typedef`, you are no worse off.

Default Arguments

C++ enables the use of default arguments, so that the caller of a function need not pass all parameters. Any unspecified parameters use a default value specified in the function declaration. Here is an example of a function that has default arguments:

```
extern void *Alloc(int numBytes, Boolean useMFMem = false);
```

Listed below are the rules for default arguments:

1. You can call these functions with a varied number of arguments. Using the above declaration, the `Alloc` function can be called with two arguments. This first is:

   ```
   ptr = Alloc(1024, false);
   ```

   Or, it can be called with:

   ```
   ptr = Alloc(1024, true);
   ```

   The function also can be called with just one argument:

   ```
   ptr = Alloc(1024);
   ```

In the last case, the second parameter, `useMFMem`, defaults to false.

2. Only trailing arguments can have defaults. Thus, the following is incorrect:

```
extern void *Alloc(Boolean useMFMem = false, int numBytes);
  // illegal
```

3. Functions may have multiple default arguments, but they all must be together at the end:

```
extern void *NewAlloc(int numBytes, Boolean useMFMem =
  false, Boolean clearMem = false);
```

The following code is incorrect:

```
extern void *NewAlloc(int numBytes = 5, Boolean useMFMem,
  Boolean clearMem = false); // illegal
```

4. You can use defaults only in the function declaration (usually a `.h` file) and not in the definition.

Error Checking

In general, C++ compilers provide stricter error checking than C compilers. As well as finding more errors, they also usually issue more warnings. Anyone who has used C long enough should be glad to have a little more discipline in his or her life. Discussed below are some of the important ways in which the Symantec C++ compiler provides you with this additional error information.

Warnings

Historically, THINK C had no concept of warnings. There was no facility for the compiler to notify the programmer of a possible problem while still continuing to compile. The THINK Project Manager's new Compile Errors window provides a place for Symantec C++ to output warnings as well as errors.

One such warning is the `used before set` warning. If the global optimizer is turned on, Symantec C++ warns you if you are trying to use variables you have not set. Try to compile the following function:

```
void Warning(int parameter)
{
    int localVariable;

    parameter = localVariable;
}
```

The compiler generates the following warning:

```
_File "Warnings.c"; Line 8
Warning: in function Warning(int) - variable 'localVariable' used
  before set
```

These are not the sorts of warnings you should ignore. They point out logic errors in your code that you should fix.

Note, however, that these warnings are available only when the global optimizer is on. The optimizer's job, among other things, is to compute data-flow information about the lifetime of each variable and its initialization times. Because the optimizer is already gathering this information, the warnings come for free (well almost free—warnings can cause your compilation to be slightly slower).

Compile-Time Type Checking

The Symantec C++ compiler also performs more rigorous type checking than the C compiler. You can view this as good or bad, depending upon how lazy you are feeling.

In THINK C, using function prototypes and declaring all functions before you use them is optional. This is good because it is less work and appeals to the lazy side of you. Unless you are a very careful programmer, however, you are likely to end up with many errors.

C++ is much stricter. It is requires you dot your i's and cross your t's; you must use prototypes and declare your functions before use. Symantec C++ then checks function calls against their declarations to make sure you are calling routines with the correct number and types of parameters.

Type-Safe Linkage

The C++ compiler also gives you an error if the types and numbers of parameters used for the function call do not match those of the function. Consider the code in table 8.1.

Table 8.1. Code Example for Type-Safe Linkage

File a.c	File d.c
`void Bar()`	`void Foo(float f)`
`{`	`{`
`    extern void Foo(int);`	`    //_`
	`}`
`    Foo(1);`	
`}`	

In C, as in C++, both `a.c` and `d.c` compile and link correctly. Unfortunately, in C, at run time, the routine `Bar` calls `Foo`, passing the integer `1`. The routine `Foo` tries to read this as a floating-point number. Not a pretty sight, is it? At best, the code works incorrectly; at worst, it crashes.

C++ catches this error for you during linking. The compiler finds that the call to `Foo` does not match the definition of `Foo`. It reports this as a link error:

```
undefined: Foo(int)
```

This signifies that there is a call to a routine `Foo` that takes one `int` parameter, but that no such routine can be found.

Interestingly enough, this error is reported less often in Symantec C++ than in other C++ implementations. Other implementations require makefiles, which specify the dependencies of various files. With makefiles, it is easy to get the dependencies wrong (as any MPW user can tell you). Symantec C++'s Project Manager does this work for you. It keeps track of when files need to be recompiled. There are, however, two cases in which these types of problems can occur in Symantec C++:

1. You declare a function `extern` in one source file and provide the function definition in another source file (as was done in the above example to show this error). You really should declare your functions in a header (a `.h` file) file. This file is included by all source files that call the function, as well as by the file containing the function definition.

2. You are using precompiled headers. Unfortunately, the Symantec C++ Project Manager does not rebuild precompiled header files automatically. So, as you can imagine, it is possible to get into a situation where you are using an old version of a precompiled header.

As you have found, Symantec C++ notifies you if your call and function definition do not match in number or type of arguments. Thus, the worst that happens with these two cases is that the compiler whines at you to fix the code—much less drastic than causing a runtime error.

Overloaded Functions

In C, all functions in the same scope must have unique names. This can make life difficult for a programmer on a large project battling to give appropriate, short, easy-to-type names that are unique. It is even more difficult when a programmer combines two libraries, each of which has used the same name for a function. One common way programmers avoid duplication is to encode the type of arguments as part of the function name. This is the approach taken by Apple programmers for one of their functions. The following standard C function returns the square root of a floating-point number:

```
double sqrt(double);
```

Because the Apple programmers wanted a square root function that operates on `Fract` numbers (a type that holds fixed-point numbers in the range of -2 to 2), they came up with the following:

Fract FracSqrt(Fract);

You easily can see how a unique name limitation can quickly lead to a proliferation of slightly differently named functions:

```
Fract FracSqrt (Fract);
int   IntSqrt(int);
float FloatSqrt(float);
long  LongSqrt(long);
```

Ideally, you would like to name them all sqrt. C++ grants this wish. Functions can still have the same name even though the types of the arguments are different. This is called *overloading* a function. Here are some examples:

```
extern double sqrt(double);
extern Fract sqrt(Fract);
extern int sqrt(int);

double f;
...
f= sqrt(f);          // calls sqrt(double)

Fract l;
...
l = sqrt(l);         // calls sqrt(Fract)

int i;
...
i = sqrt(i);         // calls sqrt(int)
```

It is important to realize that the overloading is based on the type and number of arguments and not on the return type. Look at the following:

```
int sqrt(int);
float sqrt(int);     // illegal
```

Although the code appears to be a declaration of two overloaded functions, it actually is an error; the compiler flags it as such.

C++ treats `char`, `short`, `int`, `long`, `float`, and `double` as distinct types when used as parameters. This enables functions to be overloaded based on these distinctions (and on whether the type is `unsigned` or not).

The following code declares eight overloaded functions, each of which is named `PrintValue`. C++, using its own internal wisdom, determines which function to call based on the type of the argument to `PrintValue`.

```
void PrintValue(char c);
void PrintValue(short s);
void PrintValue(int i);
void PrintValue(long l);
void PrintValue(unsigned char c);
void PrintValue(unsigned short s);
void PrintValue(unsigned int i);
void PrintValue(unsigned long l);
```

Overloaded functions are a real boon to programmers on large projects: Not only are programmers liberated from distinct naming, but code errors are reduced. The C++ compiler figures out which function to call based on the arguments you give; you can relax and cheerfully overload functions to your heart's content.

Memory Allocation/Deallocation

In C, you allocate anddeallocate memory by using the standard library. The library is not built into the language. C++, on the other hand, builds memory management into the language with the `new` and `delete` operators. Table 8.2 shows an example of `new` and `delete` in comparison with C's use of `malloc` and `free`:

Table 8.2. Comparing new/delete with malloc/free

C	C++
`int *intPtr;`	`int *intPtr;`
`intPtr = (int *) malloc(sizeof(int));`	`intPtr = new int;`
`free(intPtr);`	`delete intPtr;`

From the table you should be able to see that using `new` has two advantages:

- You do not need to typecast the return result—it is already the right type.
- You do not need to calculate the size with `sizeof`—`new` automatically calculates the correct size.

Here is an example of using `malloc` incorrectly:

```
int *intPointer;

intPointer= (int *) malloc(sizeof(char))    // error
*intPointer= 0;
```

The code accidentally allocates only enough space for a `char`. The assignment statement may very well write past the end of the allocated memory, causing hard-to-diagnose run-time errors. Using `new`, there is no possibility for error because the compiler, rather than the programmer, computes the size needed:

```
int *intPointer;

intPointer = new int;
*intPointer = 0;
```

So, although you might be exceptionally fond of `malloc` and `free`, you should still switch to `new` and `delete` if for no other reason than to avoid the kind of mistakes shown above.

Here are some rules for using `new` and `delete`:

1. You can specify any type in the `new` statement:

   ```
   intPtr = new int;
   floatPtr = new float;
   myStructPtr = new MyStruct;
   ```

2. If you want to allocate an array, use the `new []` syntax:

   ```
   intPtr  = new int[10];
   ```

   The code above allocates a pointer to 10 integers. If you allocate an array with `new []`, you delete it with a slightly different syntax using `delete []`:

   ```
   delete [] intPtr;
   ```

3. Any time you allocate memory with `new []`, you should deallocate it with `delete []`. The `[]` in the `delete` statement specifies that the pointer has been allocated with the `[]` syntax.

4. The `delete` operator specifically enables deleting a `NULL` pointer. You can avoid checks like the following:

```
if (intPtr != NULL)
    delete intPtr;
```

Use the following replacement code:

```
delete intPtr;
```

Although you may continue to use malloc and free, you should switch to using new and delete. If you use both, be extremely careful to deallocate memory with the correct routine. If you allocate with malloc, deallocate with free. If you allocate with new, deallocate with delete.

Eliminating #define

The availability of a macro preprocessor (#define) is part of what makes C more usable than other languages like Pascal. So why, you ask, get rid of it? The answer lies in the two main uses of #define:

1. Defining named constants, such as:

   ```
   #define kTableSize 512
   ```

2. Enabling functions to be evaluated inline, rather than requiring a function call:

   ```
   #define Round(myFloat) ((int) ((myFloat) + 0.5)
   ```

C++ offers replacements for both. It provides const variables to define named constants:

```
const int kArraySize = 512;
```

C++ also replaces C's pseudo inline functions with real ones:

```
inline int Round(float myFloat)
{
    return (int) (myFloat + 0.5);
}
```

Const Variables

Those of you familiar with THINK C (and ANSI C) already know something about const variables. The THINK C compiler does not take full advantage of them, however, not allowing their use where constant expressions are needed, such as when you are defining an array. Thus, `const` variable use is relegated mostly to function prototypes, rather than as a general replacement for `#define`.

Here is the syntax for `const` variables:

```
const type name = value;
```

For comparative purposes look at a program written in C and C++. Here is the C version:

```
#define kArraySize 512

void main()
{
    int myArray[kArraySize];

    myArray[0] = 1;
}
```

While the above program compiles using both C and C++, the preferred C++ way to write it is slightly different:

```
const int kArraySize = 512;

void main()
{
    int myArray[kArraySize];

    myArray[0] = 1;
}
```

The `const` keyword signifies that the value of `kArraySize` cannot change throughout the program.

Look at why this use of `const` is better than `#define`. In C++, it is the compiler, and not the preprocessor, that replaces the uses of `kArraySize` with `512`. For the following four reasons this is favorable:

1. The compiler prevents redeclaration of the variable. For instance, many C compilers allow the following:

   ```
   #define kArraySize 512
   ...
   #define kArraySize 256
   ```

Unlike other programmers, THINK C users are fortunate in this regard because THINK C does not allow a redeclaration of a #define.

2. The variable is not substituted literally; it stays a symbol. This is enormously helpful when debugging because the compiler retains a meaningful name that shows up in error messages. If you have ever tried to decipher a program that points to a value like 512, you know that kArraySize is a much more useful name to see.

3. You are not limited to built-in types with const; you are free to use your own. For example, here is how to declare a constant Rect:

```
const Rect kEmptyRect = {0, 0, 0, 0};
```

4. const uses the same syntax as other variables. While diversity is nice, consistency makes for easier maintenance and less errors.

Clearly const variables are preferable to #define. You cannot inadvertently redeclare them, they are easier to use in debugging, and you can have types that are not built-in and that have a consistent syntax.

Inline Functions

C programmers also use #define to reduce the overhead of frequent function calls. C++ addresses this problem by creating a new type of function, the inline function. By declaring a function inline, you request that the compiler place the code of the function directly inline rather than making a function call. Here is a typical C example of #define that accomplishes this purpose:

```
#define Round(myFloat) ((int) ((myFloat) + 0.5))
```

The same goal is far easier to achieve using an inline function in C++:

```
inline int Round(float f)
{
    return (int) (myFloat + 0.5);
}
```

Inlining a function can have dramatic effects on the speed of your program. (Which, of course, is why `#define` was used for this purpose in the first place). Look at a sample program without inlines to see how inlining can speed it up.

```
#include <stream.h>
#include <Events.h>

static int Value(int i)
{
    if (i < 10)
        return 2;
    else if (i < 1000)
        return 3;
    else
        return 4;
}

void main()
{
    long startTime = TickCount();
    int total = 0;
    int i;

    for (i = 0; i < 100000; i++)
        total += Value(i);

    long endTime = TickCount();
    cout << "total = " << total << '\n' << "time = " <<
      endTime - startTime;
}
```

When run, the above program outputs the following:

```
total = 398990
time = 37
```

This is what the object code looks like:

```
Value:
00000000: 4E56 0000           LINK      A6,#$0000
00000004: 0CAE 0000 000A      CMPI.L    #$0000000A,$0008(A6)
          0008
0000000C: 6C04                BGE.S     *+$0006          ; 00000012
0000000E: 7002                MOVEQ     #$02,D0
00000010: 6010                BRA.S     *+$0012          ; 00000022
00000012: 0CAE 0000 03E8      CMPI.L    #$000003E8,$0008(A6)
          0008
0000001A: 6C04                BGE.S     *+$0006          ; 00000020
0000001C: 7003                MOVEQ     #$03,D0
0000001E: 6002                BRA.S     *+$0004          ; 00000022
00000020: 7004                MOVEQ     #$04,D0
00000022: 4E5E                UNLK      A6
00000024: 205F                MOVEA.L   (A7)+,A0
00000026: 584F                ADDQ.W    #$4,A7
00000028: 4ED0                JMP       (A0)
00000036

main:

00000000: 4E56 0000           LINK      A6,#$0000
00000004: 48E7 1F20           MOVEM.L   D3-D7/A2,-(A7)
00000008: 594F                SUBQ.W    #$4,A7
0000000A: A975                _TickCount
0000000C: 281F                MOVE.L    (A7)+,D4
0000000E: 7A00                MOVEQ     #$00,D5
00000010: 7C00                MOVEQ     #$00,D6
00000012: 0C86 0001 86A0      CMPI.L    #$000186A0,D6
00000018: 6C12                BGE.S     *+$0014          ; 0000002C
0000001A: 2F06                MOVE.L    D6,-(A7)
0000001C: 4EBA 0000           JSR       Value(int)
00000020: DA80                ADD.L     D0,D5
00000022: 5286                ADDQ.L    #$1,D6
00000024: 0C86 0001 86A0      CMPI.L    #$000186A0,D6
0000002A: 6DEE                BLT.S     *-$0010          ; 0000001A
0000002C: 594F                SUBQ.W    #$4,A7
0000002E: A975                _TickCount
00000030: 2E1F                MOVE.L    (A7)+,D7
00000032: 2007                MOVE.L    D7,D0
00000034: 9084                SUB.L     D4,D0
00000036: 2F00                MOVE.L    D0,-(A7)
```

```
00000038: 486D 0000          PEA       $0000(A5)
0000003C: 700A               MOVEQ     #$0A,D0
0000003E: 1F00               MOVE.B    D0,-(A7)
00000040: 486D 0000          PEA       $0000(A5)
00000044: 486D 0000          PEA       cout
00000048: 4EBA 0000          JSR       ostream::operator <<(const
                                         char *)
0000004C: 2440               MOVEA.L   D0,A2
0000004E: 2605               MOVE.L    D5,D3
00000050: 2F03               MOVE.L    D3,-(A7)
00000052: 2F0A               MOVE.L    A2,-(A7)
00000054: 4EBA 0000          JSR       ostream::operator <<(long)
00000058: 2F00               MOVE.L    D0,-(A7)
0000005A: 4EBA 0000          JSR       ostream::operator <<(char)
0000005E: 2F00               MOVE.L    D0,-(A7)
00000060: 4EBA 0000          JSR       ostream::operator <<(const
                                         char *)
00000064: 2F00               MOVE.L    D0,-(A7)
00000066: 4EBA 0000          JSR       ostream::operator <<(long)
0000006A: 4CDF 04F8          MOVEM.L   (A7)+,D3-D7/A2
0000006E: 4E5E               UNLK      A6
00000070: 4E75               RTS
0000007A
```

This program makes a time-consuming function call for each iteration of the loop. Inlining was created to fix just this problem. Watch what happens in the same program when `Value` is inlined:

```
#include <stream.h>
#include <Events.h>

static inline int Value(int i)
{
    if (i < 10)
        return 2;
    else if (i < 1000)
        return 3;
    else
        return 4;
}
```

```
void main()
{
    long startTime = TickCount();
    int total = 0;
    int i;

    for (i = 0; i < 100000; i++)
        total += Value(i);

    long endTime = TickCount();
    cout << "total = " << total << '\n' << "time = " <<
      endTime - startTime;
}
```

This time, when you run the program, it outputs the following:

```
total = 398990
time = 18
```

In this example, the object code looks like the following:

```
main:
00000000: 4E56 FFFC          LINK      A6,#$FFFC
00000004: 48E7 1F20          MOVEM.L   D3-D7/A2,-(A7)
00000008: 594F               SUBQ.W    #$4,A7
0000000A: A975               _TickCount
0000000C: 281F               MOVE.L    (A7)+,D4
0000000E: 7A00               MOVEQ     #$00,D5
00000010: 7C00               MOVEQ     #$00,D6
00000012: 0C86 0001 86A0     CMPI.L    #$000186A0,D6
00000018: 6C28               BGE.S     *+$002A          ; 00000042
0000001A: 2606               MOVE.L    D6,D3
0000001C: 0C86 0000 000A     CMPI.L    #$0000000A,D6
00000022: 6C04               BGE.S     *+$0006          ; 00000028
00000024: 7002               MOVEQ     #$02,D0
00000026: 600E               BRA.S     *+$0010          ; 00000036
00000028: 0C86 0000 03E8     CMPI.L    #$000003E8,D6
0000002E: 6C04               BGE.S     *+$0006          ; 00000034
00000030: 7003               MOVEQ     #$03,D0
00000032: 6002               BRA.S     *+$0004          ; 00000036
00000034: 7004               MOVEQ     #$04,D0
00000036: DA80               ADD.L     D0,D5
00000038: 5286               ADDQ.L    #$1,D6
0000003A: 0C86 0001 86A0     CMPI.L    #$000186A0,D6
```

```
00000040: 6DD8           BLT.S     *-$0026        ; 0000001A
00000042: 594F           SUBQ.W    #$4,A7
00000044: A975           _TickCount
00000046: 2E1F           MOVE.L    (A7)+,D7
00000048: 2007           MOVE.L    D7,D0
0000004A: 9084           SUB.L     D4,D0
0000004C: 2F00           MOVE.L    D0,-(A7)
0000004E: 486D 0000      PEA       $0000(A5)
00000052: 700A           MOVEQ     #$0A,D0
00000054: 1F00           MOVE.B    D0,-(A7)
00000056: 486D 0000      PEA       $0000(A5)
0000005A: 486D 0000      PEA       cout
0000005E: 4EBA 0000      JSR       ostream::operator <<(const
                                     char *)
00000062: 2440           MOVEA.L   D0,A2
00000064: 2D45 FFFC      MOVE.L    D5,$FFFC(A6)
00000068: 2F2E FFFC      MOVE.L    $FFFC(A6),-(A7)
0000006C: 2F0A           MOVE.L    A2,-(A7)
0000006E: 4EBA 0000      JSR       ostream::operator <<(long)
00000072: 2F00           MOVE.L    D0,-(A7)
00000074: 4EBA 0000      JSR       ostream::operator <<(char)
00000078: 2F00           MOVE.L    D0,-(A7)
0000007A: 4EBA 0000      JSR       ostream::operator <<(const
                                     char *)
0000007E: 2F00           MOVE.L    D0,-(A7)
00000080: 4EBA 0000      JSR       ostream::operator <<(long)
00000084: 4CDF 04F8      MOVEM.L   (A7)+,D3-D7/A2
00000088: 4E5E           UNLK      A6
0000008A: 4E75           RTS
00000094
```

Note that the `Value` function is not in the object code. Instead, the `main` routine directly includes the code within the for loop.

By adding this one word (`inline`) to your program, you cut the running time by more than 50 percent. Admittedly, this is an unusual example. It does point out, however, that inlining functions can have dramatic performance effects on a program.

Before you get too attached to inline functions, you need to bear in mind that they are not a panacea:

1. In most cases, the `inline` keyword should be added to your program only after it is running correctly.
2. You should only use inline functions on portions of your program that consume the most time.

A well-known computing rule of thumb, the 80-20 rule, states that 80 percent of your time is spent on 20 percent of your code. Or, if you are an optimist you can use the 90-10 version of this rule. In any event, this means that you should focus your speed-up efforts on the 20 of your code that consumes 80 percent of your performance time (the hot spots). Trying to optimize all of your code is best left to individuals who never have to ship a product. In summary, before attempting to speed up your program, determine where your program spends its time and focus your efforts there.

NOTE

To find where your program spends your time, use a profiler. Symantec C++ provides profiling tools. See chapters 9 and 12 for more information on the subject of efficient code.

Now that you have learned how to inline and about the theoretical underpinnings of when to do so, examine when to inline.

Small Functions and Inlining

Here is the first rule of inlining: The smaller the function, the better a candidate it is for inlining. Unfortunately, inlining a function can actually slow things down instead of speeding them up. Use the following rule to determine if inlining will help.

RULE

If the code emitted for an inline function is smaller than the code necessary to call it, then inlining the function is definitely better.

Making a function inline can increase the size of the code that calls it. This is especially true in extreme cases, such as when you inline a large function that is called many times in your program. Here, you end up with increased segment loading and unloading due to the larger segments. So, instead of getting speed, you actually have injected your program with a dose of molasses. If you are unclear whether inlined functions are benefitting your code, you always can measure the speed of your program after making the supposed optimization to make sure your alleged speed-up is not in reality a slow-down.

Functions That Cannot Be Inlined

Some functions cannot be inlined. Different compilers have different rules about which functions can and cannot be inlined. You should realize that, like the `register` declaration, the `inline` declaration is a suggestion (or request) to the compiler. The compiler may not always inline a function, but usually does so if you request it.

Here are some examples of functions that are not inlined by Symantec C++:

- Recursive functions (actually, the first iteration is inlined; the remainder are not)

```
inline unsigned int Factorial(unsigned int i)
{
    if (i <= 1)
        return 1;
    else
        return i * Factorial(i - 1);
}
```

- Functions with loops

```
inline unsigned int Length(char *s)
{
    unsigned int total;

    while (*s++ != '\0')
        total++;
    return total;
}
```

- Functions with `switch` statements

```
inline unsigned int FunctionWithSwitch(int i)
{
    switch (i) {
    case 1:
        return 1;
    case 2:
        return 2;
    default:
        return 6;
    }
}
```

Some C++ compilers warn you if they will not honor your inline request. Unfortunately, Symantec C++ does not provide a warning. You have to disassemble the object code to tell for sure.

Inlining Avoids #define Problems

There are a number of problems with `#define` that you can avoid by using inline functions. Some of them can be quite nasty.

- Arguments to a macro may be evaluated an incorrect number of times. Contrast this with `inline` functions whose arguments are evaluated exactly once. Multiple argument evaluations can be frightening to contemplate. For instance, look at this seemingly innocent macro definition:

```
#define Square(x) ((x) * (x))
```

After the call `Square(i++)`, `i` is incremented twice because the call expands to the following:

```
(i++) * (i++)
```

This is definitely not what you want `Square(i++)` to do. With inlining, on the other hand, you can write the following code:

```
inline int Square(int x)
{
    return x * x;
}
```

The call to `Square(i++)` correctly increments `i` exactly once.

▼ Name conflicts occur with any temporary variables. For example, a common way to swap two variables is to use a temporary variable (however, it is possible to do so without one). Here is a macro that swaps two integers:

```
#define Swap(ptr1, ptr2) \
{ \
    int tmp; \
    tmp = *(ptr1); \
    *(ptr1) = *(ptr2); \
    *(ptr2) = tmp; \
}
```

Under normal circumstances this macro works fine:

```
int x, y;
Swap(&x, &y);
```

But, look at what happens when you call this same Swap routine with a variable named tmp:

```
Swap(&tmp, &y);
```

The routine becomes the following:

```
{
    int tmp;
    tmp = *(&tmp);
    *(&tmp) = *(&y);
    *(&y) = tmp;
}
```

It swaps the value of y with the new local (uninitialized) variable tmp. Using an inline function, on the other hand, avoids this problem:

```
inline void Swap(int *ptr1, int *ptr2)
{
    int tmp;

    tmp = *ptr1;
    *ptr1 = *ptr2
    *ptr2 = tmp;
}
```

This function works neatly for both examples because the compiler renames variables as necessary within inline functions to avoid conflict. Let the compiler do the work for you.

NOTE

There is an algorithm for swapping two variables without a temporary. For the uninitiated, it consists of three exclusive OR operations. For example, to swap two variables, x and y, use the following:

```
x = x ^ y;
y = x ^ y;
x = x ^ y;
```

Precedence Problems

Suppose that you have the following `#define`:

```
#define Square(x)     x * x
```

Then the expression `1.0 / Square(2.0)` evaluates to `1.0` rather than the `0.25` you may expect. The reason for this error can be seen by examining the expression after the preprocessor is done:

```
1.0 / 2.0 * 2.0
```

Because / and * are of equal precedence and are left-associative, the expression is evaluated as follows:

```
(1.0 / 2.0) * 2.0
```

The expression becomes `0.5 * 2.0`, which equals `1.0`.

The correct way to write `Square` using a `#define` macro is to use parentheses:

```
#define Square(x)      ((x) * (x))
```

However, the best way is, again, to use an inline function:

```
inline float Square(float x)
{
    return x * x;
}
```

Conclusions about Const Variables and Inline Functions

In summary, C++ provides two mechanisms, `const` variables and `inline` functions, that reduce or completely eliminate the need for `#define` macros. `Const` variables are superior because you can use them with your own data as well as for built-in types. Furthermore, they cannot be redeclared and they are more helpful in debugging. Likewise, you should use `inline` functions over `#define` because they provide more control over your code: Their arguments cannot be evaluated in a multiple fashion, and any naming conflicts are handled by the compiler. Lastly, inline functions can give you better program performance if they are used correctly.

References

If you took a compiler construction class, you probably remember learning about the three different ways parameters are passed. Table 8.3 shows the different parameter-passing methods.

Table 8.3. Parameter-Passing Methods

Parameter-Passing Method	What Is Passed
call by value	The value of the variable is passed.
call by reference (call by address)	The address of the variable is passed.
call by name	The function acts as if the name of the variable had been replaced textually in the function.

You may remember quizzes in school with complicated functions passing different parameters in which you had to figure out what would be printed. In C, all parameters are passed by value (with the following exception).

NOTE

Well, actually not all parameters are passed by value in C. Arrays are passed by address because the value of an array name is the address of its first element. Structures are passed by value in modern C compilers and have been for quite some time. An historical tidbit is that, behind the structure value/address problem, is the first edition of Kernighan and Ritchie, in which they stated that structures are passed by address. Soon afterward, some changes were made to C (including `enums` and passing structures by value). These changes were implemented in UNIX C compilers, but not in many PC C compilers, which were based on the Kernighan and Ritchie version of the language. Thankfully, ANSI standardization has removed the Tower of Babel. The ANSI standard is that structures are passed by value.

For example, if you need a procedure called `Increment`, which increments its argument, you write it as follows:

```
void Increment(int *p)
{
    (*p)++;
}
```

You call the procedure with the following:

```
Increment(&myInteger);
```

C++ offers more flexibility; you can pass parameters one of two ways:

1. By value, just like C
2. By address, using references

Using the second method, the `Increment` procedure looks like this in C++:

```
void Increment(int &p)
{
    p++;
}
```

You can call this procedure with the following:

```
Increment(myInteger);
```

NOTE

Many FORTRAN compilers use call by reference, even when passing constants. One trick used by FORTRAN programmers is to write a routine `SetToPi` that assigns 3.14159 to its parameter. They sneakily call `SetToPi(3)` early in their program, which changes the value of the constant 3 to 3.14159. Having done this, they then can use 3 anywhere they need the value of π in their program.

How References Work

Because it is specific to C++, this book focuses on the second method of passing parameters. Here is a fuller definition of reference, as stated in the following rule.

RULE

A reference in C++ is a variable that refers to (or is another name for) some other variable.

In the sample above, the parameter `p` in `Increment` refers to `myInteger`. In both the explicit pointer case (the C example) and the reference case (the C++ example), the actual value passed to the `Increment` procedure is the address of `myInteger`. The differences between the two are listed below:

1. How the parameter is passed. With references, no `&` is required (in fact, the `&` is forbidden).
2. How the parameter is used in the procedure. With references, you do not use `*` to dereference the parameter.

The underlying code that is generated is the same in either case, however. The compiler silently adds an `&` before reference parameters in the call to the routine and silently adds an `*` to dereference each use of a reference within the routine.

References and the Const Keyword

The `const` keyword works with references in the same way it works with explicit pointer parameters. The combination of `const` and references is especially useful with large structures: You get the simpler syntax of passing by value, while having the efficiency of passing by address.

Table 8.4 shows the possible combinations of references and `const`. From these examples, you should get a better idea how `const` interacts with references and the differences between references and pointers. You also should note that with references you do not need to explicitly check for null values.

This table shows how the `const &` syntax works. The combination looks like a call by value because the caller does not need to put an explicit & in the code. However, this syntax gives you the efficiency of a call by address because only the address is passed.

Some Rules of Thumb for Reference Use

To a certain extent you need to develop your own style of reference use. Until then, the rules listed below offer a nice approach.

RULE

If the value of the variable can change within a routine, use a non-`const` pointer:

```
void AdjustTheRectangle(Rect *r, int amount)
{
    r->top += amount;
    r->bottom += amount;
}
```

Table 8.4. Reference and Const Parameters

Const	Reference Parameter	Pointer Parameter

No	`void Routine(int &i)`
	`{`
	`    i = 5;`
	`}`
	
	Call with:
	`Routine(myVar);`
	The routine can alter the value of the reference parameter. The parameter *cannot* be `NULL (0)`.
		`void Routine(int *ip)`
		`{`
		`    if (ip != NULL)`
		`        *ip = 5;`
		`}`
		Call with:
		`Routine(&myVar);` or `Routine(NULL);`
		The routine can alter the value to which the parameter points. The parameter *can* be `NULL (0)`.

Yes	`void Routine(const int &i)`
	`{`
	`    //i = 5;  not allowed`
	`    gTotal += i; // allowed`
	`}`
	
	Call with:
	`Routine(myVar);`
	The routine cannot alter the value of the reference parameter. The parameter *cannot* be `NULL (0)`.
		`void Routine(const int *ip)`
		`{`
		`    if (ip != NULL) {`
		`        // *ip = 5; not allowed`
		`        gTotal += *ip;`
		`}`
		Call with:
		`Routine(&myVar);` or `Routine(NULL);`
		The routine cannot alter the value it points to. The parameter *can* be `NULL (0)`.

RULE

If the parameter could be NULL, use a `const` pointer.

```
// prints point as (v, h)
void PrintThePointIfItExists(const Point *pointPtr)
{
    if (pointPtr!= NULL) {
        cout << "(" << pointPtr->v << ", " pointPtr->h << ")";
    }
}
```

RULE

For a small variable (one whose size is less than or equal to the size of a pointer, 4 bytes), use neither pointers nor references:

```
// sizeof(Point) == 4
// prints point as (v, h)
void PrintThePoint(Point p)
{
    cout << "(" << pointPtr->v << ", " pointPtr->h << ")";
}
```

RULE

In all other cases, use a `const` reference:

```
// sizeof(Rect) == 8
// prints rectangle as (top, left)/(bottom, right)
void PrintTheRectangle(const Rect &r)
{
    cout << "(" << r.top << ", " << r.left << ")/(" <<
      r.bottom << ", " << r.right << ")";
}
```

Adopting the style advocated in these rules has one big advantage when you are reading the code: When looking at the call to a function, only parameters preceded by an & can change, and if a parameter is preceded by an &, it probably will change.

To illustrate further the value of these rules, look at the code examples in table 8.5. This tables shows calls to two routines: `SetRectangle` (which modifies the passed-in rectangle) and `FrameRectangle` (which does not modify the passed-in rectangle). It shows them in normal C, Pascal, and the new C++ style.

Table 8.5. Three Ways of Calling Toolbox Routines

Normal C	Pascal	New C++ Style
`FrameRectangle(&r);`	`FrameRectangle(r);`	`FrameRectangle(r);`
`SetRectangle(&r, 1, 2, 3, 4);`	`SetRectangle(r, 1, 2, 3, 4);`	`SetRectangle(&r, 1, 2, 3, 4);`

Using normal C, the calls to `SetRectangle` and `FrameRectangle` look the same: Both use &. The problem here is that, without looking at the declaration (`FrameRectangle` is declared to take a `const Rect *`), you cannot tell whether or not each call modifies `r`. In the Pascal case, the problem is the same. Without looking at the declaration (`SetRectangle` is declared to take a `var Rect` parameter), you cannot tell whether each call modifies `r`. In the new C++ style, it is clear that `SetRectangle` modifies `r` because the & is present and that `FrameRectangle` does not because the & is absent.

Other Uses of References

Supporting call-by-reference parameter passing is the most common use of references, but not the only one. Other circumstances call for this type of parameter passing as well. For instance, any declaration can use the & to define a reference. Following is a simple example:

```
void main()
{
    int i = 0;
    int &r = i;      // initializes r to refer to i
    int j = 3;
```

```
    cout << i << r << j;
    r = j;          // modifies i
    cout << i << r << j;
    i = 2;
    cout << i << r << j;
}
```

Here is the output:

```
0 0 3
3 3 3
2 2 3
```

Be careful with this kind of use. You cannot write code like the following:

```
int &r;      // illegal
```

This code declares a reference variable but fails to initialize the reference. One way to understand references is to think of aliases in the Finder. When you create an alias, you have to specify what the alias represents. You cannot just create an alias for nothing and later determine what the alias represents. References are similar: When you define a reference, you must initialize it with a variable to which it refers.

You also can use references with the return type of routines. Usually, you do this so you can use function calls on the left side of assignment statements.

```
int gVar1;
int gVar2;

int &GetCorrectGlobal()
{
    if (IsDaylightSavingsTime())
        return gVar1;
    else
        return gVar2;
}
void main()
{
    GetCorrectGlobal() = 3;
}
```

This main program sets either gVar1 or gVar2 to 3, depending on whether IsDaylightSavingsTime returns true. For functions that return a reference, the reference is initialized with the variable returned from the function.

In summary, there are cases where you may prefer C++'s use of references for parameter passing over the old style of passing by value. Besides being slicker-looking they give you the following advantages:

- They are simpler to use for parameter passing (you do not need to use & and * for referencing and dereferencing).
- When combined with the const keyword, references provide simpler syntax and greater efficiency.
- References make reading code easier in many cases, especially when you adopt some simple rules for their use.

Summary

Is C++ a better C? C++ is easier to use and handles errors better—two of C's weakest areas. These reasons alone should convince you that C++ is a better C.

Error handling is a big problem in C. Although your code may compile and link, it may not do what you want it to do. Here is how C++ improves this situation:

- C++ has much more rigorous error checking. This may be the best gift of all. Yes, you are required to do much more code preparation, such as with prototyping. The results, however, are clean compiles that work the way you want them to.
- C++ has fewer I/O errors. You do not get I/O typing errors of which the compiler never informs you, such as typing %d when you meant %f. When you use the stream library, the C++ compiler figures out what kind of I/O is necessary based on the arguments you pass.
- Twilight-zone #define macros are eliminated. C++'s inline function arguments cannot be multiply evaluated, so you do not

end up with innocent looking `#define` macros like the following that produce nightmare results:

```
#define Square(x) ((x) * (x))
```

- ▼ A new comment structure reduces the potential for error. // comments do not steal portions of your code like /* */ comments can. Furthermore, you cannot forget to close // comments because they auto-terminate.

The second major area of improvement in C++ is ease of use. Many of these improvements obviously go hand in hand with better error handling. Ideally, one would want a language that is both easier to use and handles errors better—a great combination. Below is a review of the changes that make C++ easier to use:

- ▼ C++ uses simpler I/O code. With the stream library, you no longer have to write code that looks like this:

  ```
  printf("%d %d", s.i, s.j);
  ```

  On the contrary, your code is short and sweet:

  ```
  cout << s;
  ```

- ▼ Debugging is easier. Debugging is much easier with `const` variables because you can examine the values of `const` variables, something you cannot do with `#defined` constants. Similarly, you do not have to remember the special syntax of `#define`.
- ▼ C++ code is more readable. Code that mixes execution and declaration also reads much more naturally because you can group definitions of variables with the logically related code that uses them.
- ▼ Functions can be overloaded. You no longer have to create different names for identically acting functions just because they take different arguments. This frees up your creativity for icon and About box design.
- ▼ Structs are easier to use. You no longer need to typedef them; the compiler does it for you.
- ▼ Code with argument parameters passed by address is easier to read. When you use references, it is easy to tell which variables are modified, something much more difficult with C.

- Function arguments can have default values. This makes them much more flexible. You can choose whether or not to include arguments in function calls; the compiler fills in the blanks with your preset defaults.
- Memory management is easier. You can delete null pointers using `delete` (not so with `free`).

These are just the highlights of this chapter. You can start using these new C++ constructs armed with the sure and certain knowledge you are writing better C code in C++.

Exercises

1. Convert the following from ANSI C to idiomatic C++:

```
#include <string.h>
#include <stdio.h>
#include <ctype.h>

#define kArraySize 200
#define kMaxStringSize 100

typedef struct MyStruct {
    char string[kMaxStringSize];
    int count;
} MyStruct;

MyStruct gStringArray[kArraySize];

/* InitializeArray: initializes the string array to empty
  entries */
void InitializeArray()
{
    int i;

    for (i = 0; i < kArraySize; i++)
    {
        gStringArray[i].string[0]= '\0';
        gStringArray[i].count = 0;
    }
}
```

```
/* FindEntry: returns matching entry, or NULL if no matching
  entry exists */
MyStruct *FindEntry(char *key)
{
    int i;

    for (i = 0; i < kArraySize; i++)
        if (strcmp(gStringArray[i].string, key) == 0)
            return &gStringArray[i];
    return NULL;
}

/* PrintEntries: prints all nonempty entries in the array */
void PrintEntries()
{
    int i;

    for (i = 0; i < kArraySize; i++)
        if (gStringArray[i].string[0] != '\0')
            printf("%s: %d\n", gStringArray[i].string,
gStringArray[i].count);
}

/* FindEmptyEntry: returns empty entry in array or NULL if
  no empty entries */
MyStruct *FindEmptyEntry()
{
    int i;

    for (i = 0; i < kArraySize; i++)
        if (gStringArray[i].string[0] == '\0')
            return &gStringArray[i];
    return NULL;
}

/* AddString: Adds the key to the array if not present,
  otherwise increments count */
void AddString(char *key)
{
    MyStruct *s;
```

```
    s = FindEntry(key);
    if (s == NULL) {
        s = FindEmptyEntry();
        if (s == NULL)
            return;

        strcpy(s->string, key);
    }
    s->count++;
}

/* GetWord: Gets the next word from standard input */
int GetWord(char *word)
{
    int c;

    /* skip white space */
    for (c = getchar(); c != EOF && isspace(c); c =
      getchar())
        ; /* do nothing */

    if (c == EOF)
        return 0;

    while (!isspace(c)) {
        *word++ = c;
        c = getchar();
    }
    *word++ = '\0';
    ungetc(c, stdin);    /* put back the last character */
    return 1;
}

/* prints summary of input words, along with count of each
  word */
void main()
{
    char incomingWord[256];

    InitializeArray();
    while (GetWord(incomingWord))
        AddString(incomingWord);
    PrintEntries();
}
```

2. What does the following program print if the compiler uses call-by-value, call-by-reference, or call-by-name parameter passing?

```
void Foo(int i)
{
    i = 3;
}

void Bar(int i)
{
    printf("%d\n", i * i);
}

main()
{
    int j = 4;

    Bar(j);
    Foo(j);
    printf("%d\n", j);
}
```

3. *Inside Macintosh*, the official Macintosh programming documentation uses Pascal in its sample code. C programmers may find it difficult to convert from Pascal to C due to the changes they need to make in calls to the Toolbox. Here are the rules that the Pascal compiler uses when passing parameters:

    - When passing a parameter whose value changes (VAR parameters), pass the address (call by reference).
    - When passing a parameter whose value does not change, and whose size is less than or equal to 4 bytes, pass the value (call by value).
    - When passing a parameter whose value does not change, and whose size is greater than 4 bytes, pass the address (call by reference).

    Look at these rules in action for two Toolbox calls, `FrameRect` and `AddPt`. Here are their declarations in Pascal:

    ```
    Procedure FrameRect(r: Rect);
    Procedure AddPt(src: Point; VAR dst: Point);
    ```

These routines can be called from Pascal with the following code:

```
FrameRect(myRect);
AddPt(srcPoint, dstPoint);
```

The corresponding declarations in C are as follows:

```
void FrameRect(const Rect *r);
void AddPt(Point src, Point *dst);
```

They can be called with the following code:

```
FrameRect(&myRect);
AddPt(srcPoint, &dstPoint);
```

Calls from both C and Pascal end up passing the same values, although the calls look different. Give alternate declarations for `FrameRect` and `AddPt` so that calls to them can be made from C++ the same way they are called from Pascal (with no &s) and so that the actual values that are passed remain the same.

4. `memset` is a C/C++ library function that sets memory to a given character repetitively. It is called with a pointer, a size, and a character. It is most often used to set memory to 0. Write a routine called `MemorySet` that, by default, sets the memory to 0 but accepts an argument specifying some other character. Be sure to test your routine.

5. Write a routine, `Length`, that computes the length of a string. Write routines, `Length` and `Height`, that compute the horizontal and vertical measurements of a rectangle. Be sure to test your routines.

9

An Introduction to Object-Oriented Design

As you are poised on the brink of a new language, it is time to remind yourself what kind of brink it is. Moving from C to C++ (or any other object-oriented language) is not just about learning the syntax of the new features. It also means moving from a procedural to an object-oriented model of code design. There is plenty of hoopla in the industry over oopla (object-oriented programming and language application) which, no doubt, accounts for one of the reasons you are reading this book. This chapter comes *before* you are introduced to the nuts and bolts of C++ because you need to shift your mind-set out of the procedural world first.

This chapter provides an introduction to object-oriented programming (OOP) in particular and to the object-oriented model of design in general. Along the way, you receive a liberal dose of motivational discussion regarding the benefits of this model and coding style. You also get a glimpse of the practical impulses within computer programming that have given rise to the model shift.

Object-Oriented Programming

The flavor of object-oriented programming is quite different from procedural programming, and countless books have been written on this subject, many of which are worth reading. Before getting into some programming examples, it is instructive to review the motivations behind using this coding style.

Benefits of Object-Oriented Programming

Real world programmers facing recurring problems were the impulse behind the shift to object-oriented programming. As you might expect, the benefits OOP offers bear directly on its origins. The major benefits of OOP are the following:

- Object-oriented programming is more natural. Humans are categorizers. They naturally place objects into categories in their every day lives. Take, for instance, the Library of Congress—certainly a grand testament to the organizational impulse within us. It is no less appropriate to apply this principle to programming. Code becomes easier to design and reason about if programs are organized into categories of easily understandable objects. Procedural languages that use operations are somewhat less natural and, as such, are harder to use.
- Object-oriented programs are more maintainable. Object-oriented programming separates your program into objects. You can change the internal implementation or characteristics of an object without changing its external behavior or appearance. You also can add additional behaviors to some objects without affecting all objects of that type. This makes bugs easier to fix and features easier to add because the effects of changes are contained to smaller areas and thus easier to find.
- Code in object-oriented programs is more reusable. Object-oriented programming is ideally suited for real world code reuse. The ivory tower approach to programming insists that it is

feasible to pull code from a library and use it without modification. In real life, however, the problem is never exactly what existing code solves. Instead, minor (or sometimes major) changes are necessary before the code can perform the new task. OOP insists that there is no such thing as perfect library code that solves every specialized problem. Instead, it enables you to do programming by differences. You inherit some code and modify (override) the routines that you want to customize.

- Revisions in object-oriented code are quicker because less breaks when adding new features. Because code is easier to reuse and fixes affect fewer lines of code, you finish faster. This, of course, takes some time—you have got to gain some experience using OOP. It is no different than typing: Hunt-and-peck typists are no match for a good touch typist. When hunt-and-peck typists first learn touch typing, they initially are slower than they used to be. Speed then goes back up to the starting speed and eventually exceeds it. The pattern is similar with OOP. Eventually your designs and your skills advance enough that your code becomes easier to maintain and reuse.
- Object-oriented programming is more fun. Separating your program into objects makes it easier to modify one part without breaking another part. Life is more fun because, as your program becomes more malleable, you can experiment with new features that you would not have dared adding before. You are not prevented from making a change because you fear repercussions in the rest of the code. Furthermore, because code is more reusable, you do not spend your time reinventing the wheel in program after program. You instead focus on the unique challenges a particular program presents, something that is more fun.

The Genesis of Object-Oriented Programming

OOP is a natural progression that started with modules. In the beginning, there was a morass, and the morass was made of global variables and routines that haphazardly modified the globals (see fig. 9.1). The hodge-podge of arrows in this figure and the three following ones represent program calls from other parts of the program.

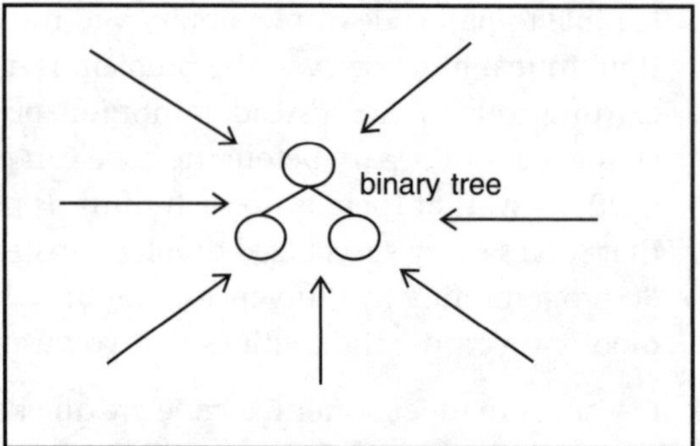

Figure 9.1. Routines haphazardly modifying a data structure.

Modular Programming

Modular programming specifies that global variables and the routines that operate on them should be broken into modules. For example, rather than having all parts of your program access the binary tree data structure, you have a few specific routines do all the accessing (see fig. 9.2). The other routines call the few.

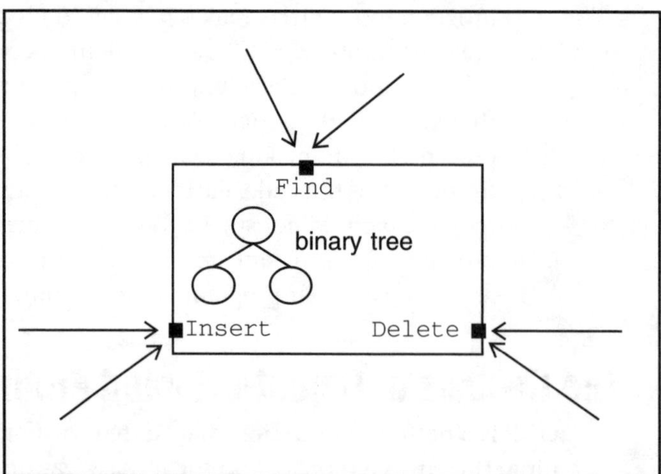

Figure 9.2. All access to binary tree through module entry points.

With modular programming, your program is better structured and more maintainable. This is handled in C with .c and .h files. You implement modules by putting defining data and routines in a .c file and exporting the specific routines in a .h file. Because the data is within a .c file, only the routines in that file can access the data. Take, for instance, the following example of a binary tree in C. The BinaryTree.h code is listed below:

```
void Insert(int key);
void Delete(int key);
int Find(int key);
```

Here is the BinaryTree.c code:

```
struct Node {
    struct Node *leftChild;
    struct Node *rightChild;
    int key;
};
static struct Node *root = NULL;

void Insert(...)
{
    ...
}
...
```

There is a major problem with modules, however. Because modules still operate on global variables, you can have only one data structure. In the above example, only one binary tree is allowed in your program. What if you need two, or five, or five hundred?

Data Types

You can extend the module by packaging the global variables from the module into a structure. This structure can then be passed to and from the module routines. A new BinaryTree.h is listed below:

```
struct Node {
    struct Node *leftChild;
    struct Node *rightChild;
    int key;
};
```

```
struct BinaryTree {
    struct Node *root;
};

void InitializeBinaryTree(struct BinaryTree *tree);
void Insert(struct BinaryTree *tree, int key);
void Delete(struct BinaryTree *tree, int key);
int Find(const struct BinaryTree *tree, int key);
```

And, here is BinaryTree.c:

```
void InitializeBinaryTree(struct BinaryTree *tree)
{
    tree->root = NULL;
}

void Insert(...)
{
    ...
}
```

This change in program structure enables multiple binary trees to form where there was only one. Unfortunately, it also enables the clients of the binary tree to modify the fields of the BinaryTree structure directly. Figure 9.3 shows the benefit of multiple binary trees, but also shows the weakness of enabling direct access to the data.

You may want to forbid such access because you know what can happen. A programmer is tempted to go to the tree and do wrong. He or she may not want to call the specified routine for fear it is too slow and directly set the data instead. Because the compiler cannot prevent direct operations on the structure, the data—and not your interface—gets used. Later on, you are unable to change the implementation of the program for fear of breaking all that code.

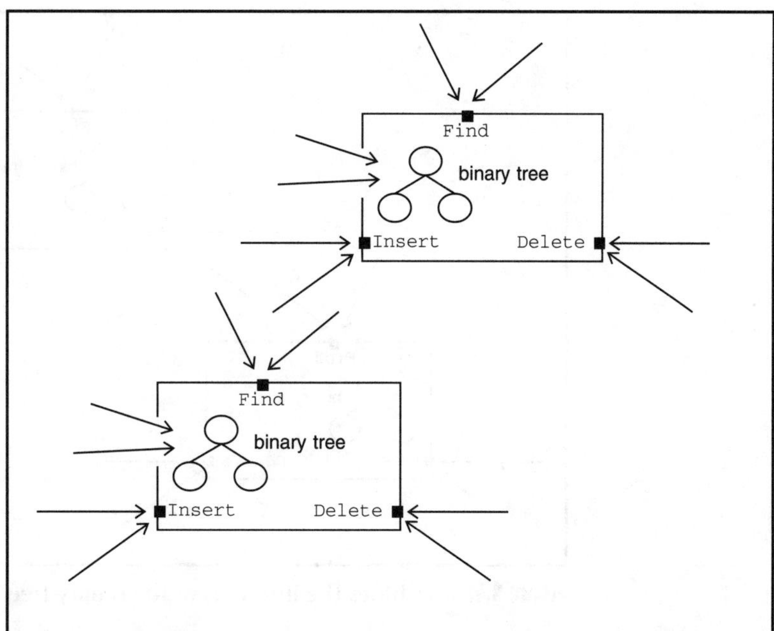

Figure 9.3. Storing a binary tree in a structure.

Data Types

Because of this, the abstract data type (ADT) was developed. It is a data structure in which all access is through procedures—no access to the data structure is allowed. This can be implemented in C by hiding the BinaryTree structure behind a pointer. The client is allowed to know only that BinaryTree is a pointer to something. Direct access to the tree is cut off forever (see fig. 9.4).

It is up to the BinaryTree module to allocate and deallocate a BinaryTree. BinaryTree.h is listed below:

```
struct BinaryTree;    /* we're not saying exactly what's in it
just yet */

struct BinaryTree *AllocateBinaryTree();
void DeallocateBinaryTree(struct BinaryTree *tree);
void Insert(struct BinaryTree *tree, int key);
void Delete(struct BinaryTree *tree, int key);
int Find(const struct BinaryTree *tree, int key);
```

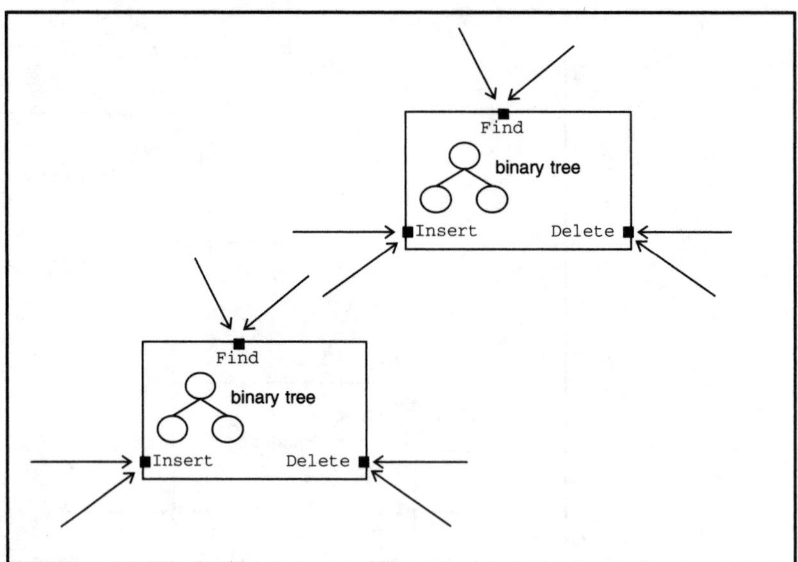

Figure 9.4. ADT hides the internals of the binary tree.

BinaryTree.c is as follow:

```
struct Node {
    struct Node *leftChild;
    struct Node *rightChild;
    int key;
};
struct BinaryTree {
    struct Node *root;
};

struct BinaryTree *AllocateBinaryTree()
{
    struct BinaryTree *tree = (struct BinaryTree *)
malloc(sizeof(BinaryTree));

    tree->root = NULL;
    return tree;
}
```

```
void DeallocateBinaryTree(struct BinaryTree *tree)
{
    free(tree);
}

void Insert(...)
{
    ...
}
```

Objects

Abstract data types can serve as the basis for a well-structured application. If you want to stop here, you can use OOP as an excellent way to create abstract data types. OOP enables you do a great deal more, however. By adding the concepts of inheritance and polymorphism, OOP gives you a new kind of type—the *class*. Variables of this type are called *objects* or *instances* of a class.

Inheritance. The concept of inheritance enables you to capture commonality among classes. For instance, there are various kinds of binary trees: red-black, AVL, and splay trees. Each kind arose in an attempt to overcome a shortcoming with standard binary trees—worst-case performance. Standard binary trees can get very unbalanced. In the worst case, a tree with *n* nodes has a depth of *n*. Searches, therefore, take linear time.

Each of these binary tree types implements `Insert` differently. Most of them do a `Find` in the same way, however. It is here that you greatly benefit from inheritance: Rather than writing each tree independently, with `Find` code duplicated, inheritance enables you to specify that each tree is derived from the same more general type. This way, each type of tree gets to inherit all the standard binary tree behavior. Moreover, a tree is free to override any general behavior for which it does not care (each overrides `Insert` differently). Extra functionality is not a problem, nor is augmenting existing behavior (for instance, splay trees must do additional work readjusting the tree during a `Find`).

NOTE

A red-black tree balances the tree by restructuring it when new nodes are inserted. Thus, a tree of *n* nodes is roughly log*n* nodes deep, and searches never take linear time. (It is called a red-black tree because each node is marked with a red or a black color. The tree is then structured so that a parent and child node do not have the same color.)

A splay (or self-adjusting) tree also tries to balance the tree. It does not attack the tree at every insertion; instead, it guarantees a balanced tree over the long run. Each time a `Find` is done, an incremental balancing is performed as well. Over time, the tree slowly becomes balanced. Although one particular search may take linear time, the average length of a search is logarithmic. The philosophy is that of doing a little house cleaning each week rather than a much larger spring cleaning each year.

Polymorphism. The second concept, polymorphism, is related to inheritance. By analogy, imagine your code request transforms itself into the very one that is required (by the object to which it is talking). Polymorphic code can make a request of a particular object, and that object's class ensures that the correct routine is called.

For example, suppose that you have red-black and splay binary tree objects and that you request an `Insert` for each one. A different `Insert` is called depending on whether the request is made of the red-black or the splay tree object.

Figure 9.5 shows the concept; each binary tree object has the same external interface (one of three entry points along the box). Internally, however, the particular function depends on the particular object.

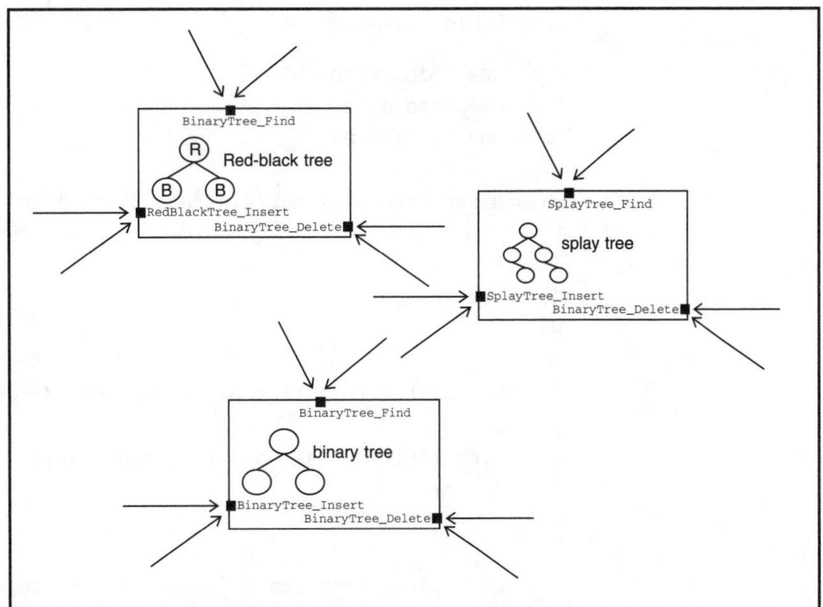

Figure 9.5. BinaryTree, RedBlackTree, and SplayTree objects.

Simulating Objects in C. You can simulate polymorphism and inheritance in C by adding function pointers to each ADT.

The following example shows binary, red-black, and splay trees; however, the actual binary tree code for each is not shown. The example focuses on showing the relationship between the different tree types. BinaryTree.h is listed below:

```
#pragma once

struct BinaryTree {
    void (*Insert)(struct BinaryTree *tree, int key);
    void (*Find)(struct BinaryTree *tree, int key);
    void (*Deallocate)(struct BinaryTree *tree);

    void *data;    /* unknown data */
};

 struct BinaryTree *AllocateBinaryTree();
```

Here is BinaryTree.c:

```
#include "BinaryTree.h"
#include <stdio.h>
#include <stdlib.h>

void BinaryTree_Deallocate(struct BinaryTree *tree)
{
    /* _ */
    free(tree);
}

void BinaryTree_Insert(struct BinaryTree *Tree, int key)
{
    printf("BinaryTree_Insert(%ld)\n", key);
    /* _ */
}

void BinaryTree_Find(struct BinaryTree *Tree, int key)
{
    printf("BinaryTree_Find(%ld)\n", key);
    /* _ */
}

struct BinaryTree *AllocateBinaryTree()
{
    struct BinaryTree *tree = (struct BinaryTree *)
      malloc(sizeof(BinaryTree));

    tree->Insert = BinaryTree_Insert;
    tree->Find = BinaryTree_Find;
    tree->Deallocate = BinaryTree_Deallocate;
    tree->data = NULL;    /* no data for now */
    return tree;
}
```

The code for RedBlackTree.h is as follows:

```
#include "BinaryTree.h"

struct BinaryTree *AllocateRedBlackTree();
```

RedBlackTree.cp is as follows:

```
#include "RedBlackTree.h"
#include <stdio.h>

void RedBlackTree_Insert(struct BinaryTree *Tree, int key)
{
    printf("RedBlackTree_Insert(%ld)\n", key);
    /* _ */
}

struct BinaryTree *AllocateRedBlackTree()
{
    struct BinaryTree *tree = AllocateBinaryTree();

    tree->Insert = RedBlackTree_Insert;
    return tree;
}
```

Listed below is SplayTree.h:

```
#include "BinaryTree.h"

struct BinaryTree *AllocateSplayTree();
```

Here is SplayTree.c:

```
#include "SplayTree.h"
#include <stdio.h>

void SplayTree_Insert(struct BinaryTree *Tree, int key)
{
    printf("SplayTree_Insert(%ld)\n", key);
    /* _ */
}

void SplayTree_Find(struct BinaryTree *Tree, int key)
{
    printf("SplayTree_Find(%ld)\n", key);
    /* _ */
}
```

```
struct BinaryTree *AllocateSplayTree()
{
    struct BinaryTree *tree = AllocateBinaryTree();

    tree->Insert = SplayTree_Insert;
    tree->Find = SplayTree_Find;
    return tree;
}
```

Finally, Main.c is listed below:

```
#include <stdio.h>
#include "BinaryTree.h"
#include "RedBlackTree.h"
#include "SplayTree.h"

void InsertInTree(BinaryTree *tree, int value)
{
    tree->Insert(tree, value);
}

void main()
{
    BinaryTree *normalBinaryTree;
    BinaryTree *redBlackTree;
    BinaryTree *splayTree;

    normalBinaryTree = AllocateBinaryTree();
    normalBinaryTree->Insert(normalBinaryTree, 5);
    normalBinaryTree->Find(normalBinaryTree, 4);

    redBlackTree = AllocateRedBlackTree();
    redBlackTree->Insert(redBlackTree, 5);
    redBlackTree->Find(redBlackTree, 4);

    splayTree = AllocateSplayTree();
    splayTree->Insert(splayTree, 5);
    splayTree->Find(splayTree, 4);

    InsertInTree(normalBinaryTree, 6);
    InsertInTree(redBlackTree, 6);
    InsertInTree(splayTree, 6);
}
```

Look carefully at this example, especially at the main program. Notice the polymorphic call to `Insert`. It invokes a different actual function based on which object it is called.

Because you can do object-oriented programming in C, you may ask yourself whether you need C++. The same question could be asked about control structures. Because you can simulate while loops, for loops, etc., in assembly, do you need a high-level language? The answer is that it always is easier to program if the language directly supports a feature rather than simulates it. Thus, an object-oriented language automatically sets up function pointers and provides easy ways to create objects.

Another important aspect of OOP is its capability to focus on what and not on how something is done. For instance, when you call a function for an object, you just specify what you want done. The object takes care of implementing your request as it sees fit. Two objects of different classes may even respond to your function call in different routines (although if two objects are in the same class, they end up in the same routine).

Object-Oriented Design

The short description of object-oriented design (OOD) is that it is a model for designing your program as a collection of classes. On a practical level, the long description occupies many shelves in the programming section of a bookstore.

Basic Rules of Object-Oriented Programming

OOD is not a subject that can be covered in these few pages. Instead, some general rules of thumb are presented.

RULE

Learn from a master designer.

Like many forms of design, the more object-oriented code you create, the better you get. Part of the way you get good, however, is by observing a master designer. While taking classes and reading books on computer programming and object-oriented design can help you on a theoretical level, there is nothing like seeing an artist in action. One of the fastest ways to become proficient in OOD is to apprentice with an expert.

RULE

Every class you create that is derived from another class must pass the "is-a" test.

Suppose that you have a base class Shape with a derived class Rectangle. To pass the "is-a" test, Rectangle is-a Shape should be true. On the other hand, because an ellipse is not a circle, you should not derive Ellipse from Circle. It is fine to derive Circle from Ellipse, however.

By following this rule, you always have derived classes that can take the place of their base classes. Because the derived class is-a base class, it can handle the same requests and carry out the same actions. It just may handle the requests differently.

If the base class guarantees some set of conditions are true after a call to one of its functions, it also better be true for derived classes. At a minimum, derived classes should guarantee those conditions are true, although they may have additional ones as well.

Likewise, if the base class requires some conditions be true before calling a particular function, any derived class should do the same.

RULE

Provide data abstractions.

Don't just wrap a bunch of variables in a class with methods to get and set their values. Instead, consider the functionality your clients need and provide it.

For example, if you are dealing with a dog class, do not just have methods that provide all the data members: for example, name, age, breed, and fang length. Instead, provide routines that your clients really want. These could range from some of the lower level ones (like those just mentioned) to higher level routines like IsMean (which uses the age, fang length, and breed data members) or IsPuppy (which uses the age data member).

RULE

Keep your methods small.

Member functions (methods) should be small and written to do one thing. Methods that try to do too much are very difficult to override. For instance, you should not have code to do both a find and a replace in one routine because it makes it very difficult to override just the find part of the code. You end up copying the code and changing the find part, but leaving the replace part.

It is better to have one routine to do the finding and another to do the replacing. If necessary, you can add a FindAndReplace routine that just calls Find and then calls Replace. Derived classes can then override Find, leaving Replace alone.

RULE

Model your objects on the real world.

If your objects are modeled on those in the real world, they react more naturally to changes. This style of design also provides an easy predictability for people not familiar with your design. How many times has a marketing person requested "one little change?" How many times has the response been "but that will cause changes to two thirds of the program!" The requested change may be little in the real world but quite large in the program. If the program were modeled after the real world, a small change in the real world would have remained small in the program.

You also should use the real world as your model domain. For chemists, the real world may be molecules; for Macintosh programmers, the real world may be windows and menus.

RULE

Use abstract classes.

Abstract classes are those that are not useful in and of themselves. Their raison d'être is to be derived. In turn, the derived classes provide the missing functionality that makes the abstract class useful. Logically, it also follows that your concrete classes should not need to be derived to be useful.

The abstract class spells out what its objects are able to do, even if derived classes must provide that behavior. For example, figure 9.6 shows a class hierarchy for some graphical objects.

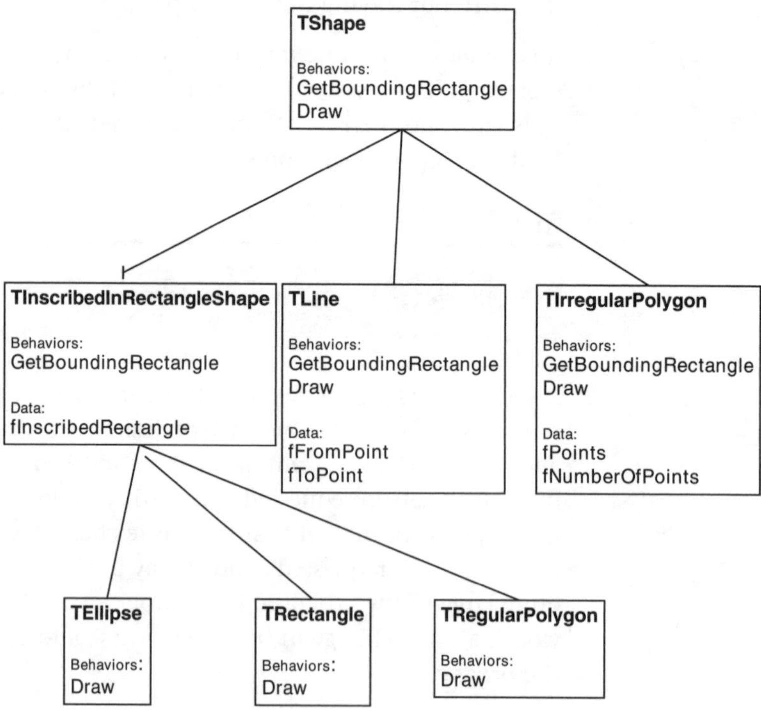

Figure 9.6. A shape class hierarchy.

Clearly, each leaf class (a class with no derived subclasses) implements Draw differently. Furthermore, `TShape` is an abstract class; it is not useful by itself. If you had a `TShape`, how would it draw? In fact, the `Draw` function of `TShape` must be overridden by derived classes to provide any actual behavior. Notice that `TInscribedInRectangleShape` is another abstract class. The others are concrete.

Even though `TShape` does not implement `Draw` or `GetBoundingRectangle`, it does declare the routines. It does this to reflect that all `TShapes` can be drawn and that all `TShapes` can return a bounding box. This declaration is useful to both readers of the program and the compiler. Any `TShape` object can be drawn. But if you, the programmer, try to call the `Draw` function for something that is not a `TShape`, you receive a compile-time error. The compiler prevents you from calling a nonexistent function on an object.

The Object-Oriented Design Process

Object-oriented design can be broken into three steps that overlap and are not strictly sequential. These steps also are influenced by the design process itself. You design a class, do something else, and come back and tweak the class design based on something you learned in the implementation. Good designers do a great deal of tweaking, and the newer you are at this the more you should tweak.

1. Identify objects. For example, in a personal financial program (like Quicken), your objects could be CheckingAccount, SavingsAccount, CreditCardAccount, Check, etc.

2. Decide on behaviors for the objects. For example, CheckingAccount and SavingsAccount must each accept deposits and support withdrawals. CheckingAccount must be able to write a check. CreditCardAccount must be able to credit a payment and debit for purchases. All the accounts need to reconcile themselves and provide the current balance. Checks must record payee, amount, data, and a memo. They also must be able to sort themselves and mark if they are cleared.

3. Create a hierarchy from your objects. Hierarchies usually are created to enable code reuse. As you find common functionality among objects, you should move it into some common base class. It is out of such movements that abstract classes are born.

For example, you can remove common functionality from CheckingAccount and SavingsAccount and create the abstract class, BankAccount. You can then move the deposit, withdrawal, reconcile, and current balance behaviors up from CheckingAccount and SavingsAccount into BankAccount. You also might want to consider creating another abstract class, Account, that is the base class of BankAccount and CreditCardAccount. Then you could move the reconcile and current balance functions up to Account from its derived classes.

Becoming familiar with good design and practicing it with examples is the best way to become proficient at OOD. Look at the design of as many object-oriented systems as you can. Read books that describe the design of systems. Design your own simple systems. With time, your design abilities will evolve.

Summary

What you gained from this chapter is idea of how object-oriented programming and design can benefit you and why they are worth the time to learn. You also learned some rules of thumb to help you in your initial attempts at this type of programming and design. C++, as an object-oriented language, is a flexible and rich language that fits well within the object-oriented model. By now, you should be convinced that this type of language is fun, so all that is left to do is learn it.

10

Getting Started with Objects

Now that you know something about the basics of object-oriented design, it is time to see how you can use what you have learned. So far you know that the fundamental structure of object-oriented programming is the object. What you also should know is that objects are not conjured out of thin air. Objects evolve from a familiar feature of C, that is, `structs`. Unlike their ancestors, however, C++ classes really are the Cadillacs of user-definable types. In this chapter, you look at how to use this important C++ feature.

You create a C program using `structs` and then do the same in C++. Along the way, you see how object orientation makes the program easier to write and control. After all, you are not learning object-oriented programming just to be a more polite team member. Where relevant, you also learn any important new Symantec C++ syntax.

Overview

Here is a more detailed look at what this chapter covers:

- You see a procedural program that uses `structs`. This program is a C program that takes a set of *x*,y coordinates. It then uses `structs` to determine and print out the length of a line.
- You create a C++ program that performs the same task as the procedural program. While writing this kind of program using objects, you also learn about C++ classes. Classes are containers for data and functions.
- You focus on how object-oriented syntax differs from procedural syntax. You also master some other object-oriented code conventions.
- You add a caching feature to both the procedural and object-oriented programs.
- You learn about access control. In C++, access control makes it much easier to deal with potential problems in programs. Access control, a serious power tool for the programmer, is great because it gives you the capability to determine who has access to data. Using C++ access control syntax, you can determine whether data access is public (anyone can access the data) or private (only the member functions of the class can access the data).
- You delve into inline functions. You learn how to use them to create efficient programs.
- You add constructors to your C++ program. A constructor is C++'s way of ensuring guaranteed default values, a luxury you have enjoyed with C global variables for years.

You are going to learn object-oriented programming in the easiest way, that is, by looking at the part of C that it evolved from—`structs`. To do this, you examine a sample program written procedurally using traditional C structures and then the same program written using object-oriented structures.

A Procedural Program

This example deals with lines that have start and end points. Here are the `struct` declarations:

```
struct PointStruct {
    int x;
    int y;
};

struct LineStruct {
    PointStruct from;
    PointStruct to;
};
```

These declarations are followed by the routines you use with these structures:

```
void SetPoint(PointStruct *p, int x, int y)
{
    p->x = x;
    p->y = y;
}

void SetLine(LineStruct *l, PointStruct from, PointStruct to)
{
    l->from = from;
    l->to = to;
}

float LineLength(const LineStruct *l)
{
    int height = l->to.x - l->from.x;
    int width = l->to.y - l->from.y;

    return sqrt(height*height + width*width);
}
```

The main program is listed below:

```
void main()
{
    LineStruct l;
    PointStruct fromPoint;
    PointStruct toPoint;
```

```
    SetPoint(&fromPoint, 1, 3);
    SetPoint(&toPoint, 4, 7);

    SetLine(&l, fromPoint, toPoint);

    cout << LineLength(&l);
}
```

Here is what this program prints out:

```
5.0
```

An Object-Oriented Program

Look at the code for the object-oriented version. (The main discussion of the new syntax and differences between the versions is in the next section of this chapter.)

The `class` types (corresponding to the procedural `struct` types) for the object-oriented case are listed below:

```
class TPoint {
public:
    void Set(int x, int y);

    int fX;
    int fY;
};

class TLine {
public:
    void Set(TPoint from, TPoint to);
    float Length();

    TPoint fFrom;
    TPoint fTo;
};
```

The member functions for the `TPoint` and `TLine` classes, which likewise correspond to the routines `SetPoint`, `SetLine`, and `LineLength` in the procedural version, are listed below:

```
void TPoint::Set(int x, int y)
{
    this->fX = x;
    this->fY = y;
}

void TLine::Set(TPoint from, TPoint to)
{
    fFrom = from;
    fTo = to;
}

float TLine::Length()
{
    int height = fTo.fX - fFrom.fX;
    int width = fTo.fY - fFrom.fY;

    return sqrt(height*height + width*width);
}
```

The main program is listed below:

```
main()
{
    TLine l;
    TPoint fromPoint;
    TPoint toPoint;

    fromPoint.Set(1, 3);
    toPoint.Set(4, 7);

    l.Set(fromPoint, toPoint);

    cout << l.Length();
}
```

This object-oriented version prints out the following:

```
5.0
```

Comparing Procedural with Object-Oriented Programs

Look at the syntax changes in the procedural and object-oriented programs as well as the new C++ language constructs.

The Descendant of Structs: The C++ Class

Following is the standard syntax for classes:

```
class ClassName {
public:
    data declarations
    function declarations
};
```

Table 10.1 shows the procedural and object-oriented versions of the point structure. In particular, it turns a sharp eye to the coupling of the functions and the data on which they operate.

Table 10.1. Procedural and Object-Oriented Points

Procedural Version	Object-Oriented Version
`struct PointStruct {`	`class TPoint {`
`    int x;`	`public:`
`    int y;`	`    void Set(int x, int y);`
`};`	`    int fX;`
	`    int fY;`
	`};`
`void SetPoint(PointStruct *p, int x, int y)`	`void TPoint::Set(int x, int y)`
`{`	`{`
`    p->x = x;`	`    this->fX = x;`
`    p->y = y;`	`    this->fY = y;`
`}`	`}`

In the procedural example, the only connection between `PointStruct` and `SetPoint` is that the procedure takes a pointer to the data as a parameter. In contrast, the object-oriented version has the procedures and the data on which they operate tightly intertwined. The `class` is the C++ language construct that binds the procedure and data.

WARNING

> `Class` declarations, like `struct` declarations, must end with a semicolon (`;`). Forgetting the semicolon is among the most common mistakes made by C++ programmers of all levels.

Member Functions and Data Members

How do you make the data and functions bind to the class? By giving the class some member functions and data members. In the above example, the member function `Set` is bound to the `TPoint` class. (There are two other member functions: `Set` and `Length`, both in `TLine`.)

Table 10.2 shows the syntax for accessing data members and calling member functions.

Table 10.2. Accessing Data Members and Member Functions

	Data Members	Member Functions
Syntax	`variable.memberName`	`variable.memberFunction(parameters)`
Examples	`fromPoint.fX`	`l.Set(fromPoint, toPoint);`
	`aLine.fFrom`	`fromPoint.Set(1, 3);`
		`toPoint.Set(4, 7);`
		`l.Length()`

Keep in mind the following important points about `class` syntax:

- When you declare variables of type `struct`, they have no special name; you just call them `struct` variables.
- On the other hand, the variables you declare of type `class` do have specific names; you call them *objects*.
- Member functions are like normal functions, except that you can invoke them only on objects. Furthermore, member functions have access to the data within the object upon which they are invoked.
- The data and the member functions that operate on them are declared together within the class.

Given these points, look at how procedural and object-oriented main programs differ from each other. Table 10.3 contrasts the procedural with the object-oriented version of the main program. The syntax in the object-oriented case for calling the `Set` member function is similar to that used for accessing a data member. Think of it as if the object has a member function imbedded in it. You access that member function just as you access data. Unlike the procedural case, you do not explicitly pass `l`. Instead, `l` is passed implicitly to the member function when you call `l.Set`.

Now that you see how the main program differs in the procedural and object-oriented cases, look at tables 10.4 and 10.5 to see the differences in writing functions as member functions. Compare the object-oriented member functions with the functions in the procedural case.

One main difference is the `::` *operator* (called the *scope resolution operator*). On the left side of the `::` is the class name; on the right side is the name of the member function.

You access the data members differently as well. Compare both versions and notice in table 10.5 that member functions automatically have access to their data members. `TLine::Set` uses the `fTo` and `fFrom` data members without specifying a structure or object before the data members.

Table 10.3. Procedural and Object-Oriented Main Programs

Procedural	Object Oriented
`void main()`	`main()`
`{`	`{`
`LineStruct l;`	`TLine l;`
`PointStruct fromPoint;`	`TPoint fromPoint;`
`PointStruct toPoint;`	`TPoint toPoint;`
`SetPoint(&fromPoint, 1, 3);`	`fromPoint.Set(1, 3);`
`SetPoint(&toPoint, 4, 7);`	`toPoint.Set(4, 7);`
`SetLine(&l, fromPoint, toPoint);`	`l.Set(fromPoint, toPoint);`
`cout << LineLength(&l);`	`cout << l.Length();`
`}`	`}`

Table 10.4. Function Definitions versus Member Function Definitions

Version	Definition
Procedural	`void SetPoint(PointStruct *p, int x, int y)`
	`void SetLine(LineStruct *l, PointStruct from, PointStruct to)`
	`float LineLength(const LineStruct *l)`
Object Oriented	`void TPoint::Set(int x, int y)`
	`void TLine::Set(TPoint from, TPoint to)`
	`float TLine::Length()`

Table 10.5. Writing a Function with and without Objects

Version	Function

Procedural	`void SetLine(LineStruct *l, PointStruct from, PointStruct to)`
	`{`
	`    l->from = from;`
	`    l->to = to;`
	`}`

Object Oriented	`void TLine::Set(TPoint from, TPoint to)`
	`{`
	`    fFrom = from;`
	`    fTo = to;`
	`}`

The this Keyword

Another important difference in the object-oriented version is the use of the `this` keyword. Look at table 10.6 and compare `TPoint::Set` with `SetPoint`.

`this` is only defined in a member function; it is a pointer to the object on which the member function is called. If you execute the following code, it calls `TLine::Set`:

```
l.Set(fromPoint, toPoint);
```

Within `TLine::Set`, `this` is a pointer to the object `l`. Therefore, `this->fFrom` refers to the data member from within `l`.

Note that using `this->` is optional when accessing data members in a member function. The only reason to do so is to distinguish between the following:

1. Accessing members (either data or functions) of this object.
2. Accessing other data (local or global) or functions (global).

Table 10.6. Setting a Procedural and an Object-Oriented Point Value

Version	Point Value

Procedural	`void SetPoint(PointStruct *p, int x, int y)`
	`{`
	`    p->x = x;`
	`    p->y = y;`
	`}`

Object Oriented	`void TPoint::Set(int x, int y)`
	`{`
	`    this->fX = x;`
	`    this->fY = y;`
	`}`

C++ Naming Conventions

There is a naming convention, however, that enables you to distinguish between these two without using `this->`. The `f` and the `T` below are examples of this naming convention:

```
void TLine::Set(TPoint from, TPoint to)
{
    fFrom = from;
    fTo = to;
}
```

Here is the convention in a nutshell:

- Label all data members with an initial `f`, global variables with an initial `g`, and local variables with another letter of your choice.
- Start class names with `T`.
- Use the scope resolution operator to call global functions with this syntax:

```
::GlobalFunction()
```

Then, if you see a `::` before a function call, it is a global function.

- If you see an object before a function call—for example, `l.Set(_)`—you know it is a member function. You see later that nothing before a function call signifies calling a member function on the object `this`.

NOTE

This naming convention, which specifies the use of `T` and `f`, is common among Macintosh C++ programmers. The larger C++ community does not share this idiosyncrasy. As is true of most conventions, it is the result of historical stickiness. In Pascal, classes were called *types* and data members were called *fields*. The initial letters just stuck around to identify types and fields long after their usage corresponded to anything meaningful. Using this convention does, however, make it easy to determine which types are classes and which variables are data members.

At this point, you might be muttering to yourself that object-oriented programming is just an alternative syntax to procedural programming—there are no real advantages. On the contrary, you just have not gotten to the fun part yet. Now that you have learned enough about the syntactical changes and new terminology, it is time to tantalize you with the advantages.

In this new syntax, all the functions you can apply to the data are embedded within the class declaration; you see them simultaneously. It is true that you can do something similar in procedural programming by declaring all functions that apply to a structure together. The problem is that there are no language police to force you to do it that way. Enforcement provides much more programming power, as you see later in this chapter.

Adding Caching

Currently, both the procedural and object-oriented versions of the program recalculate the length of lines on demand. When making many line length requests, with the same from and to points, you are obviously doing many unnecessary calculations. You can add caching of line lengths to both versions of the program to deal with this inefficiency in the code.

Caching in a Procedural Program

Proceed with the procedural program. To get this program caching correctly, make the three changes shown below. Here, as elsewhere in this book, new and changed elements are displayed in italics.

1. Add two extra fields to `LineStruct`, one to hold the cached line length, and another to tell you whether the cached length is valid:

```
struct LineStruct {
    PointStruct   from;
    PointStruct   to;
    float         cachedLength;
    Boolean       cacheIsValid;
};
```

2. Initialize the `cacheIsValid` field to false any time you set the `from` or `to` points:

```
void SetLine(LineStruct *l, PointStruct from, PointStruct
to)
{
    l->from = from;
    l->to = to;
    l->cacheIsValid = false;
}
```

3. Finally, modify `LineLength` to set the cached value, if necessary, and return the cached value:

```
float LineLength(const LineStruct *l)
{
    if (!l->cacheIsValid) {
        int height = l->to.x - l->from.x;
        int width = l->to.y - l->from.y;

        l->cachedLength = sqrt(height*height +
          width*width);
    }
    return l->cachedLength;
}
```

Caching in an Object-Oriented Program

Remember the changes you just made to the procedural code? The object-oriented program requires much the same.

1. Add two data members to the class declaration:

```
class TLine {
public:
    void Set(TPoint from, TPoint to);
    float Length();

    TPoint  fFrom;
    TPoint  fTo;
    float   fCachedLength;
    Boolean fCacheIsValid;
};
```

2. Initialize `fCacheIsValid` to false whenever setting the `from` and `to` points:

```
void TLine::Set(TPoint from, TPoint to)
{
    fFrom = from;
    fTo = to;
    fCacheIsValid = false;
}
```

3. Finally, use the cached value and set it as necessary in `TLine::Length`:

```
float TLine::Length()
{
    if (!fCacheIsValid) {
        int height = fTo.x - fFrom.x;
        int width = fTo.y - fFrom.y;

        fCachedLength = sqrt(height*height +
          width*width);
    }
    return fCachedLength;
}
```

Happily in both cases, the main program does not require changing; it just runs faster if you repetitively calculate line lengths.

Access Control

Now that the code runs more efficiently, investigate a potential problem in both programs. A problem, it turns out, that is solvable only in the object-oriented version. The problem occurs if you do not use the `SetLine` function consistently:

```
void main()
{
    LineStruct l;
    PointStruct fromPoint;
    PointStruct toPoint;

    SetPoint(&fromPoint, 1, 3);
    SetPoint(&toPoint, 4, 7);

    SetLine(&l, fromPoint, toPoint);

    cout << LineLength(&l);

    l.fromPoint.x = -33;
    cout << LineLength(&l);
}
```

Much to one's chagrin, the above code prints the wrong value in the cached case. Only in the inefficient non-cached version does it correctly output:

```
5.0
40.8999
```

In the cached version it wrongly outputs the following:

```
5.0
5.0
```

The same snag occurs in the object-oriented version if you use a similar main program that directly modifies the `fX` field of `fFromPoint` rather than using the `TLine::Set` routine.

This problem happens because the main program has bad manners. It should use the `SetLine` (`TLine::Set` in the object-oriented version) routine, but it does not do so. This obviously raises the question about what you should do with the programmer who is using your points and lines, but neglecting to use the interface you have so carefully provided. Documentation and conventions are one approach: Document the routines that you want used and chastise programmers who do not use them. If you cannot admonish strongly enough, however, there is a better approach: Make the compiler enforce your convention. Simply have the compiler refuse to compile code that does not use the interface, thereby heading off the problem before it occurs. You can perform this nifty trick by structuring your program so that it is impossible to modify lines other than through your thoughtfully provided interface.

In C++, members of a class can have any one of three levels of access control. At this point, however, only two of the three are important. They are `public` and `private`. With the `public` keyword, any function can access this member; with the `private` keyword, only member functions of this class can access this member.

There are even defaults already in place. Members are `private` (now you know why the `public` keyword was at the beginning of the `TPoint` and `TLine` classes).

Having learned about access control, it is time to fix the code so that the above problem cannot occur any more. You do this by modifying the `TLine` class declaration to make the data members private:

```
class TLine {
public:
    void Set(TPoint from, TPoint to);
    float Length();

private:
    TPoint  fFrom;
    TPoint  fTo;
    float   fCachedLength;
    Boolean fCacheIsValid;
};
```

NOTE

Conventionally, you put your public members first and then follow with your private members. This way, programmers reading your class declaration first see what they can do with the class (the public part) without having to figure out your implementation (the private part). You do not have to use the above order. In fact, you can switch back and forth from public to private if you wish:

```
class TFoo {
private:
    int    fPrivate1;

public:
    void   Public1();
    int    Public2();

private:
    void   Private();
    float  fPrivate2;
};
```

With this change in access control, the only functions in the program that can access (read or write) `fFrom`, `fTo`, `fCachedLength`, or `fCacheIsValid` are `TLine::Set` and `TLine::Length`. In other words, the only operations that the program can do with `TLine` objects are to call the `Set` member function or call the `Length` member function.

There always is somebody who wants to know what happens when you try to compile a main program that directly accesses fFrom? Take a look at the following code:

```
void main()
{
    TLine l;
    TPoint fromPoint;
    TPoint toPoint;

    fromPoint.Set(1, 3);
    toPoint.Set(4, 7);

    l.Set(fromPoint, toPoint);

    cout << l.Length();

    l.fFrom.x = -33;
    cout << l.Length();
}
```

The Symantec C++ compiler politely informs you with the following error message:

```
_File Main.cp; Line 38
Error:   member 'TLine::fFrom' of class 'TLine' is not accessible
```

Herein lies another advantage of object-oriented programming: Access control can make your C++ programs much more maintainable than their C equivalents. If you make all of your data members private (which you should), you then have a very limited number of routines that directly access those data members, that is, the member functions of that class. Your code sleuthing should improve dramatically. The following explains why:

- Tracking down errors is easier; for example, locating the value of a data member that is being corrupted requires sifting through less code.
- You can reason more easily about the effects of modifications to your data members.

For consistency's sake, you also should change the program so that the data members of the TPoint class data are private. To do so, just change the class declaration to make them private:

```
class TPoint {
public:
    void Set(int x, int y);

private:
    int fX;
    int fY;
};
```

The code does need to provide some way to access the *x* and *y* coordinates of the point because `TLine::Length` needs the values to calculate the length. To do this, you add member functions to `TPoint`, which returns those values:

```
class TPoint {
public:
    void Set(int x, int y);
    int GetX();
    int GetY();

private:
    int fX;
    int fY;
};
```

Member functions (such as `GetX` or `GetY`) that return the values of data members are called *accessors* or *getters*. Member functions that exist to modify the values of data members (like `Set`) are called *mutators* or *setters*.

In this case, the code for the accessors, `TPoint::GetX` and `TPoint::GetY`, is simple:

```
int TPoint::GetX()
{
    return fX;
}

int TPoint::GetY()
{
    return fY;
}
```

`TLine::Length` also needs to be changed to use these new accessor methods because it no longer has access to the data members directly:

```
float TLine::Length()
{
    if (!fCacheIsValid) {
        int height = fTo.GetX() - fFrom.GetX();
        int width = fTo.GetY() - fFrom.GetY();

        fCachedLength = sqrt(height*height +
          width*width);
    }
    return fCachedLength;
}
```

Now that you have controlled access to both your `TLine` and `TPoint` objects, things are shaping up rather nicely. It is time to deal with the standard objection to access control that someone invariably raises.

Inline Functions

Progress always brings forth opponents raising objections. Access control opponents ask But what about efficiency? Happily, the efficiency concern is easily addressable. By using inline functions, you get the best of both worlds: the safety of access control, with the efficiencies of direct member access.

Inline functions should appear in a header file, however, so you need to move the accessor methods to the header file that contains the `TPoint` class declaration and add the `inline` keyword before each function. Here is the correct `Point.h` header file:

```
// Point.h

#ifndef POINT_H      // prevent multiple inclusion of this file
#define POINT_H

class TPoint {
public:
    void Set(int x, int y);
    int GetX();
    int GetY();
```

```
private:
    int fX;
    int fY;
};

inline int TPoint::GetX()
{
    return fX;
}

inline int TPoint::GetY()
{
    return fY;
}
#endif
```

WARNING

> Make member functions inline only if you know they cannot change. Otherwise, modifying an inline member function requires recompiling all files that use the TLine class. This case is no different from all other optimizations, however. First, measure your code to see where it is spending time and then speed up those parts. Make sure you have a fully functional program first in any case.

Adding Constructors

There is yet another good thing about C++. As you know, there are times when you want to ensure guaranteed default values. C++ responds to this desire with *constructors*.

Simple Constructors

Constructors can make classes even easier to use. For instance, there is nothing to prevent you from writing code like the following:

```
void main()
{
    TLine l;

    cout << l.Length();
}
```

If you try to print the length of an uninitialized `TLine`, however, you get the following garbage output:

```
3282323.2382348234
```

Shouldn't `TLines` have a guaranteed default value? In C++, you ensure that objects have a default value by providing a *constructor*. A constructor is a routine that the compiler executes at the time it creates the object. You normally use it when you want reasonable default values. To see how they work, start with a constructor for `TPoint` that initializes `fX` and `fY` to default values. Listed below is the modified class declaration:

```
// Point.h
class TPoint {
public:
    TPoint();
    void Set(int x, int y);
    int GetX();
    int GetY();

private:
    int fX;
    int fY;
};
```

A constructor has the same name as its class and does not return anything. Here is the definition of the constructor:

```
TPoint::TPoint()
{    fX = fY = 0;
}
```

NOTE

> If constructors do not return anything, why don't you declare them `void`? Because you might then think you could change the return type from `void` to something else, like `int`. Having no return type at all also distinguishes them more readily from normal member functions. You will see later that *destructors* also have no return type.

The C++ compiler calls the constructor automatically whenever it creates a `TPoint`. In the program, how many times are `TPoints` created? The answer is four. Two of these are found in the main program, where you define two `TPoints`:

```
TPoint fromPoint;
TPoint toPoint;
```

Do not forget that `TLines` have `TPoints` as data members. Each `TLine` has two `TPoints`. Therefore, the following definition creates another two `TPoints`:

```
TLine l;
```

Thus, you end up with four `TPoints` in your program, each of which is automatically initialized with the `TPoint` constructor to (0,0).

If `TLine` has its `fFrom` and `fTo` data members initialized automatically to (0,0), do you still need a `TLine` constructor? Yes, because you have to initialize another data member, `fCacheIsValid`. If you do not initialize it to false, the following code might still print out garbage values:

```
TLine l;
cout << l.Length()
```

This is because the `fCacheIsValid` data member might be true; therefore, the `TLine` constructor must initialize it to false.

NOTE

Trivia question: If the `fCacheIsValid` data member is a random value, what are the odds that it is true? The answer is 255/256 (`Booleans` are `unsigned chars`, and the only value interpreted as false is zero).

When you are ready to make all of these modifications, first add the constructor to the `TLine` class declaration:

```
class TLine {
public:
    TLine();
    void Set(TPoint from, TPoint to);
    float Length();

private:
    TPoint fFrom;
    TPoint fTo;
    float fCachedLength;
    Boolean fCacheIsValid;
   };
```

Next, simply add the definition of the `TLine` constructor:

```
TLine::TLine()
{
    fCacheIsValid = false;
}
```

Use the same `main` function:

```
void main()
{
    TLine l;

    cout << l.Length();
}
```

It generates the following output:

```
0.0
```

Constructors with Parameters

Like all functions, you can overload a constructor based on the type and number of parameters. This leniency gives you the ability to make multiple constructors that initialize an object in different ways.

For instance, the main program can be much simpler if it takes advantage of constructors with parameters. First, you need a constructor to `TPoint` that takes initial *x* and *y* values. After you have it, the constructor can create a point initialized to (1,3) with the following:

```
TPoint fromPoint(1, 3);
```

This is simpler than the bulkier code you were using:

```
TPoint fromPoint;

fromPoint.Set(1, 3);
```

In fact, you can use this constructor directly within the call to `TLine::Set`. Here is the bulkier code:

```
TPoint fromPoint;
TPoint toPoint;

fromPoint.Set(1, 3);
toPoint.Set(4, 7);
l.Set(fromPoint, toPoint);
```

Instead of the code above, you can use the following:

```
l.Set(TPoint(1, 3), TPoint(4, 7));
```

This reduction in code is a big bonus. So after all that fanfare, here is the definition of such a constructor:

```
TPoint::TPoint(int x, int y)
{
    fX = x;
    fY = y;
}
```

For completeness, `TLine` also needs a constructor that takes two `TPoints` as parameters. Here is the declaration:

```
class TLine {
public:
    TLine();
    TLine(TPoint from, TPoint to);
    void Set(TPoint from, TPoint to);
    float Length();

private:
    TPoint fFrom;
    TPoint fTo;
    float fCachedLength;
    Boolean fCacheIsValid;
   };
```

Here is the definition of the constructor:

```
TLine::TLine(Point from, Point to)
{
    fFrom  = from;
    fTo = to;
    fCacheIsValid = false;
}
```

You should remember that each of your constructors may repeat certain fragments of code. In this case, both `TLine` constructors repeat `fCacheIsValid = false`. How can you encapsulate the commonality? A constructor in a class cannot call another constructor from that class. So, you can't do it that way. Both constructors can call a common member function, however, to do common initialization. In the `TLine` case, you can define a `TLine::CommonInitialization` member function that initializes `fCacheIsValid`:

```
class TLine {
...
private:
    void CommonInitialize();
...
};
...
TLine::TLine()
{
    CommonInitialize();
}
```

```
TLine::TLine(TPoint from, TPoint to)
{
    fFrom = from;
    fTo = to;
    CommonInitialize();
}

void TLine::CommonInitialize()
{
    fCacheIsValid = false;
}
```

You do not duplicate the same code in more than one constructor with this approach. While this may not look important for this class, it could be for others. You can have copious quantities of code to duplicate in some classes.

Now that you have new constructors for both `TLine` and `TPoint`, look at how much simpler you can make the main program:

```
void main()
{
    TLine l(TPoint(1, 3), TPoint(4, 7));

    cout << l.Length();
}
```

Summary

By now you know that object-oriented programming is not just more courteous than procedural programming. Examine the advantages. In C++, objects make your code better in many ways. Remember, procedural programs only have procedures that go out and pillage the structures. The result is that chaos often reigns. In the object-oriented world, on the other hand, the new class type enlivens the data, and objects can have polite, orderly interactions with other objects. When you add other features like access control, inlining functions, and constructors, it is easy to see that object-oriented code is more maintainable, easier to write, and easier to read.

The advantages do not end here, however. There is more to learn about objects and about C++. When you are ready to fully immerse yourself in object-oriented programming, dive into the next chapter.

Exercises

1. Why is `TLine::CommonInitialize` declared as private? Can you think of other cases where private member functions make sense?
2. How can you rewrite the final version of the main program so that it has only one statement, rather than two?
3. Convert the following procedural program to an equivalent (but better) object-oriented program:

```
#include <stream.h>
struct Customer {
    char name[128];
    char address[128];
};

const int kMaxEntries = 128;

Customer gCustomers[kMaxEntries];
int gNumberCustomerEntries = 0;

void InsertInDatabase(Customer &cust)
{
    if (++gNumberCustomerEntries > kMaxEntries) {
        cerr << "too many customers\n";
    } else{
        gCustomers[gNumberCustomerEntries] = cust;
    }
}

Customer *FindInDatabase(const char *name)
{
    for (int i = 0; i < gNumberCustomerEntries; i++)
        if (strcmp(gCustomers[i], name) == 0)
            return &gCustomers[i];
    return NULL;
}
```

```
main()
{
    Customer customer1 = {"Nicholas Rhodes", "1328 Clock
      Avenue" };
    Customer customer2 = {"Carolyn LaGaly", "4416 Longridge
      Avenue" };
    Customer customer3 = {"Nan Corby", "243 Park Avenue" };

    InsertInDatabase(customer1);
    InsertInDatabase(customer2);
    InsertInDatabase(customer3);

    Customer *cust;
    if ((cust = FindInDatabase("Nicholas Rhodes")) != NULL) {
        cout < "Name: " << cust.name << '\n' <<
               "Address: " << cust.address << '\n';
    } else {
        cout << "not found\n";
    }
}
```

11

A Closer Look at Objects

Objects have behaviors. You send messages to them, and they do something. However, that is not all. Objects also act like parents. They give behaviors to their children. These children are new C++ classes that inherit all of their parents' class behaviors as well as having their own unique behaviors. They are called *derived* classes. Unlike real children, however, they always follow their parents' rules.

This chapter begins with derived classes, moves on to show the power of polymorphism, and, lastly, explains dynamic memory allocation and the tricks and intricacies involved in working with objects that allocate dynamic memory.

Overview

Here is an overview of this chapter:

- ▼ You learn about derived classes, the C++ method of extending existing classes.
- ▼ You modify the caching line program from the previous chapter so it can take advantage of derived classes. You also learn the syntax that derived classes use and what behaviors you can expect from them.
- ▼ You then use the `TLine` and `TCachedLine` code to see how polymorphism works.
- ▼ You have a quick discussion of multiple inheritance. You see how to write objects that inherit from more than one base class and how they are used in C++.
- ▼ You are introduced to the special routines you must write for objects with dynamic memory. You learn why you need them and how to write them.

Derived Classes

Look again at some code from Chapter 10. There you started with a `TLine` class that was modified to support caching. While this worked, it is not the C++ way of handling the problem. You can use a more elegant approach by creating a caching `TCachingLine` class that is derived from the `TLine` base class. This section discusses how to do that. To begin, review the noncaching `TLine` class declaration from the last chapter:

```
class TLine {
public:
    TLine();
    TLine(TPoint from, TPoint to);
    virtual void Set(TPoint from, TPoint to);
    virtual TPoint GetFrom();
    virtual TPoint GetTo();
    virtual float Length();
```

```
private:
    TPoint fFrom;
    TPoint fTo;
};
```

Listed below are the class's member function definitions:

```
TLine::TLine()
{
}

TLine::TLine(TPoint from, TPoint to)
{
    fFrom = from;
    fTo = to;
 }

void Set(TPoint from, TPoint to)
{
    fFrom = from;
    fTo = to;
}

TPoint GetFrom()
{
    return fFrom;
}

TPoint GetTo()
{
    return fTo;
}

float TLine::Length()
{
    int height = fTo.GetX() - fFrom.GetX();
    int width = fTo.GetY() - fFrom.GetY();

    return sqrt(height*height + width*width);
}
```

Declaring a New Derived Class

To create a new version that uses derived classes, first declare a new class, TCachedLine:

```
class TCachedLine: public TLine {
public:
    TCachingLine();
    TCachingLine(TPoint from, TPoint to);
    virtual void Set(TPoint from, TPoint to);
    virtual float Length();

private:
    Boolean fCacheIsValid;
    float fCachedLength;
};
```

Look at the first line. It specifies that TCachingLine is derived from TLine. Here is the syntax you always should use when creating these derived classes:

```
class TDerivedClass : public TBaseClass {
```

NOTE

Always use the public keyword before the base class. The other alternatives are protected and private. Private is used only in very uncommon circumstances. Protected, on the other hand, is so rare that we have never figured out a circumstance when you should use it.

Overriding Member Functions

Look again at TCachedLine. Notice that TCachedLine redeclares both Set and Length even though they already are declared in TLine. By doing so, TCachedLine now *overrides* the original member functions provided in TLine. These new versions either totally replace or augment the original version.

TCachedLine also declares two private data members used for caching. Look at the constructors first:

```
TCachedLine::TCachedLine()
{
    InvalidateCache();
}

TCachedLine::TCachedLine(TPoint from, TPoint to) : TLine(from, to)
{
    InvalidateCache();
}
```

The first constructor invalidates the cache. Nicely enough, C++ automatically calls the constructor for the base class, `TLine`, as well as for the inherited data members (`fFrom` and `fTo`). This means you do not have to hover about and ensure that they get initialized.

You need to handle the second constructor differently, however, by calling the `TLine` constructor with arguments. You do this with an *initializer list*. Consisting of the base class name and any necessary arguments, an initializer list is separated from a constructor with a colon (`:`). You also use it to initialize data members.

Look now at the overriding features of `TCachedLine` and the functions `Set` and `Length`. Note that the override of `Set` augments the behavior of `TLine::Set`. It continues to do what `TLine::Set` does, but sets `fCacheIsValid` to false as well. The code looks like this:

```
void TCachedLine::Set(TPoint fFrom, TPoint fTo)
{
    TLine::Set(fFrom, fTo);
    fCacheIsValid = false;
}
```

The first line of this function calls the old version of `Set`, and the next line augments the old behavior. The code for `Length`, on the other hand, is only slightly more complex. If the cache is not valid, it needs to call the original version of `Length` to find the value for the cache. After that is done, it returns the cached length. The following is what `TCachedLine::Length` looks like:

```
float TCachedLine::Length()
{
    if (!fCacheIsValid) {
        fCachedLength = TLine::Length();
```

```
        fCacheIsValid = true;
    }
    return fCachedLength;
}
```

That's all there is to it. Now, you have code that caches and properly uses derived classes. There are advantages to this approach beyond just being an object-oriented approach.

Advantages of Derived Classes

What are the benefits of writing two separate classes (the derived class and the base class) instead of rewriting the original class? There are two important ones:

- ▼ You can now choose whether to use `TLine` or `TCachedLine` objects on a case-by-case basis (the tradeoff being space versus time).
- ▼ Even if you were to use only `TCachedLine`, the implementation is easier. The `TLine` class contains code relating to lines and calculating lengths, while `TCachedLine` contains caching code. This separation makes the code easier to understand and maintain.

Using the Caching Line Class

Now that you know how to write derived class code, look at how to use it:

```
void Foo(Point fromPoint, Point toPoint)
{
    TLine l(fromPoint, toPoint);
    TCachedLine cl(fromPoint, toPoint);

    l.Length();             // calls TLine::Length()
    cl.Length();            // calls TCachedLine::Length()
    l.GetFrom();            // calls TLine::GetFrom()
    cl.GetFrom()            // calls TLine::GetFrom()
}
```

Here, you can see some of the power of an object-oriented language like C++. The program calls the correct version of the member function depending upon which kind of object it needs. Thus, calling the `Length` member function for a `TLine` calls `TLine::Length`, but calling the `Length` member function for a `TCachedLine` calls `TCachedLine::Length` because `TCachedLine` overrides `Length`. Because `TCachedLine` does not override `GetFrom`, both calls to `GetFrom` call `TLine::GetFrom`.

Note that the way `TCachedLine` works when it overrides `Length` is very similar to function overloading, a feature covered in Chapter 8.

Polymorphism

Polymorphism is defined as a variable's capability to refer to one of a variety of objects. These objects belong to different classes that are members of the same superclass.

Overridden Member Functions versus Function Overloading

As in function overloading, a call to an overridden function calls the right version of a function based on the type of its arguments. There is a crucial difference, however. With overloaded functions, the compiler determines at compile time what function to call. With overridden member functions, it is not until run time that the determination is made. This tiny variation makes all the difference in the world.

Look at an example of delayed determination. An array of lines is initialized with the following code:

```
TLine       *myLines[3];
TLine       line0(TPoint(-5, 3), TPoint(50, 7));
TCachedLine line1(TPoint(6, 6), TPoint(10, 7));
TLine       line2(TPoint(2, 3), TPoint(5, 9));

myLines[0] = &line0;
myLines[1] = &line1;
myLines[2] = &line2;
```

Figure 11.1 shows what the array (and lines) looks like after the above code executes.

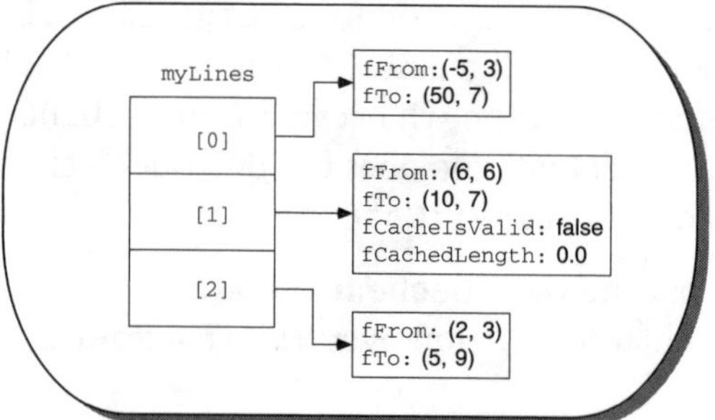

Figure 11.1. Array and lines in memory.

Look at the code that calls the `Length` member function for each line in the array:

```
void PrintLines(TLine *myLines)
{
    for (int i = 0; i < 3; i++)
        myLines[i]->Length();
}
```

When you compile `PrintLines`, all you know about the array is that it holds pointers to `TLine` objects or to some derived class of `TLine`. Here is the important part: Any derived class may override `Length`. Thus, the compiler determines to what class an object belongs and then calls the correspondingly correct `Length` function. This run-time determination is called *method lookup* or *polymorphism.*

Understanding the Power of Polymorphism

It is common practice to use object-oriented languages in conjunction with frameworks (see Chapter 15). Frameworks are normally written as a collection of classes. Unlike a standard library that has functions you call, frameworks themselves call your routines. For frameworks to do this, you must first create derived classes and then override particular member functions. Then the framework, using polymorphism, calls your overridden member function when calling that original member function.

To see how this process works in practice, look at the following code, which is a snippet of an application framework:

```
extern TView *gTheViewToDraw;
class TView {
public:
    ...
    virtual void Draw();
    ...
};
...
void TView::Draw()
{
    // do nothing
}
...
    gTheViewToDraw->Draw();
```

`TView` is a class that draws a portion of a window. The default `Draw` function does nothing; it is only when you override that it actually draws something. The global `gTheViewToDraw` holds a `TView *` with a `Draw` member function. You can have the framework call your `Draw` routine by writing a derived class:

```
class TMyView: public TView {
public:
    ...
    virtual void Draw();
    ...
};
void TMyView::Draw()
{
    code to do drawing
}
```

Next, you create a new `TMyView` and assign it to `gViewToDraw`:

```
gViewToDraw = new TMyView;
```

From this you can see how the framework calls your routines.

How Polymorphism Works

Thankfully, you do not have to understand how the compiler implements polymorphism to use it. There are a number of reasons, however, why you might want to plumb the depths of polymorphism:

- You enjoy the intellectual stimulation of seeing how a language feature is implemented (the philosophical reason).
- You are using a low-level debugger (like Macsbug) and need to trace through the compiled code (the practical reason).
- You want to better understand the time and space tradeoffs associated with using polymorphism (the efficiency reason).

If any of these reasons applies to you, read on; otherwise, you can skip this section.

How are these virtual functions implemented and run-time determinations made? Although not required by the language, most implementations of C++, including Symantec C++, use the same method. This method of dispatching virtual functions uses a *v-table,* a table of virtual pointers, for method lookup. Each object (with one virtual function or more) contains a hidden pointer to a table of function pointers. The table, in turn, contains a pointer for each virtual function. Thus, when you call a virtual function, it is transformed into an indirect function call through the table.

As an example, figure 11.2 shows a diagram of two `TLine` objects along with a `TCachedLine` object. Note that the two `TLine` objects share a copy of the `TLine` v-table (which is what you may expect because they both execute the same member functions). The pointer of the `TCachedLine` object points to a different v-table.

The `TLine::GetFrom` and `TLine::GetTo` member functions are shared by both the `TLine` objects and the `TCachedLine` object. The following code uses the objects in figure 11.2:

```
void PrintLines(TLine *myLines)
{
    for (int i = 0; i < 3; i++)
        myLines[i]->Length();
}
```

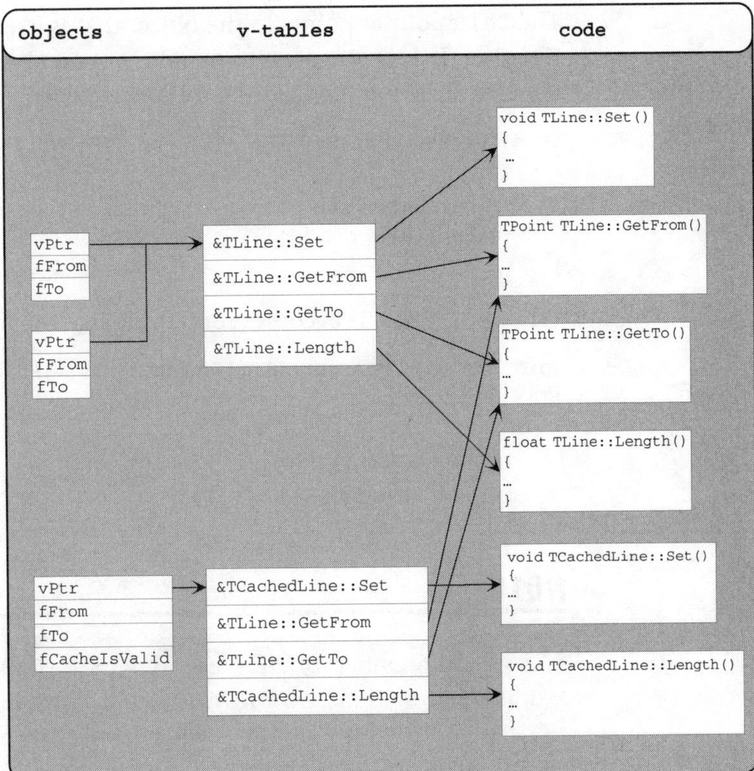

Figure 11.2. V-tables in memory.

After compilation, it ends up looking roughly like this:

```
void PrintLines(TLine *myLines)
{
    for (int i = 0; i < 3; i++)
        (*myLines[i]->vptr)[3])(myLines[i]);
}
```

Two things of special interest happen in the above code:

1. The compiler passes the `this` pointer as the parameter.
2. Every member function receives the `this` pointer as an extra (hidden) parameter.

The `this` pointer points to the object that is executing the member function. It enables access to members of an object from within a member function. Look at the following code:

```
void TCachedLine::Set(TPoint fFrom, TPoint fTo)
{
    TLine::Set(fFrom, fTo);
    fCacheIsValid = false;
}
```

When compiled, it becomes something like the following:

```
void TCachedLine::Set(TCachedLine *this, TPoint fFrom, TPoint
fTo)
{
    TLine::Set(this, fFrom, fTo);
    this->fCacheIsValid = false;
}
```

NOTE

A virtual member function uses polymorphism. Nonvirtual member functions, on the other hand, work like normal functions—the determination of which function to call is made at compile time, rather than at run time.

Multiple Inheritance

You are not restricted to a single base class. C++ enables you to supply a derived class with more than one base class (called *multiple inheritance*). Here is the syntax that enables you to set up the class:

```
class TDerivedClass: public TBaseClass1, public TBaseClass2, ...
```

With multiple inheritance, you inherit the data members and member functions from all your base classes as well. This is not a restriction, however, because you can override any of those member functions as well as provide your own.

When you use multiple inheritance, you can end up with a derivation hierarchy that is quite complex. With single inheritance, you have a simple tree structure. With multiple inheritance, on the other hand, you easily can end up with a clutter pile. Because of the problems associated with complexity, there is a debate in the object-oriented community about whether multiple inheritance should be used.

If you do employ multiple inheritance, there are ways you can minimize the complexity. One way is to use a disciplined approach to multiple base classes:

- Keep your `T` classes in a tree hierarchy.
- Define new `M` classes that modify existing behavior.
- `M` classes should have names that are adjectives.
- `T` classes should have names that are nouns.
- A derived class should have at most one `T` base class, but can have more than one `M` base class.
- The main inheritance branch is composed of the `T` classes, while the `M` classes just add additional, optional functionality.

Examples of `M` classes are `MPrintable`, `MDisplayable`, and `MWritable`. Some examples of `T` classes are `TPolygon` and `TShape`. Look at figure 11.3 to get an idea of what a well-ordered multiple inheritance structure looks like.

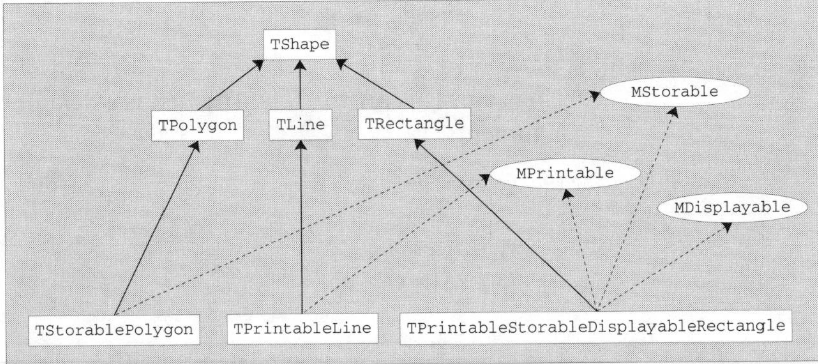

Figure 11.3. Diagram of a well-ordered multiple inheritance class hierarchy.

Using Constructors and Destructors in Dynamic Memory Allocation

You need to give special consideration to the objects you use to allocate dynamic memory. To harmonize with the rest of your code, any class that allocates dynamic memory must override a number of standard C++ member functions. To understand why this is so, create a class that allocates dynamic memory and see which member functions have to be overridden.

The TPolygon Class

The `TPolygon` class is a polygon represented as a pointer to a number of `TPoints`. Here is the initial class declaration:

```
class TPolygon {
public:
    TPolygon();
    TPolygon(const TPoint *thePoints, int numPoints);

    virtual TPoint GetNthPoint(int pointNumber);
    virtual float Length();

private:
    TPoint *fPoints;
    int fNumPoints;
};
```

There are two constructors. The first is a default constructor with no arguments:

```
TPolygon::TPolygon()
{
    fPoints = NULL;
    fNumPoints = 0;
}
```

The second is a constructor that initializes with a number of points:

```
TPolygon::TPolygon(TPoint *thePoints, int numPoints)
{
    fNumPoints = numPoints;
    if (fNumPoints == 0)
        fPoints = NULL;
```

```
    else {
        fPoints = new TPoint[fNumPoints];
        for (int i = 0; i < fNumPoints; i++)
            fPoints[i] = thePoints[i];
    }
}
```

Along with these constructors, you need to create an accessor member function that returns a requested point:

```
TPoint TPolygon::GetNthPoint(int pointNumber)
{
    if (pointNumber >= 0 && pointNumber < fNumPoints)
        return fPoints[pointNumber];
    else {
        Point emptyPoint;

        return emptyPoint;
    }
}
```

Finally, you need some code that returns the length of the perimeter of the polygon by adding together the length of each line.

```
float TPolygon::Length()
{
    float total = 0.0;

    for (int i = 0; i < fNumPoints - 1; i++) {
        TLine lineSegment(fPoints[i], fPoints[i+1]);

        total += lineSegment.Length();
    }
    return total;
}
```

Problems with Dynamic Memory

Problems with dynamic memory are important and can make for some grueling debugging. This should be reason enough to make it worth your while to allocate and dispose of memory properly. Look at some of the things that can go wrong if you get lazy with your memory handling.

You should immediately seize upon the first of the problems with the TPolygon class. Look at this function:

```
void MemoryLeak()
{
    const int kNumPoints = 3;
    TPoint somePoints[kNumPoints];
    ...
    TPolygon aPolygon(somePoints, kNumPoints);

    cout << Length =  << aPolygon.Length();
}
```

When aPolygon is constructed, it allocates a pointer to contain the points. But is this memory ever disposed of? No. This leads to the following rule for C++ objects with dynamic memory allocation.

RULE

Write a destructor when using dynamic memory allocation.

Here is an appropriate destructor for the TPolygon class. First, the declaration is as follows:

```
class TPolygon {
public:
    TPolygon();
    TPolygon(const TPoint *thePoints, int numPoints);
    virtual ~TPolygon();
...

};
```

The actual destructor code is shown below:

```
TPolygon::~TPolygon()
{
     delete fPoints;    // does nothing if fPoints is NULL
}
```

The following code shows a second type of problem. Can you ferret out the problem with the TPolygon class?

```
void Foo()
{
    ...
    TPolygon polyOne(otherPoints, 2);

    {
        TPolygon polyTwo(somePoints, 3);

        polyOne = polyTwo;
    }
    // what about polyOne now?
}
```

The problem lies in the default assignment that C++ provides. By default, assigning one object to another assigns each of the data members in turn. Consider the following example:

```
polyOne = polyTwo;
```

This code becomes the following:

```
polyOne.fNumPoints = polyTwo.fNumPoints;
polyOne.fPoints = polyTwo.fPoints;
```

This assignment leaves you with a cantankerous memory leak when the old `polyOne.fPoints` is lost. `polyOne` and `polyTwo` end up pointing to the same `TPoints`. Figure 11.4 shows a diagram of the objects before and after the assignment. As you can see, this can get nasty.

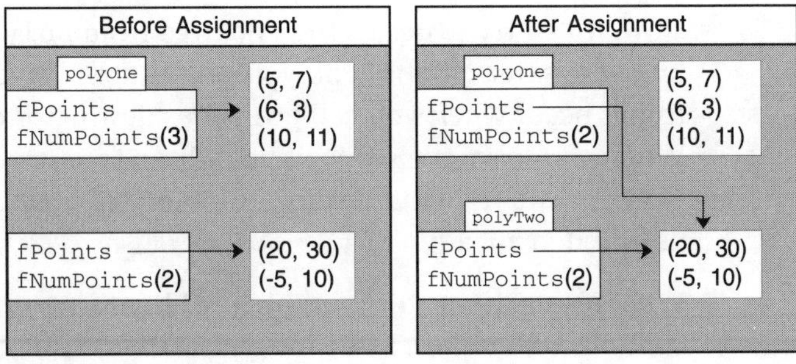

Figure 11.4. Memory leak when assigning objects.

The first problem is that the old points are not disposed of. A second problem is that both objects point to the same points. When `polyTwo` is deleted (at the end of the block it is declared in), its destructor deletes the memory for its `fPoints`. Unfortunately, this leads to `polyOne` pointing to a block of memory that has been deleted, as shown in figure 11.5.

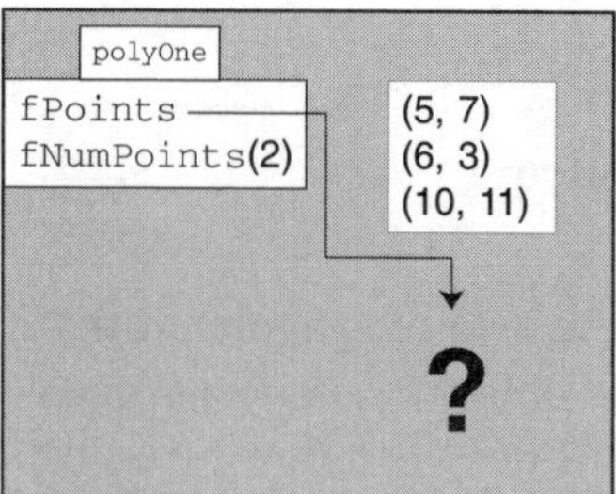

Figure 11.5. Polygons after deletion.

NOTE

It is not automatically wrong to have two objects sharing a piece of memory; it only becomes problematic when you do it unwittingly. If you intend to share memory, then this capability is an asset. In such cases, you should use a reference count to determine when to actually dispose of the shared memory.

Now, if you try to access the `fPoints` from `polyOne`, you get unknown results. Not only do you get random values, but even worse things occur when you call `polyOne`s destructor (at the end of `Foo()`). When you leave the scope of `polyOne`, its destructor deletes `fPoints`. Now you are trying to deallocate a block of memory that has been deallocated already.

What results from this grim picture? If you are very, very lucky your code always crashes. More likely, however, you have intermittent crashes.

NOTE

Here is one of the more important programmer rules of thumb: Defects causing a crash 100 percent of the time are preferred to defects that cause intermittent crashes. The rarer the crash, the harder the cause is to find. (Users probably have different preferences.)

How do you deal with this memory assignment problem? The following rule for objects should be followed when using dynamic allocation.

RULE

Override the default assignment operator.

You should provide your own function for assignment—one that can dispose of the old memory and allocate new memory for the copied data.

Here is the declaration of the assignment operator:

```
class TPolygon {
public:
    TPolygon();
    TPolygon(const TPoint *thePoints, int numPoints);
    virtual ~TPolygon();

    TPolygon &operator=(const TPolygon &poly);
...
};
```

Here is the code for the operator:

```
TPolygon &TPolygon::operator=(const TPolygon &poly)
{
    TPoint *points = NULL;
    if (poly->fNumPoints > 0) {
        points = new TPoint[poly->fNumPoints];
```

```
        for (int i = 0; i < poly->fNumPoints; i++)
            points[i] = poly->fPoints[i];
    }
    delete fPoints;
    fNumPoints = poly->fNumPoints;
    fPoints = points;
    return *this;
}
```

Now that you have taken care of the assignment operator, your code is well behaved and you have a scenario similar to that shown in figure 11.6.

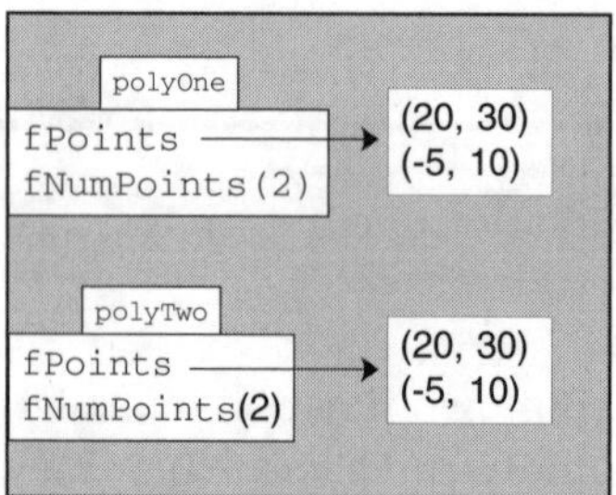

Figure 11.6. Rewritten assignment operator.

Assignment Operators Details

You should know some important facts about the assignment operator. The first point to remember is that your assignment operator should take into account the possibility of self-assignment.

This can occur in code like the following:

```
a = a;
```

Below is another example:

```
ptr = &a;
a = *ptr;
```

Because both of these assignments work with normal data types, you should write your assignment operator so that it works correctly with your objects. For instance, you wrote the assignment operator for `TPolygon` so that it works correctly in the face of self-assignment.

The second point to remember is to return the correct value. You should return a reference to a TPolygon. This enables cascading assignments like the following:

```
aPoly = bPoly = cPoly
```

To return a TPolygon & reference, use the following code:

```
return *this;
```

You are not done with memory problems yet because there are still more danger zones within the TPolygon class. When initializing one object from another, C++ uses a copy constructor. The default copy constructor initializes the data members from the copy. Here are the cases where you use such a constructor:

▼ Explicit initialization of one object from another:

```
TPolygon onePoly(anotherPoly);
```

The above example calls the copy constructor to initialize onePoly from anotherPoly.

▼ Nonreference arguments to a function:

```
// copy constructor is used to initialize aPolygon
void Bar(TPolygon aPolygon)
{
    ...
}

void Foo()
{
    ...
    TPolygon polyOne(otherPoints, 2);
    Bar(polyOne);
}
```

The above example initializes the formal parameter aPolygon with the actual parameter polyOne.

▼ To initialize the return results of functions that return an object:

```
TPolygon GetPoly()
{
    ...
```

```
        TPolygon aPoly(somePoints, 3);
        return aPoly;
    }
```

The above example calls the copy constructor to initialize the return result from aPoly.

The default copy constructors behavior of copying each data member is not sufficient. As with assignment, you need to allocate space for the points. This leads you to the third rule for objects with dynamic allocation.

RULE

Override the default copy constructor.

Here is the declaration for the copy constructor:

```
class TPolygon {
public:
    TPolygon();
    TPolygon(const TPoint *thePoints, int numPoints);
    TPolygon(const TPolygon &poly);
    virtual ~TPolygon();

    TPolygon &operator=(const TPolygon &poly);
...
};
```

Here is the constructor's implementation:

```
TPolygon::TPolygon(const TPolygon &poly)
{
    fNumPoints = poly->fNumPoints;
    if (poly->fPoints == NULL)
         fPoints = NULL;
    else {
        fPoints = new TPoint(fNumPoints);
        for (int i = 0; i < fNumPoints; i++)
            fPoints[i] = poly->fPoints[i];
    }
}
```

Review of Memory Allocation Rules

In summary, when you have a class that has dynamic memory allocation, you need to apply three rules to your code. If you forget these rules, you are almost certain to have memory problems. Here are the rules again. Tattoo them to your forehead, if necessary.

- Write a destructor.
- Override the default assignment operator.
- Override the default copy constructor.

Summary

You learned how to create derived classes and how polymorphism works and why it is so powerful. You also learned why you need to be careful when you create and use objects that allocate dynamic memory.

Having learned this much, you have now gone a long way toward understanding some of the most important differences between an object-oriented language like C++ and a procedural one like C. As you can see, manipulating objects using C++ classes is a flexible, powerful approach to coding. But as any programmer who knows more than one language can tell you, knowing the syntax of a language is not the same as being able to write good code in it. The next important topic of discussion is obvious—how to write *good* C++, that is, code that is both syntactically correct and that uses an elegant, efficient style. In other words, you need to learn how to use C++ idiomatically. You learn how to do that in Chapter 12.

12

Writing Effective C++ Code

You might as well jump in quicksand as program in C++ with a C style. While it is true that you can use C++ as a better C, you are not taking advantage of the object-oriented features. After you attempt to write object-oriented code, you may notice that many of your old C habits become more your enemies rather than your friends. Take, for instance, pointers. Like a kid who has not yet learned to talk, old-time C users point to everything. They have learned, like the toddler, that pointing is very efficient. Compared with what can be accomplished in C++ with references, however, pointers are well worth avoiding. The wizened C user who stubbornly refuses to give up C habits in C++ is no different than the kids who clamp their mouths shut and stick out their fingers instead.

If you incorporate the coding suggestions in this chapter into your work, you can be a more effective C++ programmer. Avoid the temptation to ignore or forget these suggestions, however. You may want to use the warmly familiar C methods that accomplish a task. However, using old methods in the new language is the fastest way to sink into unhappiness with both C and C++. As any speaker of multiple languages can tell you, the best way to learn a language is to go to that native country and speak nothing but that language.

Happily enough, most programmers can approach C++ first as users rather than as designers. As such, they are shielded from the more advanced features of the language. This also enables a more natural progression into the intricacies of the language. You can use classes to implement new features without worrying about how the classes are designed. Being cognizant of this reality, we have organized this chapter into two different sections. The first section is geared toward beginning C++ programmers working on a team—the clients of classes. The second section is for programmers with more experience who are taking on the role of class designers.

Both sections are loose collections of C++ tips and hints. They are not comprehensive discussions of C++ idioms or all there is to say about well designed C++. (There are several fine books on C++ design noted in Appendix E—some of which you should not be without.)

Suggestions for Class Users

The following tips help you use classes effectively in your programs.

TIP

Use pointers less often than in C.

C programs use pointers all over the place. They are used to pass large parameters and as function results. It should be no surprise by now that C++ replaces most of these uses. These alluring creatures are among the hardest for C programmers to give up, however, especially when you realize that C++ enables their continued use. You should ignore the temptation and, instead, focus on the advantages of using references.

TIP

Use references to pass large parameters.

For example, a C program frequently uses a pointer as an efficient way to pass large parameters:

```
void AFunction(const LargeStructure *s);
```

To accomplish the same result in C++, you should use a reference instead:

```
void AFunction(const LargeStructure &s);
```

TIP

Use references to return function results.

In C, you use pointers instead of values as function results. Using this method, the caller can avoid the overhead of a large value or can change what is pointed to. Thus, you might find the following example in C:

```
const LargeStructure *GetIthLargeStructure(int i);
```

You are just as likely to see this:

```
LargeStructure *GetIthLargeStructure(int i);
```

To provide the same functionality in C++, use references and do the following instead:

```
const LargeStructure &GetIthLargeStructure(int i);
```

Or, you might do this:

```
LargeStructure &GetIthLargeStructure(int i);
```

TIP

References are limited.

A problem arises, however, for NULL values. In C, it is no big deal to allow NULL as a parameter or return result—it is in the range of possible values for a pointer. This is not so for a reference.

Some programmers try to be sneaky and get around this problem by dereferencing NULL and passing a NULL reference:

```
AFunction(*NULL);     // don't do this
```

Or, they try checking the address of the return result for NULL:

```
LargeStructure &returnResult = GetIthLargeStructure(i);
if (&returnResult != NULL) {     // don't do this
    // ...
}
```

Do not use either of these methods. You have three choices in such situations:

1. Go ahead and use a pointer.
2. Pass an extra `Boolean` that states whether the function succeeded:

   ```
   Boolean success;
   LargeStructure &returnResult = GetIthLargeStructure(i,
   &success);

   if (success) {
       // ...
   }
   ```

3. Return a sentinel value that is different from all valid values:

   ```
   in some .h file:
   const kInvalidLargeStructure = {-9999,...}; // sentinel
   value

   ...

   LargeStructure &returnResult = GetIthLargeStructure(i);

   if (returnResult != kInvalidLargeStructure) {
       // ...
   }
   ```

TIP

Select whether to use default parameters or overloaded functions.

C++ provides default parameters so that callers can omit parameters. Similarly, C++ provides overloaded functions. This way you can have multiple functions of the same name with different parameter lists. In some cases, you have a choice of using one or the other of these C++ features. How do you decide between them?

Default parameters can make life easy for clients who just want default behavior from your function. You can obtain the same effect using overloaded functions, however. Look at the following example:

```
class TFoo {
public:
    enum {kDefaultOne = 5, kDefaultTwo = 7);
    void AMethod(int i, int j = kDefaultOne, int k =
kDefaultTwo);
private:
    // ...
};

// in the .cp file:
void TFoo::AMethod(int i, int j, int k)
{
    // ...
}
```

`TFoo::AMethod` requires one parameter, `i`. The remaining two parameters, `j` and `k`, are optional.

You can do the same thing with an overloaded function:

```
class TFoo {
public:
    void AMethod(int i);
    void AMethod(int i, int j);
    void AMethod(int i, int j, int k);
private:
    enum {kDefaultOne = 5, kDefaultTwo = 7);
    // ...
};
```

```
// in the .cp file:
void TFoo::AMethod(int i)
{
    AMethod(i, kDefaultOne);
}

void TFoo::AMethod(int i, int j)
{
    AMethod(i, j, kDefaultTwo);
}

void TFoo::AMethod(int i, int j, int k)
{
    // ...
}
```

By overloading `AMethod` in this manner, you let the client decide whether to call it with one, two, or three parameters.

There are tradeoffs involved in using either approach. Default parameters are less bulky and require less code. You do lose some flexibility, however, because the defaults are passed along with any other parameters at compile time by the caller. Overloaded functions, on the other hand, take more time and require additional function calls. The upside here is that missing parameters are provided at run time rather than compile time. They are not compiled into the calling code; instead, they are supplied by the overloaded functions.

In addition, overloaded functions can be overridden by a derived class to provide a different default value. Conversely, default parameters fix the default value for all time for all derived classes. The decision of which to use—default parameters or overloaded functions—can be made then depending on whether you need flexibility in the default values or run-time compilations. If you do not, use the simpler default parameters.

Issues for Class Designers

The following tips are targeted toward those of you who want to design your own classes.

TIP

Do not put inline member functions in the class declaration.

Most C++ books and articles present the implementation of a member function within the class declaration. This, of course, makes the member function inline. When you see this sort of construction, you should ask whether profiling reveals the need for this optimization. In most cases the answer is no. Can you imagine the reason for these implementations? Classes are presented this way to conserve printed space. Authors face very different optimization problems than do programmers. They want to minimize the amount of paper used. Because you do not have the same problem, you do not have the same solution.

Do not clutter your class declaration with inline member functions like the following:

```
class TManyInlines
{
public:
    TManyInlines(int i) {f1 = 3; f2 = 6; f3 = i;}
    int Get1() { return f1;}
    int Get2() { return f2;}
    int Get3() { return f3;}
    void Set1(int i) { f1 = i; }
    void Set2(int i) { f2 = i; }
    void Set3(int i) { f3 = i; }

private:
    int f1;
    int f2;
    int f3;
};
```

If your heart is absolutely set on using inline functions, use the `inline` keyword instead. Then put the implementations of your member functions directly in your header file:

```
class TManyInlines
{
public:
    TManyInlines(int i);
    int Get1();
    int Get2();
    int Get3();
    void Set1(int i);
    void Set2(int i);
    void Set3(int i);

private:
    int f1;
    int f2;
    int f3;
};

inline TManyInlines::TManyInlines(int i)
{
    f1 = 3;
    f2 = 6;
    f3 = i;
}

inline int TManyInlines::Get1()
{
    return f1;
}

inline int TManyInlines::Get2()
{
    return f2;
}

inline int TManyInlines::Get3()
{
    return f3;
}

inline void TManyInlines::Set1(int i)
{
    f1 = i;
}
```

```
inline void TManyInlines::Set2(int i)
{
   f2 = i;
}

inline void TManyInlines::Set3(int i)
{
   f3 = i;
}
```

Although this makes your header file slightly larger, it gives you the same effect as putting the code directly in your class declaration. It also has a number of additional benefits:

- The class declaration is less complex and easier to read.
- Class declaration readers do not have to be aware of the inline functions and their implementation.
- It is easier to create a document showing the interface to the class—you just delete the private parts of the class. If the code were directly in the class declaration, you would have to remove it all before creating the document.
- Most importantly, changing from inline to non-inline is a simple editing exercise. All you have to do is move the function definition into a .cp file and remove the keyword `inline`.

TIP

Use enumerations for class constants.

Most programmers find themselves in the situation of needing a class constant that they want to be evaluated at compile time. It could be for the private use of the class or for use by clients of the class. This situation poses a puzzler for beginning C++ programmers. They find it difficult to determine the right language construct to use. Is it a `const` data member? No. A `static` data member? No. Well, how about a `const static` data member? Still no.

The right answer is to use an enumeration. This example shows you how to do so for the private use of the class and for its clients:

```
class TDooHickey {
public:
    enum EOperation {eAdd, eSubtract, eMultiply, eDivide};
    enum {kCanPrint = true};
    TDooHickey(EOperation op, Boolean canPrint = !kCanPrint);

private:
    enum {kArraySize = 512};
    int     fValues[kArraySize];
};

// in a .cp file:
TDooHickey aDooHickey(TDooHickey::eAdd, TDooHickey::kCanPrint);
TDooHickey anotherDooHickey(TDooHickey::eMultiply);
```

The `e` prefix signifies a classic enumeration constant where a choice is made from a number of different possibilities. The `k` prefix signifies a constant that just happens to be implemented with an enumeration.

Note that the class name is required for these constants when outside the class. You must scope the constant with the class name using the scope resolution operator `::`. This way, it is possible for a number of classes to define the constant `eDivide`. The fact that it is nestled safely within the class prevents any conflict between the various `eDivides`.

Because enumeration constants must have integral values, this only works for constants that can be represented as integers. `Booleans` and `chars` work fine, but do not try this for constant `TPolygons`, for instance.

TIP

Use initializer lists instead of assignments.

Initializer lists contain the parameters for the constructors of the base class and the data members of the current class. These lists are present in C++ because there are certain parts of a class that are constructed before the body of the constructor executes. These two class parts are the inherited data members from the base class and the data members of the class.

An initializer list provides the mechanism for passing the parameters to the constructors of those two parts. As an example, take the following class declarations as a given:

```
class TBase {
public:
    TBase(int param1, int param2);

private:
    // ...
};

class TPolygon {
public:
    TPolygon();
    TPolygon(int numPoints, Point *points);
    TPolygon(const TPolygon &);

    TPolygon &operator=(const TPolygon &poly);

private:
    // ...
};

class TDerived: public TBase {
public:
    TDerived(int x, const TPolygon &aPoly);

private:
    int fDataMember1;
    TPolygon fPolygon;
};
```

Here is the constructor for TDerived:

```
TDerived::TDerived(int x, const TPolygon &aPoly) :
  TBase(x, TickCount()),
  fDataMember1(x * x),
  fPolygon(aPoly)
{
}
```

It uses the initializer list as a way to provide parameters for the TBase constructor and also as a way to initialize its data members, fDataMember1 and fPolygon. You might imagine that initializing data members this way is unnecessary because the constructor could have been written as follows:

```
TDerived::TDerived(int x, const TPolygon &aPoly) :
  TBase(x, TickCount())
{
    fDataMember1 = x * x;
    fPolygon = aPoly;
}
```

While it is legal to write it this way, it leads to an inefficiency. In the original correct constructor, initializing fPolygon required a call to one routine—the copy constructor (TPolygon(const TPolygon &)). This new constructor, using assignment, requires these two calls instead:

1. A call to the default constructor (TPolygon()) to initialize the polygon to a known state. This constructor is automatically called before the code within TDerived::TDerived.
2. A call to the assignment operator to assign from the polygon parameter to fPolygon.

Although one extra call may not seem like much, in some classes the default constructor may allocate memory that the assignment operator turns around and deallocates. This is useless work that consumes time.

In addition to the efficiency concerns, there are cases where data members must be initialized using an initialization list. For instance, how do you initialize a const data member? Not in the class declaration. Even if you could do it that way, all instances of your class end up with the same value for that data member. Not within the body of the constructor. It is a const, so you cannot assign to it.

To initialize a const data member, you must use an initializer list:

```
class TSanDiegoWeather {
public:
    TSanDiegoWeather(float temperature, int year);
private:
    const float fTemperature;
    const int fYear;
};
```

```
// in the .cp file:
TSanDiegoWeather::TSanDiegoWeather(float temperature, int year) :
  fTemperature(temperature),
  fYear(year)
{
  // fYear = year; // illegal
  // fTemperature = temperature; // illegal
```

Similarly, reference data members must be initialized with an initializer list.

TIP

Make classes work like built-in types.

The classes you define should function just like built-in types. Because you can assign one `int` to another, you should be able to assign one `TPolygon` to another. You can cascade assignments of `int`s (`a = b = c`); the same is expected of `TPolygon`s. Your goal is to write your classes so that they have the look and feel of built-in types. This makes users of your classes happy because they have a much easier time writing programs. You become a language god who has extended the language with a newly created species.

To make classes work this way, it is important to write a default constructor, a destructor, a copy constructor, and an assignment operator. In addition, you probably want to write an equality operator (==) and an inequality operator (`!=`).

If objects of your class can be compared, you also need to write the comparison operators: <, <=, >, and >=. You really must write all four of them. Furthermore, it is up to you to make sure that if `a < b` evaluates to true, `b > a` also does. It goes without saying that `b <= a` and `a >= b` should evaluate to false. If you break these relationships, users of the class can be quite surprised.

In general, overloading arithmetic operators is another matter. You should overload them only if your class has a numeric nature or if users of your class naturally expect them to work. It is not wise to define the + operator to mean jump, as in `theCow + theMoon`. It is far better to require clients to write `theCow.Jump(theMoon)`. On the other hand, defining the + operator to mean addition for `TPoints` is something reasonable to do.

As with gravity, it probably is best if the arithmetic operators follow the laws that users expect:

`a + b`	is equivalent to	`b + a`
`a * (b + c)`	is equivalent to	`a * b + a * c`
`a - b`	is equivalent to	`a + -(b)`

In your efforts to design class masterpieces, a good design rule is to use the principle of least surprise. Try not to startle your clients; instead, make classes fit seamlessly into their expectations. Design your classes to work exactly as users expect.

Summary

By designing your applications and writing code with certain basic C++ rules in mind, you learn to program like a veteran object-oriented coder. The rules listed in this chapter are explored at more length in Part 3 of this book, where we use the THINK Class Library to build applications.

13

The THINK Class Browser

In any large program, it is difficult to remember everything that is going on. This is true even for an object-oriented program; unless you have an eidetic memory, it can be hard to remember classes, their relationships, and the functionality they offer.

Luckily, you do not have to worry about remembering all the relationships with Symantec C++. Symantec liberates you from the limitations of your memory with the THINK Class Browser.

What Is the Browser?

The Browser is a tool that displays your class hierarchy: It shows classes and their subclasses within a graphic framework. Figure 13.1 shows an example of a Browser window displaying a C++ program.

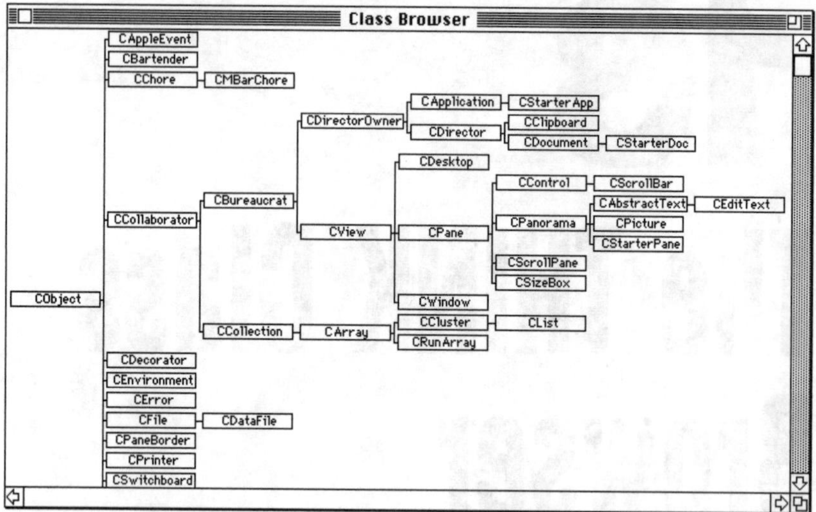

Figure 13.1. The Class Browser window.

As you can see, the Browser can be a very helpful tool to the object-oriented programmer in certain cases. The next sections discuss how to use the Browser.

Creating a Browser Window

First, you need to create some simple class declarations:

```
class TShape {
public:
    TShape();

    virtual void Draw();
};

class TQuadrilateral: public TShape {
public:
    TQuadrilateral();

    virtual int GetSideLength(int i);
    virtual int GetPerimeter();
};
```

```
class TCircle: public TShape {
public:
    TCircle();

    virtual void Draw();
};

class TSquare: public TQuadrilateral {
public:
    TSquare();

    virtual void Draw();
};
```

Now that you have these classes you can use the Browser. It is located in the Source menu. When you choose the Browser, you get a window that looks like the one in figure 13.2.

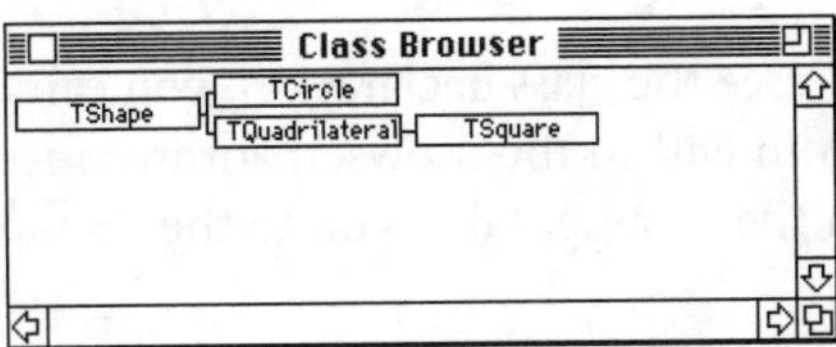

Figure 13.2. A simple Browser window.

The graphic representation displays the relationships between the classes. The `TShape` class is on the left because it has no base class. From `TShape`, two lines extend to the right to show `TShape`'s derived classes, `TCircle` and `TQuadrilateral`. Similarly, a line extends to the right of `TQuadrilateral` to its derived class, `TSquare`.

The Browser does not just display the relationships between the classes; it is an interactive tool as well. When you click on one of the classes, you get a pop-up menu of the member functions (see fig. 13.3).

Now, if you select one of the items in the pop-up, you move directly to the member function source code in the editor. For example, if you select `TShape(void)` (see fig. 13.3), the Project Manager shows you the source code for the `TShape` constructor, as shown in figure 13.4.

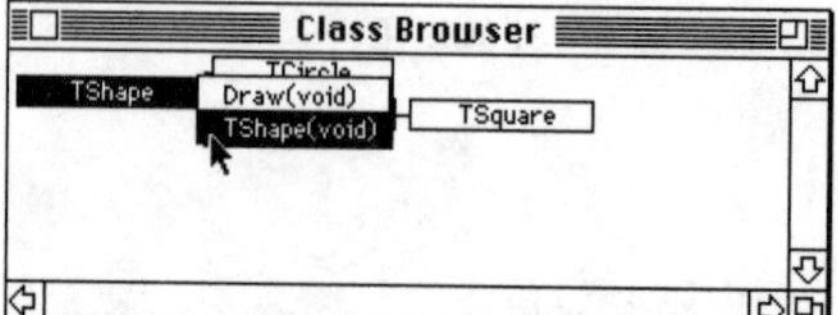

Figure 13.3. A member function pop-up.

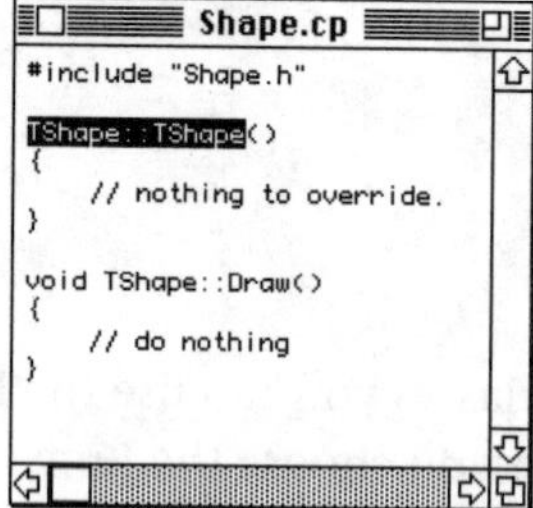

Figure 13.4. After selecting `TShape(void)` from the pop-up.

If you want to see the class declaration, you can double-click on the class name from within the Browser. For instance, double-clicking on `TShape` from the Browser takes you to the `TShape` class declaration (see fig. 13.5).

```
Shape.h
class TShape {
public:
    TShape ();

    virtual void Draw();
};

class TQuadrilateral: public TShape {
public:
    TQuadrilateral();

    virtual int GetSideLength(int i);
    virtual int GetPerimeter();
};

class TCircle: public TShape {
public:
    TCircle();

    virtual void Draw();
};

class TSquare: public TQuadrilateral {
public:
    TSquare();

    virtual void Draw();
};
```

Figure 13.5. After double-clicking `TShape` in the Browser.

Alternatively, you can use the enter or return key after selecting the class from within the Browser to get the same results.

If you want to navigate through C++ classes in the Browser, you can use the arrow keys, as shown in table 13.1.

Table 13.1. Keyboard Shortcuts in the Browser

Key	Result
↑ and ↓	Cycles between siblings of current class
←	Selects the base class of the current class
→	Selects one of the derived classes of the current class
Tab	Cycles through all of the classes

Shortcuts from the Editor

When reading code, you often need to go quickly from a function call to its corresponding source code. In the editor, holding down the option key while you double-click (option-double-click) on a function name takes you to the source code for that function. For example, if you option-double-click on a call to `GetPerimeter` (see fig. 13.6), the editor takes you to the code for `TQuadrilateral::GetPerimeter` (see fig. 13.7).

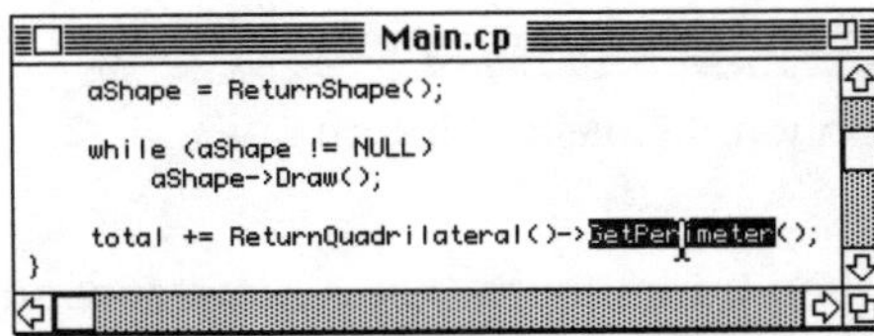

Main.cp
aShape = ReturnShape();
while (aShape != NULL)
aShape->Draw();
total += ReturnQuadrilateral()->GetPerimeter();
}

Figure 13.6. Option-double-clicking on `GetPerimeter`.

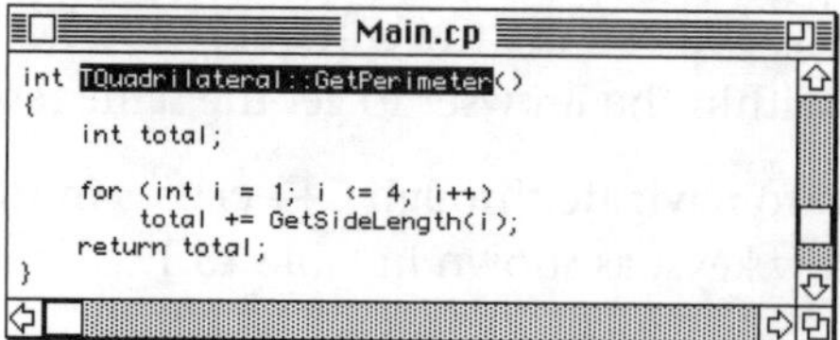
Main.cp
int TQuadrilateral::GetPerimeter()
{
int total;
for (int i = 1; i <= 4; i++)
total += GetSideLength(i);
return total;
}

Figure 13.7. After option-double-clicking on `GetPerimeter`.

Using Identically Named Functions

You may sometimes have different functions with the same name—either different classes that have member functions with the same name or overloaded functions. The next sections examine each of these cases.

Member Functions with the Same Name

Option-double-clicking on a name brings up the Class Browser window. The Browser then outlines each class that has a function with that name. Figure 13.8 shows an example of option-double-clicking on `Draw`.

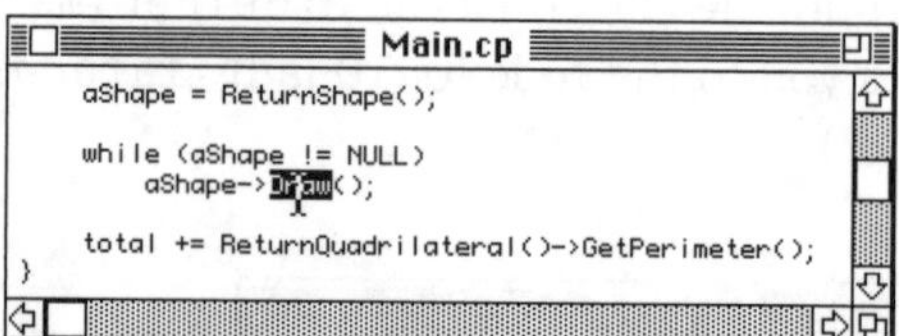
Main.cp
aShape = ReturnShape();
while (aShape != NULL)
aShape->Draw();
total += ReturnQuadrilateral()->GetPerimeter();
}

Figure 13.8. Option-double-clicking on `Draw`.

The editor then brings up the Class Browser window shown in figure 13.9. Each of the outlined classes has a `Draw` member function.

You also should note that a few standard Browser features work slightly differently. If you hit the Tab key, it cycles through the outlined classes, rather than through all classes. Similarly, double-clicking on an outlined class name takes you to the code for the `Draw` member function. For example, if you double-click on `TCircle` (see fig. 13.10), the Browser takes you to the source code for `TCircle::Draw`, as shown in figure 13.11.

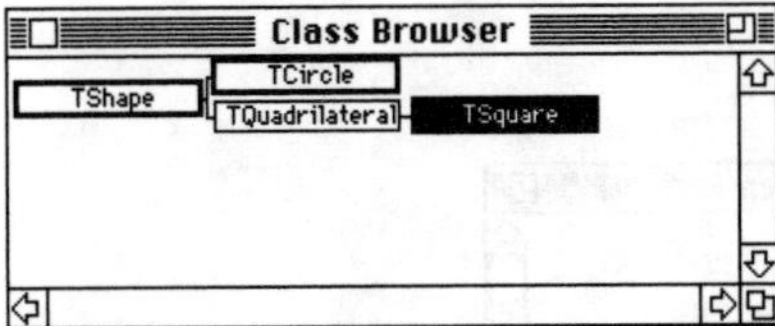

Figure 13.9. After option-double-clicking on `Draw`.

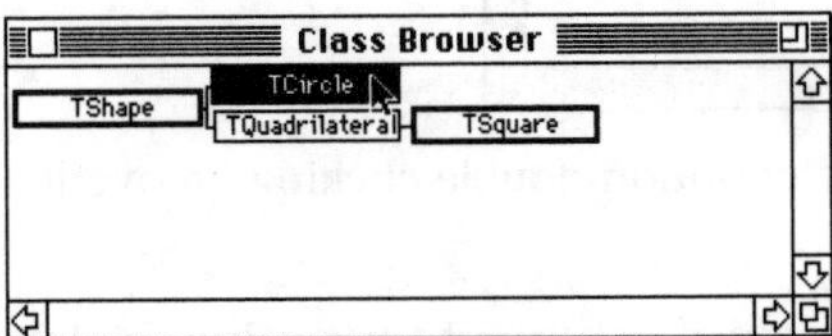

Figure 13.10. Double-clicking on `TCircle` from within the Browser.

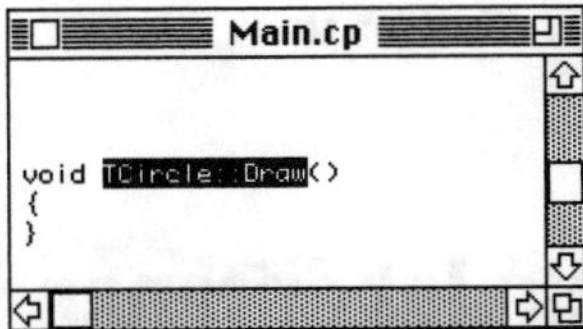

Figure 13.11. After double-clicking on `TCircle` from the Browser.

Overloaded Functions

Overloaded functions are the other case in which you can find multiple functions with the same name. If you option-double-click on a name in this case, the Browser takes you to the first overloaded function.

For example, in the following code, option-double-clicking on `Bar` takes you to the first `Bar`, as shown in figure 13.12:

```
void Bar(int i)
{
    // ...
}
```

```
void Bar()
{
    // ...
}
```

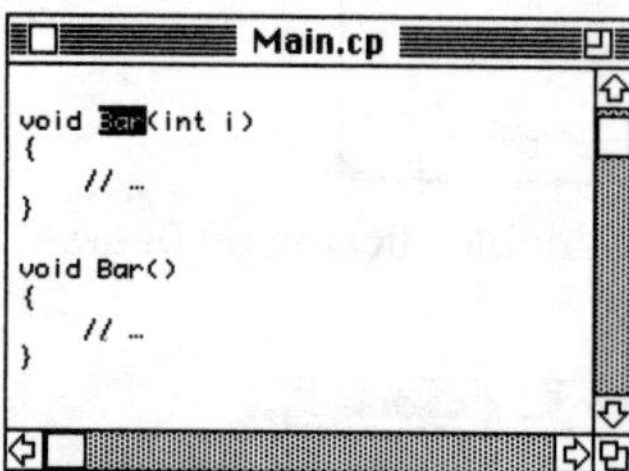

Figure 13.12. After option-double-clicking on overloaded `Bar`.

The editor provides a shortcut for getting to class declarations as well as to member functions. The shortcut is to hold down the command and option keys while double-clicking (command-option-double-click) on the name of a class. The editor then takes you to the class declaration.

Browsing with Multiple Inheritance

The Browser also works if you are using multiple inheritance. With single inheritance, the class hierarchy forms a tree (actually, a forest because the hierarchy is a collection of rooted trees). With multiple inheritance, the diagram becomes more complicated. Specifically, it forms a directed acyclic graph (DAG). It is directed because the direction of the line between classes matters. It is acyclic because there can be no cycles.

To see how this works, you first need some class declarations:

```
class TFoo {
public:
    void Foo();
};
```

```
class MBarable {
public:
    void Bar();
};

class TFooSubclass: public TFoo {
    void FooSubclass();
};

class TBarableFoo: public TFoo, public MBarable {
    void BarableFoo();
};

class MBarableSubclass: public MBarable {
    void BarableSubclass();
};
```

Figure 13.13 shows the Browser for these class declarations.

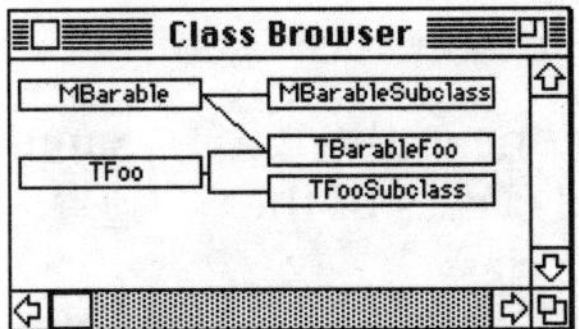

Figure 13.13. Browser with multiple inheritance.

Summary

This chapter discussed the basic features of the Browser. It is a useful tool for quickly navigating through your source code. It can help you easily locate the interrelationships between classes. All in all, the Browser is well worth mastering. To review the Browser commands, use tables 13.2 and 13.3, which show the keyboard and mouse short-cuts.

Table 13.2. Shortcuts within the Browser

Keyboard or Mouse Action	No Classes Outlined	Some Classes Outlined
Click	Shows a pop-up menu of member functions	Same
Double-click	Takes you to the class declaration	Takes you to the code for the member function on which you originally option-double-clicked
Enter/return	Takes you to the class declaration for the selected class	Takes you to the code for the member function on which you originally option-double-clicked
↑ and ↓	Cycles between siblings of the current class	Same
←	Selects the base class of the current class	Same
→	Selects one of the derived classes of the current class	Same
Tab	Cycles through all of the classes	Cycles through all of the outlined classes

Table 13.3. Double-Clicking Shortcuts within the Editor

Selected Word	Option-Dbl-Click	Cmd-Option-Dbl-Click
Class that has a constructor	Takes you to the code for the constructor	Takes you to the class declaration
Class that does not have a constructor	Takes you to the class declaration	Same
Member function found in only one class	Takes you to the code for the member function	Same

Selected Word	Option-Dbl-Click	Cmd-Option-Dbl-Click
Member function found in more than one class	Takes you to the Browser with each class with that member outlined	Same
Overloaded function	Takes you to the code for the first occurrence of the overloaded function	Same

14

The C++ Options Panels

Where would we be without options? Symantec, realizing that different C++ users have different needs, gives users a dialog of options that enables the ultimate in tailoring. In the Edit menu, you find an Options dialog that governs your C++ language settings. You learn about each option in this chapter.

Option Choices

You get your choice of five different panels in the Symantec C/C++ Options dialog. To get to the initial Options panel, select Options from the Edit Menu, as shown in figure 14.1.

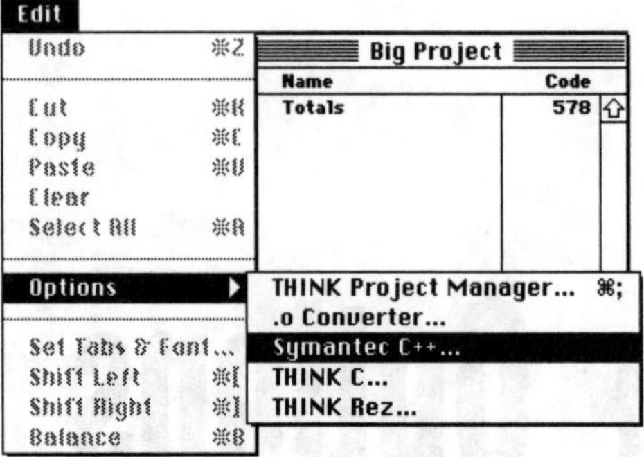

Figure 14.1. Picking Symantec C++ Options from the Edit Menu.

Selecting C++ Options gives you a choice of panels. Figure 14.2 shows you what they are.

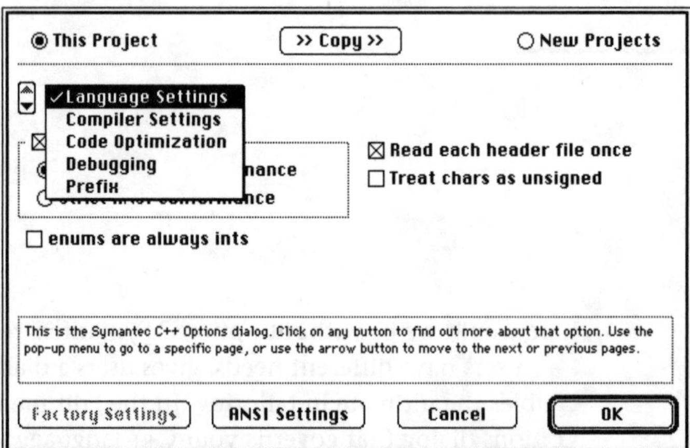

Figure 14.2. Symantec C++ Options panel choices.

Each of these five panels controls a different aspect of the C++ compiler:

- The Language Settings panel controls how the language is compiled.
- The Compiler Settings panel controls how the code is output.
- The Code Optimization panel determines how the output code is optimized.

- The Debugging panel designates whether debugging information is output with the code and how errors/warnings are treated.
- The Prefix panel shows global variable definitions and include files.

You see in figure 14.2 that there are some other buttons in the dialog. They perform the following actions:

- The Factory Settings button restores all the options in the panel to their default settings.
- The This Project button changes the settings for the current project.
- The New Projects button changes the settings for future projects.
- The Copy button copies settings from This Project to New Projects and vice versa.
- The ANSI Settings button makes your choices compatible with ANSI C (found only in the Language Settings panel).

Language Settings Panel

The first of these C++ Option panels is the Language Settings panel (shown in figure 14.3). It governs the compilation of your code.

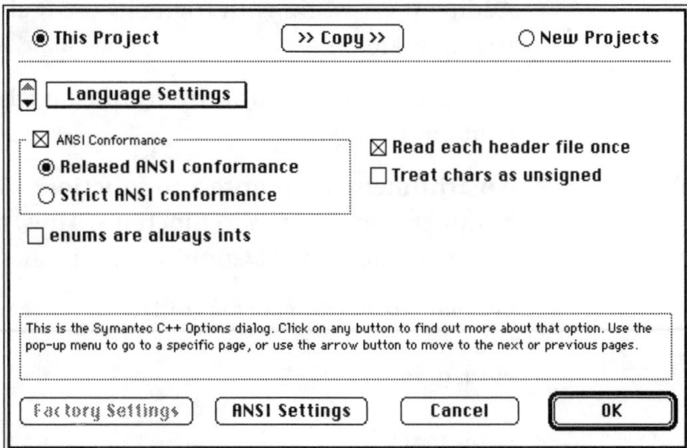

Figure 14.3. The Language Settings panel.

ANSI Conformance. In almost every way, C++ is a superset of C. Traditional C, however, has a number of features added by ANSI C that are not present in C++. To deal with this situation, you have the ANSI Conformance check box. When you check it, the C++ compiler recognizes ANSI C features. The Relaxed ANSI Conformance radio button enables all of the Symantec C++ Macintosh extensions such as the `pascal` type modifier, extended option, directions, and others. The Strict ANSI Conformance button disables all of those extensions. The items listed below should be taken into account when conforming to ANSI features:

- **Trigraphs.** Outside the United States, many computers use characters such as {, }, |, and ~ for language-specific characters like é. Because the Macintosh is an international computer, it differentiates between these characters. On other computers, however, the character { may appear on-screen as é. To deal with this problem, ANSI C added alternate forms for all but the most common (alphanumeric) characters.

  These alternate forms are all three-character sequences beginning with `??`. For example, `??'` is recognized as `^`. However, many Macintosh programs use multi-character constants that resemble trigraphs. For instance, it is common to use `'????'` as a file type. With trigraph processing on, this is recognized as `'??^` because the last three characters are read as `^`. To avoid this problem, prepend a \ to at least one of the ? characters (e.g., '`\?\?\?\?'`). Adding the \ works with trigraphs on; it also works when trigraphs are off.

  Normally, you only turn this feature on when porting code that contains trigraphs.

- **No arithmetic on pointers to functions.** ANSI C does not allow arithmetic on pointers to functions. Thus, the following code only compiles if ANSI Conformance is off:

  ```
  typedef void (*FuncPtr)(void);

  void g(void);

  void foo()
  {
  ```

```
    FuncPtr   f1 = g;
    FuncPtr    f2 = g;

    long l = f1 - f2;
}
```

- **No trailing , in enum lists.** ANSI C does not allow enumeration declarations to end in a ,. The following, therefore, does not compile if ANSI Conformance is on:

  ```
  enum {e1, e2, };
  ```

- **No binary constants.** ANSI C allows decimal, octal, and hexadecimal constants, but not binary constants like the following:

  ```
  int i = 0b1001;
  ```

- **\x must be followed by a hex digit.** Symantec C++ interprets a `\x` that is not followed by a hex number as an `x`. Because ANSI C requires that `\x` be followed by a hex digit, the following is illegal:

  ```
  char *s = "\xNN"
  ```

  If ANSI Conformance is off, the characters in `s` are '`x`,' '`N`,' '`N`,' and '`0`.'

enums are always ints. In most implementations of C and C++, enumeration variables and `ints` have the same size. In implementations of Pascal for the Macintosh, however, the size of an enumeration variable is 1, 2, or 4 bytes. This depends on the number of bytes needed to hold the range of values.

Here is the dilemma: If you turn the enums are always ints option on, you have better compatibility with other implementations of C and C++ but worse compatibility with Pascal for the Macintosh. One way to avoid this is to define your enumerations as the size of an integer regardless of the setting of this flag. Here is an example of how to do that. The following enumeration type, `Color`, uses 1 byte if this option is off and 4 bytes if this option is on:

```
enum Color {red, green, blue};
```

To guarantee that it will be 4 bytes long, add an extra enumeration constant at the end. Make sure it is large enough to force the compiler to use 4 bytes:

```
enum Color {red, green, blue, purple, bigColor = 100000};
```

You also should know that the Macintosh Toolbox header files use a technique for their enumerations so that they are 1, 2, or 4 bytes regardless of the setting of this option. For example, they define the type `GrafVerb` as follows:

```
enum {frame,paint,erase,invert,fill};
typedef unsigned char GrafVerb;
```

This defines the enumeration constants (`frame`, `paint`, `erase`, `invert`, and `fill`) separately from the type `GrafVerb`. The declaration of `GrafVerb` forces it to be 1 byte. This technique works fine in C. In C++, on the other hand, you lose some type checking. `GrafVerb` is now just an `unsigned char` rather than an enumeration. Thus, the compiler can no longer warn you about code like the following:

```
GrafVerb myGrafVerb = red;     // should be an error
```

It is enough at this point to be aware of this technique and its limitations.

Read each header file once. A common C/C++ convention is to bracket the contents of header files with `#ifndef` and `#endif` preprocessor directives so that you only have to include the contents of header files once:

```
#ifndef MYFILE_H
#define MYFILE_H
// actual contents of MyFile.h
#endif
```

If you `#include MyFile.h` more than once while compiling a particular file, the compiler ignores the actual contents of `MyFile.h` (because the compile-time variable `MYFILE_H` is defined) after the first time. You end up with a speedier compile and fewer compile errors due to the redeclaration of types or variables. You get limited speedup, however, because the compiler must preprocess the header file even when it is not compiled.

If you are after real speed, it is quicker to avoid preprocessing the file more than once. Symantec C++ provides two different ways to do this:

- ▼ Check the Read each header file once check box. The compiler then reads each header file once. This option takes advantage of the common header convention by not rereading header files that start with #ifndef and end with #endif.

- Use the once #pragma. If you use that pragma in a header file, the compiler ignores successive occurrences of #include in the header file. The above header file rewritten to use #pragma once is as follows:

```
#pragma once

// actual contents of MyFile.h
```

  You may find the pragma useful for your own header files. However, be aware that there are many header files (including the Apple header files) that do not contain the once #pragma.

Because almost all header files contain #ifndef and #endif pairs, you should normally check the Read each header file once option. This also is why it is the default.

Treat chars as unsigned. C and C++ do not determine whether char types are signed or unsigned (whether they range from -128 to 127 or from 0 to 256). Some implementations implement them as signed, while others implement them as unsigned. If you want your C/C++ code properly portable, it should work regardless of which implementation you use. Because some code may assume char types are unsigned, you need the Treat chars as unsigned option.

Normally, however, you do not check it.

That is all there is to the Language Settings panel. You will find in practice that you set up your choices only once.

Compiler Settings Panel

The second panel you can choose is the Compiler Settings panel (see fig. 14.4).

This panel contains options that affect how the compiler generates its code. Look at these choices in turn.

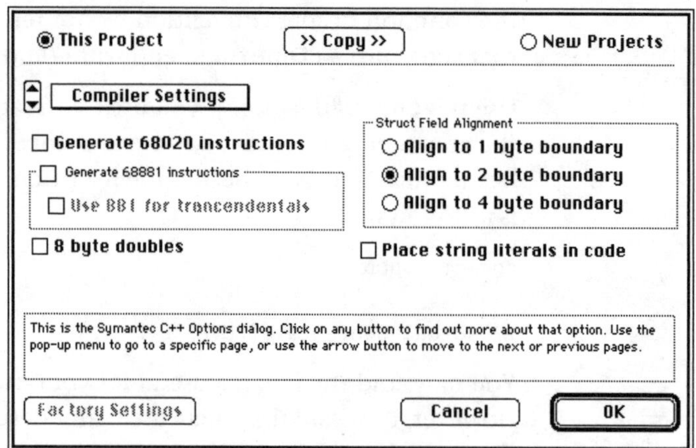

Figure 14.4. The Compiler Settings panel.

Generate 68020 instructions. Normally, Symantec C++ generates 68000 instructions, thereby enabling your code to run on any Macintosh. If the Generate 68020 instructions option is on, the compiler generates code that also uses 68020 instructions. These instructions are present on the 68020 and higher machines, but not on the earlier machines. The upshot of this is that you get snappier performance on Macintoshes with 68020, 68030, or 68040 processors, but your code cannot run on Macintoshes with the 68000 processor.

Generate 68881 instructions. For floating-point operations, Symantec C++ normally uses Standard Apple Numerics Environment (SANE) which is present on all Macintoshes. Many Macintoshes contain Motorola floating-point coprocessors that use the 68881 instruction set. SANE uses 68881 instructions if possible, reverting to software floating-point operations on Macintoshes without 68881 instructions. Although SANE uses the hardware to do floating-point calculations, using it as an intermediary to the hardware is not as fast as issuing 68881 instructions directly. Checking the Generate 68881 instructions option increases performance on machines with 68881 instructions (those with 68881 or 68882 coprocessors or those with 68040 processors), but your code cannot run on machines without 68881 instructions.

Use 881 for transcendentals. For transcendental operations (like `sin` or `cos`), you get slightly different results when using the 68881 instructions than when using SANE (only in one or two of the low-order bits). When you check the Use 881 for transcendentals option, the compiler uses 68881 instructions even for transcendental operations. Use this option only if this slight difference does not matter to you. If this option is off, the compiler uses SANE for these operations.

8 byte doubles. Symantec C++ stores the type `long double` in a format that causes floating-point operations to be bullet quick. `Long double` types are 10 bytes long if SANE is used and 12 bytes long if 68881 instructions are used.

It is surprising, but using the `long double` type is faster than using shorter floating-point types (4- or 8-byte floating-point types).

If you turn 8 byte doubles off, the type `double` is the same size as `long double` and just as fast. If you turn 8 byte doubles on, you save space for `double` variables at the expense of slowing down calculations with them.

Write your code using the type `long double` directly if you want fast floating-point operations. You should only need to change this option if you are porting code that contains references to `double` types.

Struct Field Alignment. The radio buttons in the box control field location and length in structures, unions, and classes. Here is what the choices mean:

- Align to 1 byte boundary button enables a field to start at any byte.
- Align to 2 byte boundary button enables fields of size 2 or more to begin on an even byte boundary. The size of the structure is rounded up to an even size as well.
- Align to 4 byte boundary button enables fields of size 4 or more to begin on a multiple of a 4-byte boundary. The size of the structure is rounded up to a multiple of 4 as well.

In all cases, arrays follow the alignment of their elements. Table 14.1 shows some example structures and the offsets of each field using the various options.

Table 14.1. The Effect of Struct Field Alignment

Align to 1-Byte Boundary	Align to 2-Byte Boundary	Align to 4-Byte Boundary

`struct s {`
`char a; // offset 0`
`short b; // offset 1`
`char c[2]; // offset 3`
`}; // sizeof(s) == 5`
	`struct s {`
	`char a; // offset 0`
	`short b; // offset 2`
	`char c[2]; // offset 4`
	`}; // sizeof(s) == 6`
		`struct s {`
		`char a; // offset 0`
		`short b; // offset 2`
		`char c[2]; // offset 4`
		`}; // sizeof(s) == 8`

`struct s {`
`char a; // offset 0`
`int i; // offset 1`
`char c[2]; // offset 5`
`}; // sizeof(s) == 7`
	`struct s {`
	`char a; // offset 0`
	`int i; // offset 2`
	`char c[2]; // offset 6`
	`}; // sizeof(s) == 8`
		`struct s {`
		`char a; // offset 0`
		`int i; // offset 4`
		`char c[2]; // offset 8`
		`}; // sizeof(s) == 12`

`struct s {`
`char a; // offset 0`
`double b; // offset 1`
`char c[2]; // offset 9`
`}; // sizeof(s) == 11`
	`struct s {`
	`char a; // offset 0`
	`double b; // offset 2`
	`char c[2]; // offset 10`
	`}; // sizeof(s) == 12`
		`struct s {`
		`char a; // offset 0`
		`double b; // offset 4`
		`char c[2]; // offset 12`
		`}; // sizeof(s) == 16`

`struct s {`
`char a; // offset 0`
`char b[3]; // offset 1`
`char c[2]; // offset 4`
`}; // sizeof(s) == 6`
	`struct s {`
	`char a; // offset 0`
	`char b[3]; // offset 1`
	`char c[2]; // offset 4`
	`}; // sizeof(s) == 6`
		`struct s {`
		`char a; // offset 0`
		`char b[3]; // offset 1`
		`char c[2]; // offset 4`
		`}; // sizeof(s) == 8`

Selecting anything but the 2-byte default puts you in a delicate minefield. If you want to remain compatible with the Macintosh Toolbox, you need 2-byte alignments for structures and unions because the Macintosh Toolbox assumes them.

If you are writing code that does not call the Macintosh Toolbox, you can use other alignments. 1-byte alignment utilizes memory the most efficiently, but creates code that causes a fatal address error on Macintoshes with a 68000 processor. This is because the 68000 processor cannot access multi-byte values that are on odd addresses.

Using 4-byte alignment creates code that runs faster on 68020, 68030, and 68040 machines. These machines are able to access multi-byte values on any address but run quicker with 4-byte addresses. Structures, however, take up more space.

Place string literals in code. This option defaults to off, causing string literals like "Neil" to be placed in global data space. If you check the Place string literals in code option, literals are placed within the code itself. You check this flag when you are writing stand-alone code resources (which are not able to use globals) and need to use string literals.

Code Optimization Panel

The Code Optimization panel is shown in figure 14.5. You should note that this panel has a master check box, Use Global Optimizer. If you turn this off, you get no more choices (everything else is grayed out).

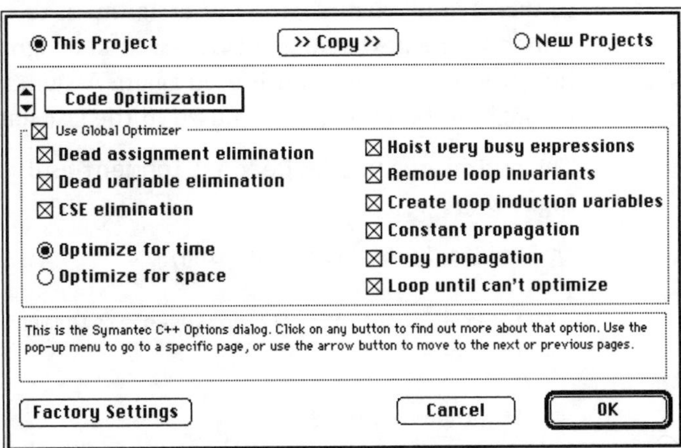

Figure 14.5. The Code Optimization panel.

Dead assignment elimination. When you check the Dead assignment elimination box, the compiler removes assignments to variables that are not subsequently used. Here is a simple example of code that does the following:

```
{
    int f = 3;

    g = f;
    f = 5;  // dead assignment, f never used afterwards
}
```

A slightly more intricate example follows:

```
int DeadAssignment(int incoming)
{
    int f = incoming;  // not dead assignment
    int  g = f+5;

    if (incoming != 3) {
        f = 3;    // dead assignment
        g = 3;  // not a dead assignment
    }
    return g * g;
}
```

In this second example, the first assignment to `f` is not dead because `f` is used in the next statement. The second assignment to `f` is dead, however, because it never is used again. Assignments to `g` remain alive throughout because `g` is even used in the last statement.

The optimizer compiles `DeadAssignment` as if you wrote the following:

```
int DeadAssignment(int incoming)
{
    int f = incoming;  // not dead assignment
    int  g = f+5;

    if (incoming != 3) {
        g = 3;  // not a dead assignment
    }
    return g * g;
}
```

To help you get a better idea of the effects of this optimization, table 14.2 shows a disassembly of the object code for `DeadAssignment` with dead assignment elimination on and off. Italics show the important differences.

Table 14.2. Effects of Dead Assignment Elimination on DeadAssignment

Dead Assignment Elimination Off				Dead Assignment Elimination On			
	LINK	A6,#$FFF8			LINK	A6,#$FFF8	
	MOVE.L	D3,-(A7)			MOVE.L	D3,-(A7)	
	MOVEQ	#$00,D0			MOVEQ	#$00,D0	
	MOVE.L	D0,$FFFC(A6)			MOVE.L	D0,$FFFC(A6)	
	MOVE.L	$0008(A6),D0			MOVE.L	$0008(A6),D0	
	MOVEQ	#$03,D3			MOVEQ	#$03,D3	
	CMP.L	D3,D0			CMP.L	D3,D0	
	BEQ.S	*+$000A	; 1E		BEQ.S	*+$0006	; 1A
	MOVE.L	D3,$FFF8(A6)					
	MOVE.L	D3,$FFFC(A6)			MOVE.L	D3,$FFFC(A6)	
1E:	MOVE.L	$FFFC(A6),D0		1A:	MOVE.L	$FFFC(A6),D0	
	MOVE.L	D0,D1			MOVE.L	D0,D1	
	JSR	ULMULT			JSR	ULMULT	
	MOVE.L	$FFF4(A6),D3			MOVE.L	$FFF4(A6),D3	
	UNLK	A6			UNLK	A6	
	MOVEA.L	(A7)+,A0			MOVEA.L	(A7)+,A0	
	ADDQ.W	#$4,A7			ADDQ.W	#$4,A7	
	JMP	(A0)			JMP	(A0)	

Dead variable elimination. The Dead variable elimination check box depends on two different optimizations that analyze the code in the same way. When you check the Dead variable elimination option, the optimizer calculates the *live range* of each automatic variable. This code range preserves the variable's value and it starts when the variable is set and ends after the last use. If a variable has an empty live range, the optimizer can eliminate it.

The optimizer also uses this computation of live range to enable variables to share space. Variables can share the same memory location if their live ranges do not overlap. The optimizer uses all this information to determine which registers to use for which variables.

A simple example of dead variable elimination is listed below:

```
{
    int f = 3;
    g = g * 2;
    f = 5;
}
```

The variable `f` is never used (its live range is empty), so the optimizer removes it, leaving the following:

```
{
    g = g * 2;
}
```

Here is a more complicated example:

```
short DeadVariable(short incoming)
{
    short k = 3;
    short l;

    short sum = incoming + incoming;

    k = 6;                          // k live

    short otherSum = k + k;         // k otherSum live
    k = otherSum;                   // k, otherSum live
    sum = 7;                        // k, sum live
    return k * sum;                 // k, sum live
}
```

The optimizer compiles the above example as if it were written as follows:

```
short DeadVariable(short incoming)
{
    short k = 3;
                                //l eliminated
    short sum;

    k = 6;                      // k live

    short otherSum = k + k;     // k otherSum live
    k = otherSum;               // k, otherSum live
    sum = 7;                    // k, sum live
    return k * sum;             // k, sum live
}
```

In addition, `sum` and `otherSum` can share the same register.

To see how this optimization works, you can look at the disassembly of the object code for `DeadVariable`. Table 14.3 shows the disassembly with dead variable elimination on and off.

Table 14.3. Effects of Dead Variable Elimination on DeadVariable

Dead Variable Elimination Off		Dead Variable Elimination On	
LINK	A6,#$FFF8	LINK	A6,#$0000
MOVEQ	#$03,D0	MOVEM.L	D3-D5,-(A7)
MOVE.W	D0,$FFF8(A6)	MOVEQ	#$03,D3
MOVE.W	$0008(A6),D0	MOVE.W	$0008(A6),D4
ADD.W	$0008(A6),D0	ADD.W	$0008(A6),D4
MOVE.W	D0,$FFFC(A6)	MOVEQ	#$06,D3
MOVEQ	#$06,D0	MOVE.W	D3,D5
MOVE.W	D0,$FFF8(A6)	ADD.W	D3,D5
MOVE.W	$FFF8(A6),D0	MOVE.W	D5,D3
ADD.W	$FFF8(A6),D0	MOVEQ	#$07,D4
MOVE.W	D0,$FFFE(A6)	MOVE.W	D3,D0
MOVE.W	D0,$FFF8(A6)	MULS.W	D4,D0

continues

Table 14.3. Continued

Dead Variable Elimination Off		Dead Variable Elimination On	
MOVEQ	#$07,D0	MOVEM.L	(A7)+,D3-D5
MOVE.W	D0,$FFFC(A6)	UNLK	A6
MOVE.W	$FFF8(A6),D0	MOVEA.L	(A7)+,A0
MULS.W	$FFFC(A6),D0	ADDQ.W	#$2,A7
UNLK	A6	JMP	(A0)
MOVEA.L	(A7)+,A0		
ADDQ.W	#$2,A7		
JMP	(A0)		

The dead variable elimination optimization works best if you also set Dead assignment elimination. The dead assignment elimination removes assignments; this decreases the live ranges of variables.

IMPORTANT

Dead variable elimination is one of the most powerful optimizations you have at your disposal because it controls variable placement into registers. Having variables in registers, rather than on the stack, significantly increases the speed of access. This is especially true if you access variables within a loop.

CSE elimination. When you select CSE (common subexpression) elimination, the optimizer removes the computations of redundant expressions. If you repeat an expression in your source code, the CSE elimination option calculates that expression once, saves it in a temporary, and then uses the precalculated value anywhere the original expression occurs. Here is an example function that repeats the expression `k * (k+2)`:

```
short Foo(short j, short k)
{
    short i = j + k * (k+2);
    short m = k * (k+2);

    return i * m;
}
```

CSE elimination computes the value of `k * (k+2)` once rather than twice. The code compiles as if it were written as follows:

```
short FooConverted(short j, short k)
{
    short tmp = k * (k+2);
    short i = j + tmp;
    short m = tmp;

    return i * m;
}
```

Table 14.4 shows a disassembly of the object code for `Foo` with CSE elimination on and off. Italics show the important differences.

Table 14.4. Effects of Common Subexpression Elimination on Foo

CSE Elimination Off		CSE Elimination On	
LINK	A6,#$0000	LINK	A6,#$FFFC
MOVEM.L	D3/D4,-(A7)	MOVEM.L	D4/D5,-(A7)
MOVE.W	$0008(A6),D3	MOVE.W	$0008(A6),D4
ADDQ.W	#$2,D3	ADDQ.W	#$2,D4
MULS.W	$0008(A6),D3	MULS.W	$0008(A6),D4
		MOVE.W	*D4,$FFFC(A6) ;store CSE*
ADD.W	$000A(A6),D3	ADD.W	$000A(A6),D4
MOVE.W	*$0008(A6),D4; recalculate CSE*	*MOVE.W*	*$FFFC(A6),D5 ;restore CSE*
ADDQ.W	*#$2,D4*		
MULS.W	*$0008(A6),D4*		
MOVE.W	D3,D0	MOVE.W	D4,D0

continues

Table 14.4. Continued

CSE Elimination Off		CSE Elimination On	
MULS.W	D4,D0	MULS.W	D5,D0
MOVEM.L	(A7)+,D3/D4	MOVEM.L	(A7)+,D4/D5
UNLK	A6	UNLK	A6
MOVEA.L	(A7)+,A0	MOVEA.L	(A7)+,A0
ADDQ.W	#$4,A7	ADDQ.W	#$4,A7
JMP	(A0)	JMP	(A0)

The example with `k * (k+2)` is one where the common subexpression is very evident. They can be much less evident, however:

```
struct MyStruct {
    char  c;
    short ints[10];
};

void Bar(MyStruct *s)
{
    for (int i = 0; i < 9; i++)
        s->ints[i] = s->ints[i+1];
}
```

Here, you get the calculation of the `ints` field within `s` done twice. CSE elimination compiles the code as if it were written as follows:

```
void BarConverted(MyStruct *s)
{
    for (int i = 0; i < 9; i++) {
        int *intPtr;

        intPtr = &s->ints[i];
        intPtr[0] = intPtr[1];
    }
}
```

Table 14.5 shows a disassembly of the object code for `Bar` with CSE elimination on and off. Italics show the important differences.

Table 14.5. Effects of Common Subexpression Elimination on Bar

CSE Elimination Off	CSE Elimination On
LINK A6,#$FFFC	LINK A6,#$FFFC
	MOVEM.L D3/D4/A2,-(A7)
MOVEQ #$00,D0	MOVEQ #$00,D0
MOVE.L D0,$FFFC(A6)	MOVE.L D0,$FFFC(A6)
CMPI.L #$00000009,$FFFC(A6)	MOVEQ #$09,D1
BGE.S *+$0030 ; 00000042	CMP.L D1,D0
	BGE.S *+$0026 ; 38
14: MOVE.L $FFFC(A6),D0	14: MOVE.L $FFFC(A6),D3
; calculate CSE &s->ints[0]	; calculate CSE &s->ints[0]
ASL.L #$1,D0	MOVEQ #$01,D4
ADD.L $0008(A6),D0	ASL.L D4,D3
MOVEA.L D0,A0	ADD.L $0008(A6),D3
	MOVEA.L D3,A2 ;
; evaluate s->ints[1]	; evaluate s->ints[1]
MOVE.W $0004(A0),D0	MOVE.W $0004(A2),D0
; calculate CSE &s->ints[0]	
MOVE.L $FFFC(A6),D1	
ASL.L #$1,D1	
ADD.L $0008(A6),D1	
MOVEA.L D1,A0	
; save into s->ints[0]	; save into s->ints[0]
MOVE.W D0,$0002(A0)	MOVE.W D0,$0002(A2)

continues

Table 14.5. Continued

CSE Elimination Off	CSE Elimination On
ADDQ.L #$1,$FFFC(A6)	ADDQ.L #$1,$FFFC(A6)
CMPI.L #$00000009,$FFFC(A6)	CMPI.L #$00000009,$FFFC(A6)
BLT.S *-$002C ; 00000014	BLT.S *-$0022 ; 14
42: UNLK A6	38: MOVEM.L (A7)+,D3/D4/A2
MOVEA.L (A7)+,A0	UNLK A6
ADDQ.W #$4,A7	MOVEA.L (A7)+,A0
JMP (A0)	ADDQ.W #$4,A7
	JMP (A0)

CSE elimination can make your code both faster and smaller by eliminating redundant calculation.

Hoist very busy expressions. This optimization is a space-saving feature. It takes code that is duplicated in more than one execution path and move it before the branch. While it does not save time, it should save code space. For example, the following code calculates the same expression in both the if and else branches:

```
int Hoist(int bool, short b, short c)
{
    short a;
    short d;

    if (bool) {
        a = b*b + 2*b*c + c*c;
    }
    else {
        d = b*b + 2*b*c + c*c;
    }
    return a * d;
}
```

With the Hoist very busy expressions option selected, the above compiles as if it were written as follows:

```
int Hoist(int bool, short b, short c)
{
    short a;
    short d;

    short tmp  = b*b + 2*b*c + c*c;
    if (bool) {
        a = temp;
    }
    else {
        d = temp;
    }
    return a * d;
}
```

Unfortunately, at the time this book went to press, the above example incorrectly compiled as if it were written like this:

```
int Hoist(int bool, short b, short c)
{
    short a;
    short d;

    short tmp  = b*b + 2*b*c + c*c;
    if (bool) {
        a = temp;
    }
    else {
        d = b*b + 2*b*c + c*c;
    }

    return a * d;
}
```

This version of the optimization does not save any space and executes more slowly if the else portion of the branch is taken. Because of this, you might not want to use this optimization unless you are sure it works correctly in your version of the software. Table 14.6 shows a disassembly of the object code for `Hoist` with the Hoist very busy expressions option on and off.

Table 14.6. Effects of Hoist Very Busy Expressions on Hoist

Hoist Very Busy Expressions Off	Hoist Very Busy Expressions On
LINK A6,#$0000	LINK A6,#$0000
MOVEM.L D4/D5,-(A7)	MOVEM.L D3-D7,-(A7)
MOVE.L $000C(A6),D0	MOVE.W $000A(A6),D3
BEQ.S *+$001E ; 0000002A	
	; temp = b*b + 2*b*c + c*c;
; d = b*b + 2*b*c + c*c;	ASL.W #$1,D3
MOVE.W $000A(A6),D4	MULS.W $0008(A6),D3
ASL.W #$1,D4	MOVE.W $0008(A6),D4
MULS.W $0008(A6),D4	MULS.W D4,D4
MOVE.W $0008(A6),D0	MOVE.W $000A(A6),D5
MULS.W D0,D0	MULS.W D5,D5
MOVE.W $000A(A6),D1	ADD.W D5,D4
MULS.W D1,D1	ADD.W D4,D3
ADD.W D1,D0	MOVE.L $000C(A6),D0
ADD.W D0,D4	BEQ.S *+$0006 ; 0000002C
BRA.S *+$001C ; 00000044	
	; a = temp
	MOVE.W D3,D6
	BRA.S *+$001C ; 00000046
; d = b*b + 2*b*c + c*c;	; temp = b*b + 2*b*c + c*c;
2A: MOVE.W $000A(A6),D5	2c: MOVE.W $000A(A6),D7
ASL.W #$1,D5	ASL.W #$1,D7
MULS.W $0008(A6),D5	MULS.W $0008(A6),D7
MOVE.W $0008(A6),D0	MOVE.W $0008(A6),D0
MULS.W D0,D0	MULS.W D0,D0

Hoist Very Busy Expressions Off			Hoist Very Busy Expressions On		
	MOVE.W	$000A(A6),D1		MOVE.W	$000A(A6),D1
	MULS.W	D1,D1		MULS.W	D1,D1
	ADD.W	D1,D0		ADD.W	D1,D0
	ADD.W	D0,D5		ADD.W	D0,D7
44:	MOVE.W	D4,D0	46:	MOVE.W	D6,D0
	EXT.L	D0		EXT.L	D0
	MOVE.W	D5,D1		MOVE.W	D7,D1
	EXT.L	D1		EXT.L	D1
	JSR	ULMULT		JSR	ULMULT
	MOVEM.L	(A7)+,D4/D5		MOVEM.L	(A7)+,D3-D7
	UNLK	A6		UNLK	A6
	MOVEA.L	(A7)+,A0		MOVEA.L	(A7)+,A0
	ADDQ.W	#$8,A7		ADDQ.W	#$8,A7
	JMP	(A0)		JMP	(A0)

Remove loop invariants. Loop invariants are expressions that do not get changed during the evaluation of a loop. Rather than evaluating the invariant each time through the loop, the optimizer evaluates the invariant once, before the loop. Thus, the optimizer moves invariant expressions out of the loop but does not delete them entirely.

Unlike some other choices, this optimization is different depending on whether you are optimizing for space or for time. Look at how each acts in turn.

Optimize for space. It is reasonably straightforward to remove loop invariants when optimizing for space. The optimizer just moves the invariant expressions before the loop. The form of the code is listed below:

```
loop {
    code using an invariant expression
}
```

This is transformed into the following:

```
temporary = invariant expression;
loop {
    code using temporary
}
```

To make this clearer, look at a specific example:

```
void Loop(register char *s, short i, short j)
{
    char c;

    while ((c = *s++) != '\0')
        func(i*j + c);
}
```

Here, `i*j` gets evaluated every time through the loop, even though it always has the same value. By removing loop invariants, the compile continues as if the following were the code:

```
void LoopConverted(register char *s, short i, short j)
{
    char c;

    short temporary = i*j;
    while ((c = *s++) != '\0')
        func(temporary + c);
}
```

Table 14.7 shows a disassembly of the object code for `Loop` with the Remove loop invariants option on and off. Italics show the important differences.

Table 14.7. Effects of Remove Loop Invariants on Loop with Space Optimization

Remove Loop Invariants Off	Remove Loop Invariants On
`    LINK      A6,#$0000`	`    LINK      A6,#$FFF8`
`    MOVEM.L   D3-D5/A2,-(A7)`	`    MOVE.W    $000A(A6),D0`
`    MOVE.W    $0008(A6),D3`	`    MULS.W    $0008(A6),D0 ; compute i * j`
`    MOVE.W    $000A(A6),D4`	`    MOVE.W    D0,$FFFC(A6)`
`    MOVEA.L   $000C(A6),A2`	`    BRA.S     *+$0014        ; 24`
`14: MOVEA.L   A2,A0`	`12: MOVE.W    $FFFC(A6),D0`
`    ADDQ.W    #$1,A2`	`    MOVE.B    $FFF8(A6),D1`
`    MOVE.B    (A0),D0`	`    EXT.W     D1`
`    MOVE.B    D0,D5`	`    ADD.W     D1,D0`
`    TST.B     D0`	`    MOVE.W    D0,-(A7)`
`    BEQ.S     *+$0012        ; 30`	`    JSR       func(short)`
`    MOVE.W    D4,D1`	`24: MOVEA.L   $000C(A6),A0`
`    MULS.W    D3,D1 ; compute i * j`	`    ADDQ.L    #$1,$000C(A6)`
`    EXT.W     D0`	`    MOVE.B    (A0),D0`
`    ADD.W     D0,D1`	`    MOVE.B    D0,$FFF8(A6)`
`    MOVE.W    D1,-(A7)`	`    TST.B     D0`
`    JSR       func(short)`	`    BNE.S     *-$0022        ; 12`
`    BRA.S     *-$001A        ; 14`	`    UNLK      A6`
`30: MOVEM.L   (A7)+,D3-D5/A2`	`    MOVEA.L   (A7)+,A0`
`    UNLK      A6`	`    ADDQ.W    #$8,A7`
`    MOVEA.L   (A7)+,A0`	`    JMP       (A0)`
`    ADDQ.W    #$8,A7`	
`    JMP       (A0)`	

Surprisingly, there are cases where this optimization can make your code run slower. When the loop body is never executed (the loop condition starts out false) and optimization is off, the compiler does not evaluate the invariant expression. On the other hand, when optimization is on, the invariant is evaluated even when the loop body is never executed. Because of this case, the optimizer acts differently when optimizing for time.

Optimize for time. When you optimize for time, the process is not as straightforward. In this case, the optimizer must evaluate invariant expressions only if the loop body executes one or more times. When the loop body does not execute, the optimizer should not evaluate the invariant expressions. Look at the following code to see how the optimizer satisfies this requirement:

```
loop {
    code using an invariant expression
}
```

This code is transformed into the following:

```
if (loop condition) {
    temporary = invariant expression;
    loop {
        code using temporary
    }
}
```

Look at a specific example:

```
void Loop(register char *s, short i, short j)
{
    char c;

    while ((c = *s++) != '\0')
        func(i*j + c);
}
```

Here, `i*j` is evaluated every time through the loop, even though it always has the same value. Checking the Remove loop invariants option, causes the code to compile as if it looked like the following:

```
void LoopConverted(register char *s, short i, short j)
{
    char c;

    if ((c = *s++) != '\0') {
        short temporary = i*j;

        do {
         func(temporary + c);
        } while ((c = *s++) != '\0');
    }
}
```

With this transformation, the compiler evaluates `i * j` only if the first character of `s` is not `\0`. If the first character is `\0`, the loop body and the evaluation of `i * j` are not executed. Table 14.8 shows a disassembly of the object code for `Loop` with the Remove loop invariants option on and off. Italics show the important differences.

You should note that, even though the optimized code has become larger, the run time is still faster in multiple loop executions. It is just as fast as the original code with a single loop execution.

Create loop induction variables. When you select the Create loop induction variables option, the optimizer searches for particular expressions. These are expressions within a loop whose values arithmetically progress as the loop iterates. The optimizer uses addition to evaluate them through each iteration of the loop.

First look at a simple and then a more complex example of using loop induction variables. You normally find these arithmetic progressions when an expression references a looping variable and derives from addition or multiplication. A simple example is the following:

```
for (i = 0; i < 10; i++)
{
    j = i * 3 + 5;
    ...
}
```

This converts to the following:

```
for (i = 0, j = 5; i < 10; i++, j += 3)
{
    ...
}
```

Table 14.8. Effects of Remove Loop Invariants on Loop with Time Optimization

Remove Loop Invariants Off	Remove Loop Invariants On
LINK A6,#$0000	LINK A6,#$FFF8
MOVEM.L D3-D5/A2,-(A7)	MOVEA.L $000C(A6),A0
MOVE.W $0008(A6),D3	ADDQ.L #$1,$000C(A6)
MOVE.W $000A(A6),D4	MOVE.B (A0),D0
MOVEA.L $000C(A6),A2	MOVE.B D0,$FFF8(A6)
14: MOVEA.L A2,A0	TST.B D0 ; if ((c = *s++) != '\0) {
ADDQ.W #$1,A2	BEQ.S *+$0032 ; 46
MOVE.B (A0),D0	MOVE.W $000A(A6),D0
MOVE.B D0,D5	MULS.W $0008(A6),D0 ; compute i * j
TST.B D0	MOVE.W D0,$FFFC(A6)
BEQ.S *+$0012 ; 30	22: MOVE.W $FFFC(A6),D0
MOVE.W D4,D1	MOVE.B $FFF8(A6),D1
MULS.W D3,D1 ; compute i * j	EXT.W D1
EXT.W D0	ADD.W D1,D0
ADD.W D0,D1	MOVE.W D0,-(A7)
MOVE.W D1,-(A7)	JSR func(short)
JSR func(short)	MOVEA.L $000C(A6),A0
BRA.S *-$001A ; 14	
30: MOVEM.L (A7)+,D3-D5/A2	ADDQ.L #$1,$000C(A6)
UNLK A6	MOVE.B (A0),D0
MOVEA.L (A7)+,A0	MOVE.B D0,$FFF8(A6)
ADDQ.W #$8,A7	TST.B D0 ; } while (_);
JMP (A0)	BNE.S *-$0022 ; 22
	46: UNLK A6
	MOVEA.L (A7)+,A0
	ADDQ.W #$8,A7
	JMP (A0)

In each case, j takes on these values: 5, 8, 11, 14, 17, 20, 23, 26, 29, and 32. In the unoptimized case, each iteration through the loop requires two operations to compute j, one addition and one multiplication. In the optimized case, each iteration requires only one addition to compute j.

The optimizer replaces a loop variable with a loop induction variable if all the following are true:

- The loop body does not use the value of the looping variable.
- The loop variable value is not used after the loop.
- Dead variable elimination is on.

For instance, if the loop is as follows:

```
for (i = 0; i < 10; i++)
{
    j = i * 3 + 5;
    Func(j);
}
```

It is converted to the following:

```
for (j = 5; j < 35; j += 3)
{
    Func(j);
}
```

Consider a more complex example of loop optimization. There is a whole class of expressions whose arithmetic progress is not obvious. This optimization is especially helpful in these cases. For instance, array access within a loop can often form an arithmetic progression.

Look at an example with arrays:

```
void ZeroArray(long *longArray) {
    for (int i = 0; i < 10; i++)
        longArray[i] = 0;
}
```

The expression `longArray[i]` forms an arithmetic progression as the loop iterates. Each time through the loop, the calculated address increases by four bytes (the size of a `long`). With loop induction on, the loop can be transformed into the following:

```
void ZeroArray(long *longArray) {
    for (int i = 0, long *tmp = &longArray[0]; i < 10; i++,
tmp++)
        *tmp = 0;
}
```

In the revised version, rather than incrementing `i` by one each time through the loop, the compiler increments `temp` by four (because ++ increments pointers by the size of the object to which they point).

Table 14.9 shows a disassembly of the object code for `ZeroArray` with Create loop induction variables on and off. Italics show the loop.

The optimized version of `ZeroArray` is slightly longer because the optimization is for time, not space. However, the inner loop is only seven instructions long, rather than the nine of the unoptimized case. Thus, the total running time of the optimized version is still faster.

Constant propagation. Constant propagation substitutes variables that have constant values with the constant values themselves. This replacement transfers these calculations from run time to compile time.

Here is an example:

```
int BytesNeeded()
{
    int numElements;
    int elementSize = sizeof(long); // equals 4

    if (elementSize > 4)
        numElements = 10;
    else
        numElements = 20;
    return  numElements * elementSize;
}
```

In `BytesNeeded`, `elementSize` has a constant value (4 with this compiler). Look at how constant propagation transforms the code:

```
int BytesNeededConverted1()
{
    int numElements;
    int elementSize = sizeof(long); // equals 4
```

```
    if (4 > 4)
        numElements = 10;
    else
        numElements = 20;
    return  numElements * 4;
}
```

Table 14.9. Effects of Create Loop Induction Variables on ZeroArray

Create Loop Induction Variables Off			Create Loop Induction Variables On		
	LINK	A6,#$FFFC		LINK	A6,#$FFF4
	MOVEQ	#$00,D0		MOVEQ	#$00,D0
	MOVE.L	D0,$FFFC(A6)		MOVE.L	D0,$FFF4(A6)
0A:	*MOVEQ*	*#$00,D0*		MOVE.L	$0008(A6),$FFF8(A6)
	MOVE.L	*$FFFC(A6),D1*		MOVEA.L	$0008(A6),A0
	ASL.L	*#$2,D1*		MOVEQ	#$28,D0
	ADD.L	*$0008(A6),D1*		ADDA.L	D0,A0
	MOVEA.L	*D1,A0*		MOVE.L	A0,$FFFC(A6)
	MOVE.L	*D0,(A0)*	*1C:*	*MOVEQ*	*#$00,D0*
	ADDQ.L	*#$1,$FFFC(A6)*		*MOVEA.L*	*$FFF8(A6),A0*
	CMPI.L	*#$0000000A,$FFFC(A6)*		*MOVE.L*	*D0,(A0)*
	BCS.S	**-$001C ; 0A*		*ADDQ.L*	*#$4,$FFF8(A6)*
	UNLK	A6		*MOVE.L*	*$FFF8(A6),D0*
	MOVEA.L	(A7)+,A0		*CMP.L*	*$FFFC(A6),D0*
	ADDQ.W	#$4,A7		*BLT.S*	**-$0014 ; 1C*
	JMP	(A0)		UNLK	A6
				MOVEA.L	(A7)+,A0
				ADDQ.W	#$4,A7
				JMP	(A0)

If you also have checked the Loop until can't optimize (covered shortly) option, the optimizer continues using constant propagation to make the following changes to this code. The optimizer calculates that `4 > 4` is false, resulting in the following:

```
int BytesNeededConverted2()
{
    int numElements;
    int elementSize = sizeof(long); // equals 4

    numElements = 20;
    return  numElements * 4;
}
```

Now `numElements` has a constant value of 20 after the assignment. Further optimization yields the following:

```
int BytesNeededConverted3()
{
    int numElements;
    int elementSize = sizeof(long); // equals 4

    numElements = 20;
    return  20 * 4;
}
```

Finally, you get this:

```
int BytesNeededConverted4()
{
    return 80;
}
```

Table 14.10 shows some disassembled code with the Constant propagation option turned on and off for the `ZeroArray` function.

Table 14.10. Effects of Constant Propagation on BytesNeeded

Constant Propagation Off	Constant Propagation On
LINK A6,#$0000	LINK A6,#$0000
MOVEM.L D3/D4,-(A7)	MOVEQ #$50,D0
MOVEQ #$04,D4	UNLK A6
MOVEQ #$04,D0	RTS
CMP.L D0,D4	
BLE.S *+$0006 ; 14	
MOVEQ #$0A,D3	
BRA.S *+$0004 ; 16	
14: MOVEQ #$14,D3	
16: MOVE.L D3,D0	
MOVE.L D4,D1	
JSR ULMULT	
MOVEM.L (A7)+,D3/D4	
UNLK A6	
RTS	

When you check the Constant propagation option, the optimizer calculates when variables hold constant values. You could have provided this same information more directly by using the `const` keyword. If you are feeling energetic, you can rewrite `BytesNeeded` to use `const` as follows:

```
int BytesNeeded()
{
    int numElements;
    const int elementSize = sizeof(long); // equals 4

    if (elementSize > 4)
        numElements = 10;
    else
        numElements = 20;
    return  numElements * elementSize;
}
```

NOTE

> `numElements` is not declared `const` because its value depends on the `if` statement. You could use code like the following:
>
> ```
> const int numElements = (elementSize > 4) ? 10 : 20;
> ```
>
> This could easily become ridiculous, however.

When you use `const` in your coding, you liberate the compiler from the optimizer; you, not the optimizer, determine which variables hold constant values. For instance, when `elementSize` is declared `const`, with copy propagation off, the code compiles as if it were written as follows:

```
int BytesNeeded()
{
    int numElements;

     numElements = 10;
     return  numElements * 4;
}
```

The resulting disassembled code, though not optimal, is better than it would be without the `const` keyword:

```
LINK      A6,#$0000
MOVE.L    D3,-(A7)
MOVEQ     #$14,D3
MOVE.L    D3,D0
ASL.L     #$2,D0
MOVE.L    $FFFC(A6),D3
UNLK      A6
RTS
```

Normally, you should keep this option on. But do not use it as a substitute for declaring constant variables `const`.

Copy propagation. The Copy propagation option is supposed to track when one variable is assigned to another. While they have the same value, the compiler uses the first variable for both. Suppose you have the following code:

```
int TestCopyPropogation(int incoming)
{
    int i = incoming;
    int j = i;
    int r = r + 1;
    return j;
}
```

When it is compiled, it is written as if it were the following:

```
int TestCopyPropogation(int incoming)
{
    int i = incoming;
    int j = i;
    int r = r + 1;
    return i;
}
```

NOTE

As this book went to press, the Copy propagation option did not produce the expected code. As a matter of fact, the option did not seem to do anything.

Loop until can't optimize. When you need the compiler to optimize your code with the unfailing loyalty of a collie dog, you should check the Loop until can't optimize option. If you do, the optimizer repetitively runs through your code implementing all possible optimizations, including those that depend on preceding ones. The optimizer stops when improvements are no longer possible. If you do not check this, the compiler only runs through the whole suite of optimizations once. As you might expect, using this option takes longer but produces better code. Look at the following sample:

```
void ZeroArray(long *longArray) {
    for (int i = 0; i < 10; i++)
        longArray[i] = 0;
}
```

Table 14.11 shows you the effect of using the Loop until can't optimize option on this function.

Table 14.11. Effects of Loop Until Can't Optimize on ZeroArray

Loop Until Can't Optimize Off	Loop Until Can't Optimize On
`LINK A6,#$0000`	`LINK A6,#$0000`
`MOVEM.L A2/A3,-(A7)`	`MOVEM.L A2/A3,-(A7)`
`MOVEQ #$00,D0`	`MOVEA.L $0008(A6),A2`
`MOVE.L D0,D1`	`MOVEA.L $0008(A6),A3`
`MULU.W #$0004,D0`	`MOVEQ #$28,D0`
`SWAP D1`	`ADDA.L D0,A3`
`MULU.W #$0004,D1`	`14: MOVEQ #$00,D0`
`SWAP D1`	`MOVE.L D0,(A2)`
`CLR.W D1`	`ADDQ.W #$4,A2`
`ADD.L D1,D0`	`CMPA.L A3,A2`
`ADD.L $0008(A6),D0`	`BLT.S *-$0008 ; 14`
`MOVEA.L D0,A2`	`MOVEM.L (A7)+,A2/A3`
`MOVEA.L $0008(A6),A3`	`UNLK A6`
`MOVEQ #$28,D0`	`MOVEA.L (A7)+,A0`
`ADDA.L D0,A3`	`ADDQ.W #$4,A7`
`2A: MOVEQ #$00,D0`	`JMP (A0)`
`MOVE.L D0,(A2)`	
`ADDQ.W #$4,A2`	
`CMPA.L A3,A2`	
`BLT.S *-$0008 ; 2A`	
`MOVEM.L (A7)+,A2/A3`	
`UNLK A6`	
`MOVEA.L (A7)+,A0`	
`ADDQ.W #$4,A7`	
`JMP (A0)`	

By turning the flag on, the optimizer devises more improvements, giving you smaller and faster code.

The Debugging Panel

The penultimate C++ options panel is the Debugging panel. It is shown in figure 14.6.

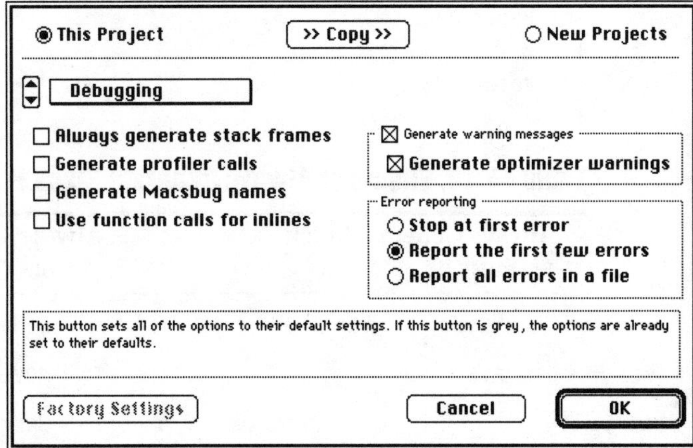

Figure 14.6. The C++ Options Debugging panel.

There are a number of different debugging options you can specify here:

- Generating stack frames.
- Generating profiler calls.
- Generating MacsBug names.
- Using functions calls for inline functions.
- Generating optimizer warnings.
- Having the compiler stop at the first error it finds.
- Having the compiler only report the first few errors it finds.
- Dumping all the errors the compiler finds into a special errors window.

Each of these options is presented in turn.

Always generate stack frames. Functions that have variables on the stack have stack space reserved using the MC68000 instruction LINK (the stack space is returned using UNLK). Functions that do not need stack space do not need a LINK/UNLK pair. Selecting the Always generate stack frames option causes the compiler to create a LINK/UNLK pair for all functions, which can make low-level debugging easier.

Table 14.12 shows the disassembly of the following code with and without this option:

```
int Return1()
{
    return 1;
}
```

Table 14.12. Effects of Always Generate Stack Frames on Return1

Always Generate Stack Frames Off		Always Generate Stack Frames On	
MOVEQ	#$01,D0	LINK	A6,#$0000
RTS		MOVEQ	#$01,D0
		UNLK	A6
		RTS	

Generate profiler calls. If you turn this option on, each function starts with a call to `_profile_`. The name of the function also is passed as an argument. Suppose you have the following code:

```
void Foo()
{
    int i = 3;
}
```

With this option on, it is compiled as if it were written as follows:

```
void Foo()
{
    _profile_("\pFoo");
    int i = 3;
}
```

This enables you to generate timing information for your code that you can then use with the Symantec C++ profile library (see the Symantec C++ Reference Manual for more information on the profile library).

Generate MacsBug names. There is a Macintosh convention used by low-level debuggers of adding the name of the function to the end of its compiled code. Traditionally, these names are called MacsBug names because they are used by the Apple low-level debugger, MacsBug. Other debuggers, like TMON, also use these function names.

Normally, source-level debuggers, like the THINK Debugger, do not need these function names because they have complete information about the relationship between compiled code and the corresponding source code. If you only use the THINK Debugger, you obviously do not need to use this option. If, however, you debug using a low-level debugger you want it on.

Table 14.13 shows the disassemblies for the following function with and without MacsBug names:

```
int MyFunction()
{
    return 32 * 7;
}
```

Table 14.13. Effects of Generate MacsBug Names on MyFunction

Generate MacsBug Names Off		Generate MacsBug Names On	
LINK	A6,#$0000	LINK	A6,#$0000
MOVE.L	#$000000E0,D0	MOVE.L	#$000000E0,D0
UNLK	A6	UNLK	A6
RTS		RTS	
		DC.B	$80+$0E, 'MyFunction__Fv', $00
		DC.W	0

NOTE

The compiler has mangled the function name from the original `MyFunction` to `MyFunction_Fv`. This is the result of C++ name mangling.

Use function calls for inlines. As you learned in Chapter 8, in C++ the `inline` keyword is a compiler request that replaces the call to a function with its actual code. When you check the Use function calls for inlines option, the compiler ignores the `inline` keyword; the function call remains a function call. This is enormously useful when you need to debug an inline function—a task that can be very difficult (e.g., how do you set a breakpoint in an inline function?). By making an inline function into a normal function, you can use the standard debugging tools.

Table 14.14 shows the disassembles of the following code with this option off and on:

```
inline short Square(short i)
{
    return i * i;
}

short FourthPower(short i)
{
    return Square(i) * Square(i);
}
```

As you would expect, when this option is off the `Square` function no longer exists in the disassembled code as a separate function. Figures 14.7 and 14.8 show the `Square` function in the THINK Debugger with the option both off and on. Note in figure 14.8 that, when the option is off, you cannot set breakpoints in `Square`. With the option on, you can.

Table 14.14. Effects of Use Function Calls for Inlines on Square

Function Calls for Inlines Off		Function Calls for Inlines On	
FourthPower:		FourthPower:	
LINK	A6,#$0000	LINK	A6,#$0000
MOVE.W	$0008(A6),D0	MOVE.L	A2,-(A7)
MULS.W	D0,D0	MOVE.W	$0008(A6),-(A7)
MULS.W	$0008(A6),D0	JSR	Square(short)
MULS.W	$0008(A6),D0	MOVEA.L	D0,A2
UNLK	A6	MOVE.W	$0008(A6),-(A7)
MOVEA.L	(A7)+,A0	JSR	Square(short)
ADDQ.W	#$2,A7	MOVE.W	D0,D1
JMP	(A0)	MOVE.L	A2,D0
		MULS.W	D1,D0
		MOVEA.L	$FFFC(A6),A2
		UNLK	A6
		MOVEA.L	(A7)+,A0
		ADDQ.W	#$2,A7
		JMP	(A0)
		Square(short):	
		LINK	A6,#$0000
		MOVE.W	$0008(A6),D0
		MULS.W	D0,D0
		UNLK	A6
		MOVEA.L	(A7)+,A0
		ADDQ.W	#$2,A7
		JMP	(A0)

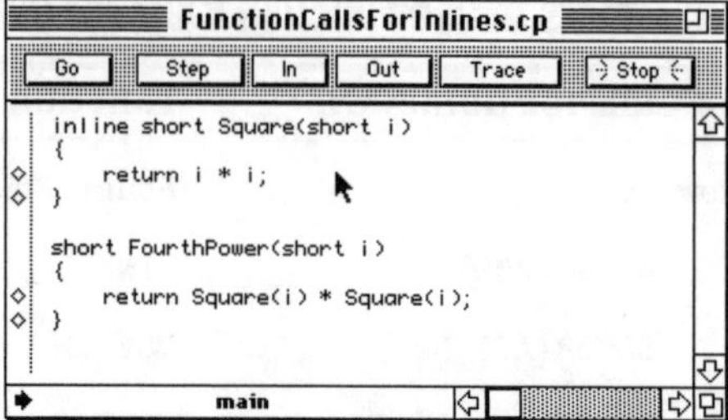

Figure 14.7. The Square function with the Use function calls for inlines option on.

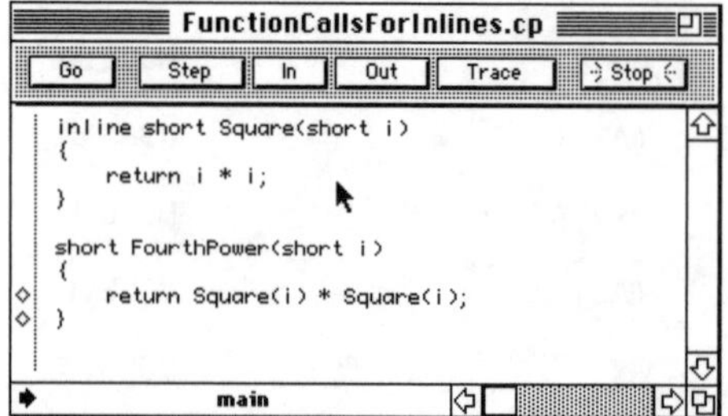

Figure 14.8. The Square function with the Use function calls for inlines option off.

Generate warning messages. Symantec C++ generates warnings for your code if you check the Generate warning messages option. This is one option you always should keep on. Compiling without warning messages makes about as much sense as studiously ignoring the traffic signs while driving on an unfamiliar windy road on a dark rainy night. If you compile without warning messages, you are ignoring potential bugs that can haunt you later.

So what do you do if you get warnings? Try to follow these rules:

- When you receive a warning, examine the code that generated it.
- If the warning reflects an error in your code, fix the code.
- If the warning is spurious, rewrite your code so that the warning is no longer generated.

In this last case, you are modifying your code so that you do not end up with files like `foo.cp` that generates 42 warnings. While files that generate spurious warnings are not bad per se, you may find it harder to notice when a warning (the 43rd one) appears that is not spurious. Think of these warnings as chaff that must be sifted through to obtain the non-spurious wheat.

Look at examples of each warning message that Symantec C++ generates. Where relevant, you see the code that generates the warning after each error message. Luckily, there are only 13 warning messages in all. Here they are.

1. The `function 'Func' is too complicated to inline` warning message.

2. The `possible unintended assignment` warning message. You can generate this warning with code like the following:

   ```
   if (a = b)
   {
       ...
   }
   ```

3. The `can't nest comments` warning message. You can do this with the following infamous line:

   ```
   /* comment /* nested comment */ */
   ```

4. The `variable '%s' used before set` warning message. This is a simple error—one you no doubt get used to seeing whenever your code looks like the following:

   ```
   void Bar()
   {
       int i;
       int j;

       j = i * 3;
   }
   ```

5. The `no tag name for struct or enum` warning message.

6. The `value of expression is not used` warning message. No doubt you usually intend an assignment here. In either case, any time you write something like the following code you get this warning:

   ```
   i == 3;
   ```

7. The `possible extraneous ';'` warning message.

8. The `very large automatic` warning message. One small typo—too many zeroes—can prove disastrous:

```
void WillOverflowStack()
{
    char bigArray[32000];

}
```

(Note that this probably will cause stack overflow.)

9. The `use delete[] rather than delete[expr], expr ignored` warning message. In the old days of C++, you used to delete arrays with the following syntax:

```
p = new SomeType[numArrayElements]
...
delete [numArrayElements] p;
```

Nowadays, you should use this:

```
p = new SomeType[numArrayElements]
...
delete [] p;
```

Thus, while the compiler accepts the older form, it fusses at you each time.

10. The `non-const reference initialized to temporary` warning message. The compiler blurts out this warning when it generates a temporary variable and the reference is initialized to the temporary. Because the reference is not `const`, you lose any changes made to the reference (only the temporary changed) and you get an error in ANSI C++. Here is an example of code that shows this:

```
void SetTo5(float &f)
{
    f = 5;
}

void Bar()
{
    int i = 3;
    SetTo5(i);
    // i is still 3
}
```

11. The `divide by 0` warning message. Compilers hate it when you attempt to divide by zero. The Symantec C++ compiler assumes you are making a mistake and badgers you any time you write the following type of code:

```
const int kTotal = 50;
const int kNumElements = 0;
const float kAveragePerElement = kTotal / kNumElements;
```

12. The `using operator++() (or —) instead of missing operator++(int)` warning message. This results in newer versions of C++ that enable separate overloading of prefix ++ (or —) and postfix ++ (or —) operators. Newer versions have operators that take an argument. This warning reminds you of old code in which both the prefix and postfix ++ (or —) called one overloaded routine. Here is an example:

```
class TBar {
public:
    TBar();

    operator++();
...
};
...
TBar aBar;

aBar++;
```

13. The `assignment to 'this' is obsolete, use X::operator new/delete` warning message. The following code generates this message:

```
class TMyClass {
public:
    TMyClass() { if (this == 0) this =
      NewPtr(sizeof(TMyClass));}
}
```

NOTE

> You are not likely to come across the last two warnings until you reach a more advanced level of C++ programming. In fact, the features that generate these warnings are not covered in this book. For completeness sake, however, you should at least see the warnings.

Generate optimizer warnings. There are additional warnings that the compiler can find if the optimizer is on. For instance, some of the information the optimizer discovers about the lifetimes of variables is useful in finding potential errors (e.g., you use a variable before you set it). To use the Generate optimizer warnings option, you must turn the optimizer on and check the Dead variable elimination option as well.

Error Reporting. THINK C only reports the first error that it finds. Nicely enough, Symantec C++ can report multiple errors. You can have errors reported three different ways:

- The Stop at first error button only reports the first error for a given file.
- The Report the first few errors button reports the first six errors in a given file.
- The Report all errors in a file button reports all the errors in a file (unless it finds an unrecoverable error).

The default is to report the first few errors. This is the best setting because one error can often cause cascading error messages. Although the compiler attempts to generate only one message for an error, you could have many, many error messages due to one actual error. When the compiler reports only the first few errors, you know that there is a limit on the number of generated messages you have to see—it's also easier on your ego.

Prefix Panel

The final C++ option panel is the Prefix panel. It is shown in figure 14.9. In this panel, you set the contents of the code you want prepended to each source file before compilation. This is where you normally define compile-time variables or project-wide include files.

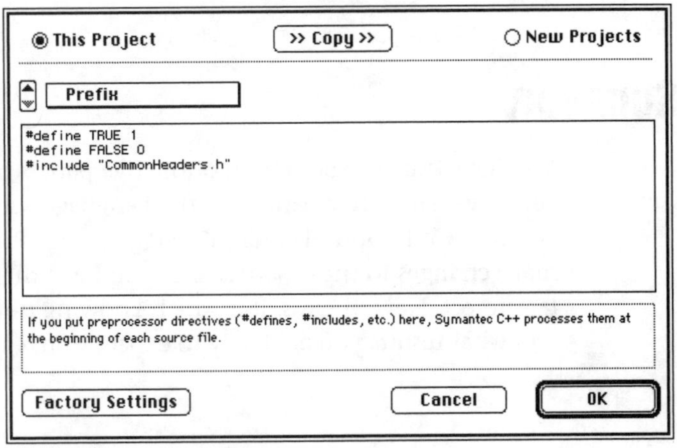

Figure 14.9. The Prefix panel.

If you look in figure 14.9 in the preprocessor window, you see directives that cause every file to have `TRUE` and `FALSE` defined and `CommonHeaders.h` included at the beginning.

Customarily, you use this panel to toggle particular compile-time flags depending on which compile you are doing. For example, you may define a compile-time flag `qDebug` that is true if you want debugging code included in your program and false if you do not. You then bracket debugging code with the following:

```
#if qDebug
    DebugStr("\pReached point A1 in the program");
#endif
```

NOTE

> If you make any changes to the contents of this panel, the compiler recompiles all your files the next time you build. Because this panel affects what the compiler includes at the beginning of each file, this always must occur.

Summary

You have learned about each of the five panels that affect your C++ compiles. These five panels are the Language Settings, Compiler Settings, Code Optimization, Debugging, and Prefix panels. You rarely make changes to these panels after you have them set up for a particular project. Nevertheless, it is worth knowing how each option works and what results you are likely to expect from each setting.

PART 3

The THINK Class Library and Other Frameworks

This is by far the most important practical section in the book. Here you use the C++ you have learned. Before doing so, however, you learn about present application frameworks and what is planned for the future in Chapter 15. Chapters 16-21 contain C++ programs that use the TCL to create a variety of object-oriented applications.

How are you going to learn to use the TCL? TCL is not presented in an abstract fashion, but in the context of coding. This can be both good and bad. It is bad because you are learning only about the parts of the TCL used in the creation of these programs. But, it is good because you see the how and when of using a framework.

15
Using a Framework

This chapter provides you with a strong incentive to use frameworks in your programming. You first see the benefits a framework can provide and then you learn about what is available.

There is more than one application framework in the Macintosh arena. Two of the most important Macintosh application frameworks, MacApp and the THINK Class Library (TCL), were released in 1985 and 1989, respectively; others have arrived since. Some of the most intriguing application frameworks are on the horizon.

What Are Frameworks?

What is a framework? The answer is simple: A framework is a collection of objects that collaborate to carry out a task.

If you call to mind a framework, you probably imagine the most common example—an *application framework*. This, of course, is a framework that includes a collection of classes that simplifies the job of creating an application. On the Macintosh programming side, application frameworks arrived late, not appearing until 1985.

The tardiness of applications frameworks for the Macintosh meant that pioneer programmers were forced to write their applications from scratch—a rather daunting task. In fact, many programmers when they came to Macintosh were amazed by how much code they had to write to create a Macintosh application. They muttered about having to call `DragWindow` to deal with user clicks in the title bar of a window. There was justification to such discontent. If a user clicked on one radio button, an application programmer had to write code to turn off the other radio buttons—a framework should have done that. Born out of this situation were application frameworks such as MacApp and the THINK Class Library.

The late appearance of Macintosh application frameworks is made even more ironic when you reflect upon one of the fundamental tenets of the Macintosh experience—all applications should look and work the same way. When you realize that much of this uniform experience is the result of enormous amounts of duplicated code present in all Macintosh applications, you should be surprised that the applications manage the uniformity that they do.

Capturing this common code in an application framework that sits above the Macintosh operating system is an obvious solution. If the user clicks in the title bar of a window, the framework calls `DragWindow`. If a user clicks on a radio button, the framework turns off all the others.

All application code must jump through the hoops of Macintosh operating system requirements. By using a framework, you rely on the framework programmer who is a hoop-jumper by nature and, thus, are freed of such tedious coding.

There is not much of a downside to letting the framework handle such tasks. If you want control, you always can assert it. A framework is object-oriented, so any programmer who wants to do something different in response to the user clicking on the title bar of a window just overrides the member function that deals with that activity.

Why Use Frameworks?

There are a number of general rules to remember when you think about whether or not to use frameworks:

- Frameworks enable you to finish your program faster. The time spent learning to use a framework is much less than it takes to write the code it handles for you. As a result, you can start working on the unique aspects of your application much sooner.
- Frameworks reduce errors in your programs. Frameworks are tested, not only by their vendor, but by all the programmers who use them. You benefit from that. In addition, frameworks are written by subject experts—programmers who know how to design classes and know their field.
- Framework enhancements benefit your program. When a framework is enhanced, your application may be able to take advantage of this simply by recompiling.
- Frameworks enable you to concentrate on your area of expertise. If you are a seismologist writing MacEarthquake, you can concentrate on designing and writing your classes (`TSanAndreasFault`, `TRichterScale`, etc.). The framework ensures that your program works on the Macintosh; you ensure that everybody is ready for the Big One.
- Using frameworks increases portability. By structuring your code correctly, you easily can port your application. You design your user interface code to be separate from the actual content of your application. Your application ends up being divided into three parts (see fig. 15.1).

  Structuring your application this way gives your content classes portability. They can be moved from one framework to another and even from one operating system to another. Your content classes can go anywhere there is a C++ compiler.

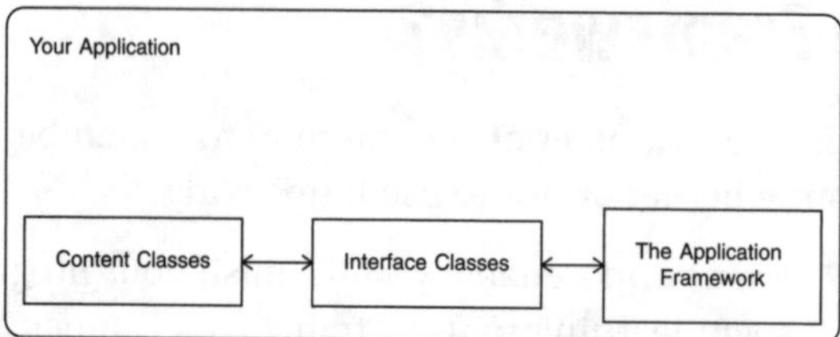

Figure 15.1. The structure of your application.

Types of Frameworks

Frameworks come in a variety of useful flavors. Besides the basic vanilla application framework, you also can create any of the following frameworks on the Macintosh:

- desk accessory frameworks
- control panel frameworks
- start-up document (INIT) frameworks
- printer driver frameworks
- device driver frameworks

A good framework for each of these items provides all the code required to produce a complete shell, but without any useful content. For example, the control panel framework could be structured to respond to mouse clicks, menu items, opening, and closing. You, the control panel programmer, need to override a handful of member functions with names like `HandleOpen`, `HandleClose`, `HandleMouseClick`, `HandleKeystroke`, etc.

The Role of Frameworks

If you approach a framework with the mind-set of a procedural programmer, you run into a brick wall. In Part 2 of this book, you learned the need to shift from a procedural point of view to an object oriented one when writing C++ code. Likewise, there is a difference between using a procedural library and a framework.

When you use a procedural library, *you* call the functions as you see fit; you are master of the universe. As an object-oriented programmer using a framework, however, you are not in charge—the framework is. You are the specialist the framework calls in when it needs your (overridden) member functions to do the job right. For example, in an application framework, you override the member function for drawing the contents of a window. The framework, in turn, calls that function whenever the window needs to be redrawn.

Choices for Application Frameworks

MacApp is by far the most robust application framework for Macintosh, although you also can create a commercial quality application with the TCL. The other application frameworks discussed here have more specialized uses.

The THINK Class Library

The THINK Class Library (TCL) is a framework from Symantec for creating Macintosh applications. There are two versions of it—one written in a subset of C++ and the other in Object Pascal. TCL ships with THINK Pascal, THINK C, and Symantec C++.

The TCL uses only a subset of C++ because it works with the THINK C+ Objects extension to C, a minimal subset of C++ that supports object-oriented programming. The TCL is constrained further by its Object Pascal version, which lacks many features that C++ (and THINK C+ Objects) supports. As a result, the TCL does not use the following C++ features:

- overloaded operators
- constructors
- destructors
- class-specific allocators and deallocators
- multiple inheritance
- nondynamic objects (objects that are not allocated with `new`)

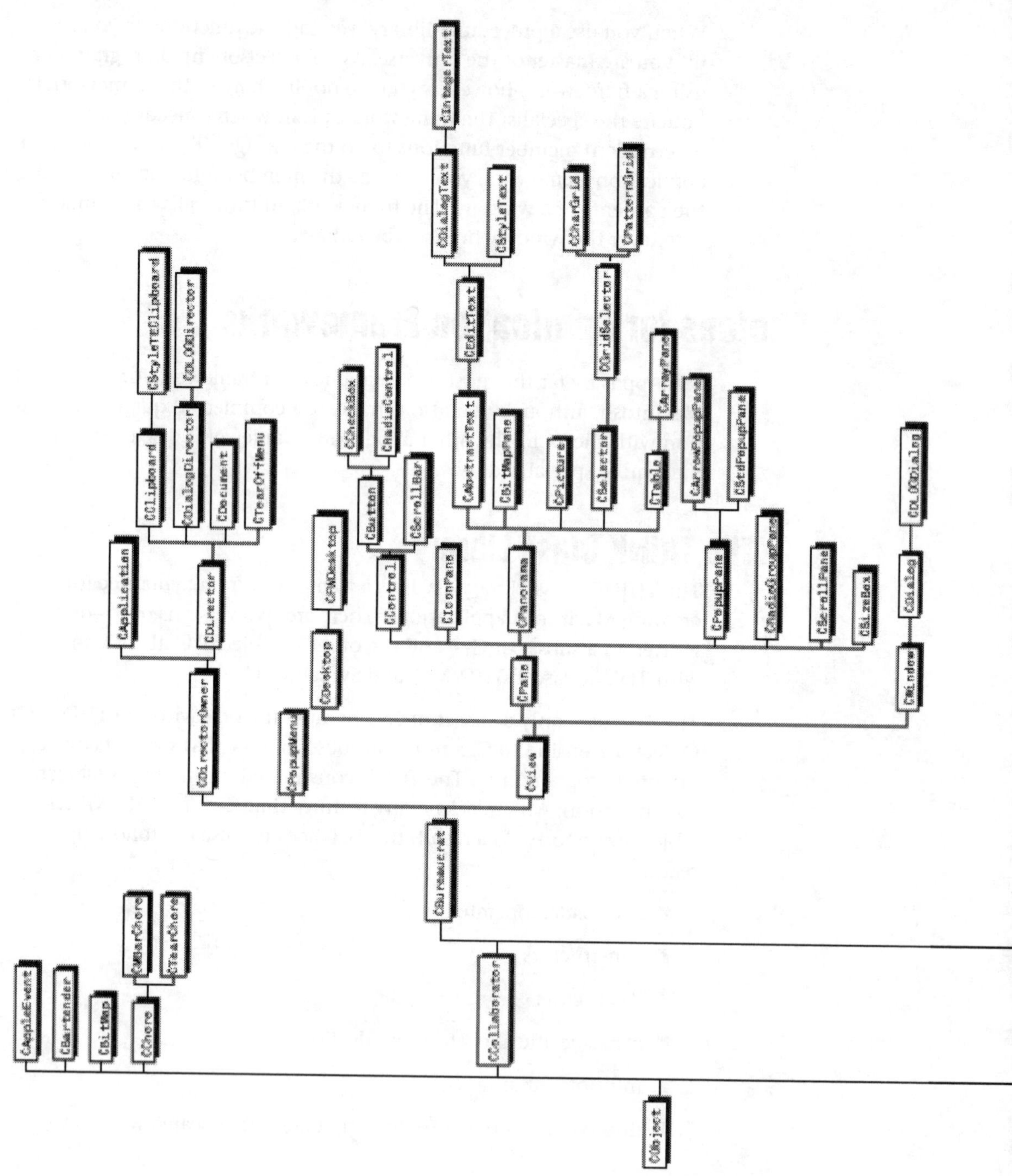

CObject
CAppleEvent
CBartender
CBitMap
CChore
CMBarChore
CTearChore
CCollaborator
CBureaucrat
CDirectorOwner
CApplication
CDirector
CClipboard
CDialogDirector
CDocument
CTearOffMenu
CStyleTEClipboard
CDLOGDirector
CPopupMenu
CView
CDesktop
CFWDesktop
CPane
CWindow
CControl
CIconPane
CPanorama
CPopupPane
CRadioGroupPane
CScrollPane
CSizeBox
CDialog
CDLOGDialog
CButton
CScrollBar
CCheckBox
CRadioControl
CAbstractText
CBitMapPane
CPicture
CSelector
CTable
CArrowPopupPane
CStdPopupPane
CArrayPane
CGridSelector
CCharGrid
CPatternGrid
CEditText
CDialogText
CStyleText
CIntegerText

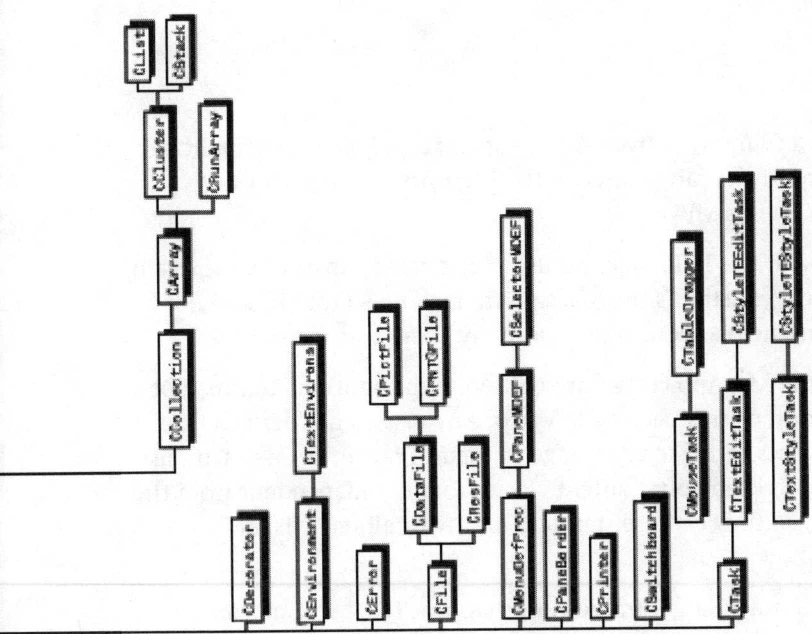

Figure 15.2. The TCL class hierarchy.

This situation is not as grim as its sounds to C++ enthusiasts. Only the TCL-derived classes in your application need to suffer these constraints. Any classes not derived from TCL can take advantage of the full power of C++. This should provide you with even further incentive to keep your content classes totally independent from the interface portion of your code—a domain more germane to the framework.

Class diagrams can help you conceptualize the scope of a framework's classes. With this in mind, look at the diagram of the TCL's class hierarchy shown in figure 15.2.

The goal of the TCL framework writers was to provide an application framework that was both easy to learn and could serve as a basis for commercial quality applications. Imagine that using the TCL is like driving a Chevrolet. It is not elegant, but it is the car you learned to drive and it dependably gets you where you need to go.

The applications in Chapters 16-21 are all written using the TCL. Appendix C contains a small reference manual for the TCL classes used in those chapters.

MacApp

MacApp is a framework from Apple for creating Macintosh applications. Currently, it can be used with either Apple MPW C++ or Symantec C++ for MPW.

As is true with the TCL, MacApp uses a restricted subset of C++. Again, Object Pascal constrains the MacApp framework so that it does not enable constructors, destructors, or many other features of C++.

Although the MacApp classes are written with these constraints, not all application classes need be affected. Any classes not derived from MacApp classes can take advantage of the full power of C++. This also is incentive to keep your content classes totally independent from the framework, so they can use standard C++ with all its bells and whistles.

MacApp is a much larger framework than the TCL. And, as you might expect, the class diagram is correspondingly more complex. Figure 15.3 shows what the MacApp class hierarchy looks like.

The creators of MacApp wanted an application framework that could be used to create bullet-proof, industrial-strength applications. As a result, using MacApp is like driving a tank. It is slow and heavy, but bullet-proof and guaranteed to get you where you want to go (by whatever means necessary).

QuickApp

QuickApp, a product from Emergent Behavior, is another Macintosh application framework. It has quite a different goal from the TCL or MacApp, however. It does not attempt to support commercial quality or commercial size applications. Instead, it focuses on rapid development and prototyping tasks. It is especially well suited for prototypes or applications that have a limited life span or audience. QuickApp compiles with Apple MPW C++, Symantec C++, and Symantec C++ for MPW.

The C++ limitations present in the TCL and MacApp disappear with QuickApp, which utilizes the full power of C++, including the following:

- constructors
- destructors
- multiple inheritance
- copy constructors
- stack-based objects

Figure 15.4 shows you the class hierarchy for QuickApp. As you can imagine, the small size makes it not only easy to learn, but extremely quick to compile.

Using QuickApp is like driving a British roadster. It is small, fast, and provides a great driving experience. It may lack some of the amenities that, while not strictly necessary, do make life easier. It also is not the best choice for developing large programs.

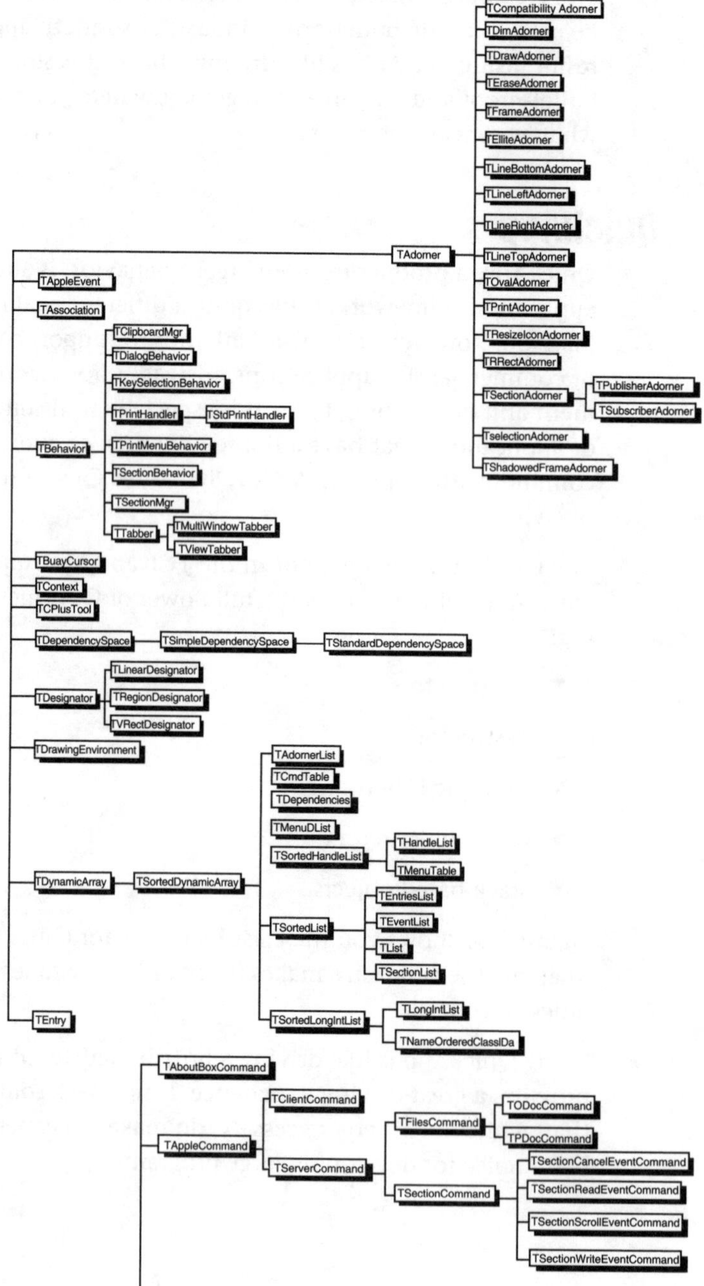

Figure 15.3. The MacApp class hierarchy.

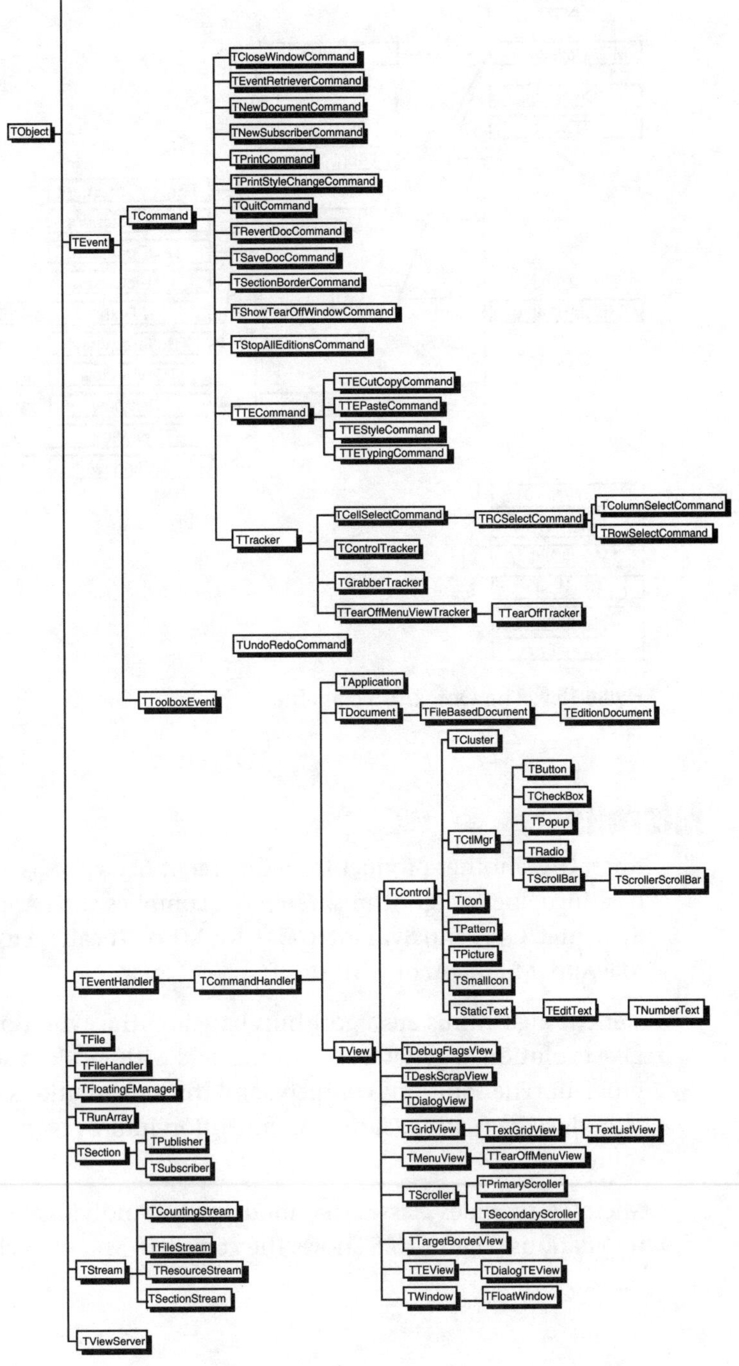
TObject
TEvent
TCommand
TCloseWindowCommand
TEventRetrieverCommand
TNewDocumentCommand
TNewSubscriberCommand
TPrintCommand
TPrintStyleChangeCommand
TQuitCommand
TRevertDocCommand
TSaveDocCommand
TSectionBorderCommand
TShowTearOffWindowCommand
TStopAllEditionsCommand
TTECommand
TTECutCopyCommand
TTEPasteCommand
TTEStyleCommand
TTETypingCommand
TTracker
TCellSelectCommand
TRCSelectCommand
TColumnSelectCommand
TRowSelectCommand
TControlTracker
TGrabberTracker
TTearOffMenuViewTracker
TTearOffTracker
TUndoRedoCommand
TToolboxEvent
TEventHandler
TCommandHandler
TApplication
TDocument
TFileBasedDocument
TEditionDocument
TView
TControl
TCluster
TCtlMgr
TButton
TCheckBox
TPopup
TRadio
TScrollBar
TScrollerScrollBar
TIcon
TPattern
TPicture
TSmallIcon
TStaticText
TEditText
TNumberText
TDebugFlagsView
TDeskScrapView
TDialogView
TGridView
TTextGridView
TTextListView
TMenuView
TTearOffMenuView
TScroller
TPrimaryScroller
TSecondaryScroller
TTargetBorderView
TTEView
TDialogTEView
TWindow
TFloatWindow
TFile
TFileHandler
TFloatingEManager
TRunArray
TSection
TPublisher
TSubscriber
TStream
TCountingStream
TFileStream
TResourceStream
TSectionStream
TViewServer

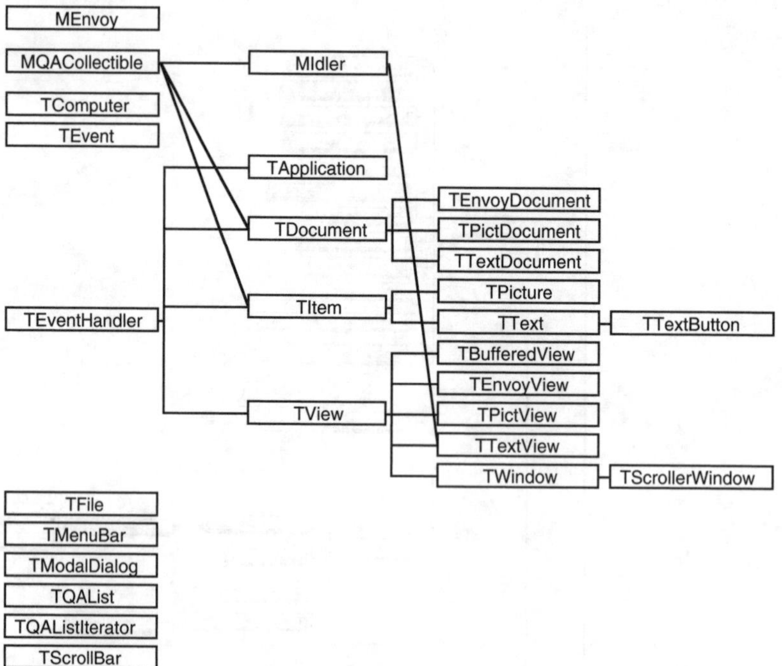

Figure 15.4. The QuickApp class hierarchy.

MicroGA

MicroGA, another product from Emergent Behavior, is a framework for creating genetic algorithms. MicroGA compiles with Apple MPW C++, Symantec C++, and Symantec C++ for MPW. It can be used with MacApp, MicroGA, or with the TCL.

Genetic algorithms are algorithms based on the evolutionary model. Like evolution, a genetic algorithm starts with random solutions to a problem. The solutions compete, and the best solutions survive and reproduce by mating. Slowly, competition improves the quality of the solutions.

MicroGA provides classes that model genes, individual solutions, and populations. Figure 15.5 shows the complete MicroGA class hierarchy.

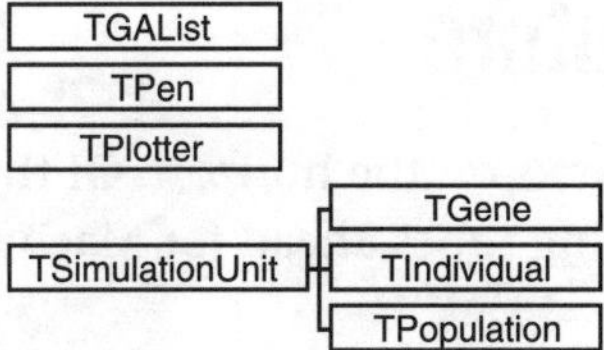

Figure 15.5. The MicroGA class hierarchy.

Physics

Emergent Behavior's final framework, Physics, is a tool for modeling physical interactions between objects. For instance, it can be used to model how the moon orbits around the earth.

Physics compiles with Apple MPW C++, Symantec C++, and Symantec C++ for MPW. It can be used with MacApp, MicroGA, or with the TCL.

Figure 15.6 shows the complete Physics class hierarchy.

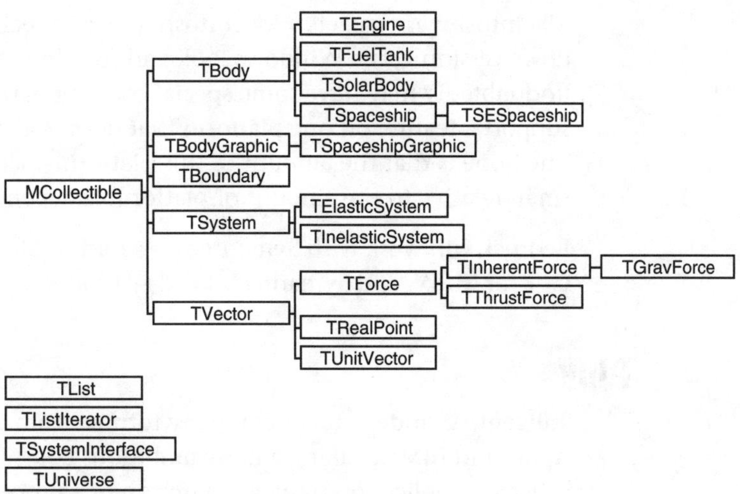

Figure 15.6. The Physics class hierarchy.

Frameworks of the Future

There are other frameworks on the horizon. Of these frameworks, two offer some very interesting times ahead for Macintosh programmers.

Bedrock

Bedrock is an application framework being developed jointly by Symantec and Apple. In some ways, it is the successor to both TCL and MacApp. By far its most distinctive feature is that it is a cross-platform application framework. Initially, it will support Macintosh and Microsoft Windows—a powerful combination.

There are a large number of developers who have created products in both Macintosh and Windows versions. The goal of the Bedrock designers is to reduce the amount of work by providing one unified application framework that runs on both platforms. Ideally, you write one version of your application using Bedrock, with no special code for either platform, and then compile it for each platform. Your Macintosh version gets a Macintosh look and feel, while your Windows version gets a Windows look and feel. In practice, however, you undoubtedly may have some special code for particular platforms to support a feature on one platform that does not exist on the other. The hope is that the amount of this platform-specific code will be small relative to the amount of platform-independent code.

Bedrock will work with Symantec C++ for the Macintosh, Symantec C++ for MPW, and Symantec's PC C++ product.

Pink

Taligent, an independent company formed from a partnership of Apple and IBM, is taking a more ambitious course. Not content to splice an application framework on top of a procedural operating system, they are writing a wholly object-oriented environment from the ground up. Everything, including the operating system, will be accessed via objects.

The product, code named Pink, will be available on a number of platforms because it was designed from the beginning to be portable.

NOTE

In the late 1980s, Apple was contemplating the future for the Macintosh operating system. As they looked at various features and possible characteristics, they wrote each one down on different colored note cards according to a feasible time frame. Blue note cards were short term, pink note cards were medium term, and red note cards were long term. The blue note cards eventually became the basis of System 7 (thus the engineers stamping out System 7 bugs were called Blue Meanies). The pink note cards became the Pink project, which is now pursued at Taligent. It makes you wonder where the red cards ended up.

Summary

Now that you have an idea of what application frameworks are and why you should use them, it is time to get down to the business of actually using them. The rest of the chapters in Part 3 use the TCL to create a variety of programs.

16

RandomRectangle: Building a Rectangle Display Program

This program will never put any of the sophisticated screen-saver programs to shame, but it does perform a simple task relatively well. It is a rectangle drawing program that does the following:

- ▼ Creates a window for the rectangles
- ▼ Draws the rectangles in that window
- ▼ Fills the rectangles with random colors
- ▼ Makes the rectangles random sizes
- ▼ Decides how often to create each new rectangle

You use the THINK Class Library to write the program in this chapter. By looking at what the program does and by reviewing the source files, you see how the TCL can be used to develop a project. You look at each new class and learn what it does. Lastly, you look at the program resources.

How RandomRectangle Works

RandomRectangle is an example of one of the simplest programs you can write with the TCL. Figure 16.1 shows a screen dump of the program. A static snapshot, such as this, fails to capture the dynamic nature of the program, which continually draws rectangles of random sizes filled with random colors. If you run RandomRectangle, you can get a good feel for what it does.

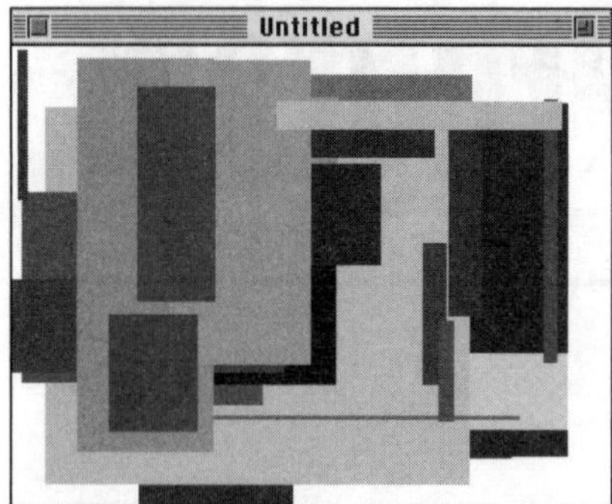

Figure 16.1. RandomRectangle at work.

When you run RandomRectangle on a non-Color QuickDraw machine, it fills the rectangles with random patterns instead of colors. Figure 16.2 shows you that version.

Because it is so small, this program is a good one to familiarize yourself with using the TCL. It also sharpens your use of machine-specific characteristics and teaches you about the system's idle time.

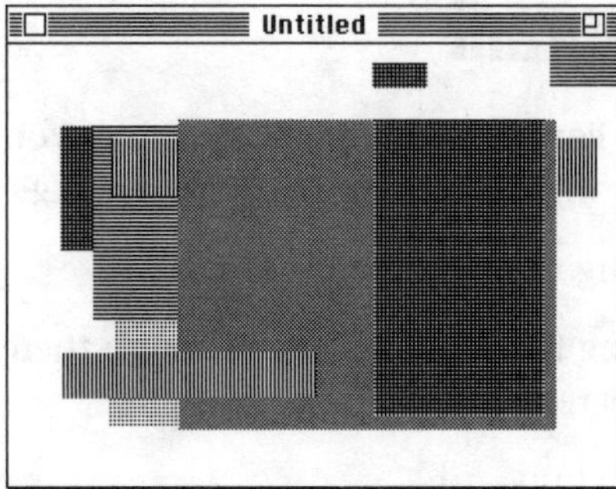

Figure 16.2. RandomRectangle at work on a machine without Color QuickDraw.

Setting Up and Compiling RandomRectangle

The first order of business is to compile and run the program. Before you can do this, however, you probably need to increase the memory partition of the THINK Project Manager. You need to allocate at least 4 megabytes to the partition to compile with the TCL.

NOTE

> To increase the partition size of the THINK Project Manager, select the Project Manager and use Get Info from the File menu of the Finder.

You need to copy the RandomRectangles folder from the source code disk. Open the RandomRectangles. project and then choose Run. (If you need help opening or running a project, refer to Chapter 1, which contains a tutorial on the Project Manager.) It takes a few minutes before the program runs because all of the files in the project need to be recompiled.

Running the Program

After you have RandomRectangles. running, you should test the program by reconnoitering through the rectangles:

- Try moving the window.
- Try resizing the window. Even though there is no grow box, the window is resizable.
- Show the clipboard.
- Notice what does not work (for instance, the About menu item does not do anything).

Later chapters provide functionality that you can use to upgrade this program. Chapter 18 gives you code that makes the About menu item work. There also is code in Chapter 19 that enables background processing even when the window is not active. Currently, the rectangles only draw if the rectangle window is active.

Inspecting the Program

This program is built upon three important classes: `TRandom`, `CRandomRectanglePane`, and `CRectangleApp`. Class diagrams help clarify the structure of these and the other classes by providing a mechanism for describing the members of a class (data and functions) as well as showing the inheritance relationship. Figure 16.3 shows you the class diagram for this application. As the diagram shows, `TRandom`, `CRandomRectanglePane`, and `CRectangleApp` are the new base classes. They are on the left and are connected by lines to their derived classes on the right.

Here are short descriptions of each of these new classes:

`TRandom`	A random number generator. This class is independent of the TCL.
`CRandomRectanglePane`	Draws the random rectangles.
`CRectangleApp`	Creates the window and the `CRandomRectanglePane` object within that window.

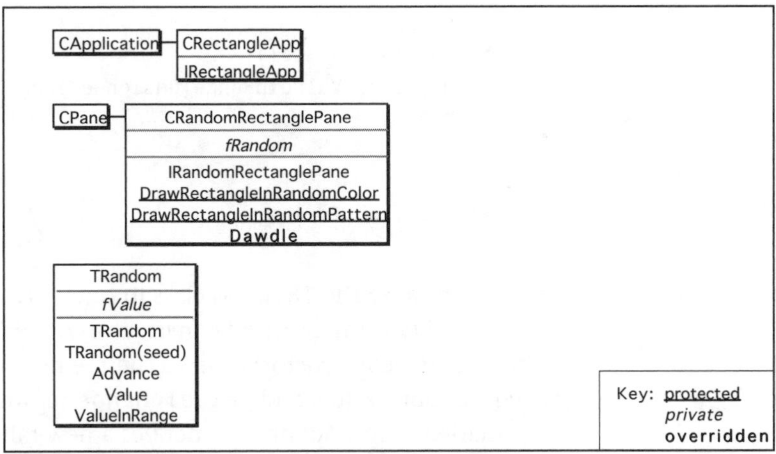

Figure 16.3. RandomRectangle's class diagram.

IMPORTANT

The THINK Class Library uses a naming convention different from that described in Chapter 10. The TCL class names begin with `C`, instead of `T`, as you might expect. There also is no particular convention for data members in the TCL. In the interests of maintaining convention, Chapters 16-21, which use the TCL, begin class names with `C` for all the classes derived from TCL classes. Please note, however, if the classes are independent of the TCL, they begin with the more standard `T`. Any new data members begin with `f`.

The TRandom Class

Look at the `TRandom` class first. The class declaration is as follows:

```
class TRandom {
public:
    TRandom();
    TRandom(unsigned long seed);
```

```
    void Advance();
    unsigned long Value();
    unsigned long ValueInRange(unsigned long low, unsigned long
      high);

private:
    unsigned long fValue;
};
```

You can initialize the TRandom class in one of two ways: with an explicit seed (with the second constructor) or with a default seed (using the first constructor). The Value member function returns the current random value, and ValueInRange returns a random value in the specified range. Advance generates a new random number.

Because this class is stand-alone, you can use it with or without the TCL. As with any good object-oriented class, its declaration does not specify how to generate the random numbers, just how to use them.

Here are the constructors for TRandom:

```
TRandom::TRandom()
{
    fValue = ::TickCount();
}

TRandom::TRandom(unsigned long seed)
{
    fValue = seed;
}
```

When you create a TRandom object, you can choose whether or not to specify a seed for the random number generator. If you do not specify a seed, the initial value is seeded with the number of ticks since machine boot time, which is a reasonably random value. You also can set a particular seed in the constructor if you wish. You might find this method useful if you want to recreate a random sequence. The routines that return values are simple. The current random value is stored in fValue, and the Value routines look like this:

```
unsigned long TRandom::Value()
{
    return fValue;
}

unsigned long TRandom::ValueInRange(unsigned long low, unsigned
long high)
{
    return (Value() % (high - low + 1)) + low;
}
```

ValueInRange returns a number in the range from low to high. In tandem with this, the Advance routine calculates the next random value:

```
void TRandom::Advance()
{
    fValue = fValue * 12345 + 6789;
}
```

This is all there is to the TRandom class. It generates random numbers and returns them to the program. Now, look at the second new class, CRandomRectanglePane.

The CRandomRectanglePane Class

In the TCL, you do your doodling or drawing in a *pane*. Panes are derived from views. These views are representations of visual objects on the screen. Views have other derived classes as well. These include windows, controls, and pictures. Furthermore, the TCL arranges views in an enclosure hierarchy, where each view has one enclosure and can enclose zero or more other views. CRandomRectanglePane exists in such a hierarchy; it is a subview of a window. This new class derives from CPane and does the job of drawing the random rectangles:

```
class CRandomRectanglePane: public CPane {
public:
    void  IRandomRectanglePane(CView *anEnclosure,
      CBureaucrat *aSupervisor, short aWidth,
      short aHeight, short aHEncl, short aVEncl,
      SizingOption aHSizing, SizingOption aVSizing);

    virtual void  Dawdle(long *maxSleep);
```

```
protected:
    virtual void    DrawRectangleInRandomColor(const Rect *r);
    virtual void    DrawRectangleInRandomPattern(const Rect *r);
private:
    TRandom         fRandom;
};
```

IMPORTANT

The TCL was originally written for Think Pascal, a language that does not have constructors or destructors. As you might expect upon hearing this news, the classes in the TCL do not use constructors and destructors. Instead, each class provides an initialization member function that consists of taking the class name and replacing the first character with an `I`. The `Dispose` member function does cleanup for an object and is used in place of a destructor.

In the above code, the initialization member function is `IRandomRectanglePane`, which requires the same parameters as `IPane`. This is all you need to know for now because each of these functions gets described in greater detail later in this chapter.

Take a look at how `CRandomRectanglePane` works and how it uses its member functions. First, you should note that it overrides its inherited member function, `Dawdle`, which is called whenever idle time is available. Idle time is available when the main event loop is receiving null events. `CRandomRectanglePane` only has one data member, `fRandom`. This is used by the drawing routines to generate random rectangles, colors, and patterns.

Initialization

The initialization member function does nothing beyond calling the initialization method of its base class:

```
void CRandomRectanglePane::IRandomRectanglePane(CView *anEnclosure,
  CBureaucrat *aSupervisor, short aWidth, short aHeight,
  short aHEncl, short aVEncl, SizingOption aHSizing,
  SizingOption aVSizing)
{
    IPane(anEnclosure, aSupervisor, aWidth, aHeight,
      aHEncl, aVEncl, aHSizing, aVSizing);
}
```

It is important to write an initialization method for each class, even when it just calls the base class. If you do this extra work, determining what member function to call to perform initialization is trivial.

Obtaining Idle Time

How does the program obtain the idle time it needs to draw the rectangles? It overrides `Dawdle`. The following code shows the mechanism:

```
void CRandomRectanglePane::Dawdle(long *maxSleep)
{
    Rect        r;
    Point       p1;
    Point       p2;
    LongRect    frameSize;

    GetFrame(&frameSize);

    p1.h = fRandom.ValueInRange(frameSize.left, frameSize.right);
    fRandom.Advance();
    p1.v = fRandom.ValueInRange(frameSize.top, frameSize.bottom);
    fRandom.Advance();
    p2.h = fRandom.ValueInRange(frameSize.left, frameSize.right);
    fRandom.Advance();
    p2.v = fRandom.ValueInRange(frameSize.top, frameSize.bottom);
    fRandom.Advance();

    ::Pt2Rect(p1, p2, &r);

    Prepare();          // prepare coordinate system for drawing
```

```
    if (gSystem.hasColorQD)
        DrawRectangleInRandomColor(&r);
    else
        DrawRectangleInRandomPattern(&r);

    *maxSleep = 20;         // one rectangle every 1/3 second
}
```

First, the `GetFrame` member function returns the bounding rectangle (size) of the pane. Unlike the standard QuickDraw 16-bit coordinate system, the TCL panes can use a 32-bit system. `GetFrame` generates a frame that is then used as the bounds to create two random points. Then, `Pt2Rect` initializes the random rectangle `r`, using the two random points as corners.

Using idle time to draw is not standard on the Macintosh. Normally, Macintosh drawing occurs as a response to update events. When an update event occurs, the program calls a pane's `Draw` member function, which issues QuickDraw calls to draw the contents of the pane.

In RandomRectangle, on the other hand, the pane is not drawing in response to update events, but rather at idle time. Because it is drawing at such an unusual time, the TCL has not prepared its coordinate system for drawing. `CRandomRectanglePane` must prepare its coordinate system on its own by calling its `Prepare` member function. This sets up the correct GrafPort, clipping, and origin.

After the pane is prepared, `Dawdle` examines the global structure `gSystem`—a TCL structure that describes the environment in which the application is running. Here are the fields of `gSystem`:

```
Boolean    hasWNE;
Boolean    hasColorQD;
Boolean    hasGestalt;
Boolean    hasAppleEvents;
Boolean    hasAliasMgr;
Boolean    hasEditionMgr;
Boolean    hasHelpMgr;
Boolean    hasScriptMgr;
Boolean    hasFPU;
short      scriptsInstalled;
short      systemVersion;
```

This variable is initialized by the TCL as part of the initialization process. `Dawdle` calls the appropriate `DrawRectangle` function based on whether this machine has Color QuickDraw.

Finally, `Dawdle` specifies in the `maxSleep` parameter how many ticks until the pane receives its next `Dawdle`. It sets `maxSleep` to 20 (three rectangles per second draw).

Drawing in a Random Pattern

`DrawRectangleInRandomPattern` draws the specified rectangle in a random pattern, which it gets from the system:

```
void CRandomRectanglePane::DrawRectangleInRandomPattern(const
  Rect *r)
{
    Pattern aPattern;

    GetIndPattern(aPattern, sysPatListID, fRandom.ValueInRange(1,
      31));
    fRandom.Advance();
    FillRect(r, aPattern);
}
```

If you look at `Dawdle`, you can see that `DrawRectangleInRandom-Pattern` only gets called if the machine does not have Color QuickDraw. This routine uses patterns as a way to distinguish the rectangles from each other on noncolor machines.

Drawing in a Random Color

Next, look at the function that colors the rectangles, `DrawRectangle-InRandomColor`:

```
void CRandomRectanglePane::DrawRectangleInRandomColor(const Rect
  *r)
{
    RGBColor     aColor;
    PixPatHandle myPixPat;
```

```
    aColor.red = fRandom.Value();
    fRandom.Advance();
    aColor.blue = fRandom.Value();
    fRandom.Advance();
    aColor.green = fRandom.Value();
    fRandom.Advance();

    myPixPat = NewPixPat();
    MakeRGBPat(myPixPat, &aColor);
    FillCRect(r, myPixPat);
    DisposPixPat(myPixPat);
}
```

Red, blue, and green (an RGB pattern) values are set in `aColor`. Next, the routine uses this pattern of colors to approximate a given color that works on displays of any bit depth.

NOTE

For those of you familiar with the standard method for drawing in color—using the Color QuickDraw call to `RGBForeColor`—this might appear a strange way to color a rectangle. It should make sense, however, when you realize that, regardless of the color, `RBGForeColor` draws in either solid black or solid white when in 1-bit mode. To avoid this, the program has `DrawRectangleInRandomColor` call `MakeRGBPat`. In 1-bit mode, this creates a black-and-white pattern that simulates the requested color.

The CRectangleApp Class

Now that you have a class that creates a random number and one that draws and colors the rectangles, you need one last class—one that creates a window and the pane for the rectangles. This new class is `CRectangleApp` and is derived from the TCL class `CApplication`.

IMPORTANT

Every TCL program needs to create a class derived from CApplication. In this case, it may not be obvious why because CRectangleApp does not override any CApplication member functions. Because most programs need such overriding (certainly any programs that support multiple documents), it is customary to always override CApplication.

The following code shows the declaration:

```
class CRectangleApp: public CApplication {
public:
    void    IRectangleApp();
};
```

CRectangleApp only has one member function, which performs initialization:

```
void CRectangleApp::IRectangleApp()
{
    const short   kExtraMasters =    1;
    const Size    kRainyDayFund =    45000;
    const Size    kCriticalBalance = 40000;
    const Size    kToolboxBalance =  20000;
    const short   kWINDResourceID =  500;
    const Boolean kWindowFloats =    TRUE;

    IApplication( kExtraMasters, kRainyDayFund,
      kCriticalBalance, kToolboxBalance);

    CDirector *aDirector = new CDirector;
    aDirector->IDirector(this);

    CWindow *aWindow = new CWindow;
    aWindow->IWindow(kWINDResourceID, !kWindowFloats, gDesktop,
       aDirector);
    aDirector->itsWindow = aWindow;

    CRandomRectanglePane *thePane = new CRandomRectanglePane;
    thePane->IRandomRectanglePane(aWindow, aDirector, 0, 0, 0, 0,
      sizELASTIC, sizELASTIC);
```

```
    thePane->FitToEnclosure(TRUE, TRUE);
    aDirector->itsGopher = thePane;
}
```

Initializing

`CRectangleApp` begins by calling the initialization of its base class `CApplication`. Listed below are its parameters and what they control:

`kExtraMasters`	The number of calls to the Toolbox routine `MoreMasters`
`kRainyDayFund`	The amount of memory reserved for low-memory conditions
`kCriticalBalance`	The amount of memory used for critical operations
`kToolboxBalance`	The amount of memory used for Toolbox operations

You use this reserved memory to ensure that TCL applications continue to function when memory space gets tight. If you need more information on memory management, you should look at the TCL documentation.

Creating the Director

All TCL applications consist of managers who control the interactions between elements. As in the real world, these *bureaucrats* have specific names, functions, and exist within a chain of command. The first manager you need to understand is the *director*—an object that handles the interactions between a window and the application. `CRectangleApp` creates just such a director and initializes it with its *supervisor*, the application.

The first object in the chain of command is the *gopher* (lowest on the totem pole). If the gopher does not handle the command, it sends it up the chain to its supervisor, the next bureaucrat in line. This processing continues until some bureaucrat handles the command. You need to remember to connect the chain of command: When you initialize a bureaucrat, you need to specify its supervisor. Be attentive to these command chains because a TCL application creates a very bureaucratic world where many objects are bureaucrats, including applications, panes, and windows.

Creating the Window

After determining the pecking order in the program, the function creates a window and initializes it. Using `kWINDResourceID`, it specifies the resource ID for the window. `!kWindowFloats` indicates that the window is not a floating window (that is, not a windoid). After initializing the window, it sets the director's data member, `itsWindow`, to point to that window.

Creating the RandomRectangle Pane

Finally, the function creates a `CRandomRectanglePane` and initializes the following:

- Its enclosure
- Its director
- Its horizontal and vertical size
- Its horizontal and vertical location within this enclosure
- Its horizontal and vertical sizing options

Note that, even though the size and location are initialized to 0, they are modified shortly. Look at the sizing options: `sizELASTIC` specifies that the pane size changes whenever the enclosure changes, and the `FitToEnclosure` member function sets the pane to the size of the window. Thus, the pane always is exactly as big as its enclosing window. `FitToEnclosure` starts it that way; `sizELASTIC` keeps it that way.

Notice also that the director's `itsGopher` data member refers to a particular bureaucrat. When the director is activated, it makes this bureaucrat the gopher. `IRectangleApp` sets this data member to the pane.

Looking at the Final Chain of Command

The chain of command after these objects have been created is as shown in figure 16.4.

Figure 16.4. The chain of command in RandomRectangle.

The chain of command is used not only for handling commands, but also for dealing with idle time. The TCL calls the `Dawdle` member function for bureaucrats in the chain. If a bureaucrat is not part of the chain of command, its `Dawdle` does not get called. If you circumvent the chain of command, the application stops working correctly. For instance, try showing the clipboard or putting the RandomRectangle application in the background. Notice that the rectangles stop drawing. This is because the chain of command is based on the active window. If the rectangle window is not active, `CRandomRectanglePane` is not the gopher and therefore does not call `Dawdle`.

NOTE

> In Chapter 19, you learn how to get the `Dawdle` routine to be called even when the pane is not part of the chain of command. The rectangles then continue drawing even if the application is in the background or the window is not active.

The Main Program

All good things must have a beginning. In this case, that is the `main` function.

```
void main()
{
    CRectangleApp *rectangleApp;

    rectangleApp = new CRectangleApp;
    rectangleApp->IRectangleApp();
    rectangleApp->Run();
    rectangleApp->Exit();
}
```

This main function is very similar to the one used for all other TCL programs. It creates a derived class called `CApplication`, initializes it, calls its `Run` member function, and then calls its `Exit` member function. The `Run` function does not return until the user chooses `Quit`; at that point, `Exit` gets a chance to do any necessary cleanup.

Resources

The resources for RandomRectangle are in Rez format. Note that quite a few of them come with the TCL. Only the resources shown below, however, are unique to this application:

```
resource 'BNDL' (128) {
    'C++1',
    0,
    {
        'FREF',
        {
                0, 128
        },
        'ICN#',
        {
                0, 128
        }
    }
};

data 'C++1' (0, "Owner resource") {
    $"00"
};

data 'FREF' (128) {
    $"4150 504C 0000 84"
};

resource 'ICN#' (128) {
    {
        $"0000 0000 0000 0000 003F FE00 0020 0200"
        $"0020 0200 03FF F200 0220 1200 0220 1200"
        $"0220 1200 0220 1200 0FFE 1200 0A22 1200"
        $"0A22 1200 0A22 1200 0BFF F200 0822 0200"
        $"083F FE00 0802 0000 0FFE",
```

```
        $"0000 0000 0000 0000 003F FE00 003F FE00"
        $"003F FE00 03FF FE00 03FF FE00 03FF FE00"
        $"03FF FE00 03FF FE00 0FFF FE00 0FFF FE00"
        $"0FFF FE00 0FFF FE00 0FFF FE00 0FFF FE00"
        $"0FFF FE00 0FFE 0000 0FFE"
    }
};
```

The `'BNDL'`, `'C++1'`, `'FREF'`, `'ICN#'`, and `'ics#'` resources are for the application's icon.

The remaining resources are part of the TCL. The only change you need to make is to the File menu. You need to remove some of the standard menu items that are not needed for RandomRectangle:

```
resource 'MENU' (2, "File", preload) {
    2,
    textMenuProc,
    0x7FFFFFFE,
    enabled,
    "File",
    {
        "Close#4", noIcon, "W", noMark, plain,
        "Quit#1", noIcon, "Q", noMark, plain
    }
};
```

Summary

You have learned that the RandomRectangle program uses three important classes: `TRandom`, `CRandomRectanglePane`, and `CRectangleApp`. `TRandom`—the only TCL-independent class—handles all the randomization for the program. `CRandomRectangle` manages the drawing of the rectangles including their size, color, and frequency. `CRectangleApp` creates the window in which the rectangles are drawn and makes sure they exist in a coherent world.

17

TextTyper: Building a Text-Editing Program

Because many Macintosh applications have some text-editing capabilities, it is worth knowing how to use the TCL to do text editing. The application that follows enables only simple editing. It does not provide features for font changing, spell checking, or even formatting the text. What it shows you, however, is how to use the TCL with text-based applications.

The TextTyper Program

The text editor, TextTyper, is a far more substantial TCL program than the RandomRectangle application. It does the following:

- Opens multiple documents.
- Creates or edits the text of a document.
- Prints a document.

Figure 17.1 shows the text-entry window and should give you a fairly good idea of TextTyper's functionality.

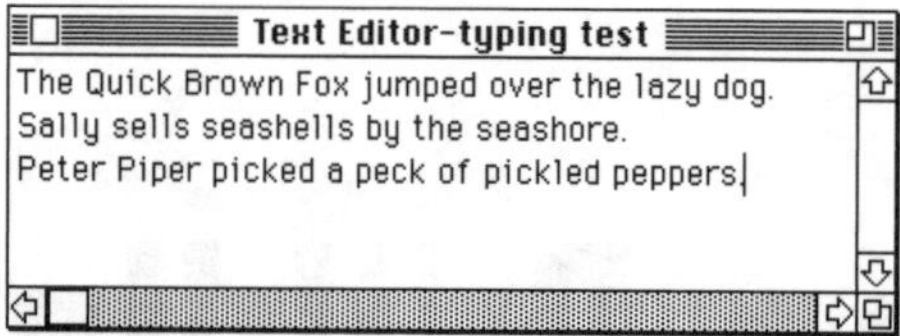

Figure 17.1. The text-entry window of TextTyper.

Compiling the Program

Copy the TextTyper folder from the source code disk. Open the TextTyper. project and then choose Run. It takes a little time for all the files in the project to recompile.

Running the Program

After TextTyper is running, take it for a test drive. Feel free to do any of the following:

- Create new files.
- Open existing text files.
- Open a large text file (greater than 32,000 characters).
- Print a text file.

What happened when you tried to open the large text file? You should have gotten the alert shown in figure 17.2. TextTyper has a limit of 32,000 characters. Because TCL text-editing classes use TextTyper, they inherit this limitation. You also might have noticed that the About box does not work. The next chapter has the code to fix this problem.

If you printed one of your text files, you should have seen that pages break between lines rather than in the middle of them. This works correctly because TextTyper deals properly with line breaks when printing.

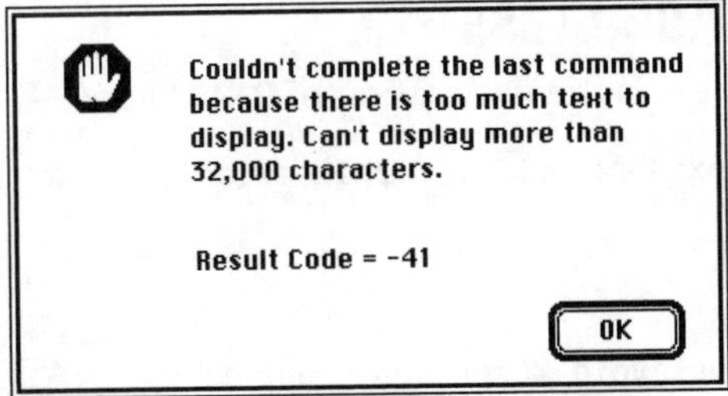

Figure 17.2. The alert from opening a big file in TextTyper.

Inspecting the Program

Now that you have manipulated the application, look at the code. Figure 17.3 shows the class diagram.

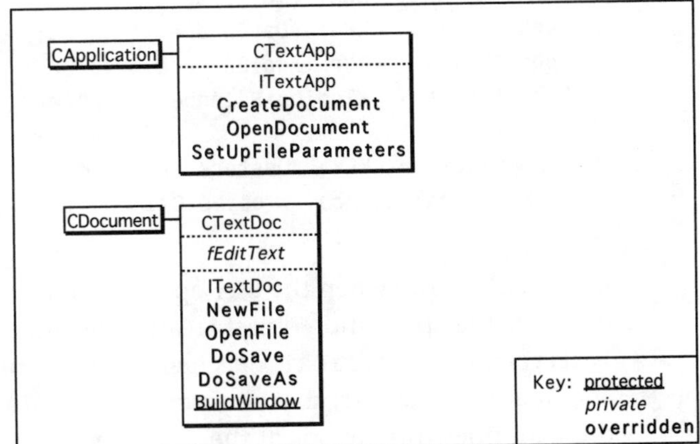

Figure 17.3. TextTyper's class diagram.

There are two new classes: `CTextApp` and `CTextDoc`. They do the following:

- `CTextApp` creates the documents and sets parameters for the Open dialog.
- `CTextDoc` creates the window and text-editing pane and reads and writes the text to disk.

The CTextApp Class

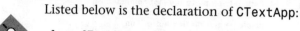

Listed below is the declaration of CTextApp:

```
class CTextApp: public CApplication {
public:
    void            ITextApp();

    virtual void    CreateDocument();
    virtual void    OpenDocument(SFReply *macReply);
    virtual void    SetUpFileParameters();
};
```

The initialization method, ITextApp, is simpler than the one in the last chapter. In TextTyper, it is the document and not the application that creates the windows.

```
void CTextApp::ITextApp()
{
    const short   kExtraMasters =    1;
    const Size    kRainyDayFund =    45000;
    const Size    kCriticalBalance = 40000;
    const Size    kToolboxBalance =  20000;

    IApplication( kExtraMasters, kRainyDayFund,
      kCriticalBalance, kToolboxBalance);
}
```

In the TCL world, when the user opens an old document or creates a new one, the application object creates a document object. In TextTyper, it is CApplication's member functions, OpenDocument and CreateDocument, that perform this job. CTextApp overrides these routines. Take a look at the simplified version of CreateDocument:

```
void CTextApp::CreateDocument()
{
    CTextDoc *theDocument = new CTextDoc;
    theDocument->ITextDoc(this);
    theDocument->NewFile();
}
```

The function creates a CTextDoc, initializes it, and then calls the NewFile member function (which you see shortly). CreateDocument is not quite complete, however, because it does not deal with the errors that might occur in `ITextDoc` or `NewFile`. These errors need to be dealt with by exception handlers.

IMPORTANT

Error handling in the TCL is based on *exceptions*, not on the error codes with which you are familiar. While this approach may seem novel to you, it is worth adopting for two reasons: First, ANSI C++ directly supports exception handling (assuring its increasing popularity); second, it makes for easier maintenance of code.

Generating Exceptions

Instead of returning error codes, the TCL uses functions that generate exceptions. Take a look at the functions that do this:

- `FailOSErr(short error)` generates an exception if the error is not `noErr`.
- `FailNIL(void *p)` is equivalent to `FailOSErr(memFullErr)` if `p` is NULL.
- `FailMemError()` is equivalent to `FailOSErr(MemError())`.
- `FailResError()` is equivalent to `FailOSErr(ResError())`.
- `FailNILRes(void* p)` generates an exception if `p` is NULL and provides a more useful error message than `FailNIL`.

Here is how exception handling works:

1. When an exception is generated, the function in progress is aborted.
2. All of the other functions currently in the call chain abort, all the way back to the main event loop.
3. Next, the TCL puts up an error alert to notify the user about what went wrong.
4. After the user responds to the alert, the main event loop continues to the next event.

Listed below are some examples:

```
Handle h;

h = ::NewHandle(20);
::FailNIL(h);

h = ::GetResource('ALRT', 128);
::FailNILRes(h);

::FailOSErr(::HandToHand(&h)); // HandToHand returns an OSErr
```

Exception-Handling Cases

It is not enough to just generate the exceptions. Sometimes you must respond to them, as in the cases where some cleanup is necessary. Table 17.1 shows some cases where exception handlers are necessary.

Table 17.1. Examples of Exceptions That Need To Be Handled

Normal Case	Exception Case
The program opens a file, reads its contents, and closes the file.	If the read fails, the file still needs to be closed.
The program creates an object, does something with it, and then disposes of it.	If the action fails, the object still needs to be disposed of.
The program locks a handle, does something with it, and unlocks it.	If the something fails, the handle still needs to be unlocked.

The TCL handles exceptions and cleanup using three macros: TRY, CATCH, and ENDTRY. Here is how you use them:

```
TRY {
    code that could generate an exception
}
CATCH
{
    code that cleans up if an exception occurs
}
ENDTRY;
```

To clarify the functioning of these macros, first examine a case that does not fail. If the code in TRY does not fail, the code in CATCH is not executed (sorry, but double negatives are like that). If CATCH is not executed, the code continues after ENDTRY. On the other hand, examine a failing case: If an exception occurs (TRY fails), the CATCH code executes. After the last line of CATCH finishes, the stack of currently executing functions is aborted all the way back to the next exception handler.

Handling Exceptions in CreateDocument

Now, imagine handling errors while trying to create a document. In the function, `CreateDocument`, if an error occurs during the initialization of the document or in the call to `NewFile`, you need to throw the document away. Here is the code you must add to `CreateDocument` to perform that action:

```
void CTextApp::CreateDocument()
{
    CTextDoc *theDocument = new CTextDoc;

    TRY
    {
        theDocument->ITextDoc(this);
        theDocument->NewFile();
    }
    CATCH
    {
        ForgetObject(theDocument);
    }
    ENDTRY;
}
```

Notice that, if either `ITextDoc` or `NewFile` cause an exception, the document is thrown away.

You add exception handling to the `OpenDocument` member function similarly:

```
void CTextApp::OpenDocument(SFReply *macReply)
{
    CTextDoc *theDocument = new CTextDoc;

    TRY
    {
        theDocument->ITextDoc(this);
        theDocument->OpenFile(macReply);
    }
    CATCH
    {
        ForgetObject(theDocument);
    }
    ENDTRY;
}
```

There are some differences between `OpenDocument` and `NewDocument`:

- The presence of the `SFReply` (obtained from the user in the Open dialog).
- The call to `OpenFile` rather than `NewFile`.

The TCL shows all the available files in an Open dialog. The user of a text-editing program, however, only wants to see the available *text* files. TextTyper, therefore, needs to modify the TCL's default behavior to show only `'TEXT'` files:

```
void CTextApp::SetUpFileParameters()
{
    CApplication::SetUpFileParameters();

    sfNumTypes = 1;
    sfFileTypes[0] = 'TEXT';
    gSignature = 'C++2';
}
```

The overriding member function augments the existing behavior of `CApplication`. It sets the data members `sfNumTypes` and `sfFileTypes`, which are later used as parameters to the Toolbox call `SFGetFile`. After this is accomplished, TextTyper only shows text files when the user selects the Open dialog.

NOTE

This is also a good place to set the signature for the application because the signature is a file-related piece of information. Alternatively, the signature could be set in ITextApp.

The CTextDoc Class

The CTextDoc class has these duties in TextTyper:

- Create the window.
- Create the panes within the window.
- Read the text from disk.
- Write the text to disk.

Listed below is the class declaration:

```
class CTextDoc: public CDocument {
public:
    void            ITextDoc(CApplication *supervisor);

    virtual void    NewFile();
    virtual void    OpenFile(SFReply *macReply);
    virtual Boolean DoSave();
    virtual Boolean DoSaveAs(SFReply *macSFReply);
protected:
    virtual void    BuildWindow();
private:
    CEditText  *fEditText;
};
```

The member functions NewFile, OpenFile, DoSave, and DoSaveAs are all overrides of CDocument member functions. BuildWindow is a utility member function that encapsulates common code from NewFile and OpenFile. The sole data member, fEditText, refers to the CEditText pane in the document's window.

Initializing CTextDoc

The initialization member function is short:

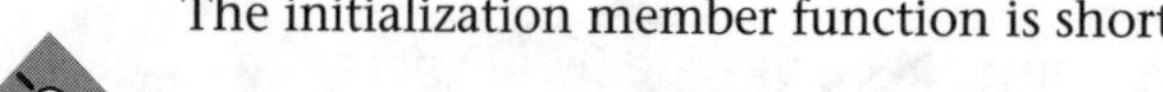

```
void CTextDoc::ITextDoc(CApplication *supervisor)
{
    const Boolean kPrintable = TRUE;

    IDocument(supervisor, kPrintable);
}
```

The second parameter to `IDocument`, `kPrintable`, specifies whether or not the document can be printed. Because a text-entry program that does not print is a bit like a fly without wings, this program has printable documents.

Creating a New File

When the user wants to create a new text document, `CTextApp` calls the member function `NewFile` (existing documents open differently). Listed below is the `NewFile` code:

```
void CTextDoc::NewFile()
{
    BuildWindow();

    Str255 wTitle;
    short wCount;
    Str255 wNumber;

    itsWindow->GetTitle(wTitle);
    wCount = gDecorator->GetWCount();
    ::NumToString(wCount, wNumber);
    ::ConcatPStrings(wTitle, "\p-");
    ::ConcatPStrings(wTitle, wNumber);
    itsWindow->SetTitle(wTitle);

    itsWindow->Select();
}
```

`NewFile` calls `BuildWindow` to create the necessary windows and panes. The TCL, by default, sets the title of new windows to the oh-so-familiar "Untitled." TextTyper is a bit more sophisticated than this, however, because it sets the titles to "Untitled-1," "Untitled-2," etc. To do this, NewFile sends a message to the global gDecorator asking how many windows have been created. It takes this number and attaches it to the end of the untitled document it just created. So the user does not have to watch a schizoid window, this title is not displayed until its Select member function is called.

Building the Window

The BuildWindow member function creates the window and the necessary panes for TextTyper:

```
void CTextDoc::BuildWindow()
{
    const short   kWINDResourceID =          500;
    const Boolean kWindowFloats =            TRUE;
    const Boolean kFitHorizontal =           TRUE;
    const Boolean kFitVertical =             TRUE;
    const Boolean kHasHorizontalScrollbar =TRUE;
    const Boolean kHasVerticalScrollbar =  TRUE;
    const Boolean kHasGrowBox =              TRUE;
    const short   kEditTextWidth =           72 * 6;
    const Boolean kRedraw =                  TRUE;

    CWindow *aWindow = new CWindow;
    aWindow->IWindow(kWINDResourceID, !kWindowFloats, gDesktop,
      this);
    itsWindow = aWindow;
    CScrollPane *theScrollPane = new CScrollPane;
    theScrollPane->IScrollPane(aWindow, this, 10, 10, 0, 0,
      sizELASTIC, sizELASTIC, kHasHorizontalScrollbar,
      kHasVerticalScrollbar, kHasGrowBox);
    theScrollPane->FitToEnclFrame(kFitHorizontal, kFitVertical);

    CEditText *thePane = new CEditText;
    thePane->IEditText(theScrollPane, this, 1, 1, 0, 0,
      sizELASTIC, sizELASTIC, kEditTextWidth);
    itsGopher = thePane;
    itsMainPane = thePane;
    fEditText = thePane;
    theScrollPane->InstallPanorama(thePane);
    thePane->FitToEnclosure(kFitHorizontal, kFitVertical);
```

```
    Rect margin;
    ::SetRect(&margin, 2, 2, -2, -2);
    thePane->ChangeSize(&margin, !kRedraw);

    gDecorator->PlaceNewWindow(itsWindow);
}
```

This is a long function, so you can examine it a bit at a time. First, peruse the declarations to get familiar with them. A more detailed discussion follows.

- `kWINDResourceID` is the ID of the `'WIND'` resource.
- `kWindowFloats` makes the window float (windoid).
- `kFitHorizontal` makes this pane the same horizontal size as its enclosure.
- `kFitVertical` makes this pane the same vertical size as its enclosure.
- `kHasHorizontalScrollbar` signals the panorama to create a horizontal scroll bar.
- `kHasVerticalScrollbar` signals the panorama to create a vertical scroll bar.
- `kHasGrowBox` ensures the panorama has a grow box.
- `kEditTextWidth` sets the allowable width of the edit text.
- `kRedraw` redraws this pane.

Now see how `BuildWindow` handles window scrolling. A TCL application uses two special panes to support scrolling: `CScrollPane` and `CPanorama`. A `CPanorama` is a scrollable `CPane`. Here is the process of creating a window:

1. `BuildWindow` creates a `CWindow`.
2. Next, it creates a `CScrollPane`, specifying horizontal and vertical scroll bars and a grow box. The `FitToEnclFrame` function resizes the scroll pane to match the size of the window.
3. Then, `BuildWindow` creates an editable text with a width of 6 inches.

4. The itsMainPane data member determines which pane prints when the user selects Print.
5. CEditText also is stored in fEditText, a CTextDoc data member. This is used for document saving.
6. The call to InstallPanorama notifies the scroll pane of its panorama (the edit text).
7. Then, the edit text is resized to fit the window.
8. The edit text is next inset by 2 pixels on each side. This way it cannot bump up against the edge of the window.
9. Finally, PlaceNewWindow staggers the window by adjusting its size and location.

NOTE

The itsGopher data member determines the chain of command. Chains of command, along with gophers, are described in detail in Chapter 16.

After BuildWindow executes, TextTyper has a new window ready for text.

Opening an Existing File

If a document already exists, then TextTyper must use a different process. CTextDoc calls its OpenFile member function to open an existing file. It is specified with an SFReply parameter:

```
void CTextDoc::OpenFile(SFReply *macReply)
{
    CDataFile    *theDataFile;
    Handle        theData;
    Str63         theName;
    OSErr         theError;
    const long    kMaxFileSize = 32000;

    theDataFile = new CDataFile;
```

```
    itsFile = theDataFile;

    theDataFile->IDataFile();
    theDataFile->SFSpecify(macReply);

    theDataFile->Open(fsRdPerm);

    TRY {
        if (theDataFile->GetLength() > kMaxFileSize)
            ::Failure(mFulErr, excExceedTELimit);
        theData = theDataFile->ReadAll();
    } CATCH {
         theDataFile->Close();
    }
    ENDTRY;

    TRY {
        theDataFile->Close();
        BuildWindow();
        fEditText->SetTextHandle(theData);
    } CATCH {
        ::DisposHandle(theData);
    }
    ENDTRY;
    ::DisposHandle(theData);

    itsFile->GetName(theName);
    itsWindow->SetTitle(theName);

    itsWindow->Select();
}
```

`CDataFile` is a TCL class that interacts with a data file on disk. Note that `OpenFile` creates a `CDataFile` and stores it in the `CDocument` data member, `itsFile`. It waits there until it is time to save the document.

When given an `SFReply`, `SFSpecify` notifies the data file of its location. `OpenFile` then opens the file, reads its data with `ReadAll`, and closes it.

Note that the code uses the exception-handling macros: `TRY`, `CATCH`, and `ENDTRY`. This exception handler, which encompasses `ReadAll`, ensures that the file is closed even if there is an error reading the file. The check for file length makes sure that the file is not too long for TextTyper.

After reading the text and closing the file, `OpenFile` builds the window. Next, it calls the `SetTextHandle` member function, which provides the text to the `CEditText` pane (the exception handler is here to dispose of the handle in case of an error).

Finally, `OpenFile` sets the title of the window appropriately and then calls `Select` to show the window to the user.

Handling the Save Option

When the user selects Save, `CDocument` calls the `DoSave` member function:

```
Boolean CTextDoc::DoSave()
{
    Handle          theData;

    if (itsFile == NULL)
        return(DoSaveFileAs());
    else {
        CDataFile *theDataFile = (CDataFile *) itsFile;

        theData = fEditText->GetTextHandle();
        theDataFile->Open(fsWrPerm);
        TRY {
            theDataFile->WriteAll(theData);
        } CATCH {
            theDataFile->Close();
        }
        ENDTRY;
        theDataFile->Close();
        dirty = FALSE;
        return(TRUE);
    }
}
```

If the user is still working with an untitled document (one not yet saved) then `DoSave` calls `DoSaveAs`. This generates a filename prompt for the user. When the file already exists, `DoSave` does the following:

- ▼ Gets the data from CEditText.
- ▼ Opens the file.
- ▼ Writes the data.
- ▼ Closes the file.

Again, an exception handler is necessary for cleanup.

After the file is saved, the file's dirty data member is reset to false. This flag enables Save and controls whether the Save changes before the closing alert dialog appears when the document is closed.

The return value of DoSave is only set to false if the user cancels the Save (as might happen if he or she cancels the SFPutFile for an untitled document).

Handling the Save As Option

When the user selects Save As, CDocument calls the member function DoSaveAs. It also passes the SFReply to specify where the document should be saved. DoSaveAs is listed below:

```
Boolean CTextDoc::DoSaveAs(SFReply *macSFReply)
{
    if (itsFile != NULL)
        itsFile->Dispose();

    CDataFile *theDataFile = new CDataFile;
    itsFile = theDataFile;
    theDataFile->IDataFile();
    theDataFile->SFSpecify(macSFReply);
    if (theDataFile->ExistsOnDisk())
        theDataFile->ThrowOut();
    theDataFile->CreateNew(gSignature, 'TEXT');

    itsWindow->SetTitle(macSFReply->fName);

    return(DoSave());
}
```

First, the itsFile data member determines if the file exists. If it already exists, then DoSaveAs disposes of it. DoSaveAs then creates a new data file and saves it in the data member itsFile.

Second, the function deals with the case of an existing file that needs replacement. If it exists, DoSaveAs deletes it. Then, it creates the new file using CreateNew. The appropriate signature and file type also are set.

Third, DoSaveAs updates the window's title to reflect the new filename. It then calls DoSave to actually write the contents of the file.

TextTyper's Main Program

Here is another very similar TCL main program:

```
void main()
{
    CTextApp     *app;

    app = new CTextApp;
    app->ITextApp();
    app->Run();
    app->Exit();
}
```

The Resources

Other than its different icons, the only new resource TextTyper has is a modified version of the edit menu:

```
resource 'MENU' (3, "Edit", preload) {
    3,
    textMenuProc,
    0x7FFFFF80,
    enabled,
    "Edit",
    {
        "Undo#16", noIcon, "Z", noMark, plain,
        "-", noIcon, noKey, noMark, plain,
        "Cut#18", noIcon, "X", noMark, plain,
        "Copy#19", noIcon, "C", noMark, plain,
        "Paste#20", noIcon, "V", noMark, plain,
        "Clear#21", noIcon, noKey, noMark, plain,
        "Select All#23", noIcon, "A", noMark, plain,
        "-", noIcon, noKey, noMark, plain,
```

```
        "Show Clipboard#22", noIcon, noKey, noMark, plain
    }
};
```

The Select All menu item has been added to the Edit menu. Notice that all the menu items have a number after them. These numbers are not displayed in the running application. They are *command numbers*, which are used within the TCL to refer to the menu item. This is a much more convenient method than using the menu ID and item number. Using command numbers enables you to modify a program more easily because you can move a menu item within a menu, or even into another menu, without recompiling your code.

Summary

TextTyper, the application featured in this chapter, has two new classes: `CTextApp` and `CTextDoc`. With these, you can use the TCL to create a program that does the following:

- ▼ Creates a new text document (`CreateDocument` and `NewFile`).
- ▼ Opens an existing document (`OpenDocument` and `OpenFile`).
- ▼ Sets up the windows to look and work correctly (`BuildWindow`).
- ▼ Names and saves a document (`DoSave` and `DoSaveAs`).

You also learned about an important new way to deal with errors: exception handling.

18

PICTPeeker: Building a Graphics-Viewing Program

The application in this chapter, PICTPeeker, is a PICT-viewing program that enables the user to open, print, cut, copy, and paste. It contains new classes that handle undo and redo as well as enable more menus. It also contains important new exception-handling classes.

The PICTPeeker Program

PICTPeeker is yet another kind of program you can build with the TCL. While still on the simpler side of the application spectrum, it nevertheless opens multiple documents and enables cut, copy, paste, and print operations. PICTPeeker is built with an augmented version of the TCL class that displays pictures. Figure 18.1 shows the application in action.

Figure 18.1. The PICTPeeker program.

Compiling and Running the Program

Copy the PICTPeeker folder from the source code disk. Open the PICTPeeker. project and choose Run. It takes a few minutes for the compiler to recompile all the files in this project.

After it is running, put the program through its paces. Feel free to try any of the following:

- ▼ Create some new files.
- ▼ Open some existing PICT files.
- ▼ Cut, copy, and paste a PICT file.
- ▼ Undo and redo what you just did.
- ▼ Show the clipboard during these operations to convince yourself it works correctly.
- ▼ Look at the About box.

After you have examined PICTPeeker, it is time to study the code.

Inspecting the Program

First, look at the class diagram in figure 18.2. Spend a few minutes studying it because there are a number of new classes.

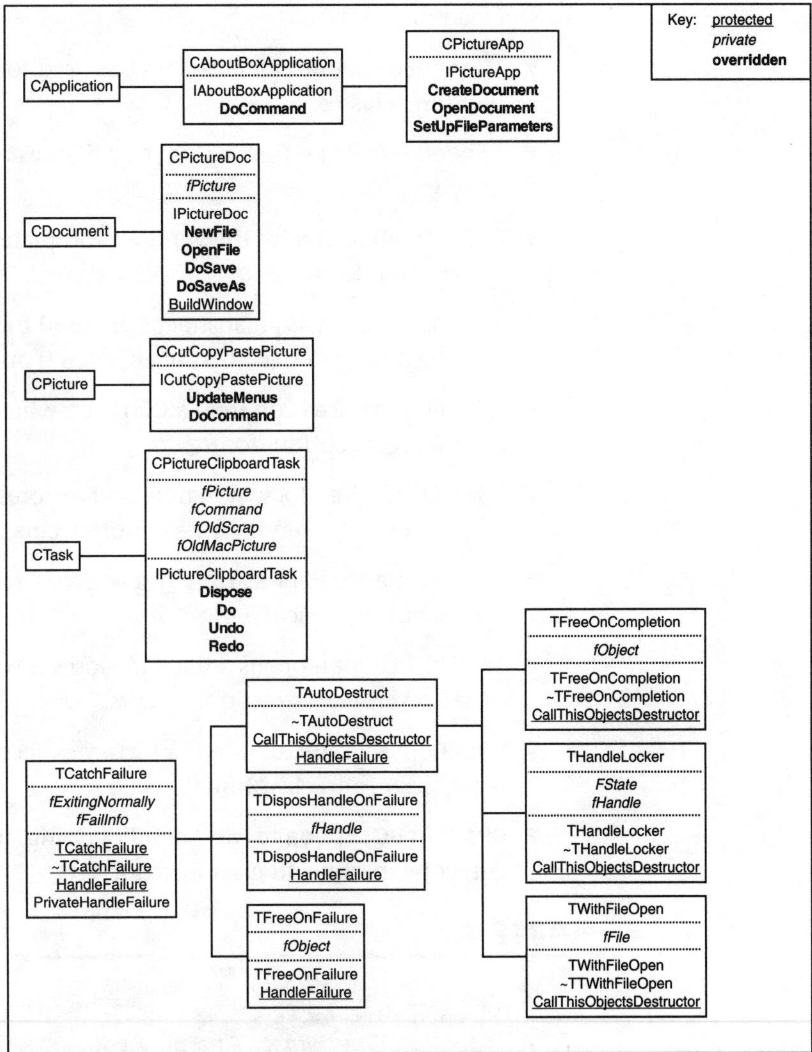

Figure 18.2. The class diagram for PICTPeeker.

Each of these classes is covered in detail later in this chapter. For now, look at the list below to get the gist of what each class controls:

- `CAboutBoxApplication` displays the About box.
- `CPictureApp` creates new documents and sets parameters for the Open dialog.
- `TCatchFailure` is an abstract class used for creating exception-handling classes.
- `TFreeOnFailure` frees a `CObject` if an exception occurs during its scope.
- `CPictureDoc` creates the window and picture pane and reads/writes the PICT to disk.
- `TAutoDestruct` is an abstract class used for stack-based objects that need their destructors called, even if an exception occurs.
- `TFreeOnCompletion` frees a `CObject` when its scope is exited, even if an exception occurs.
- `THandleLocker` locks a handle and restores its state when its scope is exited, even if an exception occurs.
- `TDisposHandleOnFailure` disposes of a handle if an exception occurs during its scope.
- `TWithFileOpen` opens a file and closes it when its scope is exited, even if an exception occurs.
- `CCutCopyPastePicture` is a picture object that supports cut, copy, paste, and clear functions.
- `CPictureClipboardTask` handles doing, undoing, and redoing cut, copy, paste, and clear functions.

NOTE

If you skipped Chapter 16, pay special attention to this note. The THINK Class Library uses a naming convention different from that described in Chapter 10. The TCL class names begin with `C`, instead of `T`, as you might expect. There also is no particular naming custom for data members in the TCL. In the interests of maintaining convention, Chapters 16-21 (which use the TCL) begin class names with C for all of the classes derived from TCL classes. Note, however, if the classes are independent of the TCL, they begin with the more standard T. Any new data members begin with f.

Look at the new class that handles the display of the About box first.

The CAboutBoxApplication Class

When the user chooses the About menu item, the CAboutBoxApplication class displays the About box. This new class also serves as the base class for PICTPeeker itself. Here is the class declaration:

```
class CAboutBoxApplication: public CApplication {
public:
    void    IAboutBoxApplication(short extraMasters,
      Size aRainyDayFund, Size aCriticalBalance,
      Size aToolboxBalance);

    virtual void   DoCommand(long theCommand);
};
```

The initialization method, IAboutBoxApplication, is quite straightforward as well:

```
void CAboutBoxApplication::IAboutBoxApplication(short extra-
  Masters, Size aRainyDayFund, Size aCriticalBalance,
  Size aToolboxBalance)
{
    IApplication(extraMasters, aRainyDayFund, aCriticalBalance,
      aToolboxBalance);
}
```

In the TCL, when a menu item is selected—whether by mouse or by a command key equivalent—the member function DoCommand is called for each bureaucrat in the chain of command. CAboutBoxApplication overrides DoCommand. It is on the lookout for the user selecting the About menu item.

```
void CAboutBoxApplication::DoCommand(long theCommand)
{
    const short kAboutBoxResourceID = 1024;

    switch (theCommand) {
    case cmdAbout:
        Str255 applicationName;
        short  appRefNum;
        Handle h;

        ::PositionDialog('ALRT', kAboutBoxResourceID);
        ::GetAppParms(applicationName, &appRefNum, &h);
        ::DisposHandle(h);
        ::ParamText(applicationName, NULL, NULL, NULL);
        Alert(kAboutBoxResourceID, NULL);
        break;
    default:
        CApplication::DoCommand(theCommand);
        break;
    }
}
```

DoCommand puts up the alert with ID 1024. This alert is customized to include the application name with the Toolbox call ParamText. The ALRT resource is shown in figure 18.3.

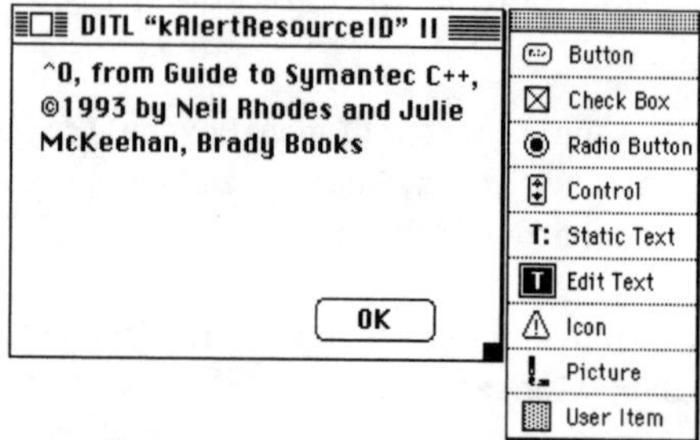

Figure 18.3. The About box alert in ResEdit.

The string ^0 in the alert is replaced with the application name by the call to ParamText. When you look at this alert in the running program it transforms into the one shown in figure 18.4.

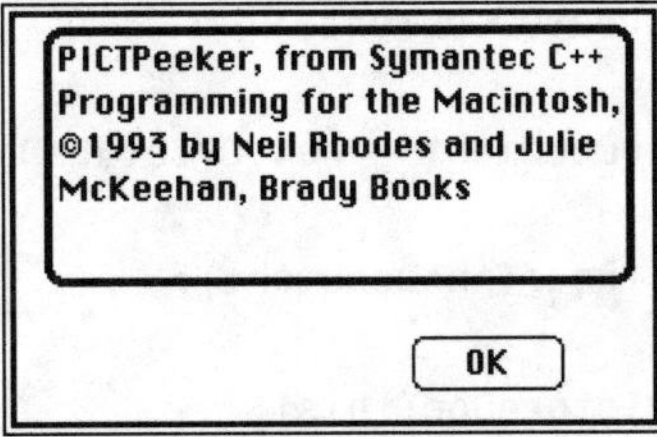

Figure 18.4. The About box alert as seen in PICTPeeker.

When the incoming command is not `cmdAbout`, the command is passed on to the default `DoCommand`.

The CPictApp Class

The `CPictApp` class takes advantage of the behavior of `CAboutBoxApplication` by deriving from it:

```
class CPictureApp: public CAboutBoxApplication {
public:
    void          IPictureApp();

    virtual void  CreateDocument();
    virtual void  OpenDocument(SFReply *macReply);
    virtual void  SetUpFileParameters();
};
```

The member functions also might look familiar. They are quite similar to the ones used in TextTyper (discussed in Chapter 17). Table 18.1 compares TextTyper's functions with those in this chapter. Listed below are `CAboutBoxApplication`'s member functions:

```
void CPictureApp::IPictureApp()
{
    const short   kExtraMasters =    1;
    const Size    kRainyDayFund =    45000;
    const Size    kCriticalBalance = 40000;
    const Size    kToolboxBalance =  20000;

    IAboutBoxApplication(kExtraMasters, kRainyDayFund,
      kCriticalBalance, kToolboxBalance);
}
```

```
void CPictureApp::CreateDocument()
{
    CPictureDoc *theDocument = new CPictureDoc;

    TFreeOnFailure freer(theDocument);

    theDocument->IPictureDoc(this);
    theDocument->NewFile();
}

void CPictureApp::OpenDocument(SFReply *macReply)
{
    CPictureDoc *theDocument = new CPictureDoc;

    TFreeOnFailure freer(theDocument);

    theDocument->IPictureDoc(this);
    theDocument->OpenFile(macReply);
}

void CPictureApp::SetUpFileParameters()
{
    CApplication::SetUpFileParameters();

    sfNumTypes = 1;
    sfFileTypes[0] = 'PICT';
    gSignature = 'C++3';
}
```

If you look at table 18.1, you see that `IPictureApp` and `ITextApp` are identical except for their names. The `SetUpFileParameters` function also is similar, except that the file type is not `'TXT'` but `'PICT'` and that PICTPeeker has a different signature. The substantial differences lie in the member function's handling of exceptions. The PICTPeeker code does not contain the exception handlers (TRY, CATCH, and ENDTRY) in `CreateDocument` and `OpenDocument`. Instead, these two routines use an object of the class `TFreeOnFailure`. The object makes sure that `theDocument` is disposed of if exceptions occur between the declaration of the object and the end of the routine.

Table 18.1. Comparing PICTPeeker with TextTyper Member Functions

<table>
<tr><th>PICTPeeker Functions</th><th>TextTyper Functions</th></tr>
<tr><td><pre>void CPictureApp::IPictureApp()
{
    const short   kExtraMasters =   1;
    const Size   kRainyDayFund =   45000;
    const Size   kCriticalBalance = 40000;
    const Size   kToolboxBalance = 20000;

    IAboutBoxApplication(kExtraMasters,
      kRainyDayFund, kCriticalBalance,
      kToolboxBalance);
}</pre></td><td><pre>void CTextApp::ITextApp()
{
    const short   kExtraMasters =   1;
    const Size   kRainyDayFund =   45000;
    const Size   kCriticalBalance = 40000;
    const Size   kToolboxBalance = 20000;

    IApplication(kExtraMasters, kRainyDayFund,
      kCriticalBalance, kToolboxBalance);
}</pre></td></tr>
<tr><td><pre>void CPictureApp::CreateDocument()
{
    CPictureDoc *theDocument = new CPictureDoc;

    TFreeOnFailure freer(theDocument);

    theDocument->IPictureDoc(this);
    theDocument->NewFile();
}</pre></td><td><pre>void CTextApp::CreateDocument()
{
    CTextDoc *theDocument = new CTextDoc;

    TRY
    {
        theDocument->ITextDoc(this);
        theDocument->NewFile();
    }
    CATCH
    {
    ForgetObject(theDocument);
    }
    ENDTRY;
}</pre></td></tr>
<tr><td><pre>void CPictureApp::OpenDocument(SFReply *macReply)
{
    CPictureDoc *theDocument = new CPictureDoc;</pre></td><td><pre>void CTextApp::OpenDocument(SFReply *macReply)
{
    CTextDoc *theDocument = new CTextDoc;</pre></td></tr>
</table>

continues

Table 18.1. Continued

<table>
<tr><th>PICTPeeker Functions</th><th>TextTyper Functions</th></tr>
<tr><td><pre>   TFreeOnFailure freer(theDocument);

    theDocument->IPictureDoc(this);
    theDocument->OpenFile(macReply);
}</pre></td><td><pre>   TRY
    {
        theDocument->ITextDoc(this);
        theDocument->OpenFile(macReply);
    }
    CATCH
    {
        ForgetObject(theDocument);
    }
    ENDTRY;
}</pre></td></tr>
<tr><td><pre>void CPictureApp::SetUpFileParameters()
{
    CApplication::SetUpFileParameters();

    sfNumTypes = 1;
    sfFileTypes[0] = 'PICT';
    gSignature = 'C++3';
}</pre></td><td><pre>void CTextApp::SetUpFileParameters()
{
    CApplication::SetUpFileParameters();

    sfNumTypes = 1;
    sfFileTypes[0] = 'TEXT';
    gSignature = 'C++2';
}</pre></td></tr>
</table>

The TFreeOnFailure Class

`TFreeOnFailure` is a new class that handles exceptions. Note that it is not derived from the TCL.

```
class TFreeOnFailure: public TCatchFailure {
public:
    TFreeOnFailure(CObject *object);
protected:
    virtual void HandleFailure(OSErr err, long message);
private:
    CObject *fObject;
};
```

```
TFreeOnFailure::TFreeOnFailure(CObject *object)
{
    fObject = object;
}

void TFreeOnFailure::HandleFailure(OSErr /*err*/, long /*message*/)
{
    if (fObject != NULL)
        fObject->Dispose();
}
```

The constructor takes a `CObject *` parameter, which it saves in `fObject`. The `HandleFailure` routine is overridden from the `TCatchFailure` base class. It is called if a failure occurs during the lifetime of the `TCatchFailure` object. Its only task is to dispose of the `fObject`.

The TCatchFailure Class

`TCatchFailure` is an abstract class that serves as a foundation for other beneficial classes. (Because it is such a useful base class, the way it works is less important than knowing how to create derived classes from it.) Take a look at how it handles exceptions. It uses a different method than the `TRY` macro. Instead of designating code within a function that handles an exception, `TCatchFailure` has a member function handle it. Listed below is the class declaration:

```
class TCatchFailure
{
protected:
    TCatchFailure();
    virtual ~TCatchFailure();
    virtual void HandleFailure(OSErr err, long message) = 0;
private:
    Boolean fExitingNormally;  // false if exiting due to failure
    pascal void PrivateHandleFailure(OSErr err, long message);
    FailInfo fFailInfo;
};
```

The HandleFailure member function is declared as a pure virtual function (=0). Derived classes always need to override it because this function has no default behavior of its own. The TFreeOnFailure derived class overrides it to dispose of an object.

Installing and Removing the Exception Handler

TCatchFailure uses the CatchFailures call to install an exception handler in its constructor:

```
TCatchFailure::TCatchFailure()
{
    ::CatchFailures(&fFailInfo, (HandlerFuncPtr)
      TCatchFailure::PrivateHandleFailure, (long) this);
    fExitingNormally = true;
}
```

After installing the exception handler, if an exception occurs, the member function TCatchFailure::PrivateHandleFailure is called.

If no exception occurs, then the destructor calls Success to remove the exception handler:

```
TCatchFailure::~TCatchFailure()
{
    if (fExitingNormally)
        ::Success();
}
```

Handling an Exception

If an exception occurs, the exception handler is executed:

```
pascal void TCatchFailure::PrivateHandleFailure(OSErr err, long
  message)
{
    fExitingNormally = false;
    HandleFailure(err, message);
}
```

PrivateHandleFailure calls HandleFailure. This is a member function that derived classes should override.

Now that you have seen how the base class is constructed, take a look at the number of classes you can build from the TCatchFailure abstract class.

The TDisposHandleOnFailure Class

The TDisposHandleOnFailure class is similar to the TFreeOnFailure class; however, rather than disposing an object in case of an exception, this class disposes a *handle*:

```
class TDisposHandleOnFailure: public TCatchFailure {
public:
    TDisposHandleOnFailure(Handle h);
protected:
    virtual void HandleFailure(OSErr err, long message);
private:
    Handle fHandle;
};
TDisposHandleOnFailure::TDisposHandleOnFailure(Handle h)
{
    fHandle = h;
}

void TDisposHandleOnFailure::HandleFailure(OSErr err, long message)
{
    if (fHandle != NULL)
        ::DisposHandle(fHandle);
}
```

You see how TDisposHandleOnFailure is used later in this chapter in CPictureDoc::OpenFile.

The TAutoDestruct Class

TAutoDestruct is another abstract class. Derived classes inherit the following behavior: If an exception occurs during the lifetime of a class, then its destructor is called. Such derived classes should not be allocated dynamically; instead, they should be declared globally or as automatic (stack-based) variables.

IMPORTANT

> ANSI C++ adds exception handling to C++. After C++ compilers implement this, the destructors of stack-based objects automatically are called when exceptions occur. This leads to the use of *resource acquisition classes,* a method of handling exceptions. These classes have constructors that acquire a resource and destructors that release the resource.

The resource acquisition class idiom is used by classes derived from TAutoDestruct:

```
class TAutoDestruct: public TCatchFailure {
public:
    virtual ~TAutoDestruct();
protected:
    virtual void HandleFailure(OSErr err, long message);
};

TAutoDestruct::~TAutoDestruct()
{
}

void TAutoDestruct::HandleFailure(OSErr /*err*/, long /*message*/
)
{
    this->~TAutoDestruct(); //explicit virtual call to destructor
}
```

The HandleFailure routine needs to call the destructor. It also must ensure that derived class destructors are called as well (that is, the call must go through the v-table).

TAutoDestruct has a number of derived classes based on it. The next sections take a look at each of these.

The TFreeOnCompletion Class

The TFreeOnCompletion class frees a CObject when its destructor is called:

```
class TFreeOnCompletion: public TAutoDestruct {
public:
    TFreeOnCompletion(CObject *object);
    virtual ~TFreeOnCompletion();

private:
    CObject *fObject;
};

TFreeOnCompletion::TFreeOnCompletion(CObject *object)
{
    fObject = object;
}

TFreeOnCompletion::~TFreeOnCompletion()
{
    if (fObject != NULL)
        fObject->Dispose();
}
```

The THandleLocker Class

The `THandleLocker` class locks a handle in its constructor and then restores the handle state when its destructor gets called:

```
class THandleLocker: public TAutoDestruct {
public:
    THandleLocker(Handle h);
    virtual ~THandleLocker();
private:
    Handle fHandle;
    char fState;
};

THandleLocker::THandleLocker(Handle h)
{
    fHandle = h;
    fState = ::HGetState(fHandle);
    ::HLock(h);
}
```

```
THandleLocker::~THandleLocker()
{
    ::HSetState(fHandle, fState);
}
```

The destructor calls `HSetState` to restore the handle's state, rather than using `HUnlock`. It performs this way because the handle cannot start out locked.

The TWithFileOpen Class

The `TWithFileOpen` class has a constructor that opens a file and destructor that closes it:

```
class TWithFileOpen: public TAutoDestruct {
public:
    TWithFileOpen(CFile *theFile, SignedByte permission);
    virtual ~TWithFileOpen();

private:
    CFile *fFile;
};

TWithFileOpen::TWithFileOpen(CFile *theFile,
  SignedByte permission)
{
    theFile->Open(permission);
    fFile = theFile;
}

TWithFileOpen::~TWithFileOpen()
{
    if (fFile != NULL)
        fFile->Close();
}
```

That is all there is to the exception classes. You can now use these sparkling new classes to simplify dealing with exceptions in other parts of the program.

The CPictureDoc Class

The CPictureDoc class is quite similar to the CTextDoc class of Chapter 17. It manipulates a PICT document, however, instead of text:

```
class CPictureDoc: public CDocument {
public:
    void           IPictureDoc(CApplication *supervisor);

    virtual void    NewFile();
    virtual void    OpenFile(SFReply *macReply);
    virtual Boolean DoSave();
    virtual Boolean DoSaveAs(SFReply *macSFReply);
protected:
    virtual void    BuildWindow();
private:
    CPicture  *fPicture;
};

void CPictureDoc::IPictureDoc(CApplication *supervisor)
{
    const Boolean kPrintable = TRUE;

    IDocument(supervisor, kPrintable);
}

void CPictureDoc::NewFile()
{
    BuildWindow();

    Str255 wTitle;
    short wCount;
    Str255 wNumber;

    itsWindow->GetTitle(wTitle);
    wCount = gDecorator->GetWCount();
    ::NumToString(wCount, wNumber);
    ::ConcatPStrings(wTitle, "\p-");
    ::ConcatPStrings(wTitle, wNumber);
    itsWindow->SetTitle(wTitle);

    itsWindow->Select();
}
```

```
void CPictureDoc::BuildWindow()
{
    const short   kWINDResourceID =        500;
    const Boolean kWindowFloats =          TRUE;
    const Boolean kFitHorizontal =         TRUE;
    const Boolean kFitVertical =           TRUE;
    const Boolean kHasHorizontalScrollbar =TRUE;
    const Boolean kHasVerticalScrollbar =  TRUE;
    const Boolean kHasGrowBox =            TRUE;
    const Boolean kRedraw =                TRUE;

    CWindow *aWindow = new CWindow;
    aWindow->IWindow(kWINDResourceID, !kWindowFloats, gDesktop,
      this);
    itsWindow = aWindow;
    CScrollPane *theScrollPane = new CScrollPane;
    theScrollPane->IScrollPane(aWindow, this, 10, 10, 0, 0,
      sizELASTIC, sizELASTIC, kHasHorizontalScrollbar,
      kHasVerticalScrollbar, kHasGrowBox);
    theScrollPane->FitToEnclFrame(kFitHorizontal, kFitVertical);

    CCutCopyPastePicture *thePane = new CCutCopyPastePicture;
    thePane->ICutCopyPastePicture(theScrollPane, this, 1, 1, 0, 0,
      sizELASTIC, sizELASTIC);
    itsGopher = thePane;
    itsMainPane = thePane;
    fPicture = thePane;
    theScrollPane->InstallPanorama(thePane);
    thePane->FitToEnclosure(kFitHorizontal, kFitVertical);

    gDecorator->PlaceNewWindow(itsWindow);
}

Boolean CPictureDoc::DoSaveAs(SFReply *macSFReply)
{
    if (itsFile != NULL)
        itsFile->Dispose();

    CDataFile *theDataFile = new CDataFile;
    itsFile = theDataFile;
    theDataFile->IDataFile();
```

```
    theDataFile->SFSpecify(macSFReply);
    if (theDataFile->ExistsOnDisk())
        theDataFile->ThrowOut();
    theDataFile->CreateNew(gSignature, 'PICT');

    itsWindow->SetTitle(macSFReply->fName);

    return(DoSave());
}
```

Look at the differences. Here, BuildWindow creates a TCutCopy-PastePicture instead of a TEditText. There are more pronounced differences in DoSave and OpenFile:

```
void CPictureDoc::OpenFile(SFReply *macReply)
{
    CDataFile    *theDataFile;
    Handle        theData;
    Str63         theName;
    OSErr         theError;

    theDataFile = new CDataFile;

    itsFile = theDataFile;

    theDataFile->IDataFile();
    theDataFile->SFSpecify(macReply);

    Handle theMacPicture = ::NewHandleCanFail(0);
    ::FailNIL(theMacPicture);
    {
        TWithFileOpen fileOpener(theDataFile, fsRdPerm);
        TDisposHandleOnFailure handleFreer(theMacPicture);

        long thePictureLength = theDataFile->GetLength() -
          kPICTHeaderLength;
        if (thePictureLength <= 0)
            ::FailOSErr(eofErr);
        theDataFile->SetMark(kPICTHeaderLength, fsFromStart);
        ::ResizeHandleCanFail(theMacPicture, thePictureLength);
        ::FailMemError();
        {
            THandleLocker lock(theMacPicture);
```

```
            theDataFile->ReadSome(*theMacPicture,
              thePictureLength);
        }
        BuildWindow();
    }
    fPicture->SetMacPicture((PicHandle) theMacPicture);

    itsFile->GetName(theName);
    itsWindow->SetTitle(theName);

    itsWindow->Select();
}

Boolean CPictureDoc::DoSave()
{
    Handle        theData;

    if (itsFile == NULL)
        return(DoSaveFileAs());
    else {
        CDataFile *theDataFile = (CDataFile *) itsFile;

        Handle theMacPicture = (Handle) fPicture->
          GetMacPicture();
        {
            TWithFileOpen fileOpener(theDataFile, fsWrPerm);
            char    zeros[kPICTHeaderLength];

            for (int i = 0; i < kPICTHeaderLength; i++)
                zeros[i] = 0;
            theDataFile->WriteSome(zeros, sizeof(zeros));
            THandleLocker lock(theMacPicture);
            theDataFile->WriteSome(*theMacPicture,
              ::GetHandleSize(theMacPicture));
        }
        dirty = FALSE;
        return(TRUE);
    }
}
```

Both DoSave and OpenFile extensively use the exception-handling classes just created. The functions are complicated further by the fact that the PICT files have a 512-byte header that must be skipped or written. The basic structure, however, is the same as the corresponding functions in CTextDoc.

The CCutCopyPastePicture Class

The CCutCopyPastePicture class is derived from the TCL class CPicture and adds support for the cut, copy, paste, and clear menu items:

```
class CCutCopyPastePicture: public CPicture {
public:
void ICutCopyPastePicture(CView *anEnclosure, CBureaucrat
  *aSupervisor, short aWidth, short aHeight, short aHEncl,
  short aVEncl, SizingOption aHSizing, SizingOption aVSizing);

   virtual void UpdateMenus();
   virtual void DoCommand(long cmd);
};
```

Its initialization method is simple:

```
void CCutCopyPastePicture::ICutCopyPastePicture(CView
  *anEnclosure, CBureaucrat *aSupervisor, short aWidth,
  short aHeight, short aHEncl, short aVEncl,
  SizingOption aHSizing, SizingOption aVSizing)
{
    IPicture(anEnclosure, aSupervisor, aWidth, aHeight,
      aHEncl, aVEncl, aHSizing, aVSizing);
}
```

It also enables the clipboard menu items:

```
void CCutCopyPastePicture::UpdateMenus()
{
    CPicture::UpdateMenus();

    if (GetMacPicture() != NULL) {
        gBartender->EnableCmd(cmdCopy);
        gBartender->EnableCmd(cmdCut);
        gBartender->EnableCmd(cmdClear);
    }
```

```
    if (gClipboard->GetData('PICT', NULL))
        gBartender->EnableCmd(cmdPaste);
}
```

UpdateMenus gets called to enable menu items when the user clicks on the menu bar (or uses a command key equivalent). The TCL dims the menu items before calls to UpdateMenus. This function also can selectively enable certain menu items and ignore the rest. The TCL ensures that ignored items remain disabled.

CBartender is a class that handles the menu bar. The global variable gBartender is the one and only CBartender object. Its member function, GetMacPicture, enables cut, copy, and clear if there is currently a picture. It also enables paste if the clipboard contains PICT data.

In tandem with UpdateMenus, CCutCopyPastePicture must actually carry out the menu commands with DoCommand:

```
void CCutCopyPastePicture::DoCommand(long cmd)
{
    switch (cmd) {
    case cmdCopy:
    case cmdCut:
    case cmdClear:
    case cmdPaste:
        CPictureClipboardTask  *clipTask = new
CPictureClipboardTask;
        {
            TFreeOnFailure freer(clipTask);

            clipTask->IPictureClipboardTask(this, cmd);
        }
        itsLastTask = clipTask;
        if (cmd == cmdCopy)
            itsSupervisor->NotifyClean(clipTask);
        else
            itsSupervisor->Notify(clipTask);
        clipTask->Do();
        break;

    default:
        CPicture::DoCommand(cmd);
    }
}
```

The class CPictureClipboardTask handles doing, undoing, and redoing of cut, copy, paste, and clear operations. DoCommand must perform the following:

- Create one of these objects.
- Initialize it.
- Tell it to do its task.

The TCL handles undo and redo using the CPane data member itsLastTask (where the member function saves its task).

Notify and NotifyClean alert the supervisor that a task is going to be executed. The document, in turn, responds to Notify by setting its dirty data member to true. NotifyClean, on the other hand, does not change dirty.

The CPictureClipboardTask Class

The actual code for CPictureClipboardTask is listed below:

```
class CPictureClipboardTask: public CTask {
public:
    void IPictureClipboardTask(CPicture *thePicture,
      long command);

    virtual void Dispose();
    virtual void Do();
    virtual void Undo();
    virtual void Redo();
private:
    CPicture *fPicture;
    long      fCommand;
    Handle    fOldScrap;
    PicHandle fOldMacPicture;
};
```

Derived classes of CTask must override Do, Undo, and Redo to carry out, undo, and redo their operations.

In this class, the data member, fOldScrap, holds the old contents of the scrap, while fOldMacPicture holds the old PicHandle in the CPicture.

Initialization Function

The initialization member function, IPictureClipboardTask, initializes the data members and then calls ITask:

```
void CPictureClipboardTask::IPictureClipboardTask(CPicture
  *thePicture, long command)
{
    fOldMacPicture = NULL;
    fOldScrap = NULL;
    fPicture = thePicture;
    fCommand = command;
    ITask(command - cmdCut + 2);  // cmdTyping is first string,
                                     cmdCut is next
}
```

The parameter to ITask is an index from the task names 'STR#' resource. This index contains text for the Undo menu. Thus, when the user chooses Cut, the Undo menu shows the text "Undo Cut," rather than the less descriptive "Undo" label.

Doing the Command

Listed below is the function that actually carries out the command:

```
void CPictureClipboardTask::Do()
{
    if (fCommand != cmdClear) {
        Handle h;

        gClipboard->GetData('PICT', &h);
        fOldScrap = h;
    }
    fOldMacPicture = fPicture->GetMacPicture();
    Redo();
}
```

Unless the command is Clear, Do saves the old clipboard. This is needed for Undo. Do then saves the current PicHandle and calls Redo, which contains the code common to both Do and Redo.

Redoing the Command

Redo is called by Do the first time a command is executed. It also is called whenever the user selects Redo:

```
void CPictureClipboardTask::Redo()
{
   if (fCommand == cmdCopy || fCommand == cmdCut) {
        gClipboard->EmptyScrap();
        gClipboard->PutData('PICT', (Handle) fOldMacPicture);
    }
    if (fCommand == cmdCut || fCommand == cmdClear) {
        fPicture->SetPosition((LongPt *) &kZeroZeroPt);
        fPicture->SetMacPicture(NULL);
    }
    if (fCommand == cmdPaste) {
        fPicture->SetPosition((LongPt *) &kZeroZeroPt);
        fPicture->SetMacPicture((PicHandle) fOldScrap);
     }
    if (fCommand != cmdCopy)
        fPicture->Refresh();
    undone = FALSE;
}
```

Redo modifies the clipboard and the picture. Lastly, it sets the CTask data member undone to FALSE, signifying the command has not been undone. This data member is, in turn, used by the Dispose function.

IMPORTANT

This is an important function, so read through this code four times, once for each different command. Be certain you understand how it works.

Undoing the Command

The member function Undo restores any change to the clipboard and any change to the PicHandle:

```
void CPictureClipboardTask::Undo()
{
   if (fCommand == cmdCopy || fCommand == cmdCut) {
        gClipboard->EmptyScrap();
        if (fOldScrap != NULL)
            gClipboard->PutData('PICT', fOldScrap);
    }
    if (fCommand != cmdCopy) {
        fPicture->SetPosition((LongPt *) &kZeroZeroPt);
        fPicture->SetMacPicture(fOldMacPicture);
        fPicture->Refresh();
    }
    undone = TRUE;
}
```

Notice that this time the CTask data member undone is set to TRUE. This signifies that the task has indeed been undone.

Disposing of Data

As a new undoable task is created, any existing undoable task is jettisoned—it is no longer undoable. When a task can no longer be undone or redone, the TCL gets rid of it by calling the member function Dispose:

```
void CPictureClipboardTask::Dispose()
{
    if (!IsUndone()) {
        switch (fCommand) {
        case cmdCut:
            ::DisposHandle((Handle) fOldMacPicture);
            ::DisposHandle(fOldScrap);
            break;
        case cmdClear:
            ::DisposHandle((Handle) fOldMacPicture);
            break;
        case cmdPaste:
            ::DisposHandle((Handle) fOldMacPicture);
            // old scrap is now the picture
            break;
        case cmdCopy:
            // old picture remains the picture
```

```
            ::DisposHandle(fOldScrap);
            break;
        }
    } else
        if (fOldScrap != NULL)
            ::DisposHandle(fOldScrap);
    CTask::Dispose();
}
```

Notice that the function disposes of data differently, depending upon what command is executed and whether the task has been undone.

PICTPeeker's Main Program

Finally, the main program arrives. By now, it should seem like an old friend:

```
void main()
{
    CPictureApp *app;

    app = new CPictureApp;
    app->IPictureApp();
    app->Run();
    app->Exit();
}
```

The Resources

Other than different icons, the only new resources are those for the About box:

```
resource 'ALRT' (1024, "kAlertResourceID") {
    {40, 40, 184, 276},
    1024,
    {    /* array: 4 elements */
        OK, visible, sound1,
        OK, visible, sound1,
        OK, visible, sound1,
        OK, visible, sound1
    }
};
```

```
resource 'DITL' (1024, "kAlertResourceID") {
    {
        {5, 12, 93, 228},
        StaticText {
            disabled, "^0, from Symantec C++ Programming for the
              Macintosh, ©1993 b"
            "y Neil Rhodes and Julie McKeehan, Brady "
            "Books"
        },
        {116, 147, 136, 205},
        Button {
            enabled,
            "OK"
        }
    }
};
```

Summary

PICTPeeker contains three important new features:

- A better way to do exception handling.
- A working About box.
- The capability to undo and redo cut, copy, paste, and clear operations.

You saw that many of PICTPeeker's functions were very similar to those used to create TextTyper in Chapter 17. You also witnessed the creation of classes for dealing with exception handling and how to use those classes.

19

Tick-Tock: Building a Clock Application

This application, Tick-Tock, is a simple desk accessory-like clock. It displays the time in digital or analog fashion. Surprising as it may seem, this small program contains valuable functionality features, such as managing idling states, creating preference files, and performing off-screen drawing. Because time waits for no one, move ahead to the program.

The Tick-Tock Program

As with previous programs in this part, Tick-Tock is built with the TCL. This program displays a working clock (in either digital or analog format) on the screen in either the foreground or background. Figure 19.1 gives you a view of time standing still in a screen dump of Tick-Tock.

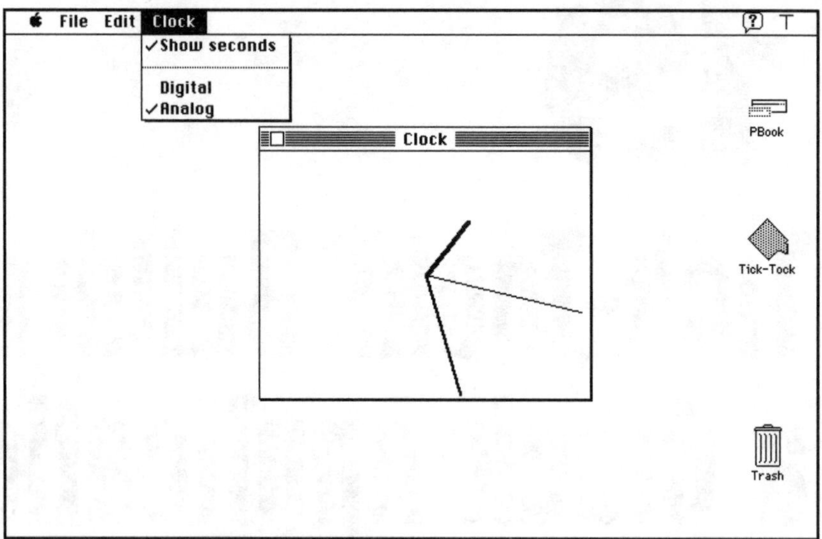

Figure 19.1. A view of time standing still in Tick-Tock.

Compiling the Program

Copy the Tick-Tock folder from the source code disk. Open the Tick-Tock. project and then choose Run. All the files in the project need to be recompiled, so this takes a few tick-tocks.

Running the Program

After you have the program running, test it out. Try the following time-tested ideas:

- Use the Clock menu to switch back and forth from digital to analog.
- Try turning the second hand on and off.
- Resize the window by dragging the lower-right corner.
- Move the Clock window, quit, and then run the program again. The window should reappear in the new location.

After you have played with the program, it is time to move on to the code.

Inspecting the Program

Figure 19.2 shows you the class diagram for Tick-Tock. As the diagram shows, there are a number of new classes.

The classes are covered in detail later in this chapter. Listed below are short descriptions to help you get started:

- `CClockApp` creates the Clock window.
- `CQuitOnCloseWindow` quits the application when the window is closed.
- `CSaveRestoreSizeWindow` saves its location and size at closing and restores it when opened.
- `CClockPane` draws the clock in either analog or digital mode.
- `CDawdleBureaucratChore` calls the clock pane's `Dawdle` member function when the clock is not the frontmost window.

The CClockApp Class

The `CClockApp` class has `CAboutBoxApplication` as its base class. As you might expect from the last chapter, the code is pretty straightforward. Listed below is the class definition:

```
class CClockApp: public CAboutBoxApplication
{
public:
    void IClockApp(void);
};
```

The initialization is similar to RandomRectangle's initialization in Chapter 16:

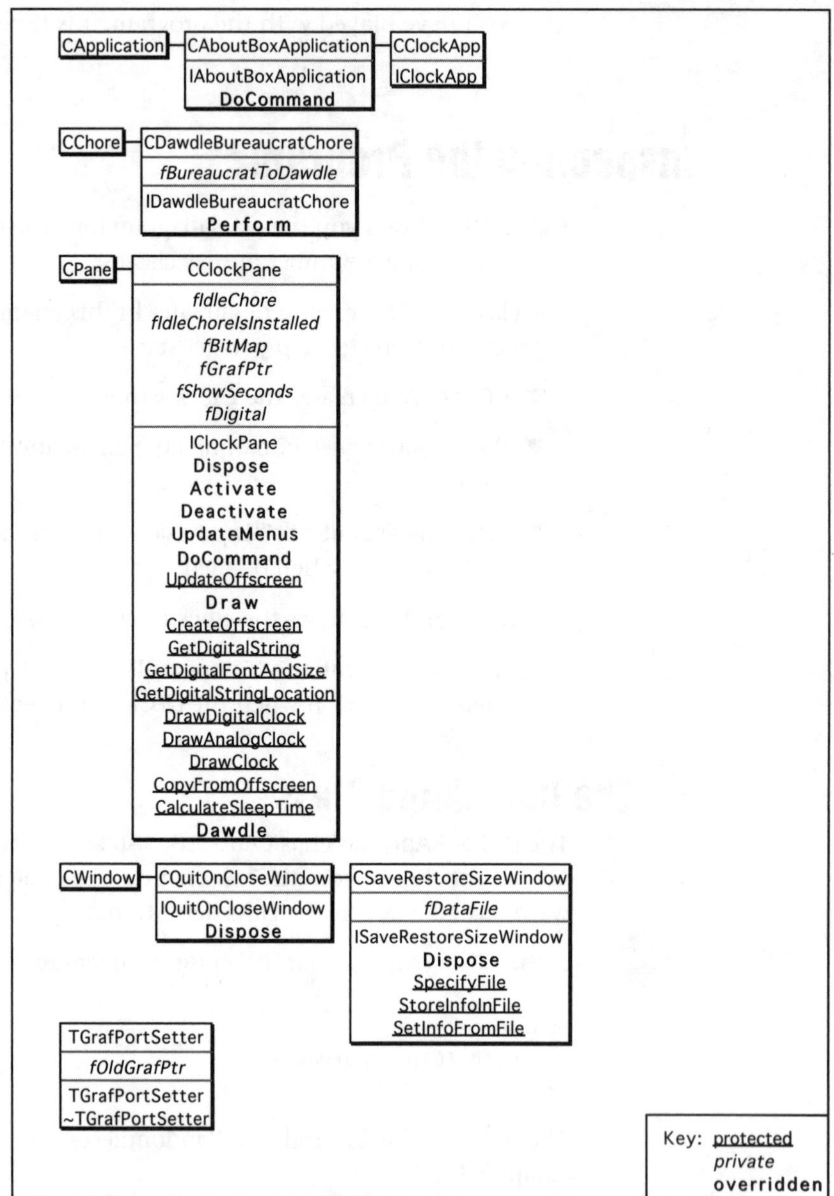

Figure 19.2. The Tick-Tock class diagram.

```
void CClockApp::IClockApp(void)
{
    const Boolean     kFloatingWindow = TRUE;
    const short       kMinWindowHeight = 30;
    const short       kMinWindowWidth = 30;

    IAboutBoxApplication(kExtraMasters, kRainyDayFund,
      kCriticalBalance, kToolboxBalance);

    CDirector *aDirector = new CDirector;
    aDirector->IDirector(this);

    CSaveRestoreSizeWindow *aWindow = new CSaveRestoreSizeWindow;
    aWindow->ISaveRestoreSizeWindow(kWINDStarter,
      !kFloatingWindow, gDesktop, aDirector);
    aDirector->itsWindow = aWindow;
    Rect sizeRect = aWindow->sizeRect;
    sizeRect.top = kMinWindowHeight;
    sizeRect.left = kMinWindowWidth;
    aWindow->SetSizeRect(&sizeRect);

    aWindow->Select();
    CClockPane *thePane = new CClockPane;
    thePane->IClockPane(aWindow, aDirector, 0, 0, 0, 0,
      sizELASTIC, sizELASTIC);
    thePane->FitToEnclosure(TRUE, TRUE);
    aDirector->itsGopher = thePane;
}
```

The only substantial difference between the two programs' initializations is the call to `SetSizeRect` for the window in Tick-Tock. This sets the minimum size to which the user can resize the window. Besides this and a few other minor differences, the initialization in this program is handled the same way as in Chapter 16.

The CQuitOnCloseWindow Class

The `CQuitOnCloseWindow` class provides desk accessory-like behavior to Tick-Tock: If you close the Clock window, the application quits. The class has two member functions:

```
class CQuitOnCloseWindow: public CWindow {
public:
    void IQuitOnCloseWindow(short WINDid, Boolean aFloating,
         CDesktop *anEnclosure, CDirector *aSupervisor);
    virtual void Dispose();
};
```

The class's initialization method is trivial:

```
void CQuitOnCloseWindow::IQuitOnCloseWindow(short WINDid, Boolean
  aFloating, CDesktop *anEnclosure, CDirector *aSupervisor)
{
    IWindow(WINDid, aFloating, anEnclosure, aSupervisor);
}
```

The `Dispose` method is not much more complex:

```
void CQuitOnCloseWindow::Dispose()
{
    CWindow::Dispose();

    gApplication->Quit();
}
```

`CWindow::Dispose` manages the normal window closing behavior, while the `Quit` member function of `CApplication` handles exiting the program altogether.

The CSaveRestoreSizeWindow Class

The `CSaveRestoreSizeWindow` class is responsible for saving the window position and location at closing and restoring them when opening. It saves this information in a preferences file that is located in the Preferences folder in the System folder. `CSaveRestoreSizeWindow` is derived from `CQuitOnCloseWindow`:

```
class CSaveRestoreSizeWindow: public CQuitOnCloseWindow {
public:

    void ISaveRestoreSizeWindow(
      short        windID,
      Boolean      aFloating,
      CDesktop     *anEnclosure,
      CDirector    *aSupervisor);
```

```
    virtual void Dispose();

protected:
    virtual void StoreInfoInFile(CDataFile *aFile);
    virtual void SetInfoFromFile(CDataFile *aFile);
    virtual void SpecifyFile(CFile *aFile);

private:
    CDataFile    *fDataFile;
};
```

CSaveRestoreSizeWindow provides an initialization function and then overrides Dispose. Next, it presents three utility functions. Last, CSaveRestoreSizeWindow stores a CDataFile as a member, which it uses to deal with the preferences file.

The class's initialization method creates the fDataFile data member and attempts to read information from the specified file:

```
void CSaveRestoreSizeWindow::ISaveRestoreSizeWindow(
  short      windID,
  Boolean    aFloating,
  CDesktop   *anEnclosure,
  CDirector  *aSupervisor)
{
    fDataFile= NULL;
    IQuitOnCloseWindow(windID, aFloating, anEnclosure,
      aSupervisor);

    fDataFile = new CDataFile;
    fDataFile->IDataFile();
    SpecifyFile(fDataFile);
    SetInfoFromFile(fDataFile);
}
```

When the window is disposed of, the member function Dispose saves the window's information to the preferences file and then removes its data member:

```
void CSaveRestoreSizeWindow::Dispose()
{
    StoreInfoInFile(fDataFile);
    ForgetObject(fDataFile);
    CQuitOnCloseWindow::Dispose();
}
```

The member function SpecifyFile specifies the location of the preferences file:

```
void CSaveRestoreSizeWindow::SpecifyFile(CFile *aFile)
{
    short vRefNum;
    long  dirID;

    FailOSErr(FindFolder(kOnSystemDisk, kPreferencesFolderType,
       kCreateFolder, &vRefNum,&dirID));
    aFile->SpecifyHFS("\pTick-Tock Preferences", vRefNum, dirID);
}
```

SpecifyFile calls FindFolder, a Toolbox routine. This routine returns in its parameters the volume reference number and directory ID of the Preferences folder on the system disk. If the directory does not exist, FindFolder creates it. SpecifyFile then sets the CFile to refer to the Tick-Tock Preferences file in the Preferences folder.

StoreInfoInFile stores the window position and location in the preferences file as a rectangle:

```
void CSaveRestoreSizeWindow::StoreInfoInFile(CDataFile *aFile)
{
    if (!aFile->ExistsOnDisk())
        aFile->CreateNew('C++5', 'PREF');

    aFile->Open(fsWrPerm);

    Rect     theWindowLocSize = macPort->portRect;

    {
        TGrafPortSetter setPort(macPort);

        ::LocalToGlobal((Point *) &theWindowLocSize.top);
        ::LocalToGlobal((Point *) &theWindowLocSize.bottom);
    }

    TRY {
        aFile->WriteSome((Ptr) &theWindowLocSize,
          sizeof(theWindowLocSize));
    }
```

```
    CATCH {
        NO_PROPAGATE;  // not writing window location isn't fatal
    }
    ENDTRY;
    aFile->Close();
}
```

If the file does not yet exist, CSaveRestoreSizeWindow creates it. It then gets the local coordinates that form the bounds of the window and converts them to global coordinates. Note that it temporarily must set the port using a TGrafPortSetter because LocalToGlobal converts based on the coordinates of the current window.

The call to WriteSome is within a TRY block. Note that you need to revert to the TRY, CATCH, and ENDTRY macros for handling exceptions in this case. This is because the CATCH portion of the exception handler is unusual—it calls NO_PROPOGATE and thereby stops the exception from propagating any further. After the exception, the code after ENDTRY is executed, and this action closes the file. If the exception had continued to propagate, it would send an alert to the user. Because this exception does not affect the functioning of the program in any substantial way, an alert is unnecessary for such a minor error.

SetInfoFromFile reads the location and size of the window from the preferences file, if it exists:

```
void CSaveRestoreSizeWindow::SetInfoFromFile(CDataFile *aFile)
{
    if (aFile->ExistsOnDisk()) {
        Rect    portRect;

        aFile->Open(fsRdPerm);

        TRY {
            aFile->ReadSome((Ptr) &portRect, sizeof(portRect));
            Move(portRect.left, portRect.top);
            ChangeSize(portRect.right - portRect.left,
              portRect.bottom - portRect.top);
        }
        CATCH {
            NO_PROPAGATE;  // not reading window loc. isn't fatal
        }
```

```
        ENDTRY;
        aFile->Close();
    }
}
```

SetInfoFromFile first checks to see if the file exists. If it finds the preferences file, it performs the following actions:

- Opens the file.
- Reads the rectangle information.
- Sets the location with Move.
- Sets the size with ChangeSize.

An exception handler is again used to prevent propagation of the error. Failing to read the stored information is not important enough to be brought to the user's attention.

The CDawdleBureaucratChore Class

The CDawdleBureaucratChore class calls the clock pane's Dawdle function, even when the clock is not the active window. The TCL's CApplication class keeps a list of idle chores whose Perform member function is called when nothing else is occurring.

NOTE

> You may remember that the rectangles in Chapter 16 stopped drawing if another window or application was brought to the front. While this might have been acceptable for the rectangles, it is not for a clock. Tick-Tock is the kind of application the user is likely to keep in a background window. If it is in the background, the user is sure to want the clock to keep ticking along.

Following is the class declaration:

```
class CDawdleBureaucratChore: public CChore {
public:
    void        IDawdleBureaucratChore(CBureaucrat *theBureaucrat);
    virtual void    Perform(long *maxSleep);

private:
    CBureaucrat     *fBureaucratToDawdle;
};
```

The class is initialized with a bureaucrat (in this program, the bureaucrat is the clock pane). `CDawdleBureaucratChore` stores that bureaucrat in a data member, `fBureaucratToDawdle`. It does so in its initialization function:

```
void CDawdleBureaucratChore::IDawdleBureaucratChore(CBureaucrat
  *theBureaucrat)
{
    fBureaucratToDawdle = theBureaucrat;
}
```

In turn, `fBureaucratToDawdle` gets used as a data member in `Perform`:

```
void CDawdleBureaucratChore::Perform(long *maxSleep)
{
    fBureaucratToDawdle->Dawdle(maxSleep);
}
```

The CClockPane Class

`CClockPane` is the class that actually draws the clock:

```
class CClockPane: public CPane {
public:
    void  IClockPane(CView *anEnclosure, CBureaucrat
      *aSupervisor,  short aWidth, short aHeight, short aHEncl,
      short aVEncl, SizingOption aHSizing, SizingOption
      aVSizing);

    virtual void   Dispose(void);

    virtual void   Draw(Rect *area);
    virtual void   Activate(void);
    virtual void   Deactivate(void);
```

```
    virtual void   Dawdle(long    *maxSleep);

    virtual void   UpdateMenus();
    virtual void   DoCommand(long theCommand);

protected:
    enum {cmdShowSeconds = 1024, cmdDigital=1025,
      cmdAnalog=1026};

    virtual void   DrawClock(const Rect &clockSize);
    virtual void   CopyFromOffscreen(const Rect &areaToCopy);
    virtual void   CreateOffscreen(const Rect &area);
    virtual void   UpdateOffscreen(const Rect &area);
    virtual long   CalculateSleepTime();
    virtual void   DrawAnalogClock(const Rect &clockSize,
      unsigned long now);
    virtual void    DrawDigitalClock(const Rect &clockSize,
      unsigned long now);
    virtual void   GetDigitalString(unsigned long now, Str255 s);
    virtual void   GetDigitalFontAndSize(const Str255 s, const
      Rect &clockSize, short *font, short *size);
    virtual void   GetDigitalStringLocation(const Str255 s, const
      Rect &clockSize, short *h, short *v);

private:

    CDawdleBureaucratChore      *fIdleChore;
    Boolean                     fIdleChoreIsInstalled;
    BitMap                      fBitMap;
    GrafPtr                     fGrafPtr;
    Boolean                     fShowSeconds;
    Boolean                     fDigital;
};
```

As you might have expected, this is a complex class that overrides a number of functions and provides some new member functions. It also stores a BitMap member and GrafPtr which it uses for off-screen drawing.

The initialization function must do a number of things:

```
void CClockPane::IClockPane(CView *anEnclosure, CBureaucrat
  *aSupervisor, short aWidth, short aHeight, short aHEncl, short
  aVEncl, SizingOption aHSizing, SizingOption aVSizing)
{
    fIdleChore = NULL;
    fIdleChoreIsInstalled = FALSE;
    fBitMap.baseAddr = NULL;
    fGrafPtr = NULL;
    SetRect(&fBitMap.bounds, 0, 0, 0, 0);

    IPane(anEnclosure, aSupervisor, aWidth, aHeight, aHEncl,
      aVEncl, aHSizing, aVSizing);

    fIdleChore = new CDawdleBureaucratChore;
    fIdleChore->IDawdleBureaucratChore(this);
    fGrafPtr = (GrafPtr) ::NewPtrCanFail(sizeof(GrafPort));
    ::FailNIL(fGrafPtr);
    ::OpenPort(fGrafPtr);

    fDigital = false;
    fShowSeconds = true;
}
```

The initialization function creates a `CDawdleBureacratChore`, but does not yet install that chore in the application's idle list—a task reserved for when the pane becomes deactivated. It also creates and opens a GrafPort that is used for off-screen drawing.

The `Dispose` function cleans up quite a bit for `CClockPane`:

```
void CClockPane::Dispose(void)
{
    if (fIdleChoreIsInstalled)
        gApplication->CancelIdleChore(fIdleChore);
    ::ForgetObject(fIdleChore);
    if (fBitMap.baseAddr != NULL)
        ::DisposPtr(fBitMap.baseAddr);
    if (fGrafPtr != NULL) {
        ::ClosePort(fGrafPtr);
        ::DisposPtr((Ptr) fGrafPtr);
    }
}
```

First, it removes the chore from the application's idle list, if it is currently installed there. It also frees memory occupied by the off-screen BitMap member and GrafPort.

`CClockPane` then uses its two member functions, `Activate` and `Deactivate`, to install and deinstall `CBureaucratDawdleChore`. The code for these two functions is simple:

```
void CClockPane::Activate(void)
{
    CPane::Activate();
    if (fIdleChoreIsInstalled) {
        gApplication->CancelIdleChore(fIdleChore);
        fIdleChoreIsInstalled = false;
      }
}

void CClockPane::Deactivate(void)
{
    CPane::Deactivate();
    gApplication->AssignIdleChore(fIdleChore);
    fIdleChoreIsInstalled = true;
}
```

These routines are called when the pane's window is activated or deactivated.

The `UpdateMenus` function handles the updating of the three menu items: Show seconds, Digital, and Analog:

```
void CClockPane::UpdateMenus()
{
    CPane::UpdateMenus();

    gBartender->EnableCmd(cmdShowSeconds);
    gBartender->EnableCmd(cmdDigital);
    gBartender->EnableCmd(cmdAnalog);

    gBartender->CheckMarkCmd(cmdShowSeconds, fShowSeconds);
    gBartender->CheckMarkCmd(cmdDigital, fDigital);
    gBartender->CheckMarkCmd(cmdAnalog, !fDigital);
}
```

UpdateMenus checkmarks the appropriate items as well as updates them. It uses CheckMarkCmd, which takes a Boolean number specifying whether to checkmark.

DoCommand actually implements the menu commands:

```
void CClockPane::DoCommand(long theCommand)
{
    switch (theCommand) {
    case cmdShowSeconds:
        fShowSeconds = !fShowSeconds;
        Refresh();
        if (fShowSeconds)
            gSleepTime = 1;     // Make Dawdle start being called
        break;

    case cmdDigital:
        if (!fDigital) {
            fDigital = TRUE;
            Refresh();
        }
        break;

    case cmdAnalog:
        if (fDigital) {
            fDigital = FALSE;
            Refresh();
        }
        break;

    default:
        CPane::DoCommand(theCommand);
        break;
    }
}
```

DoCommand sets the fShowSeconds and fDigital data members appropriately. If the data members change, the pane must be redrawn by calling the Refresh member function. This invalidates the whole pane.

The Dawdle member function performs a substantial portion of the drawing work:

```
void CClockPane::Dawdle(long *maxSleep)
{
    LongRect    frame;
    Rect    qdFrame;

    GetFrame(&frame);
    ::LongToQDRect(&frame, &qdFrame);
    UpdateOffscreen(qdFrame);

    Prepare();
    CopyFromOffscreen(qdFrame);

    *maxSleep = CalculateSleepTime();
}
```

First, `Dawdle` calls `UpdateOffscreen` to update the off-screen BitMap member with the current clock image. It then calls `CopyFromOffscreen`, which copies that image back onto the screen. `CalculateSleepTime` then determines when `Dawdle` must be called next to show a new time.

`Draw` is needed in addition to `Dawdle` because the clock's image may need refreshing due to an update event and because `Dawdle` may be called as rarely as once per minute:

```
void CClockPane::Draw(Rect *area)
{
    UpdateOffscreen(*area);
    CopyFromOffscreen(*area);
}
```

`CClockPane` uses `CalculateSleepTime` to figure out when `Dawdle` is going to need to be called next:

```
long CClockPane::CalculateSleepTime()
{
    const short kTicksPerSecond = 60;

    if (fShowSeconds)
        return kTicksPerSecond;
    else {
        unsigned long    now;
        DateTimeRec      nowDateTime;
        const short      kSecondsPerMinute = 60;
```

```
        GetDateTime(&now);
        Secs2Date(now, &nowDateTime);
        return kTicksPerSecond * (kSecondsPerMinute -
          nowDateTime.second);
    }
}
```

If the second hand is shown, `CalculateSleepTime` returns the number of ticks in a second. Otherwise, the function figures out how long it takes for the minute hand to change and returns that number of ticks.

`UpdateOffscreen` calls `CreateOffscreen`, which creates an off-screen bitmap and calls `DrawClock` to draw into it:

```
void CClockPane::UpdateOffscreen(const Rect &area)
{
    LongRect    frame;
    Rect    qdFrame;

    GetFrame(&frame);
    ::LongToQDRect(&frame, &qdFrame);
    CreateOffscreen(qdFrame);
    TGrafPortSetter setPort(fGrafPtr);
    DrawClock(qdFrame);
}
```

`CreateOffscreen` also allocates an off-screen BitMap if the size of the current BitMap is not sufficient and sets the necessary clipping and visible regions of the off-screen GrafPort:

```
void CClockPane::CreateOffscreen(const Rect &area)
{
    if (area.left != fBitMap.bounds.left ||
      area.right != fBitMap.bounds.right ||
      area.top != fBitMap.bounds.top ||
      area.bottom != fBitMap.bounds.bottom) {
        fBitMap.bounds = area;
        fBitMap.rowBytes =
      ::NumberOfBytesRoundedUpToAMultipleOf2(fBitMap.bounds.right
        - fBitMap.bounds.left);
        if (fBitMap.baseAddr != NULL)
            ::DisposPtr(fBitMap.baseAddr);
```

```
            fBitMap.baseAddr =
              ::NewPtrCanFail(fBitMap.rowBytes *
                (fBitMap.bounds.bottom - fBitMap.bounds.top));
            ::FailNIL(fBitMap.baseAddr);
            ::RectRgn(fGrafPtr->visRgn, &area);
            ::RectRgn(fGrafPtr->clipRgn, &area);
            fGrafPtr->portRect = area;

            TGrafPortSetter setPort(fGrafPtr);
            ::SetPortBits(&fBitMap);
        }
}
```

`CopyFromOffscreen` copies the off-screen bitmap to the current `GrafPort` using the Toolbox call `CopyBits`:

```
void CClockPane::CopyFromOffscreen(const Rect &areaToCopy)
{
    ::CopyBits(&fBitMap, &thePort->portBits,
      &areaToCopy, &areaToCopy, srcCopy, 0L);
}
```

`DrawClock` draws the clock by calling the appropriate routine to draw either a digital or an analog version:

```
void CClockPane::DrawClock(const Rect &clockSize)
{
    unsigned long    now;

    ::GetDateTime(&now);

    ::EraseRect(&clockSize);

    if (fDigital)
        DrawDigitalClock(clockSize, now);
    else
        DrawAnalogClock(clockSize, now);
}
```

As you might expect, `DrawAnalogClock` draws the analog version of the clock:

```
void CClockPane::DrawAnalogClock(const Rect &clockSize, unsigned
  long now)
{
    DateTimeRec     nowDateTime;
    const short     kSecondHandThickness = 1;
    const short     kMinuteHandThickness = 2;
    const short     kHourHandThickness = 3;

    ::Secs2Date(now, &nowDateTime);

    if (fShowSeconds)
        DrawLine(clockSize, ((float) nowDateTime.second) / 60.0,
          kSecondHandThickness);
    DrawLine(clockSize, nowDateTime.minute / 60.0,
      kMinuteHandThickness);

    Rect smallFrame = clockSize;  // hour hand is inscribed here
    const kHourHandSmallerConstant = 2; //1/2 size of other hands
    ::InsetRect(&smallFrame,
      (clockSize.right - clockSize.left) / (2 *
        kHourHandSmallerConstant),
      (clockSize.bottom - clockSize.top) /  (2 *
        kHourHandSmallerConstant));
    DrawLine(smallFrame, nowDateTime.hour / 12.0,
      kHourHandThickness);
}
```

`DrawAnalogClock` has a `DrawLine` member function that draws a line at a given position around the clock, inscribed in a given rectangle, with a specified line width:

```
// fractionOfCircle: 0 means straight up, .25 means to the right

void DrawLine(const Rect &frame, long double fractionOfCircle,
  short size)
{
    long double angle = 2 * 3.14159 * (1-(fractionOfCircle -
      0.25));
    short radiusX = (frame.right - frame.left) / 2;
    short radiusY = (frame.bottom - frame.top) / 2;

    short xCoord = ::Round(::cos(angle) * radiusX);
    short yCoord = ::Round(::sin(angle) * radiusY);
```

```
    ::PenSize(size, size);
    ::MoveTo(frame.left + radiusX, frame.top + radiusY);
    ::Line(xCoord, -yCoord);    // Macintosh uses Y decreasing
}
```

DrawLine figures the *x* and *y* location of the line (the hour, minute, or second hand line depending on where DrawLine is called), using fractionOfCircle to determine the angle. It then uses the Toolbox calls PenSize, MoveTo, and Line to actually do the drawing.

DrawDigitalClock, in drawing the digital version, obviously has an easier time of it than in drawing the analog version:

```
void CClockPane::DrawDigitalClock(const Rect &clockSize, unsigned
long now)
{
    Str255           nowStr;
    short            h;
    short            v;
    short            font;
    short            size;

    GetDigitalString(now, nowStr);
    GetDigitalFontAndSize(nowStr, clockSize, &font, &size);
    ::TextFont(font);
    ::TextSize(size);
    GetDigitalStringLocation(nowStr, clockSize, &h, &v);
    ::MoveTo(h, v);
    ::DrawString(nowStr);
}
```

DrawDigitalClock uses the utility member functions GetDigital-String, GetDigitalFontAndSize, and GetDigitalString-Location to determine what to draw, how big it is, and where to draw it:

```
void CClockPane::GetDigitalString(unsigned long now, Str255 s)
{
    ::IUTimeString(now, fShowSeconds, s);
}
```

```
void CClockPane::GetDigitalFontAndSize(const Str255 s, const Rect
  &clockSize, short *font, short *size)
{
    *font = geneva;
    *size = 9;
}

void CClockPane::GetDigitalStringLocation(const Str255 s, const
  Rect &clockSize, short *h, short *v)
{
    FontInfo    fInfo;

    ::GetFontInfo(&fInfo);
    short excessHeight = clockSize.bottom - clockSize.top -
      fInfo.descent - fInfo.ascent;
    if (excessHeight < 0)
        *v = clockSize.bottom;
    else
        *v = clockSize.bottom - fInfo.descent - excessHeight / 2;

    short excessWidth = clockSize.right - clockSize.left -
      ::StringWidth(s);
    if (excessWidth < 0)
        *h = clockSize.left;
    else
        *h = clockSize.left + excessWidth / 2;
}
```

Tick-Tock is a suave, international program, so the `GetDigitalString` function uses `IUTimeString`, an international utilities call. This way it can present the time correctly in all the countries to which it travels.

Tick-Tock's Main Program

After the preceding extended tour of the `CClockPane` class, it is probably refreshing to finally get to the TCL main program:

```
void main()
{
    CClockApp    *clockApp;

    clockApp = new CClockApp;
    clockApp->IClockApp();
    clockApp->Run();
    clockApp->Exit();
}
```

The Resources

Other than different icons, the only new resources are those for the Clock menu itself:

```
resource 'MENU' (4, "Clock", preload) {
    4,
    textMenuProc,
    0x7FFFFFFF,
    enabled,
    "Clock",
    {
        "Show seconds#1024", noIcon, noKey, noMark, plain,
        "-", noIcon, noKey, noMark, plain,
        "Digital#1025", noIcon, noKey, noMark, plain,
        "Analog#1026", noIcon, noKey, noMark, plain,
   }
};

resource 'MBAR' (1, preload) {
    { 1,  2, 3, 4
    }
};
```

Summary

The application in this chapter is a utility clock that keeps time in digital or analog fashion, with or without a second hand. Even when it is no longer the foreground window, Tick-Tock still keeps ticking.

More important than the application are the new programming skills you have acquired as a result of your further use of the TCL. You should now be able to do the following:

- ▼ Offer specialized menus in an application.
- ▼ Create and update preference files.
- ▼ Use the system's idle time in a more sophisticated way.
- ▼ Take advantage of desk accessory-like behavior in the TCL.
- ▼ Handle an application that continues to run in either the foreground or background.

These new skills should really add up when you look at the next programming challenge—creating a desktop calculator.

Exercises

1. If the user saves the clock on the second screen of a two-screen system and then tries to open it on a one-screen system, the clock cannot be seen. Add code to make sure the restored window position is on-screen and to move the clock back on-screen if the window position is off-screen.
2. Add a Font and Size menu to change the presentation of the digital clock.
3. Write a window definition procedure (WDEF) that draws a round window (warning: this is difficult).
4. Have the Copy menu item copy the current time in a text format that is suitable for pasting into a word-processing document.
5. Draw tick marks around the clock.
6. Draw hour markings around the clock.
7. The hour hand currently moves only at the top of the hour. So, at 1:59, the hour hand is on the 1, rather than almost on the 2. Make the hour hand move slowly, so that at 1:30 it is halfway between 1 and 2.
8. Use `GWorlds`, the preferred mechanism for off-screen drawing, for the off-screen bitmap drawing.

Exercises

20

C++ Calc: Building a Calculator

This application, C++ Calc, is a simple desktop calculator with a twist. Unlike the standard Calculator desk accessory, it calculates using the Reverse Polish Notation (RPN) system you find on a Hewlett-Packard calculator.

After you review the classes that go into the creation of C++ Calc, you will know how to do the following:

- ▼ Create content classes.
- ▼ Use and customize control classes.

C++ Calc offers a more complete application than the others in this part. The ease with which you can create a finished application in the TCL should convince you that the multiple benefits of frameworks are worth their few subtractions.

The C++ Calc Program

Take a look at figure 20.1 to get a peek at C++ Calc. As you can see, it displays a functional desktop calculator.

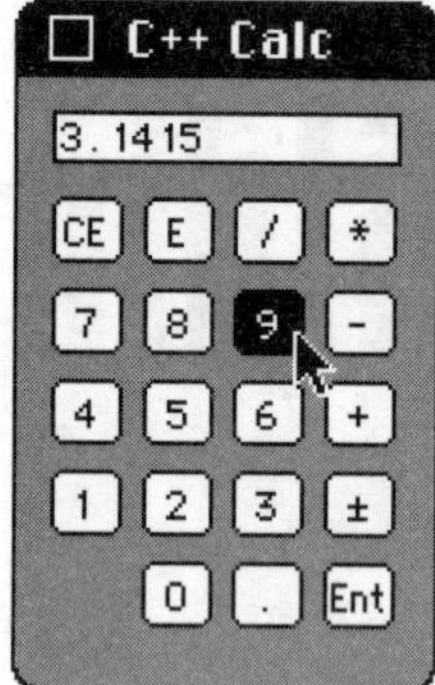

Figure 20.1. The C++ Calc calculator.

Compiling the Program

Copy the Calculator folder from the source code disk. Open the Calculator. project and then choose Run. All the files in the project need to be recompiled, and this takes a few minutes.

NOTE

Standard calculators use infix notation—the operator is in between the operands. In an infix system, the sum of 3 and 4 is represented as 3 + 4. In an RPN calculator, the calculations use postfix notation—the operator is after the two operands. In postfix, the sum of 3 and 4 is represented as 3 4 +. One of the advantages of RPN is that it makes parentheses unnecessary. The infix expression (2 + 3) × (5 ÷ 6) can be written in RPN as 2 3 + 5 6 ÷ ×.

Every calculator needs some way of knowing when you are finished entering a number. In infix, after you finish a number entry you must click the equal sign (=). In RPN, you must click the Enter key (Ent) to separate two numbers.

Running the Program

After you have C++ Calc running, check it out. You can balance your checkbook or just try the examples provided below:

- Calculate 5 - (3 + 4). The result should be 35. Click on the following calculator buttons:

```
5
Ent
3
Ent
4
+
*
```

- Calculate the same thing using the keyboard (notice that the calculator keys flash each time you type a character). Type the following:

```
5
return
3
return
4
+
*
```

- Select Copy from the Edit menu and then show the Clipboard. The value from the calculator should display in the Clipboard.
- Type the following:

```
77
```

- Clear the current number by selecting Clear, pressing the C key, or clicking the C calculator button. Then choose Paste from the Edit menu. The Clipboard contents should paste into the calculator.
- Try to calculate the old-time favorite: 1 ÷ 0. Here are the keystrokes:

```
1
Ent
0
/
```

- Calculate -1 ÷ 0. Here are the keystrokes:

```
1
±
Ent
0
/
```

- Move the calculator window, quit, and then run the program again. The window should appear in the new location.

Now that you know the ins and outs of C++ Calc, it is time to look at the code.

Inspecting the Program

Figure 20.2 shows the class diagram for the application. As you can see, there are a number of new classes.

Listed below are brief descriptions of the classes you have not seen before:

- TCalculator contains the calculator engine.
- CCalculatorApp creates the calculator window.
- CCalculatorPane stores a TCalculator object. It also contains the buttons and the numeric display. It handles keystrokes, menu items, and all communication with the `TCalculator` object.
- CFloatText creates a text field that holds a floating-point number.
- CButtonWithFontAndSize makes a button that displays in a given font and size.

The TCalculator Class

As said before, the content class of the application emulates a Hewlett-Packard calculator using Reverse Polish Notation (RPN):

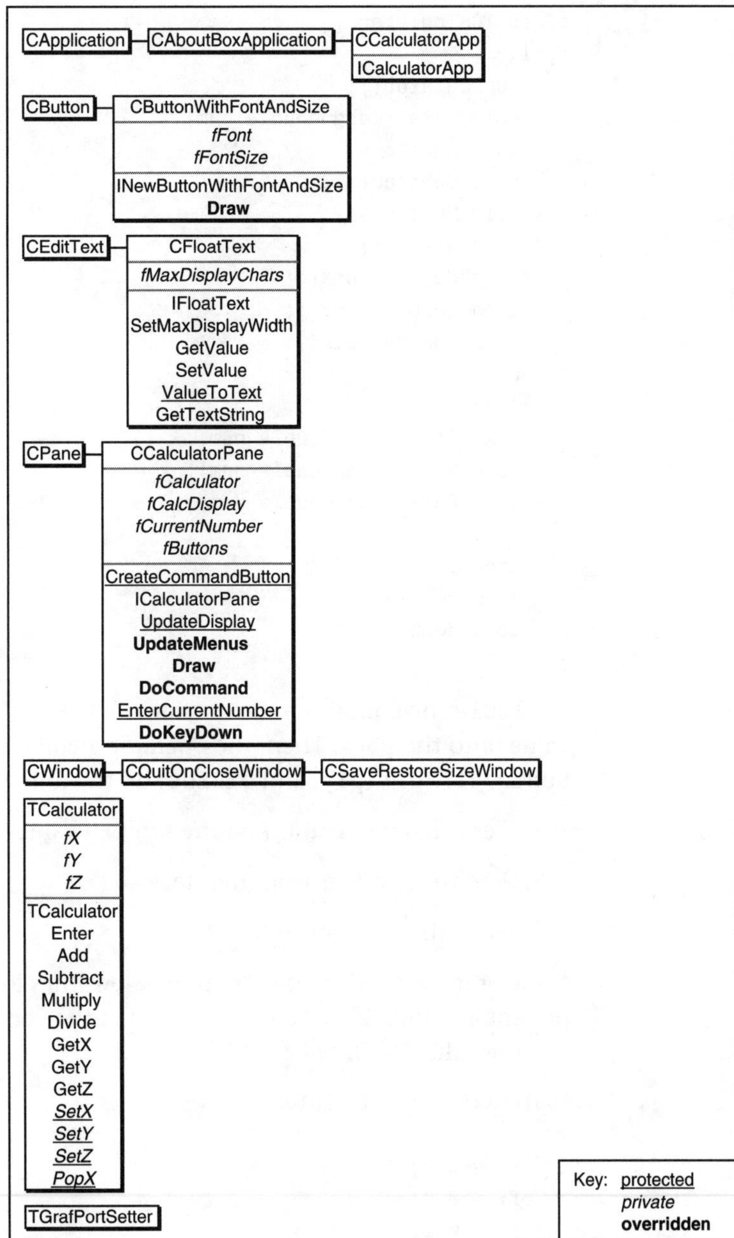

Figure 20.2. The C++ Calc class diagram.

```
class TCalculator {
public:
    TCalculator();
    void Enter(long double num);
    void Add();
    void Subtract();
    void Multiply();
    void Divide();
    long double GetX();
    long double GetY();
    long double GetZ();
private:
    long double PopX();
    void SetX(long double num);
    void SetY(long double num);
    void SetZ(long double num);

    long double    fX;
    long double    fY;
    long double    fZ;
};
```

`TCalculator` contains a three-value stack. First, `Enter` pushes a new value onto the stack. Then, the operator member functions (`Add`, `Subtract`, `Multiply`, and `Divide`) do the following:

1. Perform an operation on the top two values in the stack.
2. Pop those values from the stack.
3. Push the result onto the stack.

None of these routines is more than a few lines long and should not present any problems. Start by looking at the constructor that initializes the values to 0:

```
TCalculator::TCalculator()
{
    fX = 0.0;
    fY = 0.0;
    fZ = 0.0;
}
```

The Enter routine puts the value in the x register, pushing the remaining values:

```
void TCalculator::Enter(long double num)
{
    fZ = fY;
    fY = fX;
    fX = num;
}
```

The operators all pop two values on the stack and then return the result of the operation to the top of the stack:

```
void TCalculator::Add()
{
    long double v = PopX();
    Enter(v + PopX());
}

void TCalculator::Subtract()
{
    long double v = PopX();
    Enter(PopX() - v);
}

void TCalculator::Multiply()
{
    long double v = PopX();
    Enter(v * PopX());
}

void TCalculator::Divide()
{
    long double v = PopX();
    Enter(PopX() / v);
}
```

The setters and getters are simple:

```
long double TCalculator::GetX()
{
     return fX;
}
long double TCalculator::GetY()
{
     return fY;
}
long double TCalculator::GetZ()
{
     return fZ;
}

void TCalculator::SetX(long double num)
{
     fX = num;
}

void TCalculator::SetY(long double num)
{
     fY = num;
}

void TCalculator::SetZ(long double num)
{
     fZ = num;
}
```

The pop routine is equally simple. It returns the x value and moves the remaining values up:

```
long double TCalculator::PopX()
{
    long double v = GetX();

    fX = fY;
    fY = fZ;
    fZ = 0.0;
    return v;
}
```

Notice that, even though none of the routines are very difficult, this class still contains a working calculator engine.

NOTE

If you are unclear about how the TCalculator operations function, test the class members with a simple program using cout/cin (or scanf/printf).

The CCalculatorApp Class

The CCalculatorApp class has CAboutBoxApplication as its base class. Here is the class definition:

```
class CCalculatorApp: public CAboutBoxApplication
{
public:
    void        ICalculatorApp();
};
```

The initialization bears remarkable similarity to CClockApp's initialization in Chapter 19:

```
void CCalculatorApp::ICalculatorApp()
{
    const Boolean kFloatingWindow = TRUE;
    const short   kMinWindowHeight = 30;
    const short   kMinWindowWidth = 30;

    IAboutBoxApplication(kExtraMasters, kRainyDayFund,
      kCriticalBalance, kToolboxBalance);

    CDirector *aDirector = new CDirector;
    aDirector->IDirector(this);

    CSaveRestoreSizeWindow *aWindow = new CSaveRestoreSizeWindow;
    aWindow->ISaveRestoreSizeWindow(kWINDStarter,
      !kFloatingWindow, gDesktop, aDirector);
    aDirector->itsWindow = aWindow;

    aWindow->Select();
    CCalculatorPane *thePane = new CCalculatorPane;
    thePane->ICalculatorPane(aWindow, aDirector, 0, 0, 0, 0,
      sizELASTIC, sizELASTIC);
```

```
    thePane->FitToEnclosure(TRUE, TRUE);
    aDirector->itsGopher = thePane;
}
```

As with Tick-Tock, C++ Calc needs to use `CSaveRestoreSizeWindow` to take advantage of desk accessory-like behavior. Note that `CSaveRestoreSizeWindow` is derived from `CQuitOnCloseWindow` and, as such, gets desk accessory behavior—that is, closing the calculator window quits the application.

The CCalculatorPane Class

The `CCalculatorPane` class displays a calculator:

```
class CCalculatorPane: public CPane {
public:
    void ICalculatorPane(CView *anEnclosure,  CBureaucrat
      *aSupervisor, short aWidth, short aHeight, short aHEncl,
      short aVEncl, SizingOption aHSizing, SizingOption
      aVSizing);

    virtual void  UpdateMenus();
    virtual void  DoCommand(long theCommand);
    virtual void  DoKeyDown(char theChar, Byte keyCode,
      EventRecord *macEvent);
    virtual void  Draw(Rect *r);

protected:
    enum {cmdFirstCommand = 1025,
      cmdAdd = cmdFirstCommand, cmdMultiply, cmdDivide,
        cmdSubtract, cmdEnter,
      cmdPeriod, cmdE, cmdClearEntry, cmdChangeSign,
      cmd0, cmd1, cmd2, cmd3,
      cmd4, cmd5, cmd6, cmd7, cmd8, cmd9, cmdLastCommand = cmd9 };

    virtual void    UpdateDisplay();
    virtual void    EnterCurrentNumber();
    virtual void    CreateCommandButton(short rowNumber, short
      colNumber, long command);
```

```
private:
    TCalculator fCalculator;
    CFloatText  *fCalcDisplay;
    unsigned char fCurrentNumber[15];
    CButton     *fButtons[cmdLastCommand - cmdFirstCommand + 1];
};
```

Member Function Descriptions

Listed below is a short description of each member function:

- `ICalculatorPane` initializes the calculator pane and creates all the calculator buttons and the floating-point display.
- `UpdateMenus` enables the Clear, Copy, and Paste menu items.
- `DoCommand` implements the Clear, Copy, and Paste menu items. It also handles the commands `cmdAdd`, `cmdSubtract`, `cmd8`, and `cmd9`.
- `DoKeyDown` handles all the calculator keystrokes.
- `Draw` draws a gray background for the calculator.
- `UpdateDisplay` updates the numeric display to show the current value of the x register.
- `EnterCurrentNumber` takes any current user-entered number and enters it into the calculator.
- `CreateCommandButton` creates one of the calculator buttons with each call to this function.

`fCalculator` is the calculating engine, `fCalcDisplay` handles the numeric display of the calculator, and `fCurrentNumber` is a Pascal string that holds what the user has typed in. If the value is empty, then the numeric display shows the x register; otherwise, the numeric display shows this string. `fButtons` is an array of button objects, indexed by command number.

The ICalculatorPane Initialization Function

The initialization function, ICalculatorPane, is as follows:

```
void CCalculatorPane::ICalculatorPane(CView *anEnclosure,
  CBureaucrat *aSupervisor, short aWidth, short aHeight, short
  aHEncl, short aVEncl, SizingOption aHSizing, SizingOption
  aVSizing)
{
    const short kFloatTextWidth= 86;
    const short kFloatTextHeight = 20;
    const short kFloatTextLeftMargin = 10;


    IPane(anEnclosure, aSupervisor, aWidth, aHeight, aHEncl,
      aVEncl, aHSizing, aVSizing);

    wantsClicks = true;

    fCalcDisplay = new CFloatText;
    fCalcDisplay->IFloatText(this, aSupervisor, kFloatTextWidth,
      kFloatTextHeight, kFloatTextLeftMargin,
      kFloatTextTopMargin, sizFIXEDSTICKY, sizFIXEDSTICKY, -1);
    fCalcDisplay->Specify(kNotEditable, kNotSelectable,
      kNotStylable);
    fCalcDisplay->SetFontName("\pMonaco");
    fCalcDisplay->SetFontSize(9);
    fCalcDisplay->SetMaxDisplayWidth(sizeof(fCurrentNumber)-1);

    CPaneBorder *border = new CPaneBorder;
    border->IPaneBorder(kBorderFrame);
    border->SetPenSize(1, 1);
    fCalcDisplay->SetBorder(border);

    CreateCommandButton(5, 2, cmd0);
    CreateCommandButton(5, 3, cmdPeriod);
    CreateCommandButton(5, 4, cmdEnter);

    CreateCommandButton(4, 1, cmd1);
    CreateCommandButton(4, 2, cmd2);
    CreateCommandButton(4, 3, cmd3);
    CreateCommandButton(4, 4, cmdChangeSign);
```

```
    CreateCommandButton(3, 1, cmd4);
    CreateCommandButton(3, 2, cmd5);
    CreateCommandButton(3, 3, cmd6);
    CreateCommandButton(3, 4, cmdAdd);

    CreateCommandButton(2, 1, cmd7);
    CreateCommandButton(2, 2, cmd8);
    CreateCommandButton(2, 3, cmd9);
    CreateCommandButton(2, 4, cmdSubtract);

    CreateCommandButton(1, 1, cmdClearEntry);
    CreateCommandButton(1, 2, cmdE);
    CreateCommandButton(1, 3, cmdDivide);
    CreateCommandButton(1, 4, cmdMultiply);

    Length(fCurrentNumber) = 0;
}
```

This function calls its base initialization method and then sets its inherited data member, `wantsClicks`, to true. `wantsClicks` ensures that both this pane and subpanes accept mouse clicks.

`CFloatText` gets initialized next. This is important because a calculator that calculates, but does not show you the result, only is useful to the folks at Langley. The `CPaneBorder` frames the text as a visual nicety. `CreateCommandButton` gets called once for each button, with the row, column, and command number as parameters. Finally, `ICalculatorPane` initializes `fCurrentNumber` to an empty string.

The CreateCommandNumber Function

The Create`CommandNumber` function creates a button at the given row and column location. It also gives each button a specific command number:

```
void CCalculatorPane::CreateCommandButton(short rowNumber, short
  colNumber, long command)
{
    CButtonWithFontAndSize *aButton;
    Str255        buttonName;
    const short kButtonWidth = 18;
    const short kButtonHeight = 16;
```

```
    const short kColumnWidth = 23;
    const short kColumnHeight = 22;
    const short kLeftMargin = 9;
    const short kTopMargin = 29;
    const short kButtonTitleStringID = 1025;

    GetIndString(buttonName, kButtonTitleStringID,
      command - cmdFirstCommand + 1);
    aButton= new CButtonWithFontAndSize;
    aButton->INewButtonWithFontAndSize(kButtonWidth,
      kButtonHeight, kLeftMargin + (colNumber-1)* kColumnHeight,
      kTopMargin + (rowNumber-1) * kColumnHeight, buttonName,
      TRUE, 0, this, this, "\pGeneva", 9);
    aButton->SetClickCmd(command);
    fButtons[command - cmdFirstCommand] = aButton;
}
```

The function gets the button title from an `'STR#'` resource with the Toolbox call `GetIndString`. It then creates a `CButtonWithFont-AndSize` button at the correct location with the font Geneva 9. `CreateCommandButton` then sets the button's click command to the command number. This click command is what the button reports to its supervisor when it is clicked. Finally, `CreateCommandButton` saves the button in the `fButtons` array.

The UpdateMenus Function

`UpdateMenus` enables the Edit menu items:

```
void CCalculatorPane::UpdateMenus()
{
    CPane::UpdateMenus();

    if (Length(fCurrentNumber) > 0)
        gBartender->EnableCmd(cmdClear);
    gBartender->EnableCmd(cmdCopy);
    if (gClipboard->GetData('TEXT', NULL) > 0)
        gBartender->EnableCmd(cmdPaste);
}
```

Note that Clear is enabled only if the user has typed in a number (that is, `fCurrentNumber` is not empty). Copy always is enabled; Paste is enabled if there is text in the Clipboard.

DoCommand is the processing station for everything. When the user clicks on a button, the button sends the DoCommand message to its supervisor, the CCalculatorPane. Because it is such a large switch statement, the code is shown in pieces to make it easier to follow:

```
void CCalculatorPane::DoCommand(long theCommand)
{
    switch (theCommand) {
    case cmdCopy:
        gClipboard->EmptyScrap();
        gClipboard->PutData('TEXT', fCalcDisplay->
          GetTextHandle());
        break;
```

cmdCopy puts the current text into the Clipboard and cannot be undone (unlike PICTPeeker in Chapter 18).

cmdPaste gets the Clipboard text. It also resizes the text if it is too large to fit in the fCurrentNumber string.

```
 case cmdPaste:
        Handle h;
        Str255 s;
        gClipboard->GetData('TEXT', &h);
        if (GetHandleSize(h) > sizeof(fCurrentNumber)-1)
            SetHandleSize(h, sizeof(fCurrentNumber)-1);
        fCalcDisplay->SetTextHandle(h);
        ::DisposHandle(h);
        fCalcDisplay->GetTextString(s);
        CopyPString(s, fCurrentNumber);
        break;
```

Note that cmdPaste sets the display and the fCurrentNumber to the contents of that handle. The Paste command cannot be undone.

The Clear menu item does the same thing as clicking the clear entry (CE) button on C++ Calc. Therefore, the menu item gets redirected to be a click on the button with SimulateClick.

```
case cmdClear:
        fButtons[cmdClearEntry - cmdFirstCommand]->
          SimulateClick();
        break;
```

The clear entry item clears any user-entered number by restoring the display to the x register and clearing the `fCurrentNumber` string.

```
case cmdClearEntry:
        fCalcDisplay->SetValue(fCalculator.GetX());
        Length(fCurrentNumber) = 0;
        break;
```

Each of the operations uses `EnterCurrentNumber` to enter any number the user has typed. Each operation then tells the calculator to carry out the required computation.

```
case cmdAdd:
        this->EnterCurrentNumber();
        fCalculator.Add();
        UpdateDisplay();
        break;

case cmdSubtract:
        this->EnterCurrentNumber();
        fCalculator.Subtract();
        UpdateDisplay();
        break;

case cmdMultiply:
        this->EnterCurrentNumber();
        fCalculator.Multiply();
        UpdateDisplay();
        break;

case cmdDivide:
        this->EnterCurrentNumber();
        fCalculator.Divide();
        UpdateDisplay();
        break;
```

`UpdateDisplay` ensures that the display shows the new value of the x register.

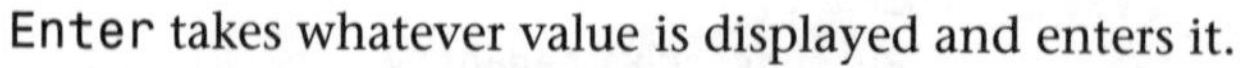

`Enter` takes whatever value is displayed and enters it.

```
case cmdEnter:
        fCalculator.Enter(fCalcDisplay->GetValue());
        Length(fCurrentNumber) = 0;
        UpdateDisplay();
        break;
```

cmdChangeSign changes the sign of the number in the display. It does this by getting the text version and then adding or removing a leading minus sign.

```
case cmdChangeSign:
        Str255 minusSign = "\p-";
        Str255 current;

        fCalcDisplay->GetTextString(current);

        if (Length(current) > 0 && current[1] == '-') {
            ::BlockMove(&current[2], &current[1],
              Length(current)-1);
            Length(current)--;
        }
        else
        {
            ::ConcatPStrings(minusSign, current);
            ::CopyPString(minusSign, current);
        }
        fCalcDisplay->SetTextString(current);
        ::CopyPString(current, fCurrentNumber);
        break;
```

Each number is converted to a string (with NumToString) and appended to the fCalcDisplay (if it fits):

```
case cmd1:
    case cmd2:
    case cmd3:
    case cmd4:
    case cmd5:
    case cmd6:
    case cmd7:
    case cmd8:
    case cmd9:
        Str31 numberAsString;

        NumToString(theCommand - cmd0, numberAsString);
        if (Length(fCurrentNumber) + Length(numberAsString) <
          sizeof(fCurrentNumber)) {
            ConcatPStrings(fCurrentNumber, numberAsString);
            fCalcDisplay->SetTextString(fCurrentNumber);
        }
        break;
```

Scientific notation is handled the same way as appending a period to a number. In each case, if the appendage does not make the string too long, it is added to the `fCurrentNumber` string. The whole string is then displayed.

```
    case cmdPeriod:
        Str31 periodString = "\p.";
        if (Length(fCurrentNumber) + Length(periodString) <
          sizeof(fCurrentNumber)) {
            ConcatPStrings(fCurrentNumber, periodString);
            fCalcDisplay->SetTextString(fCurrentNumber);
        }
        break;
    case cmdE:
        Str31 eString = "\pE";
        if (Length(fCurrentNumber) + Length(eString) <
          sizeof(fCurrentNumber)) {
            ConcatPStrings(fCurrentNumber, eString);
            fCalcDisplay->SetTextString(fCurrentNumber);
        }
        break;
```

The default case just calls the inherited version.

```
    default:
        CPane::DoCommand(theCommand);
    }
}
```

The DoKeyDown Function

`DoKeyDown` handles user commands in the form of keystrokes:

```
void CCalculatorPane::DoKeyDown(char theChar, Byte keyCode,
  EventRecord *macEvent)
{
    const kReturnChar = 13;
    const kEnterChar = 3;
    const kBackspaceChar = 8;
    long commandNumber;

    switch (theChar){
    case kBackspaceChar:
        if (Length(fCurrentNumber) == 1)
            DoCommand(cmdClearEntry);
```

```
    else if (Length(fCurrentNumber) > 1) {
        Length(fCurrentNumber)--;
        fCalcDisplay->SetTextString(fCurrentNumber);
    }
    return;
case '0':
case '1':
case '2':
case '3':
case '4':
case '5':
case '6':
case '7':
case '8':
case '9':
    commandNumber = cmd0 + theChar - '0';
    break;
case 'e':
case 'E':
    commandNumber = cmdE;
    break;
case 'c':
case 'C':
    commandNumber = cmdClearEntry;
    break;
case '.':
    commandNumber = cmdPeriod;
    break;
case '+':
    commandNumber = cmdAdd;
    break;
case '`':
case '~':
    commandNumber = cmdChangeSign;
    break;
case '-':
    commandNumber = cmdSubtract;
    break;
case '*':
    commandNumber = cmdMultiply;
    break;
```

```
        case '/':
            commandNumber = cmdDivide;
            break;
        case kReturnChar:
        case kEnterChar:
            commandNumber = cmdEnter;
            break;

        default:
            inherited::DoKeyDown(theChar, keyCode, macEvent);
            return;
        }
        fButtons[commandNumber - cmdFirstCommand]->SimulateClick();
}
```

The backspace key removes the last character from the `fCurrentDisplay` string. If `fCurrentDisplay` only has one character in it, then the backspace key, in effect, clears the entry. DoCommand gets called to clear the character.

All the other keystrokes are mapped to buttons. The switch statement calculates the correct command number, and then `DoKeyDown` calls `SimulateClick`. This, in turn, makes the appropriate button act as if it were clicked on. The ` and ~ keys are used as keyboard equivalents for ± because ± is difficult to type.

The Draw Function

The `Draw` function draws a light gray background for the buttons and display:

```
void CCalculatorPane::Draw(Rect *r)
{
    if (!gSystem.hasColorQD)
       FillRect(r, qd.ltGray);
    else {
        RGBColor     aColor;
        PixPatHandle myPixPat;

        aColor.red = aColor.green = aColor.blue = 0xaaaa;
          // light gray
        myPixPat = NewPixPat();
        MakeRGBPat(myPixPat, &aColor);
```

```
        FillCRect(r, myPixPat);
        DisposPixPat(myPixPat);
    }
}
```

To learn how to use MakeRGBPat to draw in color, see Chapter 16. Look at the discussion of DrawRectangleInRandomColor.

The UpdateDisplay Function

UpdateDisplay makes the display show the current x register:

```
void CCalculatorPane::UpdateDisplay()
{
    fCalcDisplay->SetValue(fCalculator.GetX());
}
```

The EnterCurrentNumber Function

If the user has typed a number, then EnterCurrentNumber enters it into the display:

```
void CCalculatorPane::EnterCurrentNumber()
{
    if (Length(fCurrentNumber) > 0) {
        fCalculator.Enter(fCalcDisplay->GetValue());
        Length(fCurrentNumber) = 0;
        UpdateDisplay();
    }
}
```

The CFloatText Class

The CFloatText class displays a floating-point number in a text field:

```
class CFloatText: public CEditText {
public:
    void        IFloatText(
      CView          *anEnclosure,
      CBureaucrat    *aSupervisor,
      short          aWidth,
      short          aHeight,
      short          aHEncl,
```

```
        short           aVEncl,
        SizingOption    aHSizing,
        SizingOption    aVSizing,
        short           aLineWidth);

    virtual long double GetValue();
    virtual void        SetValue(long double value);
    virtual void        GetTextString(Str255 s);
    virtual void        SetMaxDisplayWidth(short numChars);

protected:
    virtual void        ValueToText(long double value, Str255 s);
private:
    short   fMaxDisplayChars;
};
```

Note that the class stores the number as a text string, rather than as a floating-point number. Floating-point values are needed only when the user enters a number from the keyboard. The rest of the time only the text string is necessary for handling the on-screen display. Because of this, it is quicker to store numbers in text format and convert them to floating-point values as necessary.

Member Function Descriptions

Listed below are brief descriptions of the member functions:

- `IFloatText` initializes the `CFloatText` object.
- `GetValue` returns the floating-point value.
- `SetValue` sets the floating-point value.
- `GetTextString` returns the text as a string.
- `SetMaxDisplayWidth` sets the maximum number of characters in the floating-point number display.
- `ValueToText` converts a floating-point value to a string representation.
- `fMaxDisplayChars`, the only data member, stores the maximum number of characters needed to display the number.

The IFloatText Initialization Function

Here is the initialization function:

```
void CFloatText::IFloatText(
  CView         *anEnclosure,
  CBureaucrat   *aSupervisor,
  short         aWidth,
  short         aHeight,
  short         aHEncl,
  short         aVEncl,
  SizingOption  aHSizing,
  SizingOption  aVSizing,
  short         aLineWidth)
{
    IEditText(anEnclosure, aSupervisor, aWidth, aHeight, aHEncl,
      aVEncl, aHSizing, aVSizing, aLineWidth);
    SetValue(0.0);
    SetMaxDisplayWidth(8);
}
```

A newly created `CFloatText` has a value to 0 and is displayed in, at most, eight characters.

The SetMaxDisplayWidth Function

The `SetMaxDisplayWidth` function is a simple setter:

```
void CFloatText::SetMaxDisplayWidth(short numChars)
{
    fMaxDisplayChars = numChars;
}
```

The GetValue and SetValue Member Functions

The `GetValue` function converts the text to a floating-point value using the SANE call `str2num`:

```
long double CFloatText::GetValue()
{
    Str255 s;

    GetTextString(s);
    if (Length(s) == 0)
        return 0.0;
```

```
    else
        return ::str2num(s);
}
```

If the text is empty, GetValue returns 0.

The SetValue functions does the opposite. It converts the incoming floating-point number to text and saves it:

```
void CFloatText::SetValue(long double value)
{
    Str255 newString;
    Str255 existingString;

    ValueToText(value, newString);
    GetTextString(existingString);
    if (!::EqualString(newString, existingString, TRUE, TRUE))
        SetTextString(newString);
}
```

Notice the efficiency nicety: SetValue first checks to see whether the new string differs from the current string (using the Toolbox call EqualString) before saving it. This check prevents an unnecessary screen redraw for identical values.

The ValueToText routine is responsible for the actual conversion from floating-point to text numbers:

```
void CFloatText::ValueToText(long double value, Str255 s)
{
    ::sprintf((char *) s, "%.*g", fMaxDisplayChars, value);
    ::c2pstr((char *) s);
}
```

ValueToText uses the C standard library call, sprintf, to print the floating-point number value into s. The %g format determines whether to print the floating-point number in standard floating-point notation (e.g., 523.67) or scientific notation (e.g., 5.2367e2) depending on the size of the number. The .* signifies that the field width is passed as a parameter. The field width itself determines how many characters the number has when it prints out.

Because the TCL and the Toolbox only work with Pascal strings, the c2pstr call converts from a C string (with trailing zero byte) to a Pascal string (with leading length byte).

The GetTextString Function

Finally, GetTextString returns the text as a string:

```
void CFloatText::GetTextString(Str255 s)
{
    Handle h = GetTextHandle();
    *s = Min(::GetHandleSize(h), 255);
    ::BlockMove(*h, s+1, *s);
}
```

CEditText's base class, CFloatText, has no member function to return the text as a string—it only returns the text as a handle. This routine gets that handle, sets the length byte of the string (up to 255), and then uses the Toolbox call BlockMove to copy the characters from the handle to the string.

The CButtonWithFontAndSize Class

Customarily, button titles use Chicago 12 as the default font. This class enables you to vary that behavior; you can specify the font and size of the button titles:

```
class CButtonWithFontAndSize: public CButton {
public:
    void INewButtonWithFontAndSize(short aWidth, short aHeight,
      short aHEncl, short aVEncl, StringPtr title, Boolean
      fVisible, short procID, CView *anEnclosure, CBureaucrat
      *aSupervisor, StringPtr fontName, short fontSize);

    virtual void Draw(Rect *area);

private:
    short fFont;
    short fFontSize;
};
```

The initialization method converts the passed-in font name to a font number. Next, it saves both the font number and size:

```
void CButtonWithFontAndSize::INewButtonWithFontAndSize(short
  aWidth, short aHeight, short aHEncl, short aVEncl, StringPtr
  title, Boolean fVisible, short procID, CView *anEnclosure,
  CBureaucrat *aSupervisor, StringPtr fontName, short fontSize)
{
    INewButton(aWidth, aHeight, aHEncl, aVEncl, title, fVisible,
      useWFont ¦ procID, anEnclosure, aSupervisor);

    short fontNumber;
    GetFNum(fontName, &fontNumber);
    fFont = fontNumber;
    fFontSize = fontSize;
}
```

Notice that, if you change the default behavior, you also must tell the Control Manager to get font information from the `GrafPort`. `INewButtonWithFontAndSize` does this by adjusting the `procID` in `useWFont`, a the Control Manager constant. This constant specifies that the current font and size should come from the `GrafPort` (rather than using Chicago 12).

The `Draw` routine sets the font and size before calling `CButton::Draw`:

```
void CButtonWithFontAndSize::Draw(Rect *area)
{
    ::TextFont(fFont);
    ::TextSize(fFontSize);

    CButton::Draw(area);
}
```

The C++ Calc Main Program

Listed below is C++ Calc's main program:

```
void main()
{
    CCalculatorApp  *CalculatorApp;

    CalculatorApp = new CCalculatorApp;
    CalculatorApp->ICalculatorApp();
    CalculatorApp->Run();
    CalculatorApp->Exit();
}
```

The Resources

There is only one new resource (other than those needed for the icons). The 'STR#' resource contains the calculator button titles. The associated command numbers of the constants determines the order of the strings within the resource:

```
resource 'STR#' (1025, "button names", purgeable, preload) {
{
    "+",
    "*",
    "/",
    "-",
    "Ent",
    ".",
    "E",
    "CE",
    "±",
    "0",
    "1",
    "2",
    "3",
    "4",
    "5",
    "6",
    "7",
    "8",
    "9"
}
};
```

Summary

In this chapter you saw how easy it is to create a fully functional calculator using the TCL and C++. As a result of this application, you should now be able to do the following:

- Construct content classes that are separate from the interface portion of the application. The `TCalculator` class gives you a working calculator engine before you have to go about designing the interface.

- Customize control classes so that you can set particular parameters and override default behaviors you do not want.

When you calculate the time saved creating this application with C++ and the TCL, you should have plenty left over for the next challenge—creating an address book database.

Exercises

1. Save the values in the calculator when it closes and restore them when it reopens. This may require creating an abstract class from `CSaveRestoreSizeWindow`. This new class should have member functions that read and write the data in the preferences file, but do not open or close it. `CSaveRestoreSizeWindow` can then override those two member functions to read and write the window location and size. After this is done, you can create a new derived class from `CSaveRestoreSizeWindow` that overrides the two member functions to read and write the x, y, and z registers.
2. Make Copy, Paste, and Clear undoable.
3. Make Enter, +, -, *, and / undoable.
4. Add a display of the x, y, and z registers to C++ Calc.

21

AddressBook: Building an Address Database Program

Separating your user interface from the core of your application can make a great deal of sense. If the central features are independent of the user interface, they can be ported from one application framework to another or even from one platform to another.

Another advantage of this separation is increased software maintainability. When an application has all its classes designed around the user interface, every change to the interface requires reworking all of the code. It even may necessitate completely redesigning your classes. On the other hand, if you design your content classes (sometimes called the content model) based on the problem domain, you should not have to touch them when redesigning the interface. Only a change in the problem domain requires changing your content classes.

With this in mind, the application in this chapter has been bifurcated. The first part deals with creating the new C++ classes that make up the database engine and then testing them. The effort results in the DatabaseTester program—an engine test bed that tests the addresses and the database of addresses. With the engine running smoothly, the second phase adds a full-featured TCL user interface to the underlying address and database classes. This results in the AddressBook application.

Because of the limitations of the TCL, you have not seen classes that fully utilize the features of C++. However, because the content classes in this chapter are independent of the TCL, you see more advanced C++ features used. One such feature is multiple inheritance. During the interface design phase you also learn how to create modal dialogs using the TCL.

The DatabaseTester Program

It is the C++ classes that represent the database and the C++ objects that fill it that make DatabaseTester interesting. The main program, conversely, is quite simple. It just creates address book entries and adds them to a database. Before exiting, it prints out the contents of the database. Figure 21.1 shows a screen dump of this output.

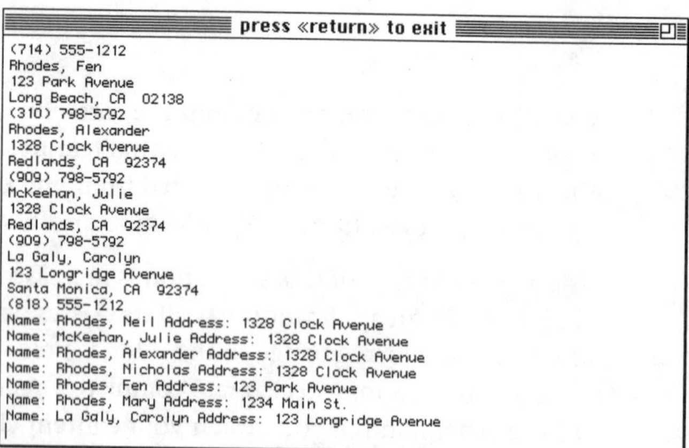

Figure 21.1. Output from the DatabaseTester program.

Compiling DatabaseTester

Copy the DatabaseTester folder from the source code disk. Open the DatabaseTester. project and select Run.

Running DatabaseTester

After you have DatabaseTester running, test it by comparing the output with the main program. Listed below are the relevant portions of the main function for comparison purposes:

```
void main()
{
    TDatabase    theDatabase;

    theDatabase.Insert(new TEntry("Rhodes, Neil", "1328 Clock
      Avenue", "Redlands", "CA", "92374", "(909) 798-5792"));
    theDatabase.Insert(new TEntry("McKeehan, Julie", "1328 Clock
      Avenue", "Redlands", "CA", "92374", "(909) 798-5792"));
    theDatabase.Insert(new TEntry("Rhodes, Alexander", "1328
      Clock Avenue", "Redlands", "CA", "92374", "(909) 798-
      5792"));
    theDatabase.Insert(new TEntry("Rhodes, Nicholas", "1328 Clock
      Avenue", "Redlands", "CA", "92374", "(909) 798-5792"));
    theDatabase.Insert(new TEntry("Rhodes, Mary", "1234 Main
      St.", "Fullerton", "CA", "92635", "(714) 555-1212"));
    theDatabase.Insert(new TEntry("Rhodes, Fen", "123 Park
      Avenue", "Long Beach", "CA", "02138", "(310) 798-5792"));
    theDatabase.Insert(new TEntry("La Galy, Carolyn", "123
      Longridge Avenue", "Santa Monica", "CA", "92374", "(818)
      555-1212"));
    PrintDatabase(theDatabase);

    FindAndPrint(theDatabase, "Rhodes, Neil");
    FindAndPrint(theDatabase, "McKeehan, Julie");
    FindAndPrint(theDatabase, "Rhodes, Alexander");
    FindAndPrint(theDatabase, "Rhodes, Nicholas");
    FindAndPrint(theDatabase, "Rhodes, Fen");
    FindAndPrint(theDatabase, "Rhodes, Mary");
    FindAndPrint(theDatabase, "La Galy, Carolyn");
}
```

Inspecting DatabaseTester

Now that you have perused the output, take a look at the application's class diagram, as shown in figure 21.2. As you can see, there are very few classes.

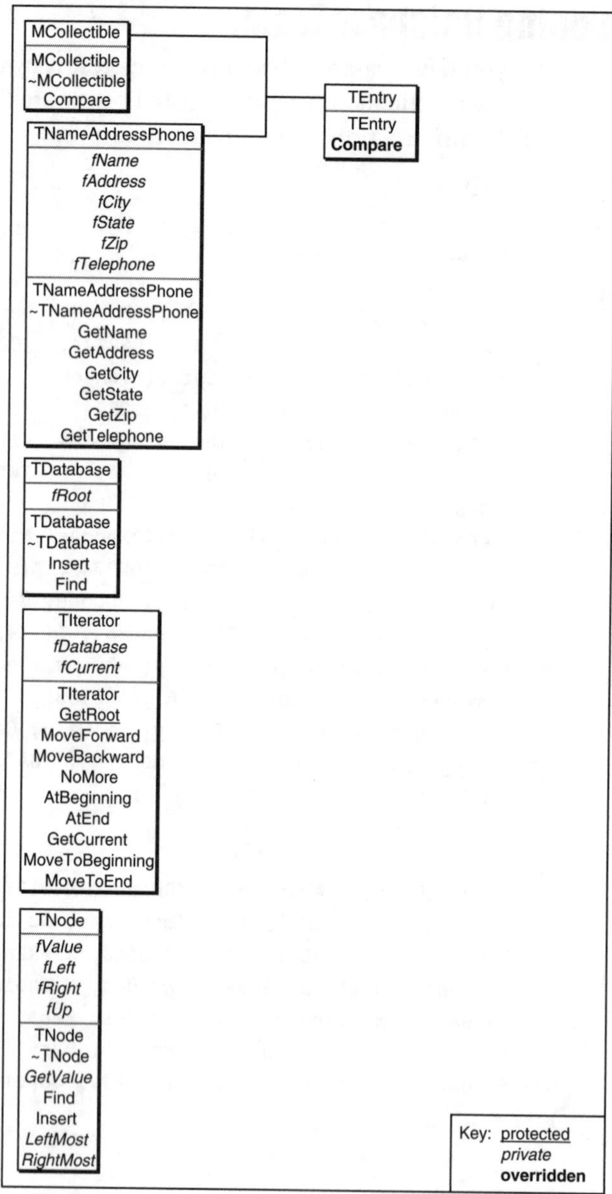

Figure 21.2. The class diagram of DatabaseTester.

Listed below are short descriptions of the classes; the details of each class are described in the following sections:

- `MCollectible` is an abstract class that represents objects that can be stored in the database.
- `TNameAddressPone` is a class that holds a name, address, and phone number.
- `TEntry` is derived from `MCollectible` and `TNameAddress-Phone`. One `TEntry` can compare itself with another `TEntry`.
- `TNode` is used in the implementation of `TDatabase`. It represents a node in a binary tree.
- `TDatabase` stores pointers to `MCollectibles`. It also provides a mechanism for finding a particular `MCollectible`.
- `TIterator` is a class that can cycle through the elements of a `TDatabase`.

The MCollectible Class

Multiple inheritance comes into play in the `MCollectible` class because its derived classes can be inserted into `TDatabase`.

IMPORTANT

Multiple inheritance is the capability to inherit the characteristics of more than one class. Recall from the discussion of multiple inheritance in Chapter 11, that a disciplined approach is needed. This approach involves using `T` (noun) classes to form trees combined with `M` (adjective) classes. Ideally, you create an `M` class, which can be combined with a `T` class at any point in the class tree. This approach provides selective functionality; each class can pick and choose from which `M` classes it derives and, therefore, what functionality it inherits.

A less favorable method of making a member function common to all classes is adding the member function to some `T` class high in the tree. This results in class bloat because more and more common functionality is added to these root classes.

This abstract class, `MCollectible`, defines a function that compares the values of two objects. Note that derived classes override this `Compare` member function.

Here is the class declaration:

```
class MCollectible {
public:
    enum {kItem1EqualItem2 = 0, kItem1LessThanItem2 = -1,
      kItem1GreaterThanItem2 = 1};
    MCollectible();
    virtual ~MCollectible();

    virtual int Compare(const MCollectible &item2) const;
};
```

The `Compare` function is declared `const`. You can call `Compare` on a `const MCollectible` object because it does not change the data members of the object.

The constructor and destructor do nothing:

```
MCollectible::MCollectible()
{
}

MCollectible::~MCollectible()
{
}
```

The `Compare` member function does a three-way comparison against another item. It determines whether an object is less than, greater than, or equal to its argument and returns that information:

```
int MCollectible::Compare(const MCollectible &item2) const
{
    if (this < &item2)
        return kItem1LessThanItem2;
    else if (this > &item2)
        return kItem1GreaterThanItem2;
    else
        return kItem1EqualItem2;
}
```

This version of Compare takes two locations in memory and compares them. Item 1 is less than item 2 if its memory location is less than item 2's memory location.

You see later on that the database class calls the Compare function to find where to insert an MCollectible in the binary tree.

The TNameAddressPhone Class

TNameAddressPhone holds name, address, and phone number information:

```
class TNameAddressPhone {
public:
    TNameAddressPhone(const char *name = NULL, const char
      *address = NULL, const char *fCity = NULL, const char
      *fState = NULL, const char *fZip = NULL, const char
      *fTelephone = NULL);
    virtual  ~TNameAddressPhone();

    const char *GetName() const;
    const char *GetAddress() const;
    const char *GetCity() const;
    const char *GetState() const;
    const char *GetZip() const;
    const char *GetTelephone() const;

private:
    char *fName;
    char *fAddress;
    char *fCity;
    char *fState;
    char *fZip;
    char *fTelephone;
};
```

TNameAddressPhone provides a constructor, a destructor, and a number of getters (i.e., GetName, GetAddress, GetCity, GetState, GetZip, and GetTelephone).

The constructor code is as follows:

```
TNameAddressPhone::TNameAddressPhone(const char *name, const char
  *address, const char *city, const char *state, const char *zip,
  const char *telephone)
{
    fName = fAddress = fCity = fState = fZip = fTelephone = NULL;

    fName = CopyOfString(name);
    fAddress = CopyOfString(address);
    fCity = CopyOfString(city);
    fState = CopyOfString(state);
    fZip = CopyOfString(zip);
    fTelephone = CopyOfString(telephone);
}
```

Note that the constructor initializes each of the data members using a utility routine, `CopyOfString`:

```
static char *CopyOfString(const char *s)
{
    if (s == NULL)
        s = "";
    char *copy;

    copy = new char[::strlen(s)+1];
    ::strcpy(copy, s);
    return copy;
}
```

All of those newly created chunks of memory for each data member also must be destroyed eventually. This, of course, is the destructor's job:

```
TNameEntryPhone::~TNameEntryPhone()
{
    delete [] fName;
    delete [] fAddress;
    delete [] fCity;
    delete [] fState;
    delete [] fZip;
    delete [] fTelephone;
}
```

Notice that the destructor uses `delete []` rather than just `delete`. This is necessary to match the allocation, which used `new[]`.

Here are all the getters (accessors) you heard about above—all perfect one-liners:

```
const char *TNameAddressPhone::GetName() const
{
    return fName;
}

const char *TNameAddressPhone::GetAddress() const
{
    return fAddress;
}

const char *TNameAddressPhone::GetCity() const
{
    return fCity;
}

const char *TNameAddressPhone::GetState() const
{
    return fState;
}

const char *TNameAddressPhone::GetZip() const
{
    return fZip;
}

const char *TNameAddressPhone::GetTelephone() const
{
    return fTelephone;
}
```

Each of these functions returns a `const char *`, which is a pointer to unmodifiable characters. Because the functions do not modify any data members of `TNameAddressPhone`, they are declared `const`.

The TEntry Class

TNameAddressPhone objects cannot be inserted into the database because they are not derived from the MCollectible class. The way to rectify the situation is to use multiple inheritance in the design of the next class. Therefore, you create a new class that derives from both TNameAddressPhone (so it can hold names, addresses, and phone numbers) and MCollectible (so it can be inserted in a TDatabase). This new class is TEntry:

```
class TEntry: public MCollectible, public TNameAddressPhone {
public:
    TEntry(const char *name = NULL, const char *address = NULL,
      const char *fCity = NULL, const char *fState = NULL,
      const char *fZip = NULL, const char *fTelephone = NULL);

    virtual int Compare(const MCollectible &item2) const;
};
```

TEntry's Compare member function overrides MCollectible::Compare and compares fName data members:

```
int TEntry::Compare(const MCollectible &item2) const
{
    int compareResult = ::strcmp(GetName(), ((TEntry &)
      item2).GetName());

    if (compareResult < 0)
        return kItem1LessThanItem2;
    else if (compareResult > 0)
        return kItem1GreaterThanItem2;
    else
        return kItem1EqualItem2;
}
```

Note that only the fName data member gets compared at this point. This is because the name is used as the key to the rest of the information. When inserting a TEntry, TDatabase calls the Compare routine to find the proper location. Compare also is used to find a TEntry.

The TNode Class

The TNode class represents one node in a binary tree:

```
class TNode {
public:
    TNode(MCollectible *value, TNode *up = NULL)
    {fRight = fLeft = NULL; fUp = up; fValue = value;}

    ~TNode() {delete fRight; delete fLeft; delete fValue;}
    void Insert(MCollectible *value);
    MCollectible *Find(const MCollectible  &key) const;

private:
    const TNode *LeftMost() const;
    const TNode *RightMost() const;

    MCollectible *GetValue() const;

    MCollectible *fValue;
    TNode *fLeft;
    TNode *fRight;
    TNode *fUp;
    friend class TIterator;
};
```

The nodes are hooked together in a binary tree, as shown in figure 21.3.

Besides its constructor and destructor, TNode has a few other functions. One function, Insert, handles the insertion of an MCollectible into the tree starting at this node. Another function, Find, attempts to locate a matching MCollectible in the tree rooted at this node. The other two member functions, LeftMost and RightMost, return the left- and rightmost subnode.

Pay special attention to the friend designation of TIterator in TNode:

```
friend class TIterator;
```

As a friend, TIterator has access to the private members of TNode. Because TIterator is tied tightly to TNode, it needs more access than a normal class does.

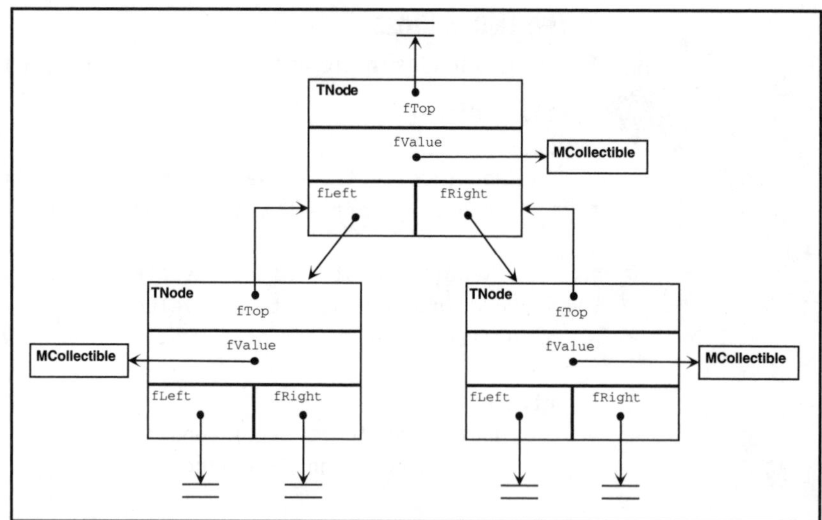

Figure 21.3. TNodes in a tree.

Listed below is the actual code for the `TNode` functions, starting with the `LeftMost` and `RightMost` routines. Notice that `LeftMost` chases the `fLeft` data member and that `RightMost` chases `fRight`.

```
const TNode *TNode::LeftMost() const
{
    const TNode *n = this;

    while (n->fLeft != NULL)
        n = n->fLeft;
    return n;
}

const TNode *TNode::RightMost() const
{
    const TNode *n = this;

    while (n->fRight != NULL)
        n = n->fRight;
    return n;
}
```

`GetValue` is a simple getter function that returns the current value in `fValue`:

```
MCollectible *TNode::GetValue() const
{
    return fValue;
}
```

`Find` finds a matching `MCollectible` in this node or a subnode:

```
MCollectible *TNode::Find(const MCollectible&key) const
{
    const TNode    *node = this;

    while (node != NULL) {
        int compareResult = node->GetValue()->Compare(key);

        if (compareResult == MCollectible::kItem1EqualItem2)
            return node->GetValue();
        else if (compareResult <= MCollectible::kItem1LessThanItem2)
            node = node->fRight;
        else
            node = node->fLeft;
    }
    return NULL;
}
```

Note that `Find` takes advantage of the fact that the nodes are sorted. For a given node, all nodes in the left subtree are less than it and all nodes in the right subtree are greater than it (see fig. 21.4).

Notice the use of the class qualifier (`MCollectible::`) before the enumeration constants `kItem1EqualItem2` and `kItem1LessThanItem2`. This is done because you must specify the originating class when using an enumeration constant that is defined in another class. Each new class defines a new scope.

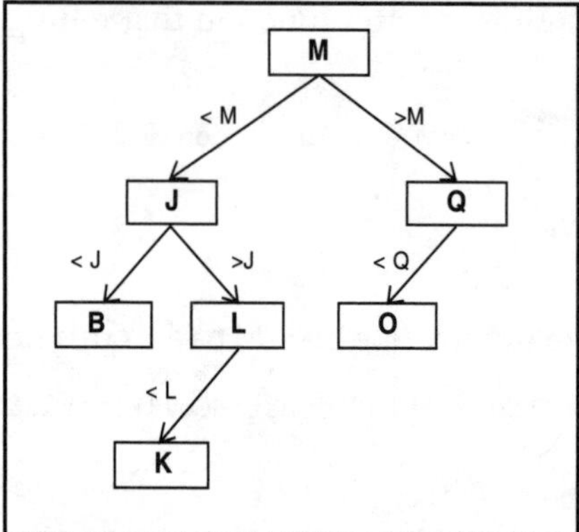

Figure 21.4. The sorting of nodes.

Next, take a look at the `Insert` routine in `TNode`:

```
void TNode::Insert(MCollectible *value)
{
	TNode	**node = &this;	// after loop: holds address
							// within previous node
							// which points to current node
	TNode	*up = NULL;		// after loop: pointer to
							// previous node

	do {
		int compareResult = (*node)->GetValue()->Compare(*value);

		up = *node;	// points at the current node

		if (compareResult == MCollectible::kItem1EqualItem2)
		{
				delete value;
				return;
		}
		else if (compareResult <= MCollectible::kItem1LessThanItem2)
			node = &(*node)->fRight;	// advance to next node
		else
			node = &(*node)->fLeft;		// advance to next node
	} while (*node != NULL);
	*node = new TNode(value, up);
}
```

After the loop is finished, the `node` variable is a pointer to either the `fLeft` or `fRight` data member, depending on where the new node needs to be placed. If an identical entry is already in the node, `Insert` deletes the value it was going to insert and then returns.

The TDatabase Class

`TDatabase` is the class that holds the database of `MCollectible` objects. These objects can be inserted or searched.

Each `TDatabase` tree looks different, depending on the order in which `MCollectible` objects were inserted. For instance, when using the names in DatabaseTester's main program and the same order of entry, you get the `TNode` tree shown in figure 21.5.

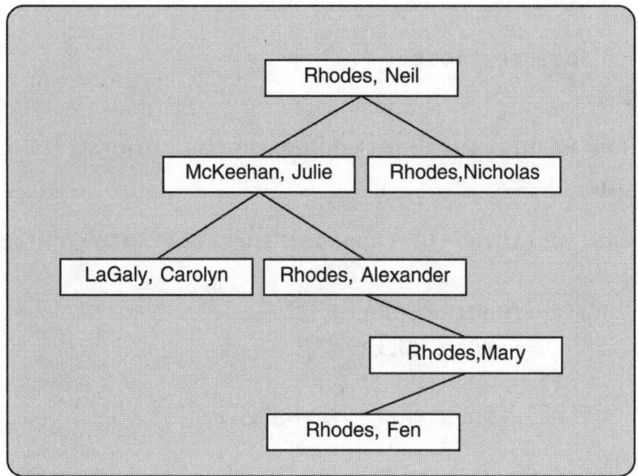

Figure 21.5. The tree of names from the main program.

The order in which you insert nodes can affect greatly the resulting tree. Can you imagine a more balanced tree holding these particular objects? (If so, see exercise 2 at the end of this chapter.)

The class declaration for `TDatabase` is as follows:

```
class TDatabase {
public:
    TDatabase();
    virtual ~TDatabase();
```

```
    void Insert(MCollectible* dataElement);
    MCollectible *Find(const MCollectible& key) const;

private:
    TNode *fRoot;
    friend class TIterator;
public:
};
```

The constructor and destructor are simple:

```
TDatabase::TDatabase()
{
    fRoot = NULL;
}

TDatabase::~TDatabase()
{
    delete fRoot;
}
```

The Find routine just delegates the chore to the root node, if there is one:

```
MCollectible *TDatabase::Find(const MCollectible& key) const
{
    if (fRoot == NULL)
        return NULL;
    else
        return fRoot->Find(key);
}
```

Similarly, the Insert routine delegates the insertion to the root node:

```
void TDatabase::Insert(MCollectible* dataElement)
{
    if (fRoot == NULL)
        fRoot = new TNode(dataElement);
    else
        fRoot->Insert(dataElement);
}
```

If there is no root node, it creates a new node and makes the new node the root node.

The TIterator Class

The `TIterator` class iterates over objects within a `TDatabase`. As it is common, data structures such as `TDatabase` should provide iteration capabilities to access each element of a data structure. This class also guarantees that the objects are visited in sorted order (sorting is imposed by the `Compare` function for the objects in the database).

There is an advantage to placing the iteration in a separate class rather than providing iteration member functions directly in `TDatabase`. With this method, you can have multiple iterators iterating over a `TDatabase` simultaneously, each at its own pace.

The declaration for `TIterator` is as follows:

```
class TIterator {
public:
    TIterator(const TDatabase &database):fDatabase(database)
      {fCurrent = NULL;}

    void MoveForward();
    void MoveBackward();
    int NoMore();
    int AtEnd();
    int AtBeginning();
    void MoveToBeginning();
    void MoveToEnd();
    MCollectible *GetCurrent();

protected:
    TNode *GetRoot();

private:
    const TDatabase &fDatabase;
    const TNode *fCurrent;
};
```

`TIterator` is initialized with the database that it iterates. For example, you use a `TIterator` to iterate in sorted order using the following code:

```
TIterator iter(aDatabase);
for (iter.MoveToBeginning(); !iter.NoMore(); iter.MoveForward()) {
    MCollectible *currentObject = iter.GetCurrent();
    ...
}
```

You similarly can iterate in reverse order:

```
TIterator iter(aDatabase);
for (iter.MoveToEnd(); !iter.NoMore(); iter.MoveBackward()) {
    MCollectible *currentObject = iter.GetCurrent();
    ...
}
```

The `fDatabase` data member contains the database over which the iterator iterates. The `fCurrent` data member points to the node where the iterator is currently processing.

The `GetRoot` and `GetCurrent` member functions are trivial:

```
TNode *TIterator::GetRoot()
{
    return fDatabase.fRoot;
}

MCollectible *TIterator::GetCurrent()
{
    if (fCurrent == NULL)
        return NULL;
    else
        return fCurrent->GetValue();
}
```

The `NoMore` function returns true at the end of the iteration and false if there are remaining elements to iterate over. It uses the fact that `fCurrent` is NULL when reaching the end of iteration.

```
int TIterator::NoMore()
{
    return fCurrent == NULL;
}
```

The first element in sorted order is the leftmost node of the root. `AtBeginning` returns true if the iterator is currently at the first (leftmost) node.

Similarly, the last element in sorted order is the rightmost node of the root. AtEnd returns true if the iterator is currently at the last (rightmost) node.

```
int TIterator::AtBeginning()
{
    return fCurrent != NULL && GetRoot()->LeftMost() == fCurrent;
}

int TIterator::AtEnd()
{
    return fCurrent != NULL && GetRoot()->RightMost() == fCurrent;
}
```

MoveToBeginning moves the iterator to the first node in the tree:

```
void TIterator::MoveToBeginning()
{
    if (GetRoot() == NULL)
        fCurrent = NULL;
    else
        fCurrent = GetRoot()->LeftMost();
}
```

MoveToEnd moves the iterator to the last node in the tree:

```
void TIterator::MoveToEnd()
{
    if (GetRoot() == NULL)
        fCurrent = NULL;
    else
        fCurrent = GetRoot()->RightMost();
}
```

MoveForward just moves to the next node in the tree.

```
void TIterator::MoveForward()
{
    if (fCurrent == NULL)
        MoveToBeginning();
    // if we have a right-hand side, the next node is the
    // left-most of our RHS)
    else if (fCurrent->fRight != NULL)
        fCurrent = fCurrent->fRight->LeftMost();
```

```
    else if (fCurrent->fUp == NULL)    // if we don't have an RHS,
                                       // and don't have an up, we're done
        fCurrent = NULL;
    else {
        // the next is our first ancestor who we are on the
        // left-hand side of
        const TNode *last;
        do {
            last = fCurrent;
            fCurrent = last->fUp;
        } while (fCurrent != NULL && fCurrent->fRight == last);
    }
}
```

MoveBackward, as you might expect, moves to the previous node in the tree:

```
void TIterator::MoveBackward()
{
    if (fCurrent == NULL)
        MoveToEnd();
    // if we have a left-hand side, the next node is the
    // right-most of our LHS
    else if (fCurrent->fLeft != NULL)
        fCurrent = fCurrent->fLeft->RightMost();
    else if (fCurrent->fUp == NULL)    // if we don't have an LHS,
                                       // and don't have an up, we're done
        fCurrent = NULL;
    else {
        // the next is our first ancestor who we are on the
           right-hand side of
        const TNode *last;
        do {
            last = fCurrent;
            fCurrent = last->fUp;
        } while (fCurrent != NULL && fCurrent->fLeft == last);
    }
}
```

If you find yourself getting lost in these last two functions, you might want to draw a small binary tree and convince yourself that the algorithms correctly find the desired node.

The DatabaseTester Main Program

This main program has more in it than most. First, it inserts some entries into a database. Next, it iterates over the database in reverse order, printing out each entry. Last, it finds entries within the database and prints them out.

```
void main()
{
    TDatabase    theDatabase;

    theDatabase.Insert(new TEntry("Rhodes, Neil", "1328 Clock
      Avenue", "Redlands", "CA", "92374", "(909) 798-5792"));
    theDatabase.Insert(new TEntry("McKeehan, Julie", "1328 Clock
      Avenue", "Redlands", "CA", "92374", "(909) 798-5792"));
    theDatabase.Insert(new TEntry("Rhodes, Alexander", "1328
      Clock Avenue", "Redlands", "CA", "92374", "(909) 798-
      5792"));
    theDatabase.Insert(new TEntry("Rhodes, Nicholas", "1328 Clock
      Avenue", "Redlands", "CA", "92374", "(909) 798-5792"));
    theDatabase.Insert(new TEntry("Rhodes, Mary", "1234 Main
      St.", "Fullerton", "CA", "92635", "(714) 555-1212"));
    theDatabase.Insert(new TEntry("Rhodes, Fen", "123 Park
      Avenue", "Long Beach", "CA", "02138", "(310) 798-5792"));
    theDatabase.Insert(new TEntry("La Galy, Carolyn", "123
      Longridge Avenue", "Santa Monica", "CA", "92374", "(818)
      555-1212"));
    PrintDatabase(theDatabase);

    FindAndPrint(theDatabase, "Rhodes, Neil");
    FindAndPrint(theDatabase, "McKeehan, Julie");
    FindAndPrint(theDatabase, "Rhodes, Alexander");
    FindAndPrint(theDatabase, "Rhodes, Nicholas");
    FindAndPrint(theDatabase, "Rhodes, Fen");
    FindAndPrint(theDatabase, "Rhodes, Mary");
    FindAndPrint(theDatabase, "La Galy, Carolyn");
}
```

Listed below are the two functions that the main program uses, `FindAndPrint` and `PrintDatabase`:

```
void FindAndPrint(const TDatabase &theDatabase, char *name)
{
    TEntry *entry = (TEntry *) theDatabase.Find(TEntry(name));
    if (entry != NULL)
        cout << "Name: " << entry->GetName() << " Address: "
          << entry->GetAddress() << '\n';
}

void PrintDatabase(const TDatabase &theDatabase)
{
    printf("Database\n:");
    TIterator iter(theDatabase);
    for (iter.MoveToEnd(); !iter.NoMore(); iter.MoveBackward()) {
        TEntry *entry = (TEntry *) iter.GetCurrent();
        if (entry)
            cout << entry->GetName() << '\n' <<
              entry->GetAddress() << '\n' <<
              entry->GetCity() << ", " << entry->GetState() << "  "
              << entry->GetZip() << '\n' <<
              entry->GetTelephone() << '\n';
    }
}
```

With these new C++ classes and main program you can see how easy it is to test the database and entry classes, without first having to create a full-blown user interface. At this point, if you want a limited form of user interaction, you can modify the main program to read input from `cin`. After you assure yourself that the engine is purring as smoothly as a kitten, it is time to turn your attention to the database interface.

The AddressBook Program

AddressBook is larger than any of the other TCL programs presented so far. With it, you can do any of the following:

- Enter names, addresses, and telephone numbers.
- Save the names and restore them.
- Browse through the entries one at a time.
- Flip to the beginning or end of the database.

If you look at figure 21.6, you see what AddressBook's main entry screen looks like. You also see the main address database positioned behind it.

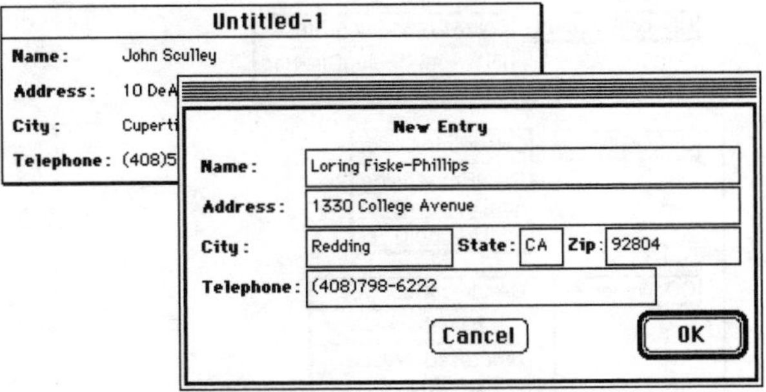

Figure 21.6. The AddressBook program.

Compiling AddressBook

Copy the AddressBook folder from the source code disk. Open the AddressBook. project and then choose Run. All the files in the project need a few minutes to recompile.

Running AddressBook

After the program is up and running, test it out by trying the following:

- Use the New Entry menu item to create some new names and addresses.
- Save your new address book in a file.
- Cycle through the address book. Go both forward and backward. Flip to the front and back of the book.
- Quit the application and then reopen your saved file.

Inspecting AddressBook

Figure 21.7 shows the class diagram for this application. As the diagram shows, there are a number of new classes as well as some with which you already should be familiar from earlier in the chapter.

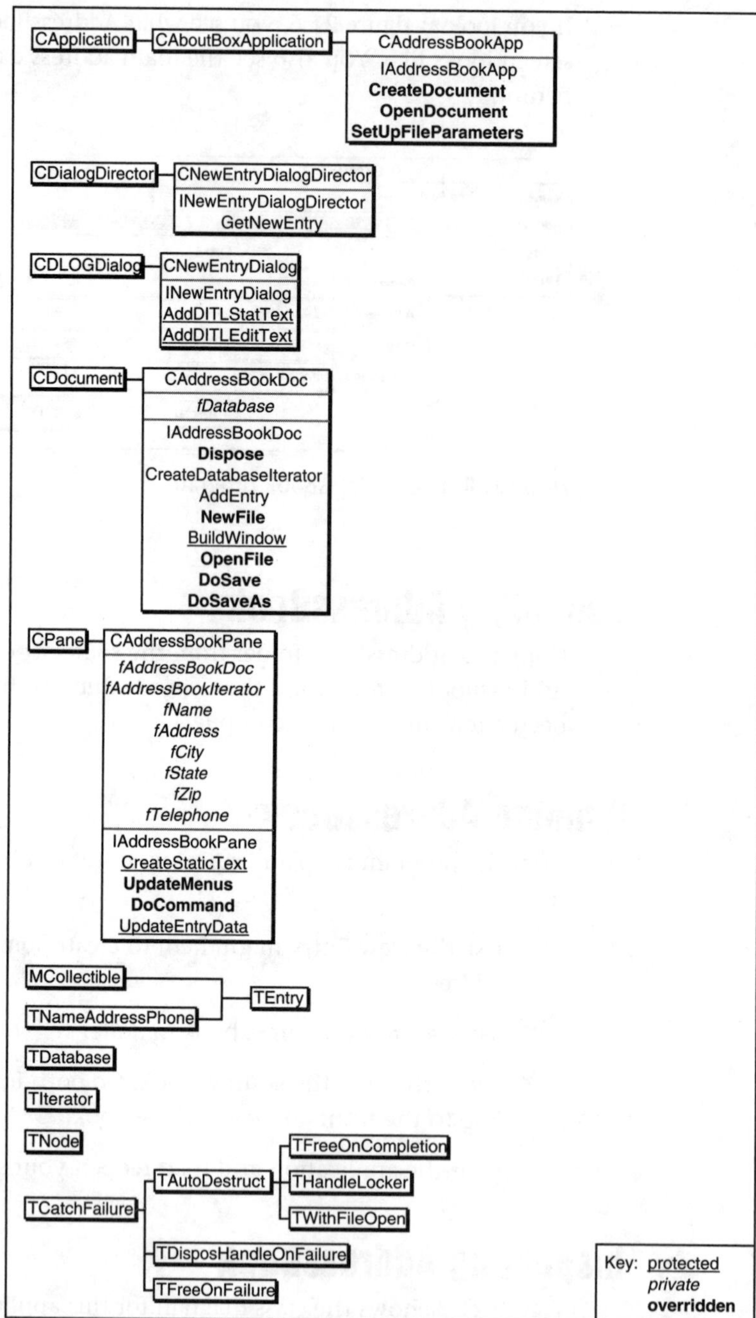

Figure 21.7. The class diagram for AddressBook.

Listed below are short descriptions of the new classes:

- CAddressBookApp creates the documents and sets up parameters for the Open dialog.
- CAddressBookDoc holds the addresses, saves them to disk, and reads them from disk. It also creates the windows and panes to display them.
- CAddressBookPane keeps track of which address is currently on display. It also handles the different database view requests and handles the New Entry menu command.
- CNewEntryDialog ensures that the New Entry dialog has the correct font and styles.
- CNewEntryDialogDirector is responsible for putting up the New Entry dialog and reading the information from the dialog to create a new entry

The CAddressBookApp Class

The CAddressBookApp class is similar to the application classes of earlier chapters:

```
class CAddressBookApp: public CAboutBoxApplication {
public:
    void            IAddressBookApp();

    virtual void    CreateDocument();
    virtual void    OpenDocument(SFReply *macReply);
    virtual void    SetUpFileParameters();
};
```

The code for the member functions should strike a familiar chord:

```
void CAddressBookApp::IAddressBookApp()
{
    const short     kExtraMasters =    1;
    const Size      kRainyDayFund =    45000;
    const Size      kCriticalBalance = 40000;
    const Size      kToolboxBalance =  20000;

    IAboutBoxApplication(kExtraMasters, kRainyDayFund,
      kCriticalBalance, kToolboxBalance);
}
```

```
void CAddressBookApp::CreateDocument()
{
    CAddressBookDoc *theDocument = new CAddressBookDoc;

    TFreeOnFailure freer(theDocument);

    theDocument->IAddressBookDoc(this);
    theDocument->NewFile();
}

void CAddressBookApp::OpenDocument(SFReply *macReply)
{
    CAddressBookDoc *theDocument = new CAddressBookDoc;

    TFreeOnFailure freer(theDocument);

    theDocument->IAddressBookDoc(this);
    theDocument->OpenFile(macReply);
}

void CAddressBookApp::SetUpFileParameters()
{
    CApplication::SetUpFileParameters();

    sfNumTypes = 1;
    sfFileTypes[0] = 'ADDR';
    gSignature = 'C++3';
}
```

The CAddressBookDoc Class

The CAddressBookDoc class does all of the following:

- Holds the database of addresses.
- Writes the addresses to disk after a Save command.
- Reads the addresses from disk on an Open command.
- Creates the window and pane that displays the addresses.

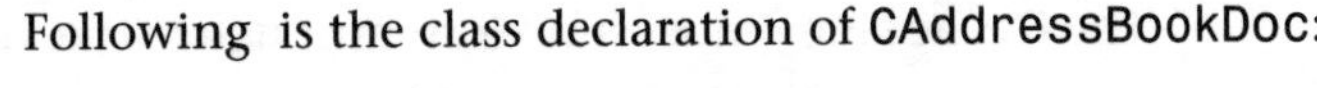

Following is the class declaration of CAddressBookDoc:

```
class CAddressBookDoc: public CDocument {
public:
    void                IAddressBookDoc(CApplication *supervisor);
    virtual void        Dispose();

    virtual void        NewFile();
    virtual void        OpenFile(SFReply *macReply);
    virtual Boolean     DoSave();
    virtual Boolean     DoSaveAs(SFReply *macSFReply);
    virtual TIterator   *CreateDatabaseIterator();
    virtual void        AddEntry(TEntry *entry);

protected:
    virtual void        BuildWindow();

private:
    TDatabase           *fDatabase;
};
```

The initialization member function, IAddressBookDoc, creates a TDatabase to hold the addresses:

```
void CAddressBookDoc::IAddressBookDoc(CApplication *supervisor)
{
    const Boolean kPrintable = TRUE;
    fDatabase = NULL;
    IDocument(supervisor, kPrintable);
    fDatabase = new TDatabase;
    ::FailNIL(fDatabase);
}
```

Notice that there is a call to FailNIL after the new. You have not seen it before because it is not necessary for TCL classes. CObject, the base class of all TCL classes, overrides the new operator so that it fails rather than returns NULL. Why is it present above? Because TDatabase does not descend from CObject, the new operator result must be checked for NULL.

The Dispose member function must delete the TDatabase:

```
void CAddressBookDoc::Dispose()
{
    delete fDatabase;

    CDocument::Dispose();
}
```

The NewFile and its member functions contain no surprises:

```
void CAddressBookDoc::NewFile()
{
    BuildWindow();

    Str255 wTitle;
    short wCount;
    Str255 wNumber;

    gDecorator->StaggerWindow(itsWindow);
    itsWindow->GetTitle(wTitle);
    wCount = gDecorator->GetWCount();
    ::NumToString(wCount, wNumber);
    ::ConcatPStrings(wTitle, "\p-");
    ::ConcatPStrings(wTitle, wNumber);
    itsWindow->SetTitle(wTitle);

    itsWindow->Select();
}
```

You have seen DoSaveAs in previous chapters as well:

```
Boolean CAddressBookDoc::DoSaveAs(SFReply *macSFReply)
{
    if (itsFile != NULL)
        itsFile->Dispose();

    CDataFile *theDataFile = new CDataFile;
    itsFile = theDataFile;
    theDataFile->IDataFile();
    theDataFile->SFSpecify(macSFReply);
    if (theDataFile->ExistsOnDisk())
        theDataFile->ThrowOut();
```

```
    theDataFile->CreateNew(gSignature, 'ADDR');

    itsWindow->SetTitle(macSFReply->fName);

    return(DoSave());
}
```

The BuildWindow member function creates the window and pane:

```
void CAddressBookDoc::BuildWindow()
{
    const short   kWINDResourceID = 500;
    const Boolean kWindowFloats = TRUE;
    const Boolean kFitHorizontal = TRUE;
    const Boolean kFitVertical = TRUE;

    CWindow *aWindow = new CWindow;
    aWindow->IWindow(kWINDResourceID, !kWindowFloats, gDesktop,
      this);
    itsWindow = aWindow;

    CAddressBookPane *thePane = new CAddressBookPane;
    thePane->IAddressBookPane(itsWindow, this, 72*6, 72*4, 0, 0,
      sizFIXEDSTICKY, sizFIXEDSTICKY);
    itsGopher = thePane;
    itsMainPane = thePane;
    thePane->FitToEnclosure(kFitHorizontal, kFitVertical);
}
```

Notice that the window is of fixed size and contains no scroll bars. A database entry screen is an example of the kind of window you might expect to find designed this way.

Take a look at how the DoSave member function saves a file:

```
Boolean CAddressBookDoc::DoSave()
{
    Handle        theData;

    if (itsFile == NULL)
        return(DoSaveFileAs());
    else {
        CDataFile *theDataFile = (CDataFile *) itsFile;
```

```
        {
            TWithFileOpen fileOpener(theDataFile, fsWrPerm);
            TIterator    iter(*fDatabase);

            for(iter.MoveToBeginning(); !iter.NoMore();
              iter.MoveForward()) {
                TEntry *curEntry = (TEntry *) iter.GetCurrent();

                WriteAString(theDataFile, curEntry->GetName());
                WriteAString(theDataFile, curEntry->
                  GetAddress());
                WriteAString(theDataFile, curEntry->GetCity());
                WriteAString(theDataFile, curEntry->GetState());
                WriteAString(theDataFile, curEntry->GetZip());
                WriteAString(theDataFile, curEntry->
                  GetAddress());
            }
        }
        dirty = FALSE;
        return(TRUE);
    }
}
```

DoSave writes out the file as a succession of entries. In turn, each entry in the file is written out as a succession of strings, and each string is written with a length byte, followed by that many bytes.

Here is the WriteAString routine that DoSave calls to write each string:

```
static void WriteAString(CDataFile *aDataFile, const char *s)
{
    unsigned char length = Min(255, strlen(s));
                    // write length(s),   s
    aDataFile->WriteSome((Ptr) &length, sizeof(length));
    aDataFile->WriteSome((Ptr) s, length);
}
```

Note the nicety of writing the strings with a leading length byte instead of with a trailing '\0' byte. This makes it easier to read in the string. (A trailing '\0' byte might necessitate reading the strings character by character.)

`OpenFile` reads in the strings and entries in the same order they were written:

```
void CAddressBookDoc::OpenFile(SFReply *macReply)
{
    CDataFile     *theDataFile;
    Handle         theData;
    Str63          theName;
    OSErr          theError;

    theDataFile = new CDataFile;
    itsFile = theDataFile;

    theDataFile->IDataFile();
    theDataFile->SFSpecify(macReply);

    {
        TWithFileOpen fileOpener(theDataFile, fsRdPerm);
        long    fileLength = theDataFile->GetLength();
        while (theDataFile->GetMark() < fileLength)
        {
            char    name[256];
            char    address[256];
            char    city[256];
            char    state[256];
            char    zip[256];
            char    telephone[256];

            ReadAString(theDataFile, name);
            ReadAString(theDataFile, address);
            ReadAString(theDataFile, city);
            ReadAString(theDataFile, state);
            ReadAString(theDataFile, zip);
            ReadAString(theDataFile, telephone);

            TEntry *newEntry = new TEntry(name, address, city,
              state, zip, telephone);
            ::FailNIL(newEntry);
            AddEntry(newEntry);
        }

        BuildWindow();
    }
```

```
    gDecorator->StaggerWindow(itsWindow);
    itsFile->GetName(theName);
    itsWindow->SetTitle(theName);

    itsWindow->Select();

    // make pane display the first entry
    itsMainPane->DoCommand(CAddressBookPane::kBeginning);
}
```

Listed below is the ReadAString routine that OpenFile uses to actually read in the information:

```
static void ReadAString(CDataFile *aDataFile, char *s)
{
    unsigned char    length;

    aDataFile->ReadSome((Ptr) &length, sizeof(length));
    aDataFile->ReadSome((Ptr) s, length);
    s[length] = '\0';
}
```

The AddEntry member function is quite simple:

```
void CAddressBookDoc::AddEntry(TEntry *anEntry)
{
    fDatabase->Insert(anEntry);
}
```

The CreateDatabaseIterator returns an iterator that iterates over the entries in the database:

```
TIterator *CAddressBookDoc::CreateDatabaseIterator()
{
    TIterator *iter;

    iter = new TIterator(*fDatabase);
    ::FailNIL(iter);
    return iter;
}
```

The CAddressBookPane Class

The CAddressBookPane class is responsible for the following:

- Ensuring that each database view menu item works. For instance, if Go Forward is selected, CAddressBookPane directs the next name in the database to be shown.
- Handling the New Entry menu item.
- Making sure that the correct entry is displayed.

CAddressBookPane does not directly display an entry. Instead, it acts as the enclosing pane for a number of CEditText objects, each of which displays a component of the entry:

```
class CAddressBookPane: public CPane {
public:
    enum {kNextEntry = 1025, kPreviousEntry = 1026,
      kBeginning=1027, kEnd=1028, kNewEntry = 1029,
      kItemStringResourceID = 1024};

    void    IAddressBookPane(CView *anEnclosure, CAddressBookDoc
      *aSupervisor, short aWidth, short aHeight, short aHEncl,
      short aVEncl,  SizingOption aHSizing, SizingOption
      aVSizing);

    virtual void    UpdateMenus();
    virtual void    DoCommand(long theCommand);

protected:
    CEditText       *CreateStaticText(short width, short height,
      short horizLocation, short verticalLocation, short itemID);
    void            UpdateEntryData();

private:
    CAddressBookDoc *fAddressBookDoc;
    TIterator        *fAddressBookIterator;
    CEditText        *fName;
    CEditText        *fAddress;
    CEditText        *fCity;
    CEditText        *fState;
    CEditText        *fZip;
    CEditText        *fTelephone;
};
```

Look at what the various member functions do. CreateStaticText creates a CEditText at the given location and of the given size. The CEditText cannot be edited and, thus, is treated as static.

```
CEditText *CAddressBookPane::CreateStaticText(short width,
  short height, short horizLocation, short verticalLocation,
  short itemID)
{
    CEditText *text;

    text = new CEditText;
    text->IEditText(this, fAddressBookDoc,
      width, height, horizLocation, verticalLocation,
      sizFIXEDSTICKY, sizFIXEDSTICKY,-1);
    text->Specify(kNotEditable, kNotSelectable, kNotStylable);
    if (itemID != 0) {
        Str255    string;

        GetIndString(string, kItemStringResourceID, itemID);
        text->SetTextString(string);
    }
    text->SetFontName("\pGeneva");
    text->SetFontSize(9);
    if (wantBold)
        text->SetFontStyle(bold);
    return text;
}
```

The last parameter, itemID, specifies an index within an 'STR#' resource. This is where the text for the object is located. Note that the text object is set to Geneva 9 point because the default Chicago 12 point is too large.

The initialization method uses CreateStaticText to create a number of text objects:

```
void CAddressBookPane::IAddressBookPane(CView *anEnclosure,
  CAddressBookDoc *anAddressBookDoc,
  short aWidth, short aHeight,
  short aHEncl, short aVEncl,
  SizingOption aHSizing, SizingOption aVSizing)
{
    const Boolean kWantBold = true;
```

```
    fAddressBookDoc = anAddressBookDoc;
    fAddressBookIterator = NULL;
    IPane(anEnclosure, anAddressBookDoc, 0, 0, aHEncl, aVEncl,
      aHSizing, aVSizing);
    fAddressBookIterator = fAddressBookDoc->
      CreateDatabaseIterator();
    fAddressBookIterator->MoveToBeginning();

    CreateStaticText(50, 20, 5, 3, 1, kWantBold);     // Name:
    CreateStaticText(60, 20, 5, 23, 2, kWantBold);    // Address:
    CreateStaticText(40, 20, 5, 43, 3, kWantBold);    // City:
    CreateStaticText(35, 20, 155, 43, 4, kWantBold); // State:
    CreateStaticText(20, 20, 220, 43, 5, kWantBold); // Zip:
    CreateStaticText(60, 20, 5, 63, 6, kWantBold);    // Phone:

    fName = CreateStaticText(250, 20, 70, 3, 0);
    fAddress = CreateStaticText(250, 20, 70, 23, 0);
    fCity = CreateStaticText(80, 20, 70, 43, 0);
    fState = CreateStaticText(20, 20, 195, 43, 0);
    fZip = CreateStaticText(80, 20, 245, 43, 0);
    fTelephone = CreateStaticText(200, 20, 70, 63, 0);
}
```

Look at what this function does. First it initializes its base class. It then creates an iterator that keeps track of which entry currently is being viewed. It also creates a number of static text items, each initialized with an entry from an 'STR#' resource. These are for the (unchanging) labels "Name:," "Address:," "City:," "State:," "Zip:," and "Telephone:." Last, the function creates some other text items—these are the ones in which the actual name, address, and other information appear. They are stored in data members.

The member function UpdateEntryData does two things: It gets the current entry and it updates the information in the on-screen text items:

```
void CAddressBookPane::UpdateEntryData()
{
    const TEntry *entry = (TEntry *) fAddressBookIterator->
      GetCurrent();
    char          name[256] = "";
    char          address[256] = "";
    char          city[256] = "";
```

```
    char        state[256] = "";
    char        zip[256] = "";
    char        phone[256] = "";

    if (entry) {
        ::strcpy(name, entry->GetName());
        ::strcpy(address, entry->GetAddress());
        ::strcpy(city, entry->GetCity());
        ::strcpy(state, entry->GetState());
        ::strcpy(zip, entry->GetZip());
        ::strcpy(phone, entry->GetTelephone());
    }
    fName->SetTextPtr(name, strlen(name));
    fAddress->SetTextPtr(address, strlen(address));
    fCity->SetTextPtr(city, strlen(city));
    fState->SetTextPtr(state, strlen(state));
    fZip->SetTextPtr(zip, strlen(zip));
    fTelephone->SetTextPtr(phone, strlen(phone));
    Refresh();
}
```

For cases where there is no current entry, `UpdateEntryData` preinitializes all of the fields to empty strings. The iterator's `GetCurrent` returns the current entry as an `MCollectible *`. Notice that a cast to `TEntry *` is necessary; you may know that the database contains `TEntry` objects, but the compiler does not. Last, `Refresh` gets called to invalidate the pane, causing the text fields to redisplay themselves with their new values.

The menus are enabled (as always) with `UpdateMenus`:

```
void CAddressBookPane::UpdateMenus()
{
    CPane::UpdateMenus();
    if (!fAddressBookIterator->AtEnd())
        gBartender->EnableCmd(kNextEntry);
    if (!fAddressBookIterator->AtBeginning())
        gBartender->EnableCmd(kPreviousEntry);
    if (!fAddressBookIterator->NoMore()) {
        gBartender->EnableCmd(kEnd);
        gBartender->EnableCmd(kBeginning);
    }
    gBartender->EnableCmd(kNewEntry);
}
```

Care is taken to make sure that Go Forward is not enabled at the end and that Go Backward is not enabled at the beginning. Go to Beginning and Go to End are enabled if there are any entries in the database. New Entry always is enabled.

The workhorse function that implements the above menu items is, as always, DoCommand:

```
void CAddressBookPane::DoCommand(long theCommand)
{
    switch (theCommand) {
    case kNewEntry:
        CNewEntryDialogDirector *aDialogDirector =
          new CNewEntryDialogDirector;
        aDialogDirector->
          INewEntryDialogDirector(fAddressBookDoc);
        TEntry *anEntry = aDialogDirector->GetNewEntry();
        aDialogDirector->Dispose();

        if (anEntry != NULL) {
            fAddressBookDoc->AddEntry(anEntry);
            // Display entry
            fAddressBookIterator->MoveToBeginning();
            for (;!fAddressBookIterator->NoMore();
              fAddressBookIterator->MoveForward())
                if (anEntry == (TEntry *) fAddressBookIterator->
                  GetCurrent())
                    break;
            UpdateEntryData();
        }
        break;
    case kNextEntry:
        fAddressBookIterator->MoveForward();
        UpdateEntryData();
        break;
    case kPreviousEntry:
        fAddressBookIterator->MoveBackward();
        UpdateEntryData();
        break;
    case kBeginning:
        fAddressBookIterator->MoveToBeginning();
        UpdateEntryData();
        break;
```

```
        case kEnd:
            fAddressBookIterator->MoveToEnd();
            UpdateEntryData();
            break;
        default:
            CPane::DoCommand(theCommand);
            break;
    }
}
```

The Go Forward, Go Backward, Go to Beginning, and Go to End menu items adjust the iterator and then call UpdateEntryData to display the new entry.

For a new entry, a CNewEntryDialogDirector function is created, which puts up an alert. It then returns the new entry (unless the user cancels the dialog). After the entry is added to the document, CNewEntryDialogDirector iterates through the entries to see to it that the new entry is the current one. This nicety ensures that new entries are shown as soon as they are completed.

The CNewEntryDialog Class

CDLOGDialog serves as the base class of CNewEntryDialog. CDLOGDialog is a class that creates the objects (text, controls, etc.) for a dialog by reading standard 'DLOG' and 'DITL' resources. These resources are used to determine what objects to create, as well as their size and locations. CDLOGDialog creates its text items in the standard dialog font: Chicago 12 point.

The class declaration for CNewEntryDialog is as follows:

```
class CNewEntryDialog: public CDLOGDialog {
public:
    enum {nameTextID = 3, addressTextID = 4, cityTextID = 5,
      stateTextID = 6, zipTextID = 7, phoneTextID = 8};

    void INewEntryDialog(short DLOGid, CDesktop *anEnclosure,
      CDirector *aSupervisor);

protected:
    CPane *AddDITLEditText( short aWidth, short aHeight,
      short hEncl, short vEncl, CView *enclosure, tDITLItem
      *ditlItem);
```

```
    CPane *AddDITLStatText( short aWidth, short aHeight,
      short hEncl, short vEncl, CView *enclosure, tDITLItem
      *ditlItem);
};
```

CNewEntryDialog uses a font different than the default; it uses Geneva 9 for edit text items and Geneva 9 bold for static text items. CNewEntryDialog does this by overriding AddDITLEditText and AddDITLStaticText. These are the CDLOGDialog routines that create panes corresponding to edit text and static text items in the 'DITL' resource. The enumeration constants refer to the index within the 'DITL' resource.

The initialization method is trivial:

```
void CNewEntryDialog::INewEntryDialog(short DLOGid, CDesktop
  *anEnclosure, CDirector *aSupervisor)
{
    IDLOGDialog(DLOGid, anEnclosure, aSupervisor);
}
```

The two routines AddDITLStatText and AddDITLEditText augment the original versions. They call the old version and then set the font, size, and, possibly, style of the resulting pane:

```
CPane *CNewEntryDialog::AddDITLStatText( short aWidth, short
  aHeight, short hEncl, short vEncl, CView *enclosure, tDITLItem
  *ditlItem)
{
    CAbstractText *result;

    result = (CAbstractText *) CDLOGDialog::AddDITLStatText(aWidth,
      aHeight, hEncl, vEncl, enclosure, ditlItem);
    result->SetFontName("\pGeneva");
    result->SetFontSize(9);
    result->SetFontStyle(bold);
    return result;
}

CPane *CNewEntryDialog::AddDITLEditText( short aWidth, short
  aHeight, short hEncl, short vEncl, CView *enclosure, tDITLItem
  *ditlItem)
```

```
{
    CAbstractText *result;

    result = (CAbstractText *) CDLOGDialog::AddDITLEditText(aWidth,
      aHeight, hEncl, vEncl, enclosure, ditlItem);
    result->SetFontName("\pGeneva");
    result->SetFontSize(9);
    return result;
}
```

The CNewEntryDialogDirector Class

The `CNewEntryDialogDirector` class is responsible for displaying the dialog and for ensuring that it acts like a modal dialog:

```
class CNewEntryDialogDirector: public CDialogDirector {
public:
    void INewEntryDialogDirector(CDirectorOwner *aSupervisor);
    TEntry *GetNewEntry();
};
```

The class has an initialization member function:

```
void CNewEntryDialogDirector::INewEntryDialogDirector
  (CDirectorOwner *aSupervisor)
{
    CNewEntryDialog *dialog;

    CDialogDirector::IDialogDirector( aSupervisor);

    dialog = new(CNewEntryDialog);
    itsWindow = dialog;

    dialog->INewEntryDialog(kNewEntryDLOGID, gDesktop, this);

    gDecorator->CenterWindow(dialog);
}
```

Notice that this initializer function creates a `CNewEntryDialog`, initializes it with the resource ID of the `'DITL'` and `'DLOG'` resources, and then calls the `CDecorator` member function `CenterWindow` to center the window appropriately.

Next is the GetNewEntry function, which displays the modal dialog, reads the information the user typed, and then creates a TEntry based on that information:

```
TEntry *CNewEntryDialogDirector::GetNewEntry()
{
    long            theCommand;

        // show the dialog

    BeginModalDialog();

        // run the dialog and return the final command.

    theCommand = DoModalDialog(cmdOK);

    if (theCommand == cmdOK)
    {
        CDialogText *dialogText;
        Str255    name;
        Str255    address;
        Str255    city;
        Str255    state;
        Str255    zip;
        Str255    phone;
        TEntry *newEntry;

        ::GetTextFromWindow(itsWindow,
          CNewEntryDialog::nameTextID, name);
        ::GetTextFromWindow(itsWindow,
          CNewEntryDialog::addressTextID,address);
        ::GetTextFromWindow(itsWindow,
          CNewEntryDialog::cityTextID, city);
        ::GetTextFromWindow(itsWindow,
          CNewEntryDialog::stateTextID, state);
        ::GetTextFromWindow(itsWindow,
          CNewEntryDialog::zipTextID, zip);
        ::GetTextFromWindow(itsWindow,
          CNewEntryDialog::phoneTextID, phone);

        newEntry = new TEntry(p2cstr(name), p2cstr(address),
          p2cstr(city), p2cstr(state), p2cstr(zip),
          p2cstr(phone));
```

```
        ::FailNIL(newEntry);
        return newEntry;
    }
    return NULL;
}
```

The parameter to DoModalDialog is the command number of the default button. For this dialog, the OK button is the default. The return result of DoModalDialog is the command number of the button pressed by the user. (Note that the buttons in the 'DITL' resource have command numbers appended to them just like menu items do.) If the user hits the OK button, the function reads each of the fields with GetTextFromWindow, creates a TEntry, and returns it.

GetTextFromWindow gets the text that the user types in by calling GetTextString:

```
static void GetTextFromWindow(CWindow *theWindow, short itemID,
  StringPtr string)
{
    CDialogText *dialogText;

    dialogText = (CDialogText *) theWindow->FindViewByID(itemID);
    ::FailNIL(dialogText);
    dialogText->GetTextString(string);
}
```

The AddressBook Main Program

With the interface and engine complete, you have a plain vanilla main program again:

```
void main()
{
    CAddressBookApp *app;

    app = new CAddressBookApp;
    app->IAddressBookApp();
    app->Run();
    app->Exit();
}
```

The Resources

The AddressBook application has three resources of note: a new 'MENU' resource; an 'MBAR' resource that includes the 'MENU' within it; and an 'STR#' resource with strings for the address pane. It also has 'DLOG' and 'DITL' resources to initialize the New Entry dialog.

```
resource 'MBAR' (1, preload) {
    { 1,  2, 3, 4
    }
};

resource 'MENU' (4, "Entries", preload) {
    4,
    textMenuProc,
    0x7FFFFFFE,
    enabled,
    "Entries",
    {
        "Go Forward#1025", noIcon, "F", noMark, plain,
        "Go Backward#1026", noIcon, "B", noMark, plain,
        "-", noIcon, noKey, noMark, plain,
        "Go to Beginning#1027", noIcon, noKey, noMark, plain,
        "Go to End#1028", noIcon, noKey, noMark, plain,
        "-", noIcon, noKey, noMark, plain,
        "New Entry#1029", noIcon, "E", noMark, plain,

    }
};
```

As always, the menu items have command numbers appended to them for reference within the program.

The 'STR#' resource contains the text for the fields in the address book pane:

```
resource 'STR#' (1024, "field names") {
    {
        "Name:",
        "Address:",
        "City:",
        "State:",
        "Zip:",
        "Telephone:"
    }
};
```

The 'DLOG' and 'DITL' resources are used to initialize the New Entry dialog:

```
resource 'DLOG' (1025, "New Entry") {
    {72, 76, 222, 404},
    movableDBoxProc,
    visible,
    noGoAway,
    0x0,
    1025,
    ""
};

resource 'DITL' (1025, "New Entry") {
    {
        {118, 265, 138, 323},
        Button {
            enabled,
            "OK#100"
        },
        {118, 139, 138, 197},
        Button {
            enabled,
            "Cancel#101"
        },
        {23, 70, 39, 320},
        EditText {
            enabled,
            "@!!255"
        },
        {46, 70, 62, 320},
        EditText {
            enabled,
            "@!255"
        },
        {69, 70, 85, 150},
        EditText {
            enabled,
            "@!255"
        },
        {69, 195, 85, 215},
        EditText {
```

```
        enabled,
        "@!5"
    },
    {69, 245, 85, 320},
    EditText {
        enabled,
        "@!10"
    },
    {92, 70, 108, 270},
    EditText {
        enabled,
        "@!255"
    },
    {46, 5, 62, 65},
    StaticText {
        disabled,
        "Address:"
    },
    {23, 5, 39, 55},
    StaticText {
        disabled,
        "Name:"
    },
    {1, 118, 19, 238},
    StaticText {
        disabled,
        "New Entry"
    },
    {69, 220, 85, 240},
    StaticText {
        disabled,
        "Zip:"
    },
    {69, 155, 85, 190},
    StaticText {
        disabled,
        "State:"
    },
    {69, 5, 85, 45},
    StaticText {
        disabled,
        "City:"
```

```
            },
            {92, 5, 108, 65},
            StaticText {
                disabled,
                "Telephone:"
            }
        }
};
```

Figure 21.8 shows what these resources look like in ResEdit.

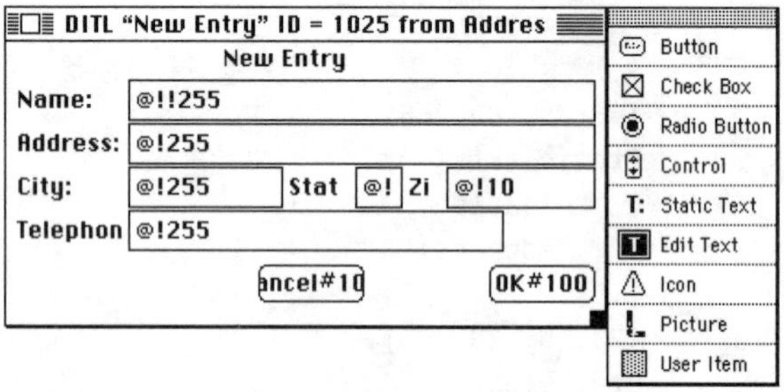

Figure 21.8. The New Entry dialog as seen in ResEdit.

Notice the OK and Cancel buttons have the command numbers appended to them. Also note the odd entries in the edit text items. When `CDITLDialog` reads edit text fields from a `'DITL'`, it looks at the first character. If the first character is an @, `CDITLDialog` treats the remainder of the string as initialization information. `@!number` specifies that the edit text holds no more than *number* characters. In this dialog, most of the edit text fields hold no more than 255 characters. The zip code field, as an exception, holds at most 10. Two ! characters (`@!!number`) specify that the field is a required one and cannot be left empty.

Summary

This chapter contains an application that was developed in two parts. First, you learned the advantages of bifurcating an application. Then, you learned how to generate content classes that take advantage of their independence from the TCL by using multiple inheritance. The second part of the development focused on the user interface, including the use of modal dialogs. After the interface was finished, it was melded to the working database with TDatabase to form a usable address book application.

Exercises

1. Add a Find menu item that brings up a dialog into which the user can type a name. If an entry matches the name, the address book pane should then display it.
2. As it is written, the binary tree has poor worst-case performance. For instance, if entries are inserted in alphabetical order (when reading from an existing file, for instance), the binary tree is completely lopsided, with each node having only one child.

   Rewrite the TDatabase class to use a balanced binary tree such as a Red-Black, an AVL, or a Splay tree.
3. AddressBook loses memory each time you create a document and then close it. The CAddressBookPane allocates a TIterator (by calling TAddressBookDoc::CreateDatabaseIterator), but never frees it. Fix this memory leak.

A

Compatability and Porting

This appendix provides broad a overview of issues related to implementing compatibility and portability features in code. MPW C++, THINK C, and standard C++ code are covered.

Converting from MPW C++

If you have been using Apple's MPW C++, there are some differences about which you may want to know.

No #pragma Segment

Symantec C++ does not recognize the following `pragma`:

```
#pragma segment segmentName
```

Segmentation in Symantec C++ is done on a file-by-file basis from the Project window.

No SingleObject

Apple C++ provides an extension to C++, `SingleObject`. This is a special class that cannot utilize multiple inheritance. Furthermore, any derived classes of this class also are prohibited from using multiple inheritance. Its advantage is that virtual function calls are slightly faster with `SingleObject` because there is no overhead for multiple inheritance.

I/O Differences with SANE

The way in which Symantec C++ outputs illegal floating-point values is different, as shown in table A.1.

Table A.1. Differences in How Nonnumbers Are Output

	Symantec C++	MPW C++
Infinity	INFINITY	INF
Negative Infinity	–INFINITY	–INF
Nonnumber	NAN or -NAN	NAN(*numeral*) or –NAN(*numeral*), where *numeral* is the NaN code

Converting from THINK C

There are differences between how THINK C and Symantec C++ handle enumeration sizes and Pascal string literals.

Enumeration Sizes

THINK C and Symantec C++ calculate the size of enumeration types differently. For example, given the following enumerations:

```
typedef enum {a=0,          k=255}        Enum1;
typedef enum {b=-128,       l=127}        Enum2;
typedef enum {c=0,          m=256}        Enum3;
typedef enum {d=-129,       n=127}        Enum4;
typedef enum {e=-32768,     o=32767}      Enum5;
typedef enum {f=0,          p=32768}      Enum6;
typedef enum {g=0,          q=32769}      Enum7;
typedef enum {x=0,          r=65535}      Enum8;
typedef enum {i=0,          s=65536}      Enum9;
typedef enum {j=-32769,     t=32767}      Enum10;
```

THINK C calculates the sizes as follows:

```
sizeof(Enum1)=2
sizeof(Enum2)=1
sizeof(Enum3)=2
sizeof(Enum4)=2
sizeof(Enum5)=2
sizeof(Enum6)=4
sizeof(Enum7)=4
sizeof(Enum8)=4
sizeof(Enum9)=4
sizeof(Enum10)=4
```

Symantec C++ and MPW C++ calculate the sizes as follows:

```
sizeof(Enum1)=1
sizeof(Enum2)=1
sizeof(Enum3)=2
sizeof(Enum4)=2
sizeof(Enum5)=2
sizeof(Enum6)=2
sizeof(Enum7)=2
sizeof(Enum8)=2
sizeof(Enum9)=4
sizeof(Enum10)=4
```

Size of Pascal String Literals

Pascal string literals (which have the form "\p*chars*") are laid out differently in memory. In Symantec C++, MPW C, and MPW C++, the following string occupies six bytes:

```
"\pNeil"
```

Listed below are the contents of six bytes:

```
5 'N' 'e' 'i' 'l' 0
```

In THINK C, on the other hand, the string is only five bytes long because it is missing the 0:

```
5 'N' 'e' 'i' 'l'
```

Differences from Standard C++

Symantec C++'s variations from standard C++ can be grouped into three categories: modifications to standard C++, extensions, and additional classes.

Modifications

In standard C++, the size of an enumeration is the same as the size of an `int`. In Symantec C++, the size of an enumeration is as big as necessary to fit the enumeration constants. Symantec C++ calculates sizes in this way for compatibility with Macintosh Pascal compilers.

You can turn off this modification with the enums are always ints check box in the Language Settings panel of the Symantec C++ Options dialog.

Extensions

Extensions are additions to Standard C++. They provide additional Macintosh functionality.

SANE Support. To support the Standard Apple Numerics Environment (SANE), Symantec C++ has added some new types to C++:

- `extended` is an 80-bit floating-point number. It is equivalent to `long double`.
- `comp` is a 64-bit integer.

You should use the type `long double` instead of `extended` so that your code is portable. If you need a 64-bit integer, your only choice is to use `comp` because there is no synonymous type.

Direct Function Calls. Direct calls are used to call traps. A direct call provides 68000 machine instructions that are executed instead of the standard jump to subroutine (JSR) call.

As an example, the Toolbox call `FrameRect` is declared as follows:

```
pascal void FrameRect(const Rect *r) = 0xA8A1;
```

The call to `FrameRect` looks like this:

```
FrameRect(&aRectangle);
```

Because `FrameRect` is a direct function call, the example gets compiled as follows:

```
PEA address of aRectangle;  // push the one parameter
FrameRect                   // the two bytes A8 and A1
```

If it were *not* a direct function call, the resulting assembly would be the following:

```
PEA address of aRectangle;  // push the one parameter
JSR FrameRect               // call the subroutine FrameRect
```

The Pascal Modifier. The `pascal` type modifier specifies that a function uses Pascal calling conventions. Most Toolbox routines use Pascal calling conventions. Therefore, these routines are declared with the `pascal` modifier. Here is an example:

```
pascal void FillRect(const Rect *r);
```

With Pascal calling conventions, parameters are pushed left to right, return results are passed on the stack (in space reserved by the caller), and the function pops the parameters off of the stack rather than the caller.

Pascal String Literals. In addition to standard string literals (like "Hello"), Symantec C++ supports Pascal string literals, which begin with \p. A Pascal string literal is one byte longer than a standard string literal. This is due to a length byte placed at the front.

For a standard string literal, "Hello" is an array with the following six bytes:

```
'H' 'e' 'l' 'l' 'o' 0
```

The corresponding Pascal string literal, "\pHello," is an array with seven bytes:

```
7 'H' 'e' 'l' 'l' 'o' 0
```

The type of a standard string literal is an array of `char`, while the type of a Pascal string literal is an array of `unsigned char`.

Additional Classes

The additional classes discussed here are abstract classes that modify how their derived classes behave.

HandleObject Class. Objects of type `HandleObject` are allocated as relocatable blocks on the heap with `NewHandle`. To preserve source code compatibility, the compiler automatically inserts an extra dereference.

Suppose you have the following code:

```
aHandleObject->fDataMember
```

It is compiled as if it were written as follows:

```
(*aHandleObject)->fDataMember
```

Objects of this type must be allocated dynamically. Thus, the following definition is illegal:

```
TMyHandleObject aHandleObject;
```

There are other restrictions placed on `HandleObjects`:

- No multiple inheritance.
- No operator overloading.
- No pointers to member functions.
- No pointers to data members.
- They only can be allocated dynamically. They must be declared as pointers and have to be allocated with `new`.

PascalObject Class. The `PascalObject` class provides objects that behave like those in Object Pascal.

Like HandleObjects, PascalObjects are relocatable blocks on the heap. In addition, calls to member functions are handled quite differently. Normally, calls to member functions are implemented using a table of function pointers stored in the object. For PascalObjects, calls to member functions are implemented by a call to a dispatch routine. To determine the actual function to call, this routine does a lookup based on the class ID stored in the object and the desired member function.

PascalObject provides some added functionality. The oops++ library provides the following:

```
void *new_by_name(char *aClassName);
char *class_name(void *anObject);
char member(void *anObject, void *aClass)
```

new_by_name takes the name of a class as an argument and returns a newly created object of that type:

```
TMyPascalObject *obj = new_by_name("TMyPascalObject");
```

class_name takes an object and returns its class:

```
printf("class name = %s\n", class_name(obj));
```

member returns 1 if anObject is an instance of aClass or of a class derived from aClass; otherwise, it returns 0.

```
if (member(obj, TMyPascalObject))
  printf("yes");
```

These routines only work for objects derived from PascalObject.

B

SourceServer and ToolServer

SourceServer and ToolServer are two utilities that can make working on large or multi-person projects easier. SourceServer is a source code control system that comes with Symantec C++. ToolServer, which must be ordered from APDA, is a stripped-down MPW that can execute tools and scripts.

This appendix introduces you to SourceServer, giving you enough information so that you can use it in your projects. You need to refer to the documentation if you want to know about advanced features. You also get a much briefer introduction to Apple's ToolServer.

SourceServer

Source code control is an important feature of a programming environment, but one that is new to the Symantec C++/THINK environment. Symantec has added source code control to the THINK Project Manager via Apple's Projector system, using the SourceServer application.

By way of introducing SourceServer, first examine the two most likely scenarios in which source code control can be useful:

- A multiple-person program. There are many development conflicts that can arise when working on a multiple-person program. One of most prevalent problems occurs when two people attempt to modify the same file at the same time. SourceServer deals with this by having Projector maintain control of the project files. Projector ensures that only one person can have write access to a file at a given time, while still enabling other people to have read-only access. Under this system, if you want to modify a file, you check it out with write access. When you are done modifying it, you check it in and retain a copy with read-only access. During the period you have it checked out, you are guaranteed that no one else can modify it.
- A program with two tracks of development. Imagine you have the typical development effort of a program that has been released as a 1.0 version and also is undergoing a major enhancement (to become a forthcoming 2.0). The enhancement engenders a long period of development, and version 1.0 needs some minor bug fix releases (versions 1.01, 1.1, etc.) before 2.0 is ready. Commonly, to deal with this, you start with two copies of 1.0—one becomes 1.01 and the other becomes 2.0. The two sets of sources diverge, and the fixes in version 1.01 quite likely are not reflected in version 2.0.

  When using Projector, all the files in the program are held in a database and the files for version 1.0 are named by a revision name (perhaps Version 1.0). Any file that needs to be modified for both 2.0 and 1.01 is *branched*. The branched version contains the 1.01 modification, while the unbranched version contains the 2.0 version. Thus, you have a project database that reflects a real-world situation—both versions were spawned from the 1.0 version. See figure B.1 for a small example of this.

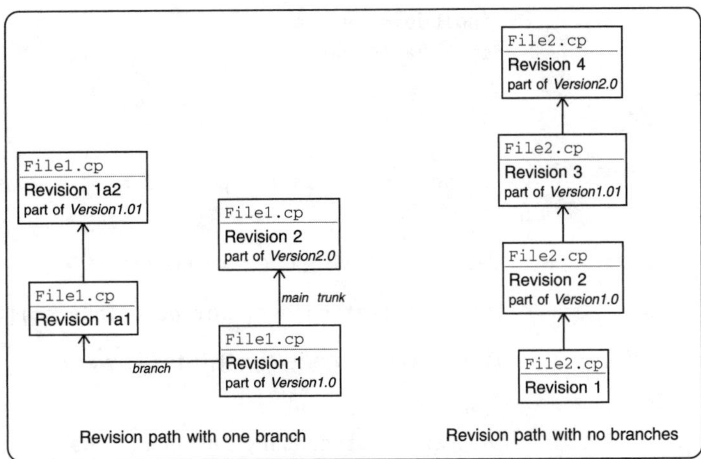

Figure B.1. A revision hierarchy with named versions.

In the past, many THINK C programmers found Projector so useful that they used MPW to get access to it. They developed their code using THINK C and then exported it to MPW for Projector. As you might expect, this system was an inconvenient solution. Apple fortuitously broke Projector out of MPW and turned it into an application—SourceServer—that responds to Projector commands via Apple Events. THINK Project Manager is a client that sends Apple Events to SourceServer in response to selections from the SourceServer menu.

Now that you know a little of its history and situations in which you might want to use it, you can learn how to handle source code control with SourceServer.

Creating a Project

First, you have to create some source files so that SourceServer has something to control. Perform the following steps:

1. Create a project within the THINK Project Manager named PowersOfTwo. .

2. Create Main.cp, Power.h, and Power.cp files. Main.cp should include the following code:

```
#include <iostream.h>
#include "Power.h"

void main()
{
    cout << "2 to the power 8 = " << Power(2, 8) << '\n';
}
```

Use the following code for Power.h:

```
int Power(int number, int powerToRaise);
```

The following code constitutes Power.cp:

```
#include "Power.h"
int Power(int number, int powerToRaise)
{
    int returnValue = 1;

    for (int i = 0; i < powerToRaise; i++)
        returnValue *= number;
    return returnValue;
}
```

3. Test the program and make sure it prints the following:

```
2 to the power 8 = 256
```

4. Load the IOStreams, ANSI++, CPlusLib, and SANE libraries. When you have finished, your project should look like the one in figure B.2.

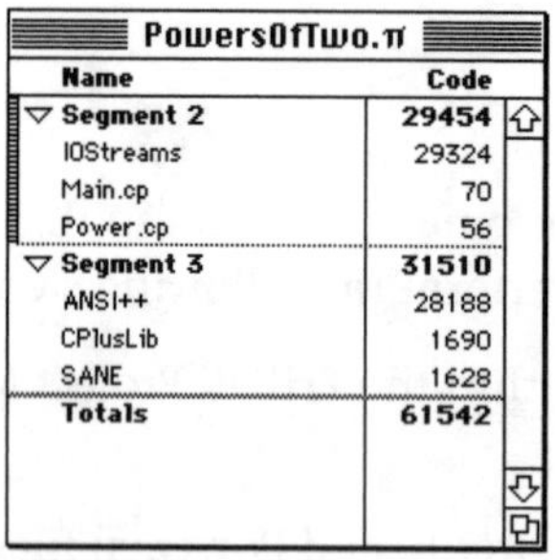

PowersOfTwo.π

Name	Code
▽ **Segment 2**	**29454**
IOStreams	29324
Main.cp	70
Power.cp	56
▽ **Segment 3**	**31510**
ANSI++	28188
CPlusLib	1690
SANE	1628
Totals	**61542**

Figure B.2. The PowersOfTwo Project window.

Launching SourceServer

All SourceServer commands are accessed from the SourceServer menu item in the Source menu. From the SourceServer menu, select Launch SourceServer (see fig. B.3).

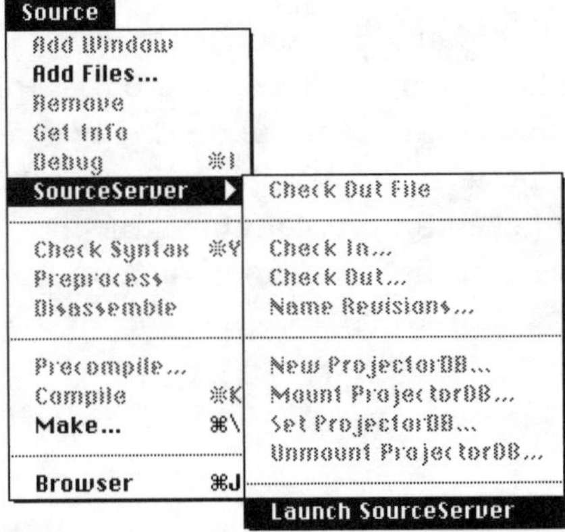

Figure B.3. Launching SourceServer.

After you launch SourceServer, verify that it is running by checking the Application menu (see fig. B.4). You should see the SourceServer icon in the menu.

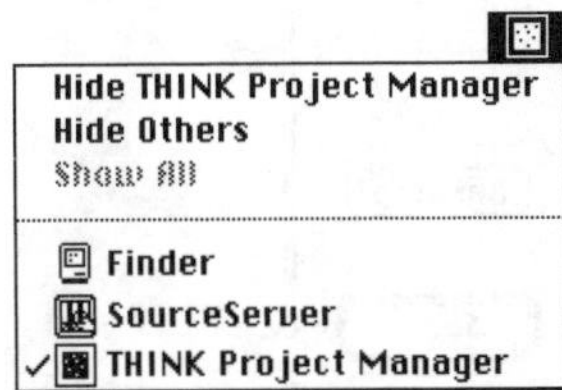

Figure B.4. Verifying that SourceServer is running.

NOTE

THINK Project Manager uses Apple Events to communicate with SourceServer and ToolServer. As a result, you must be running System 7 or later to use them.

Now, all the items in the SourceServer menu should be available. (Before selecting Launch SourceServer, they were dimmed.) Your next step is to create a Projector database for your files

WARNING

THINK Project Manager uses the term *project* to refer to the files used to build a program. Projector also uses this word to refer to a collection of files, including all the archived revisions of the files. A Projector project (also called a Projector database) is one large file containing all the revisions of all the files. To avoid confusion, throughout this discussion, the term *Projector database* is used for Projector, while the term *project* is used to mean a THINK Project Manager project.

Creating a Projector Database

Select New ProjectorDB from the SourceServer menu. Create your Projector database in the same folder as the PowersOfTwo. project and name it PowersOfTwo (see fig. B.5).

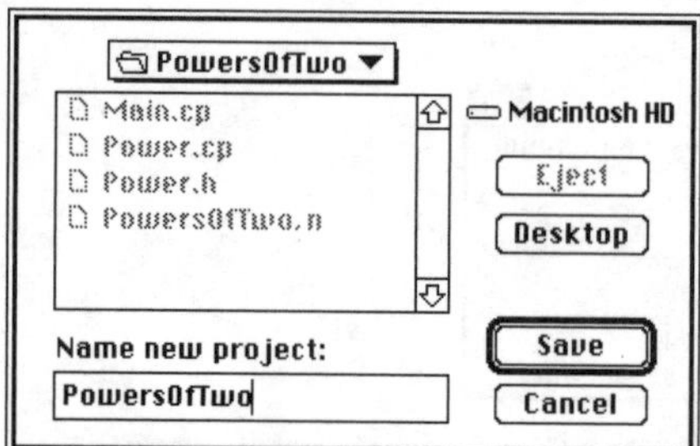

Figure B.5. Creating a new Projector database.

A dialog appears in which you can provide a comment for this Projector database. Figure B.6 shows this dialog, along with the comment you should type.

Figure B.6. The New ProjectorDB Comment dialog.

This creates a folder named PowersOfTwo, with a file in it named ProjectorDB (for Projector database). Figure B.7 shows you the folder layout.

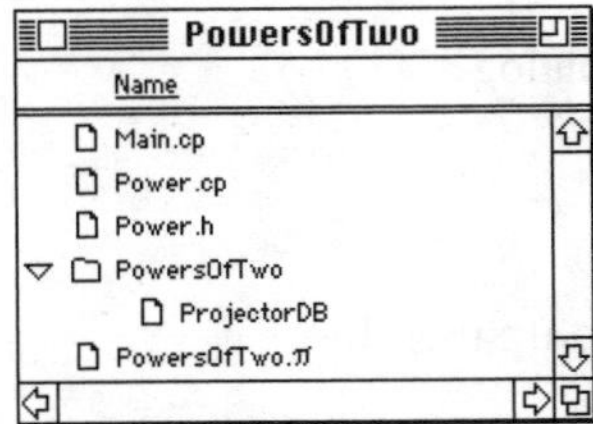

Figure B.7. The folder layout after creating the Projector database.

The SourceServer Check In Dialog

Now, you are ready to add your files to the Projector project. Select Check In from the SourceServer menu. Figure B.8 shows you the dialog you get as a result.

There are a number of names and radio buttons in this dialog. Take a look at what each one stands for.

The Project pop-up menu shown in figure B.9 contains all the mounted projects.

In the Select Files section of the dialog, you determine which files you want to check in (see fig. B.10).

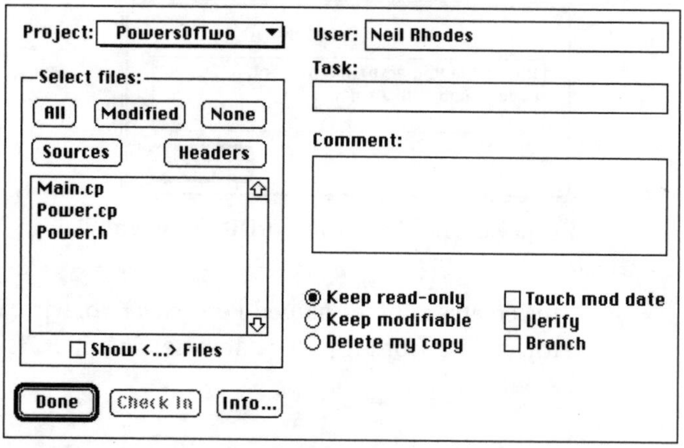

Figure B.8. The Check In dialog.

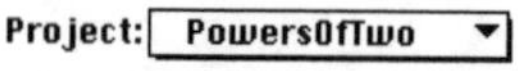

Figure B.9. The Project pop-up menu.

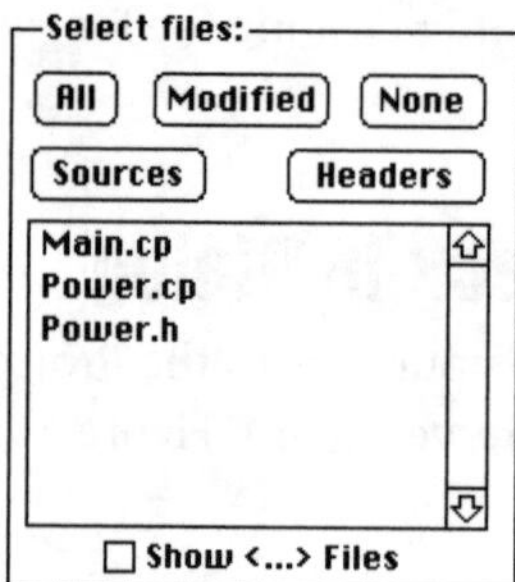

Figure B.10. The Select files section of the Check In dialog.

The options in this dialog are explained below:

- The All button selects all the files in the list.
- The Modified button selects all the files that have been modified since the last check-in.
- The None button deselects all the files in the list.
- The Sources button selects all the files that are listed in the project window (normally .cp files).

- ▼ The Headers button selects all the files that are referenced from the source files (normally .h files).
- ▼ The Show <_> Files check box, if checked, lists the files that belong to the THINK project tree (normally Macintosh or standard C++ header or TCL files).

To the right of the select files section, is the area where you enter the user name, task description, and project comment (see fig. B.11).

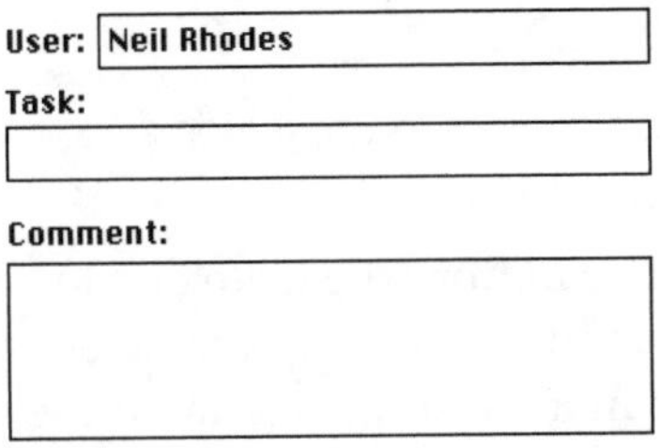

User: Neil Rhodes

Task:

Comment:

Figure B.11. User and task information portion of the dialog.

In the User field, enter the name of the user who is checking in. In the Task field, enter a short description of the task associated with this modification. You can enter a longer description of this modification in the Comment field.

Below the Comment field are the choices that affect how the files get checked in (see fig. B.12).

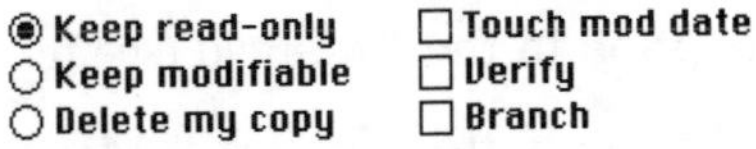

◉ Keep read-only ☐ Touch mod date
○ Keep modifiable ☐ Verify
○ Delete my copy ☐ Branch

Figure B.12. The file parameter section of the dialog.

The three radio buttons are mutually exclusive. If you select Keep read-only, after checking in, the files are checked out read-only to you. If you select Keep modifiable, after checking in, the files are checked out modifiable. If you select Delete my copy, after checking in, your copies of the files are deleted.

The three check boxes on the right control aspects of file check-in. If you select Touch mod date, SourceServer checks in the files with the current date, rather than using the modification dates of the files. If you select Verify, SourceServer double-checks the check-in by checking out each checked-in file to a temporary and comparing the temporary with the checked-in file. It aborts the check-in if the comparison reveals a difference. This is useful if you are worried about data loss. If you select Branch, the checked files are made into a new branch.

After you have set all the parameters, figure B.13 shows you the three choices that govern your next action.

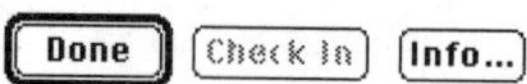

Figure B.13. The action choices in the dialog.

If you select the Done button, the dialog is closed. If you select, Check In, the files are checked in with the parameters you have set. If you select Info, you get more information about the selected files.

Now that you know what each choice entails, check in some source files.

Adding Files to the Projector Database

To check in the files you created in the PowersOfTwo project, do the following:

1. Click the All button to select all three files in the PowersOfTwo folder (or Shift-click each file to select them all).
2. Type a description in the Task field (see fig. B.14).
3. Click the Check In button (see fig. B.14).

Projector now copies the files to its database and leaves you with a copy of each file. Because the Keep read-only radio button is selected, each of the three files is now read-only.

After you leave the Check In window, open Main.cp and look at the lower-left corner. It should now look like the file in figure B.15. Main.cp should have a read-only icon in the bottom-left corner. This icon signifies that the file cannot be modified.

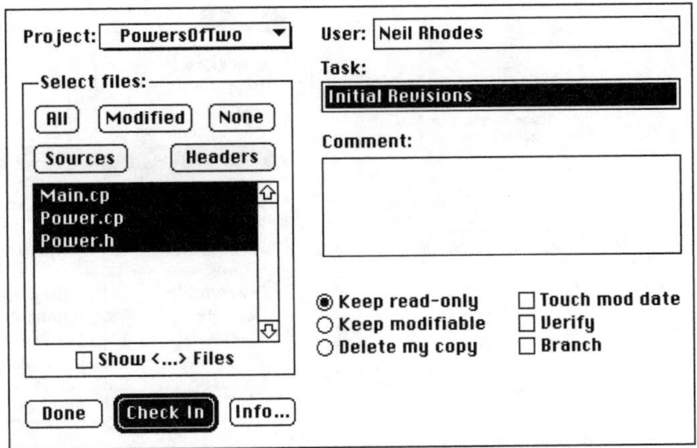

Figure B.14. Checking in three files.

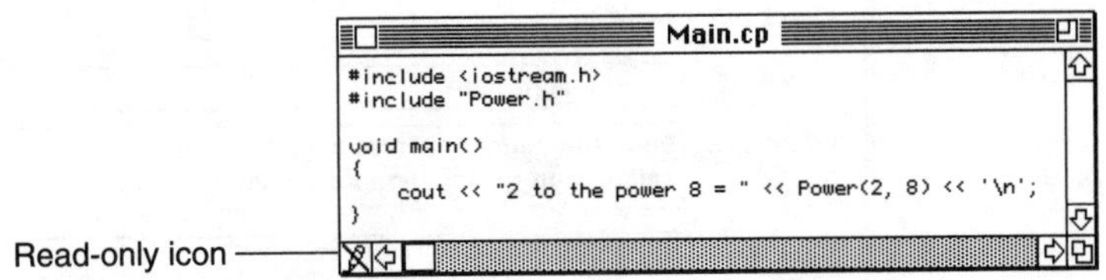

Figure B.15. A read-only file.

Checking Out a File

Now, modify Main.cp so that it calculates two numbers the user chooses, rather than 2 to the power 8. To modify the file, you need to check out a modifiable copy. To do that, make Main.cp the frontmost window and select Check Out 'Main.cp' from the SourceServer menu (see fig. B.16).

After the file is selected, you get the dialog shown in figure B.17. Fill in the Task and Comment fields and click OK.

Now, if you look at Main.cp in the THINK Project Manger, it should have a writable icon and look like the one in figure B.18.

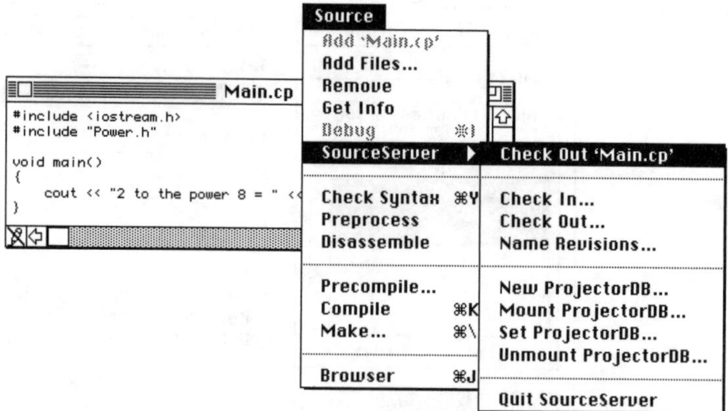

Figure B.16. Checking out Main.cp.

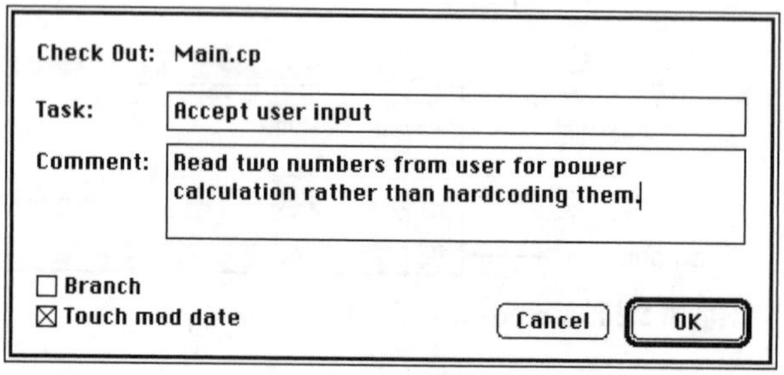

Check Out: Main.cp

Task: Accept user input

Comment: Read two numbers from user for power calculation rather than hardcoding them.

☐ Branch

☒ Touch mod date

Cancel OK

Figure B.17. The Check Out dialog.

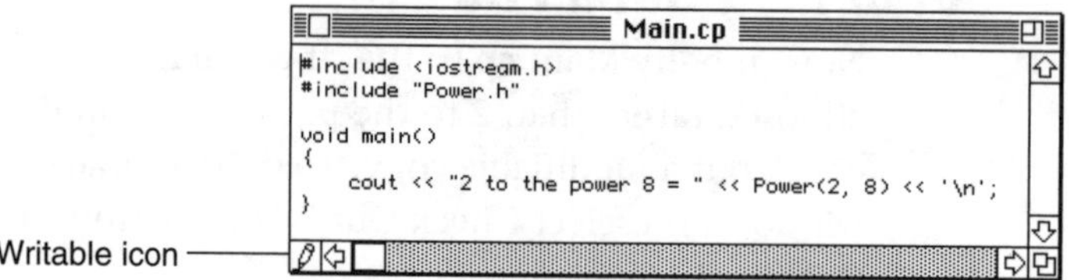

Figure B.18. File with a writable icon.

To modify Main.cp so that it can accept numbers from users and calculate their power, change it to the following:

```
#include <iostream.h>
#include "Power.h"

void main()
{
    int number;
    int power;

    cin >> number >> power;

    cout << number << " to the power " << power <<
      " = " << Power(number, power) << '\n';
}
```

Save the file using Save from the File menu.

Checking In a File

Although you could use Check In to check in the changes to Main.cp, there is an easier way. Make sure that Main.cp is the frontmost window in the THINK Project Manager and select Check In 'Main.cp' from the SourceServer menu (see fig. B.19).

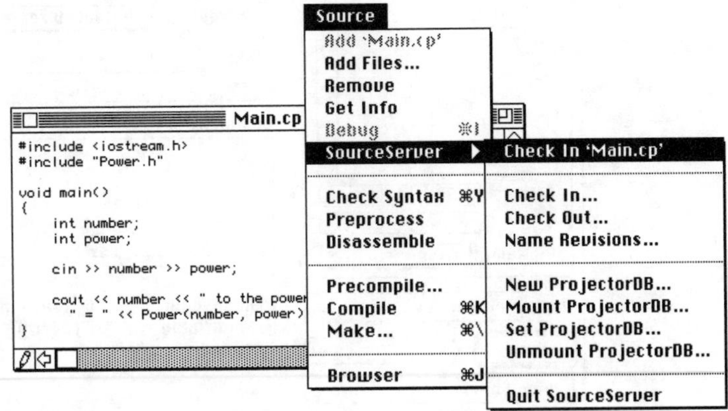

Figure B.19. Checking in the Main.cp file.

This brings up the Check In dialog where you can specify a task and command in the Task and Comment fields (see fig. B.20). Because you already specified a task and comment when checking out the file, you do not need to specify one when checking in.

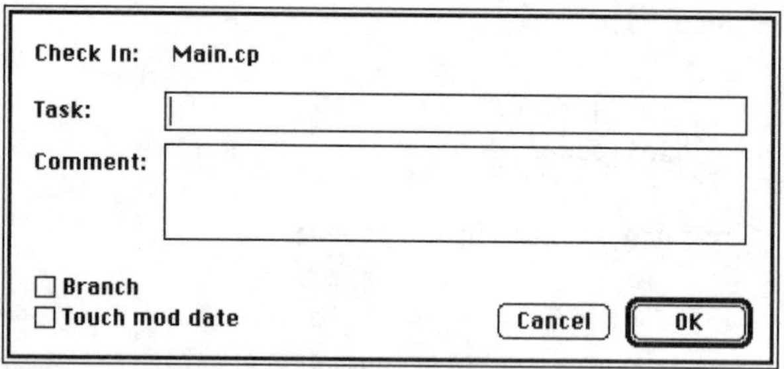

Figure B.20. The Check In dialog.

Getting Information about Revisions

Now that you have two versions of Main.cp, see how to access the information the Projector database keeps on each file. Select Check Out and double-click on Main.cp. The Check Out window shows a list of all revisions of Main.cp, as shown in figure B.21.

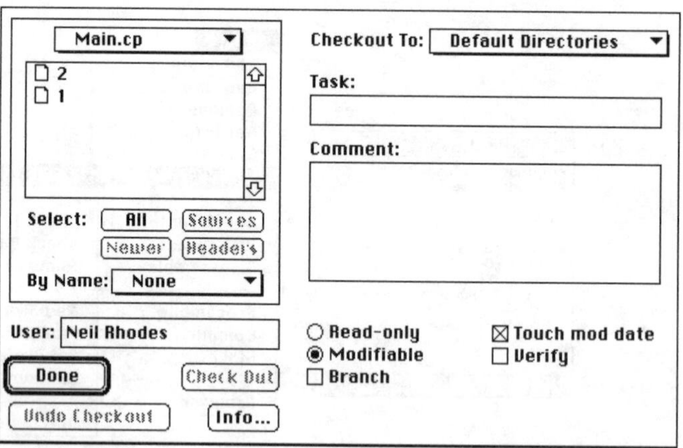

Figure B.21. The Check Out window showing the revisions of Main.cp.

Select version 2 and click the Info button (this is the version you just checked in). The window now shows you the task, comment, user, and date of that version (see fig. B.22).

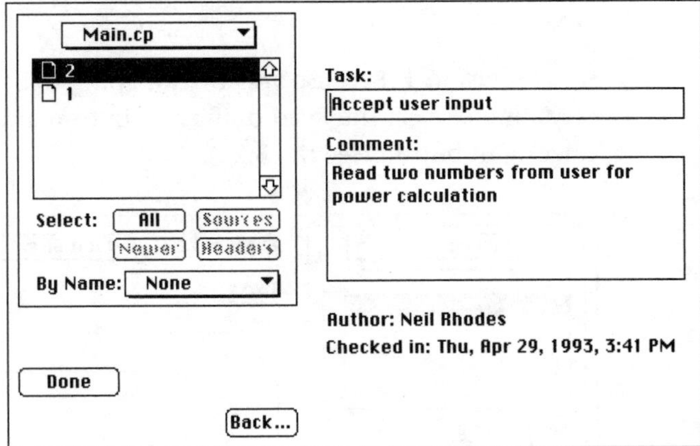

Figure B.22. The Check Out window showing information about revision 2.

Click on version 1 to see the information about that version (see fig. B.23). Note that the Task field displays "Initial revisions," the task description you typed when you initially checked in Main.cp.

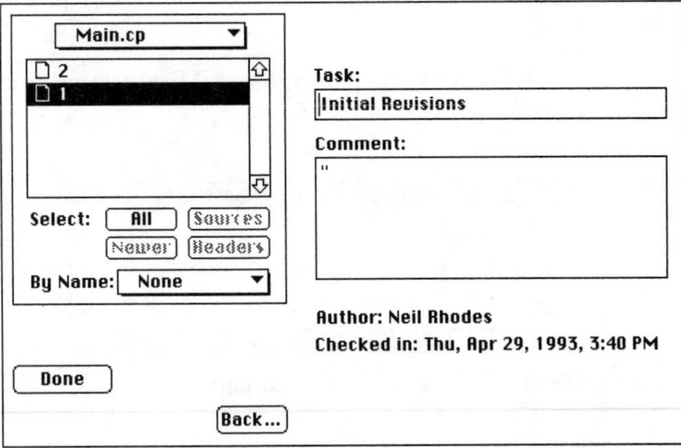

Figure B.23. The Check Out window showing information about revision 1.

Checking Out Old Versions of Files

Now that you know how to get information about each version, it is time to actually check the file out. Select Check Out and double-click on Main.cp. The Check Out window again shows a list of all revisions of Main.cp.

Select revision 1. Because you are not going to be modifying revision 1 of Main.cp, select the Read-only radio button and then click on the Check Out button (see fig. B.24).

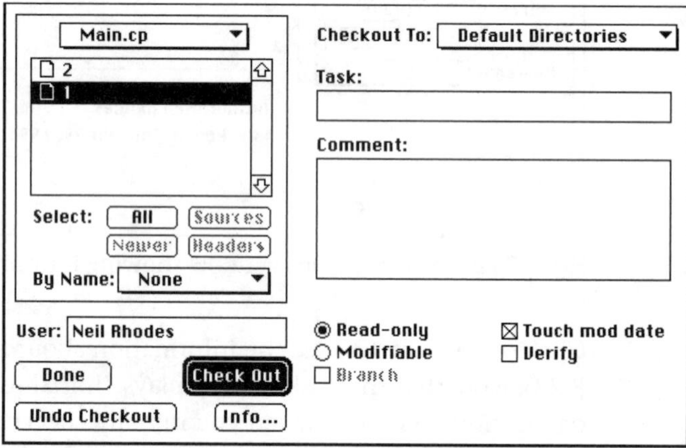

Figure B.24. Checking out revision 1 of Main.cp

Now, open Main.cp. You should find the original version of the file (see fig. B.25).

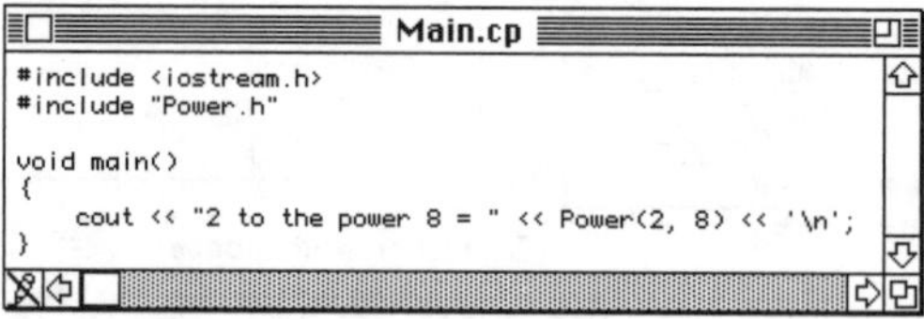

Figure B.25. Revision 1 of Main.cp

Check the file back in for now.

Checking Out on a Branch Revision

Sometimes, you need to modify a revision of a file that is not the latest. To do that, follow these steps:

1. Go to the Check Out dialog.
2. Select the revision you want to check out.
3. Select Modifiable and check Branch (see fig. B.26).

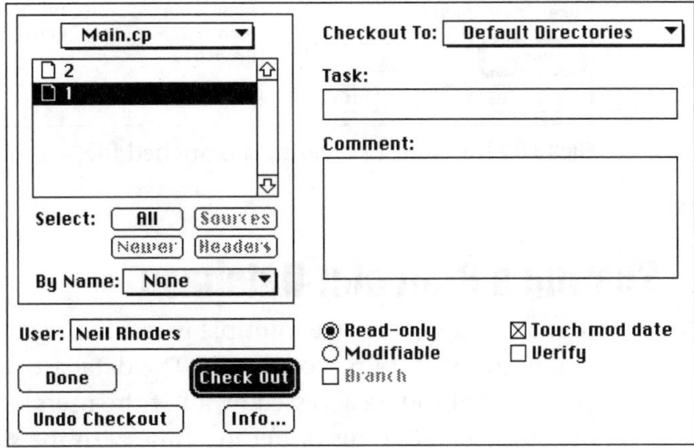

Figure B.26. Checking out a branch.

At check-in, your file is a new revision, branched off the revision you checked out. In this case, you checked out based on revision 1 and checked back in the branched revision 1a1 (see fig. B.27).

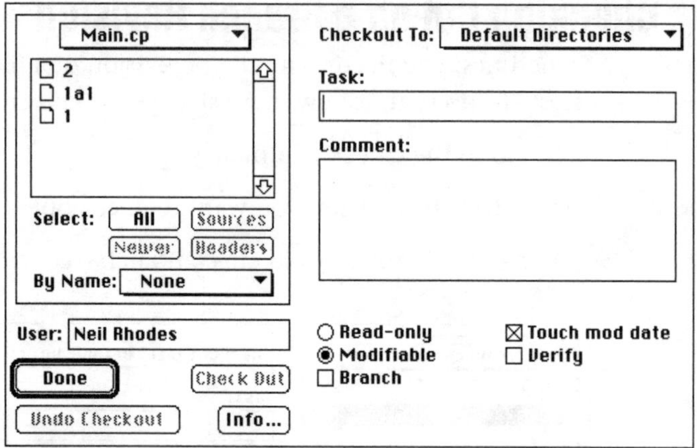

Figure B.27. Results of creating a branched file.

Sharing a Projector Database

If you are going to have multiple users sharing a Projector database, you need to set it up accordingly. The database needs to be stored on a volume that can be accessed by all of the users. Each user runs a copy of SourceServer on his or her machine with the shared database mounted. SourceServer arbitrates access to the database and ensures that only one user has a particular revision of a file checked out modifiable at any given time. SourceServer also lets you know who has checked out the file you want to use.

Modifying Files without the Projector Database

SourceServer keeps a copy of each checked-in version of a file and retrieves any version you request. To ensure that two people are not modifying the same file simultaneously, SourceServer requires that you check the file out modifiable if you want to make changes. This is all well and good, but what do you do if you want to change a file but do not have access to the Projector database? For instance, the database may be on a shared server at work, and you may be working out of the office without access to the server. THINK Project Manager deals with this by enabling you to create modified read-only versions of files.

To simulate a lack of access to the Projector database and the need to get files, do the following:

1. Quit SourceServer (using Quit SourceServer from the SourceServer menu).
2. Open Power.cp (which should be version 1).
3. Select Modify Read-Only from the File menu of the THINK Project Manager, as shown in figure B.28.

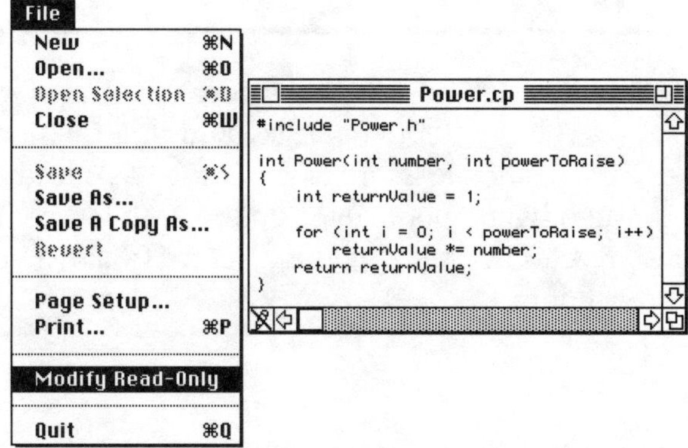

Figure B.28. Using Modify Read-Only.

Modify Read-Only marks a source file as a modified read-only copy. (Figure B.29 shows what the modified read-only icon looks like.) When you check out files this way, you can modify them. Checking them back in may be a problem, however. When the Projector database is available, you can check the file in, as long as it has not been checked out modifiable in the meantime. If the file has been checked out, it is your responsibility to merge your changes with the changes of the person who did the modifiable file check out.

By using Modify Read-Only as a shortcut, you are subverting Projector's capability to maintain file integrity. It should go without saying that you should use this shortcut only when absolutely necessary; normally, this is when the Projector database is unavailable.

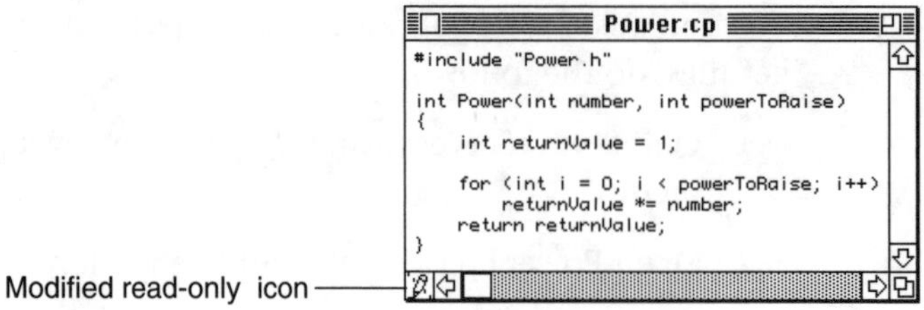

```
Power.cp
#include "Power.h"

int Power(int number, int powerToRaise)
{
    int returnValue = 1;

    for (int i = 0; i < powerToRaise; i++)
        returnValue *= number;
    return returnValue;
}
```

Modified read-only icon

Figure B.29. File with modified read-only icon.

NOTE

Projector adds a `'CKID'` resource to each file when it is checked out. The `'CKID'` resource contains information about what revision the file is and whether the file is read-only, modified read-only, or modifiable. Modify Read-Only sneaks around Projector by changing this resource from read-only to modified read-only.

Sending Commands to SourceServer

SourceServer responds to a variety of different commands. (You can find a list of all the commands in the SourceServer documentation.) To send a command to SourceServer, do the following:

1. Type the command in a window (you may want to use an empty window).
2. Select the command in the window.
3. Press control-return to send the command to SourceServer.

Figure B.30 shows a sample command that can be sent to SourceServer.

Figure B.31 shows the response that SourceServer gives to this command.

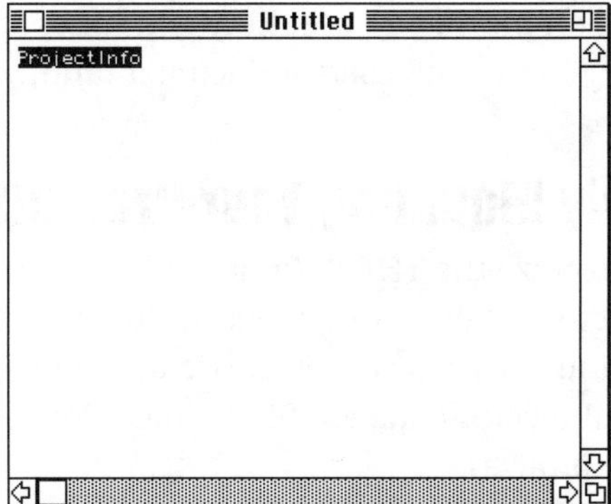

Figure B.30. Sending a command to SourceServer.

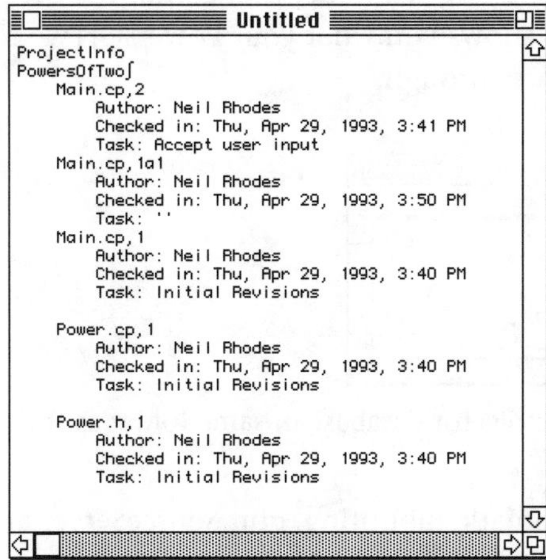

Figure B.31. Output from SourceServer command.

Here are some of the more useful commands that you might want to send SourceServer:

- `ProjectInfo` displays information about a file or files within a Projector database.
- `DeleteRevisions` deletes revisions of a file or the file itself from the Projector database.
- `TransferCKID` moves the `'CKID'` resource from one file to another.

For information on how to use these and other SourceServer commands, refer to the SourceServer documentation.

Automatically Mounting Your Projector Database

You can customize the THINK Project Manager to mount automatically a Projector database for you (as well as launch SourceServer) when you mount a project. You create this timesaving device by moving the Projector database file (named ProjectorDB) into the same folder as the project.

Try this trick by moving the ProjectorDB file located within PowersOfTwo folder to the same folder as PowersOfTwo. . You also can delete the original folder that contained the ProjectorDB file. Figure B.32 shows you what your PowersOfTwo folder should look like when you are through.

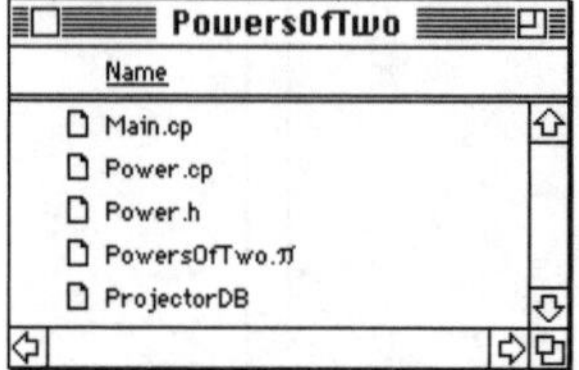

Figure B.32. Projector database in same folder as the project.

To test automatic mounting, quit SourceServer and the THINK Project Manager. Double-click on the PowersOfTwo. project to relaunch the THINK Project Manager. If everything went as expected, the THINK Project Manager should have launched SourceServer and mounted the projector database. Choose Check Out and verify that your files are listed.

This ProjectorDB file also can be an alias. If your Projector database is located on a remote machine, you can mount it automatically by creating an alias to the ProjectorDB file on the remote machine. Put the alias (which should be called ProjectorDB) in the same folder as your project. THINK Project Manager takes care of the rest.

ToolServer

As was said at the beginning of the appendix, ToolServer is a stripped-down MPW that can execute tools and scripts. ToolServer comes in its own folder, and the scripts and tools are located in subfolders. If you have ToolServer and want the THINK Project Manager to launch it automatically, create an alias to ToolServer and place the alias (which should be named ToolServer) in the Tools folder of Symantec C++. Figure B.33 shows you the setup you should have.

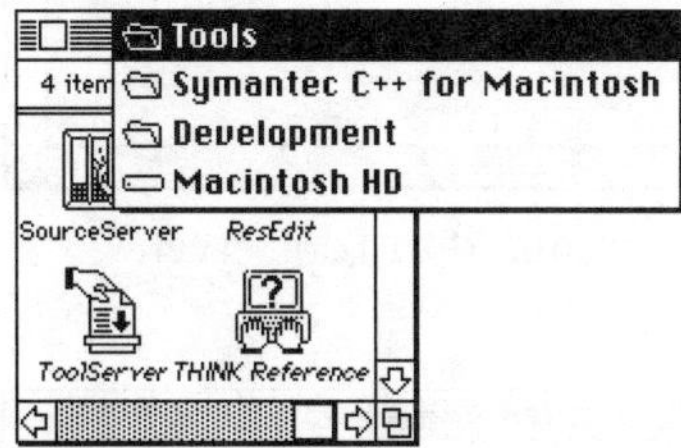

Figure B.33. ToolServer alias in the Symantec C++ Tools folder.

THINK Project Manager enables you to send commands to ToolServer. You send those commands in a fashion very similar to that of sending SourceServer commands:

1. Type a ToolServer command into a window (usually an empty untitled window).
2. Select the command.
3. Press option-return (see fig. B.34).

The results of the ToolServer command appear in the same window (see fig. B.35).

For a description of ToolServer commands, refer to the ToolServer documentation.

NOTE

ToolServer is available from the Apple Programmers and Developers Association (APDA). Call APDA at (800) 282-2732 or (716) 871-6555 for more information.

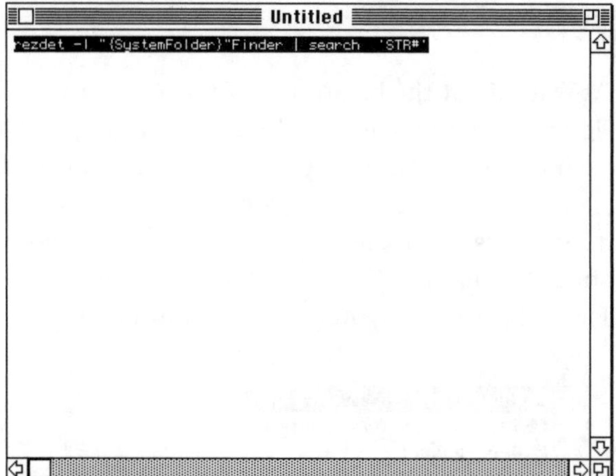

Figure B.34. Sending a command to ToolServer.

```
rezdet -l "{SystemFolder}"Finder | search  'STR#'
'STR#' (150, Purgeable) [36]
'STR#' (1250, Purgeable) [214]
'STR#' (9000, Purgeable) [486]
'STR#' (8750, Purgeable) [1024]
'STR#' (3000, Purgeable) [232]
'STR#' (20500, Purgeable) [743]
'STR#' (17250, Purgeable) [1338]
'STR#' (10500, Purgeable) [96]
'STR#' (12250, Purgeable) [341]
'STR#' (10250, Purgeable) [719]
'STR#' (11500, Purgeable) [1463]
'STR#' (17000, Purgeable) [583]
'STR#' (12000, Purgeable) [96]
'STR#' (12750, Purgeable) [1809]
'STR#' (11000, Purgeable) [414]
'STR#' (5000, Purgeable) [2823]
'STR#' (11250, Purgeable) [3569]
'STR#' (11332, Purgeable) [917]
'STR#' (11330, Purgeable) [594]
'STR#' (20750, Purgeable) [493]
'STR#' (19500, Purgeable) [53]
'STR#' (27500, Purgeable) [36]
'STR#' (10000, Purgeable) [87]
'STR#' (11750, Purgeable) [1544]
```

Figure B.35. Output from a ToolServer command.

C

A Brief TCL Reference Manual

This appendix provides a condensed reference guide for the THINK Class Library. It covers the TCL classes, member functions, data members, global variables, and global functions that are used by the programs in Part 3. It does not, however, cover any functionality not used in those chapters. For a full reference to the TCL, refer to the Symantec C++ documentation.

Class Diagram

Figure C.1 shows an abridged class diagram of the TCL classes used in this book. Not all of the intermediate classes are shown.

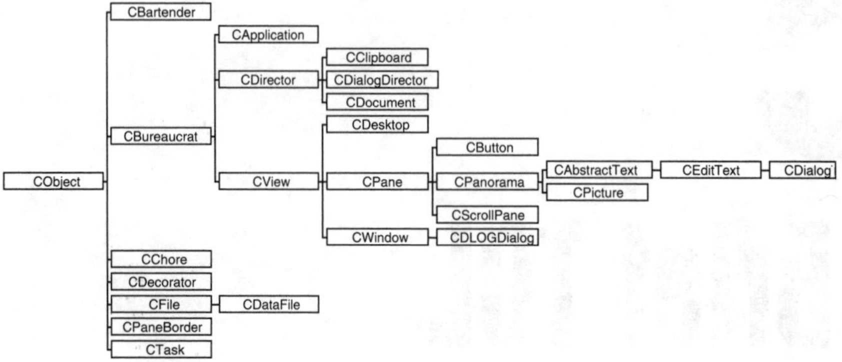

Figure C.1. An abridged TCL class hierarchy.

TCL Classes

The classes are listed alphabetically. Within each class, data members are presented first, and member functions follow alphabetically. Note that only class members used in the sample programs are shown. Within each member, the syntax is shown after the description.

CAbstractText

This is an abstract class used for displaying text. Derived classes actually implement text storage and display. This class handles the creation of tasks to type, cut, copy, and paste.

GetTextHandle. The following returns the text stored in this class as a handle. The handle should not be disposed by the caller.

```
virtual Handle GetTextHandle();
```

SetFontName. This sets the font used to display the text to `aFontName`.

```
virtual void SetFontName(Str255 aFontName);
```

SetFontSize. This sets the size of the font used to display the text to aSize.

```
virtual void SetFontSize(short aSize);
```

SetTextHandle. The following sets the text to textHand. The caller is responsible for disposing of the handle.

```
virtual void SetTextHandle(Handle textHand);
```

SetTextPtr. This sets the text to numChars characters starting at textPtr.

```
virtual void SetTextPtr(Ptr textPtr, long numChars);
```

SetTextString. This sets the text to textStr.

```
virtual void SetTextString(Str255 textStr);
```

SetFontStyle. The following sets the style of the font used to display the text to aSize.

```
virtual void SetFontStyle(short aStyle);
```

Specify. The following sets whether the text is editable (can be changed), selectable (can be selected for copying), or stylable (can use multiple fonts, styles, or sizes).

```
virtual void Specify(Boolean fEditable, Boolean fSelectable,
  Boolean fStylable);
```

CApplication

Every TCL program must create a CApplication. This is the final bureaucrat in the chain of command and handles application-wide events (like the Quit command).

sfFileTypes. This contains the file types that are shown when the user chooses Open.

```
SFTypeList sfFileTypes;
```

sfNumTypes. This contains the number of file types in sfFileTypes.

```
short sfNumTypes;
```

AssignIdleChore. This adds `theChore` to the list of idle chores. The `Perform` function of idle chores is called when there is nothing better to do (no events are available).

```
virtual void AssignIdleChore(CChore *theChore);
```

CancelIdleChore. This removes `theChore` from the list of idle chores.

```
virtual void CancelIdleChore(CChore *theChore);
```

CreateDocument. This is called when a new document is created (either by the user choosing New or when the application is first launched). You must override this routine to create a document, initialize it, and call its `NewFile` member function.

```
virtual void CreateDocument();
```

Exit. You call this routine in your main program after `TAppli-cation::Run()` returns. This function needs overriding if there is any cleanup to do when the application finishes.

```
virtual void Exit();
```

IApplication. This initializes the application object. `extraMasters` controls the number of calls to the Toolbox call `MoreMasters`. `aRainyDayFund` is the amount of memory to reserve for critical memory operations. Of that amount, `aCriticalBalance` controls the amount to use for critical operations (like quitting or saving), while `aToolboxBalance` controls the amount to use for Toolbox calls (like `CopyBits`).

```
void   IApplication(short extraMasters, Size aRainyDayFund,
  Size aCriticalBalance, Size aToolboxBalance);
```

OpenDocument. This is called when a old document is created (either by the user choosing Open or when the user opens a document from the Finder). You must override this routine to create a document, initialize it, and call its `OpenFile` member function.

```
virtual void OpenDocument(SFReply *macSFReply);
```

Run. You call this routine in your main program after initializing the application object. It runs the main event loop and does not return until the user quits.

```
virtual void Run();
```

Quit. The TCL calls this routine when the user quits. This function calls `Quit` for the directors of all open windows. Any director can return false to signify that the user has canceled the quit.

```
virtual Boolean Quit();
```

SetupFileParameters. This routine is called to set up parameters for the Toolbox `SFGetFile`. You should override this routine to set the data members `sfNumTypes` and `sfFileTypes` as well as the global variable `gSignature`.

```
virtual void SetUpFileParameters();
```

CBartender

This class controls the menu bars and menus. When an event occurs that could change the state of the menu items (for example, mouse down events may cause menu items to enable or disable), `CBartender` marks the menus as dirty. When a mouse down event on the menu bar (or a command key equivalent) occurs, `CBartender` disables and unchecks all the menu items and sends `UpdateMenus` to the chain of command.

CheckMarkCmd. This adds or removes a check mark (depending on `checked`) to the menu item with command `cmdNo`.

```
virtual void CheckMarkCmd(long cmdNo, Boolean checked);
```

EnableCmd. This enables the menu item with command `cmdNo`.

```
virtual void EnableCmd(long cmdNo);
```

CBureaucrat

A bureaucrat is an object that can handle events. Examples of bureaucrats include applications, panes, and documents. Bureaucrats can handle events like keystrokes and menu items.

Bureaucrats are arranged in a chain of command. Each bureaucrat points to a supervisor. When an event arrives, the event is sent to the first bureaucrat in the chain of command (`gGopher`). A bureaucrat can handle the event or can pass it on to its supervisor by calling its inherited member function. To make a bureaucrat the gopher, call its `BecomeGopher` function.

The chain of command is composed of bureaucrats associated with the frontmost window. Any bureaucrat not part of the frontmost window is not part of the chain of command.

Dawdle. `Dawdle` is called for bureaucrats in the chain of command during idle time. Override this function if you need to process during idle time. Set `maxSleep` to the number of ticks until your `Dawdle` is called again.

```
virtual void Dawdle(long *maxSleep);
```

DoCommand. This handles the command specified by `theCommand`. The command is commonly a menu choice or the result of the user pressing a control. Override this routine to take action when a command occurs. If the command is not one you handle, call the inherited routine.

```
virtual void DoCommand(long theCommand);
```

DoKeyDown. This is called when a key is depressed. `theChar` contains the character, while `keyCode` contains the raw key code. `macEvent` contains the actual event that you can use to check for modifier keys. Override it to handle keystrokes and call the inherited version if it is a keystroke you do not handle.

```
virtual void DoKeyDown(char theChar, Byte keyCode, EventRecord
  *macEvent);
```

Notify. You call this routine to notify a bureaucrat that a task has been completed.

```
virtual void Notify(CTask *theTask);
```

NotifyClean. You call this routine to notify a bureaucrat that a task has been completed that did not modify anything (for example, a Copy command).

```
virtual void NotifyClean(CTask *theTask);
```

UpdateMenus. You override this routine to enable and checkmark menu items that your bureaucrat handles. Make sure to call the inherited `UpdateMenus`.

```
virtual void UpdateMenus();
```

CButton

This implements a standard button. You normally do not need to derive from this class.

INewButton. This initializes the button. See `CPane::IPane` for descriptions of `aWidth`, `aHeight`, `aHEncl`, `aVEncl`, `anEnclosure`, and `aSupervisor`. The text of the button comes from `title`. If `fVisible` is false, the button is not shown. `procId` specifies the CDEF used to draw the button.

```
void INewButton( short aWidth, short aHeight, short aHEncl, short
  aVEncl, StringPtr title, Boolean fVisible, short procID, CView
  *anEnclosure, CBureaucrat *aSupervisor);
```

SetClickCmd. This sets the command number that this button sends to `DoCommand` when it is clicked.

```
virtual void SetClickCmd(long aClickCmd);
```

SimulateClick. This makes the button behave as though the user clicked it. You might call this in response to a keyboard shortcut.

```
virtual void SimulateClick();
```

CChore

This class represents an action that can be performed at idle time or immediately. Objects of this type are stored in the application in a list of chores.

Perform. Override this routine to perform whatever action your chore wants. If this is installed as an idle chore, `maxSleep` specifies how many ticks to wait before `Perform` is called again.

```
virtual voidPerform(long *maxSleep);
```

CClipboard

This handles the Macintosh Clipboard (the desk scrap). Only one object of this class exists—`gClipboard`. It also displays the clipboard in a window.

EmptyScrap. This empties out the scrap. Call this before calling PutData to write to the scrap.

```
virtual void EmptyScrap();
```

GetData. This finds data in the Clipboard of type theType and returns it as a handle in theData. It returns false if no data of the specified type is present. If you want to know whether data is there, but do not want it, you may pass 0 as the value of theData (for instance, to enable Paste in UpdateMenus). You are responsible for disposing of the returned handle.

```
virtual Boolean GetData(ResType theType, Handle *theData);
```

PutData. This puts the data in theData into the Clipboard as type theType.

```
virtual void PutData(ResType theType, Handle theData);
```

CDataFile

This class represents the data fork of a file.

GetLength. This returns the number of bytes in the file. The file must already be open.

```
virtual long GetLength();
```

IDataFile. This initializes the object.

```
void IDataFile();
```

ReadAll. This reads all the data from the file into a new handle. You must dispose of the handle that is returned.

```
virtual Handle ReadAll();
```

ReadSome. This reads howMuch bytes from the file into info.

```
virtual void ReadSome(Ptr info, long howMuch);
```

SetMark. This sets the file position to howFar bytes from fromWhere. fromWhere is one of fsFromStart, fsFromLEOF, or fsFromMark.

```
virtual void SetMark(long howFar, short fromWhere);
```

WriteAll. This writes all the data in contents to the file.

```
virtual void WriteAll(Handle contents);
```

WriteSome. This writes howMuch bytes into the file from info.

```
virtual void WriteSome(Ptr info, long howMuch);
```

CDecorator

Use this class to arrange windows on-screen. The only instance of this class is gDecorator.

CenterWindow. This centers theWindow. If theWindow is a modal dialog, it centers it in the top third of the screen.

```
virtual void CenterWindow(CWindow *theWindow);
```

GetWCount. This returns the number of windows that have been staggered or placed.

```
virtual short GetWCount();
```

PlaceNewWindow. This places theWindow in a good location on screen. It also staggers and resizes theWindow.

```
virtual void PlaceNewWindow(CWindow *theWindow);
```

StaggerWindow. This staggers theWindow so that it is offset from other windows.

```
virtual void StaggerWindow(CWindow *theWindow);
```

CDesktop

This class provides a view that represents the entire screen. There is only one instance of this class, gDesktop. This object is the enclosure of all windows.

CDialogDirector

This serves as a director for dialogs. Create one of these to control your dialogs.

BeginModalDialog. Call this routine before calling DoModalDialog.

```
virtual void BeginModalDialog();
```

DoModalDialog. This makes the dialog work modally. It only returns when the user dismisses the dialog by clicking some object with command `cmdOK` or `cmdCancel`. It returns the command number of the object that dismissed the dialog. The `defaultCmd` parameter specifies which command object is associated with the return/enter keys.

```
virtual long DoModalDialog(long defaultCmd);
```

IDialogDirector. This is the initialization function. `aSupervisor` is normally the application.

```
void IDialogDirector(CDirectorOwner *aSupervisor);
```

CDialogText

This class handles text in a dialog and knows not to handle return/enter or escape. You can set a maximum number of characters.

GetTextString. This returns the text as a string.

```
virtual void  GetTextString(StringPtr aString);
```

CDirector

This class handles communication between a window and the application. Every window must have an associated director; this is usually the document.

itsGopher. When the director's window is made active, this is the bureaucrat that should be made the gopher. This is normally some pane within the window.

```
CBureaucrat *itsGopher;
```

itsWindow. This is the window controlled by the director.

```
CWindow *itsWindow;
```

IDirector. This is the initialization function. `aSupervisor` is this director's supervisor and is normally the application.

```
void IDirector(CDirectorOwner *aSupervisor);
```

CDLOGDialog

This class is a dialog object that is initialized from a 'DLOG' and a 'DITL' resource. It creates TCL objects to correspond to dialog manager items.

AddDITLEditText. This returns a CEditText to handle an editText item from the 'DITL'. See CPane::IPane for a description of aWidth, aHeight, hEncl, vEncl, and enclosure. ditlItem contains information about the item, including its location and handle.

```
virtual CPane *AddDITLEditText(short aWidth, short aHeight, short
  hEncl, short vEncl, CView *enclosure, tDITLItem *ditlItem);
```

AddDITLStatText. This returns a noneditable CEditText to handle a staticText item from the 'DITL'. See CPane::IPane for a description of aWidth, aHeight, hEncl, vEncl, and enclosure. ditlItem contains information about the item, including its location and handle.

```
virtual CPane *AddDITLStatText(short aWidth, short aHeight, short
  hEncl, short vEncl, CView *enclosure, tDITLItem *ditlItem);
```

IDLOGDialog. This is the initialization function. DLOGid is the ID of the 'DLOG' and 'DITL'. See CPane::IPane for a description of anEnclosure and aSupervisor.

```
void IDLOGDialog(short DLOGid, CDesktop *anEnclosure, CDirector
  *aSupervisor);
```

CDocument

This object corresponds to a document on disk. Its contents are displayed in one or more windows. You normally override this class and store your data in data members.

dirty. This is true if the document has been changed since it was created or last saved; otherwise, it is false. You set this data member to false in your DoSave function. It is set to true automatically when a task is executed.

```
Boolean dirty;
```

itsFile. This is the file in which the document is saved.

```
CFile *itsFile;
```

itsMainPane. This is the main pane of the document. It is the pane that is printed when the document is printed.

```
CPane  *itsMainPane;
```

DoSave. This saves the document in `itsFile`. You should override it to write your data. If `itsFile` is 0, you need to call `DoSaveFileAs`.

```
virtual Boolean DoSave();
```

DoSaveAs. This saves the file as specified in `macSFReply`.

```
virtual Boolean DoSaveAs(SFReply *macSFReply);
```

You should override this routine to do the following:

- ▼ Delete the file if it already exists.
- ▼ Create the file on disk.
- ▼ Create a `CFile` to refer to it.
- ▼ Save the `CFile` in the data member `itsFile`.
- ▼ Call `DoSave` to actually write the file.

DoSaveFileAs. This calls the Toolbox routine `SFPutFile`. If the user cancels the dialog, it returns false. Otherwise, it calls `DoSaveAs` and returns true.

```
virtual Boolean DoSaveFileAs();
```

IDocument. This is the initialization function. `aSupervisor` is the application. `printable` specifies whether this document can be printed.

```
void IDocument(CApplication *aSupervisor, Boolean printable);
```

NewFile. This is called when the user creates a new file. You should override this routine to create a window and assign it to `itsWindow`. You also need to create panes to display in the window and assign one to `itsMainPane`.

```
virtual void NewFile(void);
```

OpenFile. This is called when the user opens an existing file.

```
virtual void OpenFile(SFReply *macSFReply);
```

You should override this routine to do the following:

- Open the file and read its data.
- Create a window and assign it to `itsWindow`.
- Create panes to display in the window and assign one to `itsMainPane`.

CEditText

This class represents a pane with editable text. It uses `TextEdit` for its editing and for a display and, therefore, shares `TextEdit`'s 32K limits: There can be no more than 32K of text, and the sum of the line heights cannot exceed 32K.

IEditText. This is the initialization function. See `CPane::IPane` for a description of `anEnclosure`, `aSupervisor`, `aWidth`, `aHeight`, `aHEncl`, `aVEncl`, `aHSizing`, and `aVSizing`. `aLineWidth` controls how wide the lines of text should be. If it is negative, the lines are the same width as the pane.

```
void IEditText(CView *anEnclosure, CBureaucrat *aSupervisor,
  short aWidth, short aHeight, short aHEncl, short aVEncl,
  SizingOption aHSizing, SizingOption aVSizing, short
  aLineWidth);
```

CFile

This is an abstract class that represents a file on disk.

Close. This closes the file.

```
virtual void Close();
```

CreateNew. This creates the file with the specified creator and file type.

```
virtual void CreateNew(OSType creator, OSType fType);
```

ExistsOnDisk. This returns true if the file exists; otherwise, it returns false.

```
virtual Boolean ExistsOnDisk();
```

GetName. This returns the name of the file.

```
virtual void GetName(Str63 theName);
```

Open. This opens the file with the specified `permission`. Permissions are the same as those of the Toolbox call `FSOpen`.

```
virtual void Open(SignedByte permission);
```

SFSpecify. This initializes the name and location of the file from `macSFReply`.

```
virtual void SFSpecify(SFReply *macSFReply);
```

SpecifyHFS. This initializes the name and location of the file from `aName`, `aVolNum`, and `aDirID`.

```
virtual void SpecifyHFS(Str63 aName, short aVolNum, long aDirID);
```

ThrowOut. This deletes the file.

```
virtual void ThrowOut();
```

CObject

This is the base class of all the TCL classes.

Dispose. This takes the place of a destructor for `CObjects`. Call this function to `delete` objects. Override this function to do whatever you normally do in a C++ destructor. Make sure it calls the inherited `Dispose`.

```
virtual void Dispose();
```

CPane

A pane is a drawable area with its own coordinate system. Drawing within windows is done in panes. Panes exist in a hierarchy; each pane has an enclosure and can enclose zero or more other panes.

ChangeSize. You call this to change the size of the pane. The values in `delta` specify by how much the pane should change on each side, with positive values specifying down and to the right. If `redraw` is true, the pane is invalidated.

```
virtual void ChangeSize(Rect *delta, Boolean redraw);
```

Draw. This draws a pane. As an optimization, only the portion of the pane intersecting area needs to be drawn. Your panes override Draw.

```
virtual void Draw(Rect *area);
```

FitToEnclFrame. This fits the pane horizontally and/or vertically (depending on horizFit and vertFit) to the frame of its enclosure. Note that the interior and frame of a view need not be the same.

```
virtual void FitToEnclFrame(Boolean horizFit, Boolean vertFit);
```

FitToEnclosure. You call this to fit the pane horizontally and/or vertically (depending on horizFit and vertFit) to the interior of its enclosure. Note that the interior and frame of a view need not be the same.

```
virtual void FitToEnclosure(Boolean horizFit, Boolean vertFit);
```

IPane. This is the initialization function. anEnclosure is the enclosing view of either a pane or a window. aSupervisor is the next bureaucrat in the chain of command and usually is the director for the window. The size of the pane is specified in aWidth and aHeight. The location of the pane within its enclosure is specified in aHEncland aVEncl.

The remaining parameters, aHSizing and aVSizing, specify what happens to this pane when its enclosure changes size. The possible values of aHSizing are sizFIXEDLeft (location from the left is fixed), sizFIXEDRIGHT (location from the right of the enclosure is fixed), sizFIXEDSTICKY (the pane scrolls with its enclosure), and sizELASTIC (the pane resizes by the same amount as its enclosure). The values for aVSizing are sizFIXEDTOP, sizFIXEDBOTTOM, sizFIXEDSTICKY, and sizELASTIC.

```
void IPane(CView *anEnclosure, CBureaucrat *aSupervisor, short
  aWidth, short aHeight, short aHEncl, short aVEncl, SizingOption
  aHSizing, SizingOption aVSizing);
```

Refresh. This invalidates the whole pane, forcing an update event.

```
virtual void Refresh();
```

SetBorder. This adds an adorning CPaneBorder.

```
virtual void SetBorder(CPaneBorder *aBorder);
```

CPaneBorder

This class draws a border around a pane.

IPaneBorder. This is the initialization function. It controls the appearance of the border. `borderFlags` can be `kBorderNone`, `kBorderLeft`, `kBorderTop`, `kBorderRight`, `kBorderBottom`, `kBorderOval`, `kBorderRoundRect`, or `kBorderFrame`.

```
void IPaneBorder(short borderFlags);
```

SetPenSize. This sets the height and width of the pen used for the border.

```
virtual void SetPenSize(short penWidth, short penHeight);
```

CPanorama

This is a pane that can be scrolled (by placing it in a `CScrollPane`).

SetPosition. This sets the scroll position to `aPosition`.

```
virtual void SetPosition(LongPt *aPosition);
```

CPicture

This is a pane that displays a picture. The picture may or may not come from a resource.

IPicture. This is the initialization function. See `CPane::IPane` for information on these parameters.

```
void IPicture(CView *anEnclosure, CBureaucrat *aSupervisor, short
  aWidth, short aHeight, short aHEncl, short aVEncl, SizingOption
  aHSizing, SizingOption aVSizing);
```

SetMacPicture. This sets `aMacPicture` as the picture. It does not dispose or release the old picture.

```
virtual voidSetMacPicture(PicHandle aMacPicture);
```

CScrollPane

This pane does scrolling for an enclosed CPanorama.

InstallPanorama. Call this routine to notify the scroll pane of its panorama.

```
virtual void InstallPanorama(CPanorama *aPanorama);
```

IScrollPane. See CPane::IPane for descriptions of anEnclosure, aSupervisor, aWidth, aHeight, aHEncl, aVEncl, aHSizing, and aVSizing. If hasHoriz is true, there is a horizontal scroll bar. If hasVert is true, there is a vertical scroll bar. If hasSizeBox is true, there is a grow icon.

```
void  IScrollPane(CView *anEnclosure, CBureaucrat *aSupervisor,
   short aWidth, short aHeight, short aHEncl, short aVEncl,
   SizingOption aHSizing, SizingOption aVSizing, Boolean hasHoriz,
   Boolean hasVert, Boolean hasSizeBox);
```

CTask

This is an abstract class that represents actions that can be done, undone, and redone. All undoable actions are implemented with tasks.

undone. This is true if the last thing done to the task was an Undo; otherwise, it is false.

```
Boolean undone;
```

Do. This carries out the initial action of the task and is called only once. Override this routine to do whatever needs to be done.

```
virtual void Do();
```

IsUndone. This returns true if the last thing done to the task was an Undo.

```
virtual Boolean IsUndone();
```

ITask. This is the initialization function. aNameIndex is an index into the 'STR#' 130 resource. This resource contains the text for the Undo/Redo menu item.

```
void ITask(short aNameIndex);
```

Redo. This redoes the action of the task. Override it to carry out a redo action.

```
virtual void Redo();
```

Undo. This undoes the action of the task. Override it to carry out an undo.

```
virtual void Undo();
```

CView

This is an abstract class representing something that can be seen on-screen. Panes and windows are both views.

wantsClicks. This is true if the view, or any subview, can accept mouse clicks.

```
Boolean wantsClicks;
```

Activate. This is called for all views within a window when that window is deactivated.

```
virtual void Activate();
```

Deactivate. This is called for all views within a window when that window is deactivated.

```
virtual void Deactivate();
```

FindViewByID. This finds the view in an enclosure hierarchy that has an ID equal to `anID`.

```
virtual CView* FindViewByID(long anID);
```

GetFrame. This returns the frame (enclosing coordinates) of the view.

```
virtual void GetFrame(LongRect *theFrame);
```

Prepare. This prepares the view for drawing. This involves setting the port, clipping, and origin. Call this routine if you are drawing at an unusual time (like within your `Dawdle` routine).

```
virtual void Prepare();
```

CWindow

This is a class that displays a standard Macintosh window.

sizeRect. The top-left coordinates specify the minimum size of the window. The bottom-right coordinates specify the maximum size.

```
Rect sizeRect;
```

ChangeSize. Use this to change the window size to `width` and `height`.

```
virtual void ChangeSize(short width, short height);
```

GetTitle. This returns the title of the window in `theTitle`.

```
virtual void GetTitle(Str255 theTitle);
```

IWindow. This is the initialization function. `WINDid` is the resource ID of the `'WIND'` resource, which contains information about the window. If the window should be a floating window, `aFloating` is true. See `CPane::IPane` for information about `anEnclosure` and `aSupervisor`.

```
void IWindow(short WINDid, Boolean aFloating, CDesktop
  *anEnclosure, CDirector *aSupervisor);
```

Move. This moves the window to the position `hGlobal`, `vGlobal` (in global coordinates).

```
virtual void Move(short hGlobal, short vGlobal);
```

Select. This brings the window to the front and makes it active.

```
virtual void Select();
```

SetSizeRect. This sets the new value of the data member `sizeRect` equal to the parameter `aSizeRect`.

```
virtual void SetSizeRect(Rect *aSizeRect);
```

SetTitle. This sets the title of the window to `theTitle`.

```
virtual void SetTitle(Str255 theTitle);
```

Global Variables

The global variables contain instances of various TCL parameters.

gDecorator. This contains the only instance of CDecorator. It is created when the TCL application initializes. For more information, see CDecorator.

```
CDecorator *gDecorator;
```

gBartender. This contains the only instance of CBartender. It is created when the TCL application initializes. For more information, see CBartender.

```
CBartender *gBartender;
```

gDesktop. This contains the only instance of CDesktop. It is created when the TCL application initializes. For more information, see CDesktop.

```
CDesktop *gDesktop;
```

gClipboard. This contains the only instance of CClipboard. It is created when the TCL application initializes. For more information, see CClipboard.

```
CClipboard *gClipboard;
```

gSignature. This contains the application signature. Initialize this variable in the initialization method of your application or in your override of TApplication::SetupFileParameters.

```
OSType gSignature;
```

Global Routines

These routines perform a number of different functions such as error handling and memory allocation.

CatchFailures. This installs handler as an exception handler until a corresponding Success call is made. If an exception occurs during that time period, handler is called with the error and message of the failure. The staticLink parameter is passed as a third parameter to handler if staticLink is not zero. If staticLink is zero, only two parameters are passed to handler.

```
typedef pascal void (*HandlerFuncPtr)( short error, long message);

pascal void CatchFailures(FailInfo *fi, HandlerFuncPtr handler,
  long staticLink);
```

ConcatPString. This appends the second string to the first string.

```
void ConcatPStrings(Str255 first, ConstStr255Param second);
```

CopyPString. This copies srcString into destString.

```
void CopyPString( ConstStr255Param srcString, Str255 destString);
```

Failure. This causes an exception that aborts the routine in progress and all other routines in the call chain. It calls exception handlers along the way. Normally, it aborts back to the main event loop, which puts up an alert based on the given error and message. It then continues, getting the next event.

```
pascal void Failure(short error, long message);
```

FailNIL. This causes a failure if p is 0.

```
pascal void FailNIL(void *p);
```

FailOSErr. This causes a failure if error is not noErr.

```
pascal void FailOSErr(short error);
```

FailMemErr. This causes a failure if MemError() is not noErr.

```
pascal void FailMemErr();
```

LongToQDRect. This converts from a 32-bit coordinate rectangle to a 16-bit coordinate rectangle by truncating.

```
pascal void LongToQDRect(LongRect *srcRect, Rect *destRect);
```

NewHandleCanFail. This allocates a handle that is size bytes big. If there is not enough memory to allocate the handle without breaching the critical reserve, it returns 0.

```
void *NewHandleCanFail(long size);
```

PositionDialog. This centers the dialog or alert specified with theType and theID according to Human Interface guidelines. The guideline is to be centered horizontally and in top third of the screen vertically. You call PositionDialog before displaying an alert or dialog.

```
void PositionDialog(ResType theType, short theID);
```

ResizeHandleCanFail. This resizes theHandle to be of size newSize. If there is not enough memory to resize without breaching the critical memory reserve, the routine does not succeed. Make sure to call either MemError or FailMemError after calling this routine.

```
void ResizeHandleCanFail(void* theHandle, long newSize);
```

SetAllocation. If canFail is true, memory allocations are not allowed to use the critical reserve. If canFail is false, memory allocations are allowed to use the critical reserve. SetAllocation returns the old setting. Use this routine to allocate memory without breaching the critical reserve. Make sure to set it back to its original value.

```
Boolean SetAllocation(Boolean canFail);
```

Success. Calls to Success are paired with calls to CatchFailures. Success removes the exception handler installed by CatchFailures. Call this routine if no error occurs within the code for which you have an exception handler installed.

```
pascal void Success();
```

Macros

These two macros handle object disposal and exception-handling routines.

ForgetObject

Call this macro with the following:

```
ForgetObject(anbject);
```

This sends anObject the Dispose message if it is not 0. It then sets anObject to 0.

Exception Handling

Use CATCH, TRY, and ENDTRY in the following way:

```
TRY {
    code which could cause an exception
}
CATCH {
    code to clean up if an exception occurs
}
ENDTRY
```

TRY installs an exception handler for the duration of the block after it. If an exception occurs during that block, control is transferred to the CATCH block. The CATCH block should do whatever cleanup is necessary. Control passes to the next installed exception handler at the end of the CATCH block.

If no exception occurs, the CATCH block is not executed.

If you do not want exceptions to continue propogating, but want to continue in the function after the CATCH block is executed, place the NO_PROPAGATE line within the CATCH block.

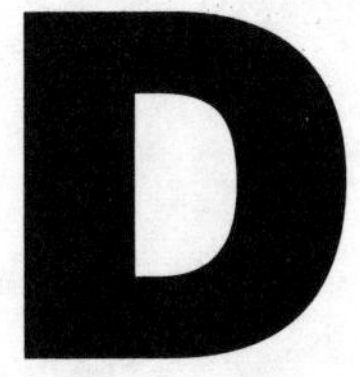

Complete Source Listings

This appendix lists the source code used for each project by chapter.

Chapter 2, MultipleFiles

Average.cp

```
#include "Average.h"
#include <SANE.h>

long double Average(double *values, int numValues)
{
    long double    total = 0.0;
    int          i;

    for (i = 0; i < numValues; i++)
        total += values[i];
    if (numValues > 0)
        return total / numValues;
    else
        return 0.0;
}
```

Main.cp

```
#include <stdio.h>
#include "Factorial.h"
#include "Reverse.h"
#include "Average.h"

void main()
{
    int    i;
    char    s[] = "Neil Rhodes";
    char     palindrome[] = "Madam, I'm Adam";
    double    values[] = {3.1, 4.1, 5.9, 15.6, 16.3, 15.7};

    for (i = 0; i < 14; i++)
        printf("Factorial(%i) = %ld\n", i, Factorial(i));

    printf("Reverse(\"%s\") = ", s);
    Reverse(s);
    printf("\"%s\"\n", s);

    printf("Reverse(\"%s\") = ", palindrome);
    Reverse(palindrome);
    printf("\"%s\"\n", palindrome);

    printf("Average() = %lf\n", Average(values, sizeof(values) / sizeof(values[0])));
}
```

Factorial.cp

```
#include "Factorial.h"

unsigned long Factorial(unsigned long n)
{
    unsigned long result = 1;
    unsigned long i;

    for (i = 2; i <= n; i++)
        result *= i;
    return result;
}
```

Reverse.cp

```
#include "Reverse.h"
#include <string.h>

static void Swap(char *c1, char *c2)
{
        char tmp;

        tmp = *c1;
        *c1 = *c2;
        *c2 = tmp;
}

void Reverse(char *s)
{
    int length = strlen(s);
    int midPoint = length / 2;
    int i;

    for (i = 0; i < midPoint; i++)
        Swap(&s[i], &s[length - i - 1]);
}
```

Average.h

```
#pragma once

long double Average(double *values, int numValues);
```

Factorial.h

```
#pragma once

unsigned long Factorial(unsigned long n);
```

Reverse.h

```
#pragma once

void Reverse(char *s);
```

Chapter 3, Errors

Average.cp

```
#include "Average.h"
#include <SANE.h>

long double Average(double *values, int numValues)
{
    long double    total = 0.0;
    int            i;

    for (i == 0; i < numValues; i++)
        total += values[i];
    if (numValues > 0)
        return total / numValues;
    else
        return;
}
```

Main.cp

```
#include <stdio.h>
#include "Reverse.h"
#include "Average.h"

void main()
{
    int     i;
    char    s[] = "Neil Rhodes";
    char    palindrome[] = "Madam, I'm Adam";
    double   values[] = {3.1, 4.1, 5.9, 15.6, 16.3, 15.7};

    printf("Reverse(\"%s\") = ", s);
    Reverse(s);
    printf("\"%s\"\n", s);

    printf("Reverse(\"%s\") = ", palindrome);
    Reverse(palindrome);
    printf("\"%s\"\n", palindrome);

    printf("Average() = %lf\n", Average(values, sizeof(values) / sizeof(values[0])));
}
```

Reverse.cp

```
#include "Reverse.h"
#include <string.h>

static void Swap(char *c1, char *c2)
{
    char tmp;

    tmp = c1;
    c1 = c2;
    c2 = tmp;
}

void Reverse(char *s)
{
    int length = strlen(s);
    int midPoint = length div 2;
    int i;

    for (i = 0; i < midPoint; i++)
        Swap(s[i], &ss[length - i - 1]);
}
```

Average.h

```
#pragma once

long double Average(double *values, int numValues);
```

Reverse.h

```
#pragma once

void Reverse(char *s);
```

Chapter 4, BinaryTree

Main.cp

```
struct BinaryTree {
    int value;
    BinaryTree *left;
    BinaryTree *right;

    BinaryTree(int v) {value = v; left = right = NULL;}
};

Boolean CheckBinaryTree(BinaryTree *aTree)
{
    if (aTree == NULL)
        return true;
    if (aTree->left != NULL) {
        if (aTree->left->value > aTree->value)
            return false;
        if (!CheckBinaryTree(aTree->left))
            return false;
    }
    if (aTree->right != NULL) {
        if (aTree->value > aTree->right->value)
            return false;
        if (!CheckBinaryTree(aTree->right))
            return false;
    }
    return TRUE;
}
```

```
BinaryTree *NewNode(int value)
{
    return new BinaryTree(value);
}

void main()
{
    /* construct binary tree by hand.
       Should really write a function to do it */
    BinaryTree *root = NULL;
    BinaryTree *node;

    node = NewNode(5);
    root = node;

    node = NewNode(3);
    root->left = node;

    node = NewNode(4);
    root->left->left = node;    /* should be root->left->right */

    node = NewNode(8);
    root->right = node;
}
```

Chapter 5, Alphabet

Main.cp

```
#include <stdio.h>
#include <Types.h>
#include <OSUtils.h>
#include <string.h>
#include <ToolUtils.h>
#include "ResourceDefinitions.h"

#define kMaxInputLine     512

/* prompt for character input */
char gPrompt[256];

/* if they type an invalid character */
char gBadCharacter[256];

/* output if they type a valid character.  This is used as the first
   argument to printf */
char gCharIsForWordTemplate[256];

Boolean FindIndexOfCharacter(char c, int *ip)
{
    const kCaseSensitive = true;
    const kDiacriticalSensitive = true;
    Str255    entry;
    int     index = 0;
    Str255  charAsString;

    charAsString[0] = 1;
    charAsString[1] = c;

    do {
        GetIndString(entry, kCharsResourceID, ++index);
    } while (Length(entry) != 0 &&
      !EqualString(charAsString, entry,
      !kCaseSensitive, !kDiacriticalSensitive));
```

```
    *ip = index;
    return Length(entry) != 0;
}

/* returns false if no more input */
Boolean HandleOneInteraction()
{
    int c;
    char    inputLine[kMaxInputLine];

    printf("\n%s", gPrompt);
    if (fgets(inputLine, sizeof(inputLine), stdin) == NULL)
        return false;
    else {
        int i;

        if (!FindIndexOfCharacter(*inputLine, &i))
            printf("%s\n", gBadCharacter);
        else {
            Str255 word;

            GetIndString(word, kWordsResourceID, i);
            printf(gCharIsForWordTemplate, *inputLine, p2cstr(word));
            putchar('\n');
        }
        return true;
    }
}

void InitializeStrings()
{
    Str255    s;

    GetIndString(s, kMiscStringsID, kPromptItem);
    strcpy(gPrompt, p2cstr(s));

    GetIndString(s, kMiscStringsID, kBadCharacterItem);
    strcpy(gBadCharacter, p2cstr(s));

    GetIndString(s, kMiscStringsID, kTemplateItem);
    strcpy(gCharIsForWordTemplate, p2cstr(s));
}

void main()
{
    InitializeStrings();

    while (HandleOneInteraction())
    {
        /* do nothing */
    }
}
```

ResourceDefinitions.h

```
#define kWordsResourceID 1024
#define kCharsResourceID 1025

#define kMiscStringsID   1026
#define kPromptItem           1
#define kBadCharacterItem     2
#define kTemplateItem         3
```

Alphabet.r

```
#include "Types.r"
#include "ResourceDefinitions.h"

resource 'STR#' (kCharsResourceID, "Characters", purgeable)
{
    {
        "a", "b", "c", "d", "e", "f", "g",
        "h", "i", "j", "k", "l", "m", "n",
        "o", "p", "q", "r", "s", "t", "u",
        "v", "w", "x", "y", "z"
    }
};

resource 'STR#' (kWordsResourceID, "Words", purgeable)
{
    {
        "Alexander",   "Barnacle", "Cornelius",
        "Daddy",       "Elephant", "Fox",
        "Gazelle",     "Horse",    "Iguana",
        "Jagular",     "Kanga",    "Limpet",
        "Mommy",       "Nicholas", "Ostrich",
        "Peacock",     "Quetzal",  "Richard",
        "Shira-kan",   "Thomas the Train", "Unicornfish",
        "Vulture",     "Walrus",   "Xirces",
        "Yo-yo",       "Zebra"
    }
};

resource 'STR#' (kMiscStringsID, "Misc", purgeable)
{
    {
        "Character? ",
        "Invalid character",
        "%c is for %s"
    }
};
```

Chapter 7, Project One

Foo.cp

```
#include <QuickDraw.h>

void Foo()
{
    Rect r = {10, 20, 50, 100};
    FrameRect(&r);
}
```

Chapter 7, Project Two

Main.cp

```
#include "FooBar++"
#include <stdio.h>

void main()
{
    printf("%d %d\n", kFoo, kBar);
}
```

Chapter 16, RandomRectangle

CRandomRectanglePane.cp

```
#include <Global.h>
#include "CRandomRectanglePane.h"

void CRandomRectanglePane::IRandomRectanglePane(CView *anEnclosure,
  CBureaucrat *aSupervisor,
  short aWidth, short aHeight,
  short aHEncl, short aVEncl,
  SizingOption aHSizing, SizingOption aVSizing)
{
    IPane(anEnclosure, aSupervisor, aWidth, aHeight,
      aHEncl, aVEncl, aHSizing, aVSizing);
}

void CRandomRectanglePane::DrawRectangleInRandomColor(const Rect *r)
{
    RGBColor     aColor;
    PixPatHandle myPixPat;

    aColor.red = fRandom.Value();
    fRandom.Advance();
    aColor.blue = fRandom.Value();
    fRandom.Advance();
    aColor.green = fRandom.Value();
    fRandom.Advance();

    myPixPat = NewPixPat();
    MakeRGBPat(myPixPat, &aColor);
    FillCRect(r, myPixPat);
    DisposPixPat(myPixPat);
}

void CRandomRectanglePane::DrawRectangleInRandomPattern(const Rect *r)
{
    Pattern    aPattern;

    GetIndPattern(aPattern, sysPatListID, fRandom.ValueInRange(1, 31));
    fRandom.Advance();
    FillRect(r, aPattern);
}

void CRandomRectanglePane::Dawdle(long *maxSleep)
{
    Rect        r;
    Point       p1;
    Point       p2;
    LongRect    frameSize;

    GetFrame(&frameSize);

    p1.h = fRandom.ValueInRange(frameSize.left, frameSize.right);
    fRandom.Advance();
    p1.v = fRandom.ValueInRange(frameSize.top, frameSize.bottom);
    fRandom.Advance();
    p2.h = fRandom.ValueInRange(frameSize.left, frameSize.right);
    fRandom.Advance();
    p2.v = fRandom.ValueInRange(frameSize.top, frameSize.bottom);
    fRandom.Advance();
```

```
    ::Pt2Rect(p1, p2, &r);

    Prepare();            // prepare coordinate system for drawing

    if (gSystem.hasColorQD)
        DrawRectangleInRandomColor(&r);
    else
        DrawRectangleInRandomPattern(&r);

    *maxSleep = 20;       // one rectangle every 1/3 second
}
```

CRectangleApp.c

```
#include "CRectangleApp.h"
#include "CRandomRectanglePane.h"
#include <CDesktop.h>
#include <CDirector.h>
#include <CWindow.h>

extern CDesktop        *gDesktop;

void CRectangleApp::IRectangleApp()
{
    const short   kExtraMasters =    1;
    const Size    kRainyDayFund =    45000;
    const Size    kCriticalBalance = 40000;
    const Size    kToolboxBalance =  20000;
    const short   kWINDResourceID =  500;
    const Boolean kWindowFloats =    TRUE;
    const Boolean kFitHorizontal =   TRUE;
    const Boolean kFitVertical =     TRUE;

    IApplication( kExtraMasters, kRainyDayFund,
      kCriticalBalance, kToolboxBalance);

    CDirector *aDirector = new CDirector;
    aDirector->IDirector(this);

    CWindow *aWindow = new CWindow;
    aWindow->IWindow(kWINDResourceID, !kWindowFloats, gDesktop, aDirector);
    aDirector->itsWindow = aWindow;

    CRandomRectanglePane *thePane = new CRandomRectanglePane;
    thePane->IRandomRectanglePane(aWindow, aDirector, 0, 0, 0, 0,
      sizELASTIC, sizELASTIC);
    thePane->FitToEnclosure(kFitHorizontal, kFitVertical);
    aDirector->itsGopher = thePane;
}
```

Rectangle.c

```
#include "CRectangleApp.h"

void main()
{
    CRectangleApp    *rectangleApp;

    rectangleApp = new CRectangleApp;
    rectangleApp->IRectangleApp();
    rectangleApp->Run();
    rectangleApp->Exit();
}
```

TRandom.cp

```
#include "TRandom.h"
#include <Events.h>

TRandom::TRandom()
{
    fValue = ::TickCount();
}

TRandom::TRandom(unsigned long seed)
{
    fValue = seed;
}

void TRandom::Advance()
{
    fValue = fValue * 12345 + 6789;
}

unsigned long TRandom::Value()
{
    return fValue;
}

unsigned long TRandom::ValueInRange(unsigned long low, unsigned long high)
{
    return (Value() % (high - low + 1)) + low;
}
```

CRandomRectanglePane.h

```
#pragma once

#include <CPane.h>
#include "TRandom.h"

class CRandomRectanglePane: public CPane {
public:
    void            IRandomRectanglePane(CView *anEnclosure,
                      CBureaucrat *aSupervisor,
                      short aWidth, short aHeight,
                      short aHEncl, short aVEncl,
                      SizingOption aHSizing, SizingOption aVSizing);

    virtual void    Dawdle(long *maxSleep);

protected:
    virtual void    DrawRectangleInRandomColor(const Rect *r);
    virtual void    DrawRectangleInRandomPattern(const Rect *r);
private:
    TRandom         fRandom;
};
```

CRectangleApp.h

```
#pragma once

#include <CApplication.h>

class CRectangleApp: public CApplication {
public:
    void    IRectangleApp();
};
```

TRandom.h

```
#pragma once

class TRandom {
public:
    TRandom();
    TRandom(unsigned long seed);

    void Advance();
    unsigned long Value();
    unsigned long ValueInRange(unsigned long low, unsigned long high);

private:
    unsigned long    fValue;
};
```

Chapter 17, TextTyper

CTextApp.cp

```
#include "CTextApp.h"
#include "CTextDoc.h"
#include <Global.h>

extern    OSType        gSignature;        // The application's signature

void CTextApp::ITextApp()
{
    const short   kExtraMasters =    1;
    const Size    kRainyDayFund =    45000;
    const Size    kCriticalBalance = 40000;
    const Size    kToolboxBalance =  20000;

    IApplication( kExtraMasters, kRainyDayFund,
      kCriticalBalance, kToolboxBalance);
}

void CTextApp::CreateDocument()
{
    CTextDoc *theDocument = new CTextDoc;

    TRY
    {
        theDocument->ITextDoc(this);
        theDocument->NewFile();
    }
    CATCH
    {
        ForgetObject(theDocument);
    }
    ENDTRY;
}

void CTextApp::OpenDocument(SFReply *macReply)
{
    CTextDoc *theDocument = new CTextDoc;

    TRY
    {
        theDocument->ITextDoc(this);
        theDocument->OpenFile(macReply);
    }
```

```
    CATCH
    {
        ForgetObject(theDocument);
    }
    ENDTRY;
}

void CTextApp::SetUpFileParameters()
{
    CApplication::SetUpFileParameters();

    sfNumTypes = 1;
    sfFileTypes[0] = 'TEXT';
    gSignature = 'C++2';
}
```

CTextDoc.cp

```
#include "CTextDoc.h"
#include <CEditText.h>
#include <CScrollPane.h>
#include <CDesktop.h>
#include <CWindow.h>
#include <CDataFile.h>
#include <CDecorator.h>
#include <TBUtilities.h>

extern CDesktop        *gDesktop;
extern OSType       gSignature;
extern CDecorator   *gDecorator;

void CTextDoc::ITextDoc(CApplication *supervisor)
{
    const Boolean kPrintable = TRUE;

    IDocument(supervisor, kPrintable);
}

void CTextDoc::NewFile()
{
    BuildWindow();

    Str255 wTitle;
    short wCount;
    Str255 wNumber;

    gDecorator->StaggerWindow(itsWindow);
    itsWindow->GetTitle(wTitle);
    wCount = gDecorator->GetWCount();
    ::NumToString(wCount, wNumber);
    ::ConcatPStrings(wTitle, "\p-");
    ::ConcatPStrings(wTitle, wNumber);
    itsWindow->SetTitle(wTitle);

    itsWindow->Select();
}

void CTextDoc::BuildWindow()
{
    const short   kWINDResourceID =        500;
    const Boolean kWindowFloats =          TRUE;
    const Boolean kFitHorizontal =         TRUE;
    const Boolean kFitVertical =           TRUE;
    const Boolean kHasHorizontalScrollbar =TRUE;
    const Boolean kHasVerticalScrollbar =  TRUE;
```

```
    const Boolean kHasGrowBox =             TRUE;
    const short   kEditTextWidth =          72 * 6;
    const Boolean kRedraw =                 TRUE;

    CWindow *aWindow = new CWindow;
    aWindow->IWindow(kWINDResourceID, !kWindowFloats, gDesktop, this);
    itsWindow = aWindow;
    CScrollPane *theScrollPane = new CScrollPane;
    theScrollPane->IScrollPane(aWindow, this, 10, 10, 0, 0,
      sizELASTIC, sizELASTIC,
      kHasHorizontalScrollbar, kHasVerticalScrollbar, kHasGrowBox);
    theScrollPane->FitToEnclFrame(kFitHorizontal, kFitVertical);

    CEditText *thePane = new CEditText;
    thePane->IEditText(theScrollPane, this, 1, 1, 0, 0,
      sizELASTIC, sizELASTIC, kEditTextWidth);
    itsGopher = thePane;
    itsMainPane = thePane;
    fEditText = thePane;
    theScrollPane->InstallPanorama(thePane);
    thePane->FitToEnclosure(kFitHorizontal, kFitVertical);
    Rect margin;
    ::SetRect(&margin, 2, 2, -2, -2);
    thePane->ChangeSize(&margin, !kRedraw);

    gDecorator->PlaceNewWindow(itsWindow);
}

void CTextDoc::OpenFile(SFReply *macReply)
{
    CDataFile     *theDataFile;
    Handle         theData;
    Str63          theName;
    OSErr          theError;
    const long     kMaxFileSize = 32000;

    theDataFile = new CDataFile;

    itsFile = theDataFile;

    theDataFile->IDataFile();
    theDataFile->SFSpecify(macReply);

    theDataFile->Open(fsRdPerm);

    TRY {
        if (theDataFile->GetLength() > kMaxFileSize)
            ::Failure(mFulErr, excExceedTELimit);
        theData = theDataFile->ReadAll();
    } CATCH {
         theDataFile->Close();
    }
    ENDTRY;

    TRY {
        theDataFile->Close();
        BuildWindow();
        fEditText->SetTextHandle(theData);
    } CATCH {
        ::DisposHandle(theData);
    }
    ENDTRY;
    ::DisposHandle(theData);
```

```
	gDecorator->StaggerWindow(itsWindow);
	itsFile->GetName(theName);
	itsWindow->SetTitle(theName);

	itsWindow->Select();
}

Boolean CTextDoc::DoSave()
{
	Handle		theData;

	if (itsFile == NULL)
		return(DoSaveFileAs());
	else {
		CDataFile *theDataFile = (CDataFile *) itsFile;

		theData = fEditText->GetTextHandle();
		theDataFile->Open(fsWrPerm);
		TRY {
			theDataFile->WriteAll(theData);
		} CATCH {
			theDataFile->Close();
		}
		ENDTRY;
		theDataFile->Close();
		dirty = FALSE;
		return(TRUE);
	}
}

Boolean CTextDoc::DoSaveAs(SFReply *macSFReply)
{
	if (itsFile != NULL)
		itsFile->Dispose();

	CDataFile *theDataFile = new CDataFile;
	itsFile = theDataFile;
	theDataFile->IDataFile();
	theDataFile->SFSpecify(macSFReply);
	if (theDataFile->ExistsOnDisk())
		theDataFile->ThrowOut();
	theDataFile->CreateNew(gSignature, 'TEXT');

	itsWindow->SetTitle(macSFReply->fName);

	return(DoSave());
}
```

Text.cp

```
#include "CTextApp.h"

void main()
{
	CTextApp	*app;

	app = new CTextApp;
	app->ITextApp();
	app->Run();
	app->Exit();
}
```

CTextApp.h

```
#pragma once

#include <CApplication.h>

class CTextApp: public CApplication {
public:
    void          ITextApp();

    virtual void  CreateDocument();
    virtual void  OpenDocument(SFReply *macReply);
    virtual void  SetUpFileParameters();
};
```

CTextDoc.h

```
#pragma once

#include <CDocument.h>
#include <CEditText.h>

class CTextDoc: public CDocument {
public:
    void            ITextDoc(CApplication *supervisor);

    virtual void    NewFile();
    virtual void    OpenFile(SFReply *macReply);
    virtual Boolean DoSave();
    virtual Boolean DoSaveAs(SFReply *macSFReply);
protected:
    virtual void    BuildWindow();
private:
    CEditText   *fEditText;
};
```

Chapter 18, PicturePeeker

CAboutBoxApplication.cp

```
#include "CAboutBoxApplication.h"
#include <SegLoad.h>

void CAboutBoxApplication::IAboutBoxApplication(short extraMasters,
  Size aRainyDayFund, Size aCriticalBalance, Size aToolboxBalance)
{
    IApplication(extraMasters,aRainyDayFund, aCriticalBalance,
      aToolboxBalance);
}

void CAboutBoxApplication::DoCommand(long theCommand)
{
    const short kAboutBoxResourceID = 1024;

    switch (theCommand) {
    case cmdAbout:
        Str255 applicationName;
        short  appRefNum;
        Handle h;

        ::PositionDialog('ALRT', kAboutBoxResourceID);
        ::GetAppParms(applicationName, &appRefNum, &h);
        ::DisposHandle(h);
        ::ParamText(applicationName, NULL, NULL, NULL);
        Alert(kAboutBoxResourceID, NULL);
        break;
```

```
    default:
        CApplication::DoCommand(theCommand);
        break;
    }
}
```

CCutCopyPastePicture.cp

```
#include "CCutCopyPastePicture.h"
#include <CBartender.h>
#include <CClipboard.h>
#include "TFailureObjects.h"
#include "CPictureClipboardTask.h"

extern CBartender *gBartender;
extern CClipboard *gClipboard;

void CCutCopyPastePicture::ICutCopyPastePicture(CView *anEnclosure,
  CBureaucrat *aSupervisor,
  short aWidth, short aHeight, short aHEncl, short aVEncl,
  SizingOption aHSizing, SizingOption aVSizing)
{
    IPicture(anEnclosure, aSupervisor, aWidth, aHeight,
      aHEncl, aVEncl, aHSizing, aVSizing);
}

void CCutCopyPastePicture::UpdateMenus()
{
    CPicture::UpdateMenus();

    if (GetMacPicture() != NULL) {
        gBartender->EnableCmd(cmdCopy);
        gBartender->EnableCmd(cmdCut);
        gBartender->EnableCmd(cmdClear);
    }

    if (gClipboard->GetData('PICT', NULL))
        gBartender->EnableCmd(cmdPaste);
}

void CCutCopyPastePicture::DoCommand(long cmd)
{
    switch (cmd) {
    case cmdCopy:
    case cmdCut:
    case cmdClear:
    case cmdPaste:
        CPictureClipboardTask  *clipTask = new CPictureClipboardTask;
        {
            TFreeOnFailure freer(clipTask);

            clipTask->IPictureClipboardTask(this, cmd);
        }
        itsLastTask = clipTask;
        if (cmd == cmdCopy)
            itsSupervisor->NotifyClean(clipTask);
        else
            itsSupervisor->Notify(clipTask);
        clipTask->Do();
        break;

    default:
        CPicture::DoCommand(cmd);
    }
}
```

CPictureApp.cp

```
#include "CPictureApp.h"
#include "CPictureDoc.h"
#include "TFailureObjects.h"
#include <Global.h>

extern    OSType        gSignature;        // The application's signature

void CPictureApp::IPictureApp()
{
    const short   kExtraMasters =    1;
    const Size    kRainyDayFund =    45000;
    const Size    kCriticalBalance = 40000;
    const Size    kToolboxBalance =  20000;

    IAboutBoxApplication(kExtraMasters, kRainyDayFund,
      kCriticalBalance, kToolboxBalance);
}

void CPictureApp::CreateDocument()
{
    CPictureDoc *theDocument = new CPictureDoc;

    TFreeOnFailure freer(theDocument);

    theDocument->IPictureDoc(this);
    theDocument->NewFile();
}

void CPictureApp::OpenDocument(SFReply *macReply)
{
    CPictureDoc *theDocument = new CPictureDoc;

    TFreeOnFailure freer(theDocument);

    theDocument->IPictureDoc(this);
    theDocument->OpenFile(macReply);
}

void CPictureApp::SetUpFileParameters()
{
    CApplication::SetUpFileParameters();

    sfNumTypes = 1;
    sfFileTypes[0] = 'PICT';
    gSignature = 'C++3';
}
```

CPictureClipboardTask.cp

```
#include "CPictureClipboardTask.h"
#include <CClipboard.h>

extern CClipboard *gClipboard;
const LongPt kZeroZeroPt = {0, 0};

void CPictureClipboardTask::IPictureClipboardTask(CPicture *thePicture,
  long command)
{
    fOldMacPicture = NULL;
    fOldScrap = NULL;
    fPicture = thePicture;
    fCommand = command;
    ITask(command - cmdCut + 2); // cmdTyping is first string, cmdCut is next
}
```

```
void CPictureClipboardTask::Dispose()
{
    if (!IsUndone()) {
        switch (fCommand) {
        case cmdCut:
            ::DisposHandle((Handle) fOldMacPicture);
            ::DisposHandle(fOldScrap);
            break;
        case cmdClear:
            ::DisposHandle((Handle) fOldMacPicture);
            break;
        case cmdPaste:
            ::DisposHandle((Handle) fOldMacPicture);
            // old scrap is now the picture
            break;
        case cmdCopy:
            // old picture remains the picture
            ::DisposHandle(fOldScrap);
            break;
        }
    } else
        if (fOldScrap != NULL)
            ::DisposHandle(fOldScrap);
    CTask::Dispose();
}

void CPictureClipboardTask::Do()
{
    if (fCommand != cmdClear) {
        Handle h;

        gClipboard->GetData('PICT', &h);
        fOldScrap = h;
    }
    fOldMacPicture = fPicture->GetMacPicture();
    Redo();
}

void CPictureClipboardTask::Undo()
{
    if (fCommand == cmdCopy || fCommand == cmdCut) {
        gClipboard->EmptyScrap();
        if (fOldScrap != NULL)
            gClipboard->PutData('PICT', fOldScrap);
    }
    if (fCommand != cmdCopy) {
        fPicture->SetPosition((LongPt *) &kZeroZeroPt);
        fPicture->SetMacPicture(fOldMacPicture);
        fPicture->Refresh();
    }
    undone = TRUE;
}

void CPictureClipboardTask::Redo()
{
    if (fCommand == cmdCopy || fCommand == cmdCut) {
        gClipboard->EmptyScrap();
        gClipboard->PutData('PICT', (Handle) fOldMacPicture);
    }
    if (fCommand == cmdCut || fCommand == cmdClear) {
        fPicture->SetPosition((LongPt *) &kZeroZeroPt);
        fPicture->SetMacPicture(NULL);
    }
```

```
    if (fCommand == cmdPaste) {
        fPicture->SetPosition((LongPt *) &kZeroZeroPt);
        fPicture->SetMacPicture((PicHandle) fOldScrap);
     }
    if (fCommand != cmdCopy)
        fPicture->Refresh();
    undone = FALSE;
}
```

CPictureDoc.cp

```
#include "CPictureDoc.h"
#include "CCutCopyPastePicture.h"
#include <CScrollPane.h>
#include <CDesktop.h>
#include <CWindow.h>
#include <CDataFile.h>
#include <CDecorator.h>
#include <TBUtilities.h>
#include "TFailureObjects.h"
#include "TDisposHandleOnFailure.h"
#include "TWithFileOpen.h"

extern CDesktop        *gDesktop;
extern OSType       gSignature;
extern CDecorator   *gDecorator;
const long    kPICTHeaderLength = 512;

void CPictureDoc::IPictureDoc(CApplication *supervisor)
{
    const Boolean kPrintable = TRUE;

    IDocument(supervisor, kPrintable);
}

void CPictureDoc::NewFile()
{
    BuildWindow();

    Str255 wTitle;
    short wCount;
    Str255 wNumber;

    itsWindow->GetTitle(wTitle);
    gDecorator->StaggerWindow(itsWindow);
    wCount = gDecorator->GetWCount();
    ::NumToString(wCount, wNumber);
    ::ConcatPStrings(wTitle, "\p-");
    ::ConcatPStrings(wTitle, wNumber);
    itsWindow->SetTitle(wTitle);

    itsWindow->Select();
}

void CPictureDoc::BuildWindow()
{
    const short   kWINDResourceID =        500;
    const Boolean kWindowFloats =          TRUE;
    const Boolean kFitHorizontal =         TRUE;
    const Boolean kFitVertical =           TRUE;
    const Boolean kHasHorizontalScrollbar =TRUE;
    const Boolean kHasVerticalScrollbar =  TRUE;
    const Boolean kHasGrowBox =            TRUE;
    const Boolean kRedraw =                TRUE;
```

```
    CWindow *aWindow = new CWindow;
    aWindow->IWindow(kWINDResourceID, !kWindowFloats, gDesktop, this);
    itsWindow = aWindow;
    CScrollPane *theScrollPane = new CScrollPane;
    theScrollPane->IScrollPane(aWindow, this, 10, 10, 0, 0,
      sizELASTIC, sizELASTIC,
      kHasHorizontalScrollbar, kHasVerticalScrollbar, kHasGrowBox);
    theScrollPane->FitToEnclFrame(kFitHorizontal, kFitVertical);

    CCutCopyPastePicture *thePane = new CCutCopyPastePicture;
    thePane->ICutCopyPastePicture(theScrollPane, this, 1, 1, 0, 0,
      sizELASTIC, sizELASTIC);
    itsGopher = thePane;
    itsMainPane = thePane;
    fPicture = thePane;
    theScrollPane->InstallPanorama(thePane);
    thePane->FitToEnclosure(kFitHorizontal, kFitVertical);

    gDecorator->PlaceNewWindow(itsWindow);
}

void CPictureDoc::OpenFile(SFReply *macReply)
{
    CDataFile    *theDataFile;
    Handle        theData;
    Str63         theName;
    OSErr         theError;

    theDataFile = new CDataFile;

    itsFile = theDataFile;

    theDataFile->IDataFile();
    theDataFile->SFSpecify(macReply);

    Handle theMacPicture = ::NewHandleCanFail(0);
    ::FailNIL(theMacPicture);
    {
        TWithFileOpen fileOpener(theDataFile, fsRdPerm);
        TDisposHandleOnFailure handleFreer(theMacPicture);

        long thePictureLength = theDataFile->GetLength() - kPICTHeaderLength;
        if (thePictureLength <= 0)
            ::FailOSErr(eofErr);
        theDataFile->SetMark(kPICTHeaderLength, fsFromStart);
        ::ResizeHandleCanFail(theMacPicture, thePictureLength);
        ::FailMemError();
        {
            THandleLocker lock(theMacPicture);
            theDataFile->ReadSome(*theMacPicture, thePictureLength);
        }
        BuildWindow();
    }
    fPicture->SetMacPicture((PicHandle) theMacPicture);

    gDecorator->StaggerWindow(itsWindow);
    itsFile->GetName(theName);
    itsWindow->SetTitle(theName);

    itsWindow->Select();
}

Boolean CPictureDoc::DoSave()
{
    Handle        theData;
```

```
    if (itsFile == NULL)
        return(DoSaveFileAs());
    else {
        CDataFile *theDataFile = (CDataFile *) itsFile;

        Handle theMacPicture = (Handle) fPicture->GetMacPicture();
        {
            TWithFileOpen fileOpener(theDataFile, fsWrPerm);
            char    zeros[kPICTHeaderLength];

            for (int i = 0; i < kPICTHeaderLength; i++)
                zeros[i] = 0;
            theDataFile->WriteSome(zeros, sizeof(zeros));
            THandleLocker lock(theMacPicture);
            theDataFile->WriteSome(
              *theMacPicture, ::GetHandleSize(theMacPicture));
        }
        dirty = FALSE;
        return(TRUE);
    }
}

Boolean CPictureDoc::DoSaveAs(SFReply *macSFReply)
{
    if (itsFile != NULL)
        itsFile->Dispose();

    CDataFile *theDataFile = new CDataFile;
    itsFile = theDataFile;
    theDataFile->IDataFile();
    theDataFile->SFSpecify(macSFReply);
    if (theDataFile->ExistsOnDisk())
        theDataFile->ThrowOut();
    theDataFile->CreateNew(gSignature, 'PICT');

    itsWindow->SetTitle(macSFReply->fName);

    return(DoSave());
}
```

Picture.cp

```
#include "CPictureApp.h"

void main()
{
    CPictureApp *app;

    app = new CPictureApp;
    app->IPictureApp();
    app->Run();
    app->Exit();
}
```

TDisposHandleOnFailure.cp

```
#include "TDisposHandleOnFailure.h"

TDisposHandleOnFailure::TDisposHandleOnFailure(Handle h)
{
    fHandle = h;
}

void TDisposHandleOnFailure::HandleFailure(OSErr err, long message)
{
    if (fHandle != NULL)
        ::DisposHandle(fHandle);
}
```

TFailureObjects.cp

```
#include "TFailureObjects.h"

TCatchFailure::TCatchFailure()
{
    ::CatchFailures(&fFailInfo,
      (HandlerFuncPtr) TCatchFailure::PrivateHandleFailure, (long) this);
    fExitingNormally = true;
}

TCatchFailure::~TCatchFailure()
{
    if (fExitingNormally)
        ::Success();
}

pascal void TCatchFailure::PrivateHandleFailure(OSErr err, long message)
{
    fExitingNormally = false;
    HandleFailure(err, message);
}

TAutoDestruct::~TAutoDestruct()
{
}

void TAutoDestruct::HandleFailure(OSErr /*err*/, long /*message*/)
{
    this->~TAutoDestruct();    // explicit virtual call to destructor
}

TFreeOnCompletion::TFreeOnCompletion(CObject *object)
{
    fObject = object;
}

TFreeOnCompletion::~TFreeOnCompletion()
{
    if (fObject != NULL)
        fObject->Dispose();
}

THandleLocker::THandleLocker(Handle h)
{
    fHandle = h;
    fState = ::HGetState(fHandle);
    ::HLock(h);
}

THandleLocker::~THandleLocker()
{
    ::HSetState(fHandle, fState);
}

TFreeOnFailure::TFreeOnFailure(CObject *object)
{
    fObject = object;
}

void TFreeOnFailure::HandleFailure(OSErr /*err*/, long /*message*/)
{
    if (fObject != NULL)
        fObject->Dispose();
}
```

TWithFileOpen.cp

```
#include "TWithFileOpen.h"

TWithFileOpen::TWithFileOpen(CFile *theFile, SignedByte permission)
{
    theFile->Open(permission);
    fFile = theFile;
}

TWithFileOpen::~TWithFileOpen()
{
    if (fFile != NULL)
        fFile->Close();
}
```

CAboutBoxApplication.h

```
#pragma once
#include <CApplication.h>

class CAboutBoxApplication: public CApplication {
public:
    void    IAboutBoxApplication(short extraMasters, Size aRainyDayFund,
              Size aCriticalBalance, Size aToolboxBalance);

    virtual void   DoCommand(long theCommand);
};
```

CCutCopyPastePicture.h

```
#pragma once

#include <CPicture.h>

class CCutCopyPastePicture: public CPicture {
public:
           void ICutCopyPastePicture(CView *anEnclosure, CBureaucrat *aSupervisor,
             short aWidth, short aHeight, short aHEncl, short aVEncl,
             SizingOption aHSizing, SizingOption aVSizing);

   virtual void UpdateMenus();
   virtual void DoCommand(long cmd);
};
```

CPictureApp.h

```
#pragma once

#include "CAboutBoxApplication.h"

class CPictureApp: public CAboutBoxApplication {
public:
    void           IPictureApp();

    virtual void  CreateDocument();
    virtual void  OpenDocument(SFReply *macReply);
    virtual void  SetUpFileParameters();

};
```

CPictureClipboardTask.h

```
#pragma once

#include <CPicture.h>
#include <CTask.h>
```

```
class CPictureClipboardTask: public CTask {
public:
    void IPictureClipboardTask(CPicture *thePicture, long command);

    virtual void Dispose();
    virtual void Do();
    virtual void Undo();
    virtual void Redo();

private:
    CPicture *fPicture;
    long      fCommand;
    Handle    fOldScrap;
    PicHandle fOldMacPicture;
};
```

CPictureDoc.h

```
#pragma once

#include <CDocument.h>
#include <CPicture.h>

class CPictureDoc: public CDocument {
public:
    void            IPictureDoc(CApplication *supervisor);

    virtual void    NewFile();
    virtual void    OpenFile(SFReply *macReply);
    virtual Boolean DoSave();
    virtual Boolean DoSaveAs(SFReply *macSFReply);
protected:
    virtual void    BuildWindow();
private:
    CPicture  *fPicture;
};
```

TDisposHandleOnFailure.h

```
#pragma once
#include "TFailureObjects.h"

// disposes the handle passed in the constructor on failure
class TDisposHandleOnFailure: public TCatchFailure {
public:
    TDisposHandleOnFailure(Handle h);
protected:
    virtual void HandleFailure(OSErr err, long message);
private:
    Handle fHandle;
};
```

TFailureObjects.h

```
#pragma once

#include <Exceptions.h>
#include <Types.h>

// abstract class which calls HandleFailure on a failure.
class TCatchFailure
{
protected:
    TCatchFailure();
    virtual ~TCatchFailure();
    virtual void HandleFailure(OSErr err, long message) = 0;    //  override this instead
```

```
private:
    Boolean    fExitingNormally;    // false if exiting due to failure
    pascal void PrivateHandleFailure(OSErr err, long message);    // don't override this!
    FailInfo    fFailInfo;
};

// abstract class which calls its destructor on a failure.
class TAutoDestruct: public TCatchFailure {
public:
    virtual ~TAutoDestruct();
protected:
    virtual void HandleFailure(OSErr err, long message);
};

// frees the object passed in the constructor on failure, or when its
// scope is exited
class TFreeOnCompletion: public TAutoDestruct {
public:
    TFreeOnCompletion(CObject *object);
    virtual ~TFreeOnCompletion();

private:
    CObject *fObject;
};

// restores the state of the handle passed in the constructor on failure, or when its
// scope is exited
class THandleLocker: public TAutoDestruct {
public:
    THandleLocker(Handle h);
    virtual ~THandleLocker();
private:
    Handle    fHandle;
    char    fState;
};

// frees the object passed in the constructor on failure
class TFreeOnFailure: public TCatchFailure {
public:
    TFreeOnFailure(CObject *object);
protected:
    virtual void HandleFailure(OSErr err, long message);
private:
    CObject *fObject;
};
```

TWithFileOpen.h

```
#pragma once

#include "TFailureObjects.h"
#include <CFile.h>
#include <Types.h>

class TWithFileOpen: public TAutoDestruct {
public:
    TWithFileOpen(CFile *theFile, SignedByte permission);
    virtual ~TWithFileOpen();


private:
    CFile *fFile;
};
```

Chapter 19, Tick-Tock

CAboutBoxApplication.cp

```
#include "CAboutBoxApplication.h"
#include <SegLoad.h>

void CAboutBoxApplication::IAboutBoxApplication(short extraMasters,
  Size aRainyDayFund, Size aCriticalBalance, Size aToolboxBalance)
{
    IApplication(extraMasters,aRainyDayFund, aCriticalBalance,
      aToolboxBalance);
}

void CAboutBoxApplication::DoCommand(long theCommand)
{
    const short kAboutBoxResourceID = 1024;

    switch (theCommand) {
    case cmdAbout:
        Str255 applicationName;
        short  appRefNum;
        Handle h;

        ::PositionDialog('ALRT', kAboutBoxResourceID);
        ::GetAppParms(applicationName, &appRefNum, &h);
        ::DisposHandle(h);
        ::ParamText(applicationName, NULL, NULL, NULL);
        Alert(kAboutBoxResourceID, NULL);
        break;
    default:
        CApplication::DoCommand(theCommand);
        break;
    }
}
```

CClockApp.cp

```
#include "CClockApp.h"
#include "CClockPane.h"
#include <CDecorator.h>
#include <CDesktop.h>
#include <CDirector.h>
#include <CScrollPane.h>
#include <Commands.h>
#include "CSaveRestoreSizeWindow.h"

const short        kExtraMasters =       1;
const Size        kRainyDayFund =    20480;
const Size        kCriticalBalance =    20480;
const Size        kToolboxBalance =    20480;

const short kWINDStarter = 500;

extern CDesktop        *gDesktop;

void CClockApp::IClockApp(void)
{
    const Boolean     kFloatingWindow = TRUE;
    const short       kMinWindowHeight = 30;
    const short       kMinWindowWidth = 30;

    IAboutBoxApplication(kExtraMasters, kRainyDayFund,
                     kCriticalBalance, kToolboxBalance);
```

```
    CDirector *aDirector = new CDirector;
    aDirector->IDirector(this);

    CSaveRestoreSizeWindow *aWindow = new CSaveRestoreSizeWindow;
    aWindow->ISaveRestoreSizeWindow(kWINDStarter, !kFloatingWindow, gDesktop, aDirector);
    aDirector->itsWindow = aWindow;
    Rect sizeRect = aWindow->sizeRect;
    sizeRect.top = kMinWindowHeight;
    sizeRect.left = kMinWindowWidth;
    aWindow->SetSizeRect(&sizeRect);

    aWindow->Select();
    CClockPane *thePane = new CClockPane;
    thePane->IClockPane(aWindow, aDirector, 0, 0, 0, 0, sizELASTIC, sizELASTIC);
    thePane->FitToEnclosure(TRUE, TRUE);
    aDirector->itsGopher = thePane;
}
```

CClockPane.cp

```
#include "CClockPane.h"
#include "CDawdleBureaucratChore.h"
#include <Global.h>
#include <Commands.h>
#include <CApplication.h>
#include <CBartender.h>
#include <Packages.h>
#include <SANE.h>
#include "Utilities.h"
#include "TGrafPortSetter.h"

extern CApplication    *gApplication;
extern CBartender     *gBartender;
extern long            gSleepTime;

void CClockPane::IClockPane(CView *anEnclosure, CBureaucrat *aSupervisor,
    short aWidth, short aHeight,
   short aHEncl, short aVEncl,
    SizingOption aHSizing, SizingOption aVSizing)
{
     fIdleChore = NULL;
     fIdleChoreIsInstalled = FALSE;
     fBitMap.baseAddr = NULL;
     fGrafPtr = NULL;
     SetRect(&fBitMap.bounds, 0, 0, 0, 0);

     IPane(anEnclosure, aSupervisor, aWidth, aHeight,
                            aHEncl, aVEncl, aHSizing, aVSizing);

     fIdleChore = new CDawdleBureaucratChore;
     fIdleChore->IDawdleBureaucratChore(this);
     fGrafPtr = (GrafPtr) ::NewPtrCanFail(sizeof(GrafPort));
     ::FailNIL(fGrafPtr);
     ::OpenPort(fGrafPtr);

     fDigital = false;
     fShowSeconds = true;
}

void CClockPane::Dispose(void)
{
     if (fIdleChoreIsInstalled)
         gApplication->CancelIdleChore(fIdleChore);
     ::ForgetObject(fIdleChore);
```

```
    if (fBitMap.baseAddr != NULL)
        ::DisposPtr(fBitMap.baseAddr);
    if (fGrafPtr != NULL) {
        ::ClosePort(fGrafPtr);
        ::DisposPtr((Ptr) fGrafPtr);
    }
}

void CClockPane::Activate(void)
{
    CPane::Activate();
    if (fIdleChoreIsInstalled) {
        gApplication->CancelIdleChore(fIdleChore);
        fIdleChoreIsInstalled = false;
    }
}

void CClockPane::Deactivate(void)
{
    CPane::Deactivate();
    gApplication->AssignIdleChore(fIdleChore);
    fIdleChoreIsInstalled = true;
}

void CClockPane::UpdateMenus()
{
    CPane::UpdateMenus();

    gBartender->EnableCmd(cmdShowSeconds);
    gBartender->EnableCmd(cmdDigital);
    gBartender->EnableCmd(cmdAnalog);

    gBartender->CheckMarkCmd(cmdShowSeconds, fShowSeconds);
    gBartender->CheckMarkCmd(cmdDigital, fDigital);
    gBartender->CheckMarkCmd(cmdAnalog, !fDigital);
}

void CClockPane::DoCommand(long theCommand)
{
    switch (theCommand) {
    case cmdShowSeconds:
        fShowSeconds = !fShowSeconds;
        Refresh();
        if (fShowSeconds)
            gSleepTime = 1;         // Make Dawdle start being called
        break;

    case cmdDigital:
        if (!fDigital) {
            fDigital = TRUE;
            Refresh();
        }
        break;

    case cmdAnalog:
        if (fDigital) {
            fDigital = FALSE;
            Refresh();
        }
        break;

    default:
        CPane::DoCommand(theCommand);
        break;
    }
}
```

```
inline short Round(float f)
{
    return (short) (f + 0.5);
}

void CClockPane::UpdateOffscreen(const Rect &area)
{
    LongRect    frame;
    Rect    qdFrame;

    GetFrame(&frame);
    ::LongToQDRect(&frame, &qdFrame);
    CreateOffscreen(qdFrame);        // we would use area, if we weren't dawdling

    TGrafPortSetter setPort(fGrafPtr);
    DrawClock(qdFrame);
}

void CClockPane::Draw(Rect *area)
{
    UpdateOffscreen(*area);
    CopyFromOffscreen(*area);
}

// fractionOfCircle: 0 means straight up, .25 means to the right
void DrawLine(const Rect &frame, long double fractionOfCircle, short size)
{
    long double angle = 2 * 3.14159 * (1-(fractionOfCircle - 0.25));
    short radiusX = (frame.right - frame.left) / 2;
    short radiusY = (frame.bottom - frame.top) / 2;

    short xCoord = ::Round(::cos(angle) * radiusX);
    short yCoord = ::Round(::sin(angle) * radiusY);

    ::PenSize(size, size);
    ::MoveTo(frame.left + radiusX, frame.top + radiusY);
    ::Line(xCoord, -yCoord);    // Macintosh uses Y decreasing
}

inline short NumberOfBytesRoundedUpToAMultipleOf2(short num)
{
    return (num + 15) / 16 * 2;
}

void CClockPane::CreateOffscreen(const Rect &area)
{
    if (area.left != fBitMap.bounds.left ||
      area.right != fBitMap.bounds.right ||
      area.top != fBitMap.bounds.top ||
      area.bottom != fBitMap.bounds.bottom) {
            fBitMap.bounds = area;
            fBitMap.rowBytes =
              ::NumberOfBytesRoundedUpToAMultipleOf2(fBitMap.bounds.right - fBitMap.bounds.left);
            if (fBitMap.baseAddr != NULL)
                ::DisposPtr(fBitMap.baseAddr);
            fBitMap.baseAddr =
              ::NewPtrCanFail(fBitMap.rowBytes * (fBitMap.bounds.bottom - fBitMap.bounds.top));
            ::FailNIL(fBitMap.baseAddr);
        ::RectRgn(fGrafPtr->visRgn, &area);
        ::RectRgn(fGrafPtr->clipRgn, &area);
        fGrafPtr->portRect = area;

        TGrafPortSetter setPort(fGrafPtr);
        ::SetPortBits(&fBitMap);
    }
}
```

```
void CClockPane::GetDigitalString(unsigned long now, Str255 s)
{
    ::IUTimeString(now, fShowSeconds, s);
}

void CClockPane::GetDigitalFontAndSize(const Str255 s, const Rect &clockSize,
  short *font, short *size)
{
    *font = geneva;
    *size = 9;
}

void CClockPane::GetDigitalStringLocation(const Str255 s, const Rect &clockSize,
  short *h, short *v)
{
    FontInfo    fInfo;

    ::GetFontInfo(&fInfo);
    short excessHeight = clockSize.bottom - clockSize.top - fInfo.descent - fInfo.ascent;
    if (excessHeight < 0)
        *v = clockSize.bottom;
    else
        *v = clockSize.bottom - fInfo.descent - excessHeight / 2;

    short excessWidth = clockSize.right - clockSize.left - ::StringWidth(s);
    if (excessWidth < 0)
        *h = clockSize.left;
    else
        *h = clockSize.left + excessWidth / 2;
}

void CClockPane::DrawDigitalClock(const Rect &clockSize, unsigned long now)
{
    Str255          nowStr;
    short           h;
    short           v;
    short           font;
    short           size;

    GetDigitalString(now, nowStr);
    GetDigitalFontAndSize(nowStr, clockSize, &font, &size);
    ::TextFont(font);
    ::TextSize(size);
    GetDigitalStringLocation(nowStr, clockSize, &h, &v);
    ::MoveTo(h, v);
    ::DrawString(nowStr);
}

void CClockPane::DrawAnalogClock(const Rect &clockSize, unsigned long now)
{
    DateTimeRec     nowDateTime;
    const short     kSecondHandThickness = 1;
    const short     kMinuteHandThickness = 2;
    const short     kHourHandThickness = 3;

    ::Secs2Date(now, &nowDateTime);

    if (fShowSeconds)
        DrawLine(clockSize, ((float) nowDateTime.second) / 60.0,
          kSecondHandThickness);
    DrawLine(clockSize, nowDateTime.minute / 60.0, kMinuteHandThickness);
```

```
    Rect smallFrame = clockSize;// hour hand will be inscribed here
    const kHourHandSmallerConstant = 2;    // half as big as other hands
    ::InsetRect(&smallFrame,
      (clockSize.right - clockSize.left) / (2 * kHourHandSmallerConstant),
      (clockSize.bottom - clockSize.top) /  (2 * kHourHandSmallerConstant));
    DrawLine(smallFrame, nowDateTime.hour / 12.0, kHourHandThickness);
}

void CClockPane::DrawClock(const Rect &clockSize)
{
    unsigned long    now;

    ::GetDateTime(&now);

    ::EraseRect(&clockSize);

    if (fDigital)
        DrawDigitalClock(clockSize, now);
    else
        DrawAnalogClock(clockSize, now);
}

void CClockPane::CopyFromOffscreen(const Rect &areaToCopy)
{
    ::CopyBits(&fBitMap, &thePort->portBits,
      &areaToCopy, &areaToCopy, srcCopy, 0L);
}

long CClockPane::CalculateSleepTime()
{
    const short kTicksPerSecond = 60;

    if (fShowSeconds)
        return kTicksPerSecond;
    else {
        unsigned long   now;
        DateTimeRec     nowDateTime;
        const short     kSecondsPerMinute = 60;

        GetDateTime(&now);
        Secs2Date(now, &nowDateTime);
        return kTicksPerSecond * (kSecondsPerMinute - nowDateTime.second);
    }
}

void CClockPane::Dawdle(long *maxSleep)
{
    LongRect    frame;
    Rect    qdFrame;

    GetFrame(&frame);
    ::LongToQDRect(&frame, &qdFrame);
    UpdateOffscreen(qdFrame);

    Prepare();
    CopyFromOffscreen(qdFrame);

    *maxSleep = CalculateSleepTime();
}
```

CDawdleBureaucratChore.cp

```
#include "CDawdleBureaucratChore.h"

void CDawdleBureaucratChore::IDawdleBureaucratChore(CBureaucrat *theBureaucrat)
{
    fBureaucratToDawdle = theBureaucrat;
}

void CDawdleBureaucratChore::Perform(long *maxSleep)
{
    fBureaucratToDawdle->Dawdle(maxSleep);
}
```

Clock.cp

```
#include "CClockApp.h"

void main()
{
    CClockApp    *clockApp;

    clockApp = new CClockApp;
    clockApp->IClockApp();
    clockApp->Run();
    clockApp->Exit();
}
```

CQuitOnCloseWindow.cp

```
#include "CQuitOnCloseWindow.h"
#include <CApplication.h>

extern CApplication *gApplication;

void CQuitOnCloseWindow::IQuitOnCloseWindow(short WINDid, Boolean aFloating,
  CDesktop *anEnclosure, CDirector *aSupervisor)
{
    IWindow(WINDid, aFloating, anEnclosure, aSupervisor);
}

void CQuitOnCloseWindow::Dispose()
{
    CWindow::Dispose();

    gApplication->Quit();
}
```

CSaveRestoreSizeWindow.cp

```
#include "CSaveRestoreSizeWindow.h"
#include <Folders.h>
#include "TGrafPortSetter.h"

void CSaveRestoreSizeWindow::ISaveRestoreSizeWindow(
  short            windID,
  Boolean        aFloating,
  CDesktop        *anEnclosure,
  CDirector        *aSupervisor)
{
    fDataFile= NULL;
    IQuitOnCloseWindow(windID, aFloating, anEnclosure, aSupervisor);

    fDataFile = new CDataFile;
    fDataFile->IDataFile();
    SpecifyFile(fDataFile);
    SetInfoFromFile(fDataFile);
}
```

```
void CSaveRestoreSizeWindow::Dispose()
{
    StoreInfoInFile(fDataFile);
    ForgetObject(fDataFile);
    CQuitOnCloseWindow::Dispose();
}

void CSaveRestoreSizeWindow::SpecifyFile(CFile *aFile)
{
    short    vRefNum;
    long     dirID;

    FailOSErr(FindFolder(kOnSystemDisk, kPreferencesFolderType,
      kCreateFolder, &vRefNum,&dirID));
    aFile->SpecifyHFS("\pTick-Tock Preferences", vRefNum, dirID);
}

void CSaveRestoreSizeWindow::StoreInfoInFile(CDataFile *aFile)
{
    if (!aFile->ExistsOnDisk())
        aFile->CreateNew('C++5', 'PREF');

    aFile->Open(fsWrPerm);

    Rect     theWindowLocSize = macPort->portRect;

    {
        TGrafPortSetter setPort(macPort);

        ::LocalToGlobal((Point *) &theWindowLocSize.top);
        ::LocalToGlobal((Point *) &theWindowLocSize.bottom);
    }

    TRY {
        aFile->WriteSome((Ptr) &theWindowLocSize, sizeof(theWindowLocSize));
    }
    CATCH {
        NO_PROPAGATE;        // not writing window location isn't fatal
    }
    ENDTRY;
    aFile->Close();
}

void CSaveRestoreSizeWindow::SetInfoFromFile(CDataFile *aFile)
{
    if (aFile->ExistsOnDisk()) {
        Rect     portRect;

        aFile->Open(fsRdPerm);

        TRY {
            aFile->ReadSome((Ptr) &portRect, sizeof(portRect));
            Move(portRect.left, portRect.top);
            ChangeSize(portRect.right - portRect.left, portRect.bottom - portRect.top);
        }
        CATCH {
            NO_PROPAGATE;        // not reading window location isn't fatal
        }
        ENDTRY;
        aFile->Close();
    }
}
```

Utilities.cp

```
#include <TCLUtilities.h>
#include "Utilities.h"

Ptr NewPtrCanFail(Size size)
{
    Ptr p;
    Boolean savedAlloc;

    savedAlloc = SetAllocation(kAllocCanFail);
    p = NewPtr(size);
    SetAllocation(savedAlloc);

    return p;
}
```

CAboutBoxApplication.h

```
#pragma once
#include <CApplication.h>

class CAboutBoxApplication: public CApplication {
public:
    void    IAboutBoxApplication(short extraMasters, Size aRainyDayFund,
              Size aCriticalBalance, Size aToolboxBalance);

    virtual void   DoCommand(long theCommand);
};
```

CClockApp.h

```
#pragma once

#include "CAboutBoxApplication.h"

class CClockApp: public CAboutBoxApplication
{
public:
    void            IClockApp(void);
};
```

CClockPane.h

```
#pragma once

#include <CPane.h>
#include <Quickdraw.h>
#include "CDawdleBureaucratChore.h"

class CClockPane: public CPane {
public:
    void            IClockPane(CView *anEnclosure, CBureaucrat *aSupervisor,
                      short aWidth, short aHeight,
                       short aHEncl, short aVEncl,
                      SizingOption aHSizing, SizingOption aVSizing);

    virtual void    Dispose(void);

    virtual void    Draw(Rect *area);
    virtual void    Activate(void);
    virtual void    Deactivate(void);

    virtual void    Dawdle(long    *maxSleep);
```

```
    virtual void    UpdateMenus();
    virtual void    DoCommand(long theCommand);

protected:
    enum {cmdShowSeconds = 1024, cmdDigital=1025, cmdAnalog=1026};

    virtual void    DrawClock(const Rect &clockSize);
    virtual void    CopyFromOffscreen(const Rect &areaToCopy);
    virtual void    CreateOffscreen(const Rect &area);
    virtual void    UpdateOffscreen(const Rect &area);
    virtual long    CalculateSleepTime();
    virtual void    DrawAnalogClock(const Rect &clockSize, unsigned long now);
    virtual void    DrawDigitalClock(const Rect &clockSize, unsigned long now);
    virtual void    GetDigitalString(unsigned long now, Str255 s);
    virtual void    GetDigitalFontAndSize(const Str255 s, const Rect &clockSize, short *font, short *size);
    virtual void    GetDigitalStringLocation(const Str255 s, const Rect &clockSize, short *h, short *v);

private:

    CDawdleBureaucratChore      *fIdleChore;
    Boolean                     fIdleChoreIsInstalled;
    BitMap                      fBitMap;
    GrafPtr                     fGrafPtr;
    Boolean                     fShowSeconds;
    Boolean                     fDigital;
};
```

CDawdleBureaucratChore.h

```
#pragma once

#include <CChore.h>
#include <CBureaucrat.h>

class CDawdleBureaucratChore: public CChore {
public:
    void            IDawdleBureaucratChore(CBureaucrat *theBureaucrat);
    virtual void    Perform(long *maxSleep);

private:
    CBureaucrat     *fBureaucratToDawdle;
};
```

CQuitOnCloseWindow.h

```
#pragma once

#include <CWindow.h>

class CQuitOnCloseWindow: public CWindow {
public:
    virtual void IQuitOnCloseWindow(short WINDid, Boolean aFloating,
                        CDesktop *anEnclosure, CDirector *aSupervisor);
    virtual void Dispose();
};
```

CSaveRestoreSizeWindow.h

```
#pragma once

#include "CQuitOnCloseWindow.h"
#include <CDataFile.h>

class CSaveRestoreSizeWindow: public CQuitOnCloseWindow {
public:
```

```
    void ISaveRestoreSizeWindow(
      short            windID,
      Boolean        aFloating,
      CDesktop        *anEnclosure,
      CDirector        *aSupervisor);

    virtual void Dispose();

protected:
    virtual void StoreInfoInFile(CDataFile *aFile);
    virtual void SetInfoFromFile(CDataFile *aFile);
    virtual void SpecifyFile(CFile *aFile);

private:
    CDataFile    *fDataFile;
};
```

Utilities.h

```
#pragma once

#include <Memory.h>

Ptr NewPtrCanFail(Size size);
```

Chapter 20, C++Calc

CAboutBoxApplication.cp

```
#include "CAboutBoxApplication.h"
#include <SegLoad.h>

void CAboutBoxApplication::IAboutBoxApplication(short extraMasters,
  Size aRainyDayFund, Size aCriticalBalance, Size aToolboxBalance)
{
    IApplication(extraMasters,aRainyDayFund, aCriticalBalance,
      aToolboxBalance);
}

void CAboutBoxApplication::DoCommand(long theCommand)
{
    const short kAboutBoxResourceID = 1024;

    switch (theCommand) {
    case cmdAbout:
        Str255 applicationName;
        short  appRefNum;
        Handle h;

        ::PositionDialog('ALRT', kAboutBoxResourceID);
        ::GetAppParms(applicationName, &appRefNum, &h);
        ::DisposHandle(h);
        ::ParamText(applicationName, NULL, NULL, NULL);
        Alert(kAboutBoxResourceID, NULL);
        break;
    default:
        CApplication::DoCommand(theCommand);
        break;
    }
}
```

Calculator.cp

```
#include "Calculator.h"

TCalculator::TCalculator()
{
    fX = 0.0;
    fY = 0.0;
    fZ = 0.0;
}

void TCalculator::Enter(long double num)
{
    fZ = fY;
    fY = fX;
    fX = num;
}

void TCalculator::Add()
{
    long double v = PopX();
    Enter(v + PopX());
}

void TCalculator::Subtract()
{
    long double v = PopX();
    Enter(PopX() - v);
}

void TCalculator::Multiply()
{
    long double v = PopX();
    Enter(v * PopX());
}

void TCalculator::Divide()
{
    long double v = PopX();
    Enter(PopX() / v);
}

long double TCalculator::GetX()
{
     return fX;
}
long double TCalculator::GetY()
{
     return fY;
}
long double TCalculator::GetZ()
{
     return fZ;
}

void TCalculator::SetX(long double num)
{
     fX = num;
}

void TCalculator::SetY(long double num)
{
     fY = num;
}
```

```
void TCalculator::SetZ(long double num)
{
     fZ = num;
}

long double TCalculator::PopX()
{
    long double v = GetX();

    fX = fY;
    fY = fZ;
    fZ = 0.0;
    return v;
}
```

CalculatorMain.cp

```
#include "CCalculatorApp.h"

void main()
{
    CCalculatorApp    *CalculatorApp;

    CalculatorApp = new CCalculatorApp;
    CalculatorApp->ICalculatorApp();
    CalculatorApp->Run();
    CalculatorApp->Exit();
}
```

CButtonWithFontAndSize.cp

```
#include "CButtonWithFontAndSize.h"

void CButtonWithFontAndSize::INewButtonWithFontAndSize(short aWidth, short aHeight,
  short aHEncl, short aVEncl,
  StringPtr title, Boolean fVisible, short procID,
  CView *anEnclosure, CBureaucrat *aSupervisor, StringPtr fontName, short fontSize)
{
    INewButton(aWidth, aHeight, aHEncl, aVEncl, title, fVisible,
      useWFont | procID, anEnclosure, aSupervisor);

    short fontNumber;
    GetFNum(fontName, &fontNumber);
    fFont = fontNumber;
    fFontSize = fontSize;
}

void CButtonWithFontAndSize::Draw(Rect *area)
{
    ::TextFont(fFont);
    ::TextSize(fFontSize);

    CButton::Draw(area);
}
```

CCalculatorApp.cp

```
#include "CCalculatorApp.h"
#include "CCalculatorPane.h"
#include <CDesktop.h>
#include <CDirector.h>
#include "CSaveRestoreSizeWindow.h"

const short        kExtraMasters =        1;
const Size        kRainyDayFund =     20480;
const Size        kCriticalBalance =    20480;
const Size        kToolboxBalance =    20480;
```

```
const short kWINDStarter = 500;

extern CDesktop        *gDesktop;

void CCalculatorApp::ICalculatorApp()
{
    const Boolean kFloatingWindow = TRUE;
    const short   kMinWindowHeight = 30;
    const short   kMinWindowWidth = 30;

    IAboutBoxApplication(kExtraMasters, kRainyDayFund,
      kCriticalBalance, kToolboxBalance);

    CDirector *aDirector = new CDirector;
    aDirector->IDirector(this);

    CSaveRestoreSizeWindow *aWindow = new CSaveRestoreSizeWindow;
    aWindow->ISaveRestoreSizeWindow(kWINDStarter, !kFloatingWindow, gDesktop,
      aDirector);
    aDirector->itsWindow = aWindow;

    aWindow->Select();
    CCalculatorPane *thePane = new CCalculatorPane;
    thePane->ICalculatorPane(aWindow, aDirector, 0, 0, 0, 0,
      sizELASTIC, sizELASTIC);
    thePane->FitToEnclosure(TRUE, TRUE);
    aDirector->itsGopher = thePane;
}
```

CCalculatorPane.cp

```
#include "CCalculatorPane.h"
#include <CBartender.h>
#include <CClipboard.h>
#include "CButtonWithFontAndSize.h"
#include <CPaneBorder.h>
#include <Global.h>

extern CBartender *gBartender;
extern CClipboard *gClipboard;

void CCalculatorPane::CreateCommandButton(short rowNumber, short colNumber, long command)
{
    CButtonWithFontAndSize *aButton;
    Str255    buttonName;
    const short kButtonWidth = 18;
    const short kButtonHeight = 16;
    const short kColumnWidth = 23;
    const short kColumnHeight = 22;
    const short kLeftMargin = 9;
    const short kTopMargin = 29;
    const short kButtonTitleStringID = 1025;

    GetIndString(buttonName, kButtonTitleStringID,
      command - cmdFirstCommand + 1);
    aButton= new CButtonWithFontAndSize;
    aButton->INewButtonWithFontAndSize(kButtonWidth, kButtonHeight,
      kLeftMargin + (colNumber-1)* kColumnHeight,
      kTopMargin + (rowNumber-1) * kColumnHeight,
      buttonName, TRUE, 0, this, this, "\pGeneva", 9);
    aButton->SetClickCmd(command);
    fButtons[command - cmdFirstCommand] = aButton;
}
```

```
void CCalculatorPane::ICalculatorPane(CView *anEnclosure, CBureaucrat *aSupervisor,
   short aWidth, short aHeight,
  short aHEncl, short aVEncl,
   SizingOption aHSizing, SizingOption aVSizing)
{
    const short kFloatTextWidth= 86;
    const short kFloatTextHeight = 20;
    const short kFloatTextLeftMargin = 10;
    const short kFloatTextTopMargin = 9;

    IPane(anEnclosure, aSupervisor, aWidth, aHeight,
                        aHEncl, aVEncl, aHSizing, aVSizing);

    wantsClicks = true;

    fCalcDisplay = new CFloatText;
    fCalcDisplay->IFloatText(this, aSupervisor,
      kFloatTextWidth, kFloatTextHeight,
      kFloatTextLeftMargin, kFloatTextTopMargin,
      sizFIXEDSTICKY, sizFIXEDSTICKY, -1);
    fCalcDisplay->Specify(kNotEditable, kNotSelectable, kNotStylable);
    fCalcDisplay->SetFontName("\pMonaco");
    fCalcDisplay->SetFontSize(9);
    fCalcDisplay->SetMaxDisplayWidth(sizeof(fCurrentNumber)-1);

    CPaneBorder *border = new CPaneBorder;
    border->IPaneBorder(kBorderFrame);
    border->SetPenSize(1, 1);
    fCalcDisplay->SetBorder(border);

    CreateCommandButton(5, 2, cmd0);
    CreateCommandButton(5, 3, cmdPeriod);
    CreateCommandButton(5, 4, cmdEnter);

    CreateCommandButton(4, 1, cmd1);
    CreateCommandButton(4, 2, cmd2);
    CreateCommandButton(4, 3, cmd3);
    CreateCommandButton(4, 4, cmdChangeSign);

    CreateCommandButton(3, 1, cmd4);
    CreateCommandButton(3, 2, cmd5);
    CreateCommandButton(3, 3, cmd6);
    CreateCommandButton(3, 4, cmdAdd);

    CreateCommandButton(2, 1, cmd7);
    CreateCommandButton(2, 2, cmd8);
    CreateCommandButton(2, 3, cmd9);
    CreateCommandButton(2, 4, cmdSubtract);

    CreateCommandButton(1, 1, cmdClearEntry);
    CreateCommandButton(1, 2, cmdE);
    CreateCommandButton(1, 3, cmdDivide);
    CreateCommandButton(1, 4, cmdMultiply);

    Length(fCurrentNumber) = 0;
}

void CCalculatorPane::UpdateDisplay()
{
    fCalcDisplay->SetValue(fCalculator.GetX());
}
```

```
void CCalculatorPane::UpdateMenus()
{
    CPane::UpdateMenus();

    if (Length(fCurrentNumber) > 0)
        gBartender->EnableCmd(cmdClear);
    gBartender->EnableCmd(cmdCopy);
    if (gClipboard->GetData('TEXT', NULL) > 0)
        gBartender->EnableCmd(cmdPaste);
}

void CCalculatorPane::Draw(Rect *r)
{
    if (!gSystem.hasColorQD)
       FillRect(r, qd.ltGray);
    else {
        RGBColor     aColor;
        PixPatHandle myPixPat;

        aColor.red = aColor.green = aColor.blue = 0xaaaa; // light gray
        myPixPat = NewPixPat();
        MakeRGBPat(myPixPat, &aColor);
        FillCRect(r, myPixPat);
        DisposPixPat(myPixPat);
    }
}

void CCalculatorPane::DoCommand(long theCommand)
{
    switch (theCommand) {
    case cmdCopy:
        gClipboard->EmptyScrap();
        gClipboard->PutData('TEXT', fCalcDisplay->GetTextHandle());
        break;

    case cmdPaste:
        Handle h;
        Str255 s;

        gClipboard->GetData('TEXT', &h);
        if (GetHandleSize(h) > sizeof(fCurrentNumber)-1)
            SetHandleSize(h, sizeof(fCurrentNumber)-1);
        fCalcDisplay->SetTextHandle(h);
        ::DisposHandle(h);
        fCalcDisplay->GetTextString(s);
        CopyPString(s, fCurrentNumber);
        break;

    case cmdClear:
        fButtons[cmdClearEntry - cmdFirstCommand]->SimulateClick();
        break;

    case cmdClearEntry:
        fCalcDisplay->SetValue(fCalculator.GetX());
        Length(fCurrentNumber) = 0;
        break;

    case cmdAdd:
        this->EnterCurrentNumber();
        fCalculator.Add();
        UpdateDisplay();
        break;
```

```
case cmdSubtract:
     this->EnterCurrentNumber();
    fCalculator.Subtract();
    UpdateDisplay();
    break;

case cmdMultiply:
    this->EnterCurrentNumber();
    fCalculator.Multiply();
    UpdateDisplay();
    break;

case cmdDivide:
    this->EnterCurrentNumber();
    fCalculator.Divide();
    UpdateDisplay();
    break;

case cmdEnter:
    fCalculator.Enter(fCalcDisplay->GetValue());
    Length(fCurrentNumber) = 0;
    UpdateDisplay();
    break;

case cmdChangeSign:
    Str255 minusSign = "\p-";
    Str255 current;

    fCalcDisplay->GetTextString(current);

    if (Length(current) > 0 && current[1] == '-') {
        ::BlockMove(&current[2], &current[1], Length(current)-1);
        Length(current)—;
    }
    else
    {
        ::ConcatPStrings(minusSign, current);
        ::CopyPString(minusSign, current);
    }
    fCalcDisplay->SetTextString(current);
    ::CopyPString(current, fCurrentNumber);
    break;

case cmd0:
case cmd1:
case cmd2:
case cmd3:
case cmd4:
case cmd5:
case cmd6:
case cmd7:
case cmd8:
case cmd9:
    Str31 numberAsString;

    NumToString(theCommand - cmd0, numberAsString);
    if (Length(fCurrentNumber) + Length(numberAsString) < sizeof(fCurrentNumber))
    {
        ConcatPStrings(fCurrentNumber, numberAsString);
        fCalcDisplay->SetTextString(fCurrentNumber);
    }
    break;
```

```
    case cmdPeriod:
        Str31 periodString = "\p.";
        if (Length(fCurrentNumber) + Length(periodString) <
          sizeof(fCurrentNumber)) {
            ConcatPStrings(fCurrentNumber, periodString);
            fCalcDisplay->SetTextString(fCurrentNumber);
        }
        break;
    case cmdE:
        Str31 eString = "\pE";
        if (Length(fCurrentNumber) + Length(eString) <
          sizeof(fCurrentNumber)) {
            ConcatPStrings(fCurrentNumber, eString);
            fCalcDisplay->SetTextString(fCurrentNumber);
        }
        break;
    default:
        CPane::DoCommand(theCommand);
    }
}

void CCalculatorPane::EnterCurrentNumber()
{
    if (Length(fCurrentNumber) > 0) {
        fCalculator.Enter(fCalcDisplay->GetValue());
        Length(fCurrentNumber) = 0;
        UpdateDisplay();
    }
}

void CCalculatorPane::DoKeyDown(char theChar, Byte keyCode, EventRecord *macEvent)
{
    const kReturnChar = 13;
    const kEnterChar = 3;
    const kBackspaceChar = 8;
    long commandNumber;

    switch (theChar){
    case kBackspaceChar:
        if (Length(fCurrentNumber) == 1)
            DoCommand(cmdClearEntry);
        else if (Length(fCurrentNumber) > 1) {
            Length(fCurrentNumber)--;
            fCalcDisplay->SetTextString(fCurrentNumber);
        }
        return;
    case '0':
    case '1':
    case '2':
    case '3':
    case '4':
    case '5':
    case '6':
    case '7':
    case '8':
    case '9':
        commandNumber = cmd0 + theChar - '0';
        break;
    case 'e':
    case 'E':
        commandNumber = cmdE;
        break;
```

```
    case 'c':
    case 'C':
        commandNumber = cmdClearEntry;
        break;
    case '.':
        commandNumber = cmdPeriod;
        break;
    case '+':
        commandNumber = cmdAdd;
        break;
    case '`':
    case '~':
        commandNumber = cmdChangeSign;
        break;
    case '-':
        commandNumber = cmdSubtract;
        break;
    case '*':
        commandNumber = cmdMultiply;
        break;
    case '/':
        commandNumber = cmdDivide;
        break;
    case kReturnChar:
    case kEnterChar:
        commandNumber = cmdEnter;
        break;

    default:
        inherited::DoKeyDown(theChar, keyCode, macEvent);
        return;
    }
    fButtons[commandNumber - cmdFirstCommand]->SimulateClick();
}
```

CFloatText.cp

```
#include "CFloatText.h"
#include <SANE.h>
#include <Packages.h>
#include <stdio.h>

 void CFloatText::IFloatText(
  CView         *anEnclosure,
  CBureaucrat   *aSupervisor,
  short         aWidth,
  short         aHeight,
  short         aHEncl,
  short         aVEncl,
  SizingOption    aHSizing,
  SizingOption    aVSizing,
 short          aLineWidth)
{
    IEditText(anEnclosure, aSupervisor, aWidth, aHeight, aHEncl, aVEncl,
      aHSizing, aVSizing, aLineWidth);
    SetValue(0.0);
    SetMaxDisplayWidth(8);
}

void CFloatText::SetMaxDisplayWidth(short numChars)
{
    fMaxDisplayChars = numChars;
}
```

```
long double CFloatText::GetValue()
{
    Str255 s;

    GetTextString(s);
    if (Length(s) == 0)
        return 0.0;
    else
        return ::str2num(s);
}

void CFloatText::SetValue(long double value)
{
    Str255 newString;
    Str255 existingString;

    ValueToText(value, newString);
    GetTextString(existingString);
    if (!::EqualString(newString, existingString, TRUE, TRUE))
        SetTextString(newString);
}

void CFloatText::ValueToText(long double value, Str255 s)
{
    ::sprintf((char *) s, "%.*g", fMaxDisplayChars, value);
    ::c2pstr((char *) s);
}

void CFloatText::GetTextString(Str255 s)
{
    Handle h =GetTextHandle();
    *s = Min(::GetHandleSize(h), 255);
    ::BlockMove(*h, s+1, *s);
}
```

CQuitOnCloseWindow.cp

```
#include "CQuitOnCloseWindow.h"
#include <CApplication.h>

extern CApplication *gApplication;

void CQuitOnCloseWindow::IQuitOnCloseWindow(short WINDid, Boolean aFloating,
  CDesktop *anEnclosure, CDirector *aSupervisor)
{
    IWindow(WINDid, aFloating, anEnclosure, aSupervisor);
}

void CQuitOnCloseWindow::Dispose()
{
    CWindow::Dispose();

    gApplication->Quit();
}
```

CSaveRestoreSizeWindow.cp

```
#include "CSaveRestoreSizeWindow.h"
#include <Folders.h>
#include "TGrafPortSetter.h"

void CSaveRestoreSizeWindow::ISaveRestoreSizeWindow(
  short           windID,
  Boolean         aFloating,
  CDesktop        *anEnclosure,
  CDirector       *aSupervisor)
```

```
{
    fDataFile= NULL;
    IQuitOnCloseWindow(windID, aFloating, anEnclosure, aSupervisor);

    fDataFile = new CDataFile;
    fDataFile->IDataFile();
    SpecifyFile(fDataFile);
    SetInfoFromFile(fDataFile);
}

void CSaveRestoreSizeWindow::Dispose()
{
    StoreInfoInFile(fDataFile);
    ForgetObject(fDataFile);
    CQuitOnCloseWindow::Dispose();
}

void CSaveRestoreSizeWindow::SpecifyFile(CFile *aFile)
{
    short    vRefNum;
    long     dirID;

    FailOSErr(FindFolder(kOnSystemDisk, kPreferencesFolderType,
      kCreateFolder, &vRefNum,&dirID));
    aFile->SpecifyHFS("\pCalculator Preferences", vRefNum, dirID);
}

void CSaveRestoreSizeWindow::StoreInfoInFile(CDataFile *aFile)
{
    if (!aFile->ExistsOnDisk())
        aFile->CreateNew('C++6', 'PREF');

    aFile->Open(fsWrPerm);

    Rect    theWindowLocSize = macPort->portRect;

    {
        TGrafPortSetter setPort(macPort);

        ::LocalToGlobal((Point *) &theWindowLocSize.top);
        ::LocalToGlobal((Point *) &theWindowLocSize.bottom);
    }

    TRY {
        aFile->WriteSome((Ptr) &theWindowLocSize, sizeof(theWindowLocSize));
    }
    CATCH {
        NO_PROPAGATE;        // not writing window location isn't fatal
    }
    ENDTRY;
    aFile->Close();
}

void CSaveRestoreSizeWindow::SetInfoFromFile(CDataFile *aFile)
{
    if (aFile->ExistsOnDisk()) {
        Rect    portRect;

        aFile->Open(fsRdPerm);

        TRY {
            aFile->ReadSome((Ptr) &portRect, sizeof(portRect));
            Move(portRect.left, portRect.top);
            ChangeSize(portRect.right - portRect.left, portRect.bottom - portRect.top);
        }
```

```
        CATCH {
            NO_PROPAGATE;         // not reading window location isn't fatal
        }
        ENDTRY;
        aFile->Close();
    }
}
```

Utilities.cp

```
#include <TCLUtilities.h>
#include "Utilities.h"

Ptr NewPtrCanFail(Size size)
{
    Ptr p;
    Boolean savedAlloc;

    savedAlloc = SetAllocation(kAllocCanFail);
    p = NewPtr(size);
    SetAllocation(savedAlloc);

    return p;
}
```

CAboutBoxApplication.h

```
#pragma once
#include <CApplication.h>

class CAboutBoxApplication: public CApplication {
public:
    void    IAboutBoxApplication(short extraMasters, Size aRainyDayFund,
                Size aCriticalBalance, Size aToolboxBalance);

    virtual void    DoCommand(long theCommand);
};
```

Calculator.h

```
#pragma once

class TCalculator {
public:
    TCalculator();
    void Enter(long double num);
    void Add();
    void Subtract();
    void Multiply();
    void Divide();
    long double GetX();
    long double GetY();
    long double GetZ();
private:
    long double PopX();
    void SetX(long double num);
    void SetY(long double num);
    void SetZ(long double num);

    long double    fX;
    long double    fY;
    long double    fZ;
};
```

CButtonWithFontAndSize.h

```
#pragma once

#include <CButton.h>

class CButtonWithFontAndSize: public CButton {
public:
    void INewButtonWithFontAndSize(short aWidth, short aHeight,
      short aHEncl, short aVEncl,
      StringPtr title, Boolean fVisible, short procID,
      CView *anEnclosure, CBureaucrat *aSupervisor,
      StringPtr fontName, short fontSize);

    virtual void Draw(Rect *area);

private:
    short fFont;
    short fFontSize;
};
```

CCalculatorApp.h

```
#pragma once

#include "CAboutBoxApplication.h"

class CCalculatorApp: public CAboutBoxApplication
{
public:
    void            ICalculatorApp();
};
```

CCalculatorPane.h

```
#pragma once
#include <CPane.h>
#include "Calculator.h"
#include "CFloatText.h"
#include <CButton.h>

class CCalculatorPane: public CPane {
public:
    void          ICalculatorPane(CView *anEnclosure,
                    CBureaucrat *aSupervisor,
                    short aWidth, short aHeight,
                    short aHEncl, short aVEncl,
                    SizingOption aHSizing, SizingOption aVSizing);

    virtual void  UpdateMenus();
    virtual void  DoCommand(long theCommand);
    virtual void  DoKeyDown(char theChar, Byte keyCode, EventRecord *macEvent);
    virtual void  Draw(Rect *r);

protected:
    enum {cmdFirstCommand = 1025,
      cmdAdd = cmdFirstCommand, cmdMultiply, cmdDivide, cmdSubtract, cmdEnter,
      cmdPeriod, cmdE, cmdClearEntry, cmdChangeSign,
      cmd0, cmd1, cmd2, cmd3,
      cmd4, cmd5, cmd6, cmd7, cmd8, cmd9, cmdLastCommand = cmd9 };

    virtual void    UpdateDisplay();
    virtual void    EnterCurrentNumber();
    virtual void    CreateCommandButton(short rowNumber, short colNumber, long command);
```

```
private:
    TCalculator fCalculator;
    CFloatText  *fCalcDisplay;
    unsigned char fCurrentNumber[15];
    CButton     *fButtons[cmdLastCommand - cmdFirstCommand + 1];
};
```

CFloatText.h

```
#pragma once

#include <CEditText.h>

class CFloatText: public CEditText {
public:
    void        IFloatText(
      CView         *anEnclosure,
      CBureaucrat   *aSupervisor,
      short         aWidth,
      short         aHeight,
      short         aHEncl,
      short         aVEncl,
      SizingOption  aHSizing,
      SizingOption  aVSizing,
      short         aLineWidth);

    virtual long double GetValue();
    virtual void        SetValue(long double value);
    virtual void        GetTextString(Str255 s);
    virtual void        SetMaxDisplayWidth(short numChars);

protected:
    virtual void        ValueToText(long double value, Str255 s);
private:
    short   fMaxDisplayChars;
};
```

CQuitOnCloseWindow.h

```
#pragma once

#include <CWindow.h>

class CQuitOnCloseWindow: public CWindow {
public:
    virtual void IQuitOnCloseWindow(short WINDid, Boolean aFloating,
                        CDesktop *anEnclosure, CDirector *aSupervisor);
    virtual void Dispose();
};
```

CSaveRestoreSizeWindow.h

```
#pragma once

#include "CQuitOnCloseWindow.h"
#include <CDataFile.h>

class CSaveRestoreSizeWindow: public CQuitOnCloseWindow {
public:

    void ISaveRestoreSizeWindow(
      short           windID,
      Boolean        aFloating,
      CDesktop        *anEnclosure,
      CDirector        *aSupervisor);
```

```
    virtual void Dispose();

protected:
    virtual void StoreInfoInFile(CDataFile *aFile);
    virtual void SetInfoFromFile(CDataFile *aFile);
    virtual void SpecifyFile(CFile *aFile);

private:
    CDataFile    *fDataFile;
};
```

Utilities.h

```
#pragma once

#include <Memory.h>

Ptr NewPtrCanFail(Size size);
```

Chapter 21, DatabaseTester

Database.cp

```
#include "Database.h"

MCollectible::MCollectible()
{
}

MCollectible::~MCollectible()
{
}

int MCollectible::Compare(const MCollectible &item2) const
{
    if (this < &item2)
        return kItem1LessThanItem2;
    else if (this > &item2)
        return kItem1GreaterThanItem2;
    else
        return kItem1EqualItem2;
}

TDatabase::TDatabase()
{
    fRoot = NULL;
}

TDatabase::~TDatabase()
{
    delete fRoot;
}

void TDatabase::Insert(MCollectible* dataElement)
{
    if (fRoot == NULL)
        fRoot = new TNode(dataElement);
    else
        fRoot->Insert(dataElement);
}
```

```
MCollectible *TDatabase::Find(const MCollectible& key) const
{
    if (fRoot == NULL)
        return NULL;
    else
        return fRoot->Find(key);
}

TNode::TNode(MCollectible *value, TNode *up)
{
    fRight = fLeft = NULL;
    fUp = up;
    fValue = value;
}

TNode::~TNode()
{
    delete fRight;
    delete fLeft;
    delete fValue;
}

MCollectible *TNode::GetValue() const
{
    return fValue;
}

MCollectible *TNode::Find(const MCollectible&key) const
{
    const TNode    *node = this;

    while (node != NULL) {
        int compareResult = node->GetValue()->Compare(key);

        if (compareResult == MCollectible::kItem1EqualItem2)
            return node->GetValue();
        else if (compareResult <= MCollectible::kItem1LessThanItem2)
            node = node->fRight;
        else
            node = node->fLeft;
    }
    return NULL;
}

void TNode::Insert(MCollectible *value)
{
    TNode    **node = &this;    // after loop: holds address within previous node
                                // which points to current node
    TNode    *up = NULL;        // after loop: pointer to previous node

    do  {
        int compareResult = (*node)->GetValue()->Compare(*value);

        up = *node;    // points at the current node

        if (compareResult == MCollectible::kItem1EqualItem2)
        {
                delete value;
                return;
        }
        else if (compareResult <= MCollectible::kItem1LessThanItem2)
```

```
            node = &(*node)->fRight;    // advance to next node
        else
            node = &(*node)->fLeft;        // advance to next node
    } while (*node != NULL);
    *node = new TNode(value, up);
}

const TNode *TNode::LeftMost() const
{
    const TNode *n = this;

    while (n->fLeft != NULL)
        n = n->fLeft;
    return n;
}

const TNode *TNode::RightMost() const
{
    const TNode *n = this;

    while (n->fRight != NULL)
        n = n->fRight;
    return n;
}

TIterator::TIterator(const TDatabase &database):
  fDatabase(database)
{
    fCurrent = NULL;
}

TNode *TIterator::GetRoot()
{
    return fDatabase.fRoot;
}

void TIterator::MoveForward()
{
    if (fCurrent == NULL)
        MoveToBeginning();
    // if we have a right-hand side, the next node is the left-most of our RHS)
    else if (fCurrent->fRight != NULL)
        fCurrent = fCurrent->fRight->LeftMost();
    else if (fCurrent->fUp == NULL)    // if we don't have a RHS, and don't have a up, we're done
        fCurrent = NULL;
    else {
        // the next is our first ancestor who we are on the left-hand-side of
        const TNode *last;
        do {
            last = fCurrent;
            fCurrent = last->fUp;
        } while (fCurrent != NULL && fCurrent->fRight == last);
    }
}

void TIterator::MoveBackward()
{
    if (fCurrent == NULL)
        MoveToEnd();
    // if we have a left-hand side, the next node is the right-most of our LHS
    else if (fCurrent->fLeft != NULL)
        fCurrent = fCurrent->fLeft->RightMost();
    else if (fCurrent->fUp == NULL)    // if we don't have a LHS, and don't have a up, we're done
        fCurrent = NULL;
```

```
    else {
        // the next is our first ancestor who we are on the right-hand-side of
        const TNode *last;
        do {
            last = fCurrent;
            fCurrent = last->fUp;
        } while (fCurrent != NULL && fCurrent->fLeft == last);
    }
}

int TIterator::NoMore()
{
    return fCurrent == NULL;
}

int TIterator::AtBeginning()
{
    return fCurrent != NULL && GetRoot()->LeftMost() == fCurrent;
}

int TIterator::AtEnd()
{
    return fCurrent != NULL && GetRoot()->RightMost() == fCurrent;
}

MCollectible *TIterator::GetCurrent()
{
    if (fCurrent == NULL)
        return NULL;
    else
        return fCurrent->GetValue();
}

void TIterator::MoveToBeginning()
{
    if (GetRoot() == NULL)
        fCurrent = NULL;
    else
        fCurrent = GetRoot()->LeftMost();
}

void TIterator::MoveToEnd()
{
    if (GetRoot() == NULL)
        fCurrent = NULL;
    else
        fCurrent = GetRoot()->RightMost();
}
```

Enry.cp

```
#include "Entry.h"
#include <string.h>

static char *CopyOfString(const char *s)
{
    if (s == NULL)
        s = "";
    char *copy;

    copy = new char[strlen(s)+1];
    ::strcpy(copy, s);
    return copy;
}
```

```
TNameAddressPhone::TNameAddressPhone(const char *name, const char *address,
  const char *city, const char *state, const char *zip, const char *telephone)
{
    fName = fAddress = fCity = fState = fZip = fTelephone = NULL;

    fName = CopyOfString(name);
    fAddress = CopyOfString(address);
    fCity = CopyOfString(city);
    fState = CopyOfString(state);
    fZip = CopyOfString(zip);
    fTelephone = CopyOfString(telephone);
}

TNameAddressPhone::~TNameAddressPhone()
{
    delete [] fName;
    delete [] fAddress;
    delete [] fCity;
    delete [] fState;
    delete [] fZip;
    delete [] fTelephone;
}

const char *TNameAddressPhone::GetName() const
{
    return fName;
}

const char *TNameAddressPhone::GetAddress() const
{
    return fAddress;
}

const char *TNameAddressPhone::GetCity() const
{
    return fCity;
}

const char *TNameAddressPhone::GetState() const
{
    return fState;
}

const char *TNameAddressPhone::GetZip() const
{
    return fZip;
}

const char *TNameAddressPhone::GetTelephone() const
{
    return fTelephone;
}

TEntry::TEntry(const char *name, const char *address, const char *city,
  const char *state, const char *zip, const char *telephone) :
  TNameAddressPhone(name, address,city, state, zip, telephone)
{
}

int TEntry::Compare(const MCollectible &item2) const
{
    int compareResult = ::strcmp(GetName(), ((TEntry &) item2).GetName());
```

```
    if (compareResult < 0)
        return kItem1LessThanItem2;
    else if (compareResult > 0)
        return kItem1GreaterThanItem2;
    else
        return kItem1EqualItem2;
}
```

Main.cp

```
#include "Database.h"
#include "Entry.h"
#include <stream.h>

void FindAndPrint(const TDatabase &theDatabase, char *name)
{
    TEntry *entry = (TEntry *) theDatabase.Find(TEntry(name));
    if (entry != NULL)
        cout << "Name: " << entry->GetName() << " Address: " << entry->GetAddress() << '\n';
}

void PrintDatabase(const TDatabase &theDatabase)
{
    printf("Database\n:");
    TIterator iter(theDatabase);
    for (iter.MoveToEnd(); !iter.NoMore(); iter.MoveBackward()) {
        TEntry *entry = (TEntry *) iter.GetCurrent();
        if (entry)
            cout << entry->GetName() << '\n' <<
              entry->GetAddress() << '\n' <<
              entry->GetCity() << ", " << entry->GetState() << "  " << entry->GetZip() << '\n' <<
              entry->GetTelephone() << '\n';
    }
}

void main()
{
    TDatabase    theDatabase;

    theDatabase.Insert(new TEntry("Rhodes, Neil", "1328 Clock Avenue",
      "Redlands", "CA", "92374", "(909) 798-5792"));
    theDatabase.Insert(new TEntry("McKeehan, Julie", "1328 Clock Avenue",
      "Redlands", "CA", "92374", "(909) 798-5792"));
    theDatabase.Insert(new TEntry("Rhodes, Alexander", "1328 Clock Avenue",
      "Redlands", "CA", "92374", "(909) 798-5792"));
    theDatabase.Insert(new TEntry("Rhodes, Nicholas", "1328 Clock Avenue",
      "Redlands", "CA", "92374", "(909) 798-5792"));
    theDatabase.Insert(new TEntry("Rhodes, Mary", "1234 Main St.",
      "Fullerton", "CA", "92635", "(714) 555-1212"));
    theDatabase.Insert(new TEntry("Rhodes, Fen", "123 Park Avenue",
      "Long Beach", "CA", "02138", "(310) 798-5792"));
    theDatabase.Insert(new TEntry("La Galy, Carolyn", "123 Longridge Avenue",
      "Santa Monica", "CA", "92374", "(818) 555-1212"));
    PrintDatabase(theDatabase);

    FindAndPrint(theDatabase, "Rhodes, Neil");
    FindAndPrint(theDatabase, "McKeehan, Julie");
    FindAndPrint(theDatabase, "Rhodes, Alexander");
    FindAndPrint(theDatabase, "Rhodes, Nicholas");
    FindAndPrint(theDatabase, "Rhodes, Fen");
    FindAndPrint(theDatabase, "Rhodes, Mary");
    FindAndPrint(theDatabase, "La Galy, Carolyn");
}
```

Database.h

```
#pragma once

class MCollectible {
public:
    enum {kItem1EqualItem2 = 0, kItem1LessThanItem2 = -1,
      kItem1GreaterThanItem2 = 1};
    MCollectible();
    virtual ~MCollectible();

    virtual int Compare(const MCollectible &item2) const;
};

class TNode {
public:
    TNode(MCollectible *value, TNode *up = NULL);
    ~TNode();

    void Insert(MCollectible *value);
    MCollectible *Find(const MCollectible  &key) const;

private:
    const TNode *LeftMost() const;
    const TNode *RightMost() const;

    MCollectible *GetValue() const;

    MCollectible *fValue;
    TNode *fLeft;
    TNode *fRight;
    TNode *fUp;
    friend class TIterator;
};

class TDatabase {
public:
    TDatabase();
    virtual ~TDatabase();

    void Insert(MCollectible* dataElement);
    MCollectible *Find(const MCollectible& key) const;

private:
    TNode *fRoot;
    friend class TIterator;
};

class TIterator {
public:
    TIterator(const TDatabase &database);

    void MoveForward();
    void MoveBackward();
    int NoMore();
    int AtEnd();
    int AtBeginning();
    void MoveToBeginning();
    void MoveToEnd();
    MCollectible *GetCurrent();
protected:
    TNode *GetRoot();
private:
    const TDatabase &fDatabase;
    const TNode     *fCurrent;
};
```

Entry.h

```
#pragma once

#include "Database.h"

class TNameAddressPhone {
public:
    TNameAddressPhone(const char *name = NULL, const char *address = NULL,
      const char *fCity = NULL, const char *fState = NULL,
      const char *fZip = NULL, const char *fTelephone = NULL);
    virtual  ~TNameAddressPhone();

    const char *GetName() const;
    const char *GetAddress() const;
    const char *GetCity() const;
    const char *GetState() const;
    const char *GetZip() const;
    const char *GetTelephone() const;

private:
    char *fName;
    char *fAddress;
    char *fCity;
    char *fState;
    char *fZip;
    char *fTelephone;
};

class TEntry: public MCollectible, public TNameAddressPhone {
public:
    TEntry(const char *name = NULL, const char *address = NULL,
      const char *fCity = NULL, const char *fState = NULL,
      const char *fZip = NULL, const char *fTelephone = NULL);

    virtual int Compare(const MCollectible &item2) const;
};
```

Chapter 21, AddressBook

AddressBook.cp

```
#include "CAddressBookApp.h"

void main()
{
    CAddressBookApp *app;

    app = new CAddressBookApp;
    app->IAddressBookApp();
    app->Run();
    app->Exit();
}
```

CAboutBoxApplication.cp

```
#include "CAboutBoxApplication.h"
#include <SegLoad.h>

void CAboutBoxApplication::IAboutBoxApplication(short extraMasters,
  Size aRainyDayFund, Size aCriticalBalance, Size aToolboxBalance)
{
    IApplication(extraMasters,aRainyDayFund, aCriticalBalance,
      aToolboxBalance);
}
```

```
void CAboutBoxApplication::DoCommand(long theCommand)
{
    const short kAboutBoxResourceID = 1024;

    switch (theCommand) {
    case cmdAbout:
        Str255 applicationName;
        short  appRefNum;
        Handle h;

        ::PositionDialog('ALRT', kAboutBoxResourceID);
        ::GetAppParms(applicationName, &appRefNum, &h);
        ::DisposHandle(h);
        ::ParamText(applicationName, NULL, NULL, NULL);
        Alert(kAboutBoxResourceID, NULL);
        break;
    default:
        CApplication::DoCommand(theCommand);
        break;
    }
}
```

CAddressBookApp.cp

```
#include "CAddressBookApp.h"
#include "CAddressBookDoc.h"
#include "TFailureObjects.h"
#include <Global.h>

extern   OSType       gSignature;       // The application's signature

void CAddressBookApp::IAddressBookApp()
{
    const short   kExtraMasters =    1;
    const Size    kRainyDayFund =    45000;
    const Size    kCriticalBalance = 40000;
    const Size    kToolboxBalance =  20000;

    IAboutBoxApplication(kExtraMasters, kRainyDayFund,
      kCriticalBalance, kToolboxBalance);
}

void CAddressBookApp::CreateDocument()
{
    CAddressBookDoc *theDocument = new CAddressBookDoc;

    TFreeOnFailure freer(theDocument);

    theDocument->IAddressBookDoc(this);
    theDocument->NewFile();
}

void CAddressBookApp::OpenDocument(SFReply *macReply)
{
    CAddressBookDoc *theDocument = new CAddressBookDoc;

    TFreeOnFailure freer(theDocument);

    theDocument->IAddressBookDoc(this);
    theDocument->OpenFile(macReply);
}

void CAddressBookApp::SetUpFileParameters()
{
    CApplication::SetUpFileParameters();
```

```
    sfNumTypes = 1;
    sfFileTypes[0] = 'ADDR';
    gSignature = 'C++3';
}
```

CAddressbookDoc.cp

```
#include "CAddressBookDoc.h"
#include "CAddressBookPane.h"
#include <CScrollPane.h>
#include <CDesktop.h>
#include <CWindow.h>
#include <CDataFile.h>
#include <CDecorator.h>
#include <TBUtilities.h>
#include "TFailureObjects.h"
#include "TWithFileOpen.h"
#include "Entry.h"
#include <String.h>

extern CDesktop        *gDesktop;
extern OSType       gSignature;
extern CDecorator   *gDecorator;
extern CBureaucrat    *gGopher;

void CAddressBookDoc::IAddressBookDoc(CApplication *supervisor)
{
    const Boolean kPrintable = TRUE;
    fDatabase = NULL;
    IDocument(supervisor, kPrintable);
    fDatabase = new TDatabase;
    ::FailNIL(fDatabase);
}

void CAddressBookDoc::Dispose()
{
    delete fDatabase;

    CDocument::Dispose();
}

TIterator *CAddressBookDoc::CreateDatabaseIterator()
{
    TIterator *iter;

    iter = new TIterator(*fDatabase);
    ::FailNIL(iter);
    return iter;
}

void CAddressBookDoc::AddEntry(TEntry *anEntry)
{
    fDatabase->Insert(anEntry);
}

void CAddressBookDoc::NewFile()
{
    BuildWindow();

    Str255 wTitle;
    short wCount;
    Str255 wNumber;
```

```
    itsWindow->GetTitle(wTitle);
    gDecorator->StaggerWindow(itsWindow);
    wCount = gDecorator->GetWCount();
    ::NumToString(wCount, wNumber);
    ::ConcatPStrings(wTitle, "\p-");
    ::ConcatPStrings(wTitle, wNumber);
    itsWindow->SetTitle(wTitle);

    itsWindow->Select();
}

void CAddressBookDoc::BuildWindow()
{
    const short   kWINDResourceID =       500;
    const Boolean kWindowFloats =         TRUE;
    const Boolean kFitHorizontal =        TRUE;
    const Boolean kFitVertical =          TRUE;

    CWindow *aWindow = new CWindow;
    aWindow->IWindow(kWINDResourceID, !kWindowFloats, gDesktop, this);
    itsWindow = aWindow;

    CAddressBookPane *thePane = new CAddressBookPane;
    thePane->IAddressBookPane(itsWindow, this, 72*6, 72*4, 0, 0,
      sizFIXEDSTICKY, sizFIXEDSTICKY);
    itsGopher = thePane;
    itsMainPane = thePane;
    thePane->FitToEnclosure(kFitHorizontal, kFitVertical);
}

static void ReadAString(CDataFile *aDataFile, char *s)
{
    unsigned char    length;

    aDataFile->ReadSome((Ptr) &length, sizeof(length));
    aDataFile->ReadSome((Ptr) s, length);
     s[length] = '\0';
}

void CAddressBookDoc::OpenFile(SFReply *macReply)
{
    CDataFile    *theDataFile;
    Handle        theData;
    Str63         theName;
    OSErr         theError;

    theDataFile = new CDataFile;
    itsFile = theDataFile;

    theDataFile->IDataFile();
    theDataFile->SFSpecify(macReply);

    {
        TWithFileOpen fileOpener(theDataFile, fsRdPerm);
        long    fileLength = theDataFile->GetLength();
        while (theDataFile->GetMark() < fileLength)
        {
            char    name[256];
            char    address[256];
            char    city[256];
            char    state[256];
            char    zip[256];
            char    telephone[256];
```

```
            ReadAString(theDataFile, name);
            ReadAString(theDataFile, address);
            ReadAString(theDataFile, city);
            ReadAString(theDataFile, state);
            ReadAString(theDataFile, zip);
            ReadAString(theDataFile, telephone);

            TEntry *newEntry = new TEntry(name, address, city, state, zip, telephone);
            ::FailNIL(newEntry);
            AddEntry(newEntry);
        }

        BuildWindow();
    }

    gDecorator->StaggerWindow(itsWindow);
    itsFile->GetName(theName);
    itsWindow->SetTitle(theName);

    itsWindow->Select();

    // make pane display the first entry
    itsMainPane->DoCommand(CAddressBookPane::kBeginning);
}

static void WriteAString(CDataFile *aDataFile, const char *s)
{
    unsigned char length = Min(255, strlen(s));
                    // write length(s),   s
    aDataFile->WriteSome((Ptr) &length, sizeof(length));
    aDataFile->WriteSome((Ptr) s, length);
}

Boolean CAddressBookDoc::DoSave()
{
    Handle        theData;

    if (itsFile == NULL)
        return(DoSaveFileAs());
    else {
        CDataFile *theDataFile = (CDataFile *) itsFile;

        {
            TWithFileOpen fileOpener(theDataFile, fsWrPerm);
            TIterator    iter(*fDatabase);

            for(iter.MoveToBeginning(); !iter.NoMore(); iter.MoveForward()) {
                TEntry *curEntry = (TEntry *) iter.GetCurrent();

                WriteAString(theDataFile, curEntry->GetName());
                WriteAString(theDataFile, curEntry->GetAddress());
                WriteAString(theDataFile, curEntry->GetCity());
                WriteAString(theDataFile, curEntry->GetState());
                WriteAString(theDataFile, curEntry->GetZip());
                WriteAString(theDataFile, curEntry->GetAddress());
            }
        }
        dirty = FALSE;
        return(TRUE);
    }
}
```

```
Boolean CAddressBookDoc::DoSaveAs(SFReply *macSFReply)
{
    if (itsFile != NULL)
        itsFile->Dispose();

    CDataFile *theDataFile = new CDataFile;
    itsFile = theDataFile;
    theDataFile->IDataFile();
    theDataFile->SFSpecify(macSFReply);
    if (theDataFile->ExistsOnDisk())
        theDataFile->ThrowOut();
    theDataFile->CreateNew(gSignature, 'ADDR');

    itsWindow->SetTitle(macSFReply->fName);

    return(DoSave());
}
```

CAddressBookPane.cp

```
#include "CAddressBookPane.h"
#include "Entry.h"
#include "CAddressBookDoc.h"
#include <QuickDraw.h>
#include <String.h>
#include <CBartender.h>
#include <CPaneBorder.h>
#include "CNewEntryDialogDirector.h"

extern CBartender *gBartender;

void CAddressBookPane::IAddressBookPane(CView *anEnclosure,
  CAddressBookDoc *anAddressBookDoc,
  short aWidth, short aHeight,
  short aHEncl, short aVEncl,
  SizingOption aHSizing, SizingOption aVSizing)
{
    const Boolean kWantBold = true;

    fAddressBookDoc = anAddressBookDoc;
    fAddressBookIterator = NULL;
    IPane(anEnclosure, anAddressBookDoc, 0, 0, aHEncl, aVEncl,
      aHSizing, aVSizing);
    fAddressBookIterator = fAddressBookDoc->CreateDatabaseIterator();
    fAddressBookIterator->MoveToBeginning();

    CreateStaticText(50, 20, 5, 3, 1, kWantBold);    // Name:
    CreateStaticText(60, 20, 5, 23, 2, kWantBold);   // Address:
    CreateStaticText(40, 20, 5, 43, 3, kWantBold);   // City:
    CreateStaticText(35, 20, 155, 43, 4, kWantBold); // State:
    CreateStaticText(20, 20, 220, 43, 5, kWantBold); // Zip:
    CreateStaticText(60, 20, 5, 63, 6, kWantBold);   // Telephone:

    fName = CreateStaticText(250, 20, 70, 3, 0);
    fAddress = CreateStaticText(250, 20, 70, 23, 0);
    fCity = CreateStaticText(80, 20, 70, 43, 0);
    fState = CreateStaticText(20, 20, 195, 43, 0);
    fZip = CreateStaticText(80, 20, 245, 43, 0);
    fTelephone = CreateStaticText(200, 20, 70, 63, 0);
}

CEditText *CAddressBookPane::CreateStaticText(short width, short height,
  short horizLocation, short verticalLocation, short itemID, Boolean wantBold)
{
    CEditText *text;
```

```
    text = new CEditText;
    text->IEditText(this, fAddressBookDoc,
        width, height, horizLocation, verticalLocation,
        sizFIXEDSTICKY, sizFIXEDSTICKY,-1);
    text->Specify(kNotEditable, kNotSelectable, kNotStylable);
    if (itemID != 0) {
        Str255    string;

        GetIndString(string, kItemStringResourceID, itemID);
        text->SetTextString(string);
    }
    text->SetFontName("\pGeneva");
    text->SetFontSize(9);
    if (wantBold)
        text->SetFontStyle(bold);
    return text;
}

void CAddressBookPane::UpdateMenus()
{
    CPane::UpdateMenus();
    if (!fAddressBookIterator->AtEnd())
        gBartender->EnableCmd(kNextEntry);
    if (!fAddressBookIterator->AtBeginning())
        gBartender->EnableCmd(kPreviousEntry);
    if (!fAddressBookIterator->NoMore()) {
        gBartender->EnableCmd(kEnd);
        gBartender->EnableCmd(kBeginning);
    }
    gBartender->EnableCmd(kNewEntry);
}

void CAddressBookPane::DoCommand(long theCommand)
{
    switch (theCommand) {
    case kNewEntry:
        CNewEntryDialogDirector *aDialogDirector = new CNewEntryDialogDirector;
        aDialogDirector->INewEntryDialogDirector(fAddressBookDoc);
        TEntry *anEntry = aDialogDirector->GetNewEntry();
        aDialogDirector->Dispose();

        if (anEntry != NULL) {
            fAddressBookDoc->AddEntry(anEntry);
            // Display entry
            fAddressBookIterator->MoveToBeginning();
            for (;!fAddressBookIterator->NoMore();
              fAddressBookIterator->MoveForward())
                if (anEntry == (TEntry *) fAddressBookIterator->GetCurrent())
                    break;
            UpdateEntryData();
        }
        break;
    case kNextEntry:
        fAddressBookIterator->MoveForward();
        UpdateEntryData();
        break;
    case kPreviousEntry:
        fAddressBookIterator->MoveBackward();
        UpdateEntryData();
        break;
    case kBeginning:
        fAddressBookIterator->MoveToBeginning();
        UpdateEntryData();
        break;
```

```
    case kEnd:
        fAddressBookIterator->MoveToEnd();
        UpdateEntryData();
        break;
    default:
        CPane::DoCommand(theCommand);
        break;
    }
}

void CAddressBookPane::UpdateEntryData()
{
    const TEntry    *entry = (TEntry *) fAddressBookIterator->GetCurrent();
    char    name[256] = "";
    char    address[256] = "";
    char    city[256] = "";
    char    state[256] = "";
    char    zip[256] = "";
    char    phone[256] = "";

    if (entry) {
        ::strcpy(name, entry->GetName());
        ::strcpy(address, entry->GetAddress());
        ::strcpy(city, entry->GetCity());
        ::strcpy(state, entry->GetState());
        ::strcpy(zip, entry->GetZip());
        ::strcpy(phone, entry->GetTelephone());
    }
    fName->SetTextPtr(name, strlen(name));
    fAddress->SetTextPtr(address, strlen(address));
    fCity->SetTextPtr(city, strlen(city));
    fState->SetTextPtr(state, strlen(state));
    fZip->SetTextPtr(zip, strlen(zip));
    fTelephone->SetTextPtr(phone, strlen(phone));
    Refresh();
}
```

CNewEntryDialog.cp

```
#include "CNewEntryDialog.h"
#include <CAbstractText.h>

void CNewEntryDialog::INewEntryDialog(short DLOGid, CDesktop *anEnclosure,
 CDirector *aSupervisor)
{
    IDLOGDialog(DLOGid, anEnclosure, aSupervisor);
}

CPane *CNewEntryDialog::AddDITLStatText( short aWidth, short aHeight,
  short hEncl, short vEncl, CView *enclosure, tDITLItem *ditlItem)
{
    CAbstractText *result;

    result = (CAbstractText *) CDLOGDialog::AddDITLStatText(aWidth, aHeight,
      hEncl, vEncl, enclosure, ditlItem);
    result->SetFontName("\pGeneva");
    result->SetFontSize(9);
    result->SetFontStyle(bold);
    return result;
}


CPane *CNewEntryDialog::AddDITLEditText( short aWidth, short aHeight,
  short hEncl, short vEncl, CView *enclosure, tDITLItem *ditlItem)
```

```
{
    CAbstractText *result;

    result = (CAbstractText *) CDLOGDialog::AddDITLEditText(aWidth, aHeight,
      hEncl, vEncl, enclosure, ditlItem);
    result->SetFontName("\pGeneva");
    result->SetFontSize(9);
    return result;
}
```

CNewEntryDialogDirector.cp

```
#include "CNewEntryDialogDirector.h"
#include <CWindow.h>
#include <CDialogText.h>
#include "CNewEntryDialog.h"
#include <CDecorator.h>
#include <CDesktop.h>

extern CDesktop *gDesktop;
extern CDecorator *gDecorator;

#define    kNewEntryDLOGID    1025    // resource ID of the DLOG resource

/******************************************************************************
 INewEntryDialogDirector


******************************************************************************/

void CNewEntryDialogDirector::INewEntryDialogDirector(
  CDirectorOwner *aSupervisor)
{
    CNewEntryDialog *dialog;

    CDialogDirector::IDialogDirector( aSupervisor);

    dialog = new(CNewEntryDialog);
    itsWindow = dialog;

    dialog->INewEntryDialog(kNewEntryDLOGID, gDesktop, this);

    gDecorator->CenterWindow(dialog);
}

static void GetTextFromWindow(CWindow *theWindow, short itemID, StringPtr string)
{
    CDialogText *dialogText;

    dialogText = (CDialogText *) theWindow->FindViewByID(itemID);
    ::FailNIL(dialogText);
    dialogText->GetTextString(string);
}

/******************************************************************************
 GetNewEntry

     Displays the modal dialog and returns a TEntry corresponding to the selection (or
     NULL if the user cancels).

******************************************************************************/
```

```
TEntry *CNewEntryDialogDirector::GetNewEntry()
{
    long            theCommand;

        // show the dialog

    BeginModalDialog();

        // run the dialog and return the final command.

    theCommand = DoModalDialog(cmdOK);

    if (theCommand == cmdOK)
    {
        CDialogText *dialogText;
        Str255    name;
        Str255    address;
        Str255    city;
        Str255    state;
        Str255    zip;
        Str255    phone;
        TEntry *newEntry;

        ::GetTextFromWindow(itsWindow, CNewEntryDialog::nameTextID, name);
        ::GetTextFromWindow(itsWindow, CNewEntryDialog::addressTextID, address);
        ::GetTextFromWindow(itsWindow, CNewEntryDialog::cityTextID, city);
        ::GetTextFromWindow(itsWindow, CNewEntryDialog::stateTextID, state);
        ::GetTextFromWindow(itsWindow, CNewEntryDialog::zipTextID, zip);
        ::GetTextFromWindow(itsWindow, CNewEntryDialog::phoneTextID, phone);

        newEntry = new TEntry(p2cstr(name), p2cstr(address), p2cstr(city),
          p2cstr(state), p2cstr(zip), p2cstr(phone));
        ::FailNIL(newEntry);
        return newEntry;
    }
    return NULL;
}
```

Database.cp

```
#include "Database.h"

MCollectible::MCollectible()
{
}

MCollectible::~MCollectible()
{
}

int MCollectible::Compare(const MCollectible &item2) const
{
    if (this < &item2)
        return kItem1LessThanItem2;
    else if (this > &item2)
        return kItem1GreaterThanItem2;
    else
        return kItem1EqualItem2;
}

TDatabase::TDatabase()
{
    fRoot = NULL;
}
```

```
TDatabase::~TDatabase()
{
    delete fRoot;
}

void TDatabase::Insert(MCollectible* dataElement)
{
    if (fRoot == NULL)
        fRoot = new TNode(dataElement);
    else
        fRoot->Insert(dataElement);
}

MCollectible *TDatabase::Find(const MCollectible& key) const
{
    if (fRoot == NULL)
        return NULL;
    else
        return fRoot->Find(key);
}

TNode::TNode(MCollectible *value, TNode *up)
{
    fRight = fLeft = NULL;
    fUp = up;
    fValue = value;
}

TNode::~TNode()
{
    delete fRight;
    delete fLeft;
    delete fValue;
}

MCollectible *TNode::GetValue() const
{
    return fValue;
}

MCollectible *TNode::Find(const MCollectible&key) const
{
    const TNode    *node = this;

    while (node != NULL) {
        int compareResult = node->GetValue()->Compare(key);

        if (compareResult == MCollectible::kItem1EqualItem2)
            return node->GetValue();
        else if (compareResult <= MCollectible::kItem1LessThanItem2)
            node = node->fRight;
        else
            node = node->fLeft;
    }
    return NULL;
}

void TNode::Insert(MCollectible *value)
{
    TNode    **node = &this;    // after loop: holds address within previous node
                                // which points to current node
    TNode    *up = NULL;        // after loop: pointer to previous node
```

```
    do  {
        int compareResult = (*node)->GetValue()->Compare(*value);

        up = *node;     // points at the current node

        if (compareResult == MCollectible::kItem1EqualItem2)
        {
                delete value;
                return;
        }
        else if (compareResult <= MCollectible::kItem1LessThanItem2)
            node = &(*node)->fRight;    // advance to next node
        else
            node = &(*node)->fLeft;        // advance to next node
    } while (*node != NULL);
    *node = new TNode(value, up);
}

const TNode *TNode::LeftMost() const
{
    const TNode *n = this;

    while (n->fLeft != NULL)
        n = n->fLeft;
    return n;
}

const TNode *TNode::RightMost() const
{
    const TNode *n = this;

    while (n->fRight != NULL)
        n = n->fRight;
    return n;
}

TIterator::TIterator(const TDatabase &database):
  fDatabase(database)
{
    fCurrent = NULL;
}

TNode *TIterator::GetRoot()
{
    return fDatabase.fRoot;
}

void TIterator::MoveForward()
{
    if (fCurrent == NULL)
        MoveToBeginning();
    // if we have a right-hand side, the next node is the left-most of our RHS)
    else if (fCurrent->fRight != NULL)
        fCurrent = fCurrent->fRight->LeftMost();
    else if (fCurrent->fUp == NULL)    // if we don't have a RHS, and don't have a up, we're done
        fCurrent = NULL;
    else {
        // the next is our first ancestor who we are on the left-hand-side of
        const TNode *last;
        do {
            last = fCurrent;
            fCurrent = last->fUp;
        } while (fCurrent != NULL && fCurrent->fRight == last);
    }
}
```

```
void TIterator::MoveBackward()
{
    if (fCurrent == NULL)
        MoveToEnd();
    // if we have a left-hand side, the next node is the right-most of our LHS
    else if (fCurrent->fLeft != NULL)
        fCurrent = fCurrent->fLeft->RightMost();
    else if (fCurrent->fUp == NULL)    // if we don't have a LHS, and don't have a up, we're done
        fCurrent = NULL;
    else {
        // the next is our first ancestor who we are on the right-hand-side of
        const TNode *last;
        do {
            last = fCurrent;
            fCurrent = last->fUp;
        } while (fCurrent != NULL && fCurrent->fLeft == last);
    }
}

int TIterator::NoMore()
{
    return fCurrent == NULL;
}

int TIterator::AtBeginning()
{
    return fCurrent != NULL && GetRoot()->LeftMost() == fCurrent;
}

int TIterator::AtEnd()
{
    return fCurrent != NULL && GetRoot()->RightMost() == fCurrent;
}

MCollectible *TIterator::GetCurrent()
{
    if (fCurrent == NULL)
        return NULL;
    else
        return fCurrent->GetValue();
}

void TIterator::MoveToBeginning()
{
    if (GetRoot() == NULL)
        fCurrent = NULL;
    else
        fCurrent = GetRoot()->LeftMost();
}

void TIterator::MoveToEnd()
{
    if (GetRoot() == NULL)
        fCurrent = NULL;
    else
        fCurrent = GetRoot()->RightMost();
}
```

Entry.cp

```
#include "Entry.h"
#include <string.h>
```

```
static char *CopyOfString(const char *s)
{
    if (s == NULL)
        s = "";
    char *copy;

    copy = new char[strlen(s)+1];
    ::strcpy(copy, s);
    return copy;
}

TNameAddressPhone::TNameAddressPhone(const char *name, const char *address,
  const char *city, const char *state, const char *zip, const char *telephone)
{
    fName = fAddress = fCity = fState = fZip = fTelephone = NULL;

    fName = CopyOfString(name);
    fAddress = CopyOfString(address);
    fCity = CopyOfString(city);
    fState = CopyOfString(state);
    fZip = CopyOfString(zip);
    fTelephone = CopyOfString(telephone);
}

TNameAddressPhone::~TNameAddressPhone()
{
    delete [] fName;
    delete [] fAddress;
    delete [] fCity;
    delete [] fState;
    delete [] fZip;
    delete [] fTelephone;
}

const char *TNameAddressPhone::GetName() const
{
    return fName;
}

const char *TNameAddressPhone::GetAddress() const
{
    return fAddress;
}

const char *TNameAddressPhone::GetCity() const
{
    return fCity;
}

const char *TNameAddressPhone::GetState() const
{
    return fState;
}

const char *TNameAddressPhone::GetZip() const
{
    return fZip;
}

const char *TNameAddressPhone::GetTelephone() const
{
    return fTelephone;
}
```

```
TEntry::TEntry(const char *name, const char *address, const char *city,
  const char *state, const char *zip, const char *telephone) :
  TNameAddressPhone(name, address,city, state, zip, telephone)
{
}

int TEntry::Compare(const MCollectible &item2) const
{
    int compareResult = ::strcmp(GetName(), ((TEntry &) item2).GetName());

    if (compareResult < 0)
        return kItem1LessThanItem2;
    else if (compareResult > 0)
        return kItem1GreaterThanItem2;
    else
        return kItem1EqualItem2;
}
```

TFailureObjects.cp

```
#include "TFailureObjects.h"

TCatchFailure::TCatchFailure()
{
    ::CatchFailures(&fFailInfo,
      (HandlerFuncPtr) TCatchFailure::PrivateHandleFailure, (long) this);
    fExitingNormally = true;
}

TCatchFailure::~TCatchFailure()
{
    if (fExitingNormally)
        ::Success();
}

pascal void TCatchFailure::PrivateHandleFailure(OSErr err, long message)
{
    fExitingNormally = false;
    HandleFailure(err, message);
}

TAutoDestruct::~TAutoDestruct()
{
}

void TAutoDestruct::HandleFailure(OSErr /*err*/, long /*message*/)
{
    this->~TAutoDestruct();    // explicit virtual call to destructor
}

TFreeOnCompletion::TFreeOnCompletion(CObject *object)
{
    fObject = object;
}

TFreeOnCompletion::~TFreeOnCompletion()
{
    if (fObject != NULL)
        fObject->Dispose();
}
```

```
THandleLocker::THandleLocker(Handle h)
{
    fHandle = h;
    fState = ::HGetState(fHandle);
    ::HLock(h);
}

THandleLocker::~THandleLocker()
{
    ::HSetState(fHandle, fState);
}

TFreeOnFailure::TFreeOnFailure(CObject *object)
{
    fObject = object;
}

void TFreeOnFailure::HandleFailure(OSErr /*err*/, long /*message*/)
{
    if (fObject != NULL)
        fObject->Dispose();
}
```

TWithFileOpen.cp

```
#include "TWithFileOpen.h"

TWithFileOpen::TWithFileOpen(CFile *theFile, SignedByte permission)
{
    theFile->Open(permission);
    fFile = theFile;
}

TWithFileOpen::~TWithFileOpen()
{
    if (fFile != NULL)
        fFile->Close();
}
```

CAboutBoxApplication.h

```
#pragma once
#include <CApplication.h>

class CAboutBoxApplication: public CApplication {
public:
    void    IAboutBoxApplication(short extraMasters, Size aRainyDayFund,
              Size aCriticalBalance, Size aToolboxBalance);

    virtual void   DoCommand(long theCommand);
};
```

CAddressBookApp.h

```
#pragma once

#include "CAboutBoxApplication.h"

class CAddressBookApp: public CAboutBoxApplication {
public:
    void          IAddressBookApp();

    virtual void  CreateDocument();
    virtual void  OpenDocument(SFReply *macReply);
    virtual void  SetUpFileParameters();
};
```

CAddressbookDoc.h

```
#pragma once

#include <CDocument.h>
#include "Database.h"
#include "Entry.h"

class CAddressBookDoc: public CDocument {
public:
    void                IAddressBookDoc(CApplication *supervisor);
    virtual void        Dispose();

    virtual void        NewFile();
    virtual void        OpenFile(SFReply *macReply);
    virtual Boolean     DoSave();
    virtual Boolean     DoSaveAs(SFReply *macSFReply);
    virtual TIterator   *CreateDatabaseIterator();
    virtual void        AddEntry(TEntry *entry);

protected:
    virtual void        BuildWindow();
private:
    TDatabase           *fDatabase;
};
```

CAddressBookPane.h

```
#pragma once
#include <CPane.h>
#include "CAddressBookDoc.h"
#include <CEditText.h>

class CAddressBookPane: public CPane {
public:
    enum {kNextEntry = 1025, kPreviousEntry = 1026,
      kBeginning=1027, kEnd=1028, kNewEntry = 1029,
      kItemStringResourceID = 1024};

    void    IAddressBookPane(CView *anEnclosure, CAddressBookDoc *aSupervisor,
                            short aWidth, short aHeight,
                            short aHEncl, short aVEncl,
                            SizingOption aHSizing, SizingOption aVSizing);

    virtual void    UpdateMenus();
    virtual void    DoCommand(long theCommand);
protected:
    CEditText       *CreateStaticText(short width, short height,
                      short horizLocation, short verticalLocation,
                      short itemID, Boolean wantBold = false);
    void            UpdateEntryData();

private:
    CAddressBookDoc *fAddressBookDoc;
    TIterator        *fAddressBookIterator;
    CEditText        *fName;
    CEditText        *fAddress;
    CEditText        *fCity;
    CEditText        *fState;
    CEditText        *fZip;
    CEditText        *fTelephone;
};
```

CNewEntryDialog.h

```
#pragma once

#include <CDLOGDialog.h>

class CNewEntryDialog: public CDLOGDialog {
public:
    enum {nameTextID = 3, addressTextID = 4, cityTextID = 5,
      stateTextID = 6, zipTextID = 7, phoneTextID = 8};

    void INewEntryDialog(short DLOGid, CDesktop *anEnclosure,
                CDirector *aSupervisor);

protected:
    CPane *CNewEntryDialog::AddDITLEditText( short aWidth, short aHeight,
      short hEncl, short vEncl, CView *enclosure, tDITLItem *ditlItem);
    CPane *CNewEntryDialog::AddDITLStatText( short aWidth, short aHeight,
      short hEncl, short vEncl, CView *enclosure, tDITLItem *ditlItem);
};
```

CNewEntryDialogDirector.h

```
#pragma once

#include <CDialogDirector.h>
#include "Entry.h"

class CNewEntryDialogDirector: public CDialogDirector {
public:
    void INewEntryDialogDirector(CDirectorOwner *aSupervisor);
    TEntry *GetNewEntry();
};
```

Database.h

```
#pragma once

class MCollectible {
public:
    enum {kItem1EqualItem2 = 0, kItem1LessThanItem2 = -1,
      kItem1GreaterThanItem2 = 1};
    MCollectible();
    virtual ~MCollectible();

    virtual int Compare(const MCollectible &item2) const;
};

class TNode {
public:
    TNode(MCollectible *value, TNode *up = NULL);
    ~TNode();

    void Insert(MCollectible *value);
    MCollectible *Find(const MCollectible  &key) const;

private:
    const TNode *LeftMost() const;
    const TNode *RightMost() const;

    MCollectible *GetValue() const;

    MCollectible *fValue;
    TNode *fLeft;
    TNode *fRight;
```

```
    TNode *fUp;
    friend class TIterator;
};

class TDatabase {
public:
    TDatabase();
    virtual ~TDatabase();

    void Insert(MCollectible* dataElement);
    MCollectible *Find(const MCollectible& key) const;

private:
    TNode *fRoot;
    friend class TIterator;
};

class TIterator {
public:
    TIterator(const TDatabase &database);

    void MoveForward();
    void MoveBackward();
    int NoMore();
    int AtEnd();
    int AtBeginning();
    void MoveToBeginning();
    void MoveToEnd();
    MCollectible *GetCurrent();
protected:
    TNode *GetRoot();
private:
    const TDatabase &fDatabase;
    const TNode     *fCurrent;
};
```

Entry.h

```
#pragma once

#include "Database.h"

class TNameAddressPhone {
public:
    TNameAddressPhone(const char *name = NULL, const char *address = NULL,
      const char *fCity = NULL, const char *fState = NULL,
      const char *fZip = NULL, const char *fTelephone = NULL);
    virtual  ~TNameAddressPhone();

    const char *GetName() const;
    const char *GetAddress() const;
    const char *GetCity() const;
    const char *GetState() const;
    const char *GetZip() const;
    const char *GetTelephone() const;

private:
    char *fName;
    char *fAddress;
    char *fCity;
    char *fState;
    char *fZip;
    char *fTelephone;
};
```

```
class TEntry: public MCollectible, public TNameAddressPhone {
public:
    TEntry(const char *name = NULL, const char *address = NULL,
      const char *fCity = NULL, const char *fState = NULL,
      const char *fZip = NULL, const char *fTelephone = NULL);

    virtual int Compare(const MCollectible &item2) const;
};
```

TFailureObjects.h

```
#pragma once

#include <Exceptions.h>
#include <Types.h>

// abstract class which calls HandleFailure on a failure.
class TCatchFailure
{
protected:
    TCatchFailure();
    virtual ~TCatchFailure();
    virtual void HandleFailure(OSErr err, long message) = 0;    //  override this instead
private:
    Boolean    fExitingNormally;    // false if exiting due to failure
    pascal void PrivateHandleFailure(OSErr err, long message);    // don't override this!
    FailInfo    fFailInfo;
};

// abstract class which calls its destructor on a failure.
class TAutoDestruct: public TCatchFailure {
public:
    virtual ~TAutoDestruct();
protected:
    virtual void HandleFailure(OSErr err, long message);
};

// frees the object passed in the constructor on failure, or when its
// scope is exited
class TFreeOnCompletion: public TAutoDestruct {
public:
    TFreeOnCompletion(CObject *object);
    virtual ~TFreeOnCompletion();

private:
    CObject *fObject;
};

// restores the state of the handle passed in the constructor on failure, or when its
// scope is exited
class THandleLocker: public TAutoDestruct {
public:
    THandleLocker(Handle h);
    virtual ~THandleLocker();
private:
    Handle    fHandle;
    char    fState;
};
```

```
// frees the object passed in the constructor on failure
class TFreeOnFailure: public TCatchFailure {
public:
    TFreeOnFailure(CObject *object);
protected:
    virtual void HandleFailure(OSErr err, long message);
private:
    CObject *fObject;
};
```

TWithFileOpen.h

```
#pragma once

#include "TFailureObjects.h"
#include <CFile.h>
#include <Types.h>

class TWithFileOpen: public TAutoDestruct {
public:
    TWithFileOpen(CFile *theFile, SignedByte permission);
    virtual ~TWithFileOpen();

private:
    CFile *fFile;
};
```

E

Annotated Bibliography

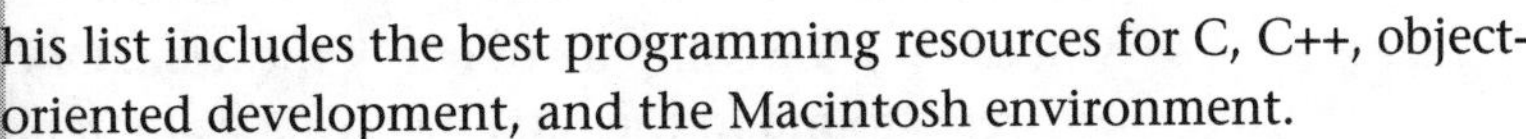

This list includes the best programming resources for C, C++, object-oriented development, and the Macintosh environment.

C Reference Material

Referred to as the white bible, the following is *the* classic text on C. If you are a C programmer, you should have it. It begins, of course, with the "Hello, world" program.

Kernighan, Brian W., and Dennis M. Ritchie. *The C Programming Language*, 2nd Edition. 1988. Prentice Hall, Englewood Cliffs, NJ. ISBN: 0-13-110370-9.

Harbison and Steele cover the intricacies of the language with emphasis on the hidden areas in C that cause problems with particular compilers. This book certainly can help you learn to write portable C code.

Harbison, Samuel P., III, and Guy L. Steele, Jr. C: *A Reference Manual*, 3rd Edition. 1991. ISBN: 0-13-110933-2.

C++ Reference Material

The following book explores a number of C++ programs that have appeared in various books and articles. It gives you a useful analysis of their design, implementation, and efficiency.

Cargill, Tom. *C++ Programming Style*. 1992. Addison-Wesley, Reading, MA. ISBN: 0-201-56365-7.

Coplien is not for the faint-hearted because each chapter is so dense it could be expanded into a book of its own. It is especially good for its presentation of the weird and wonderful things you can do with C++, such as how to make C++ dynamic like Lisp.

Coplien, James O. *Advanced C++ Programming Styles and Idioms*. 1992. Addison-Wesley, Reading, MA. ISBN:0-201-54855-0.

If you want to know whether a particular construct is allowed in C++, you can try the compiler or check the *ARM*. Of course, the one true answer is found in the *ARM*. Every C++ programmer should have a copy of this book, just as every household should have a dictionary—you do not need to know the whole book, just have it around for when definitive answers are needed.

Ellis, Margaret, and Bjarne Stroustrup. *The Annotated C++ Reference Manual*. Addison-Wesley, Reading, MA. ISBN: 0-201-51459-1.

Effective C++ is the best real world book on C++. While it does not teach you C++ features (it assumes you already know them), it does teach you how to use them and how they interact with one another. If you are a C++ programmer, you must have this book; you will refer to it often. In addition to being useful, it also is funny and entertaining.

Meyers, Scott. *Effective C++: 50 Specific Ways to Improve Your Programs and Designs.* 1992. Addison-Wesley, Reading, MA. ISBN: 0-201-56364-9.

Shapiro presents a useful set of library classes (binary trees, hash tables, and lists) that you can use in your own programs.

Shapiro, Jonathan S. *A C++ Toolkit.* 1991. Prentice Hall, Englewood Cliffs, NJ. ISBN: 0-13-127663-8.

Object-Oriented Programming

Meyer describes how OOP can be used to construct solid software. No existing language suited his needs, so he designed his own, Eiffel. The book describes why Eiffel is designed the way it is, including its support for assertions, preconditions, and postconditions. Although support is not provided explicitly for these, you still can implement them in C++. Furthermore, the programming-by-contract paradigm he presents is well worth knowing.

Meyer, Bertrand. *Object-Oriented Software Construction.* 1988. Prentice Hall, Englewood Cliffs, NJ. ISBN: 0-13-629049-3.

Object-Oriented Design

This is the book on object-oriented design. It presents not only instructions on how to design, but a number of full-sized applications in different languages: Smalltalk, CLOS, Object Pascal (on the Macintosh, using MacApp), and C++.

Booch, Grady. *Object-Oriented Design: With Applications.* 1991. Benjamin/Cummings, Redwood City, CA. ISBN: 0-8053-0091-0.

Programming

Abelson and Sussman is the textbook for the introductory programming class at MIT. Do not let that stop you, however. The book uses Scheme, a dialect of Lisp, and does so much with it that you may finally overcome your Lisp fears. It is not a Scheme textbook, however, but rather a tutorial on many different aspects of computer science. This is not something you can read in an afternoon, but it is highly recommended.

Abelson, Harold, et. al. *Structure & Interpretation of Computer Programs.* 1989. MIT Press, Cambridge, MA. ISBN: 0-262-01077-1.

Jon Bentley had a column in Communications of the ACM, the monthly publication of the Association for Computing Machinery (ACM). The ACM is the professional organization for computing professionals, so you should consider joining. Programming Pearls and More Programming Pearls are collections of the columns he wrote there. Each chapter is small, but provides some fresh ideas.

Do not optimize another program until you have read *Writing Efficient Programs.* Among other things, you learn to optimize only after your program is correct. You also are convinced that you need to do measurements to determine the effect of your optimizations.

Bentley, Jon. *Programming Pearls.* 1986. Addison-Wesley, Reading, MA. ISBN: 0-201-1033-1.

—. *More Programming Pearls: Confessions of a Coder.* 1988. Addison-Wesley, Reading, MA. ISBN: 0-201-11889-0.

—. *Writing Efficient Programs.* 1982. Prentice Hall, Englewood Cliffs, NJ. ISBN: 0-13-970244-x.

These two books—one in RATFOR (a preprocessed FORTRAN) and one in Pascal—demonstrate how to build interactive tools. If you are familiar with UNIX, you will be right at home with this tool philosophy.

Kernighan, Brian W., and P. L. Plauger. *Software Tools.* 1976. Addison-Wesley, Reading, MA. ISBN: 01-201-03669-x.

—. *Software Tools in Pascal.* 1981. Addison-Wesley, Reading, MA. ISBN: 0-201-10342-7.

Hats off to Knuth, who has published the source code to the TeX typesetting program. Read this to see how an expert computer scientist writes (and documents) code.

Knuth, Donald. *TeX (Computers & Typesetting Ser.: Vol. B)*. 1986. Addison-Wesley, Reading, MA. ISBN: 0-201-13437-3.

Any book by Weinberg is well worth reading. These three are but a sampling of his work. *Handbook of Walkthroughs, Inspections & Technical Reviews* describes how to conduct code walkthroughs and why they are important. As the book points out so well, having others pour over your code with a fine-toothed comb is the single most effective way to catch errors.

Becoming a Technical Leader: An Organic Problem-Solving Approach shows you how to become a problem solver and how to rally others around you to help generate the solutions. *Understanding the Professional Programmer* is geared more for managers than for those they manage, but is an entertaining look at programmers.

Weinberg, Gerald M., and Daniel P. Freedman. *Handbook of Walkthroughs, Inspections & Technical Reviews*, 3rd Edition. 1978. Little, Brown. ISBN: 0-933950-39-x.

Weinberg, Gerald. *Becoming a Technical Leader: An Organic Problem-Solving Approach*. Dorset House Publishing Co. ISBN: 0-932633-0201.

—. *Understanding the Professional Programmer*, Revised Edition. 1988. Dorset House Publishing Co. ISBN: 0-932633-09-9.

Macintosh

If you do not have it already, you cannot be without this series. The books are the official programming guides to Macintosh.

Apple Computer. *Inside Macintosh*. Addison-Wesley, Reading, MA.

Knaster details how the operating system works and how to debug your code in relation to it.

Knaster, Scott. *How to Write Macintosh Software: The Debugging Reference for the Macintosh*. 1992. Addison-Wesley, Reading, MA. 0-201-60805-7.

F

Disk Contents

Chapter 2, MultipleFiles

These are the files used to create the MultipleFiles project described in Chapter 2. The following files are located Average subfolder:

- Average.cp contains the source code for Average.
- Average.h contains the declaration of Average.

The following files are located in the Factorial subfolder:

- Factorial.cp contains the source code for Factorial.
- Factorial.h contains the declaration of Factorial.

The MultipleFiles folder contains three directories—Average, Factorial, and Reverse—and the following two files:

- Main.cp contains the main program.
- MultipleFiles. is the project file.

The Reverse subfolder contains the following files:

- Reverse.cp contains the source code for Reverse.
- Reverse.h contains the declaration of Reverse.

Chapter 3, Errors

These are the files used to create the Errors project described in Chapter 3. Within the Average subfolder are the following files:

- Average.cp contains the source code for Average.
- Average.h contains the declaration of Average.

The following files are located Factorial subfolder:

- Factorial.cp contains the source code for Factorial.
- Factorial.h contains the declaration of Factorial.

The Errors folder contains three directories—Average, Factorial, and Reverse—and the following two files:

- Main.cp contains the main program.
- Errors. is the project file.

Within the Reverse subfolder are the following files:

- Reverse.cp contains the source code for Reverse.
- Reverse.h contains the declaration of Reverse.

Chapter 4, Binary Tree

These are the files used to create the Binary Tree project described in Chapter 4:

- Main.cp contains the main program.
- BinaryTree. is the project file.

- TWithFileOpen.cp contains the code for `TWithFileOpen`.
- TWithFileOpen.h contains the declaration of `TWithFileOpen`.

Chapter 19, Tick-Tock

These are the project files used to create the Tick-Tock application described in Chapter 19:

- CAboutBoxApplication.cp contains the source code for `CAboutBoxApplication`.
- CAboutBoxApplication.h contains the declaration of `CAboutBoxApplication`.
- CClockApp.cp contains the source code for `CClockApp`.
- CClockApp.h contains the declaration of `CClockApp`.
- CClockPane.cp contains the source code for `CClockPane`.
- CClockPane.h contains the declaration of `CClockPane`.
- CDawdleBureaucratChore.cp contains the source code for `CDawdleBureaucratChore`.
- CDawdleBureaucratChore.h contains the declaration of `CDawdleBureaucratChore`.
- Clock.cp contains the main program.
- Clock.r contains all the resources.
- CQuitOnCloseWindow.cp contains the source code for `CQuitOnCloseWindow`.
- CQuitOnCloseWindow.h contains the declaration of `CQuitOnCloseWindow`.
- CSaveRestoreSizeWindow.cp contains the source code for `CSaveRestoreSizeWindow`.
- CSaveRestoreSizeWindow.h contains the declaration of `CSaveRestoreSizeWindow`.
- TGrafPortSetter.h contains the code (inlined) and the declaration of `TGrafPortSetter`.

Chapter 5, Alphabet

These are the files used to create the Alphabet project described in Chapter 5:

- Alphabet.r contains all the resources in Rez format. It can be added to the project.
- Alphabet. is the project file.
- Alphabet. .rsrc contains all the resources.
- AlphabetStrings.rsrc contains all the resources in binary format. It can be added to the project.
- Main.cp contains the main program.
- ResourceDefinitions.h contains the constants for resource IDs.

Chapter 7, Precompiled Headers

These are the files used to create the two Precompiled headers projects described in Chapter 7. The following files are located in the #1 subfolder:

- chap7, Proj1. is the project file.
- Foo.cp contains the main program.

Within the #2 subfolder are the following files:

- Bar.h contains the definition of `kBar`.
- chap7, Proj1.

This is the project file:

- Foo.h contains the definition of `kFoo`.
- FooBar++ is a precompiled header file.
- FooBar.cp contains the source code to create the precompiled header file.
- Main.cp contains the main program.

Chapter 16, RandomRectangle

These are the project files used to create the RandomRectangle application described in Chapter 16:

- CRandomRectanglePane.cp contains the source code for `CRandomRectanglePane`.
- CRandomRectanglePane.h contains the declaration of `CRandomRectanglePane`.
- CRectangleApp.cp contains the source code for `CRectangleApp`.
- CRectangleApp.h contains the declaration of `CRectangleApp`.
- Rectangle++. is the project file.
- Rectangle.cp contains the main program.
- Rectangle.r contains all the resources.
- TRandom.cp contains the code for `TRandom`.
- TRandom.h contains the declaration of `TRandom`.

Chapter 17, TextTyper

These are the project files used to create the TextTyper application described in Chapter 17:

- CTextApp.cp contains the source code for `CTextApp`.
- CTextApp.h contains the declaration of `CTextApp`.
- CTextDoc.cp contains the source code for `CTextDoc`.
- CTextDoc.h contains the declaration of `CTextDoc`.
- Text++. is the project file.
- Text.cp contains the main program.
- Text.r contains all the resources.

Chapter 18, PICTPeeker

These are the project files used to create the PICTPeeker application described in Chapter 18:

- CAboutBoxApplication.cp contains the source code for `CAboutBoxApplication`.
- CAboutBoxApplication.h contains the declaration of `CAboutBoxApplication`.
- CCutCopyPastePicture.cp contains the source code for `CCutCopyPastePicture`.
- CCutCopyPastePicture.h contains the declaration of `CCutCopyPastePicture`.
- CPictureApp.cp contains the source code for `CPictureApp`.
- CPictureApp.h contains the declaration of `CPictureApp`.
- CPictureClipboardTask.cp contains the source code for `CPictureClipboardTask`.
- CPictureClipboardTask.h contains the declaration of `CPictureClipboardTask`.
- CPictureDoc.cp contains the source code for `CPictureDoc`.
- CPictureDoc.h contains the declaration of `CPictureDoc`.
- Picture++. is the project file.
- Picture.cp contains the main program.
- Picture.r contains all the resources.
- TDisposHandleOnFailure.cp contains the code for `TDisposHandleOnFailure`.
- TDisposHandleOnFailure.h contains the declaration of `TDisposHandleOnFailure`.
- TFailureObjects.cp contains the code for `TFailureObjects`.
- TFailureObjects.h contains the declaration of `TFailureObjects`.

- TickTock++. is the project file.
- Utilities.cp contains the code for utility routines.
- Utilities.h contains the declaration of utility routines.

Chapter 20, C++ Calc

These are the project files used to create the C++ Calc application described in Chapter 20:

- C++ Calc++. is the project file.
- CAboutBoxApplication.cp contains the source code for `CAboutBoxApplication`.
- CAboutBoxApplication.h contains the declaration of `CAboutBoxApplication`.
- Calculator.cp contains the source code for `Calculator`.
- Calculator.h contains the declaration of `Calculator`.
- Calculator.r contains all the resources.
- CalculatorMain.cp contains the main program.
- CButtonWithFontAndSize.cp contains the source code for `CButtonWithFontAndSize`.
- CButtonWithFontAndSize.h contains the declaration of `CButtonWithFontAndSize`.
- CCalculatorApp.cp contains the source code for `CCalculatorApp`.
- CCalculatorApp.h contains the declaration of `CCalculatorApp`.
- CCalculatorPane.cp contains the source code for `CCalculatorPane`.
- CCalculatorPane.h contains the declaration of `CCalculatorPane`.
- CFloatText.cp contains the source code for `CFloatText`.
- CFloatText.h contains the declaration of `CFloatText`.

- CQuitOnCloseWindow.cp contains the source code for `CQuitOnCloseWindow`.
- CQuitOnCloseWindow.h contains the declaration of `CQuitOnCloseWindow`.
- CSaveRestoreSizeWindow.cp contains the source code for `CSaveRestoreSizeWindow`.
- CSaveRestoreSizeWindow.h contains the declaration of `CSaveRestoreSizeWindow`.
- TGrafPortSetter.h contains the code (inlined) and the declaration of `TGrafPortSetter`.

Chapter 21, AddressBook

These are the project files used to create the AddressBook application described in Chapter 21:

- AddressBook++. is the project file.
- AddressBook.cp contains the main program.
- AddressBook.r contains all the resources.
- CAboutBoxApplication.cp contains the source code for `CAboutBoxApplication`.
- CAboutBoxApplication.h contains the declaration of `CAboutBoxApplication`.
- CAddressBookApp.cp contains the source code for `CAddressBookApp`.
- CAddressBookApp.h contains the declaration of `CAddressBookApp`.
- CAddressBookDoc.c contains the declaration of `CAddressBookDoc`.
- CAddressBookDoc.cp contains the source code for `CAddressBookDoc`.
- CAddressBookDoc.h contains the declaration of `CAddressBookDoc`.

- CAddressBookPane.cp contains the source code for `CAddressBookPane`.
- CAddressBookPane.h contains the declaration of `CAddressBookPane`.
- CNewEntryDialog.cp contains the source code for `CNewEntryDialog`.
- CNewEntryDialog.h contains the declaration of `CNewEntryDialog`.
- CNewEntryDialogDirector.cp contains the source code for `CNewEntryDialogDirector`.
- CNewEntryDialogDirector.h contains the declaration of `CNewEntryDialogDirector`.
- Database.cp contains the source code for `TDatabase`.
- Database.h contains the declaration of `TDatabase`.
- Entry.cp contains the source code for `TEntry`.
- Entry.h contains the declaration of `TEntry`.
- NewEntryDialog.rsrc contains all the resources.
- TFailureObjects.cp contains the source code for `TFailureObjects`.
- TFailureObjects.h contains the declaration of `TFailureObjects`.
- TWithFileOpen.cp contains the source code for `TWithFileOpen`.
- TWithFileOpen.h contains the declaration of `TWithFileOpen`.

Chapter 21, Database Tester

These are the project files used to create the Database Tester application described in Chapter 21:

- Database.cp contains the source code for `TDatabase`.
- Database.h contains the declaration of `TDatabase`.
- Database Tester. is the project file.

- Entry.cp contains the source code for `TEntry`.
- Entry.h contains the declaration of `TEntry`.
- Main.cp contains the main program.

Appendix B, PowersOfTwo

These are the files used to create the PowersOfTwo project described in Appendix B:

- Main.cp contains the main program.
- Powers.cp contains the source code for `Powers`.
- Powers.h contains the declaration of `Powers`.
- PowersOfTwo. is the project file.
- ProjectorDB contains the Projector database of the project.

Application

The Compressed Applications.sea file is a self-expanding archive that contains the programs in Chapters 16-21.

Index

B

C

D

E

F

G

H

J–K

L

M

N

O

P

Q

R

S

T

U

V

W-Z

Symantec C++ Programming for the Macintosh
REPLACEMENT ORDER FORM

In the event that the disk bound to this book is defective, Prentice Hall Computer Publishing will send you a replacement disk free of charge.

Please fill out the information below and return this page (or a copy of this page) to the address listed below with your original disk. Please print clearly.

BOOK TITLE ______________________________ ISBN ______________

NAME ______________________________ PHONE ______________

COMPANY ______________________________ TITLE ______________

ADDRESS ______________________________

CITY ______________________________ STATE ______________ ZIP ________

Prentice Hall Computer Publishing, 11711 North College Avenue, Carmel, IN 46032. ATTN: Customer Service Department

Symantec C++ Programming for the Macintosh
LIMITED WARRANTY REGISTRATION CARD

In order to preserve your rights as provided in the limited warranty, this information must be on file with PHCP within 30 days of purchase.

Please fill in the information requested:

BOOK TITLE ______________________________ ISBN ______________

NAME ______________________________ PHONE NUMBER ______________

ADDRESS ______________________________

CITY ______________________________ STATE ______________ ZIP ________

COMPUTER BRAND & MODEL ______________ DOS VERSION ________ MEMORY ________ K

Where did you purchase this product?

DEALER NAME? ______________________________ PHONE NUMBER ______________

ADDRESS ______________________________

CITY ______________________________ STATE ______________ ZIP ________

PURCHASE DATE ______________________ PURCHASE PRICE ______________

How did you learn about this product? (Check as many as applicable.)

STORE DISPLAY ________ SALESPERSON ________ MAGAZINE ARTICLE ________ ADVERTISEMENT ________

OTHER (Please explain) ______________________________

How long have you owned or used this computer?

LESS THAN 30 DAYS ________ LESS THAN 6 MONTHS ______ 6 MONTHS TO A YEAR ______ OVER 1 YEAR ______

What is your primary use for the computer?

BUSINESS ________ PERSONAL ________ EDUCATION ________ OTHER (Please explain) ______________

Where is your computer located?

HOME ___________ OFFICE ___________ SCHOOL ___________ OTHER (Please explain) ______________

Prentice Hall Computer Publishing, 11711 North College Avenue, Carmel, IN 46032. ATTN: Customer Service Department

Important! Read Before Opening Sealed Diskette
END USER LICENSE AGREEMENT

The software in this package is provided to You on the condition that You agree with PRENTICE HALL COMPUTER PUBLISHING ("PHCP") to the terms and conditions set forth below. **Read this End User Agreement carefully. You will be bound by the terms of this agreement if you open the sealed diskette.** If You do not agree to the terms contained in this End User License Agreement, return the entire product, along with your receipt, to *Brady, Prentice Hall Computer Publishing, 15 Columbus Circle, 14th floor, New York, NY 10023, Attn: Refunds,* and your purchase price will be refunded.

PHCP grants, and You hereby accept, a personal, nonexclusive license to use this software program and associated documentation in this package, or any part of it ("Licensed Product"), subject to the following terms and conditions:

1. License

The license granted to You hereunder authorizes You to use the Licensed Product on any single computer system. A separate license, pursuant to a separate End User License Agreement, is required for any other computer system on which You intend to use the Licensed Product.

2. Term

This End User License Agreement is effective from the date of purchase by You of the Licensed Product and shall remain in force until terminated. You may terminate this End User License at any time by destroying the Licensed Product together with all copies in any form made by You or received by You. Your right to use or copy the Licensed Product will terminate if You fail to comply with any of the terms or conditions of this End User License Agreement. Upon such termination, You shall destroy the copies of the Licensed Product in your possession.

3. Restriction Against Transfer

This End User License Agreement, and the Licensed Product, may not be assigned, sublicensed, or otherwise transferred by You to another party unless the other party agrees to accept the terms and conditions of the End User License Agreement. If You transfer the Licensed Product, You must at the same time either transfer all copies, whether in printed or machine-readable form, to the same party or destroy any copies not transferred.

4. Restrictions Against Copying or Modifying the Licensed Product

The Licensed Product is copyrighted and except for certain limited uses as noted on the copyright page, may not be further copied without the prior written approval of PHCP. You may make one copy for backup purposes provided You reproduce and include the complete copyright notice on the backup copy. Any unauthorized copying is in violation of this Agreement and may also constitute a violation of the United States Copyright Law for which You could be liable in a civil or criminal lawsuit. **You may not use, transfer, copy, or otherwise reproduce the Licensed Product, or any part of it, except as expressly permitted in this End User License Agreement.**

5. Protection and Security

You shall take all reasonable steps to safeguard the Licensed Product and to ensure that no unauthorized person shall have access to it and that no unauthorized copy of any part of it in any form shall be made.

6. Limited Warranty

If You are the original consumer purchaser of a diskette and it is found to be defective in materials or workmanship (which shall not include problems relating to the nature or operation of the Licensed Product) under normal use, PHCP will replace it free of charge (or, at PHCP's option, refund your purchase price) within 30 days following the date of purchase. Following the 30-day period, and up to one year after purchase, PHCP will replace any such defective diskette upon payment of a $5 charge (or, at PHCP's option, refund your purchase price), provided that the Limited Warranty Registration Card has been filed within 30 days following the date of purchase. Any request for replacement of a defective diskette must be accompanied by the original defective diskette and proof of date of purchase and purchase price. PHCP shall have no obligation to replace a diskette (or refund your purchase price based on claims of defects in the nature or operation of the Licensed Product).

The software program is provided "as is" without warranty of any kind, either expressed or implied, including but not limited to the implied warranties of merchantability and fitness for a particular purpose. The entire risk as to the quality and performance of the program is with You. Should the program prove defective, You (and not PHCP) assume the entire cost of necessary servicing, repair or correction.

Some states do not allow the exclusion of implied warranties, so the above exclusion may not apply to You. This warrant gives You specific legal rights, and You may also have other rights which vary from state to state.

PHCP does not warrant that the functions contained in the program will meet your requirements or that the operation of the program will be uninterrupted or error free. Neither PHCP nor anyone else who has been involved in the creation of production of this product shall be liable for any direct, indirect, incidental, special, or consequential damages, whether arising out of the use or inability to use the product, or any breach of a warranty, and PHCP shall have no responsibility except to replace the diskette pursuant to this limited warranty (or, at its option, provide a refund of the purchase price).

No sales personnel or other representative of any party involved in the distribution of the Licensed Product is authorized by PHCP to make any warranties with respect to the diskette or the Licensed Product beyond those contained in this Agreement. **Oral statements do not constitute warranties**, shall not be relied upon by You, and are not part of this Agreement. The entire agreement between PHCP and You is embodied in this Agreement.

7. General

If any provision of this End User License Agreement is determined to be invalid under any applicable statute of rule of law, it shall be deemed omitted and the remaining provisions shall continue in full force and effect. This End User License Agreement is to be governed by the construed in accordance with the laws of the State of New York.

Prentice Hall Computer Publishing and the authors make no warranties, express or implied in connection with the software, and expressly exclude all warranties of fitness for a particular purpose. Prentice Hall Computer Publishing and the authors shall have no liability for consequential, incidental, or exemplary damages.

Chapter 5, Alphabet

These are the files used to create the Alphabet project described in Chapter 5:

- Alphabet.r contains all the resources in Rez format. It can be added to the project.
- Alphabet. is the project file.
- Alphabet. .rsrc contains all the resources.
- AlphabetStrings.rsrc contains all the resources in binary format. It can be added to the project.
- Main.cp contains the main program.
- ResourceDefinitions.h contains the constants for resource IDs.

Chapter 7, Precompiled Headers

These are the files used to create the two Precompiled headers projects described in Chapter 7. The following files are located in the #1 subfolder:

- chap7, Proj1. is the project file.
- Foo.cp contains the main program.

Within the #2 subfolder are the following files:

- Bar.h contains the definition of `kBar`.
- chap7, Proj1.

This is the project file:

- Foo.h contains the definition of `kFoo`.
- FooBar++ is a precompiled header file.
- FooBar.cp contains the source code to create the precompiled header file.
- Main.cp contains the main program.

Chapter 16, RandomRectangle

These are the project files used to create the RandomRectangle application described in Chapter 16:

- CRandomRectanglePane.cp contains the source code for `CRandomRectanglePane`.
- CRandomRectanglePane.h contains the declaration of `CRandomRectanglePane`.
- CRectangleApp.cp contains the source code for `CRectangleApp`.
- CRectangleApp.h contains the declaration of `CRectangleApp`.
- Rectangle++. is the project file.
- Rectangle.cp contains the main program.
- Rectangle.r contains all the resources.
- TRandom.cp contains the code for `TRandom`.
- TRandom.h contains the declaration of `TRandom`.

Chapter 17, TextTyper

These are the project files used to create the TextTyper application described in Chapter 17:

- CTextApp.cp contains the source code for `CTextApp`.
- CTextApp.h contains the declaration of `CTextApp`.
- CTextDoc.cp contains the source code for `CTextDoc`.
- CTextDoc.h contains the declaration of `CTextDoc`.
- Text++. is the project file.
- Text.cp contains the main program.
- Text.r contains all the resources.

Chapter 18, PICTPeeker

These are the project files used to create the PICTPeeker application described in Chapter 18:

- CAboutBoxApplication.cp contains the source code for `CAboutBoxApplication`.
- CAboutBoxApplication.h contains the declaration of `CAboutBoxApplication`.
- CCutCopyPastePicture.cp contains the source code for `CCutCopyPastePicture`.
- CCutCopyPastePicture.h contains the declaration of `CCutCopyPastePicture`.
- CPictureApp.cp contains the source code for `CPictureApp`.
- CPictureApp.h contains the declaration of `CPictureApp`.
- CPictureClipboardTask.cp contains the source code for `CPictureClipboardTask`.
- CPictureClipboardTask.h contains the declaration of `CPictureClipboardTask`.
- CPictureDoc.cp contains the source code for `CPictureDoc`.
- CPictureDoc.h contains the declaration of `CPictureDoc`.
- Picture++. is the project file.
- Picture.cp contains the main program.
- Picture.r contains all the resources.
- TDisposHandleOnFailure.cp contains the code for `TDisposHandleOnFailure`.
- TDisposHandleOnFailure.h contains the declaration of `TDisposHandleOnFailure`.
- TFailureObjects.cp contains the code for `TFailureObjects`.
- TFailureObjects.h contains the declaration of `TFailureObjects`.

- TWithFileOpen.cp contains the code for `TWithFileOpen`.
- TWithFileOpen.h contains the declaration of `TWithFileOpen`.

Chapter 19, Tick-Tock

These are the project files used to create the Tick-Tock application described in Chapter 19:

- CAboutBoxApplication.cp contains the source code for `CAboutBoxApplication`.
- CAboutBoxApplication.h contains the declaration of `CAboutBoxApplication`.
- CClockApp.cp contains the source code for `CClockApp`.
- CClockApp.h contains the declaration of `CClockApp`.
- CClockPane.cp contains the source code for `CClockPane`.
- CClockPane.h contains the declaration of `CClockPane`.
- CDawdleBureaucratChore.cp contains the source code for `CDawdleBureaucratChore`.
- CDawdleBureaucratChore.h contains the declaration of `CDawdleBureaucratChore`.
- Clock.cp contains the main program.
- Clock.r contains all the resources.
- CQuitOnCloseWindow.cp contains the source code for `CQuitOnCloseWindow`.
- CQuitOnCloseWindow.h contains the declaration of `CQuitOnCloseWindow`.
- CSaveRestoreSizeWindow.cp contains the source code for `CSaveRestoreSizeWindow`.
- CSaveRestoreSizeWindow.h contains the declaration of `CSaveRestoreSizeWindow`.
- TGrafPortSetter.h contains the code (inlined) and the declaration of `TGrafPortSetter`.